Jean-Christophe Liebeskind

Chinese Business Law

Jean-Christophe Liebeskind
Attorney-at-Law, Geneva, Solicitor, England & Wales, LL.M. (LSE), DipICArb, FCIArb

Chinese Business Law

Stämpfli Publishers

Bibliographic information published by the Deutsche Nationalbibliothek
Bibliographic information published by the German National Library
The German National Library lists this publication in the German National Bibliography; detailed bibliographic data are available on the Internet at http://dnb.d-nb.de.

ISBN 978-3-7272-3533-7

The following edition is available in
our online bookshop www.staempflirecht.ch:

E-Book ISBN 978-3-7272-2804-9

For questions regarding product safety
Producer: Stämpfli Publishers Ltd., Wölflistrasse 1, CH-3001 Bern,
verlag@staempfli.ch, www.staempflirecht.ch
EU Importer: Brockhaus Commission GmbH, Kreidlerstrasse 9, DE-70806 Kornwestheim,
gpsr@brocom.de, www.brocom.de

Der Schreiber steht für unseren Anspruch, gemeinsam mit unseren Autorinnen und Autoren relevante und herausragende Inhalte zu produzieren.

FSC www.fsc.org
MIX
Papier aus verantwortungsvollen Quellen
FSC® C083411

Foreword

This book focuses on the foundations of Chinese business law applying to foreign investors in and foreign parties trading with China. It mainly comments, to that extent, foreign investment law, relevant parts of the Chinese Civil Code, including the general principles of civil law and of the law of obligations, contract law and the law of liability, both contractual and for illicit acts, as well as the Labor Contract Law, which is the only major nominate contract not included in the Code; the Company Law governing the limited liability enterprise and the shareholding company; the Law on the Partnership Enterprise; the law governing foreign representative offices; and the regime applying the former joint-ventures, now abolished; it also briefly addresses variable interests entities.

The Foreign Investment Law (FIL) was promulgated in 2019 and has been effective since 2020. It was followed by the Chinese Civil Code, promulgated in 2020 and effective since 2021, and the Company Law (2023 Revision), revised in 2023 and effective since 2024. Together, these three laws form the core of the reform of Chinese business law for both domestic investors and, as far as the FIL is concerned, foreign investors. While Chinese law is a continuous process, it can be said that the aforementioned promulgation sequence achieves, by conforming with the latest global standards, the major overhaul of Chinese law undertaken since the Opening from 1978 and its acceleration as of China's accession to the World Trade Organization in 2001.

The full effects of the reform only apply since as recently as one year ago, i.e., as of 1 January 2025, with the end of the transitional period granted to foreign-invested enterprises under the Foreign Investment Law to transform into one the domestic forms of enterprise, thus achieving the level playing field between foreign and domestic investors aimed at by the Chinese legislator. Some commentaries anticipated such reform, this book purports at commenting on its implementation.

While related secondary legislation is mentioned as appropriate, it is not detailed in this book, whose scope it would exceed. Moreover, a large part of it, such as intellectual property law, competition law, tender law, consumer protection law, etc. is anterior to those reforms and has already been abundantly commented.

Owing to the author's education and qualifications, this book adopts a comparative approach with Swiss law, although not systematically, but rather opportunistically, whenever the issue at stake appears relevant enough within its scope. It does not mean in any way that this book is exclusively intended to Swiss lawyers: indeed, the concepts used in Swiss law are comparable in most respect to other civil (as opposed to common-) law systems, namely, of other continental European jurisdictions, while the terminology in English, French and German will no doubt prove useful to most continental European lawyers. Even though many of such concepts may differ from common law, Anglo-Saxon lawyers will nevertheless be comforted by the great care paid to clarifying the Chinese legal terminology in English, and to point at differences between civil law systems, to which Chinese law pertains in the first place, and common law. Likewise, Chinese lawyers may, conversely, find it useful to be able to explain concepts of Chinese law in English, French and German language to their western counterparts.

Terminology is not the least challenging issue posed by Chinese law, not to say, arguably, one of the main ones. Chinese is not only exceedingly difficult to read for foreign lawyers; printed translations are more often than not crippled with errors, many of which are material, while online automatic translation, however convenient, hardly achieves better results. This issue is worsened by the multiple equivalent expressions available in foreign languages, including conceptual variations between civil and common law. Sources of confusion, which can potentially lead to dire consequences, are endless. The author took great care to dispel potential misunderstandings by equating them with comparable notions in English, French and German and discussing translation issues, as well as by providing the names in Chinese of all laws, etc. and of selected legal institutions mentioned in this book, for the sake of accuracy. All Chinese expressions are followed by their pinyin transliteration, enabling foreign readers who are not proficient in Chinese to communicate with their Chinese counterparts.

A table of abbreviations or acronyms, of Chinese locutions sorted in English and in pinyin, of Latin locutions, of Chinese and Swiss laws, of treaties and other legal or regulatory basis mentioned in this book, as well as a selected bibliography in Chinese, Swiss and international law, are available on the beginning; an index in English is available at the end.

The laws, etc. referred to in this book have been considered as per their status on 31 December 2025, although some notable additions posterior to that date may have been mentioned.

This book will inevitably contain mistakes. All errors are the author's. Readers are invited to signal them at john.liebeskind@jcliebeskind.com.

Acknowledgements

I wish to express my gratitude, in particular, to my grandfather, Prof.Dr. Wolfgang-Amadeus Liebeskind (†), former Dean of the Faculty of Law of the University of Geneva; to my father, Dr.med. Bernard Liebeskind (†); to Prof.Dr. Herbert Schönle (†), Ordinary Professor of Law, University of Geneva; to Prof.Dr. Dominique Poncet (†), Founding Partner of my former law firm Poncet Turrettini Amaudruz Neyroud in Geneva; to Dominique Warluzel (†), former Partner at Poncet Turrettini Amaudruz Neyroud; to Prof.Dr. Pierre Lalive (†), Founding Partner of my former law firm Lalive & Partners in Geneva; to Michael Schneider, Founding Partner at Lalive & Partners; to Xing Xiusong 邢修松, Founding Partner of my Chinese law firm Global Law Office 环球律师事务所 hánqiú lǜshī shìwùsuǒ in China; to Zhang Xin, Ph.D. 张昕, Partner at Global Law Office in Beijing; to Gu Weiwei 顾伟伟, Partner at Global Law Office in Shanghai; to James Zimmerman, Partner at Loeb & Loeb in Beijing, Chairman of AmCham China and author of "China Law Deskbook" (ABA ed.); to Fanny Nguyen, Partner at Lefèvre Pelletier & Associés (LPA Law) in Paris and Shanghai; to Dr.iur. Zheng Jun 郑军, Lecturer at the University of Fribourg; to Fanny Weiss, manager at my publisher, Staempfli Éditions S.A. in Bern; and to any individual having contributed to this book whom I may not have mentioned.

About the Author

Jean-Christophe Liebeskind (A.K.A. John Liebeskind and Li Jian 李剑), LL.M. (LSE), avocat (barreau de Genève), Solicitor, England & Wales (non-practicing), DipICArb (CIArb), FCIArb, is a Swiss lawyer. He qualified both as Swiss attorney-at-law in Geneva and as English Solicitor in London, holds a Master of Laws from the London School of Economics, and earned a diploma of international commercial arbitration, and fellowship, from the Chartered Institute of Arbitrators. John practices Switzerland since 1988 and in China since 2003. He gained additional expertise in foreign investment while chairing SwissCham, the Swiss Chamber of Commerce in China. He practices in China with Global Law Office 环球律师事务所 hánqiú lǜshī shìwùsuǒ, a Chinese law firm, since 2008, and in Switzerland with Swisslegal Rouiller & Partners. Before coming to China, John worked with Lalive & Partners in Geneva, a law firm dedicated to international arbitration. John advises foreign and Chinese clients in international commercial matters, in particular foreign investment in and trade with China, both for transactions and dispute resolution. He can be reached at liebeskind@swisslegal.ch and his blog consulted at www.jcliebeskind.com.

Summary Contents

Detailed Contents

Table of abbreviations

A.K.A.	also known as
ACFTU	All-China Federation of Trade Unions
ADB	Asian Development Bank
ADR	alternative dispute resolution
AIC	Administration for Industry & Commerce [abolished]
alt.	alternative name
AMAC	Asset Management Association of China
AMR	Administration for Market Regulation
ATF	arrêt du tribunal fédéral, ruling of the Swiss Federal Supreme Court
BIT	bilateral investment treaty
BSE	Beijing Stock Exchange
C&F	Cost and Freight
CBIRC	China Banking & Insurance Regulatory Commission
CEO	Chief Executive Officer
cf.	*confer* (compare)
CFO	Chief Financial Officer
CHF	Swiss francs
China	People's Republic of China
CIETAC	China International Economic and Trade Arbitration Commission
CIF	Cost, Insurance and Freight
CIRDI	Centre international pour le règlement des différends relatifs aux investissements
CJV	Contractual (or Cooperative) Joint-venture
CNY	Chinese yuan
CO	Code des obligations
CPA	certified public accountant

CPC	Code de procédure civile
CPP	Code de procédure pénale
CR	Commentaire romand
CSL	Cybersecurity Law
CSRC	China Securities Regulatory Commission
DC	documentary credit
DDC	Agency for Development & Cooperation [Switzerland]
DSL	Data Security Law
EBRD	European Bank for Reconstruction & Development
EJV	Equity Joint-venture
EN	European Norms
ERS	Enterprise Registration System
ESOP	employees stock ownership plan
EU	European Union
FDI	foreign direct investment
Fedlex	[Swiss official database for federal law]
FESCO	Beijing Foreign Enterprise Human Resource Service Co.
FF	Feuille fédérale
ff.	and following
FIDIC	International Federation of Consulting Engineers
FIE	foreign-invested enterprise
FIL	Foreign Investment Law
Fr.	French language
FSG	Shanghai Foreign Service (Group) Co., Ltd.
FTA	Free Trade Agreement
GACC	General Administration of Customs
GCMS	Global Construction Measurement Standards
Ger.	German language

GM	General Manager
GPS	global positioning system
HK$	Hong Kong dollar
HKD	Hong Kong dollar
HKEX	Hong Kong Stock Exchange
ibid.	*ibidem*
IBRD	International Bank for Reconstruction & Development
ICC	International Chamber of Commerce
ICSID	International Center for the Settlement of Investment Disputes
id.	*idem*
IDA	International Development Association
IFC	International Finance Corporation
IM	instant messaging
IMD	International Institute for Management Development
IPO	initial public offering
IPR	intellectual property rights
ISO	International Standardization Organization
IT	information technology
JG	construction industry (standards)
JT	Journal des tribunaux
JV	Joint-venture
Lat.	Latin language
LC	letter of credit
LCIA	London Court of Arbitration
LDIP	Loi sur le droit international privé
LP	Loi sur la poursuite et la faillite
LPR	Loan Prime Rate
MFN	most-favored nation

MIGA	Multilateral Investment Guarantee Agency
MOFCOM	Ministry of Commerce
MOHURD	Ministry of Housing & Urban-Rural Development
MOP	Macanese pataca
MOP$	Macanese pataca
NAFMII	National Association of Financial Market Institutional Investors
NBS	National Bureau of Statistics
NDRC	National Development & Reform Commission
NECIPS	National Enterprise Credit Information Publicity System
NFRA	National Financial Regulatory Administration
NGO	non-governmental organization
No., Nos	number, numbers
NPC	National People's Congress
OR	Obligationenrecht
ORC	Ordonnance sur le registre du commerce
P	Macanese pataca
PBOC	People's Bank of China
PIPL	Personal Information Protection Law
POA	power of attorney
PRC	People's Republic of China
R&D	research & development
RICS	Royal Institution of Chartered Surveyors
RMB	renminbi
RO	representative office
RS	Recueil systématique
SAC	Standardization Administration of China
SAFE	State Administration for Foreign Exchange

SAIC	State Administration for Industry & Commerce [abolished]
SAMR	State Administration for Market Regulation
SAR	Special Administrative Region
SBLC	standby letter of credit
seco	State Secretariat for Economic Affairs
SEZ	Special Economic Zone
short	short name
SIA	Swiss Society of Engineers & Architects
SMS	short messaging system
SOE	State-owned enterprise
SPC	Supreme People's Court
SPV	special purpose vehicle
SSE	Shanghai Stock Exchange
STA	State Tax Administration
Swisslex	[official database of Swiss laws]
SZSE	Shenzhen Stock Exchange
UN	United Nations
UNCTAD	United Nations Conference on Trade & Development
VAT	value-added tax
VIE	variable interest entity
Vol.	volume
WFOE	Wholly Foreign-owned Enterprise
WTO	World Trade Organization
Zh.	(Simplified) Chinese language

Table of Chinese Locutions in English

This table lists the translation of the Chinese locutions used in this book in simplified Chinese together with their transliteration in pinyin, sorted by alphabetical order in *English*. For the sorting by their alphabetical order in pinyin, see next table.

acceptance inspection	进行验收	jìnxíng yànshōu
Administration for Market Regulation (AMR)	市场监督管理局	shìchǎng jiāndū guǎnlǐ jú
agency	代理	dàilǐ
agreement	协议	xiéyì
All-China Federation of Trade Unions (ACFTU)	中华全国总工会	zhōnghuá quánguó zǒng gōnghuì)
allocation	划拨	huàbō
amendment	修正	xiūzhèng
assignment	出让	chūràng
association	社会团体	shèhuì tuántǐ
assurance (quality-)	质量保证	zhìliàng bǎozhèng
assurance, guarantee or security	担保	dānbǎo
auctioning	拍卖	pāimài
basic provisions	基本规定	jīběn guīdìng
bidding	投标	tóubiāo
board	会	huì
board of directors	董事会	dǒngshìhuì
branch	分支	fēnzhī
branch office	分支机构	fēnzhī jīgòu
brokerage contract	行纪合同	xíng jì hétóng
building and construction engineering (JG)	建筑工程	jiànzhú gōngchéng
business license	营业执照	yíngyè zhízhào

cargo transportation contract [s. freight transportation]		
certificate, title certificate, ownership certificate	权属书	quán shǔ shū
chairman (of the board of directors)	董事长	dǒngshì zhǎng
chapter	章	zhāng
Civil Code	民法典	mínfǎ diǎn
civil liability	民事责任	mínshì zérèn
collateral	担保物	dānbǎo wù
collective (labor) contract	集体合同	jítǐ hétóng
collective property	集体所有	jítǐ suǒyǒu
company	公司	gōngsī
company deputy manager	公司副经理	gōngsī fù jīnglǐ
company merger	公司合并	gōngsī hébìng
complaint mechanism	投诉工作机制	tóusù gōngzuò jīzhì
concrete or conclusive evidence	确切证据	quèqiè zhèngjù
condition(s)	条件	tiáojiàn
construction industry standards	建筑行业标准	jiànzhú hángyè biāozhǔn
construction project contract	建设工程合同	jiànshè gōngchéng hétóng
construction usufruct	建设用地使用权	jiànshè yòngdì shǐyòng quán
construction usufruct	违约责任	jiànshè yòngdì shǐyòng quán
contract	合同	hétóng

contract, agreement	合同	héhuǒ
contractor	承揽人	chénglǎn rén
Contractual Joint-venture [s. Sino-Foreign Contractual Joint-venture (CJV)]		
Cooperative Joint-venture [s. Sino-Foreign Contractual Joint-venture (CJV)]		
Corp.	股份公司	gǔfèn gōngsī
corporation [s. shareholding company]		
custody contract [s. deposit]		
data	数据	shùjù
data exchange	电子数据交换	diànzǐ shùjù jiāohuàn
Departmental Information Sharing System	政务部门信息共享系统	zhèngwù bùmén xìnxī gòngxiǎng xìtǒng
[*id.*, short]	部门信息共享系统	bùmén xìnxī gòngxiǎng xìtǒng
deposit contract	保管合同	bǎoguǎn hétóng
deposit, to	提存	tícún
depositary (under a contract of deposit)	受质人	shòu zhì rén
depositary, warehouse operator	仓储人	cāng chǔ rén
depositor (under a contract of deposit)	出质人	chū zhì rén
depositor (under a contract of warehousing)	存货人	cún huò rén
deputy	副	fù
deputy general manager	副经理	fù jīnglǐ

difficult	难以	nányǐ
director (member of the board of directors)	董事	dǒngshì
dissolution, to dissolve	解散	jiěsàn
donation, contract for gift	赠与合同	zèngyǔ hétóng
eight	八	bā
electric, electronic	电	diàn
electronic	电子	diànzǐ
electronic data	电子数据	diànzǐ shùjù
electronic data message	数据电文	shùjù diànwén
e-mail	电子邮件	diànzǐ yóujiàn
employer, employing unit	用人单位	yòngrén dānwèi
employment contract	劳动合同	láodòng hétóng
enterprise	企业	qǐyè
Enterprise Registration System (ERS)	企业登记系统	qǐyè dēngjì xìtǒng
Equity Joint-venture [s. Sino-Foreign Equity Joint-venture (EJV)]		
evidence	证据	zhèngjù
exact, precise, definite, sure, true, reliable	确切	quèqiè
exchange	交换	jiāohuàn
exchange message	数据电文	shùjù diànwén
express logistic-, delivery- or courier services	快递	kuàidì
expropriation	征收	zhēngshōu
factoring contract	保理合同	bǎo lǐ hétóng

financial leasing contract	融资租赁合同	róngzī zūlìn hétóng
five	五	wǔ
foreign company	外国公司	wàiguó gōngsī
foreign investment	外商投资	wàishāng tóuzī
Foreign Investment Information Reporting System	外国投资信息报送系统	wàiguó tóuzī xìnxī bào sòng xìtǒng
foreign investment service system	外商投资服务体系	wàishāng tóuzī fúwù tǐxì
foreign investor	外国投资者	wàiguó tóuzī zhě
foreign representative office, permanent (or resident) representative offices of foreign enterprise	外国企业常驻代表机构	wàiguó qǐyè cháng zhù dàibiǎo jīgòu
foreign-invested enterprise (FIE)	外商投资企业	wàishāng tóuzī qǐyè
formation (of the shareholding company) by flotation or by fundraising	募集	mùjí
formation (of the shareholding company) by promotion	发起	fāqǐ
four	四	sì
freight transportation contract	货运合同	huòyùn hétóng
general contracting	总承包	zǒng chéngbāo
general manager	公司经理	gōngsī jīnglǐ
[*id.*, alt.]	总经理	zǒng jīnglǐ
general partnership	普通合伙	pǔtōng héhuǒ
general provisions	通则	tōngzé

[*id.*, alt.]	一般规定	yībān guīdìng
[*id.* alt.]	总则	zǒngzé
general, basic	基本	jīběn
[*id.* alt.]	一般	yībān
general, common	通	tōng
[*id.* alt.]	总	zǒng
gift, contract for [s. donation]		
Government Data Sharing	政务数据共享	zhèngwù shùjù gòngxiǎng
guarantee	担保	dānbǎo
guarantee (quality-) [s. assurance]		
guarantee contract, contract for the provision of security	担保合同	dānbǎo hétóng
guarantee contract, s. suretyship		
guaranty	保证	bǎozhèng
high duty (or degree) of care	尽到高度注意义务	jǐn dào gāodù zhùyì yìwù
improper	不正当	bù zhèngdàng
infringement	责任	zérèn
insurance for occupational or work-related diseases	工伤保险	gōngshāng bǎoxiǎn
interchange message	数据电文	shùjù diànwén
intermediary contract, s. intermediation		
intermediation contract	中介合同	zhōngjiè hétóng

interpretation (of the Supreme People's Court)	解释	jiěshì
joint-venture	经营企业	jīngyíng qǐyè
judicial interpretation(s) of the Supreme People's Court	最高人民法院解释	zuìgāo rénmín fǎyuàn jiěshì
labor contract, s. employment		
labor dispatch	劳务派遣	láowù pàiqiǎn
labor, s. work		
law	法	fǎ
lease contract	租赁合同	zūlìn hétóng
legal person	法人	hōjin
legal representative	法定代表人	fǎdìng dàibiǎo rén
liability for breach of contract	违约责任	wéiyuē zérèn
liability for illicit act ("torts")	侵权责任	qīnquán zérèn
lien	留置权	liúzhì quán
limitation of action	诉讼时效	sùsòng shíxiào
limited liability company	有限责任公司	yǒuxiàn zérèn gōngsī
limited liability partnership	有限合伙	yǒuxiàn héhuǒ
liquidated damages, payment for breach of contract	支付违约金	zhīfù wéiyuē jīn
liquidation	清算	qīngsuàn
loan contract	借款合同	jièkuǎn hétóng
loss	损失	sǔnshī
loss of profit	预期利益损失	yùqī lìyì sǔnshī

Ltd.	有限公司	yǒuxiàn gōngsī
manager	经理	jīnglǐ
mandate [contract]	委托合同	wěituō hétóng
maximum mortgage	最高额抵押权	zuìgāo é dǐyā quán
may [verb]	可能	kěnéng
measures	办法	bànfǎ
merger	合并	hébìng
merger by absorption	新设合并	xīn shè hébìng
merger by consolidation	吸收合并	xīshōu hébìng
message	邮件	yóujiàn
mortgage	抵押权	dǐyā quán
multimodal transportation contract	多式联运合同	duō shì liányùn hétóng
National Enterprise Credit Information Publicity System (NECIPS)	企业信用信息公示系统	qǐyè xìnyòng xìnxī gōngshì xìtǒng
[*id.*, short]	国家企业信用信息公示系统	qǐyè dēngjì xìtǒng
[*id.*, short]	企信网	qǐ xìn wǎng
negotiorum gestio	无因管理	wú yīn guǎnlǐ
nine	九	jiǔ
notice	通知	tōngzhī
notice by registration	登记对抗主义	dēngjì duìkàng zhǔyì
nullity	无效	wúxiào
nullity, to rescind	撤销	chèxiāo
[numeral prefix]	第	dì
one	一	yī
open bidding	公开竞价	gōngkāi jìngjià
or	或者	huòzhě
ordinary mortgage	一般抵押权	yībān dǐyā quán

ownership	权属	quán shǔ
part, book	编	biān
partnership agreement	合伙协议	héhuǒ xiéyì
partnership contract	合伙合同	héhuǒ hétóng
partnership enterprise	合伙企业	héhuǒ qǐyè
part-time employment	非全日制用工	fēi quánrì zhì yònggōng
passenger transportation contract	客运合同	kèyùn hétóng
payment for breach of contract [s. liquidated damages]		
penetration, principle of (piercing the corporate veil)	透析原则	tòuxī yuánzé
piercing the corporate veil [s. penetration, principle of]		
pledge	质权	zhì quán) in
pledge of movable	动产质权	dòngchǎn zhì quán
possession	占有	zhànyǒu
prescription (extinctive-), limitation of action	诉讼时效	susòng shíxiào
profit	利益	lìyì
promoters	发起人	fāqǐ rén
property rights	物权	wù quán
property, ownership	所有权	suǒyǒuquán
provision of security, contract for the [s. guarantee contract]		

Provisions (of the Supreme People's Court)	规定	guīdìng
quasi-contracts	准合同	zhǔn hétóng
quasi-management without true mandate	不真正无因管理	bù zhēnzhèng wú yīn guǎnlǐ
real right of property	所有权	suǒyǒuquán
real rights	物权	wù quán
regulation(s)	条例	tiáolì
renminbi	人民币	rénmínbì
request of confirmation of right	请求确认权利	qǐngqiú quèrèn quánlì
requisition	征用	zhēngyòng
revision	修订	xiūdìng
revocation	解除	jiěchú
rules, provisions	则	zé
safekeeping contract, s. deposit	保管合同	bǎoguǎn hétóng
sale contract, purchase and sale contract	买卖合同	mǎimài hétóng
sale or assignment by auction	拍卖	pāimài
sale or assignment by tender	招标	zhāobiāo
seal	章	zhāng
section, title	节	jié
security in property	担保物权	dānbǎo wù quán
servitude	地役权	dì yì quán
seven	七	qī
shall	应当	yīngdāng
shareholders	股东	gǔdōng

shareholding company, stockholding company, corporation	股份有限公司	gǔfèn yǒuxiàn gōngsī
should	应该	yīnggāi
Sino-Foreign Contractual Joint-venture (CJV)	中外合作经营企业合同	zhōngwài hézuò jīngyíng qǐyè hétóng
Sino-Foreign Cooperative Joint-venture [s. Sino-Foreign Contractual Joint-venture (CJV)]		
Sino-Foreign Equity Joint-venture (EJV)	中外合资经营企业合同	zhōngwài hézī jīngyíng qǐyè hétóng
Sino-foreign joint-venture (JV)	中外经营企业	zhōngwài jīngyíng qǐyè
six	六	liù
specialized general partnership	特殊普通合伙	tèshū pǔtōng héhuǒ
State Administration for Industry & Commerce (SAIC)	国家工商行政管理总局	guójiā gōngshāng xíngzhèng guǎnlǐ zǒngjú
State Administration for Market Regulation (SAMR)	国家市场监督管理总局	guójiā shìchǎng jiāndū guǎnlǐ zǒngjú
State property	国家所有	guójiā suǒyǒu
State-Owned Enterprise (SOE)	国有企业	guóyǒu qǐyè
statute of limitation [s. limitation of action]		
stockholding company [s. shareholding company]		
subscriber	认股人	rèngǔrén
subsidiary	子公司	zǐ gōngsī

substitute performance deposit	存	cún
substitute performance guarantee	定金	dìngjīn
Supreme People's Court (SPC)	最高人民	zuìgāo rénmín
suretyship contract	保证合同	bǎozhèng hétóng
system	系统	xìtǒng
technical consulting contract	技术咨询合同	jìshù zīxún hétóng
technical services contract	技术服务合同	jìshù fúwù hétóng
technical training contract	技术培训合同	jìshù péixùn hétóng
technology cooperative development contract	合作开发合同	hézuò kāifā hétóng
technology development contract	技术开发合同	jìshù kāifā hétóng
technology entrusted (or commissioned) development contract	委托开发合同	wěituō kāifā hétóng
technology intermediation contract	技术中介合同	jìshù zhōngjiè hétóng
technology license contract	技术许可合同	jìshù xǔkě hétóng
technology transfer contract	技术转让合同	jìshù zhuǎnràng hétóng
ten	十	shí
tendering	招标	zhāobiāo
termination, to terminate	终止	zhōngzhǐ
three	三	sān

timely	及时	jíshí
title, s. section		
to cancel	取消	qǔxiāo
to know	知道	zhīdào
to resign	辞	cí
to resign (alternative expression)	辞去	cíqù
torts [s. liability for illicit acts]		
transportation contract	运输合同	yùnshū hétóng
true intent	真实意思	zhēnshí yìsi
two	二	èr
Uniform Registration Platform for Security Interests over Movable Assets and Rights	中国人民银行征信中心动产融资统一登记公示系统	zhōngguó rénmíng yínháng zhēng xìn zhōngxīn dòngchǎn róngzī tǒngyī dēngjì gōngshì xìtǒng
unjust enrichment	不当得利	bùdāng dé lì
unlawful or improper management without mandate	不适法无因管理	bùshì fǎ wú yīn guǎnlǐ
usufruct	用益物权	yòngyì wù quán
vacate, to; dispose of, to	提存	tícún
validity	效力	xiàolì
validity, valid	有效	yǒuxiào
variable interests entity [s. VIE]		
VIE (variable interests entity)	实际控制	shíjì kòngzhì
VIE (contractual control arrangement architecture)	协议控制架构	xiéyì kòngzhì jiàgòu

VIE (contractual control arrangement structure)	协议控制结构	xiéyì kòngzhì jiégòu
VIE (contractual control arrangement)	协议控制安排	xiéyì kòngzhì ānpái
VIE (contractual control)	协议控制	xiéyì kòngzhì
VIE (variable benefit or interest entity)	可变利益实体	kě biàn lìyì zhǔtǐ
VIE (variable rights or interest entity)	可变权益实体	kě biàn quányì shítǐ
VIE (VIE architecture)	VIE 架构	VIE jiàgòu
VIE (VIE structure)	VIE 结构	VIE jiégòu
visually	有形地	yǒuxíngdì
warehousing contract	仓储合同	cāngchú hétóng
Wholly Foreign-owned Enterprise (WFOE)	外资企业	wàizī qǐyè
within a reasonable period	合理期限内	hélǐ qíxiàn nèi
work	劳动	láodòng
work, contract for	承揽合同	chénglǎn hétóng
yuan	元	yuán

Table of Chinese Locutions in Pinyin

This table lists the translation of the Chinese locutions used in this book in simplified Chinese together with their transliteration in pinyin, sorted by alphabetical order in *pinyin*. For the sorting by their alphabetical order in English, see preceding table.

bā	八	eight
bànfǎ	办法	measures
bǎo lǐ hétóng	保理合同	factoring contract
bǎoguǎn hétóng	保管合同	deposit contract
bǎoguǎn hétóng	保管合同	safekeeping contract, s. deposit
bǎozhèng	保证	guaranty
bǎozhèng hétóng	保证合同	suretyship contract
biān	编	part, book
bù zhèngdàng	不正当	improper
bù zhēnzhèng wú yīn guǎnlǐ	不真正无因管理	quasi-management without true mandate
bùdāng dé lì	不当得利	unjust enrichment
bùmén xìnxī gòngxiǎng xìtǒng)	部门信息共享系统	Departmental Information Sharing System [short name]
bùshì fǎ wú yīn guǎnlǐ	不适法无因管理	unlawful or improper management without mandate
cāng chǔ rén	仓储人	depositary, warehouse operator
cāngchú hétóng	仓储合同	warehousing contract
chénglǎn hétóng	承揽合同	work, contract for
chénglǎn rén	承揽人	contractor
chèxiāo	撤销	nullity, to rescind
chū zhì rén	出质人	depositor (under a contract of deposit)

chūràng	出让	assignment
cí	辞	to resign
cíqù	辞去	to resign (alternative expression)
cún	存	substitute performance deposit
cún huò rén	存货人	depositor (under a contract of warehousing)
dàilǐ	代理	agency
dānbǎo	担保	assurance, guarantee or security
dānbǎo	担保	guarantee
dānbǎo hétóng	担保合同	guarantee contract, contract for the provision of security
dānbǎo wù	担保物	collateral
dānbǎo wù quán	担保物权	security in property
dēngjì duìkàng zhǔyì	登记对抗主义	notice by registration
dì	第	numeral prefix
dì yì quán	地役权	servitude
diàn	电	electric, electronic
diànzǐ	电子	electronic
diànzǐ shùjù	电子数据	electronic data
diànzǐ shùjù jiāohuàn	电子数据交换	data exchange
diànzǐ yóujiàn	电子邮件	e-mail
dìngjīn	定金	substitute performance guarantee
dǐyā quán	抵押权	mortgage
dòngchǎn zhì quán	动产质权	pledge of movable
dǒngshì	董事	director (member of the board of directors)

dǒngshì zhǎng	董事长	chairman (of the board of directors)
dǒngshìhuì	董事会	board of directors
duō shì liányùn hétóng	多式联运合同	multimodal transportation contract
èr	二	two
fǎ	法	law
fǎdìng dàibiǎo rén	法定代表人	legal representative
fāqǐ	发起	formation (of the shareholding company) by promotion
fāqǐ rén	发起人	promoters
fēi quánrì zhì yònggōng	非全日制用工	part-time employment
fēnzhī	分支	branch
fēnzhī jīgòu	分支机构	branch office
fù	副	deputy
fù jīnglǐ	副经理	deputy general manager
gōngkāi jìngjià	公开竞价	open bidding
gōngshāng bǎoxiǎn	工伤保险	insurance for occupational or work-related diseases
gōngsī	公司	company
gōngsī fù jīnglǐ	公司副经理	company deputy manager
gōngsī hébìng	公司合并	company merger
gōngsī jīnglǐ	公司经理	general manager
gǔdōng	股东	shareholders
gǔfèn gōngsī	股份公司	Corp.
gǔfèn yǒuxiàn gōngsī	股份有限公司	shareholding company, stockholding company, corporation
guīdìng	规定	provisions (of the Supreme People's Court)

guójiā gōngshāng xíngzhèng guǎnlǐ zǒngjú	国家工商行政管理总局	State Administration for Industry & Commerce (SAIC)
guójiā shìchǎng jiāndū guǎnlǐ zǒngjú	国家市场监督管理总局	State Administration for Market Regulation (SAMR)
guójiā suǒyǒu	国家所有	State property
guóyǒu qǐyè	国有企业	State-Owned Enterprise (SOE)
hébìng	合并	merger
héhuǒ	合同	contract, agreement
héhuǒ hétóng	合伙合同	partnership contract
héhuǒ qǐyè	合伙企业	partnership enterprise
héhuǒ xiéyì	合伙协议	partnership agreement
hélǐ qíxiàn nèi	合理期限内	within a reasonable period
hétóng	合同	contract
hézuò kāifā hétóng	合作开发合同	technology cooperative development contract
hōjin	法人	legal person
huàbō	划拨	allocation
huì	会	board
huòyùn hétóng	货运合同	freight transportation contract
huòzhě	或者	or
jiànshè gōngchéng hétóng	建设工程合同	construction project contract
jiànshè yòngdì shǐyòng quán	建设用地使用权	construction usufruct
jiànshè yòngdì shǐyòng quán	违约责任	construction usufruct
jiànzhú gōngchéng	建筑工程	building and construction engineering (JG)

jiànzhú hángyè biāozhǔn	建筑行业标准	construction industry standards
jiāohuàn	交换	exchange
jīběn	基本	general, basic
jīběn guīdìng	基本规定	basic provisions
jié	节	section, title
jiěchú	解除	revocation
jièkuǎn hétóng	借款合同	loan contract
jiěsàn	解散	dissolution, to dissolve
jiěshì	解释	interpretation (of the Supreme People's Court)
jǐn dào gāodù zhùyì yìwù	尽到高度注意义务	high duty (or degree) of care
jīnglǐ	经理	manager
jīngyíng qǐyè	经营企业	joint-venture
jìnxíng yànshōu	进行验收	acceptance inspection
jíshí	及时	timely
jìshù fúwù hétóng	技术服务合同	technical services contract
jìshù kāifā hétóng	技术开发合同	technology development contract
jìshù péixùn hétóng	技术培训合同	technical training contract
jìshù xǔkě hétóng	技术许可合同	technology license contract
jìshù zhōngjiè hétóng	技术中介合同	technology intermediation contract
jìshù zhuǎnràng hétóng	技术转让合同	technology transfer contract
jìshù zīxún hétóng	技术咨询合同	technical consulting contract
jítǐ hétóng	集体合同	collective (labor) contract
jítǐ suǒyǒu	集体所有	collective property

jiǔ	九	nine
kě biàn lìyì zhǔtǐ	可变利益实体	VIE (variable benefit or interest entity)
kě biàn quányì shítǐ	可变权益实体	VIE (variable rights or interest entity)
kěnéng	可能	may [verb]
kèyùn hétóng	客运合同	passenger transportation contract
kuàidì	快递	express logistic-, delivery- or courier services
láodòng	劳动	work
láodòng hétóng	劳动合同	employment contract
láowù pàiqiǎn	劳务派遣	labor dispatch
liù	六	six
liúzhì quán	留置权	lien
lìyì	利益	profit
mǎimài hétóng	买卖合同	sale contract, purchase and sale contract
mínfǎ diǎn	民法典	Civil Code
mínshì zérèn	民事责任	civil liability
mùjí	募集	formation (of the shareholding company) by flotation or by fundraising
nányǐ	难以	difficult
pāimài	拍卖	auctioning
pāimài	拍卖	sale or assignment by auction
pǔtōng héhuǒ	普通合伙	general partnership
qī	七	seven
qǐngqiú quèrèn quánlì	请求确认权利	request of confirmation of right

qīngsuàn	清算	liquidation
qīnquán zérèn	侵权责任	liability for illicit act ("torts")
qǐyè	企业	enterprise
qǐyè dēngjì xìtǒng	企业登记系统	Enterprise Registration System (ERS)
qǐyè dēngjì xìtǒng	国家企业信用信息公示系统	National Enterprise Credit Information Publicity System (NECIPS) [short name]
qǐ xìn wǎng	企信网	National Enterprise Credit Information Publicity System (NECIPS) [short name]
qǐyè xìnyòng xìnxī gōngshì xìtǒng	企业信用信息公示系统	National Enterprise Credit Information Publicity System (NECIPS)
quán shǔ	权属	ownership
quán shǔ shū	权属书	certificate, title certificate, ownership certificate
quèqiè	确切	exact, precise, definite, sure, true, reliable
quèqiè zhèngjù	确切证据	concrete or conclusive evidence
qǔxiāo	取消	to cancel
rèngǔrén	认股人	subscriber
rénmínbì	人民币	renminbi
róngzī zūlìn hétóng	融资租赁合同	financial leasing contract
sān	三	three
shèhuì tuántǐ	社会团体	association
shí	十	ten
shìchǎng jiāndū guǎnlǐ jú	市场监督管理局	Administration for Market Regulation (AMR)

shíjì kòngzhì	实际控制	VIE
shòu zhì rén	受质人	depositary (under a contract of deposit)
shùjù	数据	data
shùjù diànwén	数据电文	electronic data message
shùjù diànwén	数据电文	Exchange or interchange message
sì	四	four
sǔnshī	损失	loss
suǒyǒuquán	所有权	property, ownership
suǒyǒuquán	所有权	real right of property
susòng shíxiào	诉讼时效	prescription (extinctive-), limitation of action
sùsòng shíxiào	诉讼时效	limitation of action
tèshū pǔtōng héhuǒ	特殊普通合伙	specialized general partnership
tiáojiàn	条件	condition(s)
tiáolì	条例	regulation(s)
tícún	提存	deposit, to
tícún	提存	vacate, to; dispose of, to
tōng	通	general, common
tōngzé	通则	general provisions
tōngzhī	通知	notice
tóubiāo	投标	bidding
tóusù gōngzuò jīzhì	投诉工作机制	complaint mechanism
tòuxī yuánzé	透析原则	principle of penetration (piercing the corporate veil)
VIE jiàgòu	VIE 架构	VIE (VIE architecture)
VIE jiégòu	VIE 结构	VIE (VIE structure)

wàiguó gōngsī	外国公司	foreign company
wàiguó qǐyè cháng zhù dàibiǎo jīgòu	外国企业常驻代表机构	foreign representative office, permanent (or resident) representative offices of foreign enterprise
wàiguó tóuzī xìnxī bào sòng xìtǒng	外国投资信息报送系统	Foreign Investment Information Reporting System
wàiguó tóuzī zhě	外国投资者	foreign investor
wàishāng tóuzī	外商投资	foreign investment
wàishāng tóuzī fúwù tǐxì	外商投资服务体系	foreign investment service system
wàishāng tóuzī qǐyè	外商投资企业	foreign-invested enterprise (FIE)
wàizī qǐyè	外资企业	Wholly Foreign-owned Enterprise (WFOE), foreign invested enterprise
wěituō hétóng	委托合同	mandate (contract)
wěituō kāifā hétóng	委托开发合同	technology entrusted (or commissioned) development contract
wéiyuē zérèn	违约责任	liability for breach of contract
wǔ	五	five
wù quán	物权	property rights
wù quán	物权	real rights
wú yīn guǎnlǐ	无因管理	*negotiorum gestio*
wúxiào	无效	nullity
xiàolì	效力	validity
xiéyì	协议	agreement
xiéyì kòngzhì	协议控制	VIE (contractual control)

xiéyì kòngzhì ānpái	协议控制安排	VIE (contractual control arrangement)
xiéyì kòngzhì jiàgòu	协议控制架构	VIE (contractual control arrangement architecture)
xiéyì kòngzhì jiégòu	协议控制结构	VIE (contractual control arrangement structure)
xīn shè hébìng	新设合并	merger by absorption
xíng jì hétóng	行纪合同	brokerage contract
xīshōu hébìng	吸收合并	merger by consolidation
xìtǒng	系统	system
xiūdìng	修订	revision
xiūzhèng	修正	amendment
yī	一	one
yībān	一般	general, basic (alternative expression)
yībān dǐyā quán	一般抵押权	ordinary mortgage
yībān guīdìng	一般规定	general provisions (alternative expression)
yīngdāng	应当	shall
yīnggāi	应该	should
yíngyè zhízhào	营业执照	business license
yòngrén dānwèi	用人单位	employer, employing unit
yòngyì wù quán	用益物权	usufruct
yóujiàn	邮件	message
yǒuxiàn gōngsī	有限公司	Ltd.
yǒuxiàn héhuǒ	有限合伙	limited liability partnership
yǒuxiàn zérèn gōngsī	有限责任公司	limited liability company
yǒuxiào	有效	validity, valid

yǒuxíngdì	有形地	visually
yuán	元	yuan
yùnshū hétóng	运输合同	transportation contract
yùqī lìyì sǔnshī	预期利益损失	loss of profit
zé	则	rules, provisions
zèngyǔ hétóng	赠与合同	donation, contract for gift
zérèn	责任	infringement
zhāng	章	chapter
zhāng	章	seal
zhànyǒu	占有	possession
zhāobiāo	招标	sale or assignment by tender
zhāobiāo	招标	tendering
zhèngjù	证据	evidence
zhēngshōu	征收	expropriation
zhèngwù bùmén xìnxī gòngxiǎng xìtǒng	政务部门信息共享系统	Departmental Information Sharing System
zhèngwù shùjù gòngxiǎng	政务数据共享	Government Data Sharing
zhēngyòng	征用	requisition
zhēnshí yìsi	真实意思	true intent
zhì quán	质权	pledge
zhīdào	知道	to know
zhīfù wéiyuē jīn	支付违约金	liquidated damages, payment for breach of contract
zhìliàng bǎozhèng	质量保证	assurance (quality-)
zhōngguó rénmíng yínháng zhēng xìn zhōngxīn dòngchǎn róngzī tǒngyī dēngjì gōngshì xìtǒng	中国人民银行征信中心动产融资统一登记公示系统	Uniform Registration Platform for Security Interests over Movable Assets and Rights

zhōnghuá quánguó zǒng gōnghuì)	中华全国总工会	All-China Federation of Trade Unions (ACFTU)
zhōngjiè hétóng	中介合同	intermediation contract
zhōngwài hézī jīngyíng qǐyè hétóng	中外合资经营企业合同	Sino-Foreign Equity Joint-venture (EJV)
zhōngwài hézuò jīngyíng qǐyè hétóng	中外合作经营企业合同	Sino-Foreign Contractual Joint-venture (CJV)
zhōngwài jīngyíng qǐyè	中外经营企业	Sino-foreign joint-venture (JV)
zhōngzhǐ	终止	termination, to terminate
zhǔn hétóng	准合同	quasi-contracts
zǐ gōngsī	子公司	subsidiary
zǒng	总	general, common (alternative expression)
zǒng chéngbāo	总承包	general contracting
zǒng jīnglǐ	总经理	general manager (alternative expression)
zǒngzé	总则	general provisions (alternative expression)
zuìgāo é dǐyā quán	最高额抵押权	maximum mortgage
zuìgāo rénmín	最高人民	Supreme People's Court (SPC)
zuìgāo rénmín fǎyuàn jiěshì	最高人民法院解释	judicial interpretation(s) of the Supreme People's Court
zūlìn hétóng	租赁合同	lease contract

Table of Latin Locutions

This table lists the Latin locutions used in this book, sorted by alphabetical order in Latin.

a contrario	on the contrary
a fortiori	all the more
a posteriori	subsequently
ab initio	from the outset
actio quanti minoris	price reduction claim (of the goods sold under the contract of sale and the warranty for defects)
actio redhibitoria	revocation claim (of the contract of sale under the warranty for defects)
ad	about
ad hoc	specific
ad minima	at least
aliud	other thing
bona fide	good faith
causa finita	cause having ceased to exist
causa non secuta	cause having not occurred
caveat	warning
cf. (*confer*)	compare
clausula rebus sic stantibus	change of circumstances doctrine
corpus	body
corpus iuris	body of laws
culpa in eligendo et instruendo	fault in selecting and instructing
cura in eligendo, instruendo et custodiendo	fault in selecting, instructing and supervising
damnum emergens	effective damage
de jure	by law

dies a quo	start day (for computing time limitations)
essentialiae	essential elements (of a contract)
etc. (etcaetera)	and so one and so forth
exceptio non adimpleti contractus	performance exemption
falsus procurator	agent or representative without power
falsus procurator	agent (representative) without power
forum	judiciary competence
fructus, fructi	fruit, fruits
fundum	land
ibid.	the same (reference)
id.	the same (as above)
in fine	at the end
intuitu personae	strictly personal
lato sensu	in the wide sense
lato sensu	in the wide sense
leges speciales	special laws
lex generalis	general law
lex specialis	special law
lex specialis derogat legi generali	special laws prevail over general ones
locus rei sitae	location of an immovable
lucrum cessans	loss of profit
mala fide	bad faith
modus procedendi	process
mutatis mutandis	once the necessary changes have been made
negotiorum gestio	management of another's affairs without a mandate
numerus clausus	close-ended list

pacta sunt servanda	treaties are binding
per annum	yearly
per se	as such
prima facie	on its face
primus inter pares	first among peers
pro rata	in proportion of, proportionally to
proprietas	property, ownership
proprio motu	by its own motion
quantum	amount (of compensation)
qui tacet consentire videtur	who keeps silent consents
quorum	minimum threshold of participants
ratione loci	local (competence)
ratione materiae	material (competence)
rebus sic stantibus	as things then stood
res	thing
sic	as is
sine causa	without a cause
status quo ante	original state
stricto sensu	in the narrow or strict sense
traditio	transfer of property by delivery
verbatim	literally

Table of Statutes

I. Chinese Law

This table lists the Chinese statutes mentioned in this book; it has no pretense to be comprehensive. Statutes are first mentioned by their name in English[1]; then by their official name in Chinese followed by their transliteration in pinyin. They are listed under the chapter in which they are mentioned, and subjectively sorted by relevance, then alphabetically by keywords. Keywords are signaled in bold print. Status on 31 December 2025, unless mentioned otherwise.

A. Foreign Investment Law

Foreign Investment Law of the People's Republic of China 中华人民共和国外商投资法 zhōnghuá rénmín gònghéguó wàishāng tóuzī fǎ, Order No. 26 of the President of the People's Republic of China, issued by the National People's Congress on 15 March 2019 effective 1 January 2020.

Special Administrative Measures (**Negative List**) for the Access of Foreign Investment (2024) 外商投资准入特别管理措施 (负面清单) (2024 年版) wàishāng tóuzī zhǔn rù tèbié guǎnlǐ cuòshī (fùmiàn qīngdān) (2024 niánbǎn), Order No. 23 issued by the National Development & Reform Commission and the Ministry of Commerce on 6 September 2024 effective 1 November 2024.

Notice on Establishing a **Security Review** System for Foreign Investors' Mergers and Acquisitions of Domestic Enterprises 国务院办公厅关于建立外国投资者并购境内企业安全审查制度的通知(国办发(2011)6 号) guówùyuàn bàngōng tīng guānyú jiànlì wàiguó tóuzī zhě bìnggòu jìngnèi qǐyè ānquán shěnchá zhìdù de tōngzhī (guó bàn fā (2011) 6 hào), Circular No. 6 (2011) issued by the General Office of the State Council on 3 February 2011 effective 5 March 2011.

Interim Provisions on the **Takeover of Domestic Enterprises by Foreign Investors** (2006 Revision) 关于外国投资者并购境内企业的规定(2006 修订) guānyú wàiguó tóuzī zhě bìnggòu jìngnèi qǐyè de guīdìng (2006 xiūdìng), issued by the Ministry of Commerce State-owned Asset Supervision & Administration Commission of the State Council, the State Taxation Administration, the State Administration for Industry & Commerce (dissolved), the China

[1] Chinese statutes' English names are not official; they may not literally reflect their official Chinese name and may vary from one translation to the other. Whenever so, they have been subjectively selected by the author.

Securities Regulatory Commission and the State Administration of Foreign Exchange on 8 August 2006 effective 8 September 2006, revised by the Decision of the Ministry of Commerce on Amending the Provisions on the Merger or Acquisition of Domestic Enterprises by Foreign Investors issued on 22 June 2009 effective 22 June 2009.

Anti-monopoly Law of the People's Republic of China (2022 Amendment) 中华人民共和国反垄断法(2022 修正) zhōnghuá rénmín gònghéguó fǎn lǒngduàn fǎ (2022 xiūzhèng), Order No. 116 of the President of the People's Republic of China issued by the Standing Committee of the National People's Congress on 24 June 2022 effective 1 August 2022.

Regulation on the Administration of **Commercial Franchises** 商业特许经营管理条例 shāngyè tèxǔ jīngyíng guǎnlǐ tiáolì, Order of the State Council No. 485 issued by the State Council on 6 February 2007 effective 1 May 2007.

Regulation on the Administration of **Foreign Law Firms'** Representative Offices in China (2024 Revision) 外国律师事务所驻华代表机构管理条例(2024 修订) wàiguó lǜshī shìwù suǒ zhù huá dàibiǎo jīgòu guǎnlǐ tiáolì (2024 xiūdìng), Order No. 797 of the State Council, issued by the State Council on 6 December 2024 effective 20 February 2025.

Private Sector Promotion Law of the People's Republic of China 中华人民共和国民营经济促进法 zhōnghuá rénmín gònghéguó mínyíng jīngjì cùjìn fǎ, Order of the President of the People's Republic of China No. 46, issued by the Standing Committee of the National People's Congress on 30 April 2025 effective 20 May 2025.

B. Civil Law

Constitution of the People's Republic of China (2018 Amendment) 中华人民共和国宪法(2018 修正) zhōnghuá rénmín gònghéguó xiànfǎ (2018 xiūzhèng), Announcement No. 1 of the National People's Congress of the People's Republic of China issued by the National People's Congress on 3 November 2018 effective immediately.

Civil Code of the People's Republic of China 中华人民共和国民法典 zhōnghuá rénmín gònghéguó mínfǎ diǎn, Order No. 45 of the President of the People's Republic of China, issued by the National People's Congress on 28 May 2020 effective 1 January 2021.

Civil Procedure Law of the People's Republic of China (2023 Amendment) 中华人民共和国民事诉讼法(2023 修正) zhōnghuá rénmín gònghéguó mínshì sùsòng fǎ (2023 xiūzhèng) issued by the Standing Committee of the

National People's Congress on 9 April 1991, last amended on 9 September 2023 and effective 1 January 2024.

Advertising Law of the People's Republic of China (2021 Amendment) 中华人民共和国广告法(2021 修正) zhōnghuá rénmín gònghéguó guǎnggào fǎ (2021 xiūzhèng), Order No. 49 of the President of the People's Republic of China, issued by the Standing Committee of the National People's Congress on 29 April 2021 effective immediately.

Anti-Unfair Competition Law of the People's Republic of China (2025 Revision) 中华人民共和国反不正当竞争法(2025 修订) zhōnghuá rénmín gònghéguó fǎn bú zhèngdàng jìngzhēng fǎ (2025 xiūdìng), Order No. 50 of the President of the People's Republic of China, issued by the Standing Committee of the National People's Congress on 27 June 2025 effective 15 October 2025.

Law of the People's Republic of China on the Protection of **Consumer Rights** and Interests (2013 Amendment) 中华人民共和国消费者权益保护法(2013 修正) zhōnghuá rénmín gònghéguó xiāofèi zhě quányì bǎohù fǎ, Order No. 7 of the President of the People's Republic of China, issued by the Standing Committee of the National People's Congress on 25 October 2013 and effective 15 March 2014.

Law on the Protection of **Consumer Rights** and Interests of the People's Republic of China (2013 Amendment) 中华人民共和国消费者权益保护法(2013 修正) zhōnghuá rénmín gònghéguó xiāofèi zhě quányì bǎohù fǎ (2013 xiūzhèng), Order No. 7 of the President of the People's Republic of China, issued by the Standing Committee of the National People's Congress on 25 October 2013 effective 15 March 2014.

Cybersecurity Law of the People's Republic of China (2025 Amendment) 中华人民共和国网络安全法(2025 修正) zhōnghuá rénmín gònghéguó wǎnluò ānquán fǎ (2025 xiūzhèng), Order No. 61 of the President of the People's Republic of China, issued by the Standing Committee of the National People's Congress on 28 October 2025 effective 1 January 2026.

Data Security Law of the People's Republic of China 中华人民共和国数据安全法 Zhōnghuá rénmín gònghéguó shùjù ānquán fǎ, Order No. 84 of the President of the People's Republic of China, issued by the Standing Committee of the National People's Congress on 10 June 2021 effective 1 September 2021.

Law of the People's Republic of China on the Administration of Activities of Overseas **Non-Governmental Organizations** within the Territory of China (2017 Amendment) 中华人民共和国境外非政府组织境内活动管理法(2017 修正) zhōnghuá rénmín gònghéguó jìngwài fēi zhèngfǔ zǔzhī jìngnèi huódòng guǎnlǐ fǎ (2017 xiūzhèng), Order No. 81 of the President of the People's

Republic of China, issued by the Standing Committee of the National People's Congress on 4 November 2017 effective 5 November 2017.

Personal Information Protection Law of the People's Republic of China 中华人民共和国个人信息保护法 zhōnghuá rénmín gònghéguó gèrén xìnxī bǎohù fǎ, Order No. 91 of the President of the People's Republic of China, issued by the Standing Committee of the National People's Congress on 20 August 2021 effective 1 November 2021.

Product Quality Law of the People's Republic of China (2018 Amendment) 中华人民共和国产品质量法(2018 修正) zhōnghuá rénmín gònghéguó chǎnpǐn zhí liáng fǎ (2018 xiūzhèng), Order No. 22 of the President of the People's Republic of China, issued by the Standing Committee of the National People's Congress on 29 December 2018 effective 29 December 2018.

Pricing Law of the People's Republic of China 中华人民共和国价格法 zhōnghuá rénmín gònghéguó jiàgé fǎ, Order No. 92 of the President of the People's Republic of China, issued by the Standing Committee of the National People's Congress on 29 December 1997 effective 1 May 1998.

C. Real Rights

Land Management Law of the People's Republic of China 中华人民共和国土地管理法 zhōnghuá rénmín gònghéguó tǔdì guǎnlǐ fǎ, Order No. 32 of the President of the People's Republic of China, issued by the National People's Congress Standing Committee on 26 August 2019 effective 1 January 2020.

Interim Regulation of the People's Republic of China Concerning the Assignment and Transfer of the Right to the Use of the **State-owned Land** in the Urban Areas (2020 Revision) 中华人民共和国城镇国有土地使用权出让和转让暂行条例(2020 修订) zhōnghuá rénmín gònghéguó chéngzhèn guóyǒu tǔdì shǐyòng quán chūràng hé zhuǎnràng zhànxíng tiáolì (2020 xiūdìng), Order No. 732 of the State Council of the People's Republic of China, issued on 29 November 2020 effective immediately.

D. Contract Law

1. In General

Civil Code, Third Book, Title One, General Rules, s. Civil Law.

Contract Law of the People's Republic of China 中华人民共和国合同法 zhōnghuá rénmín gònghéguó hétóng fǎ, Order No. 15 of the President of the

People's Republic of China, issued by the National People's Congress on 15 March 1999 effective as of 1 October 1999 [**repealed** by the Civil Code as of 1 January 2021].

Interpretation of the Supreme People's Court on Several Issues Concerning the Application of the **General Provisions of the Contract Law** of the Civil Code of the People's Republic of China (Fa Shi No. 13) 最高人民法院关于适用(中华人民共和国民法典)合同编通则若干问题的解释 (法释 13 号) zuìgāo rénmínfǎyuàn guānyú shìyòng (zhōnghuá rénmín gònghéguó mín fǎ diǎn) hé-tóng biān tōngzé ruògān wèntí de jiěshì (fǎ shì 13 hào), Interpretation No. 13 [2023] issued on 4 December 2023 effective 5 December 2023.
Interpretation of the Supreme People's Court on Several Issues concerning the Application of Law to the Calculation of **Interest on Debt** for the Period of Deferred Performance in the Enforcement Procedure 最高人民法院关于执行程序中计算迟延履行期间的债务利息适用法律若干问题的解释 zuìgāo rénmín fǎyuàn guānyú zhíxíng chéngxù zhòng jìsuàn chíyán lǚxíng qíjiān de zhàiwù lìxí shìyòng fǎlǜ ruògān wèntí de jiěshì, Interpretation No. 8 [2014] issued on 7 July 2014 effective 1 August 2014.

Official Reply of the Supreme People's Court Regarding the Basis of Calculation for the Interest on **Overdue Payments in a Foreign Currency** or Hong Kong, Macao, or Taiwan Currency 最高人民法院关于外币及港澳台货币逾期付款利息计算标准的批复 zuìgāo rénmín fǎyuàn guānyú wàibì jí gǎng'ào tái huòbì yúqí fùkuǎn lìxí jìsuàn biāozhǔn dì pīfù, Interpretation No. 2 [2025] issued on 12 February 2025 effective 13 February 2025.

2. *Special Contracts*

a. In General

Civil Code, Third Book, Title Two, Typical Contracts, s. Civil Law.

b. Mandate

Notice of the Supreme People's Court on Issuing the Provisions on **Case Guidance** 最高人民法院印发《关于案例指导工作的规定》的通知 zuìgāo rénmín fǎyuàn yìnfā "guānyú ànlì zhǐdǎo gōngzuò de guīdìng" de tōngzhī, Notice 51 [2010] issued on 26 November 2010 effective immediately.

c. Transportation

Civil Aviation Law of the People's Republic of China (2021 Amendment) 中华人民共和国民用航空法(2021 修正) zhōnghuá rénmín gònghéguó mínyòng hángkōng fǎ (2021 xiūzhèng), Order No. 56 of the President of the People's Republic of China, issued by the Standing Committee of the National People's Congress on 29 April 2021 effective immediately.

List of **Dangerous Goods** 危险货物品名表 wéixiǎn huò wùpǐn míngbiǎo (GB 12268-2025) issued by the State Administration for Market Regulation and the Standardization Administration of China effective 1 October 2025.

Classification and Codes of **Dangerous Goods** 危险货物分类和代码 wéixiǎn huòwù fēnlèi hé dàimǎ (GB 6944-2025) issued by the State Administration for Market Regulation and the Standardization Administration of China effective 1 October 2025.

Regulations of the People's Republic of China on **International Ocean Shipping** (2025 Revision) 中华人民共和国国际海运条例(2025 修订) zhōnghuá rénmín gònghéguó guójì hǎiyùn tiáolì (2025 xiūdìng), Order No. 817 of the State Council of the People's Republic of China, issued by the same on 28 September 2025 effective immediately.

Maritime Code of the People's Republic of China 中华人民共和国海商法 zhōnghuá rénmín gònghéguó hǎi shāngfǎ, Order No. 64 of the President Of the People's Republic of China, issued by the Standing Committee of the Seventh National People's Congress on 7 November 1992 effective 1 July 1993.

Railways Law of the People's Republic of China (2015 Amendment) 中华人民共和国铁路法(2015 修正) zhōnghuá rénmín gònghéguó tiělù fǎ (2015 xiūzhèng), Order No. 25 of the President of the People's Republic of China, issued by the Standing Committee of the National People's Congress Date on 24 April 2015 effective immediately.

Road Traffic Safety Law of the People's Republic of China (2021 Amendment) 中华人民共和国道路交通安全法(2021 修正) zhōnghuá rénmín gònghéguó dàolù jiāotōng ānquán fǎ (2021 xiūzhèng), Order No. 81 of the President Of the People's Republic of China, issued by the Standing Committee of the National People's Congress on 29 April 2021 effective immediately.

d. Construction

Construction Law of the People's Republic of China (2019 Amendment) 中华人民共和国建筑法(2019 修正) zhōnghuá rénmín gònghéguó jiànzhú fǎ (2019 xiūzhèng), Order No. 29 of the President of the People's Republic of

China, issued by the Standing Committee of the National People's Congress on 23 April 2019 effective immediately.

Interpretation (I) by the Supreme People's Court on Issues Concerning the Application of the Law in the Trial of Cases Involving Disputes over **Construction Contracts** for Construction Projects 最高人民法院关于审理建设工程施工合同纠纷案件适用法律问题的解释(一) zuìgāo rénmín fǎyuàn guānyú shěnlǐ jiànshè gōngchéng shīgōng hétóng jiūfēn ànjiàn shìyòng fǎlǜ wèntí de jiěshì (yī), Interpretation No. 25 [2020] issued on 29 December 2020 effective 1 January 2021.

Tendering and Bidding Law of the People's Republic of China (2017 Amendment) 中华人民共和国招标投标法(2017 修正) zhōnghuá rénmín gònghéguó zhāobiāo tóubiāo fǎ (2017 xiūzhèng), Order No. 86 of the President of the People's Republic of China, issued by the Standing Committee of the National People's Congress on 27 December 2017 effective 28 December 2017.

e. Technology

Foreign Trade Law of the People's Republic of China (2022 Amendment) 中华人民共和国对外贸易法(2022 修正) zhōnghuá rénmín gònghéguó duìwài màoyì fǎ (2022 xiūzhèng), Order No. 58 of the President of the People's Republic of China, issued by the Standing Committee of the National People's Congress on 30 December 2022 effective immediately.

Regulation of the People's Republic of China on the Administration of **Import and Export of Technologies** (2020 Revision) 中华人民共和国技术进出口管理条例(2020 修订) zhōnghuá rénmín gònghéguó jìshù jìn chūkǒu guǎnlǐ tiáolì (2020 xiūdìng), Order No. 732 of the State Council, issued by the same on 29 November 2020 effective immediately.

Anti-monopoly Law, s. Foreign Investment Law.

Copyright Law of the People's Republic of China (2020 Amendment) 中华人民共和国著作权法(2020 修正) zhōnghuá rénmín gònghéguó zhùzuòquán fǎ (2020 xiūzhèng), Order No. 62 of the President of the People's Republic of China, issued by the Standing Committee of the National People's Congress on 11 November 2020 effective 1 June 2021.

Regulation of the People's Republic of China on the Protection of **Integrated Circuits** Layout Design 中华人民共和国集成电路布图设计保护条例 zhōnghuá rénmín gònghéguó jíchéng diànlù bù tú shèjì bǎohù tiáolì, Order No. 300 of the State Council, issued by the same on 2 April 2001 effective 1 October 2001.

Regulation of the People's Republic of China on the Protection of **New Plant Varieties** (2025 Revision) 中华人民共和国植物新品种保护条例(2025 修订) zhōnghuá rénmín gònghéguó zhíwù xīn pǐnzhǒng bǎohù tiáolì (2025 xiūdìng), Order No. 807 of the State Council, issued by the same on 29 April 2025 effective 1 June 2025.

Patent Law of the People's Republic of China (2020 Amendment) 中华人民共和国专利法(2020 修正) zhōnghuá rénmín gònghéguó zhuānlì fǎ (2020 xiūzhèng), Order No. 55 of the President of the People's Republic of China, issued by the Standing Committee of the National People's Congress on 7 October 2020 effective 1 June 2021.

Seed Law of the People's Republic of China (2021 Amendment) 中华人民共和国种子法(2021 修正) zhōnghuá rénmín gònghéguó zhǒngzǐ fǎ (2021 xiūzhèng), Order No. 105 of the President of the People's Republic of China, issued by the Standing Committee of the National People's Congress on 24 December 2021 effective 1 March 2022.

Trademark Law of the People's Republic of China (2019 Amendment) 中华人民共和国商标法(2019 修正) zhōnghuá rénmín gònghéguó shāngbiāo fǎ (2019 xiūzhèng), Order No. 29 of the President of the People's Republic of China, issued by the Standing Committee of the National People's Congress on 23 April 2019 effective 1 November 2019.

Vocational Education Law of the People's Republic of China (2022 Revision) 中华人民共和国职业教育法(2022 修订) zhōnghuá rénmín gònghéguó zhíyè jiàoyù fǎ (2022 xiūdìng), Order No. 112 of the President of the People's Republic of China, issued by the Standing Committee of the National People's Congress on 20 April 2022 effective as of 1 May 2022.

E. Deposit

Law on **Commercial Banks** of the People's Republic of China on (2015 Amendment) 中华人民共和国商业银行法(2015 修正) zhōnghuá rénmín gònghéguó shāngyè yínháng fǎ (2015 xiūzhèng), Order No. 34 of the President of the People's Republic of China, issued by the Standing Committee of the National People's Congress on 29 August 2015 effective 1 October 2015.

F. Employment

Labor Contract Law of the People's Republic of China (2012 Amendment) 中华人民共和国劳动合同法(2012 修正) zhōnghuá rénmín gònghéguó láodòng hétóng fǎ (2012 xiūzhèng), Order No. 73 of the President of the People's Republic of China, issued by the Standing Committee of the National People's Congress on 28 December 2012 effective 1 July 2013.

Labor Law of the People's Republic of China (2018 Amendment) 中华人民共和国劳动法(2018 修正) zhōnghuá rénmín gònghéguó láodòng fǎ (2018 xiūzhèng), Order No. 24 of the President of the People's Republic of China, issued by the Standing Committee of the National People's Congress on 29 December 2018 effective immediately.

Regulation on **Public Holidays** for National Annual Festivals and Memorial Days (2024 Revision) 全国年节及纪念日放假办法(2024 修订) quánguó nián jié jí jìniàn rì fàngjià bànfǎ (2024 xiūdìng, Order No. 795 of the State Council, of the People's Republic of China, issued by the same on 10 November 2024 effective 1 January 2025.

Trade Union Law of the People's Republic of China (2021 Amendment) 中华人民共和国工会法(2021 修正) zhōnghuá rénmín gònghéguó gōnghuì fǎ (2021 xiūzhèng), Order No. 107 of the President of the People's Republic of China issued by the Standing Committee of the National People's Congress on 24 December 2021 effective as of 1 January 2022.

Interpretation (I) by the Supreme People's Court of Issues Concerning the Application of Law in the **Trial of Labor Disputes** Cases 最高人民法院关于审理劳动争议案件适用法律问题的解释(一) zuìgāo rénmín fǎyuàn guānyú shěnlǐ láodòng zhēngyì ànjiàn shìyòng fǎlǜ wèntí de jiěshì (yī), Interpretation No. 26 [2020] issued on 29 December 2020 effective 1 January 2021 [**partially repealed or invalided** by Interpretation II below].

Interpretation (II) by the Supreme People's Court of Issues Concerning the Application of Law in the **Trial of Labor Disputes** Cases 最高人民法院关于审理劳动争议案件适用法律问题的解释(二) zuìgāo rénmín fǎyuàn guānyú shěnlǐ láodòng zhēngyì ànjiàn shìyòng fǎlǜ wèntí de jiěshì (èr), Interpretation No. 12 [2025] of the Supreme People's Court issued on 31 July 2025 effective 1 September 2025.

Regulation on **Work-Related Injury Insurance** (2010 Revision) 工伤保险条例(2010 修订) gōngshāng bǎoxiǎn tiáolì (2010 xiūdìng), Order No. 375 of the State Council, issued by the same on 20 December 2010 effective 1 January 2011.

G. Company Law

Company Law of the People's Republic of China (2023 Revision) 中华人民共和国公司法(2023 修订), Order No. 15 of the President of the People's Republic of China, issued by the Standing Committee of the National People's Congress on 29 December 2023 effective 1 July 2024.

Partnership Enterprise Law of the People's Republic of China (2006 Revision) 中华人民共和国合伙企业法(2006 修订) zhōnghuá rénmín gònghéguó héhuǒ qǐyè fǎ (2006 xiūdìng), Order No. 55 of the President of the People's Republic of China, issued by the Standing Committee of the National People's Congress on 27 August 2006 effective 1 June 2007.

Regulation on the Administration of Registration of Resident **Representative Offices** of Foreign Enterprises (2024 Revision) 外国企业常驻代表机构登记管理条例(2024 修订) wàiguó qǐyè cháng zhù dàibiǎo jīgòu dēngjì guǎnlǐ tiáolì (2024 xiūdìng), Order No. 777 of the State Council issued by the same on 10 March 2024 effective 1 May 2024.

Law on Chinese-Foreign **Contractual Joint-ventures** (2017 Amendment) 中华人民共和国中外合作经营企业法(2017 修正) zhōnghuá rénmín gònghéguó zhōngwài hézuò jīngyíng qǐyè fǎ (2017 xiūzhèng), Order No. 4 of the President of the People's Republic of China, issued by the Standing Committee of the National People's Congress on 4 November 2017 effective 5 November 2017 [**repealed** by the Foreign Investment Law of 15 March 2019 as of 1 January 2020; cited as "CJV Law"].

Detailed Rules for the Implementation of the Law of the People's Republic of China on Sino-Foreign **Contractual Joint-ventures** 中华人民共和国中外合作经营企业法实施细则 zhōnghuá rénmín gònghéguó zhōngwài hézuò jīngyíng qǐyè fǎ shíshī xìzé, issued by the Ministry of Foreign Trade & Economic Cooperation on 4 September 1995 effective 4 September 1995 [**repealed** by the Foreign Investment Law of 15 March 2019 as of 1 January 2020].

Law on Chinese-Foreign **Equity Joint-ventures** (2016 Amendment) 中华人民共和国中外合资经营企业法(2016 修正) zhōnghuá rénmín gònghéguó zhōngwài hézī jīngyíng qǐyè fǎ (2016 xiūzhèng), Order No. 51 of the President of the People's Republic of China, issued by the Standing Committee of the National People's Congress on 3 September 2016 effective 1 October 2016 [**repealed** by the Foreign Investment Law of 15 March 2019 as of 1 January 2020; cited as "EJV Law"].

Accounting Law of the People's Republic of China (2017 Amendment) 中华人民共和国会计法(2017 修正) zhōnghuá rénmín gònghéguó kuàijì fǎ (2017 xiūzhèng) Order No. 81 of the President of the People's Republic of China, issued by the Standing Committee of the National People's Congress on 4 November 2017 effective 5 November 2017.

Provisions of the Supreme People's Court on Several Issues concerning the **Application of the Company Law** of the People's Republic of China (I) (2014 Amendment) 最高人民法院关于适用《中华人民共和国公司法》若干问题的规定 (一) (2014 修正) zuìgāo rénmín fǎyuàn guānyú shìyòng "zhōnghuá rénmín gònghéguó gōngsī fǎ" ruògān wèntí de guīdìng (yī) (2014 xiūzhèng), Interpretation No. 2 [2014] issued on 20 February 2014 effective 1 March 2014 ["Interpretation I"].

Provisions of the Supreme People's Court on Several Issues concerning the **Application of the Company Law** of the People's Republic of China (II) (2020 Amendment) 最高人民法院关于适用《中华人民共和国公司法》若干问题的规定（二）(2020 修正) zuìgāo rénmín fǎyuàn guānyú shìyòng "zhōnghuá rénmín gònghéguó gōngsī fǎ" ruògān wèntí de guīdìng (èr) (2020 xiūzhèng), Interpretation No. 18 [2020] issued on 29 December 2020 effective 1 January 2021 ["Interpretation II"].

Provisions of the Supreme People's Court on Several Issues concerning the **Application of the Company Law** of the People's Republic of China (III) (2020 Amendment) 最高人民法院关于适用《中华人民共和国公司法》若干问题的规定（三）(2020 修正) zuìgāo rénmín fǎyuàn guānyú shìyòng "zhōnghuá rénmín gònghéguó gōngsī fǎ" ruògān wèntí de guīdìng (sān) (2020 xiūzhèng), Interpretation No. 18 [2020] issued on 29 December 2020 effective 1 January 2021 ["Interpretation III"].

Provisions of the Supreme People's Court on Several Issues concerning the **Application of the Company Law** of the People's Republic of China (IV) Revised 最高人民法院关于适用《中华人民共和国公司法》若干问题的规定(四) zuìgāo rénmín fǎyuàn guānyú shìyòng "zhōnghuá rénmín gònghéguó gōngsī fǎ" ruògān wèntí de guīdìng (sì), Interpretation No. 16 [2017] issued on 25 August 2017 effective 1 September 2017 ["Interpretation IV[2]"].

Provisions of the Supreme People's Court on Several Issues Concerning the **Application of the Company Law** of the People's Republic of China (V) Revised 最高人民法院关于适用《中华人民共和国公司法》若干问题的规定(五) zuìgāo rénmín fǎyuàn guānyú shìyòng "zhōnghuá rénmín gònghéguó gōngsī fǎ" ruògān wèntí de guīdìng (wǔ), Interpretation No. 7 [2019] issued on 28 April 2019 effective 29 April 2019 ["Interpretation V[3]"].

---

2 The Roman numbering of these Provisions is consistent with the applicable official naming conventions of Chinese law; it may not correspond to their chronological order.

3 S. preceding note.

Assets Appraisal Law of the People's Republic of China, 中华人民共和国资产评估法, zhōnghuá rénmín gònghéguó zīchǎn pínggū fǎ, Order No. 46 of the President of the People's Republic of China issued by the Standing Committee of the National People's Congress on 2 February 2016 effective 1 December 2016.

Law of the People's Republic of China on **Certified Public Accountants** (2014 Amendment) 中华人民共和国注册会计师法(2014 修正) zhōnghuá rénmín gònghéguó zhùcè kuàijìshī fǎ (2014 xiūzhèng), Order No. 14 of the President of the People's Republic of China, issued by the Standing Committee of the National People's Congress on 31 August 2014 effective immediately.

Code of **Corporate Governance for Listed Companies** (2018 Revision) 上市公司治理准则(2018 修订) shàngshì gōngsī zhìlǐ zhǔnzé (2018 xiūdìng), Announcement No. 29 [2018] issued by the China Securities Regulatory Commission on 30 September 2018 effective immediately.

Notice on Matters Related to Macro-Prudential Management of **Cross-Border Financing** 中国人民银行关于全口径跨境融资宏观审慎管理有关事宜的通知 zhōngguó rénmíng yínháng guānyú quán kǒujìng kuà jìng róngzī hóngguān shěnshèn guǎnlǐ yǒuguān shìyí de tōngzhī, Notice No. 9 [2017] issued by the People's Bank of China on 11 January 2017 effective immediately.

Notice on Adjusting the Macro-Prudential Adjustment Parameter for **Cross-border Financing** of Enterprises 中国人民银行、国家外汇管理局关于调整企业跨境融资宏观审慎调节参数的通知 zhōngguó rénmíng yínháng, guójiā wàihuì guǎnlǐ jú guānyú tiáozhěng qǐyè kuà jìng róngzī hóngguān shěnshèn tiáojié cān shǔ de tōngzhī, Notice No. 5 [2021] issued by the People's Bank of China and the State Administration of Foreign Exchange on 7 January 2021 effective immediately.

Enterprise Bankruptcy Law of the People's Republic of China 中华人民共和国企业破产法 zhōnghuá rénmín gònghéguó qǐyè pòchǎn fǎ, issued by the Standing Committee of the National People's Congress of 27 August 2006 effective 1 June 2007.

Measures for the Administration of **Information Disclosure by Listed Companies** (2025 Revision) 上市公司信息披露管理办法(2025 修订) shàngshì gōngsī xìnxī pīlù guǎnlǐ bànfǎ (2025 xiūdìng), Order No. 226 issued by the China Securities Regulatory Commission on 26 March 2025 effective 1 July 2025.

Several Provisions of the Supreme People's Court on Issuing the Information on the **List of Dishonest Judgment Debtors** (2017Amendment) 最高人民法院关于公布失信被执行人名单信息的若干规定(2017 修正) zuìgāo rénmín fǎyuàn guānyú gōngbù shīxìn bèi zhíxíng rén míngdān xìnxī de ruògān guīdìng

(2017 xiūzhèng), Interpretation No. 7 [2017] issued on 28 February 2017 effective 1 May 2017.

Law of the People's Republic of China on the Administration of Activities of **Overseas Non-Governmental Organizations** within the Territory of China (2017 Amendment) 中华人民共和国境外非政府组织境内活动管理法(2017 修正) zhōnghuá rénmín gònghéguó jìngwài fēi zhèngfǔ zǔzhī jìngnèi huódòng guǎnlǐ fǎ (2017 xiūzhèng) [A.K.A. "Foreign NGOs Law"], Order No. 44 of the President of the People's Republic of China, issued by the Standing Committee of the National People's Congress on 4 April 2017 effective 5 November 2017.

Notice on Matters Related to **Macro-Prudential Management** of Cross-Border Financing 中国人民银行关于全口径跨境融资宏观审慎管理有关事宜的通知(银发(2017)9 号) zhōngguó rénmíng yínháng guānyú quán kǒujìng kuà jìng róngzī hóngguān shěnshèn guǎnlǐ yǒuguān shìyí de tōngzhī (yínfà (2017) 9 hào), issued of the People's Bank of China on 11 January 2017 effective 12 January 2017.

Provisional Regulations on the **Proportion of Registered Capital to Total Amount of Investment** of Sino-Foreign Joint-ventures 关于中外合资经营企业注册资本与投资总额比例的暂行规定 guānyú zhōngwài hézī jīngyíng qǐyè zhùcè zīběn yǔ tóuzī zǒng'é bǐlì de zhàn háng guīdìng, Provisional Regulations No. 38 [1987] issued by the State Administration for Industry & Commerce (dissolved) on 1 March 1987 effective immediately.

Provisional Regulations on the Proportion of **Registered Capital** to Total Investment of Sino-Foreign Joint-ventures 国家工商行政管理局关于中外合资经营企业注册资本与投资总额比例的暂行规定 (工商企字(1987)第 38 号) guójiā gōngshāng háng zhèng guǎnlǐ jú guānyú zhōngwài hézī jīngyíng qǐyè zhùcè zīběn yǔ tóuzī zǒng'é bǐlì de zhàn háng guīdìng (gōngshāng qǐ zì (1987) dì 38 hào), issued by the Ministry of Commerce and the State Administration of Foreign Exchange on 17 February 1987 effective 1 March 1987.

Securities Law of the People's Republic of China (2019 Revision) 中华人民共和国证券法(2019 修订) zhōnghuá rénmín gònghéguó zhèngquàn fǎ (2019 xiūdìng, Order No. 37 of the President of the People's Republic of China, issued by the Standing Committee of the National People's Congress on 28 December 2019 effective 1 March 2020.

Securities **Investment Fund Law** of the People's Republic of China 中华人民共和国证券投资基金法 zhōnghuá rénmín gònghéguó zhèngquàn tóuzī jījīn fǎ issued by the Standing Committee of the National People's Congress on 24 April 2015 effective immediately.

Provisional Measures on Supervision and Administration of **Private Equity Investment Funds** 私募投资基金监督管理暂行办法 sīmù tóuzī jījīn jiāndū guǎnlǐ zhànxíng bànfǎ, Order No. 105 issued by the China Securities Regulatory Commission (CSRC) on 21 August 2014 effective immediately.

Regulation on Supervision and Administration of **Private Equity Investment Funds 私募投资基金监督管理条例** sīmù tóuzī jījīn jiāndū guǎnlǐ tiáolì, Decree No.762 issued by the State Council on 3 July 2023 effective 1 September 2023.

Announcement on the Promulgation of the Measures for Registration and Filing of **Private Equity Investment Funds 私募投资基金登记备案办法** sīmù tóuzī jījīn dēngjì bèi'àn bànfǎ (Zhong Ji Xie Fa [2023] No. 5) issued by the Asset Management Association of China (AMAC) on 24 February 2024 effective 1 May 2023.

Measures for the Administration of the **Takeover of Listed Companies** (2025 Amendment) 上市公司收购管理办法(2025 修正) shàngshì gōngsī shōugòu guǎnlǐ bànfǎ (2025 xiūzhèng), Order No. 227 issued by the China Securities Regulatory Commission on 27 March 2025 effective immediately.

Securities and Futures Laws Application Opinion No. 19, Opinion on the Application of Articles 13 and 14 of the Measures for the Administration of the **Takeover of Listed Companies** 《证券期货法律适用意见第 19 号——〈上市公司收购管理办法〉第十三条、第十四条的适用意见》 zhèngquàn qíhuò fǎlǜ shìyòng yìjiàn dì 19 hào – "shàngshì gōngsī shōugòu guǎnlǐ bànfǎ" dì shísān tiáo, dì shísì tiáo de shìyòng yìjiàn", Opinion No. 19 issued by the China Securities Regulatory Commission on 10 January 2025 effective immediately.

Interim Provisions on the **Takeover of Domestic Enterprises by Foreign Investors**, s. Foreign Investment Law.

Guidelines on the **Trustee Business** for Non-Financial Enterprise Debt Financing Instruments in the Interbank Bond Market (Trial) 银行间债券市场非金融企业债务融资工具受托管理人业务指引（试行） yínháng jiān zhàiquàn shìchǎng fēi jīnróng qǐyè zhàiwù róngzī gōngjù shòutuō guǎnlǐ rén yèwù zhǐyǐn (shìxíng) issued by the National Association of Financial Market Institutional Investors on 27 December 2019.

H. Private International Law

Law of the People's Republic of China on the **Choice of Law for Foreign-related Civil Relationships 中华人民共和国涉外民事关系法律适用法** zhōnghuá rénmín gònghéguó shèwài mínshì guānxì fǎlǜ shìyòng fǎ, Order No. 36 of the President of the People's Republic of China, issued by the

Standing Committee of the National People's Congress on 28 October 2010 effective 1 April 2011.

Provisions of the Supreme People's Court on Several Issues Concerning **Jurisdiction in Foreign-Related Civil and Commercial Cases** (Fa Shi [2022] No. 18) 最高人民法院关于涉外民商事案件管辖若干问题的规定法释 (2022) 18号 zuìgāo rénmín fǎyuàn guānyú shèwài mín shāngshì ànjiàn guǎnxiá ruògān wèntí de guīdìng fǎ shì (2022) 18 hào, Provisions No. 18 [2022] issued on 14 November 2022 effective 1 January 2023.

II. Swiss Law

This table lists the Swiss statutes mentioned in this book; it has no pretense to be comprehensive. Statutes are first mentioned by their name in English[4]; then by their official name in French and in German. They are subjectively sorted by relevance, then alphabetically by keywords. Keywords are signaled in bold print. Each statute is followed by its reference to the official federal collection of Swiss laws (RS). Status on 31 December 2025, unless mentioned otherwise.

Swiss Civil Code; Fr.: Code civil suisse (CC); Ger.: Schweizerisches Zivilgesetzbuch (ZGB) issued on 10 December 1907; status as of 1 January 2024; RS 210.

Federal Law on the Amendment of the Swiss Civil Code (Part Five: Obligations Law) [A.K.A. **Swiss Code of Obligations**]; Fr.: Loi fédérale complétant le Code civil suisse (Livre cinquième : Droit des obligations) [A.K.A. Code des obligations; CO]; Ger.: Bundesgesetz betreffend die Ergänzung des Schweizerischen Zivilgesetzbuches (Fünfter Teil: Obligationenrecht) [A.K.A. Obligationenrecht; OR] issued on 30 March 1911; status as of 1 January 2024; RS 220.

Swiss Code of **Civil Procedure**; Fr.: Code de procédure civile (CPC); Ger.: Schweizerische Zivilprozessordnung (ZPO) issued on 19 December 2008; status as of 1 January 2025; RS 272.

Swiss Criminal Code; Fr.: Code pénal suisse [CP]; Ger. Schweizerisches Strafgesetzbuch [StGB] issued on 21 December 1937; status as of 1 January 2026; RS 311.0.

---

4 Swiss statutes' English names are not official; they correspond to the semi-official translation found on Swisslex, whenever available (s. below note 88); if not, they have been freely translated by the author.

Swiss Code of **Criminal Procedure**; Fr.: Code de procédure pénale suisse (CPP); Ger.: Strafprozessordnung (Strafprozessordnung, StPO) issued on 5 October 2025; status as of 1 April 2025; RS 312.0.

Federal Law on **Debt Recovery and Bankruptcy**; Fr.: Loi sur la poursuite pour dettes et la faillite (LP); Ger.: Bundesgesetz über Schuldbetreibung und Konkurs (SchKG) issued on 11 April 1889; RS 281.1.

Federal Law on **Private International Law** [A.K.A. Federal Act on Private International Law (PILA)]; Fr.: Loi fédérale sur le droit international privé (LDIP) : Ger.: Bundesgesetz über das Internationale Privatrecht (IPRG) issued on 18 December 1987 effective 1 January 1989; status as of 1 January 2025; RS 291.

Ordinance on the **Register of Commerce**; Fr.: Ordonnance sur le registre du commerce (ORC); Ger.: Handelsregisterverordnung (HRegV) issued on 17 October 2007; status as of 1 January 2025; RS 221.411.

Federal Law on **Consumer Credit;** Fr.: Loi fédérale sur le crédit à la consommation (LCC); Ger.: Bundesgesetz über den Konsumkredit (KKG) issued on 23 March 2001; status as of 1 September 2023; RS 221.214.1.

Federal Law on Certification Services in the Field of Electronic Signatures and other Applications of Digital Certificates (**Electronic Signature Law**); Fr.: Loi fédérale sur les services de certification dans le domaine de la signature électronique et des autres applications des certificats numériques ((Loi sur la signature électronique, SCSE); Ger.: Bundesgesetz über Zertifizierungsdienste im Bereich der elektronischen Signatur und anderer Anwendungen digitaler Zertifikate (Bundesgesetz über die elektronische Signatur, ZertES) issued on 18 March 2016; status as of 1 January 2020; RS 943.03.

Federal Law on **Monetary Unit and Means of Payment**; Fr.: Loi fédérale sur l'unité monétaire et les moyens de paiement (LUMMP); Ger.: Bundesgesetz über die Währung und die Zahlungsmittel (WZG) issued on 22 December 1999; status as of 1 January 2020; RS 941.10.

III. International Law

This table lists international statutes mentioned in this book; it has no pretense to be comprehensive. Statutes are listed under the chapter in which they are mentioned, and subjectively sorted by relevance, then alphabetically by keywords. Keywords are signaled in bold print. Status on 31 December 2025.

A. Multilateral Treaties

1. Direct Foreign Investment

Convention on the Settlement of Investment Disputes Between States and Nationals of Other States made in Washington on 18 March 1965 (**ICSID Convention**); Fr.: Convention du 18 mars 1965 pour le règlement des différends relatifs aux investissements entre États et ressortissants d'autres États (**Convention du CIRDI**); Ger.: Übereinkommen zur Beilegung von Investitionsstreitigkeiten zwischen Staaten und Angehörigen anderer Staaten; signed by China on 9 February 1990 effective as of 6 February 1993; signed by Switzerland on 22 September 1967 effective as of 14 June 1968; RS 0.975.2.

The World Bank Group, Report to the Development Committee and Guidelines on the **Treatment of Foreign Direct Investment** *in*: Legal Framework for the Treatment of Foreign Investment, Vol. II [A.K.A. "1992 World Bank Report" and "1992 World Bank Guidelines"].

Financial Accounting Standards Board (FASB) Accounting Standards Codification (ASC), **Generally Accepted Accounting Principles (GAAP) standards**.

2. Sale

United Nations **Convention on Contracts for the International Sale of Goods** (Vienna, 1980) (CISG), adopted on 11 April 1980 and entered into force as of 1 January 1988.

UN Convention on the **Limitation Period in the International Sale of Goods** made in New York on 14 June 1974 effective 1 August 1988; Fr.: Convention sur la prescription en matière de vente internationale de Marchandises [**signed neither by China nor by Switzerland**].

CISG Advisory Council Opinion No. 4, Contracts for the **Sale of Goods to Be Manufactured or Produced and Mixed Contracts** (Article 3 CISG), issued on 24 October 2004.

CISG Advisory Council Opinion No. 16, **Exclusion of the CISG** under Article 6, issued on 30 May 2014.

3. *Transportation*

International Convention for the Unification of Certain Rules of Law relating to **Bills of Lading** made in Brussels on 25 August 1924 as amended by First Protocol of 23 February 1968 and Second Protocol of 21 December 1979; Fr.: Convention internationale pour l'unification de certaines règles en matière de connaissement; Ger.: Internationales Übereinkommen zur einheitlichen Feststellung einzelner Regeln über die Konnossemente; approved by the Swiss parliament on 17 March 1942 effective 28 November 1954; RS 0.747.354.11 [**carriage of goods by sea**; A.K.A. "Hague-Visby Rules"; **not signed by China**].

Convention for the Unification of Certain Rules Relating to International **Carriage by Air** made in Warsaw on 12 October 1929; Fr.: Convention pour l'unification de certaines règles relatives au transport aérien international; Ger.: Abkommen zur Vereinheitlichung von Regeln über die Beförderung im internationalen Luftverkehr; signed by the Republic of China 12 October 1929 effective as of 13 February 1933 and acceded by the People's Republic of China on 20 July 1958 effective as of 18 October 1958; approved by the Swiss parliament on 22 March 1934 effective 7 August 1934; RS 0.748.410.

Convention for the Unification of Certain Rules for International **Carriage by Air** made in Montreal on 28 May 1999; Fr.: Convention pour l'unification de certaines règles relatives au transport aérien international; Ger.: Übereinkommen zur Vereinheitlichung bestimmter Vorschriften über die Beförderung im internationalen Luftverkehr; signed by China on 28 May 1999 effective 31 July 2005; approved by the Swiss parliament on 17 December 2004 effective 5 September 2005; RS 0.748.411.

Convention Concerning International **Carriage by Rail** (COTIF) of 9 May 1980 amended by the Protocol of 3 June 1999 made in Vilnius on 3 June 1999 (Vilnius Protocol; COTIF 1999); Fr. Convention relative aux transports internationaux ferroviaires dans la teneur du Protocole de modification du 3 juin 1999 (COTIF); Ger.: Übereinkommen über den internationalen Eisenbahnverkehr in der Fassung des Änderungsprotokolls vom 3. Juni 1999 (COTIF); approved by the Swiss parliament on 14 December 2001 effective 1 July 2006; RS 0.742.403.12 [**not signed by China**].

Convention on the Contract for the International **Carriage of Goods by Road** (CMR) made in Geneva on 19 May 1956; Fr.: Convention relative au contrat de transport international de marchandises par route (CMR); Ger.: Übereinkommen über den Beförderungsvertrag im internationalen Strassengüterverkehr (CMR); signed by Switzerland on 19 May 1956 effective as of 28 May 1970; RS 0.741.611 [**not signed by China**].

Convention on International **Transport of Goods** Under Cover of **TIR Carnets** made in Geneva on 14 November 1975; Fr.: Convention douanière relative au transport international de marchandises sous le couvert de carnets TIR (Convention TIR); Ger.: Zollabkommen über den internationalen Warentransport mit Carnets TIR (TIR-Abkommen); signed by China on 5 July 2016 effective as of 5 January 2017; approved by the Swiss Parliament on 27 September 1977 effective as of 3 August 1978; RS 0.631.252.512.

23rd UN Model Regulations on the Transport of **Dangerous Goods** adopted Committee of Experts on the Transport of Dangerous Goods and on the Globally Harmonized System of Classification and Labelling of Chemicals (11th session) in Geneva on 9 December 2022 (UN Model Regulations Rev. 23 (2023)).

4. Other Treaties

UNIDROIT Convention on **International Financial Leasing** made in Ottawa in 1988 [**signed neither by China, nor by Switzerland**].

Convention of 5 October 1961 Abolishing the Requirement of **Legalisation** for Foreign Public Documents made in The Hague on 5 October 1961, Fr.: Convention supprimant l'exigence de la légalisation des actes publics étrangers; Ger.: Übereinkommen zur Befreiung ausländischer öffentlicher Urkunden von der Beglaubigung; signed by China on 8 March 2023 effective 7 November 2023; approved by the Swiss parliament on 27 April 1972 effective 11 March 1973; RS 0.172.030.4.

B. Sino-Swiss Treaties

Agreement between the Swiss Federal Council and the Government of the People's Republic of China on the **Promotion and Reciprocal Protection of Investments**; Fr. (original version): Accord entre le Conseil fédéral suisse et le Gouvernement de la République populaire de Chine concernant la promotion et la protection réciproque des investissements; Ger.: Abkommen zwischen dem Schweizerischen Bundesrat und der Regierung der Volksrepublik China über die Förderung und den gegenseitigen Schutz von Investitionen; signed on 27 January 2009 effective as of 13 April 2010; RS 0.975.224.9.

Free Trade Agreement Between the Swiss Confederation and the People's Republic of China; 瑞士联邦和中华人民共和国自由贸易协定 ruìshì liánbāng hé zhōnghuá rénmín gònghéguó zìyóu màoyì xiédìng; Fr.: Accord de libre-échange entre la Confédération suisse et la République populaire de

Chine ; Ger.: Freihandelsabkommen zwischen der Schweizerischen Eidgenossenschaft und der Volksrepublik China; signed on 6 July 2013 effective 1 July 2014; RS 0.946.292.492.

Agreement on **Scientific and Technical Cooperation** Between the Swiss Confederation and the People's Republic of China; Fr.: Accord de coopération scientifique et technique entre la Confédération suisse et la République populaire de Chine; Ger.: Abkommen zwischen der Schweizerischen Eidgenossenschaft und der Volksrepublik China über wissenschaftlich-technische Zusammenarbeit; signed on 24 February 1989 effective immediately; RS 0.974.224.9.

Agreement on **Social Security** Between Switzerland and the People's Republic of China; Fr.: Convention de sécurité sociale entre le Gouvernement de la Confédération suisse et le Gouvernement de la République populaire de Chine; Ger.: Abkommen zwischen der Regierung der Schweizerischen Eidgenossenschaft und der Regierung der Volksrepublik China über soziale Sicherheit; signed on 30 September 2015 effective 19 June 2017; RS 0.831.109.249.1.

Bibliography

I. Chinese Law

This bibliography selectively lists works published relatively recently in western languages on Chinese business law. It has no pretense to be comprehensive. When English bibliography is not available or scarce, works in Chinese may exceptionally be cited. They are sorted within each subject-matter, from the most to the less recent, then by alphabetical order of their author, first author or editor. While all authors are sorted by alphabetical order of their surname, western authors are mentioned by their given name first, followed by their surname while, following the Asian convention, authors bearing a Chinese name are mentioned by their surname first, followed by their given name; Asian authors' names using a western given name follow the western standard: for example, PETER [given name] MUCHLINSKI [surname]; WEI [surname] SHEN [given name]; JOSHUA [given name] LI [surname]. Works relevant for more than one subject-matter may be cited more than once. Status on 31 December 2025, unless mentioned otherwise.

A. Foreign Investment Law

PETER C. HSU *et al.*, The Foreign Investment Law: A Commentary, Springer, 2022.

WEI SHEN, Protection of Foreign Investment in China: Evolving Dynamics of Law and Policy, Kluwer Law International, 2022.

NICHOLAS F. RUNNELS, China's New Foreign Investment Law: Analysis and Implications, NYU Journal of International Law & Politics, 2021.

SHAN WENHUA/GONG JIYE, China's Foreign Investment Law: A Commentary on the 2019 FIL and Its Impact, Brill Nijhoff, 2021.

LI JI *et al.*, Chinese Foreign Direct Investment Law *in*: Perspectives on Chinese Business and Law, Cambridge University Press, 2018.

China and International Investment Law *in*: Oxford Handbook of International Investment Law, PETER MUCHLINSKI *et al.* (eds.), Oxford University Press, 2013.

B. Civil Law

LI BEI/OLIVIER VIX/MICHEL GRIMALDI/MARIE GORÉ/CHARLES GIJSBERS, Code civil de la République populaire de Chine, 1st ed., LexisNexis, 2024.

Understanding the Chinese Civil Code: A Comparative Perspective, various authors, Hugo Grotius Institute, Brill, 2024.

Chinese Civil code, The Specific Parts, A Handbook, BU YUANSHI (ed.), Beck München 2023.

JIANG HAO, The Making of the Chinese Civil Code: Historical Development and Comparative Analysis, Cambridge University Press, 2023.

HUANG MEIHUA/DAI CHENXIA DU PLESSIS, Comparative Perspectives on the Chinese Civil Code: Property Law Across Cultures. Routledge, 2022.

Der Besondere Teil des neuen chinesischen Zivilgesetzbuches, Zwischen Tradition und Moderne, THOMAS M.J. MÖLLERS/LI HAO (eds.), Nomos, Baden-Baden 2022.

中国民法典评注（共 7 篇 12 册）王利明主编，出版社:法律出版社，出版时间:2022 年 zhōngguó mínfǎ diǎn píngzhù (gòng 7 piān 12 cè) wánglìmíng zhǔbiān, chūbǎn shè: fǎlǜ chūbǎn shè, chūbǎn shíjiān:2022 nián; Commentary of the Chinese Civil Code (7 parts, 12 volumes), WANG LIMING (ed.), Law Press 2022[5].

The Civil Code of the People's Republic of China: English Translation, various authors, translated by the School of Foreign Languages, Southwest University of Political Science and Law, William S. Hein & Co., Inc./Wells Information Services Inc., 2022.

JACQUES HENRI [A.K.A. James] HERBOTS, The Chinese New Civil Code and the Law of Contract, China-EU Law Journal, Springer, Heidelberg 2021, 7:39-49.

The Civil Code of the People's Republic of China: English Translation with Judicial Interpretations, Supreme People's Court of China, Brill Nijhoff, 2021.

The Civil Code of the People's Republic of China: English Translation, WAN MENG (ed.), China University of Political Science and Law Press, 2021.

民法典评注，作者:中国社会科学院法学研究所，孙宪忠，朱广新主编，出版社:中国法治出版社，出版时间:2020 年 10 月 mínfǎ diǎn píngzhù, zuòzhě: zhōngguó shèhuì kēxuéyuàn fǎxué yánjiū suǒ, sūnxiànzhōng,

5 This commentary is not available in English; the informal translation of its title is provided for convenience.

zhūguǎngxīn zhǔbiān, chūbǎn shè: zhōngguó fǎzhì chūbǎn shè, chūbǎn shíjiān:2020 nián 10 yuè; Commentary of the Civil Code, Institute of Law, Chinese Academy of Social Sciences (ed.), SUN XIANZHONG/ZHU GUANGXIN (eds.), China Legal Publishing House, 2020[6].

BU YUANSHI, Chinese Civil Code, The General Part, A Handbook, Beck, München 2019.

Handbuch des chinesischen Zivilprozessrechts, Analyse und Materialien, KNUT BENJAMIN PISSLER (ed.), Mohr Siebeck, Tübingen 2018.

C. Business Law in General

1. General Works

Perspectives on Chinese Business and Law, JOSHUA LI/HANS VAN LOON (eds.), Intersentia/Cambridge University Press, 2018.

SHEN WEI, Chinese Business Law: Narrative & Commentary, Wolters Kluwer, Hong Kong 2016.

JAMES M. ZIMMERMAN, China Law Deskbook, A Legal Guide for Foreign-invested Enterprises, 4th ed., American Bar Association, 2014.

BU YUANSHI, Chinese Business Law, Hart Publishing, 2013.

Chinese Business Law, BU YUANSHI (ed.), Beck München 2010.

PAUL THALER, Chinese Business Law, Stämpfli, Bern 2009.

2. Special Topics

Chinese Internet Law, ZHANG CHU (ed.), William S. Hein, New York 2019.

JEAN-CHRISTOPHE [A.K.A. John] LIEBESKIND, The PRC Exchange Control: Compliance and Circumvention, *in*: Jusletter, 27 Novembre 2017.

CRISTIANO RIZZI/LI GUO/JOSEPH CHRISTIAN, Mergers and Acquisitions and Takeovers in China, A Legal and Cultural Guide to New Forms of Investment, Wolters Kluwer, The Netherlands 2012.

---

6 S. note 5.

OWEN NEE, Shareholder Agreements and Joint-ventures in China, Thomson Reuters/West, 2010.

TU HONG, Foreign Exchange Control in China, Kluwer Law, The Hague 2004.

D. Real rights

Property Acquisition *in*: Property Law in China, Cambridge University Press, 2025.

DAI YONGJUN, Examples from the English Translation of Terms in the Book of Real Rights, China University of Political Science and Law Journal, 2024.

CATHERINE SHEPHARD, Property Law in China, Cambridge University Press, 2024.

GAO ZHENYU/JIANG WENXI/REN HAOHAN/WANG KEMIN/WU YUEZHI, Mortgage Prepayments in China and Monetary Policy Transmission, S&P Global Market Intelligence, 1 October 2024, https://ssrn.com/abstract=4972487 or http://dx.doi.org/10.2139/ssrn.4972487.

ZHOU ZHIHUA, The Development of Mortgage Finance in China: The Implications of International Experiences in: China Perspectives 2015/4 (2015), pp. 51-61.

CHEN LEI, A Structural Analysis of Chinese Mortgage Law, https://www.researchgate.net/publication/228164742_A_Structural_Analysis_of_Chinese_Mortgage_Law, 2010.

GEORG M. REHM, The New Chinese Property Rights Law: An Evaluation from a Continental European Perspective, Columbia Journal of Asian Law, 2009.

DENG YONGHENG /DELLA ZHENG/LING CHANGFENG, An Early Assessment of Residential Mortgage Performance in China, https://lusk.usc.edu/sites/default/files/working_papers/wp_2004-1001.pdf, 2004.

G. C. S. LIN/S. P. S. HO, China's Land Resources and Land-Use Change: Insights from the 1996 Land Survey, 2003.

JOHN ALSEN, An Introduction to Chinese Property Law, Journal of Chinese Law, 1992.

E. Contract Law

Comparison with Civil Code: Contracts, Contract Law of the People's Republic of China, Peking University, https://www.pkulaw.com/en_law/2367b1767194112cbdfb.html, (last accessed 31 December 2025) [comparative table between the Contract Law and the Civil Code].

WEI WEN, Formality, Freedom of Contract and China's New Civil Code: A Legal Reform Recommendation for Land Sale Contracts, [2022] U. PA. ASIAN L. REV. 332.

LARRY A. DIMATTEO/LIU JING/JIANG HAO, Chinese Contract Law: Civil and Common Law Perspectives, Cambridge University Press, 2021.

JACQUES HENRI [A.K.A. James] HERBOTS, The Chinese New Civil Code and the Law of Contract, China-EU Law Journal, Springer, Heidelberg 2021, 7:39-49.

ZHANG MO, Chinese Contract Law, Theory and Practice, Brill Nijhoff, Leiden/Boston 2020.

MIMI ZHOU, Chinese Contract Law and the 2020 Civil Code, LexisNexis, Hong Kong 2020.

Contract Formation under Chinese Law *in*: Chinese Commercial Law, GRAHAM ELLIOTT/FU JIAN (eds.), Oxford University Press, 2018.

Chinese Contract Law, LARRY DIMATTEO/CHEN LEI *et al.*, Cambridge University Press, 2017.

F. Employment

Landmark Labor Law Cases in China, An In-Depth Analysis, DONG BAOHUA (ed.), Wolters Kluwer, The Netherlands 2019.

Droit social chinois, HAN ZHUANG (ed.), Dalloz/Juriscope, 2018.

LI WEN PEI, Labor Law in China, Chinese Workers Publishing House 中国工人出版社 Zhōngguó gōngrén chūbǎn shè, 2015.

RONALD C. BROWN, Understanding Labor and Employment Law in China, Cambridge University Press, 2012.

NILS SEIBERT, Die Begründung und Beendigung von Arbeitsverhaltnissen und Arbeitsvertragen, Eine Darstellung und Analyse der chinesischen Rechtslage, Peter Lang, Frankfurt am Main 2012.

SHEN JIE, Labour Disputes and Their Resolution in China, Chandos Publishing, Oxford 2007.

G. Liability for Illicit Acts ("Torts")

CAO YANG, Chinese Tort Law in the Era of the Civil Code *in*: The Making of the Chinese Civil Code, Cambridge University Press, 2023.

RACHEL E. STERN, Conceptions of Fairness in Chinese Tort Cases, Modern China, 2023.

GEORGE W. CONK, Tort Liability: Section 7 of the Civil Code of the People's Republic of China, SSRN, 2020.

MAURO BUSSANI *et al.*, Chinese Tort Law: Between Tradition and Modernity *in*: Comparative Tort Law, Edward Elgar, 2019.

ZHANG WEI, Understanding the Law of Torts in China: A Political Economy Perspective, University of Pennsylvania Asian Law Review, 2017.

LI XIANG/JIN JIGANG, Concise Chinese Tort Laws, Springer, Heidelberg 2014.

H. Company Law

YAN MING, China's Company Law Reform: An Experiment in Stakeholder Governance, Oxford Business Law Blog/Taylor & Francis, 2025.

YAN MING, Operationalising Stakeholder Governance: Lessons from China's Company Law, Asia Pacific Law Review, 2025.

ZHU GUOHUI, Understanding Chinese Company Law, Hong Kong University Press, 3rd ed., 2023.

The Law of Business Organizations: A Concise Introduction to Corporate, Partnership, and LLC Law in China, various authors, Brill Nijhoff, 2022.

LUTZ-CHRISTIAN WOLFF, Mergers & Acquisitions in China: Law and Practice, Wolters Kluwer, 5th ed., Hong Kong 2020.

Chinese Company Law *in*: Perspectives on Chinese Business and Law, LI JI *et al.* (eds.), Cambridge University Press, 2018.

SHEN WEI, Chinese Business Law: Narrative & Commentary, Wolters Kluwer Hong Kong, 2016.

Corporate Governance and Legal Reform in China, RANDALL PEERENBOOM (ed.), Sweet & Maxwell, 2010.

II. Swiss Law

This bibliography contains the references to works on Swiss law mentioned in this book, as well as selected authoritative general works corresponding to its chapters. It has no pretense to be comprehensive. They are sorted within each subject-matter from the most to the less recent, then by alphabetical order of their author, first author or editor. Status on 31 December 2025.

A. Civil Law

BLAISE CARRON/SABRINA GAURON-CARLIN, CC & CO annotés, Helbing Lichtenhahn, 12th ed. (2024).

Commentaire romand, Code des obligations II (Art. 530-1186 CO; Art. 120-141 LIMF; LFus/LTI), ALAIN MACALUSO/LAURENT MOREILLON/NICOLAS QUELOZ/NATHALIE DONGOIS (eds.), 3rd ed., 2024.

PIERRE TERCIER/PASCAL PICHONNAZ, Le droit des obligations, 7th ed., Schulthess, 2024.

Commentaire romand, Code civil I (Art. 1-456 CC), PASCAL PICHONNAZ (éd.), BÉNÉDICT FOËX *et al.*, Helbing Lichtenhahn, 2nd ed., 2023.

Zürcher Kommentar, Obligationenrecht, ROGER ZELTNER/IRENE FURRER *et al.*, Schulthess, (continuous ed.; last update 2022).

Basler Kommentar, Obligationenrecht I (Art. 1-529 OR), EUGEN SCHMIDLIN/BÉNÉDICT FOËX *et al.*, Helbing Lichtenhahn, 3rd ed., 2021.

Commentaire romand, LUC THÉVENOZ/FRANZ WERRO (eds.), Code des obligations I (Art. 1-529 CO), 3rd ed., Helbing & Lichtenhahn, Basel 2021 [cited as "Commentaire romand/CO I"].

Berner Kommentar. Obligationenrecht (OR), ANDREAS ABEGG/PETER TUOR *et al.*, Stämpfli, 4th ed., 2020.

Schweizerisches Obligationenrecht Allgemeiner Teil, PETER GAUCH/WALTER R. SCHLUEP/JÖRG SCHMID/SUSAN EMMENEGGER, 11th ed., Schulthess, 2020.

Basler Kommentar, Zivilgesetzbuch I (Art. 1-456 ZGB), BÉNÉDICT FOËX/ANDREAS LIENHARD *et al.* (ed.), Helbing Lichtenhahn, 3rd ed., 2019.

Commentaire romand, Code civil II (Art. 457-977 CC), PASCAL PICHONNAZ (ed.)/BÉNÉDICT FOËX *et al.*, Helbing Lichtenhahn, 1st ed., 2016.

FELIX DASSER, Punitive damages: Vom "fremden Fötzel" zum "Miteidgenoss"? SJZ 96/2000 p. 101.

PETER GAUCH/WALTER R. SCHLUEP/PIERRE TERCIER, Partie générale du droit des obligations, Schulthess, 1st ed., Zurich 1982 [cited as GAUCH/SCHLUEP/TERCIER].

WALTHER J. HABSCHEID, Droit judiciaire privé suisse, Georg, Geneva 1981.

B. Real Rights

S. above, Civil Law.

PAUL-HENRI STEINAUER, Schweizerisches Sachenrecht, Stämpfli, 7th ed., 2022.

Basler Kommentar. Zivilgesetzbuch II/3 : Sachenrecht II (art. 730-915 : Dingliche Rechte), EUGEN SCHMIDLIN *et al.*, Helbing Lichtenhahn, 3rd ed., 2021.

AMÉDÉO WERMELINGER, La propriété par étages, commentaire des art. 712a-712t CC, Schulthess, 4th ed., 2021.

Basler Kommentar, Zivilgesetzbuch II/2 : Sachenrecht I (art. 641-712 CC : Eigentum), BÉNÉDICT FOËX/PIERRE TERCIER *et al.*, Helbing Lichtenhahn, 3rd ed., 2020.

Berner Kommentar, ZGB IV : Sachenrecht (art. 641-977), ANDREAS ABEGG/PETER TUOR, Stämpfli, 4th ed., 2019.

PAUL-HENRI STEINAUER, Les droits réels, 5th ed., Stämpfli, Bern 2012.

C. Contract Law

S. above, Civil Law.

PIERRE TERCIER/BLAISE CARRON, Les contrats spéciaux, 6th ed., Schulthess, 2025.

MARIE-NOËLLE VENTURI-ZEN-RUFFINEN, La résiliation pour justes motifs des contrats de durée, thesis, Université de Fribourg, Schulthess Zurich/Basel/Geneva 2007.

D. Employment

S. above, Contract Law.

Commentaire du contrat de travail (art. 319-362 CO), JEAN-PHILIPPE DUNAND/ PASCAL MAHON (eds.), Schulthess, 2nd ed., 2023.

E. Liability for Illicit Acts ("Torts")

S. above, Civil Law.

FRANÇOIS BOHNET *et al.*, Commentaire pratique, actions civiles, vol. II : CO – Responsabilité civile, Helbing Lichtenhahn, 1st ed., 2023.

PETER FORSTMOSER/FRANK VISCHER, Schweizerisches Haftpflichtrecht, Helbing Lichtenhahn, 3rd ed., 2019.

HENRI DESCHENAUX/PIERRE TERCIER, La responsabilité civile, 2nd ed., Staempfli, 1982.

F. Company Law

FRANÇOIS BELLANGER/PASCAL PICHONNAZ *et al.*, Précis de droit des sociétés, Helbing Lichtenhahn, 6th ed., 2025.

Zürcher Kommentar zu OR und ZGB: Gesellschaftsrecht, ROGER ZELTNER/ IRENE FURRER, Schulthess (continuous ed.; last updated 2025).

PETER FORSTMOSER/GEORG VON SEGESSER/ANDREAS ABEGG, Schweizerisches Gesellschaftsrecht, Stämpfli, 11th ed., 2024.

Commentaire romand, Code des obligations II (art. 620 ss CO : sociétés), ALAIN MACALUSO *et al.* (eds.), Helbing Lichtenhahn, 3rd ed., 2024.

NICOLAS ROUILLER, Droit des sociétés, Staempfli, 2024.

Berner Kommentar. Obligationenrecht, Band VI/2 : Gesellschaftsrecht II (art. 620 ff.: A.G./GmbH), PETER TUOR/EUGEN SCHMIDLIN *et al.*, Stämpfli, 5th ed., 2023.

Berner Kommentar. Obligationenrecht, Band VI/1 : Gesellschaftsrecht I (art. 530-620 CO: Personengesellschaften, einfache Gesellschaft), ANDREAS ABEGG *et al.*, Stämpfli, 3rd ed., 2022.

NICOLAS ROUILLER/MARC BAUERN/ROBERT BERNET/COLETTE LASSERRE ROUILLER, La société anonyme suisse, Stampfli, 3rd ed., 2022.

Basler Kommentar, Obligationenrecht, Band VI: Gesellschaftsrecht, BÉNÉDICT FOËX *et al.*, Helbing Lichtenhahn, 3rd ed., 2021.

PETER FORSTMOSER/FRANÇOIS KNOEPFLER *et al.*, Droit suisse des sociétés, Stämpfli/Schulthess, 2015.

III. International Law

This bibliography contains the references to works on international law mentioned in this book, as well as selected authoritative general works corresponding to international business law, foreign direct investment law and international sale. It has no pretense to be comprehensive. They are sorted within each subject-matter from the most to the less recent, then by alphabetical order of their author, first author or editor. Status on 31 December 2025.

A. Business Law in General

NICOLAS ROUILLER, International Business Law, 2nd ed., Schulthess, Geneva/Zurich 2025.

B. Foreign Investment Law

CAMPBELL MCLACHLAN/LAURENCE SHORE/MATTHEW WEINIGER, International Investment Arbitration: Substantive Principles, 2nd ed., Oxford University Press, 2017.

M. SORNARAJAH, The International Law on Foreign Investment. 4th ed., Cambridge University Press, 2017.

The Oxford Handbook of International Investment Law, PETER MUCHLINSKI/FEDERICO ORTINO/CHRISTOPH SCHREUER (eds.), Oxford University Press, 2008.

JEAN-CHRISTOPHE [A.K.A. John] LIEBESKIND, The Legal Framework of Swiss International Trade and Investments, Part II: Protection, Vol. 7 No. 3-4 The Journal of World Investment & Trade, 2006.

JEAN-CHRISTOPHE [A.K.A. John] LIEBESKIND, The Legal Framework of Swiss International Trade and Investments, Part I: Promotion, Vol. 7 No. 3-4 The Journal of World Investment & Trade, 2006.

JEAN-CHRISTOPHE [A.K.A. John] LIEBESKIND, One-Hundred-Two Swiss Bilateral Investment Treaties: An Overview Of Investor-Host State Dispute Settlement Clauses, 19 ASA Special Series 81, 2002.

CHRISTOPH H. SCHREUER, The ICSID Convention: A Commentary, Cambridge University Press, 2001.

United Nations Conference on Trade and Development (UNCTAD), Most-Favoured-Nation Treatment, UNCTAD Series, on issues in international investment agreements, United Nations, New York and Geneva 1999.

C. Sale

MADILYNN O'HARA, Exclusion on Whose Terms?: The Harm of Upholding Implied Exclusions Under Article 6 of the Convention on the International Sale of Goods, The Michigan Journal of International Law, February 2025.

INGEBORG SCHWENZER/ULRICH G. SCHLECHTRIEM, Commentary on the UN Convention on the International Sale of Goods (CISG), 5th ed., Oxford University Press, Oxford 2022.

Legal Guide to Uniform Instruments in the Area of International Commercial Contracts, with a Focus on Sales, UNCITRAL/The Hague Conference on Private International Law/UNIDROIT, 2021.

JOSEPH M. LOOKOFSKY, Understanding the CISG: A Compact Guide to the 1980 United Nations Convention on Contracts for the International Sale of Goods, Kluwer Law International, 5th ed., 2020.

The CISG and its Impact on International Commercial Law, FRANCO FERRARI (ed.), Sellier European Law Publishers, 2017.

CHRISTOPH J. H. BERGER/BENJAMIN LEISINGER, CISG Basics, Eleven International Publishing, 2017.

PETER HUBER/ALASTAIR MULLIS, The CISG: A New Textbook for Students and Practitioners, Sellier European Law Publishers, 2007.

PETER SCHLECHTRIEM, Commentary on the UN Convention on the International Sale of Goods (CISG), Clarendon Press, 1998.

Chap. 1 Foreign Investment Law

§1. Introduction

On 15 March 2019, China passed the Foreign Investment Law (FIL) 中华人民共和国外商投资法 zhōnghuá rénmín gònghéguó wàishāng tóuzī fǎ, a landmark legislation aimed at promoting, protecting and managing foreign investment on its territory (Art. 1). The law has come into force on 1 January 2020, and has been deploying its effects fully as of 1 January 2025, after a transitional period of five years (Art. 42)[7]. 1

The FIL is remarkable in several respects. First, it is the first time that the Chinese legislator provides its foreign investment regime, which so far had been subject to a multitude of uncoordinated secondary legislation, with a comprehensive legal basis[8]. 2

Second, even though foreign investors may sometimes still struggle to reconcile the law with reality, the FIL unambiguously states the Chinese government's intent to "open to the outside world"[9] by promoting and protecting foreign investment and to achieve such goal by fostering a "stable, transparent and predictable market" (Art. 3§2). In doing so, the law incorporates all the guarantees now generally acknowledged by the international community in foreign direct investment laws and treaties[10]. 3

Third, such goal is primarily to be achieved by establishing "fairness" or "fair competition" (Art. 3§2), i.e., a level playing field between foreign and domestic investors. The FIL reiterates this core principle on several occasions throughout the law, thereby emphasizing its importance. By doing so, the legislator 4

---

7 On the transitional period, s. below §§32, 1764, 1842, 2321 and 2322 as well as note 968.

8 There is currently no such law in Switzerland; however, a draft law has been proposed in 2023, is currently pending before the legislatives bodies, and gives rise to some controversies, s. Loi fédérale sur l'examen des investissements étrangers (LEIE), FF 2024 125.

9 This intent is even expressed twice, at FIL Art. 1 and 3§2.

10 These guarantees, which are typically included in bilateral investment treaties, among others, mainly include provisions related to the encouragement and admission of foreign direct investment; its protection; fair and equitable treatment; most-favored-nation treatment; free movement of capital; expropriation; and dispute resolution. S. JEAN-CHRISTOPHE [A.K.A. John] LIEBESKIND, The Legal Framework of Swiss International Trade and Investments, Part I: Promotion, Vol. 7 No. 3-4 The Journal of World Investment & Trade, 2006, pp. 337 ff. S. also below, Chap. 1 §6.III., The Sino-Swiss Bilateral Investment Treaty.

addresses the main concern expressed by the foreign investors' community over the past decades.

5 The FIL is divided into three main chapters: promotion, protection and management. These are complemented by three secondary chapters containing common provisions: an opening chapter containing general or introductive provisions, a final chapter containing "supplemental" provisions, and a chapter on liability containing provisions applying to the violations of certain provisions contained in the main chapters. The following sections will follow the structure of the main chapters of the law.

§2. Definition of "Foreign Investment"

6 For the purpose of the FIL, "foreign investment" (外商投资 wàishāng tóuzī) is defined as the investment activities carried out directly or indirectly by foreign investors (外国投资者 wàiguó tóuzī zhě), i.e., foreign natural persons, foreign enterprises or other foreign organizations (Art. 2). The law lists four circumstances amounting to foreign investment: foreign investors, independently or jointly with other investors, setting up a foreign-invested enterprise in China; foreign investors acquiring shares, equities or similar rights or interests in a Chinese domestic company; foreign investors, independently or jointly with other investors, investing in a new project in China; or investment through other legal means (*ibid.*)

7 "Foreign-invested enterprise" (FIE) 外商投资企业 wàishāng tóuzī qǐyè is defined as an enterprise legally registered in China, which is wholly or partly invested by foreign investors. It is not to be confused with "foreign company" (外国公司 wàiguó gōngsī), which the Company Law defines as a company formed out of China under Chinese laws (Company Law, Art. 243; s. below §2178) and whose branches in China are specifically governed by Chapter 13 of the same (s. below Chap. 9 §64.XI, Branches of Foreign Companies).

8 Expressions such as "indirect", "similar", "interests", "project" and "other legal means" leave ample discretion to the authorities. Practice, especially as of 2025, will provide further guidance on their interpretation. Meanwhile, considering the historically conservative stance of the Chinese authorities, it is advisable to assume that the FIL applies extensively.

§3. Promotion

Mirroring the FIL's general goal, the law starts by reaffirming the application of the principle of *equality* between domestic enterprises and FIEs by affirming that the State's policies supporting enterprise development also apply to FIEs (Art. 9). This general principle is specifically reaffirmed throughout the law[11]. It applies both to rights and duties. 9

The law stresses another important goal, which is the *simplification* of administrative procedures or "red tape". The authorities shall do so by applying the principles of "convenience, efficiency, and transparency" (Art. 19). While this new policy is intended to address one of foreign investors' main concerns, future will tell the extent to which it will be effectively implemented[12]. This commitment is expressed, in particular, about *company registration* procedures (Company Law, Art. 41), as the time needed for the incorporation of a company in China is notoriously longer than that needed in most other major jurisdictions for direct foreign investment, notably in Hong Kong[13]. Recently, the Chinese legislator issued a *Private Sector Promotion Law* which strives at cutting more red tape and ensuring fair competition for private companies against State-owned enterprises (SOEs) to the effect of stimulating the private sector. It is hoped that this law, which also applies to FIEs, will also benefit the latter. 10

The promotion of a safe business environment requires legal certainty, which in turn requires the laws, regulations, measures, policies, etc. to be published. As far as foreign investors are concerned, the FIL expressly provides for the timely *publication* of foreign investment-related regulations, as well as adjudications (Art. 10§2). The law reiterates this requirement in connection with the prohibition of *undue State interference* (Art. 24; s. below §23). 11

The FIL even goes one step further by mandating the competent authorities to *consult* with the foreign investors community in anticipation of draft laws and regulations related to foreign investment (Art. 11§1). Such consultation 12

---

11 Other than the specific provisions discussed below, s., for example, FIL Art. 15 (standards), Art. 17 (public fund raising) and Art. 16 (procurement).

12 In 2024, China was ranked 14th on the IMD World Competitiveness Ranking as compared to Singapore (1st), Switzerland (2nd), Hong Kong (5th), Taiwan (8th) and the U.S.A. (12th).

13 On average, it is generally estimated that six months are needed for the registration of a company in China, as compared to 48 hours in Hong Kong; urgent registration in China seldom succeeds in reducing that time to less than three months. While a Special Administrative Region (SAR) of the People's Republic of China, Hong Kong maintains a legal order separate from that of the Mainland.

regularly take place in the form of invitations for comments directed at the foreign chambers of commerce and similar organizations in China[14].

13 The law further provides for a "foreign investment service system" (外商投资服务体系 wàishāng tóuzī fúwù tǐxì) to provide foreign investors with "consultation and services" related to laws, regulations, policies, measures and information related to investment projects (Art. 11). The list is not exhaustive. The extent to which this "system" has been or will be implemented is unclear. In practice, general, foreign investment-related information remains provided by the State Administration for Market Regulation (SAMR) 国家工商行政管理总局 guójiā gōngshāng xíngzhèng guǎnlǐ zǒngjú[15], which redirects to more specialized or to local authorities, and the latter, namely, the local Administration for Market Regulation (AMR) 市场监督管理局 shìchǎng jiāndū guǎnlǐ jú outlets, together with other local agencies, are expressly mandated by the law to promote and regulate foreign investment at their level and within their area of competence (Art. 18).

14 Unlike for other "systems" referred to by the FIL[16], the State has not (yet) established a centralized, unified, comprehensive "foreign investment service system"[17]. While, as noted above, the related information is, generally speaking, made available by the various authorities dealing with foreign investment, it is done in an heteroclite, rather than systematic, manner: insofar, it can be said that that "system" does not (yet) exist as such and is, rather, to be understood as an injunction from the central government to the lower level authorities to use their best endeavors to implement it locally. Company and creditworthiness registration are also part of the system (s. below, Chap. 1 §5.V, Registration).

15 Multilateral and bilateral investment *treaties* are expressly acknowledged in the law (Art. 13) and will be discussed further down (s. Chap. 1 §6, International Law).

---

14 S. below, Chap. 1 §4, Protection, about FIL Art. 26.

15 The State Administration for Market Regulation (SAMR) is the national regulatory authority responsible for business registration and market supervision. It has replaced former the State Administration for Industry & Commerce (SAIC). In March 2018, SAIC was merged into the newly created SAMR as part of a broader reform of Chinese government institutions. SAMR has taken over the functions of the former SAIC. It has local branches known as Administration for Market Regulation (AMR). As of the time of printing, AMR's website, https://www.samr.gov.cn (status on 31 December 2025), was only available in Chinese.

16 About other systems, s. below §§52ff.

17 The Chinese government has announced that it would build a comprehensive system to manage its public data by 2030. One can speculate that such system will incorporate the systems mentioned above (s. South China Morning Post, China sets out ambitious timeline for comprehensive data-sharing system by 2030, 10 October 2024).

§4. Protection

The FIL clearly enunciates the State's commitment to protect foreign investment (Art. 5). Such duty applies from top to bottom of the government (Art. 7). 16

It also affirms the principle of the most favorable treatment now generally embedded in international direct foreign investment law[18], both in the form of *national treatment*, i.e., purporting at ensuring equality of treatment between foreign and domestic (i.e., Chinese investors investing in China) investors (Art. 4§2), and in that of the *most-favorable-nation treatment* (MFN)[19] proper, i.e., ensuring the equality of treatment between foreign investors in China and Chinese investors abroad[20] (Art. 4§3). 17

National treatment only applies provided the foreign investment is not restricted or prohibited under the *Negative List*[21]. Generally speaking, the FIL recalls that foreign investors and enterprises must comply with the law (Art. 6). 18

The FIL affirms the prohibition of arbitrary *expropriation* generally embedded in public international law. However, according to same principles, expropriation is exceptionally permissible, provided in rests on a legal basis, serves the public interest, and is compensated by reasonable indemnity paid timely (Art. 20)[22]. This provision applies to both expropriation (征收 zhēngshōu) and *requisition* (征用 zhēngyòng)[23]. 19

The law further guarantees the free, *outward remittance* of all monies owned, held or earned in China by foreign investors (art. 21). It mentions expressly capital contributions, profit, capital gains, income from assets disposal, intellectual property rights, royalties, indemnities, compensation and income from liquidation. This list is not exhaustive. Such freedom applies both to foreign 20

---

18 S., for example, United Nations Conference on Trade and Development (UNCTAD), Most-favored-Nation Treatment, UNCTAD Series on Issues in International Investment Agreements, United Nations, New York and Geneva 1999.

19 The most-favored nation (MFN) clause, as typically found in bilateral investment promotion and protection treaties, is a provision that ensures a foreign investor from one treaty party receives treatment no less favorable than the treatment the host State accords to investors from any third country in comparable circumstances.

20 S. also below, Chap. 1 §5.II, The Negative List, and Chap. 1 §6, International Law.

21 S. below Chap. 1 §5.II, The Negative List.

22 On damage valuation, s. below §§1663ff.

23 Expropriation results in the permanent control, by the State, of the expropriated assets, and the transfer of their property from their former owner to the State, while requisition implies a temporary seizure or use, also for public interest, without transfer of ownership, typically in emergency situations; it also entitles the requisitioned party to indemnification. About the regime of requisitions in the Chinese Civil Code, s. further below (§407).

currencies and Chinese yuan (A.K.A. renminbi). Moreover, it also applies to domestic remittances. Any such transaction must be legal: in practice, it means first and foremost that any outward remittance must comply with *exchange control*[24], which is strictly enforced in China.

21 Addressing one of the main concerns of the foreign investors' community, the FIL also protects *intellectual property* (Art. 22§1). Beyond its introductive statement, which is largely declarative in nature, this provision represents a major departure from the former policy inasmuch as, before the FIL, the law practically compelled foreign investors to disclose their technology or intellectual property to the authorities by compelling them to submit their joint-venture (JV) agreement or contract to the local registration authorities for examination, approval and registration[25]. Foreign investors had long complained that such disclosure often resulted in leaks and eventually abuses of their intellectual property rights (IPR). In a stark contrast, the FIL now proclaims that the State "encourages" technical cooperation carried out according to "voluntary" principles. The conditions for technical cooperation shall be "negotiated and determined by all parties to the investment on equal basis pursuant to the principle of fairness". Finally administrative organs "and their staff members", which the law expressly mentions, "shall not use administrative means to force the transfer of technology" (art. 22§2), thus explicitly addressing the concern described above.

22 *Trade secrets*, however, do not quite enjoy the same level of guarantees as IPR[26], neither under the generally accepted standards in international law, nor under the FIL, especially since the registration of certain transactions, which might result in the disclosure of commercial secrets, may still be compulsory[27]; yet the FIL still mandates the authorities to protect them (Art. 23)[28].

---

24 Exchange control is not covered in this book. S., for example, JEAN-CHRISTOPHE [A.K.A. John] LIEBESKIND, The PRC Exchange Control: Compliance and Circumvention, *in*: Jusletter 27 Novembre 2017; s. also TU HONG, Foreign Exchange Control in China, Kluwer Law, The Hague 2004.

25 S. Law on Sino-Foreign Equity Joint-Ventures, Art. 3; Law on Sino-Foreign Contractual Joint-Ventures, Art. 5. Both have been repelled by the Foreign Investment Law, s. below §§30ff.

26 The IPR are mentioned here in the narrow or formal sense, i.e., trademarks, patents and copyrights.

27 S., for example, the mandatory registration of franchising contracts (Regulation on the Administration of Commercial Franchises, Art. 8) which may contain both IPR (such as trademarks or copyrights) and trade secrets (such as lists of clients, know-how, etc.) S. also below, §438.

28 Know-how and commercial or trade secrets are also protected under other laws however, namely, the Anti-unfair Competition Law (Art. 10), and by contractual confidentiality clauses, such as in the contract of employment (s. below, §§1493ff.)

A further significant development addressing another major concern of the foreign investors' community is the prohibition of *undue or arbitrary State interference*, now expressly embedded in the law (Art. 24). The FIL thus recalls that administrative decisions and measures must rest on a legal basis, and that the authorities must not, directly or indirectly, illegitimately impair foreign investment, i.e., set barriers to market entry or exit[29]. Inasmuch, the law restates the core tenet of the World Trade Organization (which China joined in 2001) which, although primarily aimed at trade, also applies, to a lesser extent, to FDI[30]. This negative injunction is mirrored by a positive one requiring the authorities to abide to the policy and contractual commitments made to foreign investors (Art. 25). 23

Mirroring this guarantee, the FIL expressly provides for the sanctioning of civil servants in case of *abuse of power* (Art. 39). This wide-encompassing provision applies to any such infringement, including but not limited to dereliction of duty, personal enrichment and trade secrets disclosure. Such liability can be administrative, civil or criminal, as the case may be. 24

In order to facilitate foreign investors' access to remedies in case of infringement, by the State, of the guarantees offered above, or of "concerns" or "problems" in such investors' dealings with the authorities, the FIL sets up a "complaint mechanism" (投诉工作机制 tóusù gōngzuò jīzhì) entrusted with promptly handling such complaints (Art. 26). In addition to offering access to the already existing ordinary judicial administrative remedies, the law specifies that the complaint mechanism authorities may do so, namely, by coordinating and improving the relevant policies and measures. Considering that lack of coordination and inadequate policies are both tangible and frequent issues met by foreign investors, but rarely amount to infringements strictly speaking, thus fail to qualify for administrative judiciary remedies, such "mechanism" is welcome.[31] 25

As such, *reconsideration*[32] is expressly mentioned. While reconsideration is already embedded in Chinese administrative law, in practice it is not always 26

[29] This prohibition is reflected in Art. 130 of the Chinese Civil Code, which directs it at any third party (which includes the State) interfering with the exercise of a civil subject's civil rights, s. below §177.

[30] S. JEAN-CHRISTOPHE [A.K.A. John] LIEBESKIND, The Legal Framework of Swiss International Trade and Investments, Part I: Promotion, Vol. 7 No. 3-4 The Journal of World Investment & Trade, 2006, pp. 331-332 and note 7.

[31] About other foreign investment-related remedies, s. also below, Chap. 1 §6, International Law.

[32] In contrast with a judicial remedy, i.e., filing a case before an administrative tribunal, a request for reconsideration is processed by the same authority which issued the decision

embraced by the authorities. The FIL and the complaint mechanism now ensure that foreign investors will enjoy a secure access to it. However, as with the "foreign investment service system", time will test the implementation of the "complaint mechanism", which so far still needs to get past the stage of mere policy statement.

27 The last provision of the chapter on protection contained in the FIL affirms the right of *foreign chambers of commerce* to exist and safeguard the interests of their members (Art. 27)[33]. Historically, foreign chambers of commerce have been, and still are, playing a significant role in China: they are regularly consulted and, if not always, heard by the authorities[34].

§5. Management

28 The Chinese government's objective is not only to promote or protect foreign investment, but also to manage or control it. Thus, under the chapter title of "investment management" or "investment administration", the FIL both incorporates preexisting features of the government's foreign investment control framework and creates (or transform existing ones into-) new ones.

29 The novelty introduced by the FIL is that, where in the past such requirements were scattered around in several uncoordinated laws and regulations that are hard to identify and connect for foreign investors, it now regroups, clearly lists and purports at coordinating these requirements for the first time. Even if these prescriptions remain general in nature, they are welcome inasmuch as they contribute to improving the legal certainty surrounding the foreign investment legal and regulatory environment.

I. Corporate Form

30 The most notable change contained in the "Investment Management" section of the FIL is that it requires FIEs, which so far had typically existed in the form of a Joint-venture (JV), be it either an Equity Joint-venture (EJV) or a Contractual (or Cooperative) Joint-venture (CJV), or of a Wholly Foreign-owned

or took the measure whose reconsideration the subject (here, the foreign investor) of the decision or measure is requesting.

33 S. also the Foreign Trade Law which provides that "foreign trade dealers may establish or join relevant associations or chambers of commerce in accordance with law." (Art. 55).

34 About the general obligation of the authorities to consult with the foreign investors community, s. above §12.

Enterprise (WFOE), to *transform* themselves into one of the forms made available to domestic investors by the Company Law, i.e., a limited liability company or a shareholding company, or into a partnership (Art. 31).

This change is consistent with the new foreign investment regime insofar as it purports at establishing a *level playing field* for both foreign and domestic investors. As such, FIEs will not enjoy anymore the special status which those dedicated laws had granted them so far. Generally speaking, with some exemptions, they will not enjoy the privileges once granted to foreign investors such as favorable tax treatment, etc., either. 31

The three laws applying to FIEs until the inception of the FIL were abolished by the same as of its promulgation, i.e., on 1 January 2020 (Art. 42§1). However, foreign invested enterprises were granted a five-year transitional period, until 31 December 2024, to transform themselves. During that period, they continued to be governed by those same laws, notwithstanding they have been repealed (Art. 42§2)[35]. 32

The implications of such transformation, which are significant, will be discussed in the chapters of this book outlining company law (s. below Chap. 9 §64, The PRC Company Law; Chap. 9 §65, The Partnership Enterprise; and Chap. 9 §66, Joint-ventures). The law applicable to the transitory period, which as noted has now ended, was governed by Art. 467§2 of the Chinese Civil Code, equally discussed in the chapter of this book on JVs. 33

II. The Negative List

The Negative List (long name: Negative List for Foreign Investment Access 外商投资准入负面清单 wàishāng tóuzī zhǔnrù fùmiàn qīngdān; short name: Negative List 负面清单 fùmiàn qīngdān; FIL Art. 4§1) is a cornerstone of China's foreign investment policy. The Chinese market is divided into sectors or industries falling in any of the following three *categories*: encouraged, restricted, or prohibited. The two latter are exhaustively itemized in the Negative List; anything not falling in the List is encouraged. 34

As far as the first, *encouraged* category is concerned, while the Negative List, as its name suggests, only contains restricted and prohibited areas, in contrast, as noted, foreign investors may invest freely in certain other areas where, as expressly mentioned in the FIL, the Chinese government "encourages" them to do so, hence the third, so-called "encouraged" category. They may do so 35

35 S. also above, note 7.

without restriction, i.e., they may enjoy the full ownership of their FIE, or the majority of their venture with Chinese partners.

36 Such freedom may apply to certain industries or regions (FIL Art. 13 and 14). In that case, foreign investors may enjoy certain *preferential policies*, which typically take the form of Special Economic Zones (SEZ)[36]. Inasmuch, the FIL maintains a derogation from the principle of equality between foreign and domestic investors, to the benefit of foreign investors.

37 Restrictions in the second, *restricted* category are specifically defined in the Negative List (FIL Art. 28§2) and may be expressed in the form of minimum Chinese shareholding[37], maximum foreign shareholding[38] (while both, however restricting the foreign investment, may, in certain cases, allow it to hold a majority share nevertheless), or generically of Chinese shareholding control[39]. Such control may be absolute or relative, i.e., in the latter case, limited to certain aspects of the business[40] or otherwise qualified[41]. Restrictions may also be expressed in the form of senior management requirements (Negative List, Art. 1§1 *in fine*).

38 The third, *prohibited* category rules out any form of foreign investment, whether direct or indirect[42] (FIL, Art. 28§1). It typically applies to strategic

36 Such policies, which may apply to certain industries (e.g., high-tech), fields (e.g., mining), regions (e.g., bonded areas), etc., and be launched in the form of pilot projects before being promoted nationwide or locally , are numerous and will not be covered in this book.

37 For example, "the Chinese shareholding ... shall not be lower than 34%" (Negative List, Serial No. 1).

38 For example, "the investment by a foreign investor and is affiliated enterprise shall not exceed 25%" (Negative List, Serial No. 11.

39 For example, "...shall be controlled by Chinese shareholders" (Negative List, Serial No. 6).

40 For example, "The construction and operation of civil airports shall be subject to relative control by Chinese shareholders. Foreign parties shall not participate in the construction and operation of airport control tower." (Negative List, Serial No. 12).

41 For example, " the Internet public information release services is prohibited. (Services already liberalized by China under its commitments upon accession to the World Trade Organization shall be excluded from the foregoing services.)" (Negative List, Serial No. 15). Or: "...shall be limited to the forms of Sino-foreign equity joint-ventures." (*ibid.*, Serial No. 17).

42 Such restrictions and prohibitions may, to some extent, be circumvented by using a variable interest entity (VIE) which, although tolerated, currently evolve in a regulatory grey zone (s. below Chap. 9 §68, Variable Interests Entities).

industries or fields such as defense, big data, etc. However, limited exemptions may be specified[43].

The List recalls that fields not included shall be managed according to the principle of *equal treatment* of domestic and foreign investment (FIL, Art. 4§2, 1st sentence and s. above, §9). However, the restricted and prohibited categories derogate from that principle (*ibid.*, 2nd sentence). Foreign investment not falling in either the restricted and the prohibited category is to be treated equally with domestic investments (*ibid.*, last sentence and FIL, Art. 28§3). 39

A purported foreign investment not complying with the List shall not be issued a *business license* (Negative List, Art. 4; s. below Chap. 1 §5.IV, Business License and §§1824ff.) A Chinese company *merging* with or acquiring a foreign company will be regarded as a FIE and, as such, must comply with the List (Negative List, Art. 7). Some other fields may not be regulated by the List but may be restricted anyway by other specific regulations (the List mentions finance and culture as examples; Negative List, Art. 8). 40

In case of *violation* of the FIL, i.e., if a foreign investor invests in a field prohibited by the Negative List (which in practice may realistically occur only if it oversteps the boundaries of its Business License, as it would not have been issued it for investing in a prohibited field), the authority will order it to stop and restore the pre-investment status, which will involve disposing of any shares of assets forming such investment as well as any other measures to that effect. Any gains will be confiscated (FIL Art. 36§1). 41

If such investment encroaches is a restricted field, the authority will order the investor to correct the situation until it fits back in the boundaries of the Business License. If the investor fails to do so, or fails to do so in a timely manner, it will be treated like an investment in a prohibited field (FIL Art. 36§2). 42

The same applies if, although not trespassing on a restricted or prohibited field, the investor does not comply with other provisions of the Negative List (FIL Art. 36§3). 43

In contrast, the List contains a *most favorable treatment* clause (s. above §17 and note 19) by which foreign investors may claim the benefit of a more favorable treatment under certain regional economic cooperation schemes, of which the List mentions three: the Mainland & Hong Kong Closer Economic Partnership Arrangement, the Mainland & Macau Closer Economic Partnership Arrangement, the Cross-strait Economic Cooperation Framework Agreement, as well as, generically, pilot free trade zones (s. above §36 and note 36). In 44

[43] For example, "...remote geological sensing ... is prohibited. (Mining right holders carrying out works within the scope of their mining right shall not be restricted by this special management measure.)" (Negative List, Serial No. 21).

addition, the clause also applies to the international treaties China has concluded or acceded to (Negative List, Art. 9; s. below Chap. 1 §6, International Law). Thus, this provision mirrors and details the general principle affirmed by the FIL (s. above, Chap. 1 §4, Protection).

45 The latest Negative List, Edition 2024, was issued in September 2024 effective 1 November 2024; it replaced the 2021 Edition. It is regularly updated, however. In principle, although tacitly, new editions repeal the former one and do not question existing investments admitted under the prior editions, in accordance with the commitments taken in the FIL to protect foreign investors' legitimate rights and expectations (Art. 1 and 3§2). The latest edition confirms China's engagement towards the liberalization of China's market (cf. FIL Art. 1, 1st phrase). In addition, the government has issued a wealth of secondary legislation, which exceeds the scope of this book.

III. Pre-approval

46 Like in the past, foreign investors must apply to the competent authority and be pre-approved before they can apply for a business license and eventually operate. The FIL expressly recalls this requirement (Art. 29). Such authority will check whether the purported investment is permitted under the Negative List. As it does so, it may approve it, request complementary information or amendments, or reject it. Such checks extend beyond the Negative List to the related applicable legal and regulatory requirements, which may be numerous and complex.

47 However, as noted above, foreign investors are protected under the guarantees of equal treatment, legality and facilitation promoted by the FIL: therefore, any such request or rejection must rest on a *legal basis*; absent it, foreign investors may challenge arbitrary decisions or formalistic requirements under the complaint mechanism setup by the FIL (s. above §25) or through ordinary administrative judiciary remedies. Nevertheless, one should keep in mind that the Negative List and the FIL leave a certain, not to say ample, degree of discretion to the authorities, which the aggrieved foreign investor will only be able to challenge if it can prove that the authority made an *arbitrary* use of it: to reach such threshold is not easy.

48 Foreign investors must apply before the local outlet of the AMR[44]. They generally entrust a local third party, typically, a lawyer, an agent or a (future) local employee[45] to do so on their behalf.

---

[44] The application is now exclusively filed online.

[45] The foreign investor will only be legally capable of employ such third-party after the FIE has been registered and issued a business license. Meanwhile, such "employee"

IV. Business License

Unlike in other jurisdictions, including Switzerland, any commercial activity is subject, in China, to the preliminary issuance of a *business license* (营业执照 yíngyè zhízhào). Therefore, once the AMR has preapproved the foreign investment, the investor must apply for such license (Art. 30§1). The law further recalls that the principle of equality (s. above §§9 and 39) also applies to the review, by the authority, of the foreign investors' business license application, i.e., that foreign and domestic investors shall be treated equally in that respect (Art. 30§2). 49

It is important to note that the legal existence of a FIE starts from the issuance of the business license.[46] The business license is discussed in more detail further down in this book about company law (s. below §§1824ff.) 50

V. Registration

Once the business license has been issued, the foreign investor must comply with extensive record filing with a number of agencies of the Chinese government (Art. 29). Such registration includes *ad minima* the tax authority (commonly known as the Tax Bureau) and the State Administration for Exchange Control (SAFE). Additional registrations may apply depending on the FIE activity[47]. 51

The FIL established the *Foreign Investment Information Reporting System* (外国投资信息报送系统 wàiguó tóuzī xìnxī bào sòng xìtǒng; Art. 34§1), which is an administrative framework that requires FIEs to submit detailed investment information to the Chinese authorities. This system has replaced the previous record-filing process and aims at supporting policy-making, improving services, and enhancing investment protection. 52

Foreign investors and FIEs must register, apply for changes, and report information such as annual operations, etc. through the *Enterprise Registration System* (ERS) 企业登记系统 qǐyè dēngjì xìtǒng and the *National Enterprise Credit Information Publicity System* (NECIPS) 国家企业信用信息公示系统 qǐyè dēngjì xìtǒng (Art. 34§1). 53

---

will be typically hired as agent under a contract of mandate (s. below Chap. 5 §30, Mandate).

[46] Civil Code, Art. 59; s. below, §128; s. also Company Law, Art. 33§1 and below, §§1824ff.

[47] For example, trading registration, customs registration, e-port registration, etc.

54 ERS and NECIPS are two distinct, but related, systems that serve different purposes: the ERS is specifically intended for business entity information, while NECIPS covers a broad range of government information. Although being distinct, these systems can overlap, as information from the ERS may be made available through the broader NECIPS.

55 Those systems are shared among the authorities through yet another system known as the *Departmental Information Sharing System* as (政务部门信息共享系统 zhèngwù bùmén xìnxī gòngxiǎng xìtǒng), A.K.A. *Government Data Sharing* (政务数据共享 zhèngwù shùjù gòngxiǎng), purporting at dispensing the applicants to have to resubmit information already submitted, thus addressing an old frustration of foreign investors (Art. 34). These systems are detailed further down in this book (s. §1822).

56 Failure to register, or to update an existing registration, may trigger an order to comply issued by the competent authority; persistent failure, or failure to comply in a timely manner, may result in a fine (Art. 37).

57 Violation of the law or regulations by a foreign investor shall, after having been handled by the authorities, be recorded in the "credit information system" (Art. 38). While this provision refers to "any" such violation, it also refers to the applicable secondary legislation, as the case may be. One should assume that minor violations may not be recorded, subject to the degree of discretion the authorities may retain in that regard.

58 Besides, the "credit information system" mentioned in this provision is not to be understood as yet another system in addition to the systems described above, but as a broad reference to the same, in particular to NECIPS. Be that as it may, this provision is intended to act as a deterrent. As a matter of fact, NECIPS is routinely consulted by potential investors in case of purported merger or acquisition. ERS and NECIPS can be said to be the Chinese equivalent of the *register of commerce* or of companies known in most other jurisdictions.

59 *Company registration* in general (not limited to FIEs) is further discussed below in the company law chapter of this book (s. Chap. 9 §64.II.D, Company Registration).

VI. Record Filing

60 The FIL also mandates foreign investors to comply with certain record filing obligations (Art. 29). Although closely related, *record filing* is to be distinguished from *registration* (for the latter, s. above Chap. 1 §5.V, Registration). Registration is to be complied with from the outset, immediately after the issuance of the business license, and does not recur. In contrast, record filing is

periodical in nature and is to be complied with yearly, at the end of each civil or accounting year, or after a corporate change, depending on its subject-matter.

The record filing requirement bears on the FIE's operational and financial data, which the foreign investors must file with the competent authority, depending on the data's nature. The FIL only contains a general reminder of the record filing requirement; it further refers to secondary legislation for the detail[48]. 61

The record filing requirement is not unlimited. The information requested must be *necessary* (Art. 34§2). This provision can be seen as a particular expression of the general duty imposed on the authorities to protect trade secrets (Art. 23; s. above §22). 62

While larger, well-established companies may do it themselves, new, smaller, inexperienced FIEs usually mandate a specialized agency to do it on their behalf, not only for saving the trouble, but also to avoid fines in case of non- or untimely compliance. 63

VII. Reviews

In addition to the review of the future foreign invested company application occurring in view of its preapproval *before* it can register, the FIL provides for additional reviews *after* the company's registration. Again, *reviews* are not to be confused with *record filing*. Unlike the latter, reviews are not periodical; they take place after the registration, on an opportunistic basis, when triggered by a specific event. 64

The principle of such reviews is contained in the same provision as record filing (Art. 29). The FIL further specifically mentions two types of reviews: the *national security* and the *anti-monopoly* reviews. 65

The *national security* review (Art. 35§1) may occur after the foreign company has been registered. As its name suggests, it is concerned with any activity[49] purported by the FIE which may threaten national security. If so, a national 66

---

48 Such authorities and data are, mainly: SAMR: annual reports (operational and financial), changes in company registration; Ministry of Commerce (MOFCOM): investment information, equity and shareholder changes; State Tax Administration (STA): tax filings (corporate income tax, value-added tax (VAT), etc.); SAFE: foreign exchange transactions and capital flow; National Bureau of Statistics (NBS): statistical reporting (where applicable).

49 The concern addressed by the national security review is echoed, among other provisions, in *contract law* by Art. 534 of the Chinese Civil Code which provides that the authorities retain a right of "supervision" and of "disposition" in case the performance of a contract endanger the "national", "social" and "public" interest (s. below §680).

security review will be conducted. Inasmuch, to some extent, this review doubles with the Negative List, since the latter already rules out industries or areas which are deemed to be contrary to China's higher interests and is therefore designed to catch the fishes that went through the net's meshes.

67 Until then, the national security review was regulated by the *Notice on Establishing a Security Review System for Foreign Investors' Mergers and Acquisitions of Domestic Enterprises*. The incorporation of the review in the FIL increases its significance by, on the one hand, giving it a stronger legal basis by elevating it in the legal hierarchy and, on the other, by potentially, however silently, expanding it beyond mergers and acquisitions to all foreign investment (s. above §8).

68 In addition, the FIL further strengthens the authority of the national security review by providing that any decision rendered upon completion of the review is final, i.e., not subject to appeal, provided, however, that the principle of legality has been respected (Art. 35§2).

69 Although the FIL does not provide detail, the competent authority is the National Development & Reform Commission (NDRC) 中华人民共和国国家发展和改革委员会 zhōnghuá rénmín gònghéguó guójiā fāzhǎn hé gǎigé wěiyuánhuì.

70 The *anti-monopoly* review is governed by the Anti-monopoly Law to which the FIL expressly refers, without providing details (Art. 33). Such review is subject to a turnover threshold above which the business operators (i.e., the foreign investors only if both parties to the transaction are foreigners, or foreign investors together with domestic ones, if any) considering a merger, an acquisition or any other business transaction amounting to a market concentration relevant to the Chinese economy must notify the Chinese anti-monopoly authority. The anti-monopoly review only occurs in case a purported or existing transaction results in a market concentration.

71 If so, or if those operators omit to and the authority becomes aware of it anyway, the authority may decide to conduct an anti-monopoly review, to which those operators, including the foreign investors, must subject the transaction at stake. Failure to comply with the anti-monopoly laws and regulations is sanctioned by stiff penalties[50].

---

[50] Anti-monopoly law is not covered by this book.

VIII. Derogations

The FIL contains a derogation for regulations or measures applicable to the financial industry. If they depart from the FIL, the former shall prevail (Art. 41). By doing so, the Chinese legislator signals that it places the interests of the State related to the financial industry above the protection of foreign investment. 72

§6. International Law

I. Introduction

At least two international instruments must be mentioned in relation with Chinese FIL: the first, the so-called Washington or ICSID Convention, is multilateral; the other, as far as Sino-Swiss relations are concerned, is the Sino-Swiss BIT. 73

II. The Washington Convention (ICSID)

The Convention on the Settlement of Investment Disputes Between States and Nationals of Other States (short named the Washington Convention[51] or the ICSID Convention) established, under the auspices of the World Bank, the *International Center for the Settlement of Investment Disputes* (ICSID) in 1966. 74

ICSID is an autonomous international organization. However, it has close links with the World Bank[52]. All of ICSID's member-States are also members of the Bank. Both China and Switzerland are[53]. 75

ICSID, which is seated within the World Bank compound in Washington, D.C., U.S.A., provides remedies or "facilities" for the conciliation and the arbitration of disputes related to the investments, by nationals of one member-State, in the country of another member State. Therefore, the Washington Convention can apply to disputes between a Swiss investor (or an investor being a national of another member-State) and China about that investor's investment in China. In 76

---

51 The Convention was signed at the seat of the World Bank in Washington, D.C., U.S.A.

52 The World Bank is an agency of the UN.

53 Switzerland joined the Washington Convention from its inception in 1967; China joined in 1990 and the Convention entered into force in China in 1993.

addition to arbitration and conciliation, ICSID also offers a number of alternative dispute resolution (ADR) facilities.

77 The Center's jurisdiction is subject to the parties' consent (Art. 25§1). Moreover, China has limited the scope of the Convention to "disputes over compensation resulting from expropriation and nationalization"[54]. In contrast, China has not subjected the recourse to the Convention to the exhaustion of local administrative or judicial remedies.[55]

78 *Damage compensation* under the World Bank's guidelines is discussed further down in this book with the liability for illicit acts (s. §§1663ff.)

III. The Sino-Swiss Bilateral Investment Treaty

79 China and Switzerland are bound by a bilateral investment treaty (BIT), i.e., an agreement on the promotion and the reciprocal protection of FDIs[56]. This treaty was signed on 27 January 2009; it became effective on 13 April 2010.

80 It is the third of its kind: a first, so-called friendship treaty had been signed as soon as 1918[57], whereas a trade agreement was subsequently signed in 1974[58]. As a matter of fact, neither the 1918 nor the 1974 treaty were concerned with FDI, which was simply not a topic between those two countries at the time; however, these treaties did contribute to establishing a benevolent environment for the development of commercial relationships between the two countries. In contrast, the 2009 treaty is a genuine BIT. Yet however obsolete and effectively

---

54 On damage valuation, s. below §§2339ff.

55 S. International Center for the Settlement of Investment Disputes, Contracting States and Measures Taken by Them for the Purpose of the Convention (28 October 2022).

56 Long name: "Agreement between the Swiss Federal Council and the Government of the People's Republic of China on the Promotion and Reciprocal Protection of Investments". The version in English language is not available on Fedlex. Fr. (original version): Accord entre le Conseil fédéral suisse et le Gouvernement de la République populaire de Chine concernant la promotion et la protection réciproque des investissements; Ger.: Abkommen zwischen dem Schweizerischen Bundesrat und der Regierung der Volksrepublik China über die Förderung und den gegenseitigen Schutz von Investitionen.

57 Fr. (original version): Traité d'amitié entre la République de la Confédération suisse et la République de Chine; Ger.: Freundschaftsvertrag zwischen der Schweiz und der Republik China; signed on 13 June 1918 effective 8 October 1919; RS 11 583 (no version in English language available).

58 Fr. (original version): Accord de commerce entre la Confédération suisse et la République populaire de Chine; Ger.: Handelsabkommen zwischen der Schweizerischen Eidgenossenschaft und der Volksrepublik China; signed on 20 December 1974 effective 30 April 1975; RS 0.946.292.491 (no version in English language available).

replaced by subsequent, modern treaties[59], both the 1918 and the 1974 treaties are still in force.

While a BIT makes certain remedies available to the parties, i.e., the foreign investor and the host State, to a foreign investment, unlike the ICSID Convention, it is not only concerned by dispute resolution, but also by foreign investment promotion. The following features pertaining to the Sino-Swiss BIT deserve being mentioned. 81

"Investment" and "investor" (BIT, Art. 1§1 and 1§2) are defined in much greater detail than in the PRC FIL (Art. 2), which potentially may be helpful in case of disagreement between a Swiss investor and the Chinese authorities as to the scope of these notions. Revenue[60] is also defined (BIT, Art. 1§3).[61] 82

It is noteworthy that the Sino-Swiss BIT may apply to investment made not only after but also *before* it entered into force, in 2010. However, the BIT does not apply to disputes whose cause arose before it became effective (Art. 2). 83

The Sino-Swiss BIT also mentions the right of the investor to repatriate profit (Art. 5[62]) with comparatively more accuracy than the PRC FIL (Art. 21). 84

The same could be said about expropriation (or nationalization) (BIT Art. 6; PRC FIL, Art. 20), whose legality and fair and timely indemnification the treaty guarantees[63]. Moreover, the BIT contains an additional guarantee by which the host State commits to indemnify the investor of the other country in case of damage resulting from a war (Art. 7[64]). 85

The Sino-Swiss BIT further contains other guarantees which generally mirror those contained in the PRC FIL and those now generally acknowledged by the international community in FDI[65]. 86

Finally, the Sino-Swiss BIT provides the parties with detailed remedies in the event of *disputes*. Its main features are as follows. The BIT offers two separate disputes mechanism between a Swiss investor and the Chinese authorities, or a 87

---

59 Notably, as far as trade is concerned, the World Trade Organization (WTO) treaties, s. below §97.

60 Revenue is translated as "returns" in the version in English language of the BIT.

61 So is "territory" (BIT Art. 1§4).

62 The repatriation of profit is mentioned, in the Sino-Swiss BIT, under the title "Transfers".

63 On damage valuation, s. below §§2339ff.

64 Such indemnification is mentioned, in the Sino-Swiss BIT, under the title "Compensation for Losses".

65 S. above note 10.

Chinese investor and the Swiss authorities (Art. 11[66]) on the one hand, and Switzerland and China (Art. 12[67]) on the other[68]. In this book, we are primarily concerned with the first mechanism, specifically disputes between a Swiss investor and the competent Chinese authorities brought by the investor against the authority.

88 Art. 11 of the BIT offers the investor the choice between local, judicial or administrative remedies before the competent Chinese courts or administrative authorities, or arbitration. However, like for the ICSID Convention[69], while arbitration is, under the Sino-Swiss BIT, equally an attractive option, such investor may only choose so provided its Chinese governmental counterpart so consents (Art. 11§3).

89 While such reservation may be perceived as effectively depriving China's commitment of much of its substance, it would be wrong to draw that conclusion. China is not required to give reasons for its refusal; yet from a diplomatic perspective, it could not do so systematically, without reason, for futile reasons, or merely in order to secure an unfair advantage, without calling into question its commitment to the international order and, more specifically, to Sino-Swiss relations.

90 In any event, a Swiss investor could rely on certain guarantees contained in the Sino-Swiss BIT even if it were to proceed before Chinese courts.

91 Certain provisions of the Sino-Swiss BIT are detailed in a Protocol supplementing the BIT[70].

IV. Other Treaties

92 In addition to the treaties mentioned above, Switzerland has signed innumerable more and is a member of numerous organizations dedicated to international,

---

66 Such mechanism is mentioned, in the Sino-Swiss BIT, under the title "Disputes between a Contracting Party and an investor of the other Contracting Party".

67 Such mechanism is mentioned, in the Sino-Swiss BIT, under the title "Disputes between the Contracting Parties".

68 Disputes between States over direct investment occur in case of *diplomatic protection*, i.e., when a State vests in the rights of one of its national investors in the other country because it considers that the interests at stake merge with its sovereignty; in such case, the investor is not a party to the proceedings. S. John LIEBESKIND, The Legal Framework of Swiss International Trade and Investments, Part II: Protection, pp. 487 ff.

69 S. above §77.

70 The Protocol is appended to the main treaty.

be it multilateral or bilateral, development and cooperation.[71] Most of them are exclusively intended to State-parties and do not confer any direct rights to investors. Moreover, China is only one country among Switzerland's many State counterparts and has not necessarily signed the same multilateral treaties like Switzerland. Yet some of these treaties deserve to be mentioned.

As far as *multilateral* treaties or organizations are concerned, both China and Switzerland are member of the *Asian Development Bank* (ADB). Most developing countries[72] are funded, sometimes heavily, by a regional bank like the ADB. Generally closely related to, but independent from the UN[73], these regional banks focus on developing economies. 93

On the Swiss side, the regional banks' counterparts are seco and the DDC[74]. Provided Switzerland is a member, as is the case for the ADB, Swiss investors have the right to tender for development projects and apply for loans. Such projects are regularly located in China[75] and are, therefore, open to Swiss investors. Even though private investors are often unaware of them, these institutions manage considerable funds and are very active. 94

Among the many organizations pertaining to the UN, which Switzerland joined only in 2002, the *World Bank* is one of the UN specialized agencies and its development bank[76]. Three of its institutions, the *International Bank for Reconstruction & Development* (which is the Bank itself), the *International Development Association* (IDA) and the *International Finance Corporation* (IFC) offer to Swiss investors, on a multilateral scale, opportunities comparable to the regional banks mentioned above. 95

---

[71] For a list of these treaties and organizations, s. RS 0.97 which breaks down in Development and Cooperation in General (RS 0.970), Multilateral Financial Aid (RS 0.972), Aid to Certain Countries (0.973), Scientific and Technical Cooperation (RS 0.974), Investment Protection (RS 0.975) and Bretton Woods Institutions (RS 0.979).

[72] The ADB still classifies China as a "developing member country".

[73] S. below §95.

[74] The development and co-operation policy of Switzerland is entrusted to both the Swiss government's Agency for Development & Cooperation (DDC) and to the Economic Cooperation to Development Division of its State Secretariat for Economic Affairs (seco).

[75] S. https://www.adb.org/where-we-work/prc.

[76] A specialized institution of the UN, the World Bank is in fact a group, the World Bank Group, consisting of five institutions: the International Bank for Reconstruction & Development (IBRD) (not to be mixed up with the European Bank for Reconstruction & Development (EBRD), the International Development Association (IDA), the International Finance Corporation (IFC), the Multilateral Investment Guarantee Agency (MIGA), and the International Centre for Settlement of Investment disputes (ICSID) (for the latter, s. above Chap. 1 §6.II. Switzerland is a member of all of them. S. RS 0.972.2-4 and 0.975.1-2.

96 Speaking of *bilateral* treaties, other than the Sino-Swiss BIT discussed above, China and Switzerland have signed an agreement on *scientific and technical cooperation*. This agreement was signed in 1989, i.e., somehow half-way between the Treaty of Commerce of 1974 and the BIT of 2009. It is very short and, as its name makes clear, limited to scientific or technical exchanges between the two countries, typically in the form of delegations visiting each other and collaborating on a project-basis. While not designed for investment proper, it planted the seeds for the promotion of FDIs (s. Art. 1§1 and Art. 4) and has proven efficient in paving their way. It is still in force today and apt to support any such cooperation.

97 For the sake of preventing any misunderstanding, the *Sino-Swiss Free Trade Agreement* (FTA; s. below §§876ff.) does not apply to FDI but, as its name makes clear, to trade only. So do the agreements oversighted by the World Trade Organization (WTO; *ibid.)* Notably, the strenuous attempts to conclude a multilateral agreement on FDI, tentatively known as the Multilateral Agreement on Investment (MAI), under the auspices of WTO, known as the *Doha Rounds*, has failed;[77] there are currently no plans to revive it. Finally, the *OECD Codes* promoted by the Organisation for Economic Co-Operation and Development and are regarded, absent the MAI, as the most important multilateral set of rules on FDI[78], is irrelevant as far as China is concerned, since it is not a member of OECD.

77 S. Jean-Christophe [A.K.A. John] LIEBESKIND, The Legal Framework of Swiss International Trade and Investments, Part I: Promotion, "The Policy Framework for Investment (PFI)", p. 354.

78 *Ibid.*, pp. 352 ff.

Chap. 2 General Provisions of Civil Law

§7. Introduction

The Chinese Civil Code 民法典 mínfǎ diǎn entered into force on 1 January 2021. It can be regarded as of the most significant milestone in the development of China's modern *corpus iuris*. It is one of the few Chinese laws bearing the name of "code"[79], which outlines its preeminence in the hierarchy of laws. 98

As such, it has *replaced* and simultaneously *repealed* a raft of disparate laws, the substance of which was revised and which are now gathered under one same code. These laws include, notably, for our purpose, the General Principles of Civil Law, the General Rules of Civil Law, the Contract Law, the Real Rights Law, the Liability for Illicit Act ("Torts") Law and the Guarantee Law[80] (Chinese Civil Code, Art. 1260). 99

China is a civil law jurisdiction (as opposed to the Anglo-Saxon common law jurisdictions[81]) since the birth of the Republic of China at the downfall of the last emperor and the Qing Dynasty in 1911. As such, it relies on codification like the continental European tradition[82]. Inasmuch, it is comparable, in many respects, to Swiss law[83]. The latter fact justifies, among other things, the comparative, however not systematic, approach of this book. 100

The Chinese Civil Code has been gradually drafted in the form of separate laws which were eventually aggregated in the 2021 Code. Starting in 1986 with the *General Principles of Civil Law* (revised and reenacted in 2017 under the title of *General Provisions of Civil Law*), its most prominent components over time 101

---

[79] Besides the Maritime Code, the Chinese government has, in 2025, been calling for public comments on a purported Ecological and Environmental Code.

[80] They also include the Marriage Law, the Succession Law and the Adoption Law, which are not covered in this book.

[81] Civil law systems rely primarily on comprehensive written codes and statutes as the main source of law. Common law systems, on the other hand, place greater emphasis on case law and judicial precedents (or jurisprudence) as a source of law, in addition to statutes. Chinese law does borrow, however, to a limited extent, certain modern legal concepts typical of the common law jurisdictions which, whenever relevant, will be discussed elsewhere in this book. *Contra*, s. JACQUES HENRI [A.K.A. James] HERBOTS, The Chinese New Civil Code and the Law of Contract, China-EU Law Journal, Springer, Heidelberg 2021, 7:39-49, p. 43.

[82] For a history of the codification of civil law in China, s., for example, *ibid.*, pp. 39-40.

[83] Swiss law is among the sources from which Chinese law drew inspiration, among other foreign sources, including German and Japanese law (*ibid.*, p. 40).

included (but were not limited to) the law of contracts (1999), the law on property and real rights (2007), tort law (2009) and private international law (2010).

102 The Code does not fundamentally alter the preexisting laws it aggregates. Nevertheless, it incorporated the jurisprudence of the Supreme People's Court (SPC) 最高人民 zuìgāo rénmín[84], i.e., its so-called judicial interpretations 最高人民法院解释 zuìgāo rénmín fǎyuàn jiěshì which it treated as a source of law on equal footing with statutory law[85].

103 The most prominent feature of the Chinese Civil Code is its legitimatization of private law by which, unlike in the past[86], public and private interests are now treated equally. This development is consistent with the amendment of the Constitution which, in 2004, held that *private property* is inviolable (then Art. 22; now Art. 13§1 and 2): the Civil Code now clearly acknowledges that "property rights of the State, of collectives and private individuals along with property rights of others receive equal protection under the law; no organization or individual shall infringe these rights." (Art. 207).

104 The Chinese Civil Code systematically integrates all the basic norms regulating civil law[87]. It compares in most respects to the Swiss Civil Code[88] and to the Swiss Code of Obligations (Fr.: CO; Ger.: OR)[89]. It is divided in seven Books: General Provisions, Property, Contracts, Personality Rights, Family Law, Succession, and Liability for Illicit Acts (Torts).

105 While the Chinese Civil Code can be said to be equivalent to the Swiss Civil Code and the Swiss Code of Obligations, the former differs from the latter in some respects, both structure- and content wise. Thus, where the Chinese Civil Code is divided in books like the Swiss Civil Code (including its Fifth Book, the Code of Obligations), the former does not contain a book on obligations

---

84 The SPC is the last instance of the Chinese judicial system. It compares to the Federal Tribunal in Switzerland.

85 S. HERBOTS (s. above note 81), pp. 40-41.

86 After the Revolution in 1949, private law was abolished and private interests deprived of protection. Both were then gradually reintroduced. S. *ibid.*, pp. 41-42.

87 Simply said, civil law regulates the legal relationships between individuals or corporations, as compared to administrative law, which regulates the relationships between the State and those individuals or corporations, and public law, which governs the activity of the State.

88 However not legally binding, a version in English language of the Swiss Civil Code is available on Swisslex, the official database of Swiss laws.

89 Although commonly referred to in French as Code of Obligations (Fr. "Code des obligation" or CO), Swiss law does not name it as such: it is the Fifth Book of the Civil Code and is literally titled "Law of Obligations" (although translated as "Code of Obligations" on Swisslex); it is commonly, and correctly, referred to in German as "Obligationenrecht" or OR however.

like the latter. Instead, the Chinese Civil Code contains a book on contracts, and on liability for illicit acts.

Speaking of those books of the Chinese Civil Code corresponding to the Swiss *Civil* Code (*stricto sensu*, i.e., without the Code of Obligations), the book titled General Provisions of the Chinese Code roughly corresponds to the Preliminary Title of the Swiss one. The Second Book on property or real rights of the Chinese Code corresponds to the Fourth Book on real rights (Fr.: "droit réels"; Ger.: "Sachenrecht") of the Swiss Code. The Fourth Book on Personality Rights of the Chinese Code correspond to the First Book on the law of persons of the Swiss Code. The Fifth Book on marriage and family of the Chinese Code corresponds to the Second Book on family of the Swiss Code. Finally, the Sixth Book on succession of the Chinese Code corresponds to the Third Book of the same name of the Swiss Code. 106

As far as the *Swiss Code of* Obligations is concerned, as noted, the Chinese Civil Code does not contain a book on obligations like the Swiss one. Instead, the Chinese Civil Code contains a book on general provisions of civil law (which also applies, to some extent, to obligations), on contracts, and on liability for illicit acts. The first, on contracts, which is the Third Book, corresponds to the First Part on "General Provisions" (of obligations) and to the Second Part on "Various Forms of Contracts" (Fr.: "Des diverses espèces de contrats"; Ger.: "Die einzelnen Vertragsverhältnisse") of the Swiss Code of Obligations. 107

However, the First Part (Title One) of the Swiss Code of Obligations also contains the regime of liability for illicit acts and quasi-contracts (*negotiorum gestio* and unjust enrichment), while the former topic corresponds to the Seventh Book of the Chinese Civil Code, and the latter forms the last title (Title Three) and the two last chapters of its Third Book of contract law. 108

Moreover, from the perspective of *liability*, in Swiss law, all three main sources of liability, liability for illicit acts, contractual liability and quasi-contracts are contained in the First Part of the Code of Obligations (Title One on the formation of obligations, complemented, for contractual liability, by Title Two on performance), while in the Chinese Civil Code these sources are scattered in the First Book on general provisions (Chap. 8), in the Third Book of contract law (last chapter of Title One on general rules) and in the Seventh Book on liability for illicit acts. The Chinese and the Swiss regimes will be compared in more detail further down in this book. 109

In addition, the following subject-matters are treated in the Swiss Code of Obligations, but not in the Chinese Civil Code: *company law*, which is the Third Part of the Swiss Code of Obligations (Fr.: " Des sociétés commerciales et de la société coopérative"; Ger. " Die Handelsgesellschaften und die Genossenschaft"), is primarily governed, in China, by the Company Law, as well as the 110

Partnership Enterprise Law[90]. The Chinese Code does regulate the partnership *contract* however (Art. 967 ff.), thus matching the simple partnership (Fr.: "société simple"; Ger.: "einfache Gesellschaft") of the Swiss Code of Obligations (Art. 530 ff.) In addition, the Chinese Code contains, in its First Book about general provisions, a Chapter 3 about legal persons which corresponds to Title Two (Fr.: "Des personnes morales"; Ger.: "Die juristischen Personen") of the First Book of the Swiss Civil Code on the law of persons.

111 Likewise, the Swiss Code of Obligations contains two more chapters which find no equivalent in the Chinese Civil Code: a Fourth Part on the *commercial register, business names and commercial accounting*, and a Fifth Part on *negotiable securities*.

112 The Chinese Civil Code is divided several *parts* which are, hierarchically, books (编 biān), titles (分编 fēn biān), chapters (章 zhāng), sections (节 jié), and articles (条 tiáo). Although the corresponding translations may vary, the one proposed here reflect those generally, although not only, used in English, in particular in western civil law jurisdictions[91], and is the one we will use throughout this book. The numbering of chapters is continuous throughout each book; it is not interrupted by titles. Those parts are preceded by their numbering in Chinese[92], which is itself signaled by the prefix 第 dì, that is not translated in English.

§8. General Provisions (of Civil Law)

113 The First Book of the Chinese Civil Code on general provisions contains ten chapters. Beyond the first chapter which contains "basic" provisions, the subject-matters of the other "general" provisions range from natural persons (Chap. 1) to legal persons (Chap. 2), unincorporated organizations (Chap. 3), civil rights (Chap. 5), legal (also translated as juristic or juridical) acts (Chap. 6), agency (or representation) (Chap. 7), civil liability (Chap. 8), limitation of actions (or extinctive prescription) (Chap. 9) and the calculation of time periods (Chap. 10).

---

90 The Wholly Foreign-Owned Enterprise Law, the Equity Joint-Venture Law and the Cooperative Joint-Venture Law have been abolished as of 1 January 2020 with the inception of the Foreign Investment Law, s. above Chap. 1 §5.I, Corporate Form.

91 Comparatively, the Swiss Civil Code is divided in books (the Code of Obligations forming its Fifth Book, s. above note 89), parts, titles, and chapters; chapters are divided according to the following marginal format: A, I, 1, a; this internal division does not exist in the Chinese Civil Code.

92 One 一 yī, two 二 èr, three 三 sān, four 四 sì, five 五 wǔ, six 六 liù, seven 七 qī, eight 八 bā, nine 九 jiǔ, ten 十 shí.

In addition, the Chinese Civil Code contains, at its very end, under the "Supplementary Provisions" final chapter (not numbered), one interpretative provision of general application (Art. 1259; s. below §232), while its last provision mentions which laws it replaces (Art. 1260; s. above §99). 114

While not all these general provisions are necessarily of immediate concern to foreign investors, several deserve attention, nevertheless. 115

I. Basic Provisions (Within the General Provisions)

Basic provisions[93] do not exactly identify with general provisions: Chapter 1 (Art. 1 to 12) contains basic provisions within the First Book of the Code on general provisions. They assert the fundamental *purpose* of civil law which is to protect the civil subjects' right and to regulate their relationship in accordance with its core values (Art. 1). These *rights* are broadly defined as including personal rights, property rights and other rights (Art. 3), while those *values* include equality among those subjects (Art. 2 and 4), freedom of will (Art. 5)[94], fairness and reasonableness (Art. 6), good faith[95], honesty and honor (Art. 7), compliance with the law and public order (which includes the social and the economic order) and morals (Art. 1 and 8). Such values are shared by Swiss law[96]. In addition, the Code emphasizes its support of socialism with Chinese characteristics and socialist core values (Art. 1). Another progressive value 116

[93] The consistency or systematic of the original titles of certain parts of the Chinese Civil Code is questionable and, by all means, not obvious. The First Book of the Code on general provisions of civil law (Art. 1 ff.) is titled 总则 zǒngzé, but Title One on general provisions of the Third Book on contract law (Art. 463 ff.) is titled 通则 tōngzé. Where in both cases, 则 zé stands for "rules" or similar meanings (including "provisions"), it is unclear why 总 zǒng was chosen as qualifier in the first and 通 tōng in the second, while both can be translated as "general" or other similar meanings (such as "common"). Likewise, Chapter 1 on basic provisions of the First Book is titled 基本规定 jīběn guīdìng, but Chapter 1 (Art. 463 ff.) on general provisions of the Third Book is titled 一般规定 yībān guīdìng. Again, where in both cases 规定 guīdìng stands for "provisions", both 基本 jīběn and 一般 yībān can equally be translated as "general" or other similar meanings (such as "basic"). Translations also result in all kinds of combinations. We do not believe that those nuances have any legal significance.

[94] This principle is reiterated at Art. 130 (s. below §177). On *contractual* freedom, s. below §554.

[95] On good faith in contractual performance, s. Art. 509§2 and below, §615.

[96] These core principles rest, in Swiss law, on the first articles of the Swiss Civil Code, i.e., on the literally fundamental notion and general duty of *good faith* (CC Art. 2§1 and 3), whose negative corollary is that the *abuse of a right* (notion also known in doctrine as "abuse of right" or "abuse of law"; Fr.: "abus de droit"; Ger.: "Rechtsmissbrauch") is not protected by the law (CC Art. 2§2).

worth being noted, let alone because it is not to be found in the Swiss Civil Code, is the protection of the environment (Art. 9).

117 The Code also, importantly, restates the principle *lex specialis derogat leges generali*, pursuant to which specific laws prevail over the general provisions of the Code (Art. 11), as well as its territorial scope, i.e., that it applies to activities carried out in China (unless the law provides otherwise; Art. 12).

118 As will be pointed out in this book, however general in nature, all these provisions apply, in one way or the other, to foreign investors in the form of concrete applications, and are, therefore, available to them.

II. Natural Persons

119 Chapter 2 (Art. 13 to 56) of the First Book of the Chinese Civil Code addresses natural persons, as opposed to legal persons which are governed by the next chapter. It is divided in four sections covering capacity for civil rights and capacity for civil conducts; guardianship; declarations of missing persons and of death of persons; and individual businesses and lease holding farm households. Only a handful of these provisions, which are briefly commented below, are of potential interest to foreign investors.

120 The first provision of Chapter 2 on natural persons enunciates that the *domicile* of a natural person shall be the place where his residence is registered or the place where he or she usually resides (Art. 25). This provision matters, among other things, for the determination of the forum or local competence of a court. As far as foreign investors may be concerned, that may prove relevant in disputes such as labor disputes, where the place of domicile of the worker commands it, or in disputes related to leases (namely, to the household of an expatriate or local worker), where the place of the tenant prevails.

121 The last section of the chapter governs *individual businesses* (Art. 54 to 56). It is primarily intended to farm households and small family businesses, for which it provides special rules in case of debt collection. Art. 54 provides that an individual business means a business run by a natural person who has been legally registered to engage in individual or commercial operation; it does not expressly rule out foreign investors. The FIL (Art. 31) mandates that FIEs shall be governed by the Company Law, the Partnership Enterprise Law "and other relevant laws". Neither the Civil Code nor the Foreign Enterprises Law expressly preclude a foreign investor from registering as an individual business. However, we believe that, in practice, the authority would reject a foreign investor's application to register as individual business and direct him to register

as a stockholding company, a limited liability company or a partnership enterprise.

The other provisions related to natural persons are general in nature and not of direct interest to foreign investors. 122

III. Legal Persons

Chapter 3 on legal persons (法人 hōjin; Art. 57 to 108) of the First Book of the Civil Code on general provisions is of great significance to FIEs. It is divided in four sections: general provisions, for-profit legal persons, non-profit legal persons, and special legal persons. 123

In China, generally speaking, aside a limited number of very specific, seldom used *forms* which are generally out of the reach of foreign investors[97] and exceed the scope of this book[98], only the limited liability company, the shareholding company and the partnership enterprise enjoy legal personality, all of which will be outlined in detail further down in this book (s. below Chap. 9, Company Law), can register as a company and are accessible to foreign investors. Yet Art. 57 to 101 are of general application and encompass all aspects related to legal persons beyond those most common forms. 124

For the sake of clarity, the ensuing presentation does not follow the sections used by the law, which we have elected to restructure by subjectively dividing the provisions they contain in seven subsections (which the law does not) or themes: establishment, changes, legal representation, liability, termination, and legal persons categories and unincorporated organizations. 125

All the principles set out in this chapter of the Code are reflected and further developed in Chinese company law and will be discussed later in this book. In this respect, the Civil Code provisions are to be regarded as *lex generalis*, while the rules of company law, by elaborating upon them and, where applicable, derogating from them, operate as *lex specialis*. 126

---

[97] Such forms include: SOEs (which take the form of a limited liability company or of a shareholding company; s. below Chap. 9 §64.V, Special Provisions on the Organizational Structure of State-owned Companies); sole proprietorships (which can register but do not enjoy a legal personality separate from its owner, and can only be registered by Chinese citizens; s. below §1758); representative offices (which must be registered but do not enjoy legal personality; s. below Chap. 9 §67, Representative Offices); very specific forms of collective, township and village enterprises (s. below §423), including the cooperative (s. below §1756); as well as associations (s. below §152). This list is not exhaustive.

[98] S. below Chap. 9 §63, Introduction.

A. *Establishment*

127 The Chinese Civil Code defines a legal person as an organization enjoying *civil capacity* (Art. 57). In order to exist, it must have its own name, structure, domicile and assets (Art. 58§2), and meet the conditions set forth by the law for its establishment (Art. 58§§ 1 and 3).

128 A legal person shall start to exist after it has been established (Art. 59). For an FIE, it shall mean having gone through the various *registration* requirements described in general terms by the FIL (s. above Chap. 1 §5.V, Registration). The tipping point from which the FIE will be deemed to exist will be the issuance of the business license (s. below §§1824ff.) The civil capacity of a legal person shall start automatically and simultaneously with its existence. Likewise, such civil capacity will end with that legal person's existence (Art. 59; *ibid.*)

129 Art. 63 defines the *domicile* of a legal person as being deemed to be at its main offices location, thus echoing Art. 25 for natural persons (s. above §120) and the Company Law (Company Law, Art. 8 and below, §1772). Again, this provision matters, among other things, for the determination of the forum or local competence of a court.

130 A legal person may establish *branches*, whose establishment must be compliant, like that of their principal (Art. 74§1). Branches are specifically governed by the Company Law, namely its Art. 13 (s. below §§1783ff.), while *foreign* branches are regulated by its Chapter 13 (s. below Chap. 9 §64.XI, Branches of Foreign Companies).

B. *Changes*

131 Section 3 on legal persons contains several provisions related to changes to the status of a legal person in the course of its existence. The changes at stake are all those impacting the information recorded with the legal person's *registration* (Art. 64; s. above Chap. 1 §5.V, Registration). Any such change must be duly filed with the registration authority. The law protects the good faith of third parties if such registration is inaccurate or out-of-date (Art. 65).

132 Legal persons' registrations must be made available to the public; it must be so timely, which means that such information must be actual (Art. 66). Although the Code does not specify it, this is to occur in the first place through the legal person's registration on the ERS mentioned, as far as FIEs are concerned, in the FIL, and its related systems (s. above Chap. 1 §5.V, Registration).

C. *Legal Representative*

A legal person is represented by its legal representative (法定代表人 fădìng dàibiăo rén). The represented party is generally known as the *principal* and the representative one as the *agent*. Representation is a complex, multifold topic. Chapter 3 on legal persons of the First Book on general provisions of the Chinese Civil Code contains the basis of representation (Art. 61 and 62). This legal relationship is further developed in Chapter 7 on *agency* (Art. 161 ff.; s. below Chap. 2 §11, Agency) of the same book. Because the power to represent a third party is, by definition, conferred to the effect of performing some task on behalf of the principal, and because whenever a third party entrusted with some task is frequently empowered to represent the principal to that effect, representation is closely related, but distinct from, although frequently, but erroneously confused with, the *mandate*, which is governed by Chapter 23 (Art. 919 ff.) of the Third Book on contract law (s. below Chap. 5 §30, Mandate; on the distinction between representation and the mandate, s. below §§275ff. and §§1055ff.) Finally, and even though this brief outline is not comprehensive, representation is further developed in *company law*. 133

The Company Law applies to the *limited liability company* and the *shareholding company*, towards which representation plays, in practice, a major role. As far as the latter is concerned, the legal representative was briefly addressed by Art. 13 of the former *Company Law* (2018 Amendment), whose current version was revised in 2023 (s. below Chap. 9 §63, Company Law, Introduction). Meanwhile, the Chinese Civil Code was enacted in 2020 and addressed the legal representative in Chapter 4 on legal persons of the First Book on general provisions of the Chinese Civil Code (Art. 61 and 62). By doing so, the legislator provides the Company Law with a legal basis in a law of superior rank which, as far as the legal representative was concerned, had been somewhat lacking so far. 134

Thus, while Art. 61 of the Chinese Civil Code mostly clarifies Art. 13 of the old Company Law, Art. 62 of the Chinese Civil Code complements it by addressing the related liabilities. Eventually, in the Company Law (2023 Revision), the legislator replaced the old Art. 13 by a new Art. 10 which mostly paraphrases Art. 61 of the Chinese Civil Code, and added a new Art. 11 which develops the liability principles established by Art. 62 of the Chinese Civil Code as well as by the general regimes of agency and related civil liability it contains (s. below §§1774ff.) In other words, although posterior to the original Company Law, the Chinese Civil Code contains the basis of the provisions on the legal representative of a legal person outlined in the current Company Law. 135

While admittedly of limited practical relevance, this somewhat tedious historical reminder remains useful for two reasons: first, it helps understanding the 136 relationship between the Code and the Company Law as far as the legal representation of a legal person, which is very significant in practice, is concerned. Second, it is relevant because the application of the latest Company Law, although effective as of 1 July 2024, is actually gradual, so that some aspects of the precedent 2018 Amendment version may still apply[99].

137 That said, it should be reminded that the Company Law applies to the limited liability company and the shareholding company. The representation of *other types of companies* is governed by their own regimes and will be addressed below (s. Chap. 9 §65ff.) The general regime of the Chinese Civil Code, i.e., Art. 61, 62 and 161 ff., applies to all of them. All the representation sub-regimes mentioned in this introduction will be outlined further down in this book with the main regime to which they pertain.

138 Art. 61 and 62 of the Chinese Civil Code enshrine the core principles of the law of representation: after having defined the legal representative (Art. 61 § 1), they state that the deeds of the agent performed towards a third party on behalf of the principal bind the latter to the third party, but that, if the agent exceeded his power (in which case it is known as *falsus procurator*), those deeds do not bind the third party of good faith (Art. 62§§ 2 and 3). The principal is further liable for the damage caused by his agent (Art. 62). These regulations are further detailed in Chapter 7 on agency of the First Book on general provisions of the Chinese Civil Code, which we discuss further down (s. below Chap. 2 §11, Agency). Moreover, as explained (s. above §§134 to 136), they are reciprocated in Art. 10 and 11 of the Company Law.

D. Liability

139 The Chinese Civil Code is concerned about the various liabilities related to a legal person throughout its section on general provisions. It grounds the basic principle according to which a legal person bears liability "with all its assets" (Art. 60); however, it does not enunciates the conditions to which such liability is subject, which are to be found in the special liability regimes following the general regime of civil liability in the wide sense, i.e., liability for illicit acts, contractual liability and other sources of liability, are detailed in other parts of the Code and will be discussed further down in this book[100].

---

99 S. above note 7.

100 On civil liability in general, s. below Chap. 2 §12, Civil Liability; on contractual liability, s. below Chap. 4 §27, Liability for Breach of Contract; on liability for illicit acts, s. below Chap. 8 , Liability for Illicit Acts ("Torts")
; specific liability regimes are outlined throughout the other chapters, as the case may be.

As a matter of fact, with few exceptions, the principle set forth by Art. 60 finds limited application since most FIEs take the corporate form of a capital corporation (shareholding company or limited liability company), whose liability is limited up to its registered capital, which in practice is often below the totality of their assets. Corporate liability will be discussed further down in this book, in the chapter on company law (s. below Chap. 9 §64.XII, Liability of the Company). 140

With respect to the legal person's *establishment*, the Code also provides for the liability of the third party establishing the legal person (Art. 75), and of the liquidation group in case of *liquidation* (s. next chapter) (Art. 70§3). 141

In case of *merger*, that liability will be transferred to the entity resulting from the merger, whereas in case of *division*, the resulting entities will assume joint liability, unless they have agreed otherwise (Art. 67). 142

Art. 74§2 provides that, even if a *branch*[101] operates in its own name, the liability resulting from its deeds shall be borne by its principal. Alternatively, the assets of the branch may be used for meeting any such liability; however, the assets of its principal shall be used for covering any portion not covered by the branch's assets (Art. 74§2). 143

E. *Termination*

Chapter 3 on legal persons of the First Book of the Chinese Civil Code provides that the existence of a legal person shall end or "terminate"[102] in two main 144

---

[101] Generally speaking, a *branch* (分支 fēnzhī or 分支机构, fēnzhī jīgòu, branch office; Fr.: "succursale"; Ger.: "Niederlassung") does not enjoy a legal personality independently from its principal, which is liable for the debts of its branches; in contrast, a *subsidiary* (子公司 zǐ gōngsī; Fr.: "filiale"; Ger.: "Tochtergesellschaft") does possess a legal personality independently from its principal, from which it is legally independent and with which it only forms a common economic entity; therefore, unlike for branches, the principal is not liable for the debts of its subsidiaries. In that respect, the Chinese and the Swiss regimes are similar. The literal translation of "branch" in French, "branche", is not used in Swiss French legal language and may, in the common French language, point indistinctively either at a "succursale" or at a "filiale".

[102] Art. 68 of the Civil Code use the characters or expression 终止 zhōngzhǐ, which can be both a substantive ("termination") or a verb ("to terminate"); it is, depending of the version of the translation in English language, alternatively translated, in the context of Art. 68, in the active form as "shall terminate" or in the passive form as "shall be terminated", suggesting that the end of a legal person's existence can occur either automatically, or as a consequence of the law or of the legal person's articles of association, or by the will of the legal person, or by an official decision. As the cases listed by Art. 69 show, every one of these situations may occur.

circumstances: in case of dissolution, and in case of bankruptcy (Art. 68). The termination of a *legal person* is not to be confused neither with that of *juristic acts*, which is governed by another chapter of the Code (s. below §243 and, generally, Chap. 2 §10.IV, Validity of Juristic Acts), nor with that of *contracts* (s. below Chap. 4 §26, Termination), even though certain legal persons may be of a contractual or quasi-contractual nature[103].

145 *Dissolution*[104] shall occur in case of a series of circumstances which the Code also lists (Art. 69). These include: statutory dissolution (resulting from the legal person's article of association), namely, because the legal person has reached the end of its statutory duration, or because of some other provision providing for its dissolution; voluntary dissolution (resulting from a resolution of the legal person's organs); necessary dissolution (resulting from its transformation through merger or division); and mandatory dissolution (resulting from the law or from a judicial or administrative order, such as the revocation of the legal person's registration or of its business license). Both Art, 68 and 69, as well as Art. 69, item 4 (mandatory dissolution) expressly reserve other cases provided for by the law.

146 In the event a legal person is to be dissolved and before it can be so, it must be liquidated. The *liquidation*[105] regime is provided by Art. 70 to 72. Other than in case of merger or division, a "liquidation group" or a committee of some sort must be immediately established to that end (Art. 70). The liquidation must comply with the applicable laws and the articles of association. In the absence of other specific laws, the Company Law applies. A legal person may not continue to operate during its liquidation. Its remaining assets, if they are to be dealt with according to the articles of association, any topical resolution of its governing body, or the law, as applicable (Art. 72). Liquidation ends with the *deregistration* of the legal person, which is, symmetrically to the beginning of its existence, the tipping point at which its existence shall end (Art. 72).

147 As provided Art. 68, *bankruptcy* also results in the end of a legal person's existence once its liquidation and deregistration have been completed (Art. 73). The liquidation of a bankrupt legal person is a bankruptcy liquidation (as opposed to the ordinary liquidation provided for by Art. 70 to 72) and is subject to the bankruptcy laws and regulations.

---

[103] Namely, the contractual joint-venture (now abolished as corporate form; s. below Chap. 9 §66, Joint-ventures) and the partnership enterprise (s. below Chap. 9 §65, The Partnership Enterprise). About the notion of "quasi-contract", s. below note 490.

[104] "Dissolution" or "to dissolve" is expressed by 解散 jiěsàn.

[105] "Liquidation" or "to liquidate" is expressed by 清算 qīngsuàn.

F. Legal Persons Categories and Unincorporated Organizations

After having outlined general provisions on legal persons, the Chinese Civil Code, in the next three sections, details three categories or subtypes of legal persons: for-profit legal persons (Sect. 2); non-profit legal persons (Sect. 3) and special legal persons (Sect. 4). Unincorporated organizations are addressed by the Code in its following chapter (Chap. 4). 148

A *for-profit legal person* (Sect. 2) means a legal person established for the purpose of making profit and distributing profit to its shareholders and other investors (Art. 76§1). They mainly consist in limited liability companies and shareholding companies, which the Code expressly mentions, while reserving "other enterprises" (Art. 76§2). As a matter of fact, "other enterprises", as far as FIEs are concerned, are limited to partnership enterprises, under the law of the same name. 149

Sect. 2 on for-profit legal persons mirrors the Company Law promulgated less than two years before the Code was, whose basic principles it recalls without any significant addition. These principles will be discussed in the company law chapter of this book. 150

The definition of *non-profit legal person* (Sect. 3) is, unsurprisingly, the opposite of that of for-profit legal persons, i.e., a legal person which is established for public benefit purposes or other non-profit purposes and does not distribute the profit it obtained to its investors, founders or members (Art. 87§1). 151

The Code further lists, as non-profit legal persons, "among others", "public institutions, social organizations, foundations and social service agencies." (Art. 87§2). They are also known as *associations* (社会团体 shèhuì tuántǐ), which are typically industry- or professional associations. 152

Arguably, this section may also apply to *foreign chamber of commerce*, which are expressly authorized by the FIL (Art. 27)[106], and to *foreign non-governmental organizations* (NGOs)[107], provided they are legally registered. Both are strongly regulated by secondary legislation. However non-profit, 153

---

106 S. above §27.

107 As of 2017, NGOs are primarily governed by the Law on the Administration of Activities of Overseas Non-Governmental Organizations within the Territory of China (2017 Amendment) (A.K:A. "Foreign NGOs Law"). That law has increased government oversight and control over their activities, reflecting China's emphasis on national security and social stability. While the law provides a legal framework to foreign NGOs, it has also strongly constrained their registration and operations. The Foreign NGO Law also applies to foreign chambers of commerce.

representative offices of FIEs do not enjoy legal personality (s. below Chap. 9 §67, Representative Offices) and do, therefore, not fall into that category.

154 As with for-profit legal persons, the section deals with non-profit legal persons establishment, organization, liability, termination, liquidation and other features typical of non-profit organizations, such as the right for donors to ask questions (Art. 94§1), and to petition the court to cancel decisions of the organization they disagree with (Art. 94§2).

155 *Special persons* (Sect. 4) are defined as the legal persons of government organs, the legal persons of rural collective economic organizations, the legal persons of cooperative economic organizations in urban and rural areas, and the legal persons of so-called "grassroots" self-governing people's organizations (Art. 96). They are intended to domestic organizations and of no concern to foreign investors.

156 *Unincorporated organizations*[108] (Chinese Civil Code, Chapter 3, First Book, Chap. 4) are defined as organizations without the status of a legal person but able to conduct civil activities in their own name in accordance with the law (Art. 102§1). They include, "among others", "individual businesses (or sole proprietorships), partnerships, professional service organizations without the status of a legal person" (Art. 102§2).

157 Among unincorporated organizations, the *partnership* is to be distinguished from the partnership *enterprise*. The partnership is a contract regulated by the Third Book of contracts of the Civil Code (Art. 967 ff.), whereas the partnership enterprise is a corporation governed by the law of the same name (s. below Chap. 5 §41, Partnership Contract and Chap. 9 §65, The Partnership Enterprise). As such, the (contract of) partnership (A.K.A. "partnership business") does not, by definition, as an unincorporated organization, enjoy legal personality, whereas the partnership enterprise does.

158 *Incorporation* is not to be confused with *registration*. "Incorporated" describes an organization that is sufficiently structured for the law to recognize it as having a legal personality separate from that of its founders, investors, and governing bodies. In contrast, "unincorporated" qualifies a smaller organization or business which is not sophisticated enough to be acknowledged legal personality on its own.

159 Under the Civil Code, unincorporated organization are mandated to register and obtain the authorities' approval "as required by the law" (Art. 103). That explains why unincorporated businesses, such as, for example, licensing

[108] Unincorporated organizations (Zh.: 非法人组织 fēi fǎrén zǔzhī) is also occasionally (and inaccurately) translated in English as "non-legal persons".

agreements in the form of franchise networks[109] or technology transfers[110] which, however contractual, often amount to unincorporated organizations and are, therefore, mandated to register even though they are not set up in the form of a incorporated company.

The regulation of unincorporated organizations is of no direct concern to foreign investors, since the latter are subject to extensive registration requirements anyway (s. above Chap. 1 §5.V, Registration) and are mandated by the FIL to give their enterprise one of the forms made available to domestic investors by the Company Law, i.e., of a limited liability company or a shareholding company, or of a partnership enterprise (FIL, Art. 31). 160

As the examples above suggest, however, the regulation of unincorporated organizations may nevertheless be of indirect concern to foreign parties, since they may typically be a party to such unincorporated organizations (e.g., as member of a foreign chamber of commerce). 161

Likewise, the notion of *incorporation* is not to be confused with that of *legal personality*. While unincorporated organizations do not enjoy unrestricted legal personality like incorporated organizations, they do enjoy certain features resembling those typical of legal personality. Thus, an unincorporated organization "may engage in civil activities in its own name" (Art. 102). It further may designate representatives which it may empower to perform legal or civil acts on its behalf (Art. 105). 162

In that sense, the *foreign representative office* deserves a special mention since, however subject to strong registration and record filing requirements, it does not enjoy legal personality but is nevertheless exceptionally acknowledged limited rights akin to enjoying it. Foreign representative offices are presented further below (s. Chap. 9 §67, Representative Offices). 163

Chap. 4 also provides for the unincorporated organization's *liquidation* and *dissolution* in a way comparable to incorporated ones (Art. 106 and 107); it further refers to the general provisions on legal persons (Sect. 1 of Chap. 3) for any matter it does not regulate (Art. 108). 164

However, unlike for incorporated organizations which typically bear limited liability (s. above §140), those quasi-incorporated organizations features granted to unincorporated organizations reach their limit whenever the *liability* of the unincorporated organization is sought after: whenever so, the investors or founders of a non-legal-person organization shall bear unlimited liability for the debts of said organization, if its assets are insufficient to pay off its debts (Art. 104). 165

---

[109] S. above note 29.
[110] S. below §§1315 and 1316.

§9. Civil Rights

166 In Chapter 5 of its First Book on general provisions (Art. 109 to 132), after having defined civil subjects, the Chinese Civil Code defines basic civil rights. Whereas Chapter 1 also provides for basic civil rights, it can be said to focus on *principles* applying to any type of basic civil rights, whereas Chapter 5 focuses on the *types* of civil rights protected by those principles. Inasmuch, there is some overlap between these two chapters.

167 While some provisions of Chapter 5 are primarily intended for natural persons and are, therefore, not of direct concern to FIEs, several other provisions are of interest to them since they, however indirectly, imply potential consequences significant enough to be mentioned.

168 The first four articles of this chapter address so-called *personal rights*. Among these, Art. 110§2 acknowledges that legal persons and unincorporated organizations are entitled to the *right to one's name, to reputation and to honor*. These rights, which were traditionally intended to natural persons, are thus expressly extended to companies[111].

169 These guarantees are of particular significance in case of smearing or damage to the economic *reputation* of a company by competitors or consumers, which can cause considerable damage to the company so unfairly targeted[112]. Smearing was already prohibited, among others, by the Anti-unfair Competition Law (Art. 11), but the inclusion of this guarantee in the Civil Code elevates its status.

---

111 Inasmuch Chinese law is more progressive than Swiss law (CC Art. 28 ff.) which expressly protects the personal rights of natural persons, but only implicitly those of legal persons to which they were eventually extended by the jurisprudence of the Swiss Federal Court (ATF 108 II 241 = JT 1984 I 66). The rights so protected include professional and economic life (ATF 129 III 715 = JT 2004 I 271; ATF 137 II 431) and the so-called intimate economic sphere (business secrets) (ATF 64 II 162 = JT 1938 I 522) to which legal entities are entitled (ATF 197 II 97 = JT 1972 I 242).

112 In China, smearing has recently been resorted to on several occasions, some of them highly publicized, by unscrupulous competitors typically using proxies disguised in disgruntled consumers, sometimes resulting in boycotts, thus inflicting the target major economic damage, but also hampering China's reputation as a safe market place. Political issues opposing the foreign investor's country to China have also been involved in other cases, leading to the same result. Such considerations may have contributed to motivate the Chinese legislator to strengthen the protection of companies' reputation. S., for example, the dispute which opposed Danone to its JV partner Wahaha in or around 2007; Carrefour's political boycott as of 2008; the 2008 melamine incident, a food safety scandal involving melamine-contaminated milk and infant formula, which primarily involving Sanlu, a Chinese company to which Nestlé was not related, but which impacted Nestlé anyway.

Personal rights further relate to *data protection*. While the protection of economic reputation is mostly providing FIEs with a right, that of personal data is imposing them an obligation which can be quite constraining. The personal information of a natural person is protected by law. As such, Art. 111 mandates any organization or individual needing to obtain the personal information of other persons to obtain it legally and to ensure its confidentiality. Symmetrically, it is prohibited to illegally collect, use, process, or transmit it, and not only to sell it, but even the purchase it, as well as to provide or publish such data. 170

Inasmuch the Civil Code remarkably embraces the evolution of the digital economy as a whole by embedding data protection[113] in a basic law. As far as personal data is concerned, the Code, by provides a legal basis, however posterior, to the Personal Information Protection Law promulgated in 2021, thus strengthening its significance. 171

The next set of provisions (Art. 113 to 117) concerns *property*. It reaffirms the right to property already mentioned in the first articles of the Code (Art. 3; s. above §§103 and 116) and defines its various aspects. Art. 117 clearly sets the conditions for *expropriation* along the standards generally accepted by public international law, i.e., that it shall rest on a legal basis, meet public interest and be fairly compensated[114]. Property is further detailed in the Second Book of the Code (s. below Chap. 3 §16, Property). 172

The *sources of obligations* (s. above §109) are listed in the following set of provisions (Art. 118 to 122). As in Swiss law, they include contracts (Art. 119), liability for illicit act (Art. 120), *negotiorum gestio* (Art. 121), unjust enrichment (Art. 122), the two latter also being known as quasi-contracts, and the law (Art. 118§2 *in fine*)[115]. 173

As a consequence, the Code expressly acknowledges *creditors' rights* resulting therefrom, which can consist in an obligation to do or not to do (Art. 118§2). 174

It further entitles civil subjects to *intellectual property rights*, the subject matter of which it lists (Art. 123)[116]. There is no such acknowledgement in the Swiss Civil Code; by doing so, the Chinese Civil Code attests both of the major 175

---

113 China's data protection policy resulted, in 2021, in a comprehensive legal framework resting mainly on the Personal Information Protection Law (PIPL), the Cybersecurity Law (CSL; revised in 2025 effective 1 January 2026) and the Data Security Law (DSL).

114 On damage valuation, s. below §§1662ff.

115 The law, as source of obligations, is also implied as such at Art. 2 and 129.

116 IPR are mainly protected by the Patent Law, the Trademark Law and the Copyright Law, as well as, to a lesser extent, by the Anti-unfair Competition Law. Intellectual property law is not covered by this book.

significance IPR have gained in the modern economy, and of its progressive outlook due to its recent promulgation.

176 Among other rights of potential interest to foreign investors, the Code also reserves the protection of *consumer rights* (Art. 128)[117].

177 Finally, the last set of provisions (Art. 129 to 132) reiterates general principles such as the *exercise of civil rights* (including civil juristic acts, which the Code detail in the next chapter), legality (Art. 129), freedom of will (Art. 130, 1st phrase)[118], the prohibition of third party interference[119] in the exercise of civil rights (Art. 130 *in fine*), compliance with both legal and contractual obligations (Art. 131), and the prohibition of abusing civil rights to the detriment of the public interest or of private interests (Art. 132).

178 Chinese law details all these rights in secondary legislation or judiciary interpretations, much of it were already existing before the Code was promulgated. However, as noted above, by mentioning them in the Code, the Chinese legislator strengthened them by providing them with a legal sound basis and elevating their status in the legal hierarchy.

§10. Civil Juristic Acts

I. Introduction

179 A juristic[120] act is a *declaration of will* by which a civil subject, expressing its intention[121], gives birth to a civil right, modifies or ends it. It is one of the three

---

[117] Consumer rights are protected by a vast legal framework whose main components are the Consumer Protection Law, the Product Quality Law, the Advertising Law, the Pricing Law, the Anti-unfair Competition Law, and industry specific laws and regulations. Recently all these laws have been comprehensively extended to online transactions. Consumer protection law is not covered by this book.

[118] Freedom of will is already asserted in the basic provisions or the general rules of the Chinese Civil Code by Art. 5 (s. below §116). On *contractual* freedom, s. below §554.

[119] Including from the State, s. FIL Art. 24 and above §§11 and 23.

[120] "Juristic" is also translated, in English, as "juridical"; these qualifiers are synonyms. We use the first in this book. They translate as "juridique" in French and "rechtlich" in German.

[121] Beyond subtle semantic nuances, in the context of juristic acts, in legal language, *declaration* and *expression* are generally considered to be equivalent; so are *will* and *intention.* Both are used indifferently in the various translations of the Civil Code from Chinese to English, most commonly combined as *declaration of will* and *expression of intention.* In English, while *intention* and *intent* are generally equivalent, "intent" conveys a stronger determination than "intention" does.

ways the Chinese Civil Code defines in the preceding chapter (Art. 129). The two others are, secondly, certain *behaviors*[122] which, while not being an express declaration of will, are deemed to amount to the same and cause effects similar like a juristic act and, thirdly, certain *events* other than the two first ways, to which the law attaches similar effects. Eventually Art. 129 reserves a fourth possibility, i.e., "other means" prescribed by law, without defining them.

However general in nature, juristic acts are of fundamental importance to foreign investors, since they must understand the legal consequences Chinese law attaches to their declarations or behaviors, or to certain events. 180

The First Book of the Code dedicates a whole chapter to civil juristic acts (Chapter 6; Art. 133 to 160). It is divided into four sections dealing with general provisions, the notion of declaration of will, the validity of civil juristic acts, and conditional acts. 181

II. General Provisions (on Civil Juristic Acts)

The first section on "general provisions"[123] (Art. 133 to 136) contain only four provisions of general application throughout Chapter 6 on civil juristic acts. A civil juristic act can be formed by a unilateral, bilateral or multilateral *declaration of will* (Art. 134§1). In the case of a company, including a FIE, its declaration of will is expressed by a *resolution*; whenever such a resolution is issued, it will form a civil juristic act, provided it was reached in compliance with its articles of association and the law (Art. 134§2). 182

A civil juristic act does not need to be in written *form*; it can also be *oral* (Art. 135). Moreover, this provision reserves "other forms": one may think, namely, at certain behaviors (s. above §179). Unless such form is *mandatory* by law, in which case it may be *qualified* (e.g., executed by a notary public) and on which the *validity* of a juristic act may depend (e.g., contract of immovable sale), the parties are *free* to agree on it; that it typically the case when the parties mandate changes to a contract to be agreed upon in writing, or on the form they should notify each other certain events, for example, termination. 183

Speaking of companies, one can conceive oral juristic acts in case the resolution from which it originates has been voted orally by its voting rights holders, 184

[122] Such an act is generally known, in legal English, as "conclusive act" or "concluding act"; in Swiss law, in French language as "acte concluant" and in German language as " konkludentes Verhalten".

[123] On terminology issues, s. above note 93.

or in an "other form" such as voting by show of hands; an oral act can also result from an oral statement made by a company's representative[124].

185 A civil juristic act becomes legally *valid* immediately after it was formed; however, its validity may be *suspended* or *differed* by law or by the will of the parties (Art. 136§1). Such a situation is conceivable in case that validity is subject to a suspensive or resolutory *condition*, i.e., the occurrence of a certain event or the disappearance of some circumstance.

186 Finally, a civil juristic act cannot be *altered* or *terminated* unless such alteration or termination[125] complies with the law or is carried out with the other party's consent (Art. 136§2).

187 In the following chapters, we often compare Chinese and Swiss law. Yet in the Chinese Civil Code, civil juristic acts are addressed in the First Book of the Code on general provisions, not in the Third on contract, whereas in Swiss law they are only addressed in the Code of Obligations about the formation of *contractual* obligations[126]. Yet as noted, Chapter 6 of the Chinese Civil Code is not limited to contracts. Still, contrary to appearances, nor is the Swiss Code of Obligations: its Art. 7 extends the general provisions of the Code of Obligations to other matters of civil law.

III. Declarations of Will

188 This second section on declarations of will (Art. 137 to 142) of Chapter 6 on civil juristic acts details, with a focus on the declaration of will as compared to other juristic acts, most of the principles already mentioned in the preceding section on general provisions.

189 It is worth stressing at this stage that, unlike the Swiss Civil Code and the civil codes of most western jurisdictions indeed, which are much older[127], the Chinese Civil Code embraces the formidable development in communication techniques and the coming of the digital economy or society, which were simply unthinkable at the time those foreign codes were drafted, and whose most

124 On representation, s. above §133 and references.

125 On termination, s. below Chap. 2 §10.IV, Validity of Juristic Acts.

126 Those provisions are to be found in the First Part of the Swiss Code of Obligations on general provisions, First Title on formation of obligations, Chapter 1 on contractual obligations, Section E on contractual subject-matter (Art. 19 to 22) and F on vitiated consent (Art. 23 to 31). The two other chapters of that title relate to liability for illicit acts and unjust enrichment.

127 The Swiss Civil Code was promulgated in 1907 and the Swiss Code of Obligations in 1911.

recent revisions still fall short to fully apprehend[128]. Insofar, this part of the Chinese Civil Code can be said to be better, in the sense that it is more adequate to the effect of regulating modern transactions, than the Swiss Civil Code and other western codes.

In contrast, because of the relative youth of the Chinese post-Opening *corpus* 190
iuris, above all, of the Civil Code promulgated as recently as 2020, of the extremely rapid pace of the development of modern Chinese law, of the sheer size of China as a jurisdiction, of the fact that the jurisprudence of the People's Supreme Court is not, or not comprehensively, readily accessible to the public, and of the language barrier, there is a relatively small pool, if at all, of authoritative, comprehensive, up-to-date scholastic commentaries and published jurisprudence to support the interpretation[129] of the Chinese Civil Code, as well as Chinese law in general, let alone in English or other foreign languages.

Conversely, while the Swiss Civil Code may not reflect the latest standards, 191
there is an abundant, established, easily accessible legal material[130] for facilitating the understanding of the law. Considering that the Chinese and the Swiss Civil Code are comparable in many respects, the practitioner may keep in mind that, where a Chinese commentary or jurisprudence may not be readily available, Swiss doctrine and jurisprudence may help in providing clarity, even if, evidently, not directly applicable in China. Also, where the Swiss Civil Code may be outdated, the jurisprudence of Swiss courts has generally provided for bridging the gap[131].

In this set of provisions, the Chinese Civil Code uses the somewhat obscure 192
expression of "intention expressed by mean of dialogue" (or "declaration of will made by dialogue"), which it opposes to an intention *not* expressed or a declaration *not* made by dialogue[132].

---

128 The latest revision or stand of the Swiss Civil Code, including the Swiss Code of Obligations, at the time of writing this book became effective as of 1 January 2024; it still left the provisions discussed in this section in their original version of 1911, however.

129 On the Interpretations of the People's Supreme Court, s. above §102.

130 In particular, the jurisprudence published by the Federal Tribunal since 1954 is freely accessible on Swisslex (s. above note 89). Pre-1954 jurisprudence from the inception of the Federal Tribunal as of 1875 is freely available on a website managed by the University of Bern.

131 S., for example, BLAISE CARRON/SABRINA GAURON-CARLIN, CC & CO annotés, Helbing Lichtenhahn, 12th ed., 2024, which comprehensively outlines, article by article, the basic jurisprudence of the Swiss Federal Supreme Court throughout the Swiss Civil Code and the Code of Obligations contains other selected basic laws and is regularly updated.

132 Compare the two subsections of Art. 137.

193 This distinction is not to be confused with that which Swiss law operates between an offer to contract extended in the *presence* (which would arguably compare to "dialog") or, on the contrary, the *absence* (which would arguably compare to "non-dialog") of the parties (CO Art. 4 and 5). Indeed, the latter provisions apply to the formation of contracts and is, therefore, limited in scope[133]; furthermore, their effects differ from those of Art. 137 of the Chinese Civil Code.

194 Mostly, CO Art. 4 and 5, which were drafted at a time when simultaneous[134] distant communications hardly existed, are focused on the parties' (physical) *presence*, taking for granted that simultaneous distant communication was not possible whenever the parties were absent or distant. The only concession these provisions made to modernity was to provide for contracts concluded by *phone*, which were (and still are) deemed to have been entered into in the parties' presence (CO Art. 4§2)[135].

195 By comparison, Chinese law, taking into account the evolution of distant communications, focuses on the *simultaneity* of communication or "dialogue": a declaration is deemed to be made "by dialogue" if it was simultaneously (i.e., at the same time it was emitted[136]) received by the recipient; on the contrary, it is deemed to be made by "non-dialogue" if it was not simultaneously received by the recipient.

196 That said, according to the Chinese Civil Code, a declaration of will made "by dialogue" becomes valid *when its recipient becomes aware of its content* (Art. 137). What Art. 137§1 of the Chinese Civil Code implies by "becoming aware" is not immediately clear. This provision actually uses the verb 知道 zhīdào which literally translates as "to know". Therefore, one can assume that it suffices that the recipient *hears* the emitter's declaration and understands its meaning, which it shall be deemed to have provided such declaration was *clear* enough, that is to say, unambiguous, for the latter to be valid[137]. This understanding rests on *interpretation*, which is addressed further down in the same section of the Code (s. below §§218ff.)

---

133 However, s. above §187.

134 By "simultaneous", we mean that the declaration is received at the same time it is emitted.

135 Indeed, although the parties to a phone communication are not in presence of each other, their declarations are simultaneously emitted and received.

136 S. above note 134.

137 These two cumulative conditions would prevent the validity of a declaration, however simultaneous, where, for example, the call is so bad that the recipient does only hear part of it, or where the meaning of the declaration is ambiguous, for example, "maybe" instead of "yes".

In contrast, a declaration made "by non-dialogue" becomes effective *when it reaches its recipient* (Art. 137§2 1st sentence). 197

Inasmuch, a declaration made face-to-face, by land line phone or by mobile phone, by IM call or by videocall is simultaneous or made "by dialogue"[138]; the same declaration made in writing, whether by post mail or courier, e-mail, SMS or IM text message is not immediate and, therefore, amounts to "non-dialogue". Likewise, a voicemail, even IM voicemails, however exchanged in rapid succession like WeChat or WhatsApp permit, would not, arguably, because of the time lag, however short and infrequent, between the emission and the reception of each declaration or message, amount to "immediate" declaration and would, consequently, also qualify as "non-dialog". 198

The Chinese Civil Code further qualifies the effects of a declaration by non-dialogue in the form of *data message*, i.e., at the time of writing this book, mainly, by e-mail, by SMS or by IM message, but not only, since that definition is flexible enough to accommodate other types of communications[139]. 199

If a declaration of will by non-dialog is in the form of data message, and the recipient has designated a specific system to receive it, the declaration shall become valid *at the time when the data message enters that system* (Art. 137§2, 2nd sentence). What it means in practice is that, when the recipient has given the sender his e-mail address or his mobile phone number, the declaration will be deemed as valid the instant the message (e-mail, SMS or IM) is sent. In other words, provided the address or the number is correct, the message will be deemed to have reached its recipient; the latter, not the sender, will bear the burden of proof it did not receive the message, provided the sender proves it has sent it[140]. 200

---

[138] The same qualification would arguably apply to the many automated pre-recorded notifications by phone (e.g., when the low balance limit of the recipient's bank account balance is reached, etc.) which are typical in China.

[139] The notion of "data message" is open-ended and would arguably also extend to now obsolete communication means such as Morse messages, telegrams, telex and faxes; to current but less obvious means such as online transactions (online purchases, online banking, etc.) pop-ups (on websites, programs and applications or "app"), push messages (on smartphones and apps), etc., as well as to, potentially, yet unknown future means.

[140] The proof that the message was sent will be easily provided in the form of the sent time embedded in the header of sent e-mail, or by the log of the sent message in the sender's smartphone. If so, the recipient will face a much taller challenge to prove that it did not receive that message despite its address or number was correct. Such proofs may be more challenging to bring for both parties in case of apps, etc., however, which is not a mundane concern given the formidable prevalence of the now all-encompassing the e-economy has quicky gained in today's China.

201 By "system", one mostly understands the recipient's domain (for e-mails), its mobile phone operator's network (for SMS[141]) or its IM provider[142]. Practically, as noted above, such system shall be deemed to have been "entered" the instant the sender sends the message. Moreover, like "data message", "system" is a notion flexible enough to potentially extend to other types of communication systems[143].

202 In the absence of such a designation, the declaration of will shall become valid when the recipient *knows or should have known* that the message has entered its system (Art. 137§2, 3rd sentence). Practically again, what this provision anticipates is the case where the parties have not agreed to communicate by e-mail or text messages, i.e., more specifically, that the recipient has not told the sender to do so and has not given it its e-mail address or mobile phone number, but that the sender sends the recipient an e-mail or a text message anyway. In such case, the recipient will not be deemed to have received the message the instant it was sent (and the corresponding declaration will, therefore, not become simultaneously valid); it will only be so deemed when the recipient effectively becomes aware that such message was sent to him.

203 However, in order to prevent a recipient from abusing this provision by indefinitely claiming that it did not know it had received the message, even though it could have read it in due time, the law further provides that the declaration also becomes effective when the recipient *should have known* that it had received the message containing it. As a matter of fact, at a time when anyone can read its e-mails or IM messages at any time almost anywhere on one's smartphone, a recipient attempting to prove that it should not have known about

---

141 SMS are seldom used nowadays, before all by Chinese users, who almost universally switched to WeChat. Be that as it may, the foreign user must keep in mind that the reliance of cross-border SMS to and from China is inconsistent, thus exposing them to the risk of invalidity of their declaration. About IM, s. below note 143.

142 On the terminology related to electronic data exchange, s. below §§208ff.

143 At the time of writing this book, the most popular IM providers are WhatsApp in the West, including Switzerland, and WeChat in China. WhatsApp is officially banned in China; it is still accessible however, but inconsistently. WhatsApp's relatively distant competitor Telegram is also banned in China and, unlike WhatsApp, appears to be consistently inaccessible. WeChat is consistently accessible in the West. Therefore, foreigners who deal by IM would be well advised to use WeChat, as WhatsApp and Telegram would open the way to challenges as to whether a data message entered the system. About proofs, s. also below §207.

such message[144], if not immediately, shortly after it was sent, will face a tall challenge once again[145].

Likewise, even though Art. 137§2 is silent about it, we believe that, despite the presumption it contains, the recipient of an *unclear* data message, however deemed to have received it, would be protected by Art. 137§1, which subjects the validity of a declaration to its understanding by its recipient[146]. In other words, an incomprehensible declaration of will by non-dialog or data message would not be valid even though it reached or was deemed to have reached its recipient[147]. 204

Finally, the last sentence of Art. 137§2 provides that the parties may agree otherwise. Inasmuch, this provision mirrors Art. 135 (s. above §183), reflecting itself Art. 5 (s. above §116), which already reserves the parties' freedom[148]. 205

To summarize, *in practice*, most of time, a declaration of will to a recipient, whether in person, by phone, by e-mail or by WeChat[149], will be valid immediately, unless it is unclear. 206

As a practical consequence, the foreign investor, and any author or recipient of a declaration of will of some legal significance, would be well advised to keep record of it for the sake of meeting the burden of *proof*, as the case may be. While archiving is evident with printed documents, it proves much more elusive with electronic data[150]. Therefore, it is worth remembering that any party 207

---

144 China's mobile network coverage was of 99.5% as of 2016 already, so that it is unlikely that a defense pretending that there was no coverage would succeed. So would the defense that the recipient's smartphone battery was discharged, at a time when to carry a (functioning) smartphone is generally regarded as almost akin to the obligation to carry an identity document; in any event, such negligence would be faulty.

145 S. above note 140.

146 S. above §196 and note 137.

147 The literal and structural interpretation of Art. 137 may give the impression that its subsection 1 applies to dialogue and subsection 2 to nondialogue and that, therefore, the second condition set forth by subsection 1, awareness, only applies to dialogue, not to both dialogue and non-dialogue. Yet we submit that, from a teleological interpretation point of view, it can hardly have been the intention of the Chinese legislator that a declaration, however incomprehensible, becomes valid by virtue of the simple fact that it was made by non-dialogue and reached (or deemed to have reached) its recipient. This understanding is supported by Art. 142§1 on interpretation, s. below §212ff.

148 On contractual freedom, s. WEI WEN, Formality, Freedom of Contract and China's New Civil Code: A Legal Reform Recommendation for Land Sale Contracts, [2022] U. PA. ASIAN L. REV. 332.

149 About SMS, s. above note 141.

150 Among the risks related to the archiving of electronic data, one may mention automatic archiving, which deletes messages after a certain time, cannot always be set by users, and can be very short for IM messaging systems such as WeChat and WhatsApp; the

bearing the burden of proof of a declaration of will in the form of electronic data finding itself unable to provide it shall face the consequences[151].

208 At this point, it is worth clarifying the *terminology* used by the Code with respect to electronic communications, which can be confusing, especially since it does not seem to be unified throughout the Code, and because translations vary and are often inaccurate.

209 "Electronic" (in the sense of the "e-" in, namely, e-mail) is expressed, in Chinese, by the qualifier 电子 diànzǐ, but also by the suffix 电 diàn (which also means "electric"; in Chinese, the distinction between electric and electronic is contextual and not as clear as in western languages); "message" by 邮件 yóujiàn; "data" by 数据 shùjù; "system" by 系统 xìtǒng; "exchange (or interchange)" by 交换 jiāohuàn. Thus, "e-mail" is expressed by 电子邮件 diànzǐ yóujiàn; "electronic data" by 电子数据 diànzǐ shùjù; and "electronic data message" by 数据电文 shùjù diànwén. Likewise, the law refers to the "systems" designed to (send or) receive such data as 系统 xìtǒng, and to "exchange" data as 电子数据交换 diànzǐ shùjù jiāohuàn.

210 "Electronic data message" is a generic expression; the e-mail is a specific form of electronic data message, and the only one expressly mentioned by the Code, but not the only one: SMS and IM messages are other such forms, even though they are not expressly mentioned by the Code. "System" and "exchange" are both generic too and can refer to notions as diverse as an e-mail provider or a stock exchange platform. Both the Code and their translations add to the confusion, in the sense that they often seem to indiscriminately use "electronic message", "data message", "electronic data message", "data exchange" and "e-mail".

211 For the purpose of civil legal relationships, this perplexing language can be, tentatively, summed up as follows: electronic systems process electronic data and exchange it in electronic messages between parties emitting and receiving declarations of will. While arguably lacking in uniformity and consistency, the Code is to be understood in a generic manner, so as to encompass not only the multiple forms electronic communications may take today, but also those they may take in the future.

---

impossibility to structure (in folders and subfolders) the archiving of IM messages like for e-mails, which complicates their search; viruses, which may destroy or corrupt data; and hacking, which may result in stolen or inaccessible data. This list is not exhaustive. IM has grown so popular in China that it has taken over e-mailing to a large extent, even in legal transactions, proportionally expanding the associated risks. Among other protective measures, it is advisable to backup in a more stable form (e.g., by taking a screenshot) any IM message containing a legally significant declaration of will.

151 About IM, s. also above note 143.

Whenever declarations of will through the exchange of electronic data messages aim at the *conclusion of a contract*, the Code supplements the general regime outlined above with specific rules applying to the form, time and place of the conclusion of contracts so concluded (s. below Chap. 4 §22, Validity, and note 341). 212

It is worth adding that the use of electronic communication by the stakeholders of a company to the effect of adopting resolutions (which is one form of expression of will by a legal civil subject) is also expressly embraced by Chinese *company law* (Company Law, Art. 24; s. below §1795). 213

This section of the Code has been so far concerned with declarations of will involving at least two parties, i.e., an author and a recipient (or more). Whenever there is *no recipient* (e.g., a letter or written statement "to whom it may concern"), the declaration of will becomes valid upon *completion* of its expression (Art. 138), i.e., when it has met a recipient which became aware of and understood it. 214

Likewise, an intention expressed by means of *announcement* (e.g., an invitation to tender) becomes valid when the announcement is *published* (Art. 139). 215

A declaration of will may be explicit or implicit (Art. 138§1). However, the popular saying "qui tacet consentire videtur" (who keeps silent consents)[152] does not apply: tacit or *silent acceptance* will only be deemed if provided by law or agreed between the parties. The law even extends the latter derogation to the case where such silent acceptance conforms to the *business practice* between the parties (Art. 138§2). In such cases, although the Code does not expressly state so, the party relying on such a practice must, pursuant to the general rules of evidence (s. below §1638), bear the burden of proving its existence. 216

An author may only withdraw its declaration of will provided such *withdrawal* reached the recipient before or at the same time the original declaration reaches the latter (Art. 141). 217

Last but not least, the last provision of this section of the Code (Art. 142) contains rules of *interpretation* of the declarations of will, whenever their meaning is unclear or disputed. Given the extended significance of interpretative rules, Art. 142 must be regarded as of paramount importance. 218

The first paragraph of Art. 142 addresses communication between two (or more) parties (*bi- or multilateral* declarations); the second where there is no counterpart (*unilateral* declarations). 219

152 Fr.: "Qui ne dit mot consent"; Ger.: "Wer schweigt, stimmt zu".

220 Although mentioned at the end, the commanding principle applying to both bi-, multi- and unilateral declarations, and from which all the other elements derive, is *good faith*, in accordance with Art. 7 (s. above §116); the same applies in Swiss law[153].

221 That said, the first element mentioned by the first subsection of Art. 142 (bi- or multilateral declarations), "*words and phrases*[154]", is the only one which is not entirely common to both bi- (or multi-) lateral and unilateral declarations. This element or *mean* of interpretation can be equated, in Swiss law, to *literal interpretation*, which prevails over other means or rules: according to a well-established doctrine and jurisprudence, in Swiss law, when the literal meaning of a declaration is clear, it shall not be further interpreted.

222 The second paragraph (unilateral declarations) does refer to "words and phrases" too: however, it *weakens* their significance by stating that "they should not be completely adhered to". Arguably, the reasoning behind is that, because such declaration was not forged by the interaction between two parties, its wording, which is unilateral and, as such, potentially more tainted by the subjectivity of its unique author, should be given less significance than more objective elements, such as the relevant provisions and terms, and the purpose and nature of the act.

223 In addition to good faith and "words and phrases", in both cases (bi- or multi- and unilateral declarations), where the intention purportedly expressed by the declaration of will is unclear, it shall be determined taking into account the following remaining elements: "the relevant provisions and terms used", "the purpose and nature of the act" and "common practices".

224 The "relevant provisions and terms[155] used" overlaps with the "words and phrases", while arguably focusing on the legal language contained in a declaration, as compared to general language.

225 In contrast, the "purpose and nature of the act" as well as "common practices" expands the scope of interpretation beyond the literal meaning of the declaration at stake by considering certain *circumstances* surrounding the declaration, i.e., the purpose and the nature of the act intended by the declaration, and the business practices generally established within the business community related to the subject-matter.

---

[153] Good faith is prominently mentioned on the very beginning of the Swiss Civil Code, at Art. 2§1.

[154] "Phrase" in English is, for French speakers, a false friend: it does not mean "phrase", i.e., full sentence as in French, but refers to the part of a sentence.

[155] "Term" in English is, for French speakers, another false friend: it does not mean "terme" or wording, but provision or condition.

In this respect too, Chinese and Swiss law are comparable, inasmuch as the elements mentioned in the preceding paragraph pertain to what Swiss doctrine qualifies as "complementary means of interpretation", "complementary elements" or "*complementary interpretation*" which, as their name suggests, complement literal interpretation as a primary mean[156]. Since they are only complementary, literal interpretation keeps prevailing, as noted above (s. §217)[157]. 226

Where both literal and complementary interpretation fail to clarify the declaration's author will, Art. 142 implies, by mentioning it at the end of the other interpretation means, that one shall resort to *good faith interpretation.* 227

Good faith interpretation is at the core of the Swiss doctrine and jurisprudence on interpretation, when a declaration of will cannot be interpreted by literal and complementary interpretation. It has taken the form of the *principle of reliance* (Fr. "principe de la confiance"; Ger. "Vertrauensprinzip")[158]. According to the same, a declaration of will (which cannot be clarified through literal or complementary interpretation) must be interpreted according to the meaning its recipient could and should have given it, *in accordance with the rules of good faith*[159]. While Art. 142 of the Chinese Civil Code does not elaborate, we believe that there are no significant differences between Chinese and Swiss law in this respect. 228

The principles of interpretation of Art. 142 are applicable to *contractual interpretation* by virtue of Art. 466§1, which also contains a special rule applying to *bilingual contracts*. Art. 466 is complemented by Art. 510 which enables the parties to *supplement* the contract whenever secondary elements are unclear or missing, and recourse to interpretation if they fail to agree on such supplements; such *supplemental contractual interpretation rules* are contained in Art. 510 *in fine* and Art. 511 (s. below §§618ff.; on the combination of these sets of rules, s. below §§622 and 623). 229

That said, the Chinese Civil Code may be regarded as more elaborate than the Swiss Civil Code insofar as the latter only mentions good faith as a most general principle[160]; it does neither specifically relate it to declarations of will, nor does it detail other means of interpretation, which were developed by Swiss 230

---

156 S., for example, GAUCH/SCHLUEP/TERCIER, §§ 845-848.

157 *Ibid.*, § 848.

158 *Ibid.*, § 191. However firmly established, this principle is expressed nowhere as such in Swiss law but has been derived by Swiss doctrine and jurisprudence from the principle of good faith.

159 *Ibid.*, §§ 185 ff., 345 ff. and 846 ff. While this principle originally applies to the declaration of will, Swiss doctrine and jurisprudence extended it to *contractual* declarations, of which it became a foundation.

160 S. above note 153.

doctrine and jurisprudence. By comparison, the Chinese Civil Code, albeit succinctly, provides a more explicit statutory framework for interpretation.

231 In contrast, Swiss law has generated an immense body of doctrine and jurisprudence in this regard. Chinese law relies, among other things, on the related interpretation of the SPC but, as noted elsewhere in this book, scholastic commentaries, including access to the same, may be somewhat limited, while the jurisprudence of the SPC is often not readily available, especially to foreign lawyers. However, given the similarity of such principles in Chinese and Swiss law, the Swiss practitioner may find it useful to draw inspiration from Swiss law, even though it does evidently not apply in China[161].

232 Finally, despite the Chinese Civil Code addresses them in its very last chapter on *supplemental provisions*, which only contains two of them, interpretation is the place where it is sensible to mention that Art. 1259 provides *definitions* for the following expressions relating to *numerals* or figures: thus, "above", "below", "within" and "expiry" shall include the given numeral; in contrast, "less than", "more than" and "beyond" shall exclude it.

IV. Validity of Juristic Acts

233 Section 3 on the validity of civil juristic acts (Art. 143 to 160) of Chapter 6 on juristic acts of the First Book of the Chinese Civil Code on general provisions is concerned by both the validity and the invalidity of juristic acts.

234 In general, and without expanding into semantic or legal theory, there are two *types* of invalidity: from the inception and occurring later on. Invalidity from the inception is known in legal Latin as *ab initio* ("from the start") or *ex tunc* ("from then") whereas, if it occurs later, it is said to occur *ex nunc* ("from now").

235 "Valid" is also expressed by "effective". An act which is invalid *ab initio* is said to be, in legal English, "invalid", "null" or "void" (or, frequently, however redundant, as "null and void"); an act which only becomes invalid from a later point in time is said to be "ineffective"[162], "invalidated"[163], "annulled",

161 Yet the invocation of Swiss law before a Chinese court as a *fact* for interpreting the will of a Swiss party in a Sino-Swiss transaction, however governed by Chinese law, would not be incompatible with Art 142§1 of the Chinese Civil Code, and is conceivable indeed.

162 S. next note.

163 However inaccurate, "invalid" is also frequently used, in English, for actually expressing "invalidated".

"dissolved", "cancelled", "abrogated", "terminated" or "revoked", depending of the context. This list is not exhaustive.

Whenever addressing invalidity, Section 3 is only concerned by *nullity*, not annulment. 236

Nullity can occur in two ways: either *passively*, i.e., *de jure* (by law), or *actively*, because the act was "rescinded", i.e., by an (other) act of rescission. 237

In both cases, whenever null, the act is deemed to be invalid *ex tunc*, i.e., never to have come into legal existence, or never to have deployed legal effects[164]. 238

However, in those cases where the law provides for rescission, the act is legally valid until pronounced rescinded by a judiciary authority (or an arbitration tribunal) or, in those cases where the law provides for it, a party to such act. Until it is, or if it is not, the act will be legally valid. In contrast, as soon as it is rescinded, the rescission will be deemed to deploy *ex tunc* effects, i.e., the act will be deemed never to have legally existed[165]. 239

There is ample room for confusion among the translation of the related *terminology* between Chinese, English, French and German; however tedious, because the legal effects resulting from the wording considered can significantly vary, it is important to gain some awareness of those issues. 240

Chinese law uses the word 效力 xiàolì (cf. section title), or 有效 yǒuxiào (cf. Art. 143§1 *in fine*), which can be either a word or an adjective, to convey the notion of *validity*. In case of *nullity*, i.e., *ex tunc*, where an act is passively found to be null, nullity is expressed by 无效 wúxiào (cf. Art. 157). Where nullity actively results from rescission, to rescind translates as 撤销 chèxiāo (cf. Art. 155). 241

Comparatively, *annulment*, i.e., invalidity *ex nunc*, calls for another distinction, which specifically applies to contracts: it can occur either for a term, or earlier. It typically occurs for a *term* when, for example, a fixed-term contract reaches its agreed term. Alternatively, annulment may occur *earlier* than such term, most of the time when either party seriously violates the contract, but also in other cases, for example, when the other party files for bankruptcy. Whenever 242

---

164 Arguably, an act which is deemed never to have come into existence should be said to be invalid, whereas an act which did come into existence but is legally deemed never to have deployed legal effects should be said to be ineffective, but these distinction are somehow blurred and overlap: indeed, Art. 157 attributes the same legal effects to "invalid" and "ineffective" acts.

165 Among other things, this consequence opens the door to a claim for unjust enrichment, as the case may be, s. below Chap. 7 §55, Unjust Enrichment.

so, such annulment may be effective immediately, or at the expiry of the revocation advance notice.

243 Annulment for a *term*, whether passive or active (s. next paragraph), is generally expressed in English, as its etymology makes clear, by "termination"; *early*[166] annulment is generally expressed by "revocation" or "termination *for a cause*". The Chinese Civil Code expresses "to terminate" *stricto sensu* by 终止 zhōngzhǐ[167] (cf. Art. 557), and "to revoke" by 解除 jiěchú (cf. Art. 563§1)[168].

244 The notions of term and early termination recoup with, but are not identical to, those of *passive* (A.K.A. "automatic" or "indirect") and *active* (or "direct") termination. Ordinary termination occurs passively or automatically, by the mere expiry of the contract's fix term, while early termination is actively caused by one party. The notions of passive and active termination are theoretical and can blur however, as discussed below about contractual termination (s. below §717).

245 As noted, Section 3, which belongs to Chapter 6 on juristic acts of the First Book of the Code on general provisions, is concerned by *nullity*, not annulment. Yet for the sake of preventing confusion with the neighboring notion of *annulment*, which the Code addresses later on, mainly, in Chapter 7 on termination of the Third Book on contract law (Art. 557 ff.), it is appropriate to draw the reader's attention on these notions at this early stage.

246 The risk of confusion is aggravated by the fact that alternative expressions abound (s. above §235), thus increasing in turn that of inaccurate translations. Thus, as noted, to declare an act's *nullity* (无效 wúxiào) is correctly translated, in English, by "to rescind" (撤销 chèxiāo). In Swiss law, it is expressed, in French, by "résoudre" or "se départir" and, in German, by "zurücktreten" (where "zurücktreten" literally translates as "to step back"; cf. CO Art. 107§2, 3rd option[169]) or, occasionally, by "wandeln" (s., e.g., CO Art. 205 ff.)

247 Both ordinary, whether passive or active, and early *annulment* in the generic sense may be expressed, in English, by "to terminate"; however, early termination is generally expressed by termination "for a cause" or "revocation". In contrast, in Swiss law, ordinary, early, active and passive termination are

166 "Termination" is also used, however, for open-ended contracts which, absent any pre-agreed term by definition, cannot occur "early" (cf., e.g., Art. 563§2 and below §732; and Labor Contract Law, Art. 37 and below §1533).

167 About related translation issues, s. above note 102.

168 About the use of these expressions in the context of the end of a labor relationship, s. below Chap. 6 §49, Termination and Revocation. About alternative expressions, s. also below, notes 198 and 199.

169 S. below §§ 266 ff.

distinguished, although inconsistently, in both languages: ordinary and passive termination is expressed by "prendre fin" in French and "endigen" in German (s., e.g., CO Art. 334§1); ordinary and active termination by "résilier" and "kündigen" (s., e.g. CO Art. 335§1). However, while early termination is also expressed, in French, by "résilier" (s., e.g., CO Art. 337 ff.), German language uses "auflösen" (*ibid.*; compare CO Art. 334§1 *in fine* and 3 as well as CO Art. 335§1 with CO Art. 337 ff.)

Comparatively, Chinese law uses 终止 zhōngzhǐ for ordinary and passive ter- 248
mination (s., e.g., Labor Contract Law, Art. 44) and 解除 jiěchú both for early- (*ibid.*, Art. 38) and ordinary active (*ibid.*, Art. 37) termination. Inasmuch 解除 jiěchú compares to the terminology used in Swiss French legal language ("résilier"), while its translation both in English (to terminate in case of ordinary active termination, to terminate for a cause, or to revoke, both in case of ordinary active termination and of early termination) and in German (kündigen or auflösen) is ambiguous.

Finally, one should recall that "valid" and "invalid" (效力 xiàolì or 有效 249
yǒuxiào, 无效 wúxiào; Fr.: "valide", "invalide"; Ger.: "gültig", "ungültig") may apply both in case of nullity and annullability. In this book, we will use the expressions mentioned in this paragraph. The use of these specific words and verbs throughout the Chinese Civil Code is consistent; their translation in English, however, is not, and a serious issue calling for closer attention indeed.

A civil juristic act is *valid* if its author enjoys civil capacity, if its intention is 250
true, if the act complies with the law, and if the latter does neither disturb the public order nor offend morals (Art. 143). If any of these conditions is unmet, the act is invalid (s. below §253)[170].

Civil capacity, which is the capacity of performing valid civil juristic acts, of 251
which children are deprived until they reach legal adulthood, and adults may be deprived by judicial decision if they are judged irresponsible (Art. 145), is not to be confused with *agency* or the capacity to represent a third party, which is regulated in the next section of the Code.

As explained above (s. §239), an act may be null either automatically or after 252
it has been rescinded (or "voided", which is equivalent in legal English). Recission can either be pronounced by a court (or an arbitration tribunal) but also, as already provided for by Art. 136§2 (s. above §186), by agreement between the parties to a civil juristic act.

---

[170] About invalid standard contractual clauses, in particular contractual liability exemption clauses, s. below §§596 and 610.

253 The Code provides for *automatic* nullity in five cases, four of which result from the lack of any of the conditions listed by Art. 143 (s. above §235): the lack of civil capacity (Art. 143, item 1 and Art. 144), false intention (Art. 143, item 2 and 146)[171], illegality (Art. 143, item 3 and 153), and disturbance to the public order and offense to morals (Art. 143, item 3)[172].

254 The only other case not already mentioned under Art. 143 is *malicious collusion* harming a third party (Art. 154)[173].

255 All the other cases addressed by Section 3 of the Code are subject to *recission*, which shall be pronounced by a court or an arbitration tribunal upon application of the interested party. These are: substantial misunderstanding (Art. 147)[174], fraud (Art. 148 and 149)[175], coercion or duress (Art. 150)[176], and unfair advantage (Art. 151)[177].

---

171 Unlike fraud (Art. 148), false intention involves both parties to a juristic act: it addresses simulated acts purporting at concealing another act, where the latter is the only one intended. In contrast, in case of *fraud*, one party deceives another (s. below §255 and note 175).

172 Art. 143, item 3 and 153 of the Chinese Civil Code (legality, public order and morals) compare with Art. 20§1 of the Swiss Code of Obligations. While useful comparisons between Chinese and Swiss law can be drawn in other cases, the notions of public order and morals substantially differ from one jurisdiction to the other, however. S. also below, §680.

173 The same applies in case of representation, s. below note 195.

174 Art. 147 of the Chinese Civil Code (substantial misunderstanding) compares with Art. 23 and 24 of the Swiss Code of Obligations ("fundamental error"; Fr.: "erreur essentielle"; Ger.: "wesentlicher Irrtum").

175 Art. 148 of the Chinese Civil Code (fraud) compares with Art. 28 of the Swiss Code of Obligations (fraud; Fr."dol"; Ger.: "Absichtliche Täuschung"). The difference between Art. 148 and 149 of the Chinese Civil Code is that Art. 148 involves two parties while Art. 149 involves three. Specifically, in the first case, the fraudster's counterparty is simultaneously the deceived party and the victim. In the second, the fraudster's counterparty is only deceived, but not the victim: a third party is. In the latter case, if the deceived party subsequently becomes or should have become aware of the fraud, the victim is entitled to apply for rescinding the act. CO Art. 28 does not address the situation contemplated by Art. 149 of the Chinese Civil Code. The latter provision also implies that, if the deceived party was not, and should not have been, aware of the fraud, the victim is not entitled to apply for rescission; however, the victim would have the right to claim compensation to the fraudster under the regime of liability for illicit acts (s. below, Chap. 8 , Liability for Illicit Acts ("Torts")

176 Art. 150 of the Chinese Civil Code (coercion or duress) compares with Art. 29 and 30 of the Swiss Code of Obligations ("duress"; Fr.: "crainte fondée"; Ger.: "Furchterregung").

177 Art. 151 of the Chinese Civil Code (unfair advantage) compares with Art. 21 of the Swiss Code of Obligations ("unfair advantage"; Fr.: "lésion"; Ger.: "Übervorteilung").

The right of rescission *extinguishes* in two cases: in case of limitation, or if that party renounces using it, either explicitly or implicitly (Art. 152). Such renunciation effectively amounts to *ratification* of the aggrieved party's consent (*ibid.*, § 1, item 3). While Swiss law expressly refers to ratification (CO Art. 31[178]), Art. 152 of the Chinese Civil Code does not explicitly name it as such, although it provides for the same cause and effect. 256

Limitation of action is subject to a relative and an absolute limit: to a relative limit of one year from the day a party has known or should have known the cause of rescission (Art. 152§1, item 1, 1st phrase; shortened to ninety days in case of misunderstanding; *ibid.*, 2nd phrase) or from the day coercion ended (*ibid.*, item 2), and to an absolute limit of five years in any case (*ibid.*, § 2). As noted in the preceding paragraph, the victim's express or implied conduct may amount to an implicit waiver (*ibid.*, § 1, item 3). 257

Partial invalidity is acknowledged by Art. 156, by providing that where any part of a civil juristic act becomes invalid, the validity of the remaining part of said act shall not be affected and shall continue to be valid. 258

Art. 157 regulates *liability* and compensation for damage resulting from invalidity: the author or faulty party shall return any property or, if it is not possible, compensate for any such damage; if both parties are faulty, liabilities shall be shared, unless the law provides otherwise. 259

Chapter 6 on juristic acts of the First Book on general provisions of the Chinese Civil Code further applies to *contracts*. In particular, Section 3 on the validity of juristic acts also governs their *validity*. Chapter 3 on the validity of contracts (Art. 502 ff.) of the Third Book on contract law only contains a limited number of provisions specifically applying to certain cases of contractual invalidity (s. below Chap. 4 §22, Validity, §§602ff.) Other than those, it relies on the general regime contained in the general provisions of the Code. 260

In that respect, it is worth noting that the structure of the Chinese Civil Code differs from that of the Swiss one: in the latter, contractual invalidity is primarily governed by Chapter 1 on contracts of the First Title of the Swiss Code of Obligations on the formation of obligations[179], not in the general part of the Swiss Civil Code, which refers to the Code of Obligations for the conclusion, the effects and the extinction of contracts (including contractual invalidity), and provides that the related provisions also apply to civil law (CC Art. 7). To that 261

---

178 CO Art. 31 is titled "consent flaws covered by the ratification of the contract" (Fr.: "vices du consentement couverts par la ratification du contrat"; Ger.: "Aufhebung des Mangels durch Genehmigung des Vertrages").

179 As noted above in this chapter, cases of contractual nullity are addressed, in the Swiss Code of Obligations, by CO Art. 20§1, 21, 23, 24 and 28 to 31 (s. above notes 172ff.)

extent, it can be said that, comparatively, the structure of the Chinese and the Swiss codes is reversed.

V. Juristic Acts Subject to Conditions or Terms

262 Art. 158 to 160 address *conditions* (条件 tiáojiàn) precedent and subsequent[180] and their timely (non-)performance. Such conditions apply to the *existence* of a juristic act, unless the nature of the act does not permit it (Art. 158, 1st sentence). A condition precedent subjects the *birth* of the act to the fulfilment of the condition, while that of a condition subsequent causes the *extinction* of the act it applies to (*ibid.*, 2nd sentence). Either condition can be subject to a *time limit* (Art. 160).

263 If a party prevents or, on the contrary, provokes the fulfilment of a condition in *bad faith*, said condition shall be deemed to have been met or, on the contrary, unmet (Art. 159).

§11. Agency

I. Introduction

264 Agency (代理 dàilǐ) or *representation* (about terminology issues, s. next section, Chap. 2 §11.II, Distinctions and Translation Issues) is the legal relationship which results from the situation by which a natural or a legal person, the principal, is represented by another party, the agent, which can also be a natural or a legal person, towards a third party. The agency regime regulates the tripartite legal effects of representation between the principal, the agent and the third party.

265 A natural person can represent or be represented by another natural person (e.g., an attorney representing his natural person client at court); a natural person can represent a legal person (typically, directors of a company representing the latter, e.g., at the general meeting of shareholders) or be represented by a legal person (e.g., a bank representing its natural person client in a transaction); finally a legal person can represent or be represented by another legal person (e.g., a bank representing its corporate client in a transaction). However

180 Condition precedent translates, in Swiss legal French, as "condition suspensive" (CO Art. 151) and subsequent as "condition résolutoire" (CO Art. 154); in Swiss legal German as "Aufschiebende Bedingung" and "Auflösende Bedingung"; conditions in general are governed by CO Art. 151 to 157.

universal, experience tells that the legal significance of agency escapes to most of those who are implicated in it. China, where foreign investors are typically represented by local employees, is no exception, quite on the contrary.

Because agency can occur in any other contractual relationship whenever one of the parties to the main contractual relationship represents the other towards a third party, it is regulated in the general part of the Civil Code, rather than as a special contract. 266

The agency regime is difficult to grasp because it is scattered around in three sets of regulations, whereas the third one is subdivided in subsets. The first two sets are to be found in the First Book of the Civil Code about general provisions. The *first set*, which is contained in the general provisions section of the chapter on legal persons, briefly addresses the legal representative of a legal person, which is one form of agency (Art. 61 and 62; s. above Chap. 2 §8.III.C, Legal Representative); it is complemented by the Company Law (namely, Art. 10 and 11; s. below §§1774ff.) The *second set*, which is the subject matter of this section, further details agency in a chapter of the Code entirely dedicated to representation (Chap. 7, Art. 161 to 175). 267

As for the *third set*, agency, given its pervasive use, is also specifically regulated by certain contracts which, while serving another purpose, put some emphasis on representation, even though it is not their main purpose; they may, therefore, also contain subsets of provisions regulating it. Those features will be highlighted throughout this book[181]. 268

The general regime of agency complements any special regulations which may be contained in other laws. However, in accordance with the principle *lex specialis derogat legi generali* (Art. 11; s. above §117), in case of contradiction, such special regulations would take precedence over the general ones. 269

As noted, the problematic of representation is universal. It is limited neither to Chinese nor to Swiss law. This chapter will focus on the salient features of Chinese law of representation and, where appropriate, to comparable features of Swiss law. For a more detailed discussion of representation, be it in Chinese or Swiss law, in international[182] business law and practice, the reader is invited to consult specialized literature. 270

---

181 S. below, for example, the mandate (§§1003 and 1005) and the contract of intermediation (§1048). About the distinction between agency and the mandate, s. below §§275ff.

182 About representation in international business law, s., for example, NICOLAS ROUILLER, International Business Law, 2nd ed., Schulthess, Geneva/Zurich 2025, p. 249 ff., Agency-representation.

271 The Swiss regime of representation compares in most respect to the Chinese one. It is regulated by Art. 32 ff. of the Swiss Code of Obligations[183].

272 Chapter 7 of the Chinese Civil Code on agency (Art. 161 to 175) is divided in three sections: the first contains general provisions; the last is concerned with the end of the representation; the middle section applies to direct and voluntary agency as opposed to statutory agency.

273 With *direct agency*, the agent acts on behalf of the principal, whereas in *indirect agency*, it acts in its name, but for the principal[184]. With *voluntary agency*, representation is agreed between the principal and the agent[185], whereas with *statutory agency*, representation is mandated by law (Art. 163). In other words, this chapter of the Code mainly applies to voluntary agency; however, the few provisions of the general section and one provision of the last section on expiry do also apply to statutory agency, which is otherwise and mainly regulated by the laws mandating it[186]. Voluntary agency is designated in the Chinese Civil Code as "agency by mandate"[187] or "entrusted agency".

II. Distinctions and Translation Issues

274 Before addressing agency in Chinese law, it is necessary to clarify the confusing terminology surrounding the institution of agency, both in legal English and in Swiss legal French and German.

275 Agency closely resembles the contract of *mandate*, with which it overlaps. Agency, which is contained in the general part both of the Chinese Civil Code (Art. 161 to 172; s. below Chap. 5 §30, Mandate) and the Swiss Code of Obligations (Art. 32 to 40) is, as its structural location suggests, a general feature of the law which can apply on top of, or in parallel to any other legal, typically

---

183 The Swiss regime, which dates back to over a century, has produced an abundant body of doctrine and jurisprudence. Therefore, because of the similarity between the Chinese and the Swiss regimes, the latter may provide a useful source of inspiration whenever, due to the recent promulgation of the Chinese Civil Code, Chinese sources may be scarce, or difficult to access for foreign lawyers.

184 On indirect agency and similar institutions, s. below Chap. 2 §11.II, "Distinctions and Translation Issues".

185 Most cases of voluntary agency are of contractual nature; however, it would be wrong to call it contractual agency: voluntary agency extends to the wider field of civil juristic acts, which may include other, non-contractual cases of representation (about Swiss law, s. Commentaire romand/CO I, *ad* Art. 32 No. 6).

186 In Swiss law, CO Art. 40 reserves special provisions applying to the powers of company representatives.

187 About terminological confusion related to "agency" and "mandate", s. next section.

civil, contractual or administrative relationship. Mandate is a special, nominate or typical contract, both in Chinese (Chinese Civil Code, Art. 919 ff.) and Swiss law (CO Art. 394 ff.)

While agency focuses on the power of the agent to represent another, the mandate focuses on the undertaking by which the agent conducts a certain business or provides certain services for the mandator; the agent's power can extend beyond the principal's mere representation to certain features akin to the mandate, while the agent's mandate can contain (or not), and if so be limited to, the power to represent the mandator. Both will be discussed in more detail below and further down in this book. 276

Representation in the narrow sense as regulated in the general provisions of the Chinese Civil Code (Chap. 7, Art. 161 to 172) is expressed by 代理 dàilǐ. The contract of *mandate* as regulated in the Third Book of the Chinese Civil Code on contracts (Chap. 23, Art. 919 ff.) is expressed by 委托合同 wěituō hétóng. Part of the confusion stems out of the fact that both are translated, in legal English, by "agency", which is proper for both representation and mandate. In contrast, "representation" only relates to 代理 dàilǐ, while "mandate" only relates to 委托合同 wěituō hétóng. Moreover, mandate is also translated by "entrustment" which, however less common than "mandate" or "agency", is correct, nevertheless. 277

Representation and mandate can both be literally translated, in common French, as "représentation" and "mandat", which is straightforward. They translate in Swiss legal German as "Vertretung" and "Auftrag". However, another translation issue arises with the translation of "representation" in the semi-official translation in English of the OR[188], which does not use "representation" but "agency". Moreover, while that translation generally uses "mandate" for the contract of the same name, it also occasionally uses "agency" within the chapter dedicated to the mandate (s. CO Art. 400). 278

Further issues arise due to the fact that agency literally translates, in common French, as "agence" and, in common German, as "Agentur". Yet "agence" or "Agentur" relate to a special contract which is, in Swiss law, a subtype of the mandate generally speaking but which, while not distant from the mandate proper, is not a mandate in the narrow sense, but another contract on its own right, i.e., "le contrat d'agence" or "der Agenturvertrag" (CO Art. 418a ff.) 279

To make it worse, "le contrat d'agence" or "der Agenturvertrag" is translated, in the semi-official English version of the Swiss Code of Obligations, by "the agency contract", thus creating a confusion between representation and the contract of agency. The latter will be discussed in the contract law chapter of 280

[188] S. above note 88.

this book. Suffices it to say, at this stage, that it is distinct from the representation of Art. 161 to 172 and from the mandate of Art. 919 ff. of the Chinese Civil Code.

281 Also, despite its name could arguably suggest, the *entrustment* contract (which, as noted, is an alternate translation for mandate) does not equate to and, indeed, has nothing to do with the contract for *safekeeping*, *bailment* or *custody,* which are alternative translations for the contract of *deposit* (保管合同 bǎoguǎn hétóng) (Chinese Civil Code, Art. 888 ff.) The contract of deposit corresponds, in Swiss law, to "le dépôt" in French and "der Hinterlegungsvertrag" in German (CO Art. 472 ff.)

282 The lesson to draw from the foregoing, which is, as the reader can see throughout this book, not limited to the issues identified above, is that translation issues are prevalent, and that translations cannot be trusted: the *content* of the contract or legal relationship considered alone shall determine its nature and the legal regime applying to it[189].

283 The contracts mentioned above will only be addressed in this chapter as far as representation is concerned, and as appropriate. Other than that, they will be discussed in the contract law chapters of this book (s. below Chap. 4, General Provisions of Contract Law, and Chap. 5, Special Contracts). In particular, because a preliminary description of those typical contracts is required, further terminology and equivalences issues will be addressed about the *mandate*, the contract of *brokerage*, the contract of *intermediation* and, yet another time, agency, at the end of the chapter on the contract of intermediation (s. below §§1055ff.)

III. Powers of Agency and Agents Without Power

284 Chapter 12 on agency (Art. 161 to 175) is divided into three sections: general provisions (Art. 161 to 164), entrusted agency (Art. 165 to 172), and expiry (Art. 173 to 175). The Chinese Civil Code distinguishes *entrusted* agency, which is of a contractual nature, from *statutory* agency, which is provided by the law (Art. 163). It only details the former, in Section 2, however. This chapter of this book does not follow the structure of the Code: instead, in this section, it will address the core principles governing powers of agency and agents

189 The Swiss Code of Obligations expressly prescribes that only the genuine intention of the parties are decisive; the names or expressions they may have used, either mistakenly or deliberately, are not (CO Art. 18§1). There is no equivalent provision in the Chinese Civil Code, even though the same can be deducted from its general principles, namely, of interpretation (s. above §§218ff.)

without powers; the next section will cover ancillary issues including sub-agency, liability, expiry and other provisions applying to agency.

The law of representation is concerned by the two sides of the same coin: the legal consequences of representation whenever the agent is properly empowered, and whenever it is not. The latter case subdivides into two subcases: whether the third-party knew about it, or not. The three core principles resulting thereof are outlined below. 285

The *first* core principle applies whenever the agent is *properly empowered*: if so, a civil juristic act performed by an agent in the principal's name within the scope of the power of agency is *effective* (Art. 162). This principle[190] is softened by various exceptions however, which the Code describes in the main section on contractual agency. Art. 170 extends this principle to legal persons. 286

The first article of Section 2 on entrusted agency specifies that the power of attorney (POA) empowering the agent must clearly state the agent's name, the agency's subject matter, the power's scope and its term, and that it must be signed or sealed[191] by the principal (Art. 165). As the beginning of this provision implies, a written power is not compulsory however: an agent can be orally, yet legally empowered. However, the position of this provision, which focuses on written powers, on the very top of the section, silently signals the pre-eminence of written powers over oral instructions. 287

In practice, the importance of representation and of clear powers cannot be understated, although it is more than often misunderstood, let alone overlooked: while oral powers are legal, the burden of proof will be on the shoulder of whichever party prevails itself of them, where such proof will generally be much more challenging to bring than a clear POA. 288

Moreover, even in case of written powers, the latter are frequently too vague, outdated, unlimited or insufficiently limited as to their scope and duration, or suffer from some informality (invalid signature, missing seal, inauthentic copy, etc.), thus favoring disputes. Also, principals neglect more often than not to destroy outdated POAs or to withdraw them after use, which frequently leads to abuses. Therefore, principals, typically foreign investors instructing local agents, would be well advised to pay close attention to such powers and to monitor, review and update them regularly, as well as to destroy or withdraw them in due time. 289

Whenever the agent is not or *not properly empowered* (*falsus procurator*), the law poses two more principles, depending on whether the third-party had 290

[190] This principle, which can be said to be universal, also applies in Swiss law (s. CO Art. 32§1).

[191] On the legal significance of signatures and seals in China, s. below §581.

reasons to believe, or not, that the agent was empowered, while in reality it was not. The lack of powers can result from the fact that the agent has no powers at all, has exceeded its powers, that its powers have expired, or that such powers are invalid for some other reason.

291 If so, the *second* core principle of the law of representation is that the principal is *also bound* if the third party *had reasons to believe* that the agent was properly empowered (Art. 172)[192]. Art. 170§2 extends this principle to legal persons: while this provision does not expressly mention it, it points at the powers of directors registered on public records (s. below §1816); any third-party believing them shall be deemed to be of good faith, hence will be protected by this provision. This principle is reiterated at Art. 504 in connection with contractual validity (s. below §608).

292 The situation envisioned by Art. 172 is, namely, when the principal has informed the third-party (directly or by remitting the agent a POA) or the public (by publishing such powers on public records) of the agent's powers, then restricted or terminated them, but neglected to inform that third-party (directly or by amending or withdrawing the POA) or the public (by amending public records)[193].

293 The *third* core principle also applies when the agent is not or not properly empowered, but when the third-party *had no reason to believe* that the agent was properly empowered. If so, the principal is *not bound* by the deeds of its agent (without powers) (Art. 171§1).

294 In the latter case, the law gives the third-party a chance to salvage the act by urging the principal to ratify it within thirty days. If so, the third party must formally notify the principal accordingly; the 30 days start from the principal's acceptance of the notification. If the *principal* refuses to do so, it will not be bound; likewise, if it does not reply, its silence shall amount to a refusal. If it accepts, it will be bound (Art. 171§2)[194].

295 After having urged the principal to ratify, and before the principal has done so within thirty days, the *third-party* may change its mind and spontaneously rescind the act, in which case the parties will not be bound (as if the act had never been performed), even though the principal ratifies before the thirtieth day, but after the rescission (Art. 171§2). To be clear, if the third party does nothing at all, the parties shall not be bound, as already noted.

296 Moreover, Chapter 6 on the validity of contracts of the Third Book on contract law provides at Art. 503 that, in case the *falsus procurator* has concluded a

---

192 This principle is reflected, in Swiss law, by CO Art. 34§3.

193 About the abuse of POAs the principal neglected to destroy or withdraw, s. above §289.

194 This principle is reflected, in Swiss law, by CO Art. 34§1.

contract, such ratification may be *implied* if the other party had already commenced to perform or had accepted the *falsus procurator*'s performance (s. below §607). The same regime is mirrored in that governing the mandate (Art. 925; s. below §1016).

IV. Sub-agency, Liability, Expiry and Other Provisions

297 *Sub-agency*, i.e., when the agent entrusts itself another (sub-)agent, is governed by a set of specific rules: the agent must be authorized by the principal to do so; alternatively, if the (main) agent entrusted a sub-agent without the principal's authorization, the sub-agency will still be valid if the main agent subsequently managed to obtain the principal's ratification (Art. 169§1).

298 In addition to the cases were the principal is bound towards the third-party, which have been outlined in the preceding section, the Code provides for several representation-related cases of *liability* which are scattered around the chapter on representation: of the agent towards the principal (Art. 164§1), of the agent and the third-party towards the principal (Art. 164§2)[195], of the agent and the principal towards others (Art. 167), and of the agent and the third-party towards others (Art. 171§4).

299 Liability in case of *sub-agency* is governed by additional, specific rules: whenever the principal has authorized the (main) agent to (sub-)entrust a (sub-)agent, the (main) agent's liability is limited to the care with which it selected and instructed the sub-agent (*culpa in eligendo et instruendo*; Art. 169§2). In other words, if the sub-agent does not perform or does not perform properly, the (main) agent shall not be liable towards the principal or the third-party provided it diligently selected and instructed the sub-agent[196]. If, however, the (main) agent was not authorized by the principal to entrust a sub-agent, or if the principal did not subsequently ratify the sub-agency, the main agent shall be liable for any damage caused by the sub-agent (Art. 169§2).

300 The main agent shall be exempted, however, in case of *negotiorum gestio*, i.e, if, in case of urgency, the main agent had no choice but entrusting a sub-agent for safeguarding the principal's interests and did so in good faith in the principal's best interest (Art. 169§3). This exemption is a special case of *negotiorum*

---

195 Art. 164§2, which applies to *malicious collusion*, is a special case of the general principle posed by Art. 154 for juristic acts (s. above §254).

196 The same solution prevails in Swiss law; however, it is not contained in the law of representation, but in that of mandate (CO Art. 399§2). It is reiterated in the Chinese Civil Code in the regime governing the mandate (Art. 923).

gestio, which the Chinese Civil Code otherwise addresses generically at Chapter 28 of the Third Book (Art. 979 ff.)

301 The main section of the chapter of the Chinese Civil Code on representation otherwise provides for a few more *special cases*, including: acts which the principal may not entrust to an agent (Art. 161); joint agency (Art. 166); acts performed by the agent with itself on behalf of the principal (Art. 168§1); and, when the agent represents more than one principal, acts performed by the agent on behalf of one principal together with acts performed for other principals (Art. 168§2), where the two latter are subject to the ratification of both principals[197].

302 The last section of the Chinese Civil Code on agency is concerned by the end of the agency. The Code lists expiry cases both for voluntary (Art. 173) and statutory (Art. 175) agency. It is further concerned by the survival of the agency in case of death of the principal (Art. 174).

303 A voluntary agency ends when the mandate is completed, the powers expire, the principal[198] or the agent[199] revokes them or dies, the agent loses its civil capacity, or when the legal or non-legal person principal is dissolved (Art. 173).

304 After the death (or dissolution, s. Art. 174§2) of the principal, the agency survives nevertheless if the agent is not aware and should not be aware of such death (or dissolution), the principal's legal successors ratify the agent's acts, the power expressly extends beyond death or dissolution, or acts initiated after the death or dissolution must carry on in the interest of the principal's legal successors (Art. 174).

305 Contractual representation is further detailed in Art. 48-50 of the Third Book of the Code on Contract Law.

306 As already noted, the general features of the Chinese law of representation compare in most respect with Swiss law, which has produced an abundant *corpus* of jurisprudence and literature from which, however not directly applicable to Chinese law, the Swiss practitioner may usefully draw guidance.

---

197 The drafting of Art. 168§2 is somewhat confusing insofar as it suggests that the act at stake were to be performed by the agent "together with other principals"; however, what this provision undoubtedly aims at are s acts performed by the agent alone, but on behalf of two or more principals simultaneously.

198 Art. 173, item 2 uses the verb 取消 qǔxiāo to express "to cancel": s. preceding note.

199 Art. 173, item 2 uses the verb 辞去 cíqù (or 辞 cí) to express "to resign" even though, agency being of a contractual nature, such cancellation arguably amounts to a revocation, which is usually expressed by 解除 jiěchú (s. above §243 and below §717).

§12. Civil Liability

I. Introduction

A sound understanding of Chinese civil liability law is facilitated by an introduction to its basic notions, its sources, terminology and legal systematic, which we will complement with selected comparisons with Swiss law. 307

The *notion* of "liability" refers to the obligation imposed to a civil subject to repair the damage it caused to another. "Civil" liability relates to private law, as opposed to criminal liability, administrative liability (towards the State) or public liability (of the State)[200]. 308

There are several *sources* of civil liability *lato sensu* in Chinese law, the main of which can be reduced to five, four of which are primarily (but not only) contained in the Civil Code: Chapter 9 titled "civil liability" 民事责任 mínshì zérèn (Art. 60[201] and 176 ff.) of the First Book of the Code on general provisions; Chapter 8 titled "liability for breach of contracts" 违约责任 wéiyuē zérèn (Art. 577 ff.) of the Third Book on contracts ; Title Three titled "quasi-contracts" 准合同 zhǔn hétóng (Art. 979 ff.) of the same Book; and the Seventh Book on liability for illicit acts (often but inaccurately translated as "tort liability") 侵权责任 qīnquán zérèn (Art. 1164 ff.) Together with other provisions of the Code not pertaining to the regimes mentioned so far, various provisions or regimes contained in other special laws form the fifth source of civil liability, referred to by Art. 118§2 *in fine* as "other legal provisions" (s. above §174). 309

Again, the *terminology* related to these notions and its translation gives rise to confusion, namely, as compared to Swiss and other foreign laws or systems, and calls for clarification. 310

"Civil liability" in Chinese law is used in its wide sense or *lato sensu*, i.e, it covers both *contractual* and *extracontractual* (or noncontractual-) liability. In contrast, in Swiss law, "civil liability" only applies to liability *for illicit acts;* to add to the confusion, in Chinese law, the latter is generally translated as "*tort* liability". 311

While there seems to be a consensus for translating 侵权责任 qīnquán zérèn by "*tort* liability"[202], the term of "tort" or "torts", its derivatives and the notion 312

[200] About the relationship between these liabilities, s. below §333.

[201] S. above §139.

[202] Even though 侵权责任 qīnquán zérèn is translated as "tort liability" in the most common translations of the Chinese Civil Code in English, 责任 zérèn litterally translates as "infringement": as such, "liability for infringement" would be a more accurate

to which they refer actually pertain to *common law*, not to the civil law system from which Chinese law stems. Even though there are similarities between civil liability (or liability for illicit acts) in the narrow sense or *stricto sensu* and torts, there are also significant differences[203]. Practically, it is also easier, in English, to refer to the short name of "torts" than to the somewhat cumbersome expression "liability for illicit acts". Yet Chinese liability for illicit acts indisputably identifies with civil law systems, not with common law. Therefore, one should understand that the use of the terminology "tort liability" as generally translated from the Chinese Civil Code is limited to avoiding the confusion between civil liability *lato sensu* and civil liability (for illicit acts) *stricto sensu*, but that the regime of so-called "tort liability" in the Chinese Civil Code identifies with civil liability (for illicit acts) *stricto sensu* as understood in civil-, not in common law systems.

313 The terminology used in Swiss law does not help to dissipate such confusion. As noted, in Swiss law, "civil liability" relates to liability for illicit acts, also commonly known as "*Aquilian* liability" (from its denomination in Roman law) or "*delictual* liability". Civil liability (law) *lato sensu* is simply referred to, among Swiss lawyers, as "the law of liability". Contractual liability is literally known as such.

314 To add to the confusion, while the terminology mentioned in the preceding paragraph is universally known among Swiss lawyers, the Swiss Code of Obligations does not contain chapters straightforwardly titled "civil liability" and "contractual liability"; in addition, their location in the Code's structure is difficult to identify: thus, civil liability is to be found is the First Part of the Code of Obligations, First Title on the formation of obligations, Chapter 2 on "obligations resulting from an illicit act" (CO Art. 41 ff.) None of these titles uses the word "liability"; only the marginal title to Art. 41 mentions "conditions of liability".

315 Likewise, both the terminology and location of the contractual liability regime are, for the non-Swiss lawyer, challenging to find in the Swiss Code of Obligations: it is located in the same part, but under the Second Title on the effects of obligations, Chapter 2 on the effects of the nonperformance of obligations (Art. 97 ff.) Again, none of these titles use the word "liability", while the

---

translation; it would also near the expression of "obligations resulting from an illicit act" used by the Swiss Code of Obligations for noncontractual liability (s. below §1633).

203 In essence, while all torts fall under the umbrella of non-contractual liability, not all forms of non-contractual liability are necessarily torts. Common law "torts" and civil law "liability for illicit acts" both address non-contractual civil wrongs causing harm, but differ in structure, sources, and scope. Details can be found in specialized literature.

marginal title to Art. 97 mentions "nonperformance"; it is only its marginal subtitle which, eventually, mentions "debtor's liability".

Even though *noncontractual* liability is sometimes used for referring to liability for illicit acts, it does not equate to the latter: noncontractual liability also extends to *negotiorum gestio* (s. below Chap. 7 §54, Negotiorum Gestio) and unjust enrichment (s. below Chap. 7 §55, Unjust Enrichment). Known as "quasi-contracts", they are, as such, equally noncontractual sources of obligations or liability, but governed elsewhere in both the Chinese and the Swiss civil codes. 316

Once terminology issues have been clarified, the *legal systematic* or structure of the Chinese law of liability is easier to understand: civil liability, i.e., Chapter 8 of the First Book of the Chinese Civil Code, acts as the general part for the special parts which are both contractual liability, i.e., Chapter 8 of the Third Book, and liability for illicit acts, i.e., the Seventh Book, that is, for general principles and, by default, whenever either of the special parts are silent. Swiss lawyers may note that there is no equivalent for such a general part in the Swiss Civil Code, which as outlined above contains two, not three main regimes only: that of liability for illicit acts and contractual liability. However, the Swiss Civil Code expressly provides that the regime of liability for illicit acts doubles a general regime, i.e., that its provisions may, therefore, apply whenever the contractual liability regime is silent (s. CO Art. 99§3), where the Chinese Civil Code only implies it (s., e.g., Art. 186 and 179§1). 317

To recapitulate, "tort liability" in the Chinese Civil Code (Art. 1164 ff.) corresponds to "civil liability" (CO Art. 41 ff.) in common Swiss legal language; "liability for breach of contracts" in the Chinese Civil Code (Art. 577 ff.) corresponds to "contractual liability" (CO Art. 97 ff.) in common Swiss legal language; finally, "civil liability" in the Chinese Civil Code (Art. 176 ff.) contains general principles which apply both to noncontractual and contractual liability. 318

II. Civil Liability

The first provision of Chapter 8 (Art. 176 to 187) of the First Book of the Chinese Civil Code only states that civil subjects shall bear civil liabilities in accordance with the law (Art. 176). The foundation of liability to which it refers is to be found in Chapter 3 on legal persons, which states that a legal person shall independently bear civil liability with all its assets (Art. 60; s. above §139). However, like Art. 60, Art. 176 does not enunciate the conditions to which liability is subject, which are to be found in special liability regimes. 319

Nevertheless, Art. 176 complements Art. 60 by adding that civil liability can also be consensually *agreed* between the parties concerned. As such, it is 320 another particular case of Art. 5, 130 and 131, all of which provide for civil subjects' contractual freedom[204].

321 The general regime of liability contained in this chapter of the Chinese Civil Code addresses three main issues common to all types of liability: remedies, joint and several liability, and exonerating facts.

322 *Remedies* include but are not limited to the following (Art. 179§1): cessation of infringements, removal of obstacles, elimination of danger, return of property, restoration to original condition, repair, reworking or replacement, resumption of performance, compensation for loss, payment for breach of contract[205], elimination of adverse effects, rehabilitation of reputation, and extension of apology.

323 The Code further expressly legitimates *punitive damages*[206] provided, however, that they are grounded on a legal basis contained in another law (Art. 179§2). Punitive damages typically pertain to common law[207]. The inclusion of punitive damages in the Chinese Civil Code illustrates the modern outlook of Chinese law which, even though such institution belongs to civil law systems, accommodates certain features of common law whenever these are widespread, however not universal, in international legal practice. Punitive damages are not to be confused with *liquidated damages*[208], which are provided for by Art. 585 (s. below §§818ff.)

324 The remedies outlined above (incl. punitive damages) can be applied individually or in *combination* (Art. 179§3).

---

204 S. below §554.

205 Art. 179§1, item 9. The expression used in this provision, 支付违约金 zhīfù wéiyuē jīn, is also frequently translated as "payment of liquidated damages". However, this translation is erroneous: literally, it should translate as "payment for breach of contract", s. below §812). About *liquidated damages*, which are a distinct notion, s. below §§818ff.

206 Unlike liquidated damages which are pre-agreed, punitive damages are awarded by a court (or an arbitral tribunal); their purpose is punitive and deterrent: they go beyond compensating the injured party and are awarded in addition to actual (or compensatory) damages.

207 In Swiss law, punitive damages are governed by the same set of provisions than liquidated damages (CO Art. 160 to 163); however, they are subject to stricter conditions than liquidated damages. Generally speaking, Swiss law is more reluctant than common law jurisdictions, in particular the U.S., to admit punitive damages, and sets tighter limits: namely, the Swiss judge may reduce their amount if he deems them excessive (CO Art. 163§3). For a detailed discussion, s., for example, FELIX DASSER, Punitive damages: Vom "fremden Fötzel" zum "Miteidgenoss"?, SJZ 96/2000 p. 101.

208 S. above note 206.

Although contractual liability is expressly mentioned (incl. liquidated damages) in the general regime, it is detailed in Chapter 8 (Art. 577 ff.) of the Third Book of the Chinese Civil Code and will be discussed later in this book with the law of contracts (s. below Chap. 4 §27, Liability for Breach of Contract). Contractual liability is mentioned twice in Chapter 8 on civil liability: other than at Art. 179§1, item 9, it is also at Art. 186, which entitles the victim of a damage resulting from a contractual breach to rely either on the contractual liability regime or on that of liability for illicit acts for seeking compensation[209]. 325

Certain circumstances *exonerate* the author of the damage from its liability or *mitigate* it. They include force majeure, self-defense, emergency and *negotiorum gestio*. 326

Force majeure, a notion which is more than often misunderstood and abusively invoked, means any objective circumstance that is *unforeseeable, inevitable, and insurmountable* (Art. 180)[210]. If any of those conditions is not met, the author shall face liability[211]. *Self-defense* is subject to proportionality (Art. 181). 327

Emergency (or urgency), which is addressed in two non-continuous provisions (Art. 182 and 184) and, in between, *negotiorum gestio* (Art. 183; s. below Chap. 7 §54, Negotiorum Gestio), exonerate the author of liability or limit the latter under certain conditions, which are subjective, i.e., left to the parties' or to the judge's appreciation. 328

Whenever two or more civil subjects cause damage together, if the law provides for it[212] or if the parties so agree[213], the authors may face *joint and several liability*[214]. This regime does not only apply if several authors have caused damage to a third party, but also if they have, together, *mutually* caused damage to each other. 329

---

209 Swiss law does not offer such choice but applies the noncontractual liability regime as a supplement to the contractual regime whenever the latter is silent, s. above §317.

210 About the *clausula rebus sic stantibus*, s. below §672.

211 On force majeure as a cause of contractual termination, s. Art. 563§1, item 1 and below §724; as a mitigating or exonerating circumstance of contractual liability, s. Art. 590 and below, §834.

212 Swiss law automatically provides for joint and several liability whenever two or more authors caused a damage together (CO Art. 50§1).

213 Chinese law may prohibit the parties to agree to be jointly and severally liable; however, s., for example, Company Law Art. 14§2 (s. below §1787).

214 Joint and several liability is known, in Swiss legal French, as "responsabilité solidaire" and, in Swiss legal German, as "gemeinsame Verantwortlichkeit". However, the Swiss Code of Obligation refers to it as "plural liability" (Fr. "responsabilité plurale"; Ger. "Haftung mehrerer"; CO Art. 50).

330 If so, the latter is governed by two provisions: the first prescribes that, if the law provides for proportional liability, each author is liable proportionally to its share if such share can be determined; if not, such shares shall be equally divided (Art. 177). The rule for such sharing is given in the two first sentences of Art. 178§2.

331 The second provides that the victim may claim full compensation to any (or some) of them[215] (Art. 178§1; external liability), while the author(s) sought is or are entitled, in turn, to claim its or their share to its or their co-authors[216] (Art. 178§2, last sentence; internal liability).

332 The regime of joint and several liability is extended to *contractual performance* and developed accordingly by Art. 518 ff. (s. below §§634ff.)

333 Finally, two provisions address the *relationships* between the various liability regimes: we have already seen that Art. 186 entitles the victim of a contractual breach to rely either on contractual liability or on liability for illicit acts[217]. In addition, Art. 187 regulates the relationship between civil, administrative and criminal liability: whenever an author faces administrative or criminal liability along with civil liability, the two former shall not affect the latter. Moreover, if its assets are insufficient for covering all two or three, they shall cover civil liability in priority.

§13. Limitation of Action

I. Introduction

334 Simply put, a limitation of action[218] is a time limit or deadline within which a claimant must file its claim before a court (or an arbitration tribunal[219]) before

---

215 The same rule prevails in Swiss law, where it is implied by CO Art. 50§1.

216 Whenever several authors have caused a damage together, but answer on different liability grounds (illicit act, contract or the law), Swiss law fixes the order of priority in which they are to internally bear its compensation (CO Art. 51). S. also below, liability for illicit acts (§1548).

217 S. above §325.

218 Limitations of action are also widely known as "statutes of limitation" in common law systems, especially in the U.S.

219 From this point onwards, in this chapter, any reference to a court shall but understood as meaning "a court *or an arbitration tribunal*". Arbitration tribunals, provided they comply with national law, are empowered to issue decisions known as awards which are enforceable like judgments issued by a judiciary authority, i.e., a tribunal, a court, or a judiciary administrative authority. S. also below, §358.

it expires; if it neglects to, it shall be deprived (or "barred") of the right it claims.

Such time limits vary, sometimes vastly, depending on the circumstances of the case, and from one jurisdiction to another. Therefore, although claimants are generally represented by a lawyer before a court, foreign investors in China would be well advised to familiarize themselves with such limits in order to be able to instruct their lawyer timely, should they ever have to consider filing a claim. 335

The law of time limitations entails complexities so that, in order to gain a sound understanding of its regime under Chinese law, some notions and distinctions must be clarified. Thus, the expiry of a legal time limit can be said to pertain to two *types*, resulting in two radically contrasting consequences: either such expiry deprives the claimant from its right to claim its right before a court, but *not* of its underlying right (the right it intended to claim before the court, A.K.A. *subjective right* since, however tentatively asserted, it was not confirmed by a court); or said expiry *does* deprive the claimant from its underlying right forever. 336

The first type of time limit is known in civil law systems as *prescription*; the second as *forfeiture*. Chapter 9 of the First Book of the Chinese Civil Code on general provisions addresses prescription only. That chapter is titled 诉讼时效 susòng shíxiào, which is accurately translated as "extinctive prescription" or "limitation of action" in some authoritative translations, but more vaguely, thus deceivingly indeed, translated as "statutes of limitation" in others, typically in U.S. translations. Forfeiture is addressed on a case by case basis elsewhere in Chinese law (s., e.g., below §§1848, 2066 and 2201). 337

Swiss law contains an entire section on prescription (CO Art. 127 ff.) That section of the Swiss Code of Obligations does not address forfeiture either, which like in Chinese law is scattered around Swiss law[220]. The distinction is well known among Swiss lawyers, however. 338

---

[220] Prescription literally translates, in legal Swiss French, as "prescription"; in legal Swiss German as "Ersitzung". Forfeiture translates in legal Swiss French as "péremption"; in legal Swiss German as "Verwirkung". However, the use of "péremption" has been criticized by some French speaking scholars who prefer to use "déchéance" which were, arguably, a more accurate translation of "forfeiture", because "péremption" may be confused with another type of time limit in certain judiciary proceedings that end the proceedings after a certain time while preserving the right of the claimant to re-file its claim (Fr. "péremption procédurale" or "péremption d'instance"; s. WALTHER J. HABSCHEID, Droit judiciaire privé suisse, Georg, Geneva 1981. pp. 202-203; s. also Commentaire romand/CO I *ad* Art. 127, No. 6 and note 27.

339 Simply put again, once *prescription* has been reached, the claimant may not re-file its claim; yet it is still entitled to invoke its claim as a *defense* in case its counterparty files itself a counterclaim against the former claimant. Such defense is known as "recoupment" or "offsetting" in common law, or as "compensation" (s. below §350), as literally translated from Swiss legal French, or "Verrechnung" in Swiss legal German (CO Art. 120 ff.)[221] In contrast, in case of *forfeiture*, the holder of a forfeited right shall never be entitled to invoke it, whether by filing a claim or as a defense, after forfeiture has been reached.

II. Limitations of Action

340 The *general* or default limitation of action for a *civil* claim in Chinese law is prescribed by the Chinese Civil Code and is of *three years*[222] (Art. 188§1). It is subject to numerous accommodations and exemptions, which we discuss below, however.

341 To start with, this deadline is subject to qualification. First, the three-years limit is *subjective*, i.e., it starts to run from the day the claimant becomes or should have become aware of its right. Second, the Code further sets an *objective* limit of *20 years* since that right was infringed (Art. 188§2, 2nd sentence), meaning that the claimant will be deprived of the right to file a claim even if it became aware of the infringement more than 20 years after it was caused. Third, notwithstanding the above, "under special circumstances", the court may decide to *extend* the (three or 20-) years limit upon application by the claimant (ibid., 3rd sentence).

342 Other laws may provide for special time limits however (Art. 197§1). Notably (but not only), is it worth noting that the Chinese Civil Code provides for the following selected special limitations of action (the following enumeration is not exhaustive).

343 *First*, as noted, the right of *rescission* provided for in Art. 143 ff. on the effectiveness of civil acts (s. above Chap. 2 §10.IV, Validity of Juristic Acts) is governed by a *subjective* limitation of action of *one year* from when the right holder became or ought to have become aware of the cause of rescission (Art. 152§1, item 1) or the coercion ended (Art. 152§1, item 2), and to an *objective* limit of *five years* from that cause (Art. 152§2); the subjective limit is shortened to *ninety days* in case of substantial misunderstanding (Art. 152§1, item 1).

---

221 About offsetting in case of termination, s. below §759.
222 This time limit was extended from two to three years as of 1 October 2017.

Second, the right of claim to the return of the original *property* shall extinguish, if the possessor fails to exercise it within *one year* from the date of the encroachment (Art. 463§2). 344

Third, *preservation* claims to the effect of revoking a debtor's acts from disposing of its assets purporting at affecting the realization of its creditor's claims are subject to a limitation of action of *one year* from the day the creditor was aware or should have been aware of such acts (Art. 538 to 541). 345

And *fourth*, for contracts of *international sale of goods* and for contracts for the *import or the export of technology*, the Code extends the general limitation of action to *four years* (Art. 594)[223]. 346

Absent any special provision to the contrary, the general limit of three years of Art. 188§1 also applies by default both to contractual and noncontractual claims, including liability for illicit acts, *negotiorum gestio* and unjust enrichment. 347

The general limit of three years provided by the Chinese Civil Code is in stark contrast with Swiss law as far as *contractual liability* is concerned, since the latter provides for a much longer limit of *ten years* (CO Art. 127). The (subjective[224]) limitation of action for claims resulting from liability for illicit acts (or "civil liability" as known in Swiss law) is identical though, i.e., of three years (CO Art. 60§1) too[225]; it also applies to *negotiorum gestio* (CO Art. 60§1 and 67§1[226]) and to unjust enrichment (CO Art. 67§1). 348

Limitation of action is not to be confused with the limitation applying to *contractual termination for a cause*, which is not to be filed before a court, but to be notified to the counterparty within one year from the cause of termination, 349

---

[223] This departure from the general limitation conforms with Art. 8 of the Convention on the Limitation Period in the International Sale of Goods of 14 June 1974 (entered into force on 1 August 1988) which is a treaty ancillary to the United Nations Convention on Contracts for the International Sale of Goods of 11 April 1980 (CISG) effective in China as of 1 January 1988. Under certain conditions, that limitation can be extended up to ten years (Art. 23 of the Convention on Limitation Period in the International Sale of Goods). Although both China and Switzerland signed the CISG, neither did sign the Convention on the Limitation; however, both adjusted their national law accordingly. On the CISG, s. below Chap. 5 §29.II, The Vienna Convention (CISG). This limitation of action is not to be confused with the time limit for inspecting the goods (Art. 620) and notifying the seller of any inconformity of the sold goods (Art. 621), which are not limitations of action.

[224] The objective time limit is of ten years (CO Art. 60§1 *in fine*).

[225] In Swiss law, the general limitation of action for civil liability claims was extended from one to three years as of 1 January 2020.

[226] CO Art. 60§1 applies to CO Art. 423§1 (profit; ATF 126 III 382 = JT 2000 I 520) and CO Art. 67§1 applies to CO Art. 423§2 (bad faith; ATF 86 II 18).

unless the law or the contract provides, or the parties have agreed, otherwise (Art. 563; s. below §§723ff.)

350 As generally noted (s. above §339), Art. 192§1 provides that the holder of a time-barred right may still invoke it as a *defense* against its counterparty whenever the latter were to file a claim against the former. However, such defense may not be used if the debtor agrees to perform after the limitation (Art. 192§2, 1st sentence). Moreover, once the debtor has performed, it may not claim back its performance from the time-barred claimant (*ibid.*, last sentence), because the debtor's performance is deemed to have compensated the time-barred claim. In other words, if party A owes 250 to party B and party A neglected to timely file against party B, while party B owes 100 to party A and party B subsequently files timely against party A, party A shall not be entitled to claim compensation as a defense for refusing to pay the whole 250 if, eventually, party B voluntarily pays 100 to party A; likewise, party B will not be entitled to claim back those 100 from party A because the latter owes 250 to party B (party B is entitled to claim the remaining 150 from party A however[227]).

351 The time limits mentioned above suffer numerous accommodations and exemptions: they may be suspended, discontinued, or not apply. *Suspension* means that the time count shall stop with the occurrence of certain events and resume *from the suspension* whenever such event ceases; discontinuation means that the time count shall stop with the occurrence of certain events and resume *from the beginning* whenever such event ceases. Some other claims are *exempt* from time limits altogether.

352 *Suspension* events include force majeure[228], no or limited civil capacity, death, subjugation or "other obstacles" preventing a claimant to file (Art. 194). *Discontinuation* events include a request to perform, the debtor's agreement to perform, and the filing of a claim or events with effects similar to filing[229]. Limitation of action *does not apply* to claims for discontinuance of infringements, removal of obstacles or elimination of dangers, immovable or registered property claims or similar rights (Art. 196).

227 Art. 192§2, last sentence does not expressly spell out that latter consequence, which is an implication resulting from the general principles of the law of obligations.

228 S. Art. 180§2 and above §327.

229 In Swiss law, an "order to pay" (Fr.: "commandement de payer"; Ger.: "Zahlungsbefehl"; Art. 69 ff. of the Swiss Federal Law on Debt Recovery and Bankruptcy) which is sent, on an official form, upon request of the creditor, by the bankruptcy office to the debtor, typically amounts to such request and discontinues the limitation of action (CO Art. 135§2). These is no equivalent to such procedure in Chinese law; such request is typically formed by a letter, preferably a lawyer's letter, sent to the debtor.

The Code further contains numerous provisions on the *calculation of time limits* which are spread out both in the chapter on limitation of actions and the next on calculation of time periods (Chap. 10, Art. 200 ff.) Other than the general rule (Art. 188; s. above §§340 and 341), the chapter contains special rules about, in particular, payments by instalments (Art. 189), revocation, rescission and "other rights" (Art. 199)[230]. 353

The difference between the calculation rules contained in Chapter 9 on limitation of actions and those on the calculation of time period contained in Chapter 10 is that the former chapter contains rules specifically applying to *judiciary remedies* (and arbitration), whereas the latter applies to the calculation of *all the time limits* contained in the law, whether related to a judicial remedy (or arbitration) or not. They define general notions such as calendar, days, months, years, hours, holidays or days off, end of the day or closing of business, and the beginning and the end of such periods. 354

The general calculation rules contained in Chapter 9 can be freely modified by the parties (Art. 204; s. also Art. 197§1 and below §348). Unless they are, these provisions are subject to other provisions of the Code (*ibid.*): in other words, they are to be regarded as *lex generalis*, whereas other provisions of the Code that may apply to the calculation of time periods are deemed to be *lex specialis*, therefore taking precedence on the general regime of Chapter 9. 355

Finally, a court will not spontaneously reject a claim filed after the limitation of action (Art. 193): such objection must be raised by the defendant. Provided the latter does, and that the main claim was belatedly filed indeed, the court shall reject the latter. A court would have to spontaneously reject a claim in case the right is *forfeited*[231] however. 356

The parties are free to agree otherwise about time limits, their calculation and the effect of their inobservance (suspension or discontinuation) (Art. 197§1). However, any agreement to that effect made *in advance* shall be deemed to be *invalid* by law (Art. 197§2). 357

Arbitration is subject to special limitation of arbitration rules if they exist and, if not, to limitation of action (Art. 198). 358

230 S. also persons without or with a limited civil capacity (Art. 190) and victims of sexual assault (Art. 191).

231 On the notion of forfeiture, s. above §§337 to 339.

Chap. 3 Real Rights

§14. Introduction

Real rights are covered by the Third Book of the Chinese Civil Code (Art. 205 to 462) It is a very dense subject-matter, running over 258 articles. We will not address it in detail or comprehensively, as to do so would far exceed the scope of this book. Nevertheless, we will comment on selected issues of interest to foreign investors. 359

The Third Book of the Code is divided in five titles: general rules, property (or ownership), usufruct, security and possession. As such, it follows the classical structure of civil law systems as far as the subject matter is concerned. However, it is worth clarifying that, while the title of that book of the Code, 物权 wù quán, is sometimes translated as "property rights", this translation is inaccurate: it literally translates as "real rights". Indeed, in civil law systems, namely, in Swiss law, "property" *stricto sensu* is only one sub-category of property rights *lato sensu*, which are correctly qualified of "real rights" (Fr.: "droits réels"; Ger, : "Sachenrecht") from the Latin root "res", the thing. 360

Civil law systems, following Roman law, mainly distinguish between *property* which, simply put, is a right entitling the right holder to use the thing, and *possession*, which is the fact of using that thing. Both are governed by specific sets of provisions, which constantly interact, but are well differentiated. 361

Other real rights (i.e., other than property *stricto sensu* and possession) form a broad group known in civil law systems as "other real rights" indeed (like in Swiss legal French: "autres droits réels") and named as such in the Chinese Civil Code[232] or, more accurately, as *limited* real rights (like in Swiss legal German: "beschränkten Dinglischen Rechte"; CC Art. 730 ff.), since those rights present features which are limited compared to property and possession. 362

Other or limited real right contain, notably but not only, *incumbrances* (Fr.: "charges"; Ger.: "Grundlasten") and *servitudes* (Fr.: "servitudes"; Ger.: "Dienstbarkeiten"). Both are subdivided in several subtypes whose specific terminology may vary from one jurisdiction to another, among which, notably, *usufruct* (Fr.: "usufruit"; Ger.: "Nutzniessung"); and *security interests* (Fr.: "charges foncières"; Ger.: "Grundlasten"), of which, mainly, the *mortgage* 363

---

232 Such reference is only incidental however, s., for example, Art. 311§3 and below §442); unlike Swiss law, the Chinese Civil Code does not dedicate a specific chapter or title to such rights, s. below §370.

(Fr.: "hypothèque"; Ger. "Grundpfandverschreibung"). *Neighboring rights* may also be mentioned along with other real rights.

364 Both property and possession distinguish between *movables* (Fr.: "meubles"; Ger.: "beweglichen Sachen") and *immovables* (Fr.: "immeubles"[233]; Ger.: "Grundstücken") (i.e., as to the latter, land, buildings and related rights), both of which are governed by different sets of provisions.

365 Moreover, property law contains distinct sub-regimes for *individual* property and *collective* property[234]. The latter subdivides into *co-property* (Fr.: "copropriété"; Ger.: "Miteigentum") and *common* property (Fr.: "propriété commune[235]"; Ger.: "Gesamteigentum")[236]; while these sub-regimes apply both to movable and immovable property, modern real law[237] added one sub-regime applying to immovables only, i.e., to property rights in *multi-property buildings* (Fr.: "propriété par étages" or PPE; Ger.: "Stockwerkeigentum"[238]).

366 Chinese law knows yet another regime for *State ownership* which, while non-existent as a separate regime or marginal in most western jurisdictions, is very significant in China, as we will see. Moreover, the notion of *collective ownership* is, under Chinese law, a specific, and widespread indeed, regime on its own, as compared to the marginal role played by collective ownership in civil law systems.

367 Finally, immovable property is subject to *registration* on a register generally known as the land or property register (Fr. "registre foncier"; Ger. "Grundbuch"): such registration is governed by a complex set of provisions, whose basic regime is also contained in the Code.

368 Among other specificities typical of Chinese law, unlike in the west, all land in China is property of the *State* and cannot be purchased: it can only be rented, for several years. This regime does not prevent the ownership of any real estate

---

233 Immovable property can be literally translated in French as "propriété immobilière"; however, the Swiss Civil code uses the alternate translation of "propriété *foncière*" (from its Latin root *fundum*, the land).

234 While "collective property" is literally translated in the Swiss Civil Code, in German, as "Gemeinschaftlisches Eigentum", it is translated, in French, as "*propriété de plusieurs sur une chose*", i.e., "property of several [owners] on one thing"; yet it is generally known, among Swiss lawyers, as "propriété collective", i.e., "collective property".

235 Also known as "main commune" (literally "common hand").

236 The main difference between co-property and common property is that, in the latter and unlike in the former, the collective owners' rights are undivided, so they must exercise them together.

237 The multi-property regime was added to the Swiss Civil Code in 1965.

238 The Swiss French and German names of theses regimes literally translate as "property by floor".

built on the land so leased. Inasmuch, this regime is closer to the *leasehold* system of *common law* than to civil law systems. Its features will be briefly presented below.

The *lease* or rental of an immovable (house, apartment, building, warehouse, 369
factory, land[239], etc.) and for a movable (vehicle, machine-tool, etc.) is not governed by real law but by the law of *contracts*, which will be extensively covered further down in this book[240].

Although the various subject-matters mentioned above are all covered both by 370
Chinese and Swiss law, they are somehow differently structured in each jurisdiction. First, while the Chinese Civil Code contains most of the matters covered both by the Swiss Civil Code and the Code of Obligations, real law is contained, in Swiss law, in the Civil Code (Fourth Book), not in the Code of Obligations. As noted above, while the topical book of the Chinese Civil Code is sometimes translated, however inaccurately (s. above §360), as "property law", it is titled "real rights" in the Swiss Civil Code. Both Chinese and Swiss law address property and other related rights first and possession last. However, the Swiss Civil Code contains a part dedicated to "other real rights" (incl. usufruct and mortgage), while the Chinese Civil Code does not[241]: like property and possession, both usufruct and mortgage are addressed under a dedicated title. In contrast, the Swiss Civil Code contains separate titles for immovable and movable property while, in the Chinese Civil Code, the related provisions are blended in the title on property. Finally, both codes contain, on the beginning of the topical book, general provisions applying to all aspects of real law.

The Second Book of the Chinese Civil Code of real rights is divided in five 371
titles: general principles, property (*stricto sensu*), usufruct, security interests and possession.

---

239 A civil subject other than the State (or a collective) can only sub-lease a land, provided such subject itself rents that land from the State (or a collective), since all land pertain to the State (or to collectives): therefore, while short-named "lease", such contract can, strictly speaking, only be a sub-lease.

240 S., in particular, the contract of lease (s. below Chap. 5 §35, Lease) and that of financial leasing (s. below Chap. 5 §36, Financial Leasing).

241 S., however, above §362 and note 232.

§15. General Principles

I. Introduction

372 General principles (Art. 205 to 239) are contained in the first title of the book on real rights and include, other than general provisions, provisions on the *existence* and the *protection* of property rights.

373 As noted, the purpose of the Code was to legitimize private law (s. above §103). As such, Art. 207 is arguably the most significant provision of the Code, since it unambiguously acknowledges *private property* by asserting the commitment of the State to equally protect both the State's and private rights. This provision rests on the Constitution (Constitution, Art. 13§§1 and 2; s. above §§103, 116 and 172), which was last amended two years before the promulgation of the Code. To measure this giant leap in China's legal history, one should keep in mind that, after the Revolution and for decades after that, private property had been abolished[242]. As such, this guarantee represents a major incentive for foreign investors.

374 This progress calls for some nuances, however. First, Art. 13 of the Constitution expressly applies to "citizens", falling short from extending to foreign investors. However, Art. 18§2, last sentence of the Constitution expressly states that the rights of *foreign investors* shall be protected by the law. In contrast, Art. 207 of the Civil Code does not specifically refer to "citizens" but extends to individuals and organizations without any reference to their nationality. Therefore, one can infer from the foregoing that the protection of private ownership does extend to foreign investors. However, the Code does not expressly state so.

375 Be that as it may, while Art. 207 provides additional comfort, that concern had been anticipated as of 1990 when China signed the *ICSID Convention* (A.K.A. Washington Convention, which it ratified in 1993), where the Convention already contains the member-States commitment to protect foreign investment[243]. Moreover, as far a Swiss investors are concerned, this commitment was reiterated in 2009 with the *Sino-Swiss BIT* (entered into force in 2010)[244].

376 A second nuance must be added by recalling that China, including its legal order, fundamentally remains a socialist economy where, notwithstanding the

---

242 For a summary historical account of the development of private law in China from the Revolution until the Civil Code, s., for example, JACQUES HENRI [A.K.A. James] HERBOTS, The Chinese New Civil Code and the Law of Contract, China-EU Law Journal, Springer, Heidelberg 2021, 7:39-49, pp. 41-42.

243 S. above Chap. 1 §6.II, The Washington Convention.

244 S. above Chap. 1 §6.III, The Sino-Swiss Bilateral Investment Treaty.

principle of equal protection of State and individual property, "public property remains dominant" (s. below §413), as affirmed by Art. 206§1 of the Code, just above Art. 207. While, in every jurisdiction, private interests are limited by the public one, it can be said that, in China, as compared to most western jurisdictions, the primacy of the State, which is entrusted with the preservation and the promotion of socialist values, is affirmed more vigorously.

The main and, indeed, a major consequence of the foregoing is that *all land pertains to the State and cannot be sold*. We develop this notion further down (s. below Chap. 3 §16.II, State-, Collective- and Private Property). 377

In addition to the foregoing, the general provisions subject the creation, alteration, transfer or extinction of *immovable* property rights to *registration*. The mandatory nature of the registration of immovables is actually contained in two separate provisions which, however consecutive, pertain to two different chapters: the first one, enunciated in the first sentence of Art. 208, which is the last of the chapter on general provisions, provides for the obligation to register immovables; the second, Art. 209§1, which is the first of the chapter on registration, proclaims that property rights shall only become valid upon completion of the registration[245]. 378

In contrast, the second sentence of Art. 208 provides that the creation or transfer of *movable* property rights occurs upon *delivery*. As noted, Art. 209§1 proclaims that the creation, alteration and extinction of property rights (without specifying whether movable or immovable) can only occur upon registration, "unless provided otherwise by law". Inasmuch, Art. 208, second sentence is the main case being "provided otherwise by law"[246]. 379

Unlike in the Swiss Civil Code, where registration is governed by a chapter clearly labelled "land register"[247], in the Chinese Civil Code, registration is contained in the next chapter of the title, i.e., Chapter 2 on the "Creation, Alteration, Transfer and Extinction of Real Rights" (Art. 209 ff.) That said, other than what we have mentioned above, the detailed regulation of registration would exceed the scope of the book and will, therefore, not be covered. 380

---

245 Although Art. 209§1 *in fine* reserves contrary provisions of the law, other than the registration of ownership of all the natural resources which are owned by the State, which may be dispensed with, some original acquisition modes (Art. 313 to 320) are conceivable, for example, accession (Art. 322).

246 There are other exemptions, s., for example, Art. 209§2, which provides that the registration of State-owned natural resources may be dispensed with.

247 S. above §359. The Vienna Convention (s. below Chap. 5 §29.II, The Vienna Convention (CISG)) does not apply to the transfer of property under a contract for the international sale of goods (s. below §§900 and 939).

II. Existence of Real Rights

381 The second chapter of the title on general principles of real rights, which we have short-titled "existence of real rights", comprehensively governs, as noted in the preceding paragraph and as its title makes clear, the *creation, alteration, transfer and extinction* of real rights, in one word the various states of real rights existence. All of them revolve around their *registration* which, although not mentioned in the chapter's title, and as also mentioned in the preceding paragraph, the chapter details. That chapter is divided in three sections: registration of immovables, delivery of movables, and other provisions.

382 As mentioned (s. above §378), the detailed regulation of registration (of immovables; Art. 209 to 223) would exceed the scope of the book and will, therefore, not be covered. Suffice it to mention that the creation, alteration, transfer or extinction of property rights shall only legally come to life upon registration, unless the law provides otherwise (Art. 209).

383 The registration requirement applies to *immovables* (s. above §§367 and 380). However, the law exceptionally prescribes such requirement for certain *movables*, even though its legal effect differs. Thus, generally speaking, registration has a *constitutive* legal effect for the creation, alteration or transfer of the property rights of immovables, but a *declarative* effect for that of movables or other rights, such as IPR, by which such registration is opposable by the registered party to *bona fide* third parties (s. below §§437 and 438).

384 The first provisions of the next section on the *delivery of movables* of Chapter 2 is of major significance for foreign traders: Art. 224 states that the creation or transfer of the property right of the movables shall become valid as of the time of their delivery, unless otherwise provided for by law. This provision is consistent with, and reiterates indeed, the general principles providing for the creation of movable property rights enunciated at Art. 208 and 209§1 (s. above §§378 and 379).

385 While pertaining to real rights, this provision is the cornerstone of the *contract for the sale of goods*, since delivery commands, under Chinese law, the transfer of the property of the goods from the seller to the buyer (s. below §899)[248].

386 The rest of the section on the delivery of movables (Art. 225 to 228) as well as the last section on other provisions (Art. 229 to 232) of the chapter on the creation, etc. of real rights both contain a small number of provisions applying to

---

248 The transfer of the property rights is not to be confused, under the contract of sale, with that of the *risks* (s. below §939).

specific cases which may not be the immediate concern of foreign investors and to which we refer the reader.

III. Protection of Real Rights

Chapter 3 on the protection of real rights is the last one of the First Title on general principles. Therefore, its provisions apply both to property and possession, as well as to other real rights. These provisions are complemented, in the special parts of the book on real rights, by provisions specifically protecting each type of real rights. 387

This chapter contains seven articles only. In case of dispute bearing on real rights, the first article (Art. 233), in a fashion typical of Chinese law, prominently encourages soft, *alternative dispute resolution* methods, which it lists in increasingly contentious order and includes conciliation, mediation and arbitration, before resorting to litigation before a court. 388

Art. 234 to 238 list the various *remedies* available to the real right holder seeking redress: confirmation of its right[249], return of the movable or immovable, removal of any impairment or danger, repair, etc. in case of damage, or compensation for damage[250]. 389

In accordance with the general principle of civil liability (s. above §324), these remedies may be used individually or in *combination* (art. 239). 390

The book on real rights of the Chinese Civil Code contains other provisions specifically protecting certain types of real rights, in particular property rights and possession. Moreover, property rights are protected by other Chinese laws and by certain international treaties. These additional provisions will be addressed later in this book in connection with the discussion of property rights and possession. 391

---

249 A "request of confirmation of right" 请求确认权利 qǐngqiú quèrèn quánlì, as it is literally known in Chinese law, corresponds, in legal French, to an "action en constatation de droit" and in legal German to a "Feststellungsklage".

250 As far as compensation for damage is concerned, Art. 238 further refers to the regime of civil liability in general; about its sources, s. above §309.

§16. Property

I. Introduction and General Provisions

392 This chapter of the Chinese Civil Code is dedicated to *property* (所有权 suŏyŏuquán) or ownership as opposed to possession (占有 zhànyŏu) and other real rights. Since both property and ownership are, in legal English, equivalent, we have elected to use "property" throughout this book to refer to property *stricto sensu*, as this word is closer from is Latin root of "proprietas" from which this legal institution derives[251]. While common law generally favors the word "ownership" instead, the regime of real rights in common law systems also differs considerably from that of civil law systems, thus providing another justification to favor "property" over "ownership" for the sake of preventing confusion between both systems. We may mitigate this redactional choice by referring to "owner" instead of the less common "proprietor" however. That said, as noted above, 所有权 suŏyŏuquán is frequently translated, in English, as "ownership", irrespective of our reservations; this latter translation is, strictly speaking, not incorrect.

393 Title Two on property of the Second Book of the Chinese Civil Code on real rights subdivides in six chapters: general provisions; State-, collective- and private property; multi-property; neighboring rights; co-property and special provisions.

394 Again, given the broad encompassing nature of the property regime, far exceeding the domain of foreign investment, we do not ambition to comment it neither exhaustively, nor in detail, but will outline its general features, and stress those which are of special interest to foreign investors.

395 The two first articles of Chapter 4[252] on *general provisions* define the scope of the right of (private) property, which includes the right to *possess*, to *use*, to *benefit* from and to *dispose* of the related movables or immovables (Art. 240), as well as that of creating *usufruct* and *security* interests (typically but not only, mortgage; Art. 241).

396 The third one has extended consequences on Chinese real estate law, as it professes the *inalterability of the property of the State* (Art. 242) which can,

[251] "Property" is also closest to its translation in legal French of "propriété", but not in German, where it is expressed by "Eigentumsrecht".

[252] The numbering of chapters throughout the book of the Chinese Civil Code to which they pertain is not interrupted by title parts but continuous (s. above §112): thus, the first chapter of the Second Title of the Second Book is numbered Chapter 4, not 1.

therefore, not be sold out. State property is discussed further down in this book (s. below Chap. 3 §16.II, *State-, Collective- and Private Property*).

397 The three last articles (Art. 243 to 245) provide for exceptions in the form of *expropriation*[253] as well as requisition[254]. Several reminders must be inserted here, in particular as far as foreign investors are concerned.

398 Generally speaking, modern Chinese law abides by the general principles of law acknowledged by the majority of the international community, which are that expropriation must be justified by the public interest, rest on a legal basis, and be fairly and timely compensated. These principles are reaffirmed throughout Chinese law, as well as in certain treaties to which China adhered.

399 Thus and *first*, these principles are affirmed in the First Book of the Code on *general provisions* (Art. 117; s. above §113).

400 *Second*, the same principles were reaffirmed in the *Foreign Investment Law* two years after the promulgation of the Chinese Civil Code (Art. 20; s. above §19), where they were more clearly articulated than in the Code. FIL Art. 20 also extends to requisition.

401 *Third*, and anyway, China had, before the Code and the FIL, adhered to the *Washington Convention*, whereby it committed to abide by those principles as protected by the Convention. As a matter of fact, while China did limit the scope of the Convention as far as it was concerned, it precisely limited it to those provisions of the Convention protecting expropriation (Art. 25§1; s. above §77) which, therefore, already protected foreign investors in China since 1993[255].

402 *Fourth*, Swiss investors were already protected by the *Sino-Swiss bilateral investment treaty* (Art. 6; s. also above §85), whose topical provisions are comparatively clearer than those to the same effect in the FIL, since 2010.

403 *Fifth* and finally, even though, whenever expropriation is alluded to, the first form of expropriation which come to mind is *land* expropriation, the latter does not apply in China, since all land is property of the State and cannot be sold, be it to foreigners or Chinese citizens. Foreign investors can buy immovable above Chinese land however, where such immovables (as well as, potentially, related

253 "Expropriation" and "nationalization" are equivalent. While Art. 243 and 244 of the Chinese Civil Code only refer to expropriation, the Washington Convention (Art. 25§1) refers indifferently to both expropriation and nationalization (s. below §388).

254 About the difference between requisition and expropriation, s. above note 23 and below §407.

255 S. above note 53.

movables, such as a production chain, machine-tools, equipment, etc.) can be expropriated, whether formally or materially.

404 The general provisions on property are expressly extended to *legal persons* (namely, companies) by the penultimate article of the next chapter on, among other things, private property (Art. 269; s. below §427).

405 Other than Art. 243§1 of the Code, the other provisions of Art. 243 and 244 are primarily intended to protect the rights of Chinese real rights holders targeted by an expropriation and to prevent expropriation-related *corruption*, which has been widespread in China as the economy was gradually liberalized and local authorities frequently abused their powers to expropriate Chinese citizen with the goal of enriching local officers instead of in the public interest.

406 These provisions are of interest to foreign investors nevertheless, since a foreign investment related to a corrupt expropriation could result in such transaction to be voided, sometimes at the cost of considerable, often not recoverable damage to the foreign investor. Therefore, foreign investors considering a transaction involving real rights potentially resulting from an expropriation would be well advised to conduct a careful review of the background of such rights before committing. Such caution is particularly warranted in transactions involving local authorities.

407 Art. 245 applies to *requisitions*. As already noted about the FIL[256], compared to expropriation and nationalization, requisition can be defined as *temporary* expropriation, i.e., a measure from the authority which temporarily deprives the real right holder from its real rights. Requisition is subject to the condition of *urgency*, which the Code describes by examples such as "rushing to rescue, providing disaster relief, or epidemic prevention and control". It must operate within the boundaries of the law. The requisitioned real right holder is entitled to compensation.

II. State-, Collective- and Private Property

408 As its title makes clear, Chapter 5 of the title on property addresses three types of property: State property, collective property and private property. It contains general principles of property rights *stricto sensu* related to those three categories of real rights holders.

409 As noted, *State property* (国家所有 guójiā suǒyǒu) is of particular significance in China since, for decades since the Revolution, private property was abolished, while only State property enjoyed legal protection. Even though private

[256] S. above note 23.

property has been gradually restored since the Opening[257] and that, notably, the proportion of State-owned or controlled enterprises has dramatically reduced, State property retains a major significance in China, which remains firmly committed to socialism (as recalled as early as in the second article of the Second Book of the Chinese Civil Code on real rights, at Art. 206§3), namely, as compared to western societies.

State property is governed by Art. 246 to 259, as well as by Art. 269, which is a common provision applying to all three types of property. 410

The assets, movable or immovable, deemed to be owned by the State are listed in Art. 247 to 254. They include, notably, all *urban land* and, as provided by the law, *suburban and rural land* (Art. 249). In other words, the Chinese Civil Code confirms that urban land belongs to the State by default, while State property of suburban and rural land must rest on another, specific legal basis. Provided that other basis exists, the Code merely affirms it. 411

However, one may not imply from the distinction above that, unless the law prescribes the opposite, suburban and rural land may be acquired by private owners, be they individuals or legal persons, Chinese citizens or foreigners: suburban and rural land is integrally owned by suburban or rural *collectives*[258], unless, as reserved by Art. 249, the law provides that it is owned by the State. The latter reservation is to be regarded as exceptional, however; generally speaking, the land in suburban and rural areas is overwhelmingly owned by local collectives[259]. 412

In other words, in China, the land is *integrally and exclusively* owned by the State or by suburban and rural collectives, and is *inalterable*[260], as affirmed by Art. 242 (s. above §396); as a consequence, it cannot be sold to private buyers, be they individuals or legal persons, Chinese citizens or foreigners. This regime is consistent with Art. 206§1 unambiguously asserting that public property remains dominant (s. above §376). 413

In contrast, immovables *above* the land can be sold to private buyers, including foreigners, subject to a form of usufruct known as *land rights* (s. below §456). These notions (incl. the conditions under which such immovables can be sold to foreigners) will be discussed below. 414

---

[257] The "Opening" started as of December 1978, when Deng Xiaoping launched the reform shifting China towards a market-oriented economy and opened it to foreign trade and investment.

[258] The notion of collectives is discussed below, s. §422.

[259] S., for example, G. C. S. Lin/S. P. S. Ho, China's Land Resources and Land-Use Change: Insights from the 1996 Land Survey, 2003, p. 69.

[260] S., however, below note 264.

415 Other assets unsurprisingly include *natural resources* (minerals, waters and sea, uninhabited islands, forests, mountains, grassland, wasteland, tidal flats, wildlife) and *infrastructures* (railways, highways, power facilities, telecommunications facilities and oil and gas pipelines), as well as national defense, cultural relics and radio frequencies[261]. Exceptions may apply if provided by law.

416 The State's right of *possession* (Art. 255) deriving from the right of property (s. below Chap. 3 §18, Possession) is extended from the State to State-owned (SOEs), controlled or invested enterprises (Art. 256), thus clarifying that the fact that the State may be a sole, majority or minority investor in a private enterprise does not deprive the latter from the right of possession; that is subject to the law which may regulate it however and, conceivably, restrict it whenever public interest justifies it.

417 Art. 257 to 259 provide for various aspects of the *protection* of State property, namely, even if not only, against corruption; as such, while focusing on State property and the right of possession resulting from it, they complement the already rather wide encompassing set of provisions contained in the first chapter on general provisions of the title on property (Art. 243 and 244; s. above §397).

418 While Art. 243 and 244 provide for the protection of *right holders* against abuses in case of expropriation, Art. 257 to 259 protects *State property* against similar abuses. Evidently, State property cannot be expropriated; the common denominator of these two sets of provisions can be said to be the fight against official *corruption*: in the first case, towards non-State civil subjects, by authorities or officers using their powers for benefiting of an abusive expropriation; in the second, towards the State, for benefiting of an abusive management of State property.

419 Again, while not of direct concern to foreign investors, these provisions may be of interest whenever those foreign investors may be the victim, directly or indirectly, of such abuses or corruption. Indeed, the FIL protects them against *abuse of power* (FIL Art. 39; s. above §24), as well as, more generally, against undue or arbitrary interference of the State[262], whereby such abuses or

---

261 The inclusion of radio frequencies implies that, under Chinese real rights, *immaterial* or intangible goods can also be the subject-matter of real rights. Such acknowledgment is not universal, however; it has been debated or disputed in other legal systems. This issue is gaining in significance in an era when the formidable expansion of digital goods and services (of which artificial intelligence is only the latest development) is transforming the global economy, not to say the society.

262 On the prohibition of interferences, s. above §§11, 23 and 177. Such undue or arbitrary interference can result in material (as opposed to formal) expropriation, among other things.

interferences could result from an infringement of Art. 257 to 259 (and, possibly, if an expropriation is involved, of Art. 243 and 244) of the Code.

Thus, the authorities must preserve and increase the value of State property (Art. 259§1), while they must manage SOEs in the interest of (all, State- and private) investors (Art. 257)[263]; *embezzlement*, looting, private division, withholding or destruction (Art. 258); dumping[264], mortgaging or any such unauthorized transaction or conspiracy to that effect, in particular on the occasion of the restructuring, merger or division of an SOE (Art. 259§2), are prohibited. If so, the authorities or officers involved shall be held liable for any such abuses[265], including *dereliction of duty* (Art. 259§1 *in fine*)[266]. 420

The level of detail of the various infringements described by Art. 243, 244, 257, 258 and 259 of the Code reflects and responds to the widespread abuses committed by officials and, typically, local authorities, as China gradually liberalized its economic and legal framework. 421

Collective property[267] (集体所有 jítǐ suǒyǒu) is regulated by the next set of articles (Art. 260 to 265). As noted, the Chinese notion of collective property, which is a pilar of Chinese real rights, is specific as compared to the generic notion of collective property in civil law systems (s. above §§365 and 366). Collectives own almost all cultivated land; besides, while the State managed to retain or be transferred large areas of sub-urban land, collectives are believed to own a majority share of it (s. above §412). 422

Art. 260 to 265 of the Code regulate property rights within the collectives. Collectives are the matter of Chinese rural citizens, villages, towns and township; as such, they are of no direct concern to foreign investors, which may, however, be impacted by collective property rights. Whenever so, the remedies foreign 423

263 This provision is of particular interest in case of JV between a foreign investor and an SOE. On JVs, s. above §§30ff. and below,Chap. 9 §66, Joint-ventures.

264 The prohibition of dumping applies to those exceptional cases where State property may be legally sold, contrary to the general principle of its inalienability, s. above §413. About dumping as an obstacle to the transfer or property, s. also below §439.

265 The liability prescribed by the Code is of a civil nature; however, in case of corruption, in China, in most cases, corruption also results in criminal liability and is harshly punished.

266 The level of details of the various infringements described by Art. 243, 244, 257, 258 and 259 of the Code reflects and responds to the widespread abuses committed by officials and, typically, local authorities as China gradually liberalized its economic and legal framework which justified the intensification of the government's fight against corruption in the recent years.

267 About the distinction with State property, s. above §412.

investors may look for are not to be found in collective property rights, but in the general regime of property, as elaborated elsewhere in the book[268].

424 *Individual property* is addressed, in this chapter of the Code, by two articles only (Art. 266 and 267). They guarantee the individual owner's right to enjoy its ownership, i.e., the rights of possession resulting from it[269] (Art. 266) and their protection (Art. 267). These guarantees extend to legal persons (namely, companies) and are detailed in the next two articles (Art. 268 and 269; s. next paragraph).

425 Art. 266 and 267 only reiterate guarantees which have already been enunciated in the general provisions of the Code, in the general principles of real rights, and in the general provisions of property rights; moreover, as far as foreign investors are concerned, they were reiterated, shortly after the promulgation of the Code, in the FIL, while they had already been provided by treaties to which China had adhered, sometimes long before the Code did (s. above §397ff.) However duplicate, these multiples statements are consistent with the structure of the law, and ought to be reassuring to foreign investors.

426 Further, the Code expressly provides that property rights owners, be they the State, collectives or individuals, have the *right to establish or to invest into companies* (Art. 268); if they invest, this provision clarifies such investor's rights, i.e., receiving benefits derived from the assets, making major decisions and selecting managers; moreover, it shall perform its duties as agreed with its co-investors, or in proportion to its investment (*ibid.*)

427 Finally the two last provisions of this chapter of the Code extend the guarantee of property rights and their protection to *legal persons* (i.e., companies or enterprises, for- or not-for-profit; Art. 269) and to social (or welfare) organizations (Art. 270).

III. Other Property-Related Rights

428 Chapters 6 to 9 of Title Two on property comprehensively cover all *other forms of property-related rights*: multi-property rights (Chap. 6), neighboring rights (Chap. 7), co-property (Chap. 8), and special provisions on the accession to property (Chap. 9). While potentially of interests to foreign investors who may engage in investing in real estate, a detailed commentary of Chapters 6 to 8

268 S., in particular, above §§388ff.

269 Art. 266 enumerates them as comprising "lawful incomes, houses, articles for daily use, tools of production, and raw and semi-finished materials"; this odd enumeration, which seems to have been primarily intended for peasant households, should be regarded as a list of examples, not as limitative or exhaustive.

would exceed the scope of this book which will, therefore, not cover them. The related notions have been described above (s. §365).

429 Chapter 9 deserves closer attention, however. Titled "special provisions on the accession to property", the majority of its eleven articles apply to *lost-and-found movables* (Art. 312 to 319) and would, therefore, arguably, only exceptionally apply. Out of the three remaining provisions however, two potentially are of general interest, and one stands out.

430 Art. 321 prescribes that the *fruits* of any (movable or immovable) property belong to the owner, save in case of usufruct, in which case they belong to the usufructuary, unless the parties agreed otherwise. As such, this provision relates to the next title on the usufruct. Because usufruct is a frequent feature of foreign investment, foreign investors ought to keep this regime in mind, as overlooking it may result in costly consequences. Usufruct is commented in the next chapter of this book.

431 Art. 322 determines the fate of the property resulting from *processing, attachment or mixing*. Although the law does not specify it, conceivably, such property can be movable or immovable. Such fate, i.e., to which party the property rights of assets resulting from processing, attachment or mixing eventually belong, is primarily to be agreed between the parties. If they abstained or omitted to do so, the law shall determine it. If the law is silent, it shall be determined according to the following two sub-principles, which are to apply in combination and be pondered or balanced against each other: first, the property (resulting from processing, attachment or mixing) shall belong to the party which makes the *main use* of it; second, the *innocent party* shall be protected[270].

432 Consequently, if a movable or immovable results from processing, attachment or mixing, its owner will be that, of the two parties involved, which has been using such resulting property the most, provided that party was not a fault. If such main use cannot be determined, or if one party was at fault, the party suffering damage from the attribution of the product's property to the other party must be compensated (Art. 322 *in fine*). Even though this provision does not expressly mention it, one can assume that it refers to the general regime of liability for illicit act (s. below Chap. 8).

433 Again, this regime is potentially significant to foreign investors engaging into processing raw materials, expanding a plant, mixing components, etc. and should, therefore, be considered and clarified while entering into a JV (s. below Chap. 9 §66, Joint-ventures), a manufacturing agreement, etc. to the effect of

270 About immovables, s. above note 245.

preventing disputes about the products resulting from the alteration of each party's property.

434 Finally, the most significant provisions of Chapter 9, and one of the key provisions of the whole title on property indeed, is Art. 311. This provision dramatically strengthen the protection already repeatedly proclaimed elsewhere in Chinese law (s. above §§397 and 417 to 419) by adding two powerful features to the mere right of obtaining compensation in case of expropriation: the owner's *right of recovery* of its property if it was unlawfully disposed of, and *ineffectiveness of the transfer* of the property right by a third party against, or absent, the will of the owner, provided certain conditions have been met.

435 Before entering into the detail of this provision, it must be emphasized that, in civil law systems, the basic protection of real rights clearly distinguishes the protection of *property* from that of *possession*: therefore, the protection of either right is embedded in two separate provisions, pertaining to separate regimes[271]: thus, Art. 311§1, 1st sentence proclaims the right to recover one's property; the protection of possession is provided by Art. 459 to 462; the latter will be commented later in this book about possession (s. below §§542ff.)

436 As far as the *right of recovery* is concerned, the first sentence of Art. 311§1 entitles the owner to recover its right of property if it was transferred away from it by a third-party enjoying no right of disposing of it. By directly providing the owner with such right of recovery, the Code implies that the owner may do so without necessarily applying before a court[272]; however, it is also implied that the owner shall exercise this right peacefully and not cause damage to a third-party[273] or disturb the public order by doing so, or else it may expose its own liability[274].

437 As far as the *ineffectiveness of the transfer* is concerned, the remainder of Art. 311§1 subjects the validity of the transfer of a property right to two additional conditions, three for immovables: first, the transferee must have been of

271 The owner's right to recover its property is known, in Swiss law, in Swiss legal French, as "revendication" and in Swiss legal German as "Herausgabeanspruch" (CC Art. 641§2); the possessor's right to recover its possession as "réintégrande" and "Besitzentziehung" (CC Art. 926 and 927). Both are cornerstones of Swiss real rights.

272 Compare, for example, with Art. 147 to 151, which expressly provide that the victim must apply to a court to obtain compensation, as opposed as seeking redress itself (s. above §250). Swiss law provides for the same solution (CC Art. 641§2).

273 Including to the infringer; however, provided such damage is rendered necessary by the infringer's deeds and proportionate, the infringer's liability shall compensate that of the owner: the general regime of liability for illicit acts (s. below Chap. 8 , Liability for Illicit Acts ("Torts") applies.

274 S. preceding note.

good faith at the time of the transfer; second, the transfer must have been performed against a *reasonable price*; and third, if the thing transferred was an immovable, such transfer must have been *registered* on the land register[275]; this requirement may also apply, although exceptionally, to certain movable assets.

Thus, for example, in case of real property and land use rights, property law requires the transfer to be registered on the land register (s. above §382); in case of patents and trademarks, assignment agreements must be registered with the China National Intellectual Property Administration or the China Trademark Office[276]; assignments under a factoring contract[277]; certain securities[278]; certain movable assets[279] must be registered as prescribed by the Chinese Civil Code or secondary legislation[280]. While as mentioned about immovables, registration has a constitutive effect (s. above §382), in the case of movables, registration has a *declarative*, not constitutive, legal effect, thus enabling the party having registered to oppose the claim of a good faith third party[281]. 438

The first condition set forth by Art. 311§1 (*bona fide* transferee) relates to the general protection that Chinese law, and civil law systems indeed, grant to good faith, i.e., in general (Art. 7 and s. above §116) and, in particular, in connection with the validity of juristic acts (Art. 143 ff. and s. above §§220ff.) While the second can also be related to certain causes of invalidity of juristic acts, it also performs an anti-corruption function by preventing *dumping*[282]. The third is a reminder of the regime of registration detailed at Art. 186ff. (s. above §§381ff.) 439

---

275 On the various authorities in charge of the registration of real rights, s. below notes 322 and 911.

276 Neither patents nor trademarks *licensing* agreements are subject to mandatory registration, only their *assignment* is; s. the Patent Law and the Trademark Law, which are not covered in this book; in case of assignment under a factoring contract, s. next note.

277 S. below §1178.

278 S. below §536; s. also preceding note.

279 For example, ships, aircrafts and motor vehicles; leased items under financial leasing (s. below §1153); goods under export control; or under bonded warehouse regime and, notably, in case of *title retention* under the contract of sale (s. below §911) of which the preceding examples are particular cases.

280 This enumeration is not exhaustive. For each of these areas of the law, the reader is invited to refer to those chapters of the book detailing the related procedures; detailed registration procedures exceed the scope of this book and will, therefore, not be covered.

281 This principle is known in Chinese law as 登记对抗主义 dēngjì duìkàng zhǔyì, i.e., "notice by registration".

282 In addition, Art. 539 protects creditors against debtors' attempts to organize their insolvency by resorting, among other things, to dumping and price inflating, by entitling the creditor to apply at court for the revocation of such acts, s. below §689. S. also above §420.

440 On the contrary, provided the transferee is of good faith, the price reasonable, the movable has been delivered[283] or the immovable registered, the property shall pass to the transferee. In other words, provided these conditions are met, the good faith of the transferee shall be *protected* even though the property may have been transferred by a non-owner third-party disposing of it against or absent the will of the original owner.

441 If so, the original owner shall be entitled to claim *compensation* from the abusive transferor (Art. 311§2).

442 Art. 311 also applies to "other real rights" *stricto sensu*[284], i.e., usufruct, etc.

443 In conclusion with respect to the protection of property, foreign investors ought to be aware that, while immovable property is relatively well protected by the registration requirement and anti-corruption policies, there is a tangible risk that movables which, as compared to immovables, can easily be disposed of, may be fraudulently sold to good faith buyers, for example, by felon employees who, even if ultimately caught, had preventively arranged their insolvency. As a result, the defrauded owner may be left more often than not without any recourse to recoup its loss. Such risks are best mitigated with sound prevention strategies.

§17. Usufruct

I. Introduction

444 Title Four of the Third Book on real rights of the Chinese Civil Code, following that on property, governs *usufruct* (用益物权 yòngyì wù quán; Art. 323 to 385). While not as extensive as the title on property, it is also substantial, with 62 articles in five chapters. Usufruct is one form of *servitude* (地役权 dì yì quán; Fr.: "servitude"; Ger. "Dienstbarkeit"), arguably, the main one. Although titled "usufruct" (Fr. "usufruit"; Ger.: "Nutzniessung"), the title also governs *other forms* of servitudes; yet the drafters of the Chinese Civil Code elected to name the whole title "usufruct", while other forms of servitudes are addressed in the last chapter of the title.

445 Further, property-related securities (notably, mortgage) are governed by the next title of the Code's book on real rights. Both servitudes, including usufruct, and securities belong to the category of "other real rights" *stricto sensu*. The

283 Cf. Art. 224; s. above §§384 to 387.

284 S. above §§362 and 370.

book on real right ends with the title on possession. There is no title or chapter on "other real rights" however (s. above §§362 and 370).

In contrast, the Swiss Civil Code dedicates a whole title to "other real rights". 446 This title is divided between one chapter on servitudes titled as such, and two chapters on securities, one for immovables and the other for movables. Usufruct is part of the chapter on servitudes; as a matter of fact, it is only part of the subsection on "other servitudes".

In the Swiss Civil Code, the chapter on servitudes also contains a subsection 447 on *land charges* (Fr.: "charges foncières"; Ger. "Grundlasten"), which the Chinese Civil Code does not: it does not operate a systemic distinction between servitudes and land charges and does not, therefore, dedicate a specific chapter or subsection to land charges.

The reason why usufruct is, structurally, given more prominence in the Chinese 448 Civil Code than in the Swiss one is, arguably, that rural usufructs have a great importance in China, while they do to a much lesser extent in Switzerland.

"Servitude" is also translated, from Chinese to English, by "easement". While 449 both expressions designate comparable legal institutions, "easement" is typically used in common law, while the notions used in civil law systems and in common law substantially differ from one another; the Chinese notion of servitude definitely best compares with that of civil law tradition.

A servitude *stricto sensu* (as understood in Swiss law) imposes a *negative* ob- 450 ligation on the owner of the servient land to tolerate certain uses or to refrain from exercising certain rights inherent to property; for example, a right of way[285] compels the owner to allow the beneficiaries of the servitude to pass over his land.

A land charge, on the other hand, can be said to be the other side of the coin: it 451 imposes a *positive* obligation on the owner to do or pay something to the beneficiary of the charge, for example, an obligation to maintain a hedge or to make a payment for the maintenance of a path. As noted, the Chinese Civil Code deals with *both* aspects, under the generic notion of servitude *lato sensu*.

II. Usufruct in General

As noted above, the title on usufruct subdivides in five chapters: on general 452 provisions, on agricultural usufruct, on construction usufruct, on residential usufruct on rural land, on the right of habitation, and on (other) servitudes.

[285] Fr.: "droit de passage"; Ger.: "Wegrecht"; CC Art. 694.

453 Agricultural usufruct (Chap. 11; Art. 330 ff.) is of no direct interest to foreign investors since agriculture is a severely restricted, if not prohibited, area for foreign investment[286] and is, therefore, mostly out of reach to them. The right of habitation (Chap. 13; Art. 362 ff.) is primarily intended to Chinese (mainly, peasants-) households and is, therefore, out of scope. Likewise, the residential usufruct on rural land (Chap. 11, Art. 330 ff.) is a specialized area which exceeds the scope of this book. Therefore, this chapter will briefly comment the first chapter (of the title on usufruct) on general provisions (Art. 323 ff.), and the last on other servitudes (Chap. 15; Art. 372 ff.); we will further outline the *construction usufruct* (Chap. 12, Art. 344 ff.) which may be of interest to foreign investors building in China, namely, for their own needs. While "*land use rights*" is commonly used to refer to various types of usufructs bearing on the land, this expression does not, strictly speaking, correspond to a specific legal notion in Chinese law.

454 The first article of the chapter on general provisions affirms the *principle* of usufruct, by which the beneficiary or usufructuary is entitled to enjoy the rights resulting from the property's possession as if it were its owner (Art. 323§1).

455 The usufruct regime applies both to *movables and immovables*, except if the nature of the institution considered only relates to a movable or an immovable.

456 Usufruct may apply to the *land*, which as explained exclusively pertains to the State or collectives, and other such natural resources (Art. 324). Whenever land or other natural resources are allocated by usufruct, the State shall be compensated by the usufructuary, and the regulation of such compensation shall rest on a legal basis. In China, they are commonly known as *land rights*, although this denomination is not used by the Chinese Civil Code.

457 The owner may not *interfere* in the use of the usufruct (Art. 326§2). If the usufruct ends or cannot be exercised as a consequence of an expropriation or confiscation of the movable or immovable being the subject-matter of the usufruct, the owner shall *compensate* the usufructuary (Art. 327).

458 The law protects *natural resources* given out in usufruct: they shall be used reasonably (Art. 326§1, 328 and 329), which implies that they shall not be depleted, and that their natural environment shall equally be protected[287].

---

286 S. above,Chap. 1 §5.II, The Negative List.

287 Natural resources given in usufruct to foreign investors in China, such as mining, are, due to their strategic significance, exceedingly rare in practice, however.

III. Construction Usufruct

A. Introduction: the Freehold and the Leasehold in Common Law

The construction usufruct is arguably the main of the few domains, if not the only one, of Chinese law which can be said to be closer to common law than from Roman law and the civil law systems stemming from it. From that point of view, in order to gain a sound understanding of the foundations of the construction usufruct in Chinese law, it is helpful to briefly describe the basic features of common law with which it compares. 459

Where Roman law (and the civil law systems from which they derive) and common law both acknowledge and rest on the distinction between property and possession, common law, as far as the property and possession of *immovables* is specifically concerned, further distinguishes, and indeed puts a strong emphasis on, two corollary notions unknown of civil law systems, which are the *freehold* and the *leasehold.* 460

While narrowly related, leasehold and freehold are two fundamental concepts of property ownership that differ significantly in terms of rights, duration, and control over the property of an immovable. *Freehold* is the most comprehensive form of property ownership in common law systems. Key characteristics of freehold include: indefinite duration; complete ownership; unrestricted rights; in its purest form[288], the owner has the right to use the property as it sees fit, subject only to the law and regulations; transferability; and tax liability. 461

Leasehold, in contrast, constitutes a more limited form of property ownership. Its key features are: fixed duration; a contractual relationship; limited rights; rent payment; and maintenance duties. 462

The main legal implications arising from those differences are that, while both create a *property interest*, a freehold is considered a stronger and more complete form of ownership; the *duration* of a freehold lasts indefinitely, while a leasehold has a defined end date; as a leasehold term shortens, the property's *value* may decrease, which is not a concern with freehold properties; a leasehold often comes with implied *legal protections* for both landlord and tenant, such as the landlord's duty to maintain habitability; and freeholders generally have more freedom to make *alterations* to their property, while leaseholders often need permission for significant changes. 463

[288] This form is known as "fee simple absolute".

464 Although common law acknowledges both leasehold and *possession*, these are, however related, distinct concepts: as explained, the leasehold is a type of real right, known in common law as an *estate*, that grants the tenant exclusive possession of an immovable property for a fixed period; it is a form of property tenure where one party acquires the right to occupy a land or a building for a given time; in common law, a leasehold estate is considered as a *property* right, even though it only involves limited rights to real property (by creating a property *interest*). Possession, on the other hand, refers to the right and ability to exercise dominion and control over the property; in the context of leasehold estates, possession is a key component, but it does not equate to ownership of the underlying real property.

465 Likewise, while common law also acknowledges the *rental lease* (of an immovable: typically, of an apartment, of a house, of offices, of a warehouse, etc.), the rental lease does not equate to a leasehold: a leasehold typically involves a longer-term agreement, often lasting for many years or even decades; a rental lease, on the other hand, is usually a shorter-term arrangement, commonly lasting for a year or less; as noted, a leasehold creates a *property interest* for the tenant, known as a leasehold estate; a rental lease primarily creates a contractual relationship between landlord and tenant[289], with less emphasis on property rights; the *transferability* of leasehold estates is generally free: the leasehold can be bought and sold on the open market, similar to freehold properties; rental leases are generally not transferable without the landlord's permission; leaseholds often come with more extensive *legal protections* and implied rights, such as the right to extend the lease or purchase the freehold; rental leases typically have fewer implied protections; in a leasehold, the tenant may have more *responsibilities for property maintenance* and improvements; in a rental lease, the landlord usually retains most maintenance responsibilities; leaseholds have a *capital value* that can appreciate or depreciate over time, depending on factors like the remaining lease term; rental leases do not typically have a separate capital value; leaseholds are often subject to *registration* with land registries, especially for longer terms, while rental leases are typically not registered. In short, leaseholds offer a more substantial and long-term interest in property compared to the more temporary nature of rental leases.

466 The leasehold system in common law originated in medieval England and evolved differently from Roman law and civil law systems due to unique historical and socio-economic factors. The English leasehold system emerged during the Middle Ages as a means for powerful landowners to generate revenue from their land without relinquishing ownership. The leasehold system in common law evolved differently from Roman law and civil law systems for several

[289] The contract of lease is, in Chinese law, a typical contract (s. below Chap. 5 §35, Lease).

reasons: in Roman law, leasehold was not considered a property right, but merely a contractual arrangement; Roman law provided limited protection to tenants beyond contractual rights against landlords; common law, over time, developed more extensive protections for tenants; common law developed a system of different "estates" or rights in land; this concept was not present in Roman law. To summarize, compared to common law, Roman law placed less emphasis on the distinction between land and other property. This led to different approaches in handling leasehold interests.

B. *The Construction Usufruct in Chinese Law*

In civil law systems, a construction usufruct is known as a *building right* (Fr.: "droit de superficie"; Ger. "Baurecht"; CC Art. 675). However, as noted in the introduction to the construction usufruct, the latter is closer to the common law leasehold than to the building right as understood in civil law systems. The reason for this is that, although for entirely different historical and socio-economic circumstances, the drafters of post-Revolution Chinese law, after having decreed that all land was property of the State, had to find a way to protect the property of anyone building atop such land, without relinquishing the property of the latter however: the solution was the construction usufruct which, inasmuch, compares to the common law leasehold better than to the civil law building right. 467

Moreover, while building rights are universal in China, since all land property is owned by the State (or collectives), they are, generally, marginal in western civil law jurisdictions, notably in Switzerland, where prospective buyers would only in exceptional circumstances run the risk, inherent to building rights, to invest in a building on a land they do not own. This is all the more so in Switzerland since very long duration building rights[290], which would be favored by prospective investors, are not listed among the real rights restrictively enumerated by the law[291]; therefore, they would risk being considered as illicit for being exceedingly long and, consequently, null and void *ab initio* under CO Art. 20[292]. 468

---

[290] Land leases with very (e.g., 99 years) or extremely (e.g., 999 years) long durations are known as *emphyteutic* leases (Fr.: "bail emphytéotique"; Ger.: "Erbpachtvertrag").

[291] This restrictive list is known as the *numerus clausus* of real rights. Real rights acknowledged by Swiss law are enumerated at CC Art. 958 and 959, which exhaustively lists which rights may be registered on the land register.

[292] S. PAUL-HENRI STEINAUER, Les droits réels, 5th ed., Stämpfli, Bern 2012, p. 565 § 120a. However, for example, 90 years-long emphyteutic leases were granted by the canton of Geneva, Switzerland, without ever being challenged. Besides, emphyteutic leases are

469 As a result, any foreign investor intending to build a plant, a warehouse or an office building in China will first have to be granted an usufruct to that effect by the State or the local collective, hence the prominent significance of this institution in China.

470 The construction usufruct (建设用地使用权 jiànshè yòngdì shǐyòng quán) is governed by Art. 344 to 361 of the Chinese Civil Code, which form Chapter 12 of the Second Book on real rights. It is defined at Art. 344, which provides that its holder shall, in accordance with the law, have the right to *possess*, use and enjoy State-owned land, including to construct buildings, structures and their ancillary facilities on it.

471 Such constructions may be built above or under ground (Art. 345).

472 A construction usufruct is enjoyed against the payment of a *fee* to the State (or the collective) (Art. 351).

473 The Code further clarifies (although only at Art. 352) the *property* rights of the construction usufruct beneficiary by asserting that the buildings, etc. which it constructed on that land belong to it. This is subject to proof to the contrary however[293].

474 The usufruct can be created by assignment, allocation or "other means" (Art. 347). The Code does not define these notions. Arguably, an *assignment* (出让 chūràng) is of contractual nature, while an *allocation* (划拨 huàbō) is an administrative act (which may further be implemented by assignment anyway). The Code further seems to distinguish allocation and assignment by providing that allocations shall be strictly controlled (Art. 347§3), while construction usufructs are subject to bidding (s. below §§474 and 475) and to being assigned (Art. 347§2 and 348§1), the contract of assignment being detailed in the next subsection (Art. 348§1). We submit that the distinction between assignment and allocation is somewhat blurred and not to be taken too rigorously, however.

475 Such *contract of assignment* shall "generally" contain the following provisions: the parties' identity and domicile; the land boundaries; the space occupied by the buildings; the use of the land and the planning conditions attached thereto; the term; the related fees and method of payment; and the dispute resolution method (Art. 348§2).

---

listed in the *numerus clausus* of certain other western civil law jurisdictions such as France where they are, therefore, legal.

293 Such proof could be brought, for example, by the third-party constructor of such buildings which is not simultaneously the beneficiary of the construction usufruct (s. below §481).

476 Among such required provisions, the *purpose* of the use of the land (Art. 348§2, item 4) is of the essence. The law mentions, along with it, in the same provision, the *planning conditions* to which the implementation of such purpose will be subjected. Any such purpose must prescribe a *rationale use* of the land. Any change is subject to the competent authority's approval (Art. 350).

477 The requirement of rationale use extends, among other things, to *natural resources saving*, the *protection of the environment* and, generally speaking, the prohibition to damage the usufruct, as well as compliance with the law (Art. 346). These requirements are consistent with the general protection granted by the Code to State property (Art. 326§1, 328 and 329 and above §458; s. also Art. 258 and 259 and above §420)[294].

478 As far as *allocations* are concerned, the Code stresses that they shall be "tightly" controlled (Art. 347§3). This provision is to be related to the government's efforts to curb undesirable or illegal appropriations of State of collective land for overambitious development plans or by unscrupulous officials for the purpose of personal enrichment[295].

479 Finally, in order to come into existence, the construction usufruct must be *registered* (Art. 349; s. above §§378 and 383), after which the registration authority will deliver a *certificate* to the beneficiary. As the parties apply for such registration, the authority will carefully check the assignment contract. Even though Art. 348§2 mentions that it shall "generally" contain the provisions it lists, it can be assumed that they are to be considered as a minimum and that any missing provision, which will be conservatively interpreted, will lead to a rejection of the application with a request to complement the contract according to the requirements of Art. 348§2. Therefore, "generally" is to be understood in the sense that such contract may (and usually will) be more detailed than Art. 348§2, but not less, that provision constituting a minimum.

480 It is interesting to note that the Code names such certificate 权属书 quán shǔ shū, which may alternatively be translated generically as "title certificate" or specifically as "ownership certificate", where 权属 quán shǔ taken in isolation translates as "ownership". Even though the latter differ from 所有权 suǒyǒuquán which is the word the Code uses for the real right of property (s. above §392), the word 权属 quán shǔ chosen by the Chinese legislator hints towards the hybrid nature (as a real right mixing both property and possession

[294] From a contractual perspective, Art. 509§1 mandates the parties to "avoid wasting resources, polluting the environment and destroying the ecology during the contract performance", s. below §617. Besides, environmental pollution and economical damage is a special case of liability for illicit acts, s. below Chap. 8 §61, Liability for Environmental Pollution and Ecological Damage.

[295] On anti-corruption policies, s. above §§405, 418ff., 439 and 443.

features) of the construction usufruct; as such, this choice suggests, once again, that the construction usufruct is closer to a leasehold than to a building right (in the civil law systems sense of this latter notion; s. above §§467 and 468).

481 It is important to note that buildings, etc. constructed on the land being the subject-matter of the usufruct must be registered as well, as mandated by Art. 208, first sentence and 209§1 (s. above §§378 and 383). Among other things, such registration may provide the proof to the contrary reserved by Art. 352 that, unlike the legal presumption set by that provision, the owner of the building, etc. is not the beneficiary of the usufruct (s. above §473).

482 The *expenses* resulting from the creation of the usufruct are to be borne by the beneficiary (Art. 351).

483 *Public tendering or auctioning* is an important feature of the construction usufruct; it is mandatory in many cases, including where land is used for: industrial, commercial, touristic, or entertaining purposes; constructing commercial residential buildings, or for other profit-making purposes, or whenever two or more (natural or legal) persons are willing to use the same land (Art. 347§2).

484 Again, the Code does not make a clear difference between tendering (招标 zhāobiāo), auctioning (拍卖 pāimài) and other open bidding methods (公开竞价 gōngkāi jìngjià[296]; cf. Art. 347§2 *in fine*); what one should take away is that the emphasis in on "open", i.e., that any such *modus procedendi* should be *public* or transparent. This requirement responds to a strident demand from the community of foreign investors in China ever since the Opening to be treated on equal footing with their Chinese counterparts; it was eventually reflected both in the Code and in the FIL (s. above §§4, 11 and 17).

485 The remainder of the chapter on construction usufruct is mostly concerned with two issues: the right of the beneficiary to dispose, mainly, transfer the usufruct (Art. 354 to 357), and its end and renewal (Art. 358 to 360).

486 As far as the right to *dispose* of the usufruct is concerned, the beneficiary may transfer the usufruct, exchange it, use it as capital contribution (e.g., as paid-off capital of a company), give it as a gift or mortgage it (Art. 354). If so, a

[296] A sale or assignment by tender (招标 zhāobiāo) involves confidential written offers submitted by a specific deadline, with the seller free to accept any offer or negotiate further. It is frequently but incorrectly translated as "bidding". Tendering is the procurement process of calling for offers; bidding (投标 tóubiāo) is the act of submitting an offer in response. A sale or assignment by auction (拍卖 pāimài) is a public, competitive process where buyers bid openly, and the property or goods are sold to the highest bidder when the auction ends.

written contract[297] must be executed. The duration of the usufruct may be shorter, but not longer. Moreover, alterations must be registered (Art. 355).

The Code further mandates that the buildings, etc. constructed on the land must be transferred, etc. with it (Art. 356), and vice versa (Art. 357). These provisions are drafted in a mandatory form and do not provide for exemptions. They do not rule them out either. One may suppose that any departure from these rules is to be consulted and negotiated with the competent authorities. Namely, issues may arise when the beneficiary of the construction usufruct and the owner of the building do not coincide (s. above §§473 and 481). 487

At the *end* of its duration, the construction usufruct *automatically renews* (Art. 359). However, the fate of the buildings, etc. constructed on the land is not necessarily linked to that of the usufruct: if agreed between the parties at the time the usufruct was created, the buildings, etc. shall be dealt with accordingly. If not, or if the agreement is unclear, such fate shall be decided according to the law[298]. 488

Even though Art. 359 provides for the automatic renewal of the construction usufruct, Art. 360 contemplates the case in which it ends anyway, at its expiry or before. This can happen, for example, if, in accordance with the agreement or the applicable law, the beneficiary voluntarily terminates it, or if the authority or the assignor do, for example, because the beneficiary did not pay the fees, because the agreement provided for a fixed duration, or because the authority expropriates it (s. next paragraph). In such case, the usufruct must be deregistered and the certificate returned to the authority. 489

The State (or the collective) may take the land back if the public interest so commands it: if so, such measure is deemed to amount to an *expropriation*, which Art. 358 mandates to be compensated as such by referring expressly to Art. 243[299] (s. above §§391ff.) 490

Art. 360 reserves specific regulations applicable to land owned by *collectives*. 491

---

297 There is no typical assignment contract in the Chinese Civil Code; such contract shall be governed by the general rules applying to the transfer of contracts contained in Chapter 6 of the Third Book of the Code on contract law (Art. 543 ff.; s. below Chap. 4 §25, Modification and Transfer).

298 Namely, the parties shall attempt to settle under Art. 510, s. below §§618ff. About interpretation, s. below §§622 and 623.

299 On damage valuation, s. below Chap. 8 §58, Damage Compensation.

492 The Code does not define the *duration* of the construction usufruct, which is set in secondary legislation[300], administrative regulations or, in certain case, by the authority. The duration varies according to the designated purpose of use. At the time of writing this book, those durations were the following: land for residential purposes: 70 years; land for industrial purposes: 50 years; land for educational, scientific and technological, cultural, health care, or sports purposes: 50 years; land for commercial, tourism, or recreational purposes: 40 years; land for combined usage or other purposes: 50 years.

493 Finally, the general provisions on usufructs (s. above Chap. 3 §17.II, Usufruct in General) apply whenever the provisions on the construction usufruct are silent or unclear.

C. Servitudes

494 Servitudes[301] (地役权 dì yì quán) are governed by Chapter 15 (Art. 372 to 385) of the book on real rights of the Chinese Civil Code. A servitude (Fr.: "servitude"; Ger.: "Dienstbarkeit"; CC Art. 655§3) grants a third-party beneficiary the right to use or access an owner's immovable property for a specific purpose, without conferring a property right to the beneficiary (Art. 372).

495 Servitudes are multiform by design and can relate to any subject-matter, for example, access to water on the neighboring property, right of passage through the neighboring property to access the beneficiary's, etc. As such, servitudes may be of concern to any foreign investor in China owning an immovable, either as existing or potential servient or dominant estate owner.

496 The immovable property of the owner granting the servitude is called the *servient* estate; that of the beneficiary, the *dominant* estate[302].

497 Servitudes must be agreed in the form of a *written contract*, whose minimum content is defined by the Code and must include the parties, the location of both estates, the purpose of the servitude and the way it shall be used; the duration of the servitude, the fees to be paid by the beneficiary to the owner[303], and the

300 Interim Regulations Concerning the Assignment and Transfer of the Right to the Use of the State-owned Land in the Urban Areas (2020 Revision), Art. 12. Rural areas are mainly governed by the Land Management Law.

301 Servitudes are also known, in English, as "easements" (s. above §449).

302 Servient estate translates in French as "fonds servant" and in German as "belastetes Grundstück"; dominant estate as "fonds dominant" and "berechtigtes Grundstück".

303 However, the easement can be granted for free, as indirectly acknowledged by Art. 384, item 2 which expressly addresses that possibility. Therefore, while the mention of the

dispute resolution method (Art. 373). A servitude becomes valid when the contract does (Art. 374, 1st sentence).

Servitudes may be registered, but *registration* is neither mandatory, nor a condition to their creation: as noted, a written contract suffices. However, when the beneficiary of a servitude fails to register it, it shall not be entitled to invoke the easement against a good faith third party (Art. 374, 2nd and 3rd sentence). If the registered servitude is altered, transferred or extinguished, the alteration must be registered (Art. 385). 498

According to what is stipulated in the contract, the mutual *rights and obligations* of the parties to a servitude consist, for the owner of the servient estate, in allowing the beneficiary to use his immovable property, and not obstruct the latter from exercising his right (Art. 375). Reciprocally, the beneficiary must use the servitude in conformity with its purpose and do its best to lighten the restrictions on the property rights of the servient estate (Art. 376). 499

The *duration* of a servitude may not exceed that of the usufruct related to either the servient or the dominant estate (Art. 377)[304]. 500

If, on the same property, a *new* usufruct is created after a servitude, the beneficiary of the new usufruct becomes tied by the servitude, be it servient or dominant (Art. 378). Conversely, the owner may not create a servitude on an existing usufruct without the consent of the usufructuary (Art. 379). 501

A servitude may be *transferred*, but it must be so with the land to which it is tied (Art. 380). Likewise, it may be *mortgaged*, but not separately (Art. 381). After the transfer, the new owner or usufructuary of the land is tied by the servitude, whether servient or dominant (Art. 382 and 383). 502

The servient owner is entitled to *revoke* the servitude if the beneficiary abuses it or fails to pay the fee, if any was agreed[305], after two reminders (Art. 384). 503

fee, let alone for stipulating that the easement is granted for free, is mandatory, its perception is not.

304 That condition does not apply in Swiss law since, most of the time, the parties own the land, unlike in China, where the land is owned by the State and granted for a limited period of time in the form of usufruct, s. above §492.

305 S. above note 303.

IV. Security in Property

A. Introduction

504 The Third Book on real rights of the Chinese Civil Code dedicates an entire title to security in property (担保物权 dānbǎo wù quán)[306]. Title Four (Art. 386 to 457) is very dense, comprising 72 articles divided into four chapters, two of which are further subdivided into two sections. While they play a major role in business law, security interests in property are a very specialized and technical subject-matter, which may not be the primary interest of foreign investors in China and exceed the scope of this book: we will, therefore, not cover them in detail. Nevertheless, in this chapter, we will briefly outline the structure and main features of that title with the goal of facilitating any further research.

505 Title Four focuses on *securities*, sometimes fully referred to as security interests in property. In other words, it does not deal indifferently with any kind of guarantees, only with *asset-based* guarantees, as opposed to debtor-based or *personal* guarantees. The latter are dealt with in the Third Book of contract with the suretyship contract (s. below §§511, 513 and 514). In other words, "security" is to be understood as an asset-based guarantee or collateral, whereas "guarantee" is a generic term which can relate either to an asset or a debtor. As a matter of fact, the Fourth Title originally reads 担保物权 dānbǎo wù quán, where 担保 dānbǎo means "guarantee"[307], 物权 wù quán "property rights" and 担保物 dānbǎo wù "collateral".

506 As noted, the title on security in property ("security") is divided in four chapters: Chapter 16 contains general provisions; Chapter 17 regulates mortgage; Chapter 18, pledge, and the last, Chapter 19, lien.

507 From the perspective of *Swiss law*, both the structure followed by the Chinese Civil Code and the English terminology used for translating it deserve clarification. Indeed, while the Chinese Civil Code addresses the *mortgage* (抵押权 dǐyā quán; Art. 394 ff.) and the *pledge* (质权 zhì quán; Art. 425 ff.) in two separate chapters, where the second on the pledge distinguishes the pledge of *movables* (*ibid.*) from that of *other* rights (Art. 440 ff.), Swiss law considers the mortgage, the pledge of movable and that of other rights altogether as pledges:

---

306 Alternative translations include "security interests", "security rights" and "security interest in property". We have chosen to refer to "security in property" in order to avoid the confusion, on one hand, with interests in the sense of return or revenue (i.e., the interest paid by the borrower to the lender on the loan extended against the security offered as collateral) and, on the other hand, with security related to assets or collaterals other than real property. See also below note 594.

307 About the difference between "guarantee" and "guaranty", s. below note 595.

in other words, while, in the translation of Chinese law, "pledge" specifically relates to the pledge of movables and other rights, in Swiss law, the mortgage is regarded as the pledge of an immovable, along with other forms of pledges, including that of movables. That said, other than that, those notions are comparable between Chinese and Swiss law.

Mortgage itself is a multiform notion whose related terminology also ought to be clarified. In Swiss law, mortgage literally translates, in French, as "hypothèque" and in German as "Grundpfandverschreibung". In reality, it covers three sub-notions, even though these latter terms are often indistinctively used to point at either of them: the mortage proper is the *security*; the financial facility borrowed or extended against that security, although generally referred to, for the sake of simplicity, as the mortgage, is actually the mortgage *loan*[308], which is not specifically referred as such in the Swiss Civil Code, but simply as "debt" (Fr.: "créance[309]"; Ger.: "Forderung"), since it can take the form of any debt, not only that of a financial loan. Finally, the *title* in which the security may be embedded in order to facilitate its liquidity is known, in French, as "cédule hypothécaire" and, in German, as "Schuldbrief"; however, there is no unanimous translation in English, which can refer to it as "mortgage note", "mortgage certificate", "mortgage bond" or "land charge certificate". 508

B. General Provisions

The first article of the chapter on general provisions affirms the basic *principle* of security by which the debt of its holder is guaranteed by the security, and the holder shall enjoy priority of compensation corresponding to the asset posted as security if the debtor fails to pay the holder (Art. 386). This equally applies to any other circumstance agreed between the parties where the security may be used. If the asset is destroyed, lost or expropriated, the holder of the security is entitled to the compensation paid by the insurance, if any, to the debtor, or by any third party which vouched for the debtor (Art. 390). Provisions of the law to the contrary are reserved. 509

The Code further provides for both *direct* and *indirect* or third-party security for the performance of any debt, i.e., securities provided by securing the 510

308 Unlike the English language, French distinguishes the loan from the perspective of the lender, where is it known as "prêt", from that of the borrower, known as "emprunt". German does not: like in English, both are known as "Darlehen".

309 Like for the debt and unlike the English language, French distinguishes the debt from the perspective of the creditor, where is it known as "créance", from that of the debor, known as "dette". Likewise, German does not: like in English, both are known as "Schuld" or "Forderung".

debtor's assets directly, or by assets made available by a third-party as security on behalf of the debtor (Art. 387). In the latter case, the third-party guarantor may ask the debtor to provide it with a *counter-guarantee*, where the latter is subject to the same legal regime as (direct) guarantees (Art. 387§2). The debtor may not *transfer* its debt without the consent of both the creditor and the guarantor (Art. 391).

511 It is once again important to note (s. above §505) that the third-party guarantee aimed at by Art. 387§2 is an *asset-based* guarantee, i.e., a security. Third-party debtor-, as opposed to asset-, based guarantees are governed, in the Third Book of the Code on contract law , by the provisions applying to the suretyship contract (Art. 681 ff.; s. below Chap. 5 §34, Suretyship).

512 The creation of security is subject to the conclusion of a *contract* (Art. 388§1). Although the Code does not specify so, and acknowledges the validity of oral contracts (Art. 135; s. above §183), practically it is not conceivable, if not as a matter of validity, then as a matter of proof, to create a security other than by written contract.

513 Art. 388 originally refers to that contract as 担保合同 dānbǎo hétóng, which literally translates as "guarantee contract" and is, therefore, deceiving since, as stressed, a guarantee can also be debtor-based, while Art. 388 applies to asset-based guarantees, or securities, only. Once again, (third-party) debtor-based guarantees are dealt with by the suretyship contract (Art. 681 ff.) Therefore, the contract mentioned at Art. 388 should be more accurately referred to as "contract for the provision of security".

514 Even though the Code expressly refers to it, Title Four does not regulate the contract for the provision of security as such. Neither does the Third Book on contracts, where it does not count among typical contracts. However, as mentioned, the latter does specifically regulate the suretyship contract (Art. 681 ff.), which is a third-party, personal, not asset-based guarantee, however.

515 Therefore, the contract for the provision of security is to be regarded as a *generic* contract not regulated as such, but whose sub-sorts are, mainly, as noted, the mortgage contract and the pledge contract.

516 Moreover, the Code expressly reserves "*other contracts* performing the function of security" (Art. 388§1), a category within which fall all the other security contacts known by finance law and practice. Among those, aside the most obvious and already mentioned loan guarantee, payments guarantee and performance guarantee, one may further mention the following common contracts: the advance payment guarantee (ensuring the return of an advance payment made to a supplier or contractor in case of default or nonperformance); the tender/bid bond guarantee (ensuring the bidder's commitment to a tender or bid process); the retention monies guarantee (providing security for the release of

final payment before the end of a retention period); the warranty bond (ensuring that goods or services will perform as specified under warranty terms); the customs and excise guarantee (allowing deferment of duties owed to tax authorities or permits transit/warehousing of goods); the corporate guarantee (a company guaranteeing the obligations of another entity, often a subsidiary); the personal guarantee (individual guaranteeing the obligations of a business or another person)[310], etc.

While this non-exhaustive list of instruments may serve general financial purposes and be of particular significance to foreign investors in China, it ought to be complemented by guarantees typically used to secure the *international sale of goods* purchased by foreign buyers to Chinese sellers: the *standby letter of credit* (SBLC; guaranteeing payment to the seller if the buyer defaults on their payment obligation) and the *documentary credit* (DC) or *letter of credit* (LC) (third-party guarantee issued by a bank on behalf of the buyer (importer) to pay the seller (exporter) a specified amount of money, provided that the seller meets certain conditions and presents the required documents)[311]: these instruments are commonly used in international trade to guarantee payment upon presentation of specified documents. The general provisions on securities of the Chinese Civil Code may also apply to them, as they arguably qualify as third-party guarantees[312] and "other contracts performing the function of guarantee". 517

In addition, while of general purpose and already mentioned above, and although less specific, the following instruments are also frequently used in connection with the international sale of goods and, whenever so, adjusted to that effect: the performance guarantee (ensuring that the seller fulfils its contractual obligations in delivering the goods as specified); the advance payment guarantee (protecting the buyer by ensuring the return of any advance payment made to the seller if the goods are not delivered as agreed) and the payment guarantee (assuring the seller that they will receive payment for the goods, even if the buyer fails to pay). 518

Other than the general provisions described above, the SBLC and the DC/LC are regulated neither in the Chinese Civil Code, nor in secondary legislation. 519

---

310 If the personal guarantee contract is provided by a third party on behalf of the debtor, it is a suretyship contract (s. above §511), which is the only typical contract among those mentioned. It may combine or overlap with any of them however (s. below §§520 to 522).

311 The difference between a SBLC and a DC/LC is that the former is activated in case of default payment, while the latter operates as primary payment method upon presentation of specified documents.

312 S. above note 310.

They are mostly regulated by the *International Chamber of Commerce* (ICC)[313].

520 Yet another time, one must keep in mind that Title Four will only apply to the "other contracts" mentioned above if they perform the "function of security" (Art. 388§1). Inasmuch, it might be difficult to determine whether a guarantee is asset-based or personal, as they may be both[314]; to attempt doing so would exceed the scope of this book and would need to be done by taking into account the specifics of the case anyway. Be that as it may, a personal guarantee containing no security element shall not be governed by the provisions of Title Four, but by the contract binding the parties and the general regime of liability for contractual nonperformance, while if such guarantee is provided by a third-party, the provisions on the suretyship contract shall apply[315].

521 Acknowledging the fact that, as stressed above, the notions of asset-based, personal and third-party guarantees may often blend into each other, the Code expressly addresses *hybrid guarantee contracts* in an effort to prevent confusion as to the rights resulting from their interactions. Thus, Art. 392 anticipates both the potential collision between asset-based and debtor-based securities, to which it further addresses that resulting from the addition of a third-party guarantor, when two of these guarantees, or all three of them, are cohabiting in the same transaction.

522 The *priority order* set by Art. 392 is the following: in case of direct guarantee, where the debtor provided both an asset-based and a debtor-based guarantee, the creditor has the right to be paid by the debtor's asset first. In case or indirect or third-party guarantee, the creditor has also the right to be paid by the third-party asset; alternatively, the creditor may ask the third-party to provide a personal guarantee, i.e., suretyship (Art. 681 ff.)[316] The parties may agree otherwise, however.

523 The guarantee contract is separate from and *ancillary* to the main contract providing for the debt secured by the guarantee (Art. 388§1, 2nd sentence). Consequently, should the main contract be proven to be null and void, so shall be the guarantee contract (Art. 388§1, last sentence). If so, the parties shall be liable towards each other according to their fault, as the case may be (Art. 388§2).

---

313 Among other things, the ICC also issues the *Incoterms* (s. below note 527).

314 If so, it would be a hybrid contract whose various elements, depending on their nature, could be governed by different legal regimes. This case is expressly contemplated by Art. 392, s. below §§521 and 522. S. also above, note 310.

315 On hybrid contracts, s. above note 314 and below §516.

316 Art. 392 *in fine* also provides that the third-party guarantor, after having fulfilled its liability towards the creditor, shall have the right to be compensated by the debtor; Art. 700 echoes this provision in connection with the suretyship contract.

The *scope of the security* is all-encompassing: it does not only cover the debt, but extends to interest, damages and other related expenses, including for the enforcement of the security, which can result in substantial costs. However, the parties may agree otherwise (Art. 389). 524

Security *extinguishes* whenever the main claim does, if the security is used as guarantee, if the creditor waives its right, or in other (unspecified) cases provided by law (Art. 393). 525

C. *Mortgage, Pledge and Lien*

As noted in the introduction to security in property (s. above §504), we will not elaborate on the mortgage, the pledge and the lien beyond the general notions and provisions outlined above, and the following short comments. 526

The *mortgage* (or pledge of an immovable; 抵押权 dǐyā quán) is governed by Chapter 17 of the Second Book on real rights (Art. 394 to 424) which is divided in two subsections: the first governs the ordinary mortgage (Art. 394 to 419), and the second the so-called "maximum mortgage" (Art. 420 to 424). That latter concept may deserve some elaboration. 527

The *ordinary* mortgage (一般抵押权 yībān dǐyā quán) addressed by the first subsection is nothing else but the traditional form of security interest by which a specific property is used to secure a fixed debt amount. In contrast, the *maximum* mortgage (最高额抵押权 zuìgāo é dǐyā quán) differs from an ordinary mortgage in several ways, inasmuch as it secures a series of debts or a *revolving credit line* up to a maximum amount[317], rather than a single fixed debt. 528

Although not specific to China, the maximum mortgage is generally known in western jurisdictions as *floating* mortgage[318], *revolving* mortgage or *flexible* mortgage; it is known in French as "crédit renouvelable" or "crédit revolving[319]" and in German as "revolvierende Hypothek" or "revolvierende Kreditfazilität". There is no specific legal basis for the maximum or floating mortgage 529

---

317 S. Art. 420, which refers to "debts to be incurred consecutively within a given period of time" as compared to Art. 394 on the ordinary mortgage, which merely refers to "the performance of an obligation".

318 Floating mortgage is not to be confused with the variable interest mortgage known in French as "hypothèque à taux variable" and in German as "variabel [*sic*] verzinsliche Hypothek" or "variable [*sic*] Hypothek". There is no specific legal basis for the variable interest mortgage in Swiss law; it is governed by the general regime of mortgages (CC Art. 824 ff.)

319 Although used in the finance practice in French, "revolving" is borrowed from English.

in Swiss law; it is governed by the general regime of mortgages (CC Art. 824 ff.)

530 The defining feature of the maximum mortgage is that the actual secured amount can fluctuate over time, as long as it does not exceed the predetermined maximum. It is particularly useful for securing periodical debts or future debts where the exact amount is not known at the time of creation. Maximum mortgages offer more flexibility for ongoing financial relationships, such as lines of credit or long-term business partnerships. The introduction of maximum mortgages in the Chinese Civil Code reflects an effort to accommodate more complex financial arrangements and provide greater flexibility in securing ongoing or future obligations.

531 If, on the contrary, the debtor exceeds the predetermined maximum and fails to pay the excess debt, the creditor or mortgagee may use the mortgaged asset for compensating its debt to the extent of such predetermined maximum (Art. 420).

532 The *pledge* of movables (动产质权 dòngchǎn zhì quán) is governed by Chapter 18 of the Second Book on real rights (Art. 425 to 446) which is divided in two subsections: the pledge of *movables*[320] (Art. 425 to 439), and the pledge of *rights* (Art. 440 to 446).

533 *Rights capable of being pledged* include bills of exchange, promissory notes, checks, bonds, certificates of deposit, warehouse receipts, bills of lading, transferable fund shares and stock rights, transferable IPR (trademarks, patents and copyrights), existing and anticipated accounts receivable, and "other property rights" as provided by law (Art. 440).

534 Finally, the *lien* (留置权 liúzhì quán) is governed by Chapter 19, which is the last chapter of the Second Book on real rights (Art. 447 to 457). Under the lien regime, if a debtor defaults, the creditor prevailing itself from the lien may retain the debtor's movables which the creditor has already been legally possessing on behalf of the debtor and shall have the right to pay itself with said movables (Art. 447§1)[321].

535 The difference between the lien and the pledge is that, in case of lien, the creditor is *already in possession* of the assets guaranteeing its debt. As noted, we will not elaborate further on the mortgage, the pledge and the lien however.

---

320 Following the structure of the Chinese Civil Code, the pledge of immovable is to be opposed to the mortgage. It is governed, in Swiss law, by CC Art. 884 ff. On the differences between the structures of the Chinese and the Swiss civil codes, s. above §533.

321 The lien is known in Swiss law, in French, as "la sûreté" and, in German, as "die Sicherheit"; unlike in the Chinese Civil Code, it is not regulated by a dedicated chapter, but throughout the Swiss Civil Code (s. e.g., CC Art. 775§2).

536 Although the Code is not specific about such requirement, mortgages and pledges must be *registered*. This requirement applies, for mortgages, both to immovables and movables and, for pledges, both for movables and rights (typically securities). It derives from Art. 386, 416 and 417 for the mortgage of immovable; Art. 386 and 395 for that of movables; Art. 427 for the pledge of movables; and of Art. 440 for the pledge of rights; furthermore, it is specifically regulated by the Securities Law and the related regulatory framework under the China Securities Regulatory Commission (CSRC)[322]. Such registration is generally recorded on the Uniform Registration Platform for Security Interests over Movable Assets and Rights (中国人民银行征信中心动产融资统一登记公示系统 zhōngguó rénmíng yínháng zhēng xìn zhōngxīn dòngchǎn róngzī tǒngyī dēngjì gōngshì xìtǒng) administered by the People's Bank of China (PBOC).

537 The lien is not subject to registration (cf. Art. 447 ff.) Registration in general has been outlined above (s. §§437 and 438).

§18. Possession

538 As explained earlier in this book in the introduction to real rights (s. above §360), civil law systems, following Roman law, mainly distinguish between *property* which, simply put, is a right entitling the right holder to use the thing, and *possession*, which is the fact of using that thing. Both are governed by specific sets of provisions, which constantly interact, but are well differentiated.

539 We have also elaborated on the hybrid case of the *leasehold* (s. above Chap. 3 §17.III.A, Introduction: the Freehold and the Leasehold in Common Law), a common law concept in-between property and possession to which the Chinese *construction usufruct* (s. above Chap. 3 §17.III, Construction Usufruct) compares (along with other usufructs which are not discussed in this book, as being of lesser concern to foreign investors in China).

540 Possession closes the Second Book of the Chinese Civil Code on real rights. Compared to Swiss law, the part which the Chinese Civil Code devotes to possession (占有 zhànyǒu) is extremely short, with only five articles (Art. 458 to 462), where Title Twenty-Four of the Swiss Civil Code on possession contains 22 (Art. 919 to 941).

---

322 Various authorities are in charge of the registration: they are mainly, for the registration of immovable mortgages, the land registry; for that of movable mortgages, the PBOC (which operates a dedicated system to that effect); and for pledges, the CSRC or the China Securities Depository & Clearing Corporation.

541 The provisions contained in this title apply by default to all forms of possession, including those recalled above, unless more specific contractual or legal regulations apply, according to the principle *lex specialis derogat leges generali* (Art. 458 and 12; s. also above §117).

542 In case of damage to the possessed asset, the possessor is only liable towards the owner (or property right holder, e.g., a usufructuary) if the possessor acted in *bad faith*. However, the good faith or *bona fide* possessor must remit the owner any indemnity received from the liable third party (namely, an insurer, or the author) up to covering the damage. Moreover, the bad faith or *mala fide* possessor shall be liable for any uncovered portion of the damage. A contract between the parties or the law may provide otherwise, i.e., they may extend such liability to good faith possessors (Art. 459 and 461).

543 Where the possession is *taken away* from its legitimate possessor by an illegitimate third-party, the latter is entitled to request the return of the possession; likewise, more specifically, if the property is *encroached* upon, it has the right to request the return of the original property; and in case of *trespass, interference*[323] *or danger*, that the infringer ceases trespassing or interfering and eliminates such danger (Art. 460 and 462§1)[324].

544 In all these cases, the infringer is *liable* for compensating for any damage (Art. 459 to 462§1). In case the possession has been taken away, the legitimate possessor is also entitled to any fruits perceived by the infringer; conversely, the legitimate possessor must indemnify the infringer for the costs of maintenance of the property, provided the latter was of good faith (Art. 460).

545 Art. 462§2 subjects such right to claim the return of the original property to a *one-year limitation* from the encroachment, however. This limit literally appears to apply to encroachment only, although it is not absolutely clear that it does not apply to the other forms of infringements mentioned above. Given the risk that the practice of Chinese courts may not yet be unified in that regard, foreign investors would be well advised to use caution and to consider that the one-year limitation applies to any form of infringement to their possession[325].

---

323 S. above note 262.

324 These remedies are consistent with the general regime of civil liability set forth by Art. 179 (s. above §335). Swiss law provides for the same rights, which entitle the possessor to apply before a court: the right to claim a possession taken away is provided by CC Art. 927; it is known in German as such, as "Klage aus Besitzentziehung", and in French by the peculiar expression of "réintégrande". The right to request the end of an interference is provided for by CC Art. 928; it is known in French as "action en raison du trouble" and in German as "Klage aus Besitzstörung".

325 Under Swiss law, the remedies provided for by CC Art. 927 and 928 are subject to an even shorter limitation, since the legitimate possessor is deprived from its right if it does

From a *Swiss* perspective, it is important to note that Chinese law offers a weaker protection to possession than Swiss law[326]: namely, Swiss law entitles the possessor, spontaneously and *proprio motu*, i.e., without or before applying to a court, both to forcefully push back any infringer and to forcefully recover any possession illegitimately taken away[327]. Even though those rights are subject to rather stringent conditions, they are not equated in Chinese law, which is probably explained by the fact that, arguably, Chinese society traditionally favors consensus and harmony: in China, the legitimate possessor can only "request" the infringer to end the infringement and repair any damage; if the latter does not voluntarily comply, the former is left with no choice but applying before a court[328]. 546

Nevertheless, one shall recall that the Chinese Civil Code does provide for a right of defense comparable to that Art. 927 of the Swiss Civil Code procures to the legitimate possessor, but that the Chinese Civil Code only makes it available to owners of a right of *property* (Art. 311§1; s. above §§435 and 436), not to possessors, however legitimate. 547

Besides, the Swiss legal regime of possession appears to be more sophisticated than that provided by the Chinese Civil Code: namely, the Swiss Civil Code operates a complex, lengthy distinction between judicial remedies aimed at protecting *possession as a fact*, and those purporting at *using possession for protecting the right from which possession stems*[329]. The Chinese Civil Code, 548

---

not claim it *immediately* after it became aware of the infringement; moreover, this limitation is subject to an absolute one-year limitation after the occurrence of the infringement (CC Art. 929). Art. 462§2 of the Chinese Civil Code is not subject to the relative limitation which would impose the claimant to file immediately after it became aware of the infringement; it is only subject to an unqualified one-year limitation. For the limitation of the claims for the protection of the right of possession, s. below note 329.

326 In contrast, the limitation of action may be shorter in Swiss law, s. preceding note.

327 These rights are known, in Swiss law, as the right of defense (Fr.: "droit de défense"; Ger.: "Abwehr von Angriffen") and is provided by CC Art. 926. The right to push back any infringement to the possession (CC Art. 926§1) is known as such in German, i.e., as "Abwehr der Eigenmacht", and in French as legitimate defense ("légitime défense"). The right to forcefully recover any possession taken away (CC Art. 926§2) is known, in French, as "droit de reprise" and, in German, as "Recht der Besitzkehrung". The use of force must be justified by the circumstances (CC Art. 926§3).

328 That is under the reservation that, in China, mediation, namely, Sate-sponsored mediation, is much more developed than in Switzerland, and actively encouraged if not practically imposed.

329 The protection by possession of the right from which it stems is provided, in Swiss law, by CC Art. 930 to 937. Swiss law addresses this issue by setting up a complex series of legal presumptions and fictions, which seem to be reduced, in the Chinese Civil Code, to the general notion of good (or bad) faith. The Swiss Civil Code further makes available, to the actual possessor, a so-called *defensive claim* (CC Art. 932), and to the

which as outlined provides for the protection of possession at Art. 460 and 462§1, seems to conflate both notions[330]. Given the extreme complexity[331] of the Swiss regime, which can be explained by ancient historical factors, and compares with that of most other western civil law jurisdictions, one may speculate that, during the elaboration of the Chinese Civil Code, the Chinese legislator may have deliberately elected to simplify the regime governing possession by submitting it to basic rules only, and to leave disputes related to detail issues to the discretion of the courts or to settlement.

549 Finally it is worth remembering that both Art. 208 and 224 provide that, unless otherwise stipulated by law, the creation or transfer of movable property rights occurs upon *delivery* (s. above §§379 and 384ff.), whereby delivery itself is completed with the transfer of possession[332].

former or allegedly dispossessed possessor, a so-called *offensive claim* known as "movable claim" (Fr.: "action mobilière"; Ger. "Besitzsrechtsklage" or "Fahrnisklage"; CC Art. 934 and 936). These remedies are subject to an (unqualified) five-years limitation (CC Art. 934§1; *cultural goods* must be claimed upon awareness of the dispossession and are subject to an absolute limitation of 30 years; CC Art. 934§2). For a detailed commentary of Swiss law on the protection of the right of possession, s., for example, PAUL-HENRI STEINAUER, Les droits réels, Staempfli, Bern 1985, p. 97 No. 10.

330 S. also above §547 however.

331 It is telling, in that respect, that the proof of the right of possession is known, in Roman law, from which the Swiss law of possession stems, as *probatio diabolica* or devilish proof.

332 The same is true in Swiss law, namely, for the delivery of goods by a transporter, s. ATF 93/1967 II 373 and STEINAUER (s. above note 329), No. 261b.

Chap. 4 General Provisions of Contract Law

§19. Introduction

Contract law is the topic of the Third Book (Art. 463 to 1163) of the Chinese Civil Code. The book is divided in two titles: Title One on general provisions, and Title Two on typical (or nominate) contracts. This chapter of the book addresses Title One; Title Two will be in the next chapter. 550

Before the Code, contract law was governed by the Contract Law of 1999. The Civil Code entirely integrated and, as such, repealed the Contract Law as of the former's promulgation (Art. 1260). However, the SPC clarified that contracts concluded under the old Contract Law remained governed by the same even after the Chinese Civil Code became effective[333]. 551

The Contract Law was incorporated without fundamental changes, which is not saying that the Civil Code did not bring any[334]: the most notable can be summarized as follows. 552

First of all, by integrating the Contract Law, the Civil Code did so in a wider legal framework including updated legal *principles* such as the general provisions of civil law or liability. 553

Notably, the Civil Code emphasizes the principle of *contractual freedom*[335] and allows for greater flexibility in contractual arrangements. This represents an evolution from the Contract Law, which had more prescriptive rules. Although the choice of the applicable law is not addressed by the Chinese Civil Code, it is the place to add that Chinese private international law also embraces freedom of *choice of law*[336]. 554

---

333 Interpretation of the Supreme People's Court on Several Issues Concerning the Application of the General Provisions of the Contract Law of the Civil Code of the People's Republic of China (Fa Shi No. 13) of 4 December 2023 effective 5 December 2023.

334 The database of Chinese law of Peking University provides a useful table comprehensively highlighting all changes, s. Comparison with Civil Code: Contracts *in*: Contract Law of the People's Republic of China 中华人民共和国合同法, [CLI Code] CLI.1.21651(EN), https://www.pkulaw.com/en_law/2367b1767194112cbdfb.html (in Chinese and on paying subscription only).

335 The principle of contractual freedom is only implied in the Third Book on contract law however; it rests on the more general principle of freedom of *will* expressed by Art. 5 and 130, s. above §§116 and 177. S. also WEI WEN, Formality, Freedom of Contract and China's New Civil Code: A Legal Reform Recommendation for Land Sale Contracts, [2022] U. PA. ASIAN L. REV. 332.

336 Chinese international private law entitles the parties to an international transaction involving a Chinese element to choose the national *applicable law* to their transaction

555 Specifically, the Civil Code introduced *new* provisions regarding the validity and enforceability of contracts, punitive damages, the concept of good faith, and specific default rules for different types of contracts; it further enhanced provisions related to consumer contracts, reflecting a growing emphasis on consumer rights and protections; and contains more detailed mechanisms for resolving disputes related to contract performance, making it clearer how parties can resolve issues.

556 Overall, the Chinese Civil Code improved the internal and external structure of the Contract Law, while modernizing it for reflecting the evolution of the economy which rapidly occurred between the promulgation of the Contract Law and that of the Code, as well as international standards.

557 A notable characteristic of both the Contract Law and the Chinese Civil Code which did not change, as compared to the pre-Chinese Civil Code regime, is that, unlike, among other western codes, the Swiss Civil Code, the *labor* contract is not contained in the Chinese Civil Code[337] (it was not in the Contract Law either), but remains governed by an entirely separate set of laws. Consequently, labor law will also be addressed separately in this book (s. below Chap. 6 , Employment
).

558 The First Title of the book on the general provisions of contract law (Art. 453 to 594) is divided into eight chapters: general rules, conclusion, validity, performance, preservation, modification and assignment, termination, and liability.

§20. General Rules

559 Chapter 1 on general rules (Art. 463 to 468) is not to be confounded with the First Title on general provisions of the book of contracts[338]. The First Title, as outlined, contains eight chapters of general application, the first of which being that on general rules, as opposed to the second title of the book on contracts, which is dedicated to special (or typical) contracts.

560 The *notion* of contract is defined as an agreement between the parties for the establishment, modification, and termination of civil legal relations (Art. 464§1). The Code further proclaims two of the core principles of

(Law on the Choice of Law for Foreign-related Civil Relationships, Art. 3), subject to mandatory provisions of Chinese law (*ibid.*, Art. 4 and 5).

337 The labor contract (Fr.: "contrat de travail"; Ger.: "Arbeitsvertrag") is governed by Chap 10 (CO Art. 319 to 362) of the Swiss Code of Obligations.

338 On terminology issues, s. above note 93.

contractual law, by which contracts are protected by law (Art. 465§1), and that they only bind their parties, unless the law provides otherwise (Art. 465§2).

Contractual interpretation is addressed by Art. 466§1, which expressly refers to Art. 142§1: the latter provision, which pertains to the chapter on civil juristic acts of the First Book on general provisions of the Code, describes the principles of interpretation applicable to all civil juristic acts (s. above §§212ff.) 561

Art. 466§1 is complemented by a second subsection addressing the contract's *language*, a common issue for foreign investors which frequently conclude contracts with Chinese parties in two (or more) languages, typically English and Chinese. Such contracts generally provide that both languages have the same legal value which, absent further guidance to resolve discrepancies, hardly helps whenever the parties have a different understanding of the same provisions of the contract, depending on the language version considered. This problem is particularly prominent with contracts between Chinese and foreign parties since, on one hand, Chinese parties, outside of large international business hubs like Beijing and Shanghai, often have a limited command of English if at all, while generally foreign parties do not have any command of Chinese; on the other hand, translation discrepancies between Chinese and western languages are more acute than among western languages which, in their majority, stem out of the same Latin roots. 562

Art. 466§2 acknowledges the peculiarity of Sino-foreign contracts by prescribing that, in such cases, even if the contract does not specify it, the languages used have the same legal weight (Art. 466§2, 1st sentence), thus preventing one language to take precedence over the other. In case of inconsistency, the contract is to be interpreted. In interpreting the relevant provisions, the parties shall pay attention, among other factors, to the *nature and purpose of the contract* as well as to *good faith*. The list is not exhaustive. Inasmuch, Art. 466§2 refers to the same principles mentioned at Art. 142§1. Therefore, one may suppose that the parties may also rest on the doctrine and jurisprudence related to the latter provision, *mutatis mutandis*. 563

The last three provisions of the chapter deal with the *scope* of application of the Third Book to certain specific areas of the law. Thus, Chapter 1 on general provisions of contract law also applies to any contracts *other* than the typical contracts governed by the Second Title of the Third Book or than contracts foreseen by other laws (Art. 467§1). 564

Art. 467§2 addresses the law applicable to *joint-ventures*. JVs are comprehensively discussed below, at the end of the chapter on company law of this book (s. Chap. 9 §66, Joint-ventures), to which we refer the reader. 565

The last provision of the chapter on general rules prioritizes the provisions governing the contractual relationship between creditor and debtor, notably, 566 contractual liability, whether in the Code or in other laws, whenever such a relationship is at stake (Art. 468)[339]. Absent such provisions, the general provisions of Chapter 1 remain applicable.

§21. Conclusion

567 Chapter 2 (Art. 469 to 501) of the Third Book on contracts governs their conclusion. According to the general theory of contracts, a contract is typically (but not only) concluded by the meeting of the *offer* by one party to conclude it, and of the latter's *acceptance* by the other, provided its form and content satisfy the minimum requirements mandated by the law (about these two notions, s. below §590). Reflecting these basic elements, Chapter 2 is roughly divided in four parts: form and content, offer, acceptance and other issues.

568 The conclusion regime is narrowly related to that of the *validity of juristic acts* (s. above Chap. 2 §10.IV, Validity of Juristic Acts, and below §592) since conclusion results from the meeting of such acts. Insofar, as noted (s. above §212), the conclusion regime complements it by extending the regime of the validity of juristic acts to that of the conclusion of contracts.

569 A contract can be concluded in writing, orally or in "any other" *form*[340] (Art. 469§1), provided the requirements otherwise posed by the law for its conclusion are met.

570 The next subsection starts by mentioning that contracts can be concluded in the form of a *letter*, which refers to the traditional form, still widely used today, of a printed document simultaneously signed in the presence of both parties or exchanged by post mail or courier. It further mentions contracts signed by telegram, telex or fax, although these forms have, in contrast, become entirely obsolete. Last but not least, this provision is remarkable insofar as it declares that *electronic data exchange (or interchange) messages* (数据电文 shùjù diànwén) qualify as *written* form (Art. 469§2). While *e-mails* (电子邮件 diànzǐ yóujiàn) are expressly mentioned, the expression "electronic data exchange (or

---

339 Swiss law contains a similar provision, although more specific, and located in its contractual liability regime: CO Art. 97§2 reserves Swiss law on debt recovery and bankruptcy. However, while that law governs both personal debts and bankruptcy, the Chinese Enterprise Bankruptcy Law only applies to the latter; the recovery of personal debts is governed by the Chinese Civil Code, namely, contract law (s. below Chap. 4 §27, Liability for Breach of Contract), judicial law and, in certain cases, by secondary legislation such as consumer protection law (s. above note 117).

340 Such other forms include *concluding behaviors*, which are expressly acknowledged by Art. 129, 2nd phrase (s. above §179).

interchange) messages", however cumbersome, is flexible enough to accommodate *other* types of electronic messages[341].

However, to qualify, such messages are subject to further *requirements*: they must "visually" (有形地 yǒuxíngdì) reflect the information they contain; moreover, they have to be accessible and readable at any time (Art. 496§2). 571

What "visually"[342] is supposed to mean is not entirely clear. However, considering that the evolution of electronic messages ever since their inception, from e-mails through SMS to instant messaging (IM), resulted in their senders ever shortening their communications, one may reasonably speculate that the message simply needs to be not only in *graphic* form (as opposed to, e.g., a voice mail; s., however, next paragraph), but also *understandable*[343]: thus, for example, a "smilie", however popular in IM messaging, would arguably not qualify as the acceptance of an offer. 572

While the visibility requirement of Art. 469§2 is welcome, one ought to keep in mind that Art. 469§1 expressly reserves *other forms* of conclusion (s. below, §581) which may be less obvious, namely, as far as electronic contracts are concerned, but significant nevertheless, given their prevalence in today's economy: one may think, for example, at the simple click by which a buyer, almost unconsciously, accepts general conditions of sales and buys a product online or, less obvious even, at any *behavior* implying such acceptance[344], such as clicking "next", or at the mere use of a service, for example, a SIM card for mobile phone communications, whose first use may imply acceptance. Besides, given that a contract can be concluded *orally* (Art. 469§1; s. above §569), a mere voicemail, for example, on WeChat, clearly expressing acceptance would suffice. 573

In this context, it is worth recalling that, comparatively, *Swiss law*, notably the Swiss Civil Code, does not comprehensively provide for neither the conclusion of contracts by e-mail (or by other electronic means), nor for declarations of will by the same means, with one limited exception: since 2016, the new Swiss law on *electronic signature* assimilates the latter to a manuscript signature 574

---

341 On the *time* of such conclusion, s. below §586; on the *place* of such conclusion, s. below §588. On *declarations of will between distant parties*, s. above Chap. 2 §10.III, Declarations of Will. On the *terminology* related to electronic data interchange messages, s. above, §§208ff.

342 有形地 yǒuxíngdì is actually translated as "tangibly" or "visibly" but, given the context, we believe that both "visually", which convey that the message should be in graphical form, and "visibly", which conveys that it should be readable or understandable, are better suited.

343 To be understandable, a visual message must be visible. On the clarity of declarations of will, s. above §204.

344 S. above note 340.

(provided it is qualified, i.e., matches the strict formal conditions set forth by the law[345]); moreover, the Swiss Code of Obligations was complemented accordingly (Art. 14§2*bis*). In contrast, the Chinese Civil Code does not specifically provide for e-signatures. Besides, Swiss jurisprudence has occasionally admitted the validity of contracts concluded by e-mail only, subject to interpretation of the declarations of will contained in e-mail exchange allegedly proving the conclusion[346]. In practice, in Switzerland as, one may safely add, in the rest of the world, declarations of will, namely, the conclusion of contracts by e-mail (and, before e-mail took over, by fax[347]) is almost universally accepted but for the most formal juristic acts, while e-signatures meeting the requirements posed by its eponymous law, which has failed to gain traction so far, are the exception.

575 As reminded (s. above §568), generally speaking, the issue of the form in which a contract is concluded is related to that of *declarations of will* (Art. 137 to 142) treated in Chapter 6 on juristic acts of the First Book of the Code on general provisions. That chapter provides detailed guidance about the validity of such declarations, whose regime also apply in contractual or precontractual relationships; we refer the reader to the related detailed discussion (s. above Chap. 2 §10.IV, Validity of Juristic Acts). Among other things, because of the relative instability of electronic data formats, one should like to stress once again the importance of properly storing *proofs* of the contract conclusion (s. above, §207).

576 The Code further describes the *content* of a contract, which should generally contain provisions related to the parties, the contract's subject-matter, quantity, quality, price, time, place and method of performance, liability and dispute resolution (Art. 470). As its wording suggests, this list is neither mandatory nor exhaustive, provided always the parties have reached an agreement on the contract's essential elements or *essentialiae*, thus defining their mutual rights and obligations.

577 Indeed, if they have not reached such an agreement, or if their agreement fails to define their mutual rights and obligations, the purported contract is incapable of deploying its effects and shall be deemed not to have been concluded. If there is uncertainty as to certain elements, the parties can either recourse to

---

[345] A mere e-mail does not satisfy such requirements. To qualify, an e-signature must be authenticated by an e-certificate issued by a provider authorized by the competent authority.

[346] S. for example, ATF 4A_241/2017 of 31 August 2018; ATF 142 III 239; on related proof requirements, s. also ATF 142 V 82; ATF 121 III 38 = JT 1995 I 377; ATF 141 III 495; ATF 145 III 199 = JT 2021 II 251.

[347] While the use of fax for concluded contracts quickly became widespread, those concluded by telex or telegram before its inception remained exceptional.

interpretation (Art. 142 and 466; s. above §§229ff., 561ff., 622 and 623) or supplement the contract (Art. 510; s. below §§618ff.)

578 The basic principle by which a contract is concluded by the meeting of offer and acceptance results from the combination of Art. 471, which provides that the parties may conclude a contract by exchanging offer and acceptance (s. above §578), and Art. 483, which adds that the contract shall be concluded at the *time* acceptance becomes effective. Once again, this issue depends itself on the time at which each party's corresponding declaration of will is deemed to be effective, that is also subject to Art. 137 to 142 on the validity of declarations of will, which the general provisions of contract law complement by extending them to the regime of the conclusion of contracts (s. above §568).

579 Be that as it may, in that regard, the Chinese Civil Code seems to be more *liberal* than the Swiss one. Indeed, one may note that the corresponding article of the Swiss Code of Obligations is the first one of the Code, thus signaling its prominence in the Swiss legal order, while Art. 471 of the Chinese one is unremarkably located somewhere in the second chapter of the book on contract law. Then, while the Swiss Code of Obligations resolutely affirms that the contract is concluded when the parties have, reciprocally and in a concordant manner, expressed their will[348] (CO Art. 1§1), the Chinese Civil Code uses a more liberal language by stating that the parties "may" (可以 kěyǐ) conclude a contract by (exchanging) offer and acceptance, while expressly reserving "any other means" (Art. 471). Moreover, the same provision adds that the parties may agree, or that the law may provide, that the contract may be concluded at another time than when the acceptance becomes effective (s. below §584). Swiss law permits both other means and the parties to agree otherwise too, but in provisions other than CO Art. 1§1. Therefore, for the reasons stated above, Swiss-, and perhaps other western lawyers, may like to consider that, for socio-cultural reasons, Chinese law may adopt a more flexible approach to the conclusion of contracts than Swiss law, and arguably than other western jurisdictions.

580 Art. 490 to 494 provides additional clarity as to the form, the time and the place of such conclusion. Art. 490§1 implies that the parties can conclude a written contract not only by affixing their *signature*, but also the (Chinese) company official seal or stamp (s. next paragraph), or the parties' fingerprint. This may be disconcerting for foreigners. Indeed, in western jurisdiction, western contracts are concluded by the signature of the parties; the company seal does not legally bind the company; while fingerprints may have been used as a substitute

[348] The semi-official translation of the Swiss Code of Obligations on Swisslex reads: "The conclusion of a contract requires a mutual expression of intent by the parties." This translation is inaccurate, however.

to signatures in a distant past, when parties may still have been illiterate, their legal value nowadays would be, in western jurisdictions, questionable, if considered at all[349].

581 In contrast, in China, much more weight is given to the company's official *seal* (章 zhāng), a round rubber stamp bearing the company registered name and applied with red ink, commonly known in English, in China, as "chop". The official seal has a mandatory format; as its name suggests, it is exclusively issued by the authority, together with the business license[350]. Other formats[351] but the official signal that the stamp is not official. A company registered in China, whether foreign invested or not, cannot, practically if not legally, do business in China or interact with the authorities without a chop.

582 While Art. 490§1 expressly admits that the parties may conclude by signing the contract (which, in the case of a Chinese company, foreign-invested or not, should be that of its legal representative or of the latter's representative duly empowered[352]), in practice, Chinese companies are expected to bind themselves by affixing their seal; a signature alone, be it by their legal representative, is generally not accepted. Likewise, let alone for preventing any issue, in practice, foreign investors would be well advised to insist on the affixing of such seal, instead of contenting themselves with a mere signature, even though the latter is legally binding.

583 Conversely, Chinese parties do frequently not understand that western companies bind themselves by the signature of one, often two authorized officers, and that the company rubber stamp has no legal value. In case of persisting misunderstanding, the foreign party is advised to produce, to its Chinese counterpart, an excerpt, if necessary legalized[353], of the register of commerce displaying the

349 A fingerprint, actually designated in Swiss law by the more flexible notion of "hand mark" (Fr.: "marque à la main"; Ger.: "Handzeichen") does amount to a binding handwritten signature in Swiss law, provided it is legalized however (CO Art. 15). They are typically used by disabled parties physically incapable of writing.

350 S. below, §§1824ff.

351 For example, an oval seal, or a seal printed with blue ink, would suggest that the stamp is not official. Moreover, because the company name is written in Chinese only, it is advisable to parties not proficient in Chinese to verify it.

352 S. below §1774.

353 China has finally signed the Convention of The Hague of 5 October 1961 Abolishing the Requirement of Legalisation for Foreign Public Documents on 8 March 2023 effective 7 November 2023, that considerably facilitates such legalization by merely applying the Apostille, which can be done instantly at any public notary office. Previously, such legalization was not only an administrative ordeal, it was also subject to a widespread lack of consensus on its recognition, namely, by Chinese courts.

signatory powers of the officers signing the contract, together with a legalization of their signature.

While incidentally addressing signature *lato sensu*, Art. 490 and 491 are primarily concerned by the *time* of the conclusion. In accordance with the reservation granted by Art. 471 *in fine* (s. above §579), they complement with two special rules the basic rule resulting from the combination of Art. 471 and 483 by which the contract shall be concluded at the time acceptance becomes effective (s. above §578). The time of conclusion is itself, once again, narrowly related to the general regime of the validity of *declarations of will* which must, therefore, also be taken into consideration (s. above Chap. 2 §10.IV, Validity of Juristic Acts) and to which the Code occasionally refers (s. below §592 and note 360). 584

Those two special cases are anticipated performance and distant acceptance. 585
Thus, other than occurring with the affixing of such signature or seal, in case of *anticipated performance*, i.e., performance before signature, conclusion occurs with such performance's acceptance (Art. 490§2).

In case of *distant conclusion* (typically by post mail, courier or e-mail), conclusion occurs at the time[354] of the signature (or acceptance) of the last party (Art. 491§1). Remarkably, the Chinese Civil Code expressly addresses the *online* offer of goods or services[355], in which case conclusion occurs when the other party places its order, unless agreed otherwise between the parties (Art. 491§2). Distant conclusion is itself, once again, narrowly related to the general regime of the validity of distant *declarations of will* which must, therefore, equally be considered (s. above Chap. 2 §10.IV, Validity of Juristic Acts). 586

The *place* of acceptance is governed by Art. 492 and 493. It matters insofar as it may command certain rights or obligations of the parties, namely, in case of dispute, the *forum* and, in international transactions, the determination of the *applicable law*[356]. The basic rule is that a contract is deemed to have been 587

354 S. above note 341.

355 The online offer of goods and services has recently, in a matter of years, become universal in China and has permeated every aspect of life, especially for small transactions paid by mobile phone through dedicated apps, namely, WeChat Pay (A.K.A. Weixin) and Alipay.

356 In case of conflict of laws, Chinese international private law, which is governed by the Law on Choice of Law for Foreign-related Civil Relationships, embraces the doctrine of *characteristic performance*, according to which, in creditor's rights disputes, the laws of the habitual residence of the party whose fulfillment of obligations can best reflect the characteristics of this contract or other laws which have the *closest relation* with this contract shall apply (Art. 41, 2nd sentence). In that respect, the place of conclusion may be considered as being a decisive factor. Beyond that general rule, the law provides for several other special cases (s. Art. 42 ff.) Swiss law, from which Chinese

concluded at the place where *acceptance* became effective (Art. 492§1). While both the form and the time of the conclusion relate to the *validity of juristic acts* (s. above §§568, 575 and 578), the place of conclusion is not covered by the latter regime; however, the time of acceptance, which in turn commands the place of conclusion, may.

588 The basic rule of Art. 492§1 is *complemented* by the following special rules: notably, in case of *contracts concluded by electronic message*, the place[357] of conclusion is that of the receiver's registered business and, absent it, residence (Art. 492§2); if by post mail or courier, it is that of the last signatory's place (Art. 493).

589 Like for the time of conclusion (s. Art. 471 *in fine* and 492§1; s. above §§579 and 586), both special rules about the place of conclusion expressly enable the parties to agree otherwise. While the general rule of Art. 492§1 does not mention such possibility, it does not preclude it either. Considering the general principle of the parties' contractual freedom[358], one may consider that the parties may depart from the general rule prescribing the place of conclusion too. Be that as it may, given that the place of conclusion may control certain rights and obligation and, in particular, the applicable law, considering the importance of the latter, the parties, especially the foreign party to a contract potentially subject to Chinese law, should be careful not to omit to specify the place of conclusion in their contract (in any case if they have not selected such applicable law), instead of leaving it to relatively complex rules they may not be familiar with.

590 Art. 471 to 478 detail the notion of offer and its content, that of an invitation to offer, the offer's time, and its withdrawal, revocation and invalidity. Acceptance is governed by Art. 479 to 489. An *offer* is an indication of intent to enter into a contract with another party (Art. 479§1, 1st sentence). *Acceptance* is an indication of the intent of an offeree to assent to an offer (Art. 479). That set of provisions further applies to the notion of acceptance, its form, time, contents, and related changes. Because these provisions are reasonably straightforward and because the general theory of contracts exceeds the scope of this book, we will not discuss them in detail and refer the reader to the law or to specialized literature. However, the following comments deserve to be made.

591 Art. 473 provides a long, although not exhaustive, list of *invitations to offer* including: auction announcements, announcements or invitations to bid,

---

law drew inspiration in that respect, provides for the same basic solution for contractual disputes under the Federal Law on Private International Law (Art. 117§1 and 2).

357 S. above note 341.

358 S. above §554.

prospectuses[359], bond offer methods, fund prospectuses, commercial advertisements and publicity, and mailed or delivered price lists. This enumeration is welcome inasmuch as the authors of such invitations may not always be aware of their legal significance, and because, consequently, their nature may be disputed.

Four provisions refer to the regime of juristic acts governed by the First Book of the Chinese Civil Code on general provisions[360]. However, as repeatedly noted above, beyond these specific references, that regime is generally applicable to the conclusion of contracts (s. §568). 592

The next set of provisions (Art. 494 to 501) of this chapter addresses *other ways* to conclude a contract but by offer and acceptance, and related cases of liability. While expressly reserving other ways to conclude a contract than by exchanging offer and acceptance, Art. 471 does not mention any. Yet one may think of the following, all of which are acceptable under Chinese law: implied contracts (contracts concluded by concluding behavior or implicit acceptance; s. Art. 138 and above §216); unilateral contracts (e.g., public offer; s. Art. 138, 139 and 142§2, and above §§214, 215 and 219; rewards, Art. 499); adhesion contracts (typically, general conditions of sale, s. next paragraph); quasi-contracts (namely, unjust enrichment and *negotiorum gestio*; s. below Chap. 7 , Quasi-contracts
); and time and material contracts (construction contracts with variable quantities). This list is not exhaustive. 593

Chapter 2 on contract conclusion mentions three such cases elsewhere, however. The first[361], which is by far the most significant in practice, is that of *standard clauses* (or terms; Art. 496 to 498), A.K.A. adhesion contracts, typically found in general conditions of sales or services. Standard clauses are characterized by the unequal bargaining power of the parties, non-negotiable terms and conditions, and a standardized format used for high-volume transactions. Because those terms are not negotiated with the weaker party but almost forced on the latter ("take it or leave it"), such contracts do not correspond to the spirit of the basic offer and acceptance method of conclusion of Art. 471 and are, therefore, to be regarded as one of the "other methods" reserved by the latter. 594

---

359 On the prospectus for the public shares offering of a shareholding company, s. below §§1904, 2007ff. and 2101ff.

360 Art. 474 (offer) and 484 (acceptance) both refer to Art. 137 about the time of a declaration. Art. 478 (offer) and 485 (acceptance) refer to Art. 141 about the withdrawal of the same.

361 The two others are Art. 494 and 499: Art. 494 envisages the case of disaster, etc., in which the State may impose certain parties to conclude contracts in the public interest, while Art. 499 that of public rewards.

595 A standard clause is defined by the following three elements: they are pre-formulated, purport at a repeated use, and do not result from a negotiation (Art. 496§1). Art. 496 protects the weaker party by subjecting the stronger one to two requirements: it does not only subject the stronger party to a general duty of fairness; moreover, the latter must draw the weaker party's attention on the terms limiting the stronger party's liability and, upon the weaker party's request, explain unclear terms. If the stronger party fails to do either, the weaker one may argue that such terms are not part of the contract (Art. 496§2).

596 The protection provided by Art. 496§2 is strengthened by Art. 497 which invalidates standard clauses whenever they result in unreasonably exempting or mitigating the stronger party's liability, aggravating that of the weaker party, or restricting or exempting the latter's rights. In addition, standards clauses shall be invalidated whenever they contravene the conditions set forth by the First Book of the Code to the validity of civil juristic acts (Art. 143 ff.; s. above §250) or to Art. 506 pertaining to the next chapter of the Code on the validity of contracts, which invalidates certain contractual liability exemption clauses (s. below §610).

597 Given that the protection extended by these provisions is subject to the qualification of the disputed clause as being unfair, the Code provides specific, additional *interpretation* rules to that effect (Art. 498), both of which favor the weaker party. Thus, such clause shall primarily be interpreted according to "common understanding". While not explicit, this statement refers to the general rules of interpretation of civil juristic acts (Art. 142; s. above §§218ff.) and of contractual interpretation (Art. 466§1; s. above §561). Where interpretation fails to yield a clear and unambiguous meaning, the interpretation most favorable to the weaker party shall prevail. Moreover, in case of discrepancy between a standard and a non-standard clause, the latter prevails.

598 While Art. 496 to 498 do not offer the weaker party an absolute protection since its invocation is subject both to proof and interpretation, given the prevalence of general conditions of sales or services in today's commercial transactions, foreign investors subject to Chinese law may want to be aware of the limits of contractual freedom with respect to standard clauses, whether on the stronger or the weaker side. Besides, this regime is to be related to that of *consumers protection*, which is comprehensive[362].

599 The last set of provisions (Art. 500 and 501) contemplates various cases of *liability* related to the conclusion of a contract. Art. 500 addresses *pre-contractual liability*, by which one party deliberately causing damage to the other during the negotiation of the contract is liable towards it.

---

362 S. above note 117.

Moreover, a party which discloses or exploits *business secrets* (or related confidential information) which came to its knowledge during contractual negotiations shall equally be liable for any damage resulting from such disclosure (Art. 501). Liability occurs whether the contract is concluded or not. Therefore, the latter case can be seen as a special case of precontractual liability. 600

Contractual liability, i.e., after the contract has been concluded and during its performance (or because of its nonperformance), is governed by Chapter 8 of the Third Book and will be outlined below (s. Chap. 4 §27, Liability for Breach of Contract). 601

§22. Validity

A concluded contract is not necessarily valid. Swiss law implies it[363], while separately subjecting its validity to a number of conditions[364]. The Chinese Civil Code, however, expressly stipulates that, unless the law provides or the parties agree otherwise, the contract becomes valid simultaneously with its *conclusion*. As outlined in the preceding section, in Chinese law, a contract is concluded at the time of one party's acceptance of the other's offer to conclude it (Art. 471 and 483; s. above §578), whereas Art. 471 *in fine* mirrors the reservation contained in Art. 502§1 *in fine* by equally providing that the parties may agree otherwise (s. above §579). Art. 490 and 491 specify two special cases of conclusion (s. above §§584 to 586). 602

Beyond the general principle of contractual validity stated above, Chapter 3 hardly elaborates on contractual *invalidity*. Instead, in the last provision of the chapter (Art. 508), it primarily refers to Chapter 6 on civil juristic acts of the First Book on general provisions of the Chinese Civil Code. While Art. 508 refers to the regime applying to civil juristic acts in general and, *mutatis mutandis*, to contracts, their invalidity is specifically governed by Title Three on the validity of juristic acts (Art. 143 ff.) of Chapter 6 of the First Book, to which we also refer the reader (s. above Chap. 2 §10.IV, Validity of Juristic Acts, in particular §§260 and 261). 603

Other than referring to the general provisions of the Code, Chapter 3 addresses a limited number of *cases* specifically applying to contractual invalidity. They 604

363 S. Commentaire romand/CO I *ad* CO Art. 1, No. 34.

364 Such conditions relate to the parties' civil capacity, the contract's formal and material validity, the parties' free consent, as well as additional conditions the parties may have agreed upon, s. Commentaire romand/CO I *ad* CO Art. 1, Nos 5 and 33.

relate to failure to obtain administrative approval, agency, liability exempting clauses and dispute resolution clauses.

605 Art. 502§2 addresses the relatively frequent case, in a country strongly regulated like China, of *failure to obtain administrative approval* where such approval is a condition for the validity of the contract at stake. In such case, the obligation to apply for such approval is not affected by the contract invalidity. This provision also applies to ancillary formalities such as related to the change, transfer and revocation of such contracts (Art. 502§3). The party failing to apply may be held liable by the other (Art. 502§2 *in fine*).

606 The three next articles (Art. 503 to 505) apply to *agency*. They do little more than mirroring the general regime of agency contain in the First Book on general provisions (Art. 161 ff.; s. above Chap. 2 §11, Agency) and complementing it with additional rules specifically applying to contracts.

607 Art. 503 addresses the *ratification* by the other party of a contract concluded with a *falsus procurator*: if the other party has already either commenced to perform the contract or accepted the agent's performance, then either is deemed to amount to ratification. As such, Art. 503 complements the express ratification requested by Art. 171§1 and 2 (s. above §294) by providing for the possibility that such ratification may be *implied.*

608 Art. 504 expressly applies to *legal representatives* concluding a contract in excess of their power, the principle contained in the general regime of agency at Art. 172, by which the principal is also bound if the third-party was of *good faith*, i.e., had no reason to believe that the agent was not properly empowered. This principle is already extended by Art. 170§2 to "legal persons' representatives" which, arguably, refers to a wider notion than that of "legal representative" *stricto sensu* (s. above §§291 and 292 and below §1774). If so, the contract is deemed to be valid.

609 Finally, Art. 505 stresses that the sole fact that the *contractual scope* exceeds the agent's powers does not suffice to invalidate the contract. Given that Art. 504 already reminds that the principal is bound towards a good faith third party, one should understand that, by further referring to the general regime governing the invalidity of juristic acts, Art. 505 serves as a reminder that the *bad faith* third-party may still request the principal to ratify the contract or invoke implied ratification (s. above §607). As such, by singling out, among the various forms in which an agent may excess his power, the excess related to the contractual scope, the purpose of Art. 505 seems to be to favor contractual validity in case of what may prove being a relatively minor excess of power by one party, without departing from the general regime applying to juristic acts.

610 Art. 506 invalidates certain contractual *liability exempting clauses*, including those resulting in physical injuries, and intentional or grossly negligent

property loss[365]. Invalidation cases of liability exemption clauses are also found in other parts of the Code, such as Art. 497, which invalidates standard clauses whenever they result in unreasonably exempt or mitigate the stronger party's liability, aggravating that of the weaker party, or restricting or exempting the latter's rights (s. above §596). Moreover, standards clauses, which typically contain liability exemption clauses, shall be invalidated whenever they contravene the conditions set forth by the First Book of the Code on the validity of civil juristic acts (Art. 143 ff.; s. above §250). Secondary legislation can provide for additional cases.

Finally, in case of contractual invalidity, the *dispute resolution clause* con- 611
tained in the invalid contract is deemed to be valid or to retain its validity (Art. 507). This applies indifferently of whether the contract never became valid, becomes invalid, is revoked, rescinded or terminated.

§23. Performance

I. Introduction and General Rules

Chapter 4 of the First Title on general rules of the Third Book on contracts of 612
the Chinese Civil Code governs contractual performance (Art. 509 to 534). As its position in the Code suggests, it contains general rules applying to all contracts; special rules are contained in the Second Title on special contracts of the Third Book.

The first subsection of the first article of the chapter embeds the foundation of 613
contractual law by proclaiming that the parties shall fulfil their respective obligations according to the contract (Art. 509§1). Obvious as it may seem, this core principle, already known in Roman law as *pacta sunt servanda*, is only implied[366] in the general part of the Swiss Code of Obligations: there is no equivalent provision, namely, in Chapter 1 on the performance of obligations of the Second Title on the effect of obligations of the general part of the Swiss Code of Obligations. The obligatory effect of contractual obligation is, in the Swiss Code of Obligation, affirmed and detailed on a contract-by-contract basis in the special part of that Code. To that extent, the Chinese Civil Code is, like for contractual validity (s. above §602), clearer than its Swiss counterpart.

---

365 The OR generally prohibits liability exemption clauses for willful misconduct or gross negligence (s. CO Art. 100§1). For particular cases, s. CO Art. 100§2 and 3 and CO Art. 101§3. This list is not exhaustive.

366 S. GAUCH/SCHLUEP/TERCIER No. 1344; Commentaire romand/CO I *ad* CO Art. 1 No. 34.

614 Although Art. 509§1 falls short from specifying it, but as implied by Art. 582, 1st sentence which governs liability in case of nonperformance (s. below §799), *any* performance not conforming with the contract shall amount to nonperformance, be it quantitative, qualitative (often known as "substandard"), untimely, or not complying with any other condition agreed upon by the parties (e.g., *intuitu personae*[367] performance).

615 The second subsection of the first article of the chapter on contractual performance of the Chinese Civil Code affirms another core principle of contract and, indeed, civil law, which is that, in performing their contractual obligations, the parties shall observe the principle of *good faith* (Art. 509§2). Inasmuch, and once again, the Chinese Civil Code, structurally, differs from the Swiss one since, while the latter expresses this principle on the beginning of the Swiss Civil Code (Art. 2§1), like the Chinese one (Art. 7, s. above §116), the Swiss Code does not repeat it in the part on contract law of the Swiss Code of Obligations, unlike the Chinese Code, which does. However, because the Swiss Code of Obligations is ancillary to the Swiss Civil Code, CC Art. 2§1 does apply to Swiss contract law[368].

616 Beyond the mere reference to good faith, Art. 509§2 elaborates by adding that the parties shall perform their *general obligations* of "notification, assistance, confidentiality, etc." according to the "nature and purpose of the contract and trade practices".

617 Moreover, the parties shall "avoid wasting resources, polluting the environment and destroying the ecology during performing the contract." This requirement reflects the recent environmental consciousness to which China has committed to adhere to and echoes similar requirements related to, namely, the usufruct (Art. 326§1, 328 and 329; s. above §458), the construction usufruct (Art. 346 and 350; s. above §477), and to liability for illicit acts, specifically for ecological pollution and economical damage (s. below Chap. 8 §61, Liability for Environmental Pollution and Ecological Damage).

II. Contractual Interpretation

618 Art. 510 offers the parties the possibility to *supplement* their contract after it has been concluded and became effective, if certain issues have not or not

367 S. below note 399.

368 Unlike CC Art. 7 which proclaims that the general principles of contract law apply in civil matters, there is, in Swiss law, no provision to the reverse, i.e., that the general principles of civil law apply to contract law or to the law of obligations. Nevertheless, the foregoing is universally accepted in Swiss law.

clearly been agreed upon. This provision mentions, as examples, quality, price or remuneration, place of performance, etc. This option is only available if the main elements or *essentialiae* of the contract have been agreed upon; it only applies to secondary elements. Indeed, unless the *essentialiae* have been agreed upon, the contract cannot be concluded[369].

619 However, if the parties fail to agree, Art. 510 and 511 offer helpful *complementary interpretation rules* for that effect. Art. 510 *in fine* mandates the parties to interpret the contract "in accordance with the relevant clauses of the contract" or based on *trade usages*. In other words, the expression "in accordance with the relevant clauses of the contract" points, like Swiss law[370], at *literal interpretation*[371] as primary method of interpretation[372].

620 As such, Art. 510 *in fine* also silently refers to Art. 466 on *contractual interpretation* which, other than special rules applying to discrepancies resulting from bilingual contracts, refers to the general rules of *interpretation of declarations of will* (Art. 142) contained in Chapter 6 on civil juristic acts of the First Book of the Chinese Civil Code on general provisions, which we discussed elsewhere in this book (s. above §§218ff., 561, 622 and 623).

621 Art. 511 complements the general rules of interpretations reminded above about unclear *quality requirements, price*[373] *or remuneration, place of performance, time limit for performance*[374], *and assumption of the cost of performance*. While this enumeration mirrors that of Art. 510, it is, as noted, not exhaustive. Therefore, whenever secondary elements need to be interpreted but are not listed at Art. 510 and 511, the general rules recalled above apply. The guidance provided by Art. 511 for each case is straightforward; therefore, rather than paraphrasing it, we refer the reader to its content.

622 The principles of *interpretation* applying to contracts reside, therefore, in several sets or rules, whose combination can prove confusing. These are, mainly, Art. 142 on declarations of will in general; Art. 466 on contractual interpretation; and Art. 510 and 511 on contractual supplementing. This list is not exhaustive, since beyond these general rules, specific interpretation rules are to

369 Those *essentialiae* are non-exhaustively listed at Art. 470; s. above §576.

370 S. GAUCH/SCHUEP/TERCIER, No. 840 ff.; Commentaire romand/CO I *ad* Art. 18, No. 25.

371 In Swiss law, literal interpretation relies on the common meaning of the contract's wording, on its special meaning, if any, within the parties' trade, and on the contractual context, namely, the contract's structure, in which such language is to be understood (systematic interpretation), s. GAUCH/SCHUEP/TERCIER, No. 840 ff. On Chinese rules of interpretation and further comparison with Swiss law rules, s. above §§218ff.

372 The contractual interpretation rules in case of modification of the contract are complemented by Art. 544, s. below §692.

373 On government-set prices, s. below Art. 513 and §630.

374 On the delivery time for online sales, s. Art. 512 and below, §§626 to 628.

be found throughout Chinese law (e.g., Art. 498, which poses special interpretation rules for standard clauses, s. above §597; or Art. 544, which applies to contractual modifications, s. below §692). The following guidelines may help to clarify the relationship between said sets.

623 If there is uncertainty about the *main* elements of the contract, the parties shall interpret their declarations of will according to Art. 142. Art. 466, 510 and 511 do not apply since they govern existing contracts, while a contract cannot come into existence unless the parties have agreed on its main elements.

624 If there is uncertainty about *secondary* elements of an existing contract, the parties may *supplement* it according to Art. 510, since this provision may apply after the contract has come into effect, i.e., after the parties have agreed on its main elements.

625 If the parties fail to supplement the contract, they shall *interpret* it according to Art. 466 (which as noted applies to contracts but refers to Art. 142 anyway) and the supplemental rules provided by Art. 510 *in fine* and 511.

626 Art. 512 remarkably embraces the new economy by addressing *online sales* and providing guidance as to the time of performance of such transactions, specifically their *time of delivery*. Even though that provision does not explicitly spell it out, one is to understand that it applies to *online sales of goods delivered by courier*[375], and to *online provision of services delivered either online*[376] *or physically*[377] after having been concluded online. Moreover, it provides for a particular case of online provision of services which are *downloads*.

627 In case of provision of services, Art. 512 does not specify whether the *time* of delivery is that of the beginning or the end of the provision of services. However, because both may matter depending on the circumstances and the legal consequences attached thereto, one may suppose that it can be either.

628 In case of online sale of goods, the delivery time is when the buyer signs the receipt. In case of online services, it is that of either the issuance of the electronic receipt, or when the buyer signs the receipt; if there is no receipt, it is the time when the services are actually provided. In case of download, it is when

---

375 Courier, or "express logistic (or delivery, or courier) services", is universally known in China as 快递 kuàidì.

376 For example, online language classes.

377 For example, online order of house cleaning services. Indeed, Art. 512 provides, in case a provision of service has been concluded online, that the related voucher may be issued either electronically (i.e., online) or physically, in the form of a printed document, which implies that, in the latter case, however sold online, the services are provided on-site, not online.

the product downloaded onto the buyer's system can be used. The parties may agree otherwise.

It is worth noting that, despite e-commerce has rapidly taken over the global economy, Swiss law is entirely deprived of such rules, which are left to general principles of contractual interpretation and the jurisprudence of Swiss courts which, absent established precedents, may lack consistency. 629

Art. 513 provides for further guidance for government-set or *official prices and pricing regulations*. While such a provision may be unusual for free market economies like Switzerland, it is relevant in a semi-commanded one like China's. Whenever the authority has imposed mandatory prices or pricing regulations, the applicable price shall be that corresponding to the time of the delivery. However, in case of late delivery and price variation in the meantime, the lower price prevails; in case of late receipt or payment, the higher one does. 630

The creditor may request the debtor to pay in the *currency* being the official currency of the place of performance (Art. 514). The official currency of the PRC is the Chinese yuan (CNY), also referred to, even in English, by its transliteration from Chinese, 人民币 rénmínbì (RMB). In Greater China, the official currency of the Hong Kong Special Administrative Region (SAR) is the Hong Kong dollar (HKD or HK$); that of the SAR of Macau, the Macanese pataca (MOP, P or MOP$). The law may mandate or the parties agree otherwise, however; moreover, the drafting of this provision ("may") makes clear that this right is at the creditor's discretion. 631

Given that the Chinese yuan in not yet freely convertible globally and because of the Chinese exchange control[378], most cross-border transactions still occur in foreign currencies, mostly U.S. dollars or euros. Yet foreign parties to a transaction with a Chinese one are advised to verify that the contractual currency (or, at least, the applicable law and its consequences on said currency[379]) is defined[380] in order to avoid any inconvenience, especially in online transactions where the place of performance may not be obvious. 632

---

378 S. above note 24.

379 In Swiss law, the currency in which a debt is to be paid is governed by CO Art. 84, which can lead to another result than Chinese law. S. also the Swiss Federal Law on Monetary Unit and Means of Payment (Fr.: Loi fédérale sur l'unité monétaire et les moyens de paiement (LUMMP); Ger.: Bundesgesetz über die Währung und die Zahlungsmittel (WZG) of 22 December 1999 which modernized CO Art. 84.

380 In practice, it is not rare to see contracts merely denominated with the dollar sign "$" with no additional indication. Yet in the Greater China region, it can point at U.S. dollars (USD), Hong Kong dollars (HKD), Singapore dollars (SGD), Macanese pataca (MOP), and is even frequently used for Chinese yuan (CNY or RMB) instead of the

III. Multiple Debts, Creditors or Debtors and Third Parties

633 Art. 515 and 516 apply to the case of *alternative debts* towards the same creditor, not to be confused with that of multiple debts, i.e., debts owed by multiple debtors or towards multiple creditors: the latter cases are governed by the next set of provisions, outlined below. Art. 515 and 516 leave the debtor free to choose which it will pay off, unless otherwise provided by the law or agreed between the parties, or such performance is impossible; in case of untimely choice, the right to choose passes to the other party[381].

634 As noted, the cases of *multiple creditors*, *multiple debtors* and, in particular, *joint and several liability* are governed by Art. 517 to 520. The last four provisions (Art. 518 to 520) apply to joint and several liability; Art. 517 applies to multiples debtors or creditors absent joint liability.

635 *Joint and several liability* is simply known, in legal French and German, as solidarity (Fr.: "solidarité"; Ger.: "Solidarität"; CO Art. 143 ff.) Even though solidarity is usually translated by "joint and several liability" in legal English, for the sake of simplicity we will use "solidarity" throughout this chapter.

636 Solidarity arises either where a single debtor is liable towards multiple creditors, each of whom is entitled to demand payment of the entire debt from that debtor, or conversely where multiple debtors are liable towards a single creditor, who may require any one of them to perform the obligation in full. Solidarity thus entitles one or some creditors (instead of all of them) to claim the whole debt, or the creditor to claim the debt to one or some debtors (instead of all of them; Art. 518§1). Even though these provisions generally address both creditors and debtors individually, Art. 521§3 expressly provides that solidarity rules for debtors apply *mutatis mutandis* to creditors.

637 Solidarity must either be prescribed by law or agreed between the parties (Art. 518§2). The principle of solidarity is already contained in the general regime of civil liability contained in the general provisions of the Code (Art. 178; s. above §§329ff.) Art. 518 to 521 extend and develop it in the ambit of contractual performance. Typically, as far as contractual liability *lato sensu*, i.e., resulting from the (non- or imperfect) performance of a contract, is concerned, solidarity is mandated in several cases of damage caused by, for example, corporate division (Art. 67§2), investment (Art. 83§2), agency (Art. 164§2 and 167), co-ownership (Art. 307), suretyship (Art. 686 ff.), contract for work (Art. 786 and 791§2), transport of goods (A.K.A. freight carriers; Art. 834),

---

yuan symbol "¥". Inasmuch, a clear reference to universally accepted currency codes (ISO 4217) like the ones mentioned here is advisable.

381 CO Art. 86 provides for a similar solution, although for *multiple*, not alternative debts.

mandate (Art. 932) and contractual partnership (Art. 973). It can also apply in case of liability for illicit acts (Art. 1168 to 1171). This list is not exhaustive; namely, solidarity can be provided in other cases, by secondary legislation.

In case there is *no solidarity* and the subject matter is *divisible*, each creditor is entitled or each debtor is liable for its share (Art. 517§1). If the subject-matter is *indivisible* or if the creditors' shares are *difficult to determine*, the subject-matter shall be divided evenly; the later rule applies both *absent and in case of solidarity* (Art. 517§2, 519§1 and 521§1). 638

Art. 519 and 520 contain several rules detailing the functioning of solidarity in specific situations. A debtor who has performed more than its share of the obligation is entitled to claim reimbursement of the excess from its co-debtors as if it were a creditor (Art. 519§1). If a debtor defaults, its outstanding share is divided among its co-debtors (Art. 519§3). If a debtor pays for the others, the claim is extinguished (Art. 520§1; the debtor remains entitled to the excess claim foreseen by Art. 519§1). If one debtor is exempted, the others are liberated to the extent of the exempted debtor's share (Art. 520§2). If the creditor becomes one of the debtors, the corresponding share is extinguished, but not the remainder of the debt of the other debtors (Art. 520§3). The delay of the creditor to collect the debt of one debtor extends to the other debtors (Art. 520§4)[382]. In case one creditor collects the whole debt, it shall pay their shares to the other creditors (Art. 521§2). 639

In certain cases, Chinese law may prohibit the parties to agree to be jointly and severally liable however (s., §, Company Law Art. 14§2 and below, §1787). 640

The next set of provisions (Art. 522 to 524) addresses contractual performance involving *third parties*, specifically two cases: when the debtor performs towards a third party instead of towards the creditor (Art. 522), and when a third party, instead of the debtor, performs the latter's obligation towards the creditor (Art. 523 and 524). 641

In any case, there must be a tripartite agreement between the creditor, the debtor and the third party. In the first case (debtor to perform towards a third party; Art. 522), in case the debtor fails to perform towards such third party, the debtor remains liable towards the *creditor*, not the third party (Art. 522§1). However, the debtor may be liable towards the *third party* if the following two conditions are fulfilled: the parties agreed or the law stipulates so, and the third party did not refuse the debtor's performance (obviously, if the third party has refused the debtor's performance, it cannot subsequently complaint that the debtor did 642

[382] Among other things, this provision may matter in case of interest, since the creditor is deprived of its right to claim it ever since it is late in accepting the debtor's performance, s. Art. 589§2 and below §833.

not perform; the third party must have expressed its refusal timely). If the debtor is liable towards the third party, the former may raise against the latter the defenses it may have against the creditor (Art. 522§2).

643 The second case (third party to perform with the creditor; Art. 523 and 524) addresses two sub-cases, depending on whether the parties (i.e., the original debtor and the creditor) have so agreed or not.

644 In the *first* sub-case (*agreement* between the parties; Art. 523), in case the third party fails to perform, the *debtor* remains liable towards the creditor. Unlike Art. 552, which provides for a similar but different institution (s. below §§701ff.), Art. 523 does not specify whether the creditor is to be part of the agreement or if, at least, it needs to be notified. Be that as it may, even though the law does not mandate so, one may safely deduce that the creditor logically needs to be either in order to prove its rights towards the third party.

645 In the *second* sub-case (*no agreement* between the parties; Art. 524), there is no agreement between the debtor and the creditor, but the third party has a *legitimate interest* to the debtor's performance. In such case, the third party has the right to spontaneously perform in the stead of the debtor, except if, due to its nature, the obligation can only be performed by the debtor (e.g., *intuitu personae* obligations[383]), the parties (in this case, the creditor and the debtor only) have so agreed, or the law prescribes otherwise. The third party's performance is subject to the creditor's acceptance however, as Art. 524 *in fine* only suggests. If the creditor does accept it, its claim against the debtor is transferred to the third party, unless, once again, the parties have agreed otherwise.

646 Art. 523 and 524 are not to be mixed with several *neighboring but distinct institutions* involving third parties performing instead of the defaulting debtor: as noted, Art. 523 applies to the case in which the debtor and a third party have agreed that the latter would perform instead of the former; Art. 524 addresses the case in which a third party has a legitimate interest to perform in place of the debtor; Art. 535 to 537 apply to subrogation, by which the creditor is entitled to substitute itself to the debtor for performing the latter's obligation when the debtor relies on the performance of a third party for performing towards the creditor (s. below §§682ff.); Art. 552 addresses the transfer or assignment of the debtor's liabilities to a third party to the extent that the latter commits to being jointly and severally liable together with the debtor towards the creditor (s. below §700); Art. 581 entitles the creditor to apply at court for a third party to perform in lieu of the debtor in case of the latter's subjective impossibility (s. below §803); the contract of suretyship (Art. 681 ff.; s. below Chap. 5 §34, Suretyship) is a typical contract by which a third party agrees with the creditor

[383] S. below note 399.

that the former shall either perform in the stead of the debtor or bear liability for nonperformance if the debtor defaults.

This enumeration is not exhaustive; it focuses on general provisions related to third party performance or guarantees. Chinese law provides for *other forms* of guarantees, often specialized, for example, the mortgage, and dedicates a whole chapter to securities in the Second Book on real law of the Chinese Civil Code (s. below Chap. 3 §17.IV, Security in Property). The other cases will be discussed below together with the chapter of the Chinese Civil Code to which they belong. The comparison between Art. 523 and 552 is discussed with the latter provision (s. below §§701ff.) 647

IV. Exceptions

The provisions outlined in this section provide for two main regimes of *exceptions* to performance, i.e., giving either party the right not to perform in case of *synalagmatic*[384] contracts: the first (Art. 525 and 526) is concerned by the *sequence* of the parties' performance and the consequences of its inobservance on said performance (s. next paragraph and ff.); the second (Art. 527 and 528) is concerned by *default*, i.e., the threat that the debtor may not perform and the protection the creditor's own performance (s. below §§659ff.) Art. 525 to 528 are complemented by Art. 529 to 532 which provide for various, comparatively minor, exceptions (s. below §678). 648

The *first exception* rests on Art. 525 and 526 which define the *sequence* of the parties' performance in synallagmatic contracts, i.e., when the parties both are creditor and debtor from each other. Art. 525 applies to the case where the parties have not agreed on such sequence, while Art. 526 applies whenever they have. It further defines the rights resulting from the inobservance of such sequence. 649

In the first case (the parties *have not agreed* on such sequence), Art. 525 mandates the parties to perform *simultaneously*[385] (Art. 525, 1st sentence). It further contains two corollaries to this principle: first, either party is entitled to reject 650

---

[384] A synallagmatic contract is bilateral, i.e., both parties have rights and obligations towards the other. In contrast, a contract can be unilateral, i.e., it can provide for an obligation for one party and a right for the other, but not for a right for the former and an obligation for the latter, for example, the contract of donation, which is not synallagmatic. Synallagmatic contracts in which the parties perform simultaneously are further known as *perfect* synallagmatic contracts, while if one party perform subsequently to the other, such contracts are known as *imperfect* synallagmatic contracts.

[385] In other words, if the parties did not agree on such sequence, the contract is deemed to be a perfect synallagmatic contract (s. preceding note).

any request from the other party that the former (the requested party) performs before the latter (the requesting party; Art. 525, 2nd sentence). Second, if the performance of the party which performed first anyway was not in compliance with the contract, the other one has the right to reject the former party's request for counter-performance (Art. 525, 3rd sentence).

651 The latter case calls for the two following developments: first, if such performance was compliant, the creditor may not refuse counter-performance, except, however and second, if *early performance* damaged it (Art. 530; s. below §678). If, on the contrary, such early performance did not damage the creditor, the latter may not reject it. In both cases, if the creditor rejects such performance despite it was not entitled to be either exception, it will find itself in default and liable towards the debtor (Art. 589§1; s. below §833). Inasmuch, in the case of early, unilateral performance of a perfect synallagmatic contracts[386], Art. 525, 3rd sentence and Art. 530 *overlap* and provide for the same solution.

652 In the second case (the parties *have agreed* on such sequence; Art. 526), if the party which was to perform first failed to do so or did not comply with the contract, the other one has the right to reject the former (defaulting) party's request for counter-performance.

653 It may be puzzling, at first sight, that Art. 525, last sentence, only refers to the debtor's imperfect performance, while Art. 526 applies both to imperfect (the debtor performs, but imperfectly) and to integral (the debtor does not perform at all) nonperformance. Indeed, as noted, Art 525 contemplates the case in which one party, despite having to perform simultaneously with the other, performs first anyway, but does so imperfectly, which gives birth to the right of the other party to withhold "correspondingly". The first party cannot fail to perform first altogether, since by definition it did not have to.

654 In contrast, under Art. 526, the party which was to perform first can either perform imperfectly or fail to perform entirely, hence the difference between these two provisions. Under Art. 525, one party is protected against integral nonperformance of the other by being entitled to reject the latter's request that the former performs first[387].

655 The regime provided by Art. 525 and 526 qualifies as *performance exception* and conforms with that known in Roman law as *exceptio in adimpleti contractus*. It corresponds, in Swiss law, to CO Art. 82, which prescribes that the

[386] S. preceding note.

[387] Non-Chinese readers should be warned that some translations of Art. 525 and 526 contain serious inaccuracies potentially leading to misunderstandings and are advised to pay close attention to their substance and context.

creditor requesting its debtor to perform must have performed itself or offered to do so[388].

It may be noted that, comparatively, even though they are formulated differently, Art. 525 and 526 of the Chinese Civil Code and Art. 82 of the Swiss Code of Obligations have the same effect. In particular, in case the parties agreed to perform simultaneously, Chinese law contemplates the situation in which one party requests the other to perform first, where the requested party may reject such request, while Swiss law contemplates that in which one party has not offered to perform, where the other may withhold its performance: in the first case, the debtor expresses its intent of not simultaneously performing; in the second, the debtor does not express its intent to simultaneously perform. 656

Both Art. 525 and 526 of the Chinese Civil Code and Art. 82 of the Swiss Code of Obligations only entitle to *suspension*, i.e., temporary nonperformance: the creditor may not invoke it if it does not intend to perform once the debtor resumes its own performance. In the latter case, the creditor must rely on the regime of contractual termination governed by Chapter 7 (Art. 557 ff.), and that of contractual liability governed by Chapter 8 of the Third Book on contract law (Art. 577 ff.; s. below Chap. 4 §27, Liability for Breach of Contract)[389]. 657

As long as the debtor does not perform, resume performance or remedy its defective performance, the creditor is entitled to withhold its own. However, as soon as the debtor complies, the creditor must *resume* its own performance. If the creditor fails to do so, it will find itself in default and liable towards the debtor, which may result in mitigating any compensation the debtor may owe the creditor (Art. 591§1; s. below §836). This also applies in case the creditor refuses to accept the debtor's performance (Art. 589§1; s. below §833). 658

The *second exception* is provided by Art. 527 and 528 and applies to *default*. It offers, in case of synallagmatic contracts, enhanced protection to the creditor by entitling it, in certain circumstances, to withhold its own performance in case the debtor merely threatens to default, even before the latter does. 659

Thus, Art. 527 gives the party first performing the right to *suspend* its performance provided it has "concrete" or "conclusive" evidence (确切证据 quèqiè zhèngjù, where 证据 zhèngjù means evidence and 确切 quèqiè can translate as 660

[388] CO Art. 82 applies primarily to perfect (s. above note 384) synallagmatic contracts (sale, rental, work, transport, mandate, warehousing, etc.), but also, to some extent, by analogy, to imperfect synallagmatic ones, for example, mandate (where the agent is entitled to use its retention right for guaranteeing the payment of its fees); labor contract; contract of sale with scaled deliveries, etc. S. Commentaire romand/CO I *ad* CO Art. 82, No. 9.

[389] In Swiss law, the creditor not intending to perform because of the debtor's default has to rely on CO Art. 97 ff. (s. below §§841ff.)

exact, precise, definite, sure, true, reliable, etc.) of three *circumstances* this provision defines, albeit loosely, or because of any other circumstances to the effect that the debtor cannot, will not or even may not perform. These three circumstances are: the serious deterioration of the debtor's business, any attempt to evade its obligations (namely, by transferring assets or withdrawing funds), or the loss of its creditworthiness.

661 The creditor only needs to prove those circumstances, but it is not requested to prove that they will inevitably result in the debtor's nonperformance. The mere *risk* that the debtor may (可能 kěnéng) not perform, as expressly mentioned by Art. 527§1, item 4, provided it rests on concrete evidence as requested by Art. 527§1, suffices to entitle the creditor to suspend.

662 It is worth noting that, in other words, Art. 527 entitles the creditor to suspend its performance even *before* the debtor actually defaults, since the latter's business may seriously deteriorate, the debtor may evade its obligations, or lose its creditworthiness even before its performance is actually due. As a matter of fact, by defining such circumstances, the Chinese legislator expressly intended to protect creditors by giving them a chance to anticipate nonperformance in cases they had serious reasons to fear it, while protecting debtors by holding creditors liable in case of abuse (s. below §669).

663 If the creditor suspends its performance, Art. 528 mandates it to "timely" *notify* the debtor accordingly (Art. 528, 1st sentence). By "timely", one is, arguably, to understand "immediately" or at least "as soon as possible", in order to prevent the occurrence of any damage unnecessarily caused to the debtor by an untimely notification. However, this provision does not expressly mandate the creditor to notify the debtor before suspending, thus suggesting that the creditor is free to notify the debtor *before or after* the suspension, provided it does so "timely". Indeed, even though Art. 528 does not expressly mention it either, untimely notification would amount to a violation of that provision, thus rendering it liable towards the debtor under the general regime of contractual liability (Art. 577 ff., s. below Chap. 4 §27, Liability).

664 The debtor then has a chance to provide the creditor with "appropriate *assurance*" for its performance. If so, the creditor must resume its own performance (Art. 528, 2nd sentence). Art. 528 does not specify which kind of "assurance" qualifies. It uses the word 担保 dānbǎo, which is alternatively translated as "assurance", "guarantee" or "security"[390]. Absent specific requirements mentioned by Art. 528, one may speculate that a mere declaration of intent, even oral, from the debtor to the creditor, by which the former commits to perform,

[390] The Chinese Civil Code uses the same word, for example, for collateral assets securing an immovable property mortgage (s. Art. 386 ff.) which are highly formal securities; nevertheless, 担保, dānbǎo can also be used in an informal sense, s. below note 595.

may qualify, provided the creditor accepts it, subject to good faith on both sides, i.e., provided the debtor's commitment is serious enough and the creditor does not reject it although it is[391]. A formal security (like, e.g., for a mortgage[392]) or financial guarantee is not required.

Art. 528 does not mention when the debtor should provide such assurance, but it should obviously do so soon enough so as not to deprive it of its intended use, subject, once again, to both parties' good faith, which in practice shall be immediately or as soon as possible. One may also suppose that the creditor may set a deadline to the debtor, provided such deadline is reasonable or set in good faith. 665

If the debtor fails to provide such assurance and persists in not performing, or if, after having provided such assurance and in spite of the latter, the debtor does not perform anyway within a "reasonable time" as expressly mentioned by Art. 528, the creditor has the right to *revoke* the contract (Art. 528, 3rd sentence). What a "reasonable time" should be is subject to the creditor's discretion, within the boundaries of good faith. 666

Art. 528 further expressly spells out that, if the debtor neither performs, nor provides said assurances within such reasonable time, it shall be deemed as being liable for faulty nonperformance, thus entitling the creditor to terminate the contract and to claim compensation for nonperformance. It is noteworthy that Art. 528 does not request that the debtor actually defaulted; provided the circumstances listed at Art. 527§1 are proven and the debtor has failed to provide adequate assurances, its nonperformance shall, by virtue of Art. 528, amount to a legal *presumption.* 667

Therefore, the creditor terminating the contract under such circumstances is entitled to invoke the debtor's contractual liability (Art. 528, 3rd sentence *in fine*) and to claim *compensation* in accordance with the regime of contractual liability governed by the next chapter of the Code (Art. 577 ff.; s. below Chap. 4 §27, Liability for Breach of Contract). 668

In contrast, the creditor itself may be liable towards the debtor for breach of contract if the former suspended its performance without *concrete evidence* that the debtor could not or may not have performed in the circumstances described at Art. 527 or of any other circumstances to the same effect (Art. 527§2). As noted, although Art. 528 does not mention it, under the general regime of contractual liability, the creditor may also be liable in case of untimely notification or termination (s. above §§663, 665 and 666). 669

391 On differences with Swiss law in this respect, s. below §§841ff.

392 S. above note 390.

670 *Swiss law* offers a comparable regime at CO Art. 83[393].

671 As mentioned, Art. 525 to 528 are complemented by Art. 529 to 532 which provide for various, comparatively minor, exceptions which are addressed in the next section (s. below §678).

V. Miscellaneous Provisions

672 The last set of provisions of Chapter 4 on performance (Art. 529 to 534) contains various exceptions, the most significant of which is arguably that known in Roman law as the *clausula rebus sic stantibus*. According to this provision (Art. 533), which incorporates in Chinese law a doctrine widely accepted both in civil and common law jurisdictions, if the circumstances in which a contract was concluded have changed so dramatically that its performance becomes strikingly unfair for one of the parties, then that party may, under certain conditions, be freed, or its burden alleviated.

673 The *clausula* is not to be confounded with *impossibility* or *force majeure* (Art. 180 and 590; s. above §327 and below §834): in the situation aimed at by the *clausula*, performance is still possible, but has become so unfair that the law allows the contract to be modified. *Clausula* cases may typically result from hyperinflation, notably where currency exchange is involved, or natural disasters, such as earthquakes or typhoons, which are not uncommon in China.

674 In order for the debtor to be entitled to invoke it, several conditions must be met: the change must have occurred *after* the contract was made; it must be *material*; it must have been *unpredictable*; it must be *exceptional*, i.e., it must not amount to a regular commercial risk considering the contract at stake; last but not least, it must result in rendering the continuation of the contractual performance *unbearably unfair* for *either party*, which is to say incompatible with the general principle of *good faith*.

675 If these conditions are met, Art. 533 incites the parties to *negotiate*; if negotiations fail, either party may apply at court or resort to arbitration for modifying or revoking the contract. Obviously, the law cannot compel the parties to settle or even negotiate; however, they may not apply to court unless they have

393 Alternatively, under Swiss law, the creditor fearing the default of its debtor may apply before a court for a preservation order ordering the debtor to deposit sureties or the attachment of its assets on the basis of the Federal Law on Debt Recovery and Bankruptcy (LP Art. 271, namely, § 1, item 2), of the Civil Procedure Law (CPC Art. 261 ff.) or of the Criminal Procedure Law (CPP Art. 238, 239§2, 240§4 and CP Art. 73). All these provisions require the creditor to face an imminent damage exceedingly difficult to repair absent such measures and, in some cases, a fraud or serious grounds to suspect it.

attempted to negotiate during a "reasonable" time (A.K.A. "cooling off period"); in other words, a Chinese court and, possibly, the arbitration tribunal, in particular if State-sponsored, may turn down the application if it finds that the parties have not displayed enough good-faith efforts to settle[394].

Once it accepts the application, the court or the arbitration tribunal may either change the contract in order to render it fair again or revoke it altogether if fairness cannot be achieved by maintaining the contract. As noted, fairness is to be measured up to the principle of good faith. 676

The *clausula* doctrine is unanimously admitted in *Swiss law*; however, it is not expressly mentioned in the law and rests on general principles, namely, good faith (CC Art. 2) and contractual interpretation (CO Art. 18)[395]. In any event, it is applied restrictively by Swiss courts. 677

Art. 529 to 532 complement Art. 525 to 528 with various *exceptions* resulting from circumstances entitling or prohibiting the debtor, the creditor or both to either suspend their performance or refuse to accept their counterparty's: after the contract is valid, no party may refuse to perform in case of *change of name or representative*, (Art. 532), except in case of *division*, *merger* or *change of domicile* rendering the debtor's performance exceedingly difficult, in which case the latter is entitled to suspend it (Art. 529); *early* (Art. 530) or *partial* (Art. 531) *performance* damageable to the creditor entitle it to refuse the debtor's performance; in both cases, additional expenses resulting thereof are to be borne by the debtor (Art. 530§2 and 531§2). 678

The relationship between Art. 530 (early performance) and Art. 525, 3rd sentence (unilateral performance in *perfect synallagmatic contracts* where the parties did not agree on the sequence of performance) has been discussed above (s. §651). 679

Finally, the authorities retain a right of "supervision" and of "disposition" in case the performance of a contract endangers the "national"[396], "social"[397] and "public"[398] interest (Art. 534). 680

---

394 S. below §§1449 and 1462.

395 S., for example, GAUCH/SCHUEP/TERCIER, Nos 895 and 1596.

396 The reference to the *national interest* echoes, in contract law, among other provisions, the national security review foreseen by the Foreign Investment Law (Art. 35§1, s. above §§66 to 68).

397 Disturbance to the *public order* and offense to *morals*, which do not equate to the "social interest" but are, arguably, two of its components, result in the nullity of the juristic act (Art. 143, item 3; s. above §253).

398 The *public interest* does not confound with the *national interest* either. It is a wide encompassing exception. It is, notably, the foundation of the right of expropriation (s. above §§19, 397ff. and 490), but can also be invoked in other cases, for example,

§24. Preservation

681 While Chapter 4 on performance of the Third Book on contacts of the Chinese Civil Code provides for certain exceptions entitling the creditor not to perform in case of default or threat of default of its debtor, Chapter 5 (Art. 535 to 542) contains provisions aimed at protecting the creditor's right to obtain its debtor's performance, hence at the *preservation* of the contract. Such rights contemplate two situations: subrogation (Art. 535 to 537), and the debtor's voluntary insolvency (Art. 538 to 542).

682 Art. 535 to 537 address a situation in which a debtor relies on the performance of a third party for performing itself, the debtor, towards the creditor: for example, a buyer (the creditor) orders certain goods from a retailer (the debtor), which the latter buys from a supplier (the third party). Therefore, while the retailer is the buyer's contractual counterpart, the supplier is not: it is the retailer's.

683 In such a situation, that set of provisions is concerned with the right of *subrogation* by which, under certain conditions, the creditor is entitled to substitute itself to the debtor for performing the latter's obligation towards itself, the creditor. Art. 535 applies to *due* debts; Art. 536 may apply to debts *before* they are due. Art. 537 details the modalities of exercising the right of subrogation. These provisions also apply to accessory rights (e.g., necessary preparatory acts, etc.)

684 Art. 536 may apply if the debtor's performance is subject to a *threat,* such as a looming limitation of action against the debtor, or the debtor's failure to have declared bankruptcy timely. These examples, which this provision expressly mentions, are not exhaustive. Although Art. 536 does not detail the conditions which such threat should meet, one may infer from the general requirement of good faith that it should be serious and imminent, while its realization should most likely result in the creditor suffering damage exceedingly difficult to repair.

685 In both cases, i.e., whether the debt is due (Art. 535) or not yet (Art. 536), the creditor is entitled to apply at court to be authorized to substitute itself to the debtor towards the latter's counterparty, and obtain from that counterparty the performance owed by the debtor to the creditor (e.g., in the example given above, the supply of the goods ordered by the creditor); alternatively, the creditor may be authorized "to perform any necessary act", such as declaring bankruptcy (Art. 536 *in fine*).

---

disaster, where the State may impose certain parties to conclude contracts (Art. 494; s. above note 361). The Code prohibits the abuse of civil rights, hence contracts, to the detriment of the public interest (Art. 132; s. above §177).

Art. 535 adds the following rights or obligations: the subrogation cannot apply to strictly personal rights[399] of the debtor (Art. 535§1 *in fine*); the subrogation is limited to *due* (as opposed to immature) debts; the subrogation's costs are to be borne by the debtor (Art. 535§2); and the counterpart may raise against the creditor any defense it may have against the debtor (Art. 535§3). 686

If the court authorizes the subrogation, the debtor's counterpart is under a duty to perform to the benefit of the creditor; it is freed towards both the debtor and the creditor once it has and the creditor has accepted its performance (Art. 537, 1st sentence). If the counterpart's performance is already subject to preservation or enforcement, or the debtor is already bankrupt, the relevant laws apply (Art. 537 *in fine*). 687

Art. 535 to 537 can be seen as a particular case of Art. 524, which entitles the creditor to perform instead of its debtor (s. above §645)[400]. The differences between *neighboring institutions* by which a third party performs in the stead of the debtor have been discussed above (s. §§646 and 647). 688

Art. 538 and 539 protect the creditor against the debtor's foul play to the effect of *voluntary insolvency*, such as waiving claims or guarantees, gratuitously transferring property, maliciously extending time limits for its performance (Art. 538), dumping sale prices, inflating purchase prices[401] or providing guarantees to the benefit of a third party (Art. 539). These two provisions do not expressly mention that the list is not exhaustive, but it seems reasonable to assume so, providing any such attempt results in the same effect. 689

In such cases, the creditor may apply at court for the *rescission* of the juristic acts resulting from any such attempt. However, in the cases aimed at by Art. 539, revocation is subject to the condition of the beneficiary's *bad faith*. Indeed, as far as a property is concerned, Art. 311§1, item 1 protects the property of the good faith transferee (subject to the other conditions set forth by Art. 311; s. above §440). 690

Said right of rescission is subject to three additional provisions (Art. 540 to 542). First, as for the debtor's counterpart performance, the right of revocation is limited to *due* debts and the *costs* resulting from its exercise are to be borne by the debtor (Art. 540). Second, it is subject to a relative *time limitation* of *one year* from the moment creditor became aware or should have become aware of 691

---

[399] Although Art. 535 does not specify the notion of "strictly personal rights", it points out at rights known in Roman law as *intuitu personae*, for example, the public performance of a musical work by a particular artist.

[400] On neighboring but distinct institutions involving third parties performing instead of the defaulting debtor, s. above §646.

[401] Art. 311§1 already prevents dumping and inflating by rendering moot bad faith attempts to transfer property at unreasonable prices, s. above §§437 and 439.

the debtor's foul play, and an absolute limitation of *five years* (Art. 541). Third, the last provision dissipates any doubt that rescission deploys effects *ex tunc* or *ab initio*, as if the act had never existed[402].

§25. Modification and Transfer

692 While Chapter 6 (Art. 543 to 556) of the Third Book on contracts is titled "Modification and Assignment of Contracts", it is overwhelmingly concerned with the latter. *Modification* is addressed by the two first articles only: the first restates the principle of contractual freedom (Art. 5 and 130; s. above §554) by stating that the parties concerned may modify a contract upon reaching consensus through consultation (Art. 543). The second is a rule of interpretation complementing the general regime of contractual interpretation[403]: a contract shall be presumed as not having been modified if such modifications are unclear (Art. 544).

693 The parties to a contract have the right to *transfer* (or "assign", which is synonymous) their rights and obligations to a third party (Art. 555), even though, somewhat oddly, given its importance in practice, this basic principle is located in the next-to-last provision of the chapter. Chapter 6 further distinguishes roughly the transfer of the creditor's rights (Art. 545 to 459) from that of the debtor's (Art. 551 to 554); it also provides for rules applicable to both.

694 Thus, a *creditor* has the right to transfer its creditor's rights, subject to certain exceptions and conditions, however. *Exceptions* are generically listed as relating to the nature of the debt, any contrary agreement between the parties, or the law (Art. 545§1). Provided none of the latter applies, the creditor is entitled to transfer its creditor's rights, subject to the conditions outlined below.

695 If the parties have agreed that the creditor shall not transfer its creditor's rights, but that the latter does so anyway, such *prohibition* shall be ineffective against the transferee, depending, however, on the nature of the debt transferred, and of whether the transferee was of good faith or not (Art. 545§2). Thus, if the debt was a *monetary* one, the transferee shall be protected, i.e., the transaction shall not be invalidated, irrespective of whether the transferee was of good or bad faith. If the debt was of a *non-monetary* nature, i.e., a good or a service, the transferee shall be protected only if it was of *good faith*, like for Art. 539 in case of voluntary insolvency (s. above §690). If not, the transaction shall be

---

402 On the notion of rescission generally, s. above Chap. 2 §10.IV, Validity of Juristic Acts.
403 S. above Chap. 4 §23.II, Contractual Interpretation.

deemed to be invalid, and the debtor remains entitled to deliver its performance to its original creditor.

In other words, if the parties to the original contract agree that the creditor shall be prohibited to transfer a monetary debt and the latter does so anyway, the creditor and the transferee, even if the latter is aware of the prohibition, i.e., was of bad faith, do not have to fear that the transfer will be invalidated; however, if the debtor suffers a damage thereof, it may have a claim for breach of contract against the creditor. Moreover, such transfer would be subject to the other conditions outlined below. The rationale of this discrepancy between the treatment of pecuniary and non-pecuniary debt can be sought in the concern of the Chinese legislator to strike a balance between, on one hand, favor the liquidity of monetary claims and, on the other hand, prevent the bad faith transfer of non-monetary claims, in particular property[404]. 696

The main *condition* for such transfer is that the creditor shall, in addition to not facing any of the exceptions mentioned above, *notify* the debtor (Art. 546§1). If the creditor fails to comply, the debtor shall not be bound. Notification is a purely declarative obligation, which is only subject to reception; the debtor does not have to agree with the transfer (unless the parties had agreed to prohibit it, s. two preceding paragraphs). Such notification, which seals the transfer, is irrevocable, unless the transferee agrees that the creditor withdraws it (Art. 546§2). 697

After the notification, the debtor is entitled to raise against the transferee any exception it may have (or would, before the transfer, have had) against the creditor (Art. 548). The law further provides specifically for one such exception: the debtor may *offset* its debt against the transferee if the latter owes the debtor and that debt relates to the same (transferred) contract. The transferee's debt must be due either simultaneously to the transfer or have matured before (Art. 549). This is consistent with the general regime of termination of contractual rights and obligations which provides for the offsetting of mutual debts (Art. 557§1, item 2; s. below §759). 698

Mirroring the right of the creditor to transfer its creditor's rights, a *debtor* has the right to transfer its debtor's obligations or liabilities (Art. 551§1). However, in order to be entitled to do so, unlike the creditor, the debtor must obtain the creditor's *consent* (*ibid.*) Such consent may not be presumed: this condition is strengthened insofar as, if the creditor has been be urged either by the debtor 699

[404] S. above §690.

or by the transferee-to-be to consent within a time limit[405] and has kept silent, it shall be deemed to have refused such consent (Art. 551§2).

700 The next article provides for the slightly different case in which a third party joins the debtor towards the latter's creditor, i.e., the third party commits to being *jointly and severally* liable along the debtor towards the latter's creditor (Art. 552)[406]. In other words, compared to Art. 551, the debtor also transfers its liability to that third party, but remains liable. In such case, the creditor must either agree about it with the debtor or at least be notified accordingly by the third party. In the latter case, the creditor may refuse, provided it does so within a reasonable time. If it consents, however silently, the creditor has the right to request both the debtor and the third party to perform jointly and severally. The third party's performance is limited to the extent of its commitment.

701 Art. 552 resembles Art. 523 (s. above §643). This comparison warrants the following remarks. *First*, the main difference between these two provisions is that, in the case of Art. 523, the debtor and the creditor agree that the third party will perform instead of the debtor, while in that of Art. 552, the debtor and the third party agree that they will be jointly and severally liable towards the creditor; moreover, Art. 552 requires the creditor to agree or be notified; it may refuse. If it accepts, the creditor may directly ask the third party to perform, like in the case of Art. 523; however, unlike Art. 523, the creditor may still ask the debtor; in the latter option, it is if the debtor defaults that the third party is jointly and severally liable[407].

702 *Second*, while Art. 523 makes clear that the third party has an obligation to perform, the debtor is liable for nonperformance if the third party defaults; comparatively, Art. 552 does not expressly refer to liability for performance or nonperformance; we submit that it may, however, be assumed that, under Art. 552, both the debtor and the third party may be liable for either party nonperformance; in both cases, they will be so jointly and severally.

703 *Third*, as noted about Art. 523, unlike Art. 552, the former provision does request the creditor neither to be party to the agreement, nor to be notified of the same, even though both are implied (s. above §644).

---

[405] Art. 551§2 specifically refers to a "reasonable" time limit. As a matter of fact, given the outcome of the creditor's silence, whether such limit is reasonable or not is irrelevant. It would be relevant if the creditor's consent, not its refusal, were to be assumed provided the time limit was reasonable.

[406] Chinese law may prohibit the parties to agree to be jointly and severally liable, however; s., for example, Company Law, Art. 14§2 (s. below §1787).

[407] On neighboring but distinct institutions involving third parties performing instead of the defaulting debtor, s. above §646.

Moreover, while Art. 523 and 552 are contained by the general part of the Third Book on contract law of the Chinese Civil Code, its special part provides for the contract of *suretyship* (Art. 681 ff.), a typical contract by which a third party agrees with the creditor that the former shall either perform in the stead of the debtor, or bear liability for nonperformance if the debtor defaults. The differences between neighboring but distinct institutions involving third parties performing instead of the defaulting debtor have been discussed above about Art. 523 (s. above §§646 and 647) and Art. 581 (s. below §803); differences with the suretyship contract will be discussed with the latter (s. below Chap. 5 §34, Suretyship). 704

Compared to *Swiss law*, Art. 523 and 552 of the Chinese Civil Code resemble Art. 111 of the Swiss Code of Obligations (Fr.: "porte-fort"; Ger.: "Vertrag zu Lasten eines Dritten"; translated into English in the semi-official version of the Swiss Code of Obligations as "guarantee of performance by third party"), but differ therefrom in some respects: CO Art. 111 literally "promises the performance of the debtor". Actually, the third party commits towards the debtor, not towards the creditor, to bear liability towards the latter for the debtor's nonperformance, while the debtor remains liable towards the creditor for performing; there is no contractual agreement between the third party and the creditor; the obligations of the third party and of that of the debtor towards the creditor are independent from one another; the third party and the debtor are not jointly and severally liable towards the creditor. Besides, the suretyship contract of the Chinese Civil Code (Art. 681 ff.; s. belowChap. 5 §34, Suretyship) can be compared, in Swiss law, to the "contract of surety" (not of "suretyship", as translated in the semi-official translation in English of the Swiss Code of Obligations; Fr.: "cautionnement"; Ger.: "Bürgschaft"; CO Art. 492 ff.)[408] 705

The regime of transfer applies both to debts or obligations and to the rights corresponding to the latter (Art. 556). Both the creditor and the debtor may transfer their debts in whole or in part (Art. 545§1 and 551§1). The transfer of a principal debt carries with it its related accessory debts, if any (Art. 547§1 and 554§1). 706

[408] In Swiss law, the distinctions between CO Art. 111, the contract of surety and other types of guarantees are no less confusing than in Chinese law and have given rise to an abundant jurisprudence: s., for example, Commentaire romand/CO I *ad* CO Art. 111, No. 19 ff.

§26. Termination

I. Introduction

707 Termination is complicated. To start with, the related terminology is confusing, and translations are rife with inaccuracies or errors. Terminology related to validity has been extensively discussed above (s. Chap. 2 §10.IV, Validity of Juristic Acts); the reader may usefully refer to it before immersing in the following chapter.

708 The relevant provisions are scattered around. They are mainly contained either in Chapter 7 of the Third Book of the Chinese Civil Code on contractual termination or in Chapter 8 on contractual liability, but not only: some typical contracts are governed by elaborate specific termination regimes, like, for example, the sale or the labor contracts.

709 In order to identify them, one has to distinguish, in the first place, between ordinary *termination* or termination in the narrow sense, and early termination, A.K.A. termination for a cause or *revocation*. The terminology related to these notions has been discussed earlier in this book (s. §§242 to 248).

710 In either case, the *remedies* they are associated with are plenty. Like termination and revocation, remedies may be contained either in Chapter 7 or 8 of the Third Book of the Code[409], in special regimes located elsewhere in the Code, or in other laws. The creditor may be entitled either to terminate or revoke unilaterally, or to request a court to do so. Remedies may consist either in compensation for nonperformance, partial, substandard or late performance (positive interest), or in negative interest[410], placing the parties in the same situation as if the contract had never been concluded; alternative remedies, such as offsetting, may apply too.

711 Other than termination occurring as a result of the contract's performance, the most common form of contractual termination in practice, *deferred termination*, following persisting default after the creditor granted the debtor an extended time limit for performing, is subject to specific conditions whose inobservance will result in the termination failing. While the Chinese regime is comparable to Swiss law and roughly provides for equivalent remedies, the comparison between the Chinese and the Swiss regimes may be confusing and is, therefore, addressed in a dedicated chapter.

---

409 S. also the general regime of civil liability (Art. 179§1; s. above §322).

410 *Negative interest* corresponds to the interest a party may have had in the contract never to have been concluded; *positive interest* that party has in the completion of that contract's performance.

Chapter 7 is the penultimate chapter of the Third Book on contracts of the Chinese Civil Code preceding contractual liability. It contains 20 articles which are roughly divided into three parts. The *first part* (Art. 557 to 561) addresses "passive" or "automatic" (ordinary) *termination*, i.e., termination occurring typically because performance has been completed or is deemed to have, or automatically results from the law, as the consequence of certain circumstances (s. above §244; on the related terminology, s. also §§247 and 248). 712

As opposed to the first part, the *second part* (Art. 562 to 569) governs termination resulting from the declaration of either of both parties, which one may label "active" (early) termination, termination for a cause or *revocation* (s. above §244; on the related terminology, s. also §§247 and 248). The second part (active termination) contains two subsets of provisions applying to the *time* of termination, and to the *liability* resulting thereof; it is especially significant because it contains the regime of *deferred termination* mentioned above, which we detail both in Chinese law and, as noted, from a comparative perspective, in Swiss law. 713

Finally, the *third part* (Art. 570 to 574) is concerned with the *deposit* of the obligations' subject matter to the effect of suspending its performance. 714

II. Automatic Termination

As explained about the validity of civil acts, the difference between ordinary and early termination is that, in the former case, the parties' performance has been completed or is deemed to have been completed, whereas in the latter, the contract is terminated before performance has been completed or deemed to have been (s. above §242). As will be shown below, while helpful for didactic purposes, these distinctions are imperfect however (s. §717). 715

In case of *automatic* or passive termination, which the Chinese Civil Code refers to as "in accordance to the law" (cf. Art. 565, 1st phrase *in fine*), the creditor's rights and obligations shall terminate in the following circumstances: both parties have *performed* all their obligations[411]; their mutual liabilities *offset* each other; the debtor has *deposited* the subject-matter of its obligation (s. 716

[411] Unlike Chinese law, Swiss law only implies that perfect performance extinguishes the contract; namely, CO Art. 114, which non-exhaustively lists some causes of contractual extinction, does not mention performance (s., e.g., GAUCH/SCHLUEP/TERCIER, Nos1170 ff. and 1843).

below Chap. 4 §26.VIII, Deposit); the creditor has *waived* its claim [412]; in case of *confusion* (i.e., the right and the corresponding obligation belong to the same civil subject[413]; Art. 557§1, items 1 to 5); as well as other circumstances provided for by the law or agreed between the parties (Art. 557§1, item 6).

717 As the examples listed by Art. 557 show, not all of them automatically or passively result from the law: the deposit by the debtor of its subject-matter or the creditor's waiver of its claim both suppose an unilateral act from the party concerned. The distinction between passive and active causes is, therefore, blurred to some extent (s. above §244), in particular where the law considers that, even though the contract has not been performed, it is *deemed* to have. Yet in case of ordinary termination, Chinese law clearly distinguishes automatic or passive from active termination or revocation since it systematically uses 终止 zhōngzhǐ (cf. Art. 557) for the first and 解除 jiěchú for the second[414] (cf. Art. 563). Be that as it may, what matters is that the legal consequences governing contractual termination in case of passive and active termination differ, as outlined below.

718 Art. 557§2 clearly states the effect or the scope of termination in case of ordinary termination, i.e., that it causes the termination of the rights and obligations contained in the terminated contract. Such termination occurs *ex nunc*, from the termination; it is not an invalidation *ab initio*[415].

719 *Accessory rights* terminate at the same time as the principal right, unless the parties agree or the law provides otherwise (Art. 559), which it does in the preceding article by reserving accessory obligations such as notification, assistance, confidentiality, recycling, etc., subject to trade practice and good faith (Art. 558).

720 The performance of *multiple debts* is governed by the regime extensively detailed by Art. 560. This provision addresses the case in which a debtor owes multiple debts identical in nature to the same creditor but cannot pay for all. In such case, Art. 560, to the explicit language of which we refer, prescribes the

412 Art. 575 provides for partial waiver unless the debtor rejects it within a reasonable time. In Swiss law, the waiver (Fr.: "remise conventionnelle"; Ger.: "Aufhebung durch Übereinkunft") is governed by CO Art. 115.

413 In Swiss law, this cause, literally known in legal Swiss French as *confusion* (Ger.: "Vereinigung"), is governed by CO Art. 118. Art. 576 of the Chinese Civil Code prohibits confusion if it damages the rights of a third party, however.

414 About alternative expressions, s. also above, notes 198 and 199.

415 About invalidation *ab initio*, s. above Chap. 4 §22, Validity (of contracts), and Chap. 2 §10.IV, Validity of Juristic Acts.

order in which such debts are to be performed, depending on the circumstances.[416]

721 When the debtor is partly insolvent and cannot wholly indemnify its creditor, the next article also provides for the debtor's payment order in case of additional damage related to nonperformance consisting in *interest* and *costs* resulting from the recovery (Art. 561). If so, this article provides for the imputation of the payment to, first, such costs, second, the interest, and third, the principal debt[417], unless the parties have provided otherwise.

III. Early Termination

722 The next set of provisions governs *early termination*, i.e., termination of the contract, *before* it has been completed, as a result of the exercise of the parties' right to do so, which can take the form of either a unilateral declaration or notice[418], or of a consensus. As mentioned, early termination or termination for a cause is usually translated, in English, by revocation and, in Chinese, by 解除 jiěchú[419].

723 The first provision of the set starts by affirming or reminding that the parties are free to terminate consensually, which is consistent with the principle of contractual freedom (Art. 562; s. above §554). Absent such agreement or consensus, the Chinese Civil Code lists four specific *causes* of termination: force majeure, refusal, delay and impossibility (Art. 563§1, items 1 to 4); other circumstances provided for by the law (*ibid.*, item 5) are also reserved, as usual. For the benefit of the discussion, we will not address them in the order in which Art. 563 lays them; instead, we will first discuss force majeure and other

416 Swiss law provides for multiple debts mainly at CO 86 and 87; however, unlike Art. 560§1 of the Chinese Civil Code, Art. CO86§1 does require the debts to be of the same nature; instead, the Swiss Code of Obligations also provides for indetermined (Art. 71) and for alternative (Art. 72) debts, which are neighboring but distinct concepts, all of which may, depending of the circumstances, combine and overlap to coincide with Art. 560 of the Chinese Civil Code.

417 Taken as a general statement of judiciary policy and compared to Swiss law, this provision is interesting inasmuch as, while Swiss law does provide, in theory, for late interest and additional damage such as recovery costs (CO Art. 104 to 106), it can be said that, in practice, creditors have frequently little choice but waiving interest when they seek to settle, while Swiss courts are notoriously reluctant to condemn debtors to realistic recovery costs.

418 S. below Chap. 4 §26.V, Termination Time.

419 About the related terminology, s. above Chap. 2 §10.IV, Validity of Juristic Acts.

impossibility cases, then refusal, followed by continuous contracts; deferred termination will be outlined in the next subsection of this chapter.

724 *Force majeure* (Art. 563§1, item 1) is defined at Art. 180§2 in Chapter 8 on civil liability of the First Book on the general provisions of the Chinese Civil Code as any objective circumstance that is unforeseeable, inevitable, and insurmountable. Thus, it must qualify as a special case of objective or absolute and subsequent *impossibility* (s. below §§802ff., in particular §805). If so, either party has the right to terminate[420]. If, however, any of those conditions is not met, the author shall face liability (s. above §327).

725 Force majeure is mirrored in the *contractual liability* regime by Art. 590§1 (s. below §833). From that latter perspective, it must be noted in particular that, while Art. 563§1, item 1 does not require any *notice* for terminating, Art. 590§1 does mandate the party unable to perform to notify the creditor to the effect of mitigating the damage. Such notification must be timely and the debtor must provide evidence of the force majeure.

726 Force majeure as addressed by Art. 563§1, item 1 is not to be confused with *other cases of impossibility* contemplated, on one hand, by Art. 563§1, item 4, which is outlined below, and, on the other, by the next chapter of the Code on contractual liability (s. below §§802ff.) Likewise, force majeure as a cause of termination ought not to be confounded with force majeure as a *mitigating or exonerating circumstance* (s. Art. 590 and below §834).

727 Art. 563§1, item 4 applies when, because of the debtor's *delay* or because of *another breach* of contract, the performance of the contract becomes impossible. In both cases, the impossibility considered must be objective or absolute (i.e., there must be no way to perform, even by entrusting a third party) and subsequent. In contrast, if the delay does *not* cause impossibility, but the debtor defaults anyway even after having been urged to perform, then the preceding subsection, i.e., item 3, not item 4, applies: such situation relates to *deferred termination*, which is outlined in the following section.

728 As mentioned, other than the first and the fourth items of Art. 563§1, the Code also addresses impossibility (other than force majeure) as a cause of termination in Chapter 8 of *liability for breach of contract.* From that latter point of view, it is worth noting that other cases of objective or absolute impossibility not amounting to force majeure, i.e., because any of the conditions listed by

420 Unlike in Chinese law, in Swiss law, objective or absolute and subsequent impossibility extinguishes the related obligation (CO Art. 119§1; Fr.: "impossibilité d'exécution"; Ger.: "Unmöglichwerden einer Leistung"; both literally translate as "performance impossibility"). Extinction is automatic; such impossibility does not merely entitle the parties to terminate.

Art. 180§2 were not met[421], entitle the creditor to a similar but lesser right, i.e., to *request the court* (or the arbitration tribunal, if the contract so provides) to terminate the contract, as opposed to terminate it unilaterally (Art. 580§1, item 1 and § 2; s. below §806).

The *difference* between Art. 563§1, item 4 and Art. 580§1, item 1 is that the former expressly refers to a breach of contract as having caused the impossibility, while the latter does not. Therefore, one may deduct, by comparing these two provisions, that, in case of impossibility, Art. 580§2 entitles the parties to apply at court (or before the arbitration tribunal) for terminating the contract irrespective of whether they have committed a fault by breaching the contract, whereas Art. 563§1 gives the right to either party to terminate unilaterally (as opposed to apply at court or before the arbitration tribunal) only if the non-terminating party has committed a *fault*. 729

Indeed, unlike Art. 580§1, item 1, the drafting of Art. 563§1, item 4 ("where either party delays performance or commits other acts in breach of contract, making it impossible to achieve the purpose of the contract") does not only expressly refer to a breach; its language goes further by implying ("commits", "making") that it was deliberate or committed by negligence, in other words, that it was faulty. Yet fault is not a condition of contractual liability; therefore, Art. 563§1, item 4 appears to subject the right of termination not only to impossibility resulting from a mere breach of contract, but also, in addition, to the condition that such breach was faulty. 730

To recapitulate, either force majeure (Art. 563§1, item 1) or a *faulty* breach of contract resulting in absolute or objective and subsequent impossibility (Art. 563§1, item 4) entitle either party to unilaterally terminate the contract, while *other* cases of objective or absolute and subsequent impossibility (Art. 580§1, item 1) give them the right to apply at court of before the arbitration tribunal for terminating. So does relative impossibility (Art. 580§2, item 2; s. below §802). Subjective impossibility, including refusal (s. next paragraph) entitles the creditor to apply at court for being authorized to request a third party to perform instead of the debtor (Art. 581; s. below §803), but 731

[421] Art. 180§2 defines force majeure as an objectively unforeseeable, unavoidable and insurmountable event. Therefore, an objective or absolute impossibility does not amount to force majeure if it was foreseeable or evitable; however, if such impossibility is absolute or objective, it is, arguably, by definition, insurmountable. Therefore, the conditions which distinguish force majeure from other cases of absolute or objective impossibility should be the two first (unforeseeable and unavoidable).

refusal is also a cause of active or direct termination. Initial impossibility is, arguably[422], a cause of nullity, not of termination.

732 The *refusal* of either party to *perform* (Art. 563§1, item 2) amounts to a case of subjective, relative and subsequent impossibility. It entitles the other party to terminate but does not exonerate the refusing party from its liability. On the contrary, it provides the creditor with an *anticipated* right to claim compensation (Art. 578; s. below §808). The refusal can be express or implied by the debtor's behavior. Alternatively, the creditor may apply to court for being authorized to request a third party to perform instead of the debtor (Art. 581; s. below §803)[423]. Moreover, the refusal of the creditor to *accept* the debtor's performance, which is nothing else but a qualified form of the refusal to perform, entitles the debtor to *deposit* (Art. 570§1, item 1; s. below §783) and results in a reversal of contractual liability (Art. 589§1; s. below §833).

733 In addition to the causes outlined above, the law further entitles either party to terminate without a cause and anytime *contracts without a term providing for continuous performance*[424]. Provided the contract qualifies as such, the terminating party must, in addition, have notified the terminated party reasonably in advance. Therefore, this provision is relevant both to the cause and to the time of termination (for the latter, s. below §749). Termination without a cause with a reasonable advance notice is typical, among other contracts, of the *mandate*, where Art. 933 (s. below §§1020 and 1022) mirrors Art. 563§2.

IV. Deferred Termination

734 Art. 563§1, item 3 provides for contractual termination by the creditor in case of *delay* of the debtor, whenever the latter has persisted to default even though the creditor extended it a reasonable time limit to perform. In other words, this provision does not only provide for deferred termination but also for *deferred*

---

422 Unlike Swiss law (CO Art. 20§1), Chinese law does not expressly enunciate that initial impossibility is a cause of nullity. We deduct that consequence from the general principles of the Chinese Civil Code on the validity of juristic acts, s. above §§250 and 253.

423 The case in which the creditor refuses to accept the debtor's performance is governed by Art. 589§2 (s. below §833).

424 Such contract is literally known, in Swiss law, as "duration contract" (Fr.: "contrat de durée"; Ger.: "Dauervertrag"). It is not specifically regulated by the law; its regime has been elaborated in doctrine: s., for example, MARIE-NOËLLE VENTURI-ZEN-RUFFINEN, La résiliation pour justes motifs des contrats de durée, thesis, Université de Fribourg, Schulthess, Zurich/Basel/Geneva 2007.

performance[425], thus salvaging the contract by avoiding immediate termination in case of default. This regime deserves sustained attention because it proves, in practice, being a cornerstone of the contractual nonperformance and liability regime.

Terminology wise, one should point out once again that deferred termination is a typical case of *revocation*, expressed in Chinese by 解除 jiěchú[426] (cf. Art. 563§1). 735

To start with and as noted above (s. §727), Art. 563§1, item 3 is to be distinguished from Art. 563§1, item 4 which also contemplates deferred performance insofar as, in the case of item 3, the delay is curable, whereas in that of item 4 it is not. As mentioned above, item 4 addresses a case of objective or absolute impossibility: performance is not possible anymore; in the case of item 3 however, it is still soon enough to perform. 736

In order to be entitled to rest termination on Art. 563§1, item 3, the creditor must have urged the defaulting debtor to perform, and the latter must have persisted in defaulting "within a reasonable period of time". Therefore, even though the Code does not explicitly set a formal *notice* requirement, it clearly implies that the creditor has to set the debtor a *time limit* for performing and that such limit must be *reasonable*. Reasonableness is subject to the usual requirement of good faith. 737

If the debtor fails to perform nevertheless, Art. 563§1, item 3 poses no further condition to the creditor's right to terminate: termination occurs automatically upon expiry of the time limit (Art. 565§1, 3rd sentence; s. below §746). Inasmuch, i.e., as far as notification is concerned, Chinese law differs from Swiss law; because of the importance of delayed performance and deferred termination in practice, we elaborate below the comparison between both jurisdictions (s. Chap. 4 §26.VII, Deferred Termination: Comparative Law). 738

In other words, however lax the requirement of an extended time limit for performing may, because of the liberal drafting of Art. 563§1, item 3, appear at first sight, it clearly results from the foregoing that the creditor is not vested with a right to immediately terminate the contract in case the debtor has not timely performed: it is the intent of the Chinese legislator that the creditor gives the belated debtor a second chance for performing indeed. Only if the debtor defaults yet another time and provided it could reasonably have been expected to do so within the time limit set by the creditor, may the latter terminate. 739

425 A performance is *delayed* when it is not provided at or within the contractually agreed time; it is *deferred* when it is provided or to be provided within the time extension granted by the creditor.

426 About the related terminology, s. above Chap. 2 §10.IV, Validity of Juristic Acts.

740 Alternatively, as outlined above among the exceptions to performance, the creditor is entitled to *suspend* its performance until the debtor resumes its own or provides appropriate assurances (Art. 527 and 528; s. above §§659).

V. Termination Time

741 While Art. 562 and 563§1 are concerned with termination causes, Art. 564 and 565 address the *time* of the termination; Art. 563§2 provides for both, however. These provisions only apply to active or *direct termination* since, in case of passive or indirect termination, the latter occurs automatically, as soon as the related circumstances are given.

742 Art. 564 applies to the *extinction* of the right to terminate, i.e., conversely, to the time limit within which the right of termination may be exercised. It distinguishes two situations: in the *first*, if such limit has been agreed between the parties or is set by law, expectedly the right of termination expires upon reaching such limit (Art. 564§1).

743 In the *second*, if, however, it has neither, i.e., a time limit for terminating has been neither agreed nor set by law, then the next subsection of Art. 564 further distinguishes two more situations: if the debtor has *urged* the creditor to terminate (or not) within a reasonable time limit and the creditor fails to terminate[427], then the creditor's right to terminate shall extinguish upon expiry of said limit (Art. 564§2 *in fine*); absent such limit, the same provision sets an absolute limit of *one year* from the date the creditor has or should have become aware of its right to terminate (Art. 564§2, 1st sentence).

744 Although the law does not expressly address it, in case of expiration, it is implied that the right of terminating may resuscitate and be exercised again, provided either the parties so agree, or there is another cause of termination (posterior to the one which the creditor failed to timely invoke) which the creditor then timely invokes.

745 In contrast, Art. 565 governs the *inception* of the termination, i.e., the point of time from which the contract is legally deemed to have terminated. Again, this

[427] The situation contemplated by Art. 564§2 *in fine*, which could be qualified of *belated termination*, is not to be confused with that of *delayed termination* addressed by Art. 563§1, item3 (s. above §§ 718 ff.): in the former case (belated termination), the creditor has the right to terminate but does not exercise it; yet the debtor may have an interest to ascertain whether the creditor will terminate or not; if so, the *debtor* may urge the creditor to use its right; if the creditor neglects to, its right to terminate extinguishes. In the latter case, the *creditor* urges the debtor to perform; it the latter fails to, the creditor is entitled to terminate.

provision contemplates several situations. First and foremost, Art. 565 is only relevant in case the creditor rests termination on the law (first case; indirect termination, s. above §§716ff.), or if it has set a time limit to the debtor (second case); indeed, there is no need for such provision in case the parties have agreed on it.

In the second case (the creditor has set a *time limit* to the debtor), termination occurs upon expiry of the time limit (Art. 565§1, 3rd sentence). In the first case (*indirect termination*) however, Art. 565 contemplates two more options, depending on whether the creditor has given notice to the debtor, or whether it has filed at court (or before an arbitration tribunal, if the contract so provides) directly. 746

In the first option (*notice*; Art. 565§1, 1st sentence), termination occurs when the notice reaches the debtor (Art. 565§1, 2nd sentence). While the law does not mention it expressly, one should assume that the notice must contain the cause of the termination, i.e., the legal basis, or at least the circumstances on which such termination rests. As mentioned above, as far as notification is concerned, we compare the Chinese and the Swiss law regimes below (s. Chap. 4 §27.V, Comparative Law). 747

In the second option (*court or arbitration filing*), termination occurs with the service to the debtor of the claim for termination (Art. 565§2). Alternatively, if the debtor objects to the termination and the creditor has not directly applied for termination, both party may apply at court (or before the arbitration tribunal) to confirm the validity of the termination (Art. 565§1 *in fine*). 748

Finally, as noted above (s. §733), Art. 563§2 applies both as a cause for termination and to the time of the same: indeed, in case of contracts without a term providing for continuous performance, either party may terminate not only without a cause, but also *anytime*, subject to the terminating party giving a reasonable advance notice to the terminated one. If the notice is unreasonable, the terminating party may be liable for any damage suffered by the terminated party as a consequence thereof, in accordance with the general regime of contractual liability or with that of typical contracts (for the mandate, s. Art. 933 *in fine*). 749

VI. Termination Liability

The next set of provisions (Art. 566 to 569) addresses certain liabilities resulting from termination. As such, these provisions are to be regarded as a *lex specialis* to the regime of liability for breach of contract governed by the next chapter of the Chinese Civil Code. Indeed, as explained, termination does not necessarily occur in case of breach of contract; it may happen for other reasons not implying or requiring one party's fault. For that reason, Chapter 7 also contains certain rules on contractual liability, which complement those of Chapter 8 750 whenever termination resulted from a breach of contract. As a matter of fact, Art. 566§2 expressly reserves the regime of liability for breach of contract.

751 The first provision of that regime, Art. 566§1, is concerned with the parties' liability for that part of the performance which had not yet been completed at the time of termination. However not obvious at first reading, but as can be inferred from its juxtaposition with the next subsection, Art. 566§2, Art. 566§1 applies indifferently both in case of termination resulting from either party's *fault*, namely, breach of contract, or not. Therefore, it also applies in case of non-faulty termination including consensual termination (Art. 562), termination because of force majeure (Art. 563§1, item 1) and, arguably, to termination because of "other circumstances provided by the law" (*ibid.*, item 5), if any, since they are not specified.

752 Art. 566§1 distinguishes between that part of the contract which had already been performed at the time of termination, from the part which had not yet. According to this provision, the parties are *freed* from performing the latter (Art. 566§1, 1st sentence). As far as the part which has been already performed is concerned, Art 556§1, 2nd sentence offers two options: either party may either request restoration of the original state (*status quo ante*), or "apply other remedial measures", arguably to mitigate the damage resulting from incomplete nonperformance, and claim damage compensation.

753 It may be noted that, even though the *status quo ante* is typically the remedy applying to nullity, not to termination, Art. 566§1 makes it available in case of termination not resulting from a contractual breach anyway.

754 Besides, damage interests are available in addition to either option (*status quo ante* or other remedial measures) since both may, and in practice inevitably will, result in additional costs. Art. 566§1 does not specify which regime of liability should apply to such. While Art. 566§2 expressly refers to the regime of contractual liability governed by Chapter 8 of the Third Book of the Chinese Civil Code, it can only apply in case of breach of contract. Likewise, if the parties were not at fault, the regime of liability for illicit acts cannot apply either. Therefore, if termination resulted from another cause than breach of contract, and if the parties were not at fault, such liability may result from the regime of *unjust enrichment* (cause having ceased to exist; s. below Chap. 7 §55, Unjust Enrichment)[428].

[428] For example, a building is destroyed by an earthquake halfway its construction. The contract for work is terminated because of force majeure. The contractor cannot pretend to be paid the price agreed for the completed work. However, the principal can re-use or sell the rubles, etc. Despite the contract has terminated and the principal did not breach it, the contractor can claim compensation for unjust enrichment.

If, however, termination did result from a breach of contract, then the parties may be liable accordingly, unless they agree otherwise (Art. 566§2). In fact, this provision simply complements the general regime provided by the first subsection by potentially allowing for *supplemental* compensation in case of breach of contract: Art. 566§2 may, therefore, apply *cumulatively* to Art. 566§1. 755

Indeed, Art. 566 also complements the general regime of contractual liability which provides for compensation in case of *nonperformance* (Art. 582, 1st sentence; s. below §799) by providing for supplemental compensation in case of damage specifically resulting from the termination, i.e., in addition to that resulting from nonperformance, irrespective of the termination. 756

Art. 566§3 further clarifies that termination does not free the *guarantor* from its undertaking to assume the debtor liability resulting from the termination, thus implicitly referring to Art. 566§1 and 2. This provision is to be understood as generic and applying to the various forms of guarantee provided throughout the Chinese Civil Code. The suretyship contract may provide otherwise however (Art. 566§3 *in fine*). 757

Likewise, termination does not affect the validity of contractual settlement clauses, in particular *liquidated damages* (Art. 567 and Art. 585; s. below §§818ff.) 758

The two last articles of the set of provisions addressing liability in case of termination govern the *offsetting* of mutual liabilities (Art. 568 and 569)[429]. They distinguish between whether those mutual liabilities are identical in nature, or not. If they are, both parties have the right to offset (Art. 568); if not, they may do so by consensus (Art. 569). In the former case however, the party intending to offset must notify the other; the latter may not subject the offsetting to conditions, such as a time limit or others (Art. 568§2). Moreover, the right to offset may be prevented by agreement between the parties, the law, or if the nature of the debts does not permit it (Art. 568§1 *in fine*). The latter objection may seem contradictory with the beginning of Art. 568§1, which entitles the parties to offset in the debts are identical in nature; however, one may conceive that, however identical in nature, such nature does not lend itself to being offset. 759

VII. Deferred Termination: Comparative Law

As noted above, because of the importance of the delayed performance and deferred termination regime in practice and the differences between Chinese and Swiss law in that respect, some comparisons may prove useful. The main 760

429 S. above §339.

differences relate to the notice requirement and the remedies available to the creditor in case of persisting default.

761 The Swiss regime is governed by CO Art. 102 to 109; it pivots around two provisions: CO Art. 102 and 107, which are complemented by CO Art. 103 to 106, 108 and 109.

762 As far as the *notice* requirement is concerned, while Chinese law does not mention a formal notification requirement, but merely asks the creditor to set the debtor a reasonable time limit for performing, then entitles the former, in case of persisting nonperformance, to terminate, Swiss law requires, in principle, subject to the exemptions mentioned below (s. §765), the creditor to notify the debtor *twice* before it can terminate (or resort to one of the other remedies offered by Swiss law, s. below §§768ff.)

763 Thus, *firstly*, in Swiss law, the creditor must notify the debtor a *formal reminder*, known in Swiss legal French as "interpellation" and in Swiss legal German as "Mahnung" (CO Art. 102§1). In order to qualify, it suffices that such reminder clearly expresses, in any way, be it in writing[430], orally or by concluding acts, the creditor's intent that the debtor performs[431]. Although CO Art. 102§1 does not mandate it, typically, the creditor sets the debtor, in the reminder, a time limit for performing.

764 *Secondly*, if, at the expiry of the time limit set according to CO Art. 102§1[432], the debtor has not performed, CO Art. 107§1 entitles the creditor to set the debtor a *time limit*[433] known, in Swiss legal French, as "grace deadline" ("délai de grâce") and, in Swiss legal German, as "subsequent deadline" ("Nachfrist") for performing. Alternatively, the creditor has the right to request a court to do so in its stead (CO Art. 107§1).

765 Under Swiss law, in principle, the creditor can only terminate after it has satisfied this double-notification requirement (the options available to the creditor in case of default following an extended time limit are discussed below, s. §§768ff.) It can escape the strict double-notification requirement of CO Art. 102§1 and 107§1 (as compared to the relatively lose requirement of

430 In practice, such reminder is generally notified in the form of a letter whose subject line mentions, in French, "mise en demeure" and, in German, "Mahnung".

431 ATF 41 II 245; ATF 129 III 535 = JT 2003 I 590.

432 In case the creditor has already set a time limit in the reminder as per CO Art. 102§1, the time limit mandated by CO Art. 107§1 will be the second one. Absent such time limit in the reminder as per CO Art. 102§1, the creditor is entitled to set the time limit mandated by CO Art. 107§1 after a reasonable time, such reasonable time being subject to good faith.

433 If the creditor has not set a time limit in the reminder as per CO Art. 102§1, it must do so as per CO Art. 107§1.

Art. 563§1, item 3 of the Chinese Civil Code) provided the *exemptions* exhaustively listed by CO Art. 102§2 and 108 are eligible, i.e., for the first notification, that the parties had agreed that the debtor was to perform as a *set date* (clause known both in legal Swiss German and French as "Fixgeschäft", literally "fix business"; CO Art. 102§2[434]) and, for the second notification, either because the debtor's behavior clearly signals that it will not perform, or because late performance would be useless to the creditor, or because the parties had agreed on a "Fixgeschäft" (CO Art. 108). An exemption from CO Art. 102§1 does not imply an exemption from CO Art. 107§1, and vice versa.

Somehow all these exemptions are mirrored in the Chinese Civil Code. The "Fixgeschäft" of Art. 102§2 and 108, item 3 of the Swiss Code of Obligations can be equated to the contractual time limit agreed between the parties as per Art. 562§2 of the Chinese Civil Code. The debtor's implicit refusal to perform is contemplated in both codes (Art. 563§1, item 2 of the Chinese Civil Code and CO Art. 108, item 1). The uselessness of late performance addressed by Art. 108, item 2 of the Swiss Code of Obligation can be derived from Art. 563§1, item 4 of the Chinese Civil Code[435]. 766

Thus, discrepancies between the Chinese and Swiss regimes relate, to start with, to *notification* requirements. Thus, in the ordinary case of delayed non-performance, Chinese law only requires one notification, while Swiss law mandates two. In both the cases of implicit refusal of the debtor and of uselessness of late performance, Chinese law does not require any notification while Swiss law mandates one. In case of "Fixgeschäft", neither Chinese nor Swiss law require any notification. 767

As far as the *remedies* available to the creditor in case of persisting default are concerned, if the debtor does not perform eventually, while Art. 563§1 of the Chinese Civil Code only entitles the creditor to terminate, the Swiss regime of delayed performance presents the creditor with *three options* (CO Art. 107§2), i.e., two main options, the first of which subdivides in two sub-options: the creditor can either *maintain* or *revoke* the contract; if it maintains the contract, it can either *insist* on the debtor's performance ("first option"), or *renounce* it ("second option"); alternatively, as noted, the creditor can choose to *rescind* the contract ("third option"). In all three cases, the creditor is entitled to claim damage interests (CO Art. 107§2 and 109§2). 768

---

434 This exemption also applies if the parties had agreed that the creditor may unilaterally fix such date subject to notifying the debtor in advance and in good faith.

435 Art. 563§1, item 4 of the Chinese Civil Code provides a cause for termination whenever the debtor's delayed performance makes it impossible to achieve the purpose of the contract.

769 The difference between the two first options on one hand and the third on the other is that, in the two first options, the *creditor remains bound* by its duty to perform or to complete its performance, whereas the third option *liberates* it from that duty. The difference between the first and the second option is that, in the first, the *debtor* (like the creditor in the two first options) *remains bound* by its duty to perform, while in the second it is *liberated* from that duty.

770 However, in the second option, the creditor enjoys a sub-option: its performance (or what is left of it, if it has already partly performed) may be transformed into a *monetary* debt to the benefit of the debtor and compensated against the latter's debt towards the creditor[436].

771 In the first option, the contract is terminated after both parties have performed; in the second option, the contract is terminated after the creditor has completed its performance and the debtor has compensated the creditor for nonperformance[437] or, in case of offsetting, after the debtor has compensated the creditor for any outstanding debt after such offsetting[438]; in the third option, the contract terminates upon the creditor's notice to the debtor that it is rescinding[439].

772 Beyond the apparent contradiction between the wording of Art. 563§1 of the Chinese Civil Code ("terminate") and that of (the effects of) Art. 107§2, first and second options of the Swiss Code of Obligations ("maintain"), the remedy provided by Art. 563§1 of the Chinese Civil Code corresponds to the *second option* of Art. 107§2 of the Swiss Code of Obligations: whenever, under either code, the creditor "terminates" the contract, the contract's existence is actually maintained until the debtor has compensated the creditor for its default, while the creditor must either complete its performance or face a reduction of the debtor's compensation; it is only once the parties have settled their mutual liabilities, in one way or the other, that the contract ends, as provided by both

---

436 This solution is not expressly mentioned by Swiss law, but unreservedly acknowledged by Swiss courts; it is known as the "theory of the difference"; in contrast, if the creditor completes its performance nevertheless, it is entitled to full compensation for the debtor's nonperformance; this solution is known as the "theory of exchange" (s., e.g., GAUCH/SCHUEP/TERCIER Nos 1775 to 1777).

437 For example, the parties exchange 150 trucks against 100 tractors. The first party delivers 40 trucks and defaults. The second party may deliver the 100 tractors anyway and ask the first party to pay for the 110 missing trucks.

438 For example, a buyer orders coal for 100; it pays 60 in advance; the seller delivers 50 and defaults; the buyer renounces the remainder of the coal and offsets the coal already delivered with the 60 it paid; the seller is still liable towards the buyer for the difference of 10; the contract terminates after the seller has paid it to the buyer.

439 The wording of CO Art. 107§2 is actually rather opaque and mostly implicit: the three-options approach described above has been proposed by the doctrine and universally adopted by the Swiss legal community ever since.

Art. 557§1, 1st item of the Chinese Civil Code and Art. 114§1 of the Swiss Code of Obligations.

That said, Art. 563§1 of the Chinese Civil Code does not provide remedies equivalent to the first and third options of Art. 107§2 of the Swiss Code of Obligations. Yet the Chinese Civil Code does not preclude them either. Indeed, nothing in Chinese law prevents the creditor, in case of persisting delayed performance, to resort to the *first option* described by Art. 107§2 of the Swiss Code of Obligations, i.e., not to terminate, but to insist on the debtor's performance while maintaining the creditor's own, as provided by Art. 579 and 580§1, 2nd phrase[440] of the Chinese Civil Code (s. below §801). 773

In Swiss law, it is now clear[441] that the *third option* of Art. 107§2 provides for *rescission*, i.e., resulting in an *ex tunc* effect by placing the parties in the same situation as if the contract had never been concluded, thus entitling the creditor to *negative damages*. Art. 563§1 of the Chinese Civil Code in contrast, by entitling the creditor to invoke the debtor's liability for breach of contract, provides for *revocation*[442] resulting in *ex nunc* effects, not for rescission. 774

While the Chinese Civil Code provides for rescission as an option in cases of direct termination other than for breach of contract (Art. 566§1 *in fine*; s. below §752), it does not in case of delayed performance, unlike in the third option of Art. 107§2 of the Swiss Code of Obligations. In other words, the third option of CO Art. 107§2, rescission, is not available under Art. 563§1, item 3 of the Chinese Civil Code. 775

The comments above about Art. 563 of the Chinese Civil Code apply *mutatis mutandis* to Art. 527 and 528 entitling the creditor to *suspend* its performance in case of threat of default of the debtor and giving the former the right to terminate in case of persisting default or if the latter does not provide it with an appropriate assurance of performance (s. above §§659ff.) 776

Finally, it may be noted that the Swiss regime of delayed performance provides for a detailed regime for *ancillary issues*, such as provisions alleviating or aggravating the liability of either party, in particular with respect to late interest 777

---

440 Art. 579 of the Chinese Civil Code entitles the creditor of a pecuniary debt to claim performance from the defaulting debtor; Art. 580§1, 1st phrase applies to the same effect to non-pecuniary debts.

441 CO 107§2, 3rd option uses the verb "se départir" in French and "zurücktreten" in German, both of which mean "to terminate" (s. above note 172). It is universally acknowledged however that this is a drafting error and that one should understand "to rescind" (s., e.g., GAUCH/SCHUEP/TERCIER, No. 1785), literally "to depart" from the contract, which is an alternative to "résoudre", generally used to express "to rescind".

442 Art. 563§1 uses the verb 解除 jiěchú, which means to terminate, not to rescind. On related terminology issues, s. above §§241ff.

(s. CO 103 to 106 and 109), which Art. 563 of the Chinese Civil Code does to a lesser extent[443].

778 In summary, subject to the exceptions mentioned above, in Chinese law, the creditor only needs to give the debtor a second chance, while Swiss law mandates a third one. If the debtor defaults anyway, the creditor is, both in Chinese and Swiss law, entitled to terminate and claim damage interests; alternatively, the creditor has the right to insist on the debtor's performance and claim compensation for late performance. However, unlike Swiss law, Chinese law does not entitle the creditor to rescind the contract (*ab initio*). Comparatively, Swiss law provides for all three remedies, i.e., continuous performance, revocation and rescission. Each of these remedies entitle the creditor to compensation (for late performance the first case, and nonperformance or positive interest[444] in the second, both in Chinese and Swiss law; in addition, Swiss law entitles to negative interest[445] in the last option and provides extensively for late interest in all three options).

779 Comparatively, the Swiss deferred performance regime expressly provides for multiple remedies, while the Chinese one only provides for one, implies a second and does not provide for the third. Also, the Swiss regime provides for detailed ancillary provisions, while the Chinese one only provides for general principles. However, generally speaking, the Swiss regime can be said to be more complicated and less pragmatic than the Chinese one, sometimes exceedingly so, as the extensive reliance of Swiss courts on elaborate doctrine and jurisprudence tends to confirm.

780 Further comparative law issues are addressed below about contractual liability (s.Chap. 4 §27.V, Comparative Law).

VIII. Deposit

781 Generically, "deposit" may correspond, in the Chinese Civil Code, to no less than three *different institutions*: deposit as a *substitute* for performance (Art. 570 ff.; s. below); deposit as a *guarantee* for performance (Art. 586 and 587; s. below Chap. 4 §27.III.B, Deposit); and deposit as a typical *contract* (Art. 888 ff.; s. below Chap. 5 §42, Deposit), where the latter may overlap with

443 Art. 561 merely provides for interest to be paid after recovery costs and before the principal debt (s. above §721).

444 S. above note 410.

445 S. preceding note.

either of the two first. However, while "deposit" may be used as a generic[446] translation for all three, the Chinese Civil Code uses three different expressions for each: 存 cún for the substitute; 定金 dìngjīn for the guarantee; and 保管 bǎoguǎn for the contract.

782 Deposit as provided under Art. 570 to 574 is a faculty offered by law to the debtor prevented from performing for a cause lying with the creditor[447]. It is available to the debtor whenever the creditor refuses to accept the debtor's performance without a cause, when its whereabouts are unknown, when he has died without having regulated his succession; or when he has lost his civil capacity and has no guardian. Other circumstances provided by law are reserved (Art. 570§1).

783 The creditor's *refusal* to accept the debtor's performance (Art. 570§1, item 1) actually amounts to the creditor's refusal to perform (by accepting the debtor's performance) and, as such, entitles the debtor to terminate without performing (Art. 563§1, item 2; s. above §732). Although the law only mentions the creditor's active refusal, we believe that this provision also applies in case of *passive* refusal, i.e., in case the creditor, while not expressly refusing the debtor's performance, does not take any measure for enabling the debtor to perform.

784 However, the debtor may have more interest in performing than not[448]. If so, the debtor has the right to deposit the goods being the subject matter of its obligation to perform, and be deemed to have performed. Besides, the creditor's refusal to accept the debtor's performance results in a reversal of contractual liability by which the creditor becomes liable of any damage its refusal may cause to the original debtor (Art. 589§1; s. below §833)[449].

785 Obviously, the deposit regime typically applies to the sale of goods and related transactions such as the *contract of deposit*, (Art. 888 ff.; s. below Chap. 5 §42, Deposit), which is a typical contract with which the deposit regime of Art. 570 ff., however closely related, is not to be confounded, as well as the contract of *warehousing* (Art. 904 ff.; s. below Chap. 5 §43, Warehousing), which is a development of the contract of deposit.

---

446 Alternative, more specific translations are also available, however. They will be mentioned in each topical chapter.

447 Deposit is known in Swiss law, in Swiss legal French, as "consignation" and in Swiss legal German as "Hinterlegung" (CO Art. 91 ff.)

448 For example, the debtor must clear the warehouse were the goods purchased by the buyer, of which it failed to take delivery, are stored.

449 Moreover, as long as the creditor delays the acceptance of the debtor's performance, the latter has no obligation to pay interest (Art. 589§2).

786 Deposit is performed by depositing the subject matter with a depositary (under a contract of deposit or warehousing[450]), which is usually a warehouse operating under a concession from the judiciary authorities to that effect. The form of the deposit depends on whether the subject matter to deposit is suitable for being deposited; in practice, suitability depends in turn on the depositary facilities; disproportionate cost may make it unsuitable. If so, the debtor is entitled to *sell or auction* the subject matter, then deposit the proceeds (Art. 570§2).

787 Deposit is deemed to have been performed when the subject matter or its proceeds are deposited (Art. 571§1); in turn, the debtor having performed the deposit is deemed to have performed the contract (Art. 571§2). In other words, subject to the general boundaries of good faith, the debtor is deemed to have performed the contract even if, typically, it sold the subject matter for less than the price paid by the creditor.

788 The debtor must immediately *notify* the creditor *after* the deposit (Art. 572). The law is, in that respect, unambiguous: provided the conditions entitling the debtor to deposit are met, the debtor has no obligation to notify the creditor before the deposit, i.e., of its intent to deposit. The risk of damage to the deposited subject matter is to be borne by the creditor (Art. 573, 1st sentence): this is consistent, in particular, with the regime of liability for breach of contract in case of refusal of the creditor to accept the debtor's performance, as reminded below (Art. 589§1; s. §833). The creditor is also liable for the debtor's related expenses; conversely, the creditor is entitled to any fruits (Art. 573 *in fine*).

789 If the creditor does not indemnify the debtor, upon request of the latter to the depositary, the latter will not allow the creditor to collect the goods unless it has either entirely indemnified the debtor or provided the latter with a guarantee (Art. 574§1). If the creditor persists in not indemnifying the debtor, the latter has the right to collect the subject matter after paying the depositary fees. The debtor has the same right if the creditor waives its right to collect. Finally, if neither the creditor, nor the debtor collects within *five years* from the deposit, the good's ownership falls to the State, after indemnification of the debtor and of the depositary, as the case may be[451]. If the creditor indemnifies the debtor,

---

450 In theory, there may, therefore, be two successive contracts of deposit or warehousing, where the nonperformance of the first may result in the conclusion of the second.

451 Art. 574§2 only mentions the creditor with respect to the five years limit, while it does not set any time limit to the debtor; therefore, one may not assume that the five years limit applies to both parties. Besides, this provision only mentions that the ownership shall fall to the State "after deduction" of the auction sale and deposit costs; it does not goes as far as stating that such costs shall be reimbursed to the debtor and the depositary; we believe that it is a reasonable assumption, however.

subject to the preceding reservations, it has the right to collect the subject matter anytime (Art. 574§1).

§27. Liability for Breach of Contract

Liability for breach of contract (违约责任 jiànshè yòngdì shǐyòng quán) is governed by Chapter 8 (Art. 577 to 594) of the Third Book of the Chinese Civil Code on contracts. As noted (s. above §310), contractual liability is one of the main sources or regimes of civil liability *lato sensu* contained in the Chinese Civil Code, the other ones being the general regime of civil liability (First Book on general provisions; Art. 60 and 176 ff.; s. above Chap. 2 §8.III.D, Liability and Chap. 2 §12.II, Civil Liability); liability for illicit acts (Seventh Book; Art. 1164 ff.; s. below Chap. 8 , Liability for Illicit Acts ("Torts")), *negotiorum gestio* (Art. 979 ff.) and unjust enrichment (Art. 985 ff.; s. below Chap. 7). 790

Moreover, contractual liability other than for breach of contract is briefly addressed in Chapter 7 on contractual termination (Art. 566§1; s. above §§750ff.) In addition to the Code, various provisions or regimes are contained in other special laws, which form another source of civil liability. *Pre-contractual liability* and liability for *business secrets* related to contractual negotiations are governed by Art. 500 and 501, which pertain to Chapter 2 on the conclusion of contracts of the Third Book of contract law (s. above §§599 and 600). 791

Although the law only implies it (s., e.g., Art. 186 and 179§1, item 9; s. also above §317), it can be assumed that the general regime of civil liability contained in Chapter 8 of the First Book of the Code on general provisions (Art. 176 ff.) applies by default to, among other liability regimes, contractual liability, provided the latter is silent or not specific enough, according to the principle *lex specialis derogat leges generali* (Art. 11; s. above §117). 792

I. Introduction

The basic principle of liability for breach of contract is enunciated by Art. 577, which prescribes that a party (the debtor) which fails to perform a contractual obligation is liable towards its contractual counterparty (the creditor). 793

The main characteristic of liability for breach of contract as compared to liability for illicit acts is that, under the former regime, *fault* is not a condition: the defective contractual party or debtor is liable for its nonperformance towards its counterparty or creditor even if it was not at fault. 794

795 Other than fault, liability for breach of contract remains subject to the other conditions to which liability for illicit acts is subject, which are a *damage* resulting from the alleged nonperformance, an illicit act, which in the ambit of liability for breach of contract takes the form of a contractual infringement or *nonperformance*, and a *causal link* between nonperformance and the damage (s. below §1641).

796 Unlike the corresponding basic provision of Swiss law on liability for breach of contract, which enumerates all three conditions (damage, nonperformance and causality), and the absence of fault as an exonerating circumstance (CO Art. 97§1), Art. 577 only implies the damage (by listing some remedies) and does not mention the fault at all. However, mitigating or exonerating circumstances are addressed in other provisions, which we will discuss below (s. below Chap. 4 §27.IV, Mitigation and Exoneration.)

797 Be that as it may, one may deduct from the general rules of Chinese civil procedure law governing to the *burden of proof* that the *creditor* bears the burden of proving the damage, nonperformance and causality, whereas the *debtor* bears that of proving any mitigating or exonerating circumstances[452]. This allocation is to be derived, namely, from Art. 67 of the Law of Civil Procedure stating that a party shall bear the burden to provide evidence supporting its claims. A logical corollary of this principle is that the other party bears the burden of proving the contrary.

798 Chapter 8 further contemplates various cases of nonperformance and provides adequate remedies for each of them. The order in which the Code addresses those cases is not obvious at first sight, however.

799 The basic case of *nonperformance* is governed by Art. 583. This provision simply provides that, in such case, the debtor shall compensate the creditor for any loss subsisting after subsequent performance (in case the debtor eventually performs), or after the remedy has been applied, if at all. Inasmuch, despite its lack of visibility in the middle of Chapter 8 on contractual liability, this provision is the *cornerstone* of contractual liability. It is complemented by Art. 582, 1st sentence, which prescribes that, in case of *incomplete* or substandard performance, the debtor shall bear liability according to the contract (Art. 509§1; s. above §613), and by Art. 566§2, which provides for supplemental compensation in case of additional damage resulting from the *termination* (s. above §§755 and 756).

800 Chapter 8 elaborates by distinguishing nonperformance cases depending on the nature of the debt and that of nonperformance. Thus, the first group (nature of

---

[452] Swiss law provides for the same rule of proof (ATF 144 III 155 = JT 2018 II 287; ATF 142 III 9; ATF 144 III 217 = JT 2018 II 334).

the debt) distinguishes *pecuniary* from *non-pecuniary* debts; the second (nature of nonperformance) distinguishes *voluntary* nonperformance, *impossible* performance, *unenforceable* performance and *incomplete* (or substandard)[453] performance. The two groups overlap.

In case of nonperformance of a *pecuniary debt*, the creditor may request payment (Art. 579)[454]. In case of *non-pecuniary debt*, the remedy depends of whether the performance is possible or not. If performance is *possible*, the creditor may request the debtor to perform (Art. 580§1, 2nd phrase). 801

Impossibility is subject to further qualification. Indeed, legally, one traditionally distinguishes *subjective* from *objective* impossibility, *relative* from *absolute* impossibility, and *initial* from *subsequent* impossibility. In case of *subjective* impossibility, the impossibility relates to the debtor's ability to perform; in case of *objective* impossibility, the impossibility relates to the nature of the obligation, which cannot be performed irrespective of the debtor's ability. In case of *relative* impossibility, the contract could be performed, but the cause preventing its performance is legally considered as akin to being impossible and is treated as such, even though performance were objectively possible. In case of *absolute* impossibility, there is no way to perform. *Initial* impossibility already exists at the time of the contract's conclusion; *subsequent* impossibility occurs after the contract has been concluded. 802

In case of *subjective* impossibility, the creditor may request a *third party* to perform in the stead of the debtor, and at the latter's costs (Art. 581)[455]. 803

The Code further considers the following impossibility cases (Art. 580§1, items 1 to 3): when performance is impossible "legally[456] or practically[457]"; 804

---

[453] Swiss law generally uses the qualifier of "imperfect" or "incorrect" instead of incomplete or substandard (performance), s. CO Art. 97§1 and, for example, CO Art. 160§1 (Fr.: "exécution imparfaite"; Ger.: "nicht richtige Erfüllung").

[454] A pecuniary debt is, by definition, never (legally) impossible, s. GAUCH/SCHLUEP/TERCIER, No. 1798.

[455] Swiss law provides for the same remedy (CO Art. 98§2). However, unlike Chinese law, that provision requests the creditor to "be authorized" to do so, which implies that the creditor must apply at court to that effect. On neighboring but distinct institutions involving third parties performing instead of the defaulting debtor, s. above §646. In case the debtor *refuses* to perform, the creditor is also entitled to terminate (Art. 563§1, item 2; s. above §732).

[456] A *legal* impossibility to perform could occur, for example, in case the import or export of some goods (e.g., rare earths or computer chips, as was the case during the Sino-U.S. import taxes rift in 2025) would be prohibited by law after the conclusion of the contract.

[457] A *practical* impossibility could conceivably occur if the chances to perform would be akin to null.

when performance cannot be enforced or only at an excessive cost; and when the creditor fails to request performance[458] timely[459]. This list is exhaustive.

805 Because, as noted above, subjective impossibility is addressed by Art. 581, because the second (exorbitance) and the third (creditor's default) cases of Art. 580 amount to *relative* impossibilities, and because Art. 580 exhaustively lists the cases deemed by law as amounting to relative impossibility, one may deduct that the first case (performance practically or legally impossible) relates to *absolute* or *objective* impossibility[460].

806 In the cases listed at Art. 580§1, either party may apply before a court (or an arbitration tribunal, provided such forum is available) for *terminating* the contract (Art. 580§2). If so, the non-performing party remains liable towards the other for any damage (Art. 580§2 *in fine*), as the case may be.

807 It must be reminded that, if the impossibility results from *faulty nonperformance*, the creditor has the right to terminate the contract without applying at court or before the arbitration tribunal (Art. 563§1, item 4; s. above §729).

808 Finally, in case either party *refuses* to perform, that is, before the contract has expired, declares its intent not to perform, the creditor has the right to ask the debtor to bear liability before the contract has even ended (Art. 578). In other words, in such case, this provision confers the creditor an *anticipated* right to claim compensation. As mentioned about termination, it is also a cause of *revocation* (Art. 563§1, item 2; s. above §731).

809 The last article of Chapter 8 on liability for breach of contract provides for a special regime for the *limitation of action* related to *contracts for the international sale of goods* and *contracts for the import and export of technology*. It extends the limitation for filing a lawsuit or applying for arbitration to *four years* (Art. 594)[461] from the ordinary limitation of three years (Art. 188)

---

458 The creditor's failure to timely request performance is not to be confused neither with that of the creditor's (active or passive) refusal of the debtor's performance (s. above §783), nor with the creditor's refusal to perform (s. above §732), nor with the general regime applying to delayed performance (s. above Chap. 4 §26.IV, Deferred Termination).

459 In case the debtor *refuses* to perform, the creditor must request performance *before* the expiry of the contract (Art. 578, s. below §582). Comparatively, in case the debtor simply *fails* to perform, Art. 580§1, item 3 implies that the creditor is to request performance "within a reasonable time". Therefore, arguably, such request *after* the expiry of the contract may be considered as untimely.

460 About *force majeure*, which is a special case of objective or absolute and subsequent impossibility, as a cause of *termination*, s. Art. 563§1, item 1 and above §724; as a *mitigating or exonerating circumstance*, s. Art. 590 and below, §834.

461 S. above §337 and note 223.

applying to civil rights as provided in Chapter 9 on limitation of actions of the First Book of the Code on general provisions.

II. Compensation

The *quantum* of compensation for contractual damage must cover both the *damnum emergens* (effective damage) and the *lucrum cessans* (loss of profit)[462] (Art. 584). However, any such quantum is subject to *reasonableness*: it may not exceed the damage which was (or should have been) foreseen by the parties when they concluded the contract as being probable in case of breach[463]. 810

Chapter 8 provides additional guidance for the determination of compensation in case of *incomplete* or substandard performance (Art. 582). If such compensation has not been agreed upon between the parties in the form of *liquidated damages* (s. below §§818ff.), the parties should seek guidance from Art. 510. The latter provision, which pertains to Chapter 4 on contractual performance of the book on contracts, enables the parties, if the contract was not clear enough, to *supplement* it with additional information to the effect of clarifying its performance. Moreover, if the parties are unable to agree, Art. 510 directs them to *interpret* the contract[464] or to follow *trade practice*. 811

If resorting to Art. 510 fails anyway, the creditor may request the debtor to compensate for the damage. Such compensation may take the form of any *remedy* that Art. 582, which complements the remedies already enumerated under the general regime of civil liability (Art. 179§1; s. above §322; s. also §710) non-exhaustively lists as repairing, remaking, replacing, returning the goods, reducing the price or remuneration, etc. However, Art. 582, in the spirit of settlement generally favored by Chinese law, urges the creditor, as it claims compensation, to be "reasonable". 812

---

[462] Art. 584 of the Chinese Civil Code uses the word 损失 sǔnshī, which translates as "loss" for expressing damage, without clearly distinguishing between *damnum emergens* and *lucrum cessans*. However, the same provision expressly refers to loss of profit (4th phrase, where "loss" is circumstantially expressed and "profit" is expressed by 利益 lìyì), entitling the creditor to claim it in addition to any "loss". Therefore, one may deduct that Art. 584 provides both for effective damage and for loss of profit. "Loss of profit" is not mentioned as such in the Code. It is generally expressed, namely, in related judicial interpretations, as 预期利益损失 yùqī lìyì sǔnshī, literally meaning "loss of expected benefits" or "foreseeable acquirable benefit loss."

[463] This test compares to the "principe de la confiance" or principle of reliance used in Swiss law for interpreting the parties' intent when the contract is unclear (s. above §228).

[464] On contractual interpretation, s. above Chap. 4 §23.II, Contractual Interpretation.

813 If the remediation urged by Art. 582 fails, Art. 583 entitles the creditor to claim *compensation* from the debtor (Art. 583; s. above §799) which, in practice, takes most of the time the form of economic compensation, i.e., the payment of a monetary indemnity from the debtor to the creditor.

814 Inasmuch, Art. 582 (incomplete or substandard performance), 583 and 584 (nonperformance) are subject to the same general requirement of reasonableness or *temperance*. In practice, it means that the creditor will often (be pressed by the tribunal, if it has been seized, to) bear part of the damage to the effect of favoring a settlement[465].

815 Damage compensation and alternative remedies are extensively discussed further down in this book about liability for illicit acts (s. below Chap. 8 §58, Damage Compensation). Unlike Swiss law, which expressly permits the analogic application of the regime of liability for illicit acts to liability for breach of contract (CO Art. 99§3), the Chinese Civil Code is silent about it. However, given the flexible approach of the Chinese legislator to remedies in case of contractual breach (s., namely, Art. 510, 577, 582 and 584), we believe that a Chinese court would consider such analogic application *mutatis mutandis*, provided it is reasonably motivated.

816 The specific case of compensation for damage resulting from unilateral alterations or the termination of contracts by a *State* to the detriment of a *foreign investor* is discussed further down in this book with the liability for illicit acts (s. §1664).

III. Performance Guarantees

817 The regime of contractual liability provides for two types of performance guarantees: liquidated damages (Art. 585) and deposit (as performance guarantee; Art. 586 and 587), while Art. 588 addresses their relationship. Both are developed below.

A. Liquidated Damages

818 Art. 585 provides for *liquidated damages*. It is a particular case of Art 176, which provides that civil liability can also be agreed between the parties concerned (s. above §320). The notion of liquidated damages calls for disambiguation, however.

---

[465] S. above note 417.

Liquidated damages are a conventional compensation by which the parties mutually agree on the compensation that the party which breaches the contract shall pay to the other[466]. They may be pre-agreed (in the contract), or agreed upon after the breach, although the expression generally refers to pre-agreed damages[467]. 819

"Liquidated damages" is the translation frequently provided for 违约金 wéiyuē jīn, namely, as used in Art. 179§1 (item 9), which lists the remedies available under the general regime of civil liability contained in the First Book of the Code (s. above §322). This is incorrect: 违约金 wéiyuē jīn actually translates literally as "breach of contract money" and is the expression used for (monetary) compensation for breach of contract, as provided by Art. 179§1, item 9. "Liquidated damages" is actually expressed by 约定的违约金 *yuēdìng de* wéiyuē jīn, literally "agreed" compensation, as mentioned at Art. 585§2, and implied in Art. 585§1, both of which provide that the parties may agree on the compensation in case of breach of contract. 820

The parties may agree either on a compensation *amount* or on a *method* for calculating such amount (Art. 585§1). However, when such amount is lower or higher[468] than the actual damage economic value, either party may apply at court (or before an arbitration tribunal, provided such forum is available) for increasing[469] or decreasing[470] it (Art. 585§2). As a result, while liquidated 821

---

466 Swiss law makes further clear that the creditor may only claim either performance, or liquidated damages (CO Art. 160§1), thus suggesting that it is precluded to claim other remedies. However, it may claim both in case of *untimely* or *delocated* performance (CO Art. 160§2; s. below note 471).

467 Even though certain translations of Art. 585 use "*pre*-agreed" before "compensation", thus suggesting that liquidated damages should have been agreed upon before the infringement, such translation is deceiving: literally, Art. 585 only refers to "agreed" compensation, which leaves both options, before or after the infringement, available.

468 In Swiss law, in case of nonperformance (or imperfect performance) liquidated damages are owed not only if the actual damage economic value is lower than the liquidated damages amount, but even if the creditor did not suffer any damage (CO 161§1), which is a major departure as compared to Chinese law. However, s. above note 470.

469 In Swiss law, the creditor may claim compensation for damage *exceeding* the liquidated damages provided it proves the debtor was at *fault* (CO Art. 161§2): in other words, under the Swiss regime of liquidated damages, this provision reintroduces the condition of fault into contractual liability.

470 In Swiss law, like in Chinese law, although the parties are free to set the liquidated damages amount (CO Art. 163§1), the judge must reduce *excessive* liquidated damages (CO 163§3). However, Swiss law further makes clear, in the liquidated damages regime, that liquidated damages may not be claimed when relating to *illicit* or immoral obligations (CO Art. 163§2; the Chinese Civil Code generally provides so at Art. 143, s. above §239). Moreover, subject to the parties' pre-agreement, liquidated damages may not be claimed either in case of *objective impossibility*.

damages facilitate the settlement of contractual breaches, they are only *relatively binding*.

822 In case liquidated damages have been agreed and paid for *delayed performance*, the party in breach is not freed from its obligation to perform after having paid the liquidated damages and must, therefore, still perform (Art. 585§3), even though such performance would be, by definition, untimely completed. In other words, liquidated damages for belated performance are not a substitute for performance[471].

823 Liquidated damages can also provide for *interest*, within certain limits however (s. below note 591).

824 Liquidated damages are not to be confused with *punitive damages* whose principle is admitted by Art. 179§2 (s. above §323).

825 Although the comparison is subject to further qualification, liquidated damages can be related, in Swiss law, to the so-called *penal clause* (CO Art. 160-163; Fr. "clause pénale"; Ger. "Konventionalstrafe"), whose regime applies both to liquidated damages[472] and to punitive damages[473].

B. *Deposit*

826 The Code further provides that the parties may agree that the debtor will remit a *deposit* to the creditor as a guarantee of the former's performance (Art. 586 and 587). As mentioned above, in English, "deposit" may actually point at three different institutions of the Chinese Civil Code (s. above §781). Art. 586 and 587, which designate such deposit as 定金 dìngjīn, are concerned with deposit as a form of *guarantee* for performance.

827 These provisions provide for several safeguards. Even though Art. 586§1 is not entirely clear, the use of the mandatory form, 由 yóu, suggests that the deposit must be agreed in writing[474]. Arguably, such agreement may take the form of a *contract of deposit* (Art. 888 ff.; s. belowChap. 5 §42, Deposit) as *lex generalis* which, as mentioned, however eponymous, is a distinct institution, and

---

471 Swiss law provides for the same solution but extends it from untimely to *delocalized* performance (CO Art. 160§2). Moreover, in both cases, the debtor has the right to prove that the payment of liquidated damages did free it from performing (CO Art. 160§3).

472 S. above notes 466 and 468 to 471.

473 S. above note 207.

474 On the requirement of the written form, s. WEI WEN, Formality, Freedom of Contract and China's New Civil Code: A Legal Reform Recommendation for Land Sale Contracts, [2022] U. PA. ASIAN L. REV. 332.

to which Art. 586 and 587 may relate as *lex specialis*. Art. 586§1 also mandates the time at which the deposit contract must be made, which is when the deposit is effectively remitted.

The deposit is limited by law to a maximum of 20% of the value of the underlying contract's performance (Art. 586§2). If the actual deposit is more or less than the agreed amount, the deposit contract shall be deemed to have been modified accordingly (*ibid.*) One may assume that this is subject to the general 20% maximum, however. 828

In order to understand the deposit regime, it is important to note that, while the deposit is made by one party to the other, the parties to the underlying contract can be *mutually* obliged towards each other, both being simultaneously debtor and creditor of the other (synallagmatic contract). In other words, the depositor is not necessarily the only debtor in the depositor-recipient (of the deposit) relationship; the recipient, its creditor, may also be its debtor at the same time. Therefore, Art. 587 provides that, once the depositor has performed, the deposit shall be either deducted from the price or refunded. If the depositor fails to perform, however, it shall be deprived of the right to be refunded. Conversely, if the recipient fails to perform towards the depositor in a case where the recipient is also the depositor's debtor, then the latter is entitled to claim the former to pay *double* the deposit. 829

However, both liability cases are subject to both parties' nonperformance resulting in an *impossibility*[475] to perform the underlying contract. Although Art. 587 does not specify it, we understand that this provision refers to *objective* impossibility. Therefore, the regime of Art. 587 implies that, as long as the impossibility is *subjective*, the creditor (whether the depositor or the recipient, as the case may be) ought to rely on the remedies provided by Art. 577 ff. (s. above §812) in case of nonperformance or incomplete performance, and that it should not be entitled to offsetting the deposit or claiming double-payment unless the underlying contract's performance has become objectively impossible. 830

Swiss law provides for similar although not identical solutions with *earnest money* (CO Art. 158§1 and 2; Fr.: "arrhes"; Ger.: "Haftgeld") and *forfeit money* (CO Art. 158§3; Fr.: "dédit"; Ger.: "Reugeld"). In both cases, one party remits the other an agreed amount of money which the recipient may keep in case of nonperformance[476]. While they are close, the differences between both institutions is that earnest money is intended as a goodwill gesture to affirm the 831

---

475 About impossibility, s. above §§802ff.

476 If so, both amount to liquidated damages (ATF 133 III 43 = JT 2007 I 226).

debtor's intent to *perform*[477], while forfeit money is intended to give the right to *either party* to *withdraw* from the underlying contract[478].

832 Under the regime of the Chinese Civil Code, if the parties have agreed *both* on liquidated damages and a deposit, the non-breaching party may choose either (Art. 588§1). If the deposit is insufficient, the receiver party may still claim compensation for the excess damage to the depositor (Art. 588§2).

IV. Mitigation and Exoneration

833 The last provisions of the chapter (Art. 589 to 594) provide for various *mitigating or exonerating circumstances*. Thus, the creditor's *refusal* to accept the debtor's performance results in a *reversal of contractual liability* by which the creditor becomes liable of any damage its refusal may cause to the original debtor (Art. 589§1)[479]. Moreover, as long as the creditor delays the acceptance of the debtor's performance, the latter has no obligation to pay interest (Art. 589§2)[480].

834 *Force majeure* (Art. 590§1), which is a case of objective subsequent impossibility[481] qualifying as a mitigating or exonerating circumstance, is already foreseen as a mitigating or exonerating circumstance in the general regime of civil liability (Art. 180; s. above §§326 and 327)[482]. In the ambit of liability for breach of contract, Art. 590§2 requests, in addition, the party which prevails itself from force majeure to *notify* the other party and to do so *timely* to the effect of mitigating the damage. In addition, the former party must provide the

---

477 In case of earnest money, if the debtor fails to perform, the creditor has the right to keep the earnest money; while if the debtor performs, the parties may agree, but do not have, to deduct the earnest money from the price. Absent such agreement, Swiss law deems that earnest money does not amount to an advance payment (CO Art. 158§2). Furthermore, in case of doubt about whether the parties have agreed earnest or forfeit money, the law deems that they have agreed on the former (CO 158§1).

478 In case of forfeit money, if the remitter withdraws, the recipient has the right to keep the forfeit money; whereas if the recipient withdraws, it must pay *double* the money to the remitter: the latter solution is, to that extent, comparable to Art. 587 of the Chinese Civil Code (s. above §829).

479 The refusal of the creditor to accept the debtor's performance also entitles the latter to deposit (Art. 570§1, item 1 and s. above §784).

480 The same applies in Swiss law, under certain conditions, s. CO Art. 91 *in fine* and 104§1. In case of solidarity between creditors while one of them is late, this provision applies to all (Art. 521§2 and s. above §639 *in fine*).

481 About impossibility, s. above §§802ff.

482 Force majeure is also a cause of contractual termination (Art. 563§1, item 1 , s. above §724).

latter with *evidence* of the force majeure: it must also do so timely. Force majeure *subsequent* to the nonperformance or delayed performance does not exonerate the debtor (Art. 590§3)[483].

Foreign investors may like to pay attention to the fact that force majeure is frequently, not to say in most cases, either abusively invoked for failure to comply with the requirements outlined above or inappropriately referred to in contracts. Typically, because, in practice, contractual parties, as they draft their purported contract, often use templates in English, which most of the time relate to common law, under which it is, unlike in civil law jurisdictions, usual, if not required, to define contractual terms, those contracts contain definitions which differ from the applicable law chosen by the parties, although that chosen law, most of the time, like Chinese law, already contains a mandatory definition of force majeure, whose invocation is subject to strict conditions. 835

As a consequence, in the best case, interpretation and conflict of laws issues may arise, while in the worst, the parties may conceive wrong expectations about their related rights and obligations, with potentially costly consequences. As far as Chinese law is concerned, a mere reference, in the contract, to Art. 590 of the Chinese Civil Code, should not only suffice, but is recommended to the effect of avoiding any discrepancy between the intended (but potentially inapplicable) contractual regime and the mandatory legal regime applying to liability for breach of contract.

The Code further mandates a *duty of mitigation*[484] by which *both parties* must not only take *remedial*, but also *preventive* mitigating measures to the effect of preventing the occurrence or the aggravation of the damage. In case of aggravation for lack of such measures, the responsible party is deprived of the right to claim compensation for the aggravated portion of the damage (Art. 591§1 *in fine*). The Code does not specify which the responsible party should be: one may assume that it is a matter of circumstances, to appreciate on a case-by-case basis. Likewise, under Art. 591§2, the "reasonable" costs of such measures are to be borne by the responsible party. 836

If *both parties* are in breach, they are *mutually liable* towards each other and shall bear respective liability (Art. 592§1)[485]. This situation reflects the basic principle posed by the general regime of civil liability for joint and several liability (s. above §329). 837

483 About the *clausula rebus sic stantibus*, s. above §672.
484 About the duty of mitigation in case of liability for *illicit acts*, s. below §1651.
485 The same solution applies in case of liability for illicit acts (s. Art. 1173 and below §1651).

838 The next subsection contemplates a slightly different situation, which is that one party is in breach and caused damage to the other, but the latter, while not being contractually in breach, is at *fault* for the occurrence of the damage anyway (*ibid.*, § 2). In other words, the situation this provision addresses is one where the contractual liability of one party meets the liability for *illicit act* of its contractual counterpart. If so, the liability of the author may be reduced (Art. 592§2).

839 If either party is in breach because of a *third party*, the breaching party shall be liable towards its non-breaching contractual counterpart under the regime of liability for breach of contract, but the third-party shall be liable towards the breaching party under the regime of liability for illicit acts (Art. 593).

840 *Liability exemption clauses* in case of physical injury or intentional or grossly negligent damage to property are deemed to be invalid (Art. 506; s. above §610).

V. Comparative Law

841 Certain features of the Swiss law regime of liability for breach of contract (CO Art. 97 ff.) compare to the Chinese one, but both regimes also differ in some important respects.

842 The foundation of liability for breach of contract is enunciated by CO Art. 97§1; certain related features of the Chinese and the Swiss regimes have been compared above (s. above Chap. 4 §26.VII, Deferred Termination: Comparative Law). However, the remedies made available by Swiss law to the creditor and the mechanism operating them are quite different.

843 As noted, like in China (Art. 577 of the Chinese Civil Code), under Swiss law (CO Art. 97§1), the breaching party is liable for the damage it caused to the other, unless it proves that it was not at fault[486].

844 That said, the main difference between the Chinese and the Swiss regimes is structural: while the Chinese Civil Code deals with the termination of the contract pursuant to nonperformance in Chapter 7, which is dedicated to contractual performance, not in Chapter 8 on liability for breach of contract, whereas the Swiss Code of Obligations addresses it together with liability for breach of

486 The Swiss Code of Obligations is more detailed than the Chinese Civil Code insofar as it adds that, if the infringed contractual obligation is an *obligation not to do*, then the debtor is liable by the mere fact of not having done so (CO Art. 98§2). In other words, this provision alleviates the burden of proving causality by not reversing it as per the ordinary rules of proof.

contract in Chapter 2 on the effects of nonperformance of the Second Book on the effects of obligations.

As a matter of fact, in the regime of liability for breach of contract, the Chinese Civil Code does briefly address termination in case of nonperformance at Art. 580§2, as noted above (s. §§729 and 731), but falls short from addressing the modalities of such termination, which are detailed in Chapter 7 on termination of the book on contract law. Incomplete (or substandard) performance is further considered at Art. 582, 1st sentence (s. above §799), but the Code fails entirely to address termination in case the remedies it prescribes fail. Again, the solution is to be found in Chapter 7. 845

In contrast, the chapter of the Swiss Code of Obligations dedicated to nonperformance (Chapter 2, effects of nonperformance, Second Book, effects of obligations; Art. 97 ff.) is divided in two parts: the first one (CO Art. 97 to 101) governs the debtor's liability in case of nonperformance, while the second (Art. 102 to 109) regulates termination as a consequence of incomplete, substandard or late (which Swiss law qualifies as "imperfect" or "incorrect"[487]) performance. As such, the second part puts much emphasis in favoring performance, while regulating termination in case nonperformance eventually persists. 846

In particular, the Swiss lawyer may be surprised to find that, in the Chinese Civil Code, Chapter 8 of the book on contracts makes no mention of the nonperformance *notice* from the creditor to the debtor, while the Swiss regime of liability for breach of contract puts much emphasis on it (CO Art. 102 to 106; Fr.: "demeure du débiteur"; Ger.: "Verzug des Schuldners"). Again, Chinese contract law addresses the notice in Chapter 7 on termination of the book on contracts of the Chinese Civil Code, not in Chapter 8. 847

That explains why we have addressed termination in Chinese contract law in our commentary of Chapter 7 (s. above Chap. 4 §26.VII, Deferred Termination: Comparative Law) to which we refer to reader, and in which we have elaborated the comparison between the Chinese and the Swiss regimes in this respect, among other things. 848

Finally, it is noteworthy that the contractual liability regime of the Chinese Civil Code does not explicitly provide for *interest*, although the general regime of civil liability indisputably, however implicitly, acknowledges it. Interest is discussed at the end of the chapter on damage compensation following that on liability for illicit acts (s. below §1673). 849

---

487 S. above note 453.

Chap. 5 Special Contracts

§28. Introduction

Traditionally, special (A.K.A. typical- or nominate-) contracts may be classified into categories, the main of which include sale, lease, labor, services (both best effort- and result-based), guarantees, partnerships, transportation, and other contracts not falling into any of these categories. Although Title Two of the Third Book on contract law of the Chinese Civil Code is dedicated to so-called typical (or nominal) contracts governs most of them, there are notable exceptions. 850

Thus, unless it was set aside, the *international sale of movables* is governed by the Vienna Convention, while the sale of *immovables* is primarily governed by the Second Book on property of the Code. 851

The *lease* of both movables and immovables takes the form of a typical contract, to the exception, however, of that of the land which, in China, takes the form of a usufruct known as *land use rights*, which are also addressed in the Second Book of the Code on property. 852

The contract of *employment* is governed by the Labor Contract Law, its Interpretations by the SPC, the Labor Law and other secondary laws. 853

Guarantees, depending on their form, may be governed either in Chapter 4 on contractual performance of Title Two on general rules of the Third Book on contract law of the Code; as far as immovables are concerned, by Title Two on security in property of the Second Book on property; or by the regime applying to certain typical contracts. 854

Partnership is governed both by the Code as a typical contract, and by the Law on the Partnership Enterprise as a corporate entity. JVs are not, as such, a form of corporate entity anymore, but a form of contractual partnership between other corporate entities; they are not governed by the former laws on JVs, which have been repelled, anymore, but by the two partnership regimes aforementioned. So are special forms of corporate structures, such as variable interest entities (VIEs). 855

Ancillary contractual institutions such as representation or *agency* are governed by a mix of provisions to be found in the general provisions on legal persons; in the agency regime contained in the First Book of the Code; in the general provisions of contract law; in the mandate, which is a typical contract, in the Third; in the Company Law; and in the various regimes of certain typical contracts. 856

857 This enumeration is not exhaustive, however, other contracts, which we may not address in this book, may be governed by other legal basis[488]. This chapter focuses on selected typical contracts contained in Title Two of the Third Book of the Code; as far as the sale is concerned, it also addresses the Vienna Convention; and includes the labor contract. The typical contracts covered in this chapter have been selected for their relevance for foreign investors; some have been left aside[489]. Those contracts, quasi-contracts[490] or contractual institutions which have been mentioned in the preceding paragraph but are not covered in this chapter (notably, although not only, the contract of employment) have been outlined in other chapters of this book: we refer the reader to the table of contents or the index to that effect.

858 Although there is no preset order, we have chosen not to follow the order in which the law addresses typical contracts; instead, we are addressing some of them on the beginning of the chapter because of their prominence in business; this order is entirely subjective. Thus, this chapter will start with the sale, followed by contracts of mandate including the mandate in general, brokerage and intermediation; financial contracts including the loan, suretyship, the lease, financial leasing and factoring; contracts of works including works in general and construction; technology contracts; partnership; and other contracts including the deposit, warehousing, and transportation. Since it is not included in the Chinese Civil Code, the labor contract will be treated last.

859 Title Two on typical contracts of the Third Book of the Code on contract law is followed by a Title Three on *negotiorum gestio* (Art. 979 ff.) and unjust enrichment (Art. 985 ff.) which are not typical contracts but *quasi-contracts*; we will address them further down in this book (s. below Chap. 7 , Quasi-contracts).

860 Not all contracts are typical. Contracts not being considered as typical and not being governed by a specific legal regime, whether contained in the Chinese Civil Code or other laws, are known as *sui generis*, of their own kind. Many of them result from the combination, sometimes complex, of typical contracts among themselves, or of typical- together with other *sui generis* contractual features, thus forming a *sui generis* contract[491]. However not typical, such

488 For example, *commercial franchises* agreements are governed by the Regulation on the Administration of Commercial Franchises.

489 Although their existence may be briefly mentioned elsewhere in this book, we will not cover the contracts for the supply and consumption of electricity, water, gas and heat (Art. 648 ff.); the donation (A.K.A. contract of gift; Art. 657 ff.); and for property services (Art. 937 ff.; s. below note 565).

490 On the notion of quasi-contract, s. below note 733.

491 S., for example, VIEs (s. below Chap. 9 §68, Variable Interests Entities).

contracts are acknowledged by Chinese law, and subject to the same general, if not special, rules.

Finally, we should like to recall that, even though this chapter is not primarily concerned with liability, while certain typical contracts may contain their own special contractual *liability* regime, those regimes are to be regarded as *leges speciales* as they complement the general contractual liability regime (s. above Chap. 4 §27, Liability for Breach of Contract) which is the *lex generalis* and to which one ought to refer for any liability matter not addressed in the typical contract regimes. 861

The same is true whenever a typical contract regime is silent about any matter of contract law governed by Title One on *general rules* of contract law including the conclusion, validity, performance, preservation, modification, transfer and termination of any typical, and any contract, even if not typical, indeed, as well as the so-called general provisions forming its first chapter (s. above Chap. 4 , General Provisions of Contract). 862

§29. Sale

I. Introduction

Under Chinese law, the contract of sale, actually named contract of purchase and sale (买卖合同 mǎimài hétóng) forms Chapter 8 (Art. 595 to 647) of the Third Book on contract law of the Chinese Civil Code. Although we will divide this chapter into thematic sections, Chapter 8 does not contain any. 863

This chapter of the book does not ambition to offer a comprehensive commentary of the contract of sale, which is a vast topic already abundantly addressed by specialized literature, but to highlight prominent features which are often misunderstood by the parties, namely, foreign buyers or sellers subject to Chinese law, sometimes with costly consequences. Nor, while it will highlight selected contrasts between Chinese law, the CISG and Swiss law because of their particular significance for foreign traders with China, will it systematically compare those three regimes: the reader is invited to consult scholarly commentaries for a comprehensive outlook. 864

The *definition* given by the law of the sale contract is that of the transfer, by the seller, of its property right to the buyer against a price paid by the latter to the former (Art. 595). Its regime applies indifferently to the sale of *movables* and *immovables*[492]. This chapter will focus on the sale of movables however, 865

[492] On the application of the CISG to immovables, s. below §893.

while signaling noteworthy differences. Likewise, they may be *material* or *immaterial*, such as, notably, for the latter, IPR[493]. In all cases however, property transfer relies primarily on the law of property and, more generally, *real rights*, both of which are governed by the Second Book of the Code (Art. 205 ff.) which we extensively commented above and to which we refer the reader (s. above Chap. 3 , Real Rights). Secondary legislation may also apply to certain types of goods, such as immovables or IPR.

866 The regime of the contract of sale contained in the Chinese Civil Code is primarily intended to commercial sales, not to *consumer sales*. Although the regime of the Code applies to consumers too[494], it is complemented by the Law on the Protection of Consumer Rights and Interests which protects them in the first place[495]. Consumer sales are not addressed in this book.

867 As far as *immovables* are concerned, one should recall at this stage, however, that, in China, the land exclusively belongs to the State and that it cannot, therefore, be sold (s. above Chap. 3 §16.II, State-, Collective- and Private Property); only constructions can, while the use of the land is to be granted in the form of *usufruct* or *land use rights* (s. above Chap. 3 §17, Usufruct), not sale. Moreover, the transfer of an immovable property is subject to stringent *formal requirements* (typically consisting in the registration of the property rights on the land register; s. above §382), while the validity of a contract purporting at the sale of a movable is not even subject to the written form (s. above §§383 and 437). Both such formal requirements and the usufruct are equally governed by real rights; they will not be elaborated in this chapter.

868 If a property right is not transferred against a price or another form of consideration but for free, it does not qualify as a sale but as a *donation*, known as a contract for gift (赠与合同 zèngyǔ hétóng), which also amounts to a contract, but is governed its own regime at Art. 657 ff. of the Chinese Civil Code.

869 *Special forms of sales* including sales in batches, by samples, by trial and by tender are briefly mentioned at the end of this chapter (s. below Chap. 5 §29.VII.B, Other Provisions).

870 The contract of sale has an immense importance in practice, not least in China, which has become the world's supplier of manufactured goods. It is no coincidence that it is the first contract mentioned in Title Two on typical contracts. Its main features generally compare with those of other civil law jurisdictions.

---

493 S. below note 514.

494 Unlike the CISG, which expressly excludes consumer sales (s. below note 509).

495 There is no such law in Swiss law. Consumer sales are governed by the ordinary regime of the contract of sale contained in the Swiss Civil Code (Art. 184 ff.) On consumer *credit*, s. below note 584.

In this chapter, while providing a general overview of the Chinese Civil Code's regime of the sale contract, we will focus on the main issues universally typical of such contract, which are the *passing of the risks* and the *warranty*[496] *for defects*[497] (s. below §873).

871 The contract's *content* is non-exhaustively described by the law as consisting in clauses such as the names, quantity, quality and price of the goods, period of performance, place and method for performance, packaging, inspection standards and methods, dispute resolution, definitions and validity (Art. 596).

872 Its *conclusion* is governed by the general provisions of contract law of the Code. Because of the formidable prevalence of *online sales* nowadays, not only in consumer sales but also in trading, the parties should pay special attention to the regime of *electronic contracts*, which is now well developed in Chinese law and has been extensively outlined above (s. Chap. 2 §10.III, Declarations of Will). In that latter respect, Swiss parties should also be aware that such an advanced regime is still entirely lacking in Swiss law.

873 The economy of a contract of sale almost universally, including in Chinese law, revolves among the following fundamental legal notions: the time, place and form of the *delivery*, which transfers the *possession* of the goods from the seller

---

[496] Although the warranty regime will be outlined below (s. below Chap. 5 §29.VI, Warranty for Defects), in order to anticipate the confusion potentially resulting from the related terminology or "false friends", it is worth to already elaborate somehow at this stage. In common English legal language, *warranty* for defects generally refers to the legal liability of the seller, whereas *guarantee* refers to the additional, contractual assurance the latter may offer the buyer in addition to the seller's legal liability. Chinese law only expressly refers to the latter (quality) guarantee or assurance (Art. 621§1 *in fine*; 质量保证 zhìliàng bǎozhèng; s. below §931). So does the CISG (s. below §935), while both generically refer to the former warranty for defects as the seller's liability for defects (s. below Chap. 5 §29.VI, Warranty for Defects). In contrast, Swiss law expressly refers to the regime of warranty for defects, but French language does not mark any difference between warranty and guarantee: the law refers to "*garantie*" for both notions (cf. CO Art. 205§1 for the warranty and 210§1 *in fine* for the guarantee), whereas German uses "*Gewährleistung*" for warranty (cf. CO Art. 205§1) and "*Haftung*" (cf. CO 210§1 *in fine*) for guarantee, which actually literally translates as liability, not guarantee. It is further to be signaled that "assurance" in French means "insurance", neither assurance nor guarantee. That difference is unambiguous in German, where insurance translates as "Versicherung".

[497] As far as terminology issues are concerned, in the context of the contract of sale, at the risk of restating the obvious, one also ought to pay particular attention not to confuse the notion of *defect*, which relates to the quality of the goods, with that of *default*, which equates to qualified nonperformance. Thus, by delivering defective goods, the seller is in default. However, in Swiss legal French, "*défaut*" exclusively refers to defect, while default translates as "*demeure*" in French and "*Verzug*" in German (cf. CO Art. 102; s. above §§512ff.); defect translates as "*Mängel*" in German.

to the buyer; the *passing of the risks*, which determines the point of time or space ahead of which the seller is legally *liable* for any damage to the goods and beyond which the buyer is (keeping in mind that delivery and passing of the risk, or possession and property, do not necessarily coincide in time or space); the transfer of the *property* of the goods from the seller to the buyer; *defects*, which is the non-conformity with the goods whose sale was agreed between the parties; and *inspection*, which is the time after delivery during which the buyer must inspect the goods and *notify* the seller of any defect in order to be entitled to any compensation. It is important to note that delivery, the passing of the risks and the transfer of property do not necessarily occur at the same time.

874 That said, the sale contract regime can be roughly divided into two main parts: the *seller's obligations*, whose main obligation consist in delivery and indemnifying the buyer in case of defect, and the *buyer's obligations*, whose main obligations consist in paying the price, inspecting the goods and notifying any such defect to the buyer. Typical issues, namely, the *passing of the risks* and the *warranty for defects*, which concern both parties, will be discussed in dedicated sections. Other, secondary issues will be briefly addressed in the last section of this chapter.

875 Before presenting the regime of the contract of sale under Chinese law however, it is important to recall that China is a contracting State to the *United Nations Convention on Contracts for the International Sale of Goods*, which entered into force in China as of 1 January 1988, and supersedes Chinese law unless the parties excluded it. It will be outlined in the next section.

876 Strictly speaking, *free trade agreements* pertain to *customs law*, which this book does not cover (s. above §97), not to the law of the contract of sale. Therefore, we will not address global trade under the rules of the *WTO*. However, considering the comparative outlook of this book, given its relevance for bilateral sales and its prominence for Sino-Swiss trade relations, one is duty bound to mention the *Sino-Swiss FTA*, whose main characteristics we briefly outline here.

877 The Sino-Swiss FTA was signed on 6 July 2013 and entered into force as of 1 July 2014. It is a comprehensive trade deal establishing preferential tariff treatment and cooperation between both countries and, remarkably, the first treaty of its kind China entered with a developed economy. It covers trade in goods and services between China and Switzerland, with a strong focus on the

first, and mainly[498] purports at the immediate elimination of tariffs which had applied so far to a majority of goods, or at their gradual reduction[499].

The FTA comprises 16 chapters with detailed provisions and 11 annexes, including tariff schedules, rules of origin, certificate of origin protocols, textiles labeling, and specific commitments on trade in services. Key chapters cover general principles, customs procedures, trade facilitation, trade remedies, technical barriers to trade, sanitary and phytosanitary measures, and economic cooperation. It also establishes mechanisms for ongoing bilateral dialogue and cooperation committees, including specialized sectoral working groups. Notably, the FTA sets a precedent by addressing *non-tariff barriers* and facilitating mutual market access for goods and services. 878

The FTA, which as noted entered into force on 1 July 2014, was initially concluded for a period of ten years; it has, therefore, theoretically expired on 30 June 2024. However, in practice, the parties keep applying it as if it were still effective, while negotiating not only its extension, but also several significant improvements. It is currently expected to be formally extended or renewed in 2026, although some uncertainties remain[500]. 879

II. The Vienna Convention (CISG)

The purpose of the UN Convention on Contracts for the International Sale of Goods, signed in Vienna in 1980 (CISG; A.K.A. UNCITRAL Convention or Vienna Convention), which resulted from the works of the United Nations Commission on International Trade Law (UNCITRAL), is to provide a modern, uniform and fair regime for contracts for the international sale of goods. 880

The Convention applies, in the first place, *ratione loci*[501], to contracts of sale of goods between parties, i.e., the seller and the buyer, whose places of business are in *different contracting States* (Art. 1§1, Litt. a). This condition is, therefore, double: first, the parties' places of business must be located in different 881

---

[498] Although the FTA mainly applies to the trade of goods and services, it extends beyond trade to investment promotion, IPR protection, environmental standards, labor cooperation, competition policy, disputes settlement, and promotes cooperation in certain areas.

[499] The FTA provides for such reduction of tariffs down to zero on most goods over a period of up to 15 years, depending on the goods considered.

[500] A future extension or renewal of the Sino-Swiss FTA will most likely be subject to parliamentary approval. It will then be subject to an optional referendum, if enough citizens or cantons request it. A mandatory referendum is also possible but less likely, unless the renewal involves constitutional amendments or exceptionally significant changes.

[501] About the Convention's scope *ratione materiae*, s. below §892.

States; second, both of them must be member State to the Convention. The place of business is a fact; whether the contract or else may mention otherwise is indifferent (*ibid.*, § 2). So is the nationality of the parties, or their civil or commercial standing (*ibid.*, § 3).

882 In that respect, it should be noted that China inserted a *reservation* to the Convention to the effect of excluding the application of the provision by which the Convention were also applicable "when the rules of private international law lead to the application of the law of a Contracting State" (Art. 1§1, Litt. b)[502]. This reservation implies that China has ruled out any exception, as may be provided for by the rules of international private law of a foreign jurisdiction, to the requirement that the parties must have their effective places of business in different contracting States.

883 At the time of writing this book, the Convention had been signed by 97 States, including China and Switzerland, and had entered into force in all but two of them. As noted, while it has, in China, entered into force as of 1 January 1988, it has in Switzerland as of 1 March 1991. Among other things, its applicability *ratione loci* depends on the location of the parties' place of business, their *choice of law* or, on the contrary, their omission to choose the applicable law.

884 Although that is often overlooked in practice, it must be stressed that, whenever each party has its place of business in a contracting State, unless they have *expressly* excluded the application of the CISG, which they have the right to (Art. 6, 1st phrase), it shall apply, i.e., it shall *supersede* the choice of a national law, if that choice did not clearly exclude the CISG. In other words, if, for example, a contract between a Chinese and a Swiss party mentions "Chinese law applicable" or "this contract is governed by Swiss law", but falls short from adding "to the exclusion of the CISG" or any other unambiguous, similar expression, absent any other clear indication that the parties intended to exclude the CISG, the latter, i.e., neither Chinese, nor Swiss law, as the case may be, shall apply, subject to the following reservations.

885 If one party has its place of business in China and the other in another member-State of the CISG, the latter applies even if the parties have elected *another* national law, i.e., other than that of either party (e.g., in the case of a Chinese and a Swiss party, French law); so does it even if that law's country is *not* a member of the CISG (e.g., in the same example, English law[503]). Finally, the same applies if the parties have *omitted* to specify the applicable law.

---

502 https://uncitral.un.org/en/texts/salegoods/conventions/sale_of_goods/cisg/status, note b.

503 Unlike France, the U.K. have not signed the CISG. Other notable non-signatories include India and South Africa. The U.S. have made reservations which the parties are advised to carefully consider, as the case may be. Finally, unlike Hong Kong, whose

If, in contrast, the counterparty of the party having its place of business in China has its own place of business in a country which has *not* signed[504] the CISG, the latter shall not apply, *even if* the parties have chosen the law of a country which *is* a CISG member-State, since China made a reservation excluding that possibility (s. above §882). The same applies if the parties have omitted to choose the applicable law, but *international private law* points at the law of a signatory country. 886

Finally, in the latter case, i.e., even if the counterparty to the party having its place of business in China has its place of business in a country which has not signed the CISG, from a Chinese perspective[505], the CISG will apply nevertheless if those parties have expressly *elected* the CISG as the law applicable to their contract, since Chinese law acknowledges the *freedom of choice* of the applicable law[506]. 887

That said, the CISG Advisory Council and prominent commentators agree that, while an explicit *exclusion* (s. above §884) is best, a clear, demonstrable intent, however by implication, to exclude, derogate to or vary from the CISG suffices; consequently, the omission of an express reference to the CISG does not, by itself, prevent such derogation, variation or exclusion, which may be *implied*: clear, mutual intent, express or implied, may be sufficient[507]. 888

It should be added, however, that, in practice, the parties not infrequently ignore, deliberately or not, the foregoing and apply either Chinese law, the law 889

member-State status is clear, the applicability of the CISG whenever the SAR Macao is involved remains uncertain; again, caution is advised about the latter.

504 Or where the CISG has not yet been ratified and has, therefore, not yet entered into force, as in the case of Ghana and Venezuela.

505 While this statement is made from the point of view of Chinese civil and international private law, freedom of choice of the applicable law is overwhelmingly, if not universally, acknowledged nowadays. However, other grounds may oppose the application of the CISG, such as its inapplicability *ratione materiae* (s. below §§892 to 894).

506 S. above notes 335 and 336.

507 CISG Advisory Council, Opinion No. 16, Exclusion of the CISG under Article 6, 30 May 2014. Such intent is to be interpreted under Art. 8 of the Convention, which provides that statements made by, and other conduct of a party are to be interpreted according to its intent where the other party knew or could not have been unaware what that intent was or, if such interpretation fails, according to the understanding that a reasonable person of the same kind as the other party would have had in the same circumstances. These guidelines compare to the *principe de la confiance* used in Swiss law and to similar principles used in Chinese law (s. above §228). That liberal approach has been criticized however: s., for example, MADILYNN O'HARA, Exclusion on Whose Terms?: The Harm of Upholding Implied Exclusions Under Article 6 of the Convention on the International Sale of Goods, The Michigan Journal of International Law, February 2025.

of the non-Chinese party, or any other law they may have chosen, even though they have not expressly excluded the CISG. That may only stand as long as the parties agree, however; in case of dispute, any court or arbitration tribunal, whether Chinese or not, may apply the CISG anyway.

890 Since most if not all[508] developed countries are member-States, it means that, unless the parties have, expressly or implicitly but unambiguously, excluded the Convention, it will almost systematically apply to contracts of sale between a Chinese and a foreign party, such as a Swiss party.

891 When it applies, the application of the CISG is limited to its scope, however. Beyond it, the national chosen law, if any, or the national law to which the rules of private international law lead, take over. The *scope* of the Convention governs the formation of the contract of sale and the rights and obligations of the seller and the buyer arising from such a contract (Art. 4, 1st sentence).

892 In contrast, subject to limited exceptions which exceed the scope of this book, the Convention does *not* apply *ratione materiae* to: the sale of certain goods including: goods for personal use, etc.[509]; sold by auction; resulting from enforcement; of financial instruments; of ships; and of electricity (Art. 2); goods manufactured with material supplied by the buyer (Art. 3§1); the provision of labor or services (*ibid.*, § 2); the validity of the contract of sale; that of any of its provisions; any related usage; the effect which the contract may have on the property in the goods sold (Art. 4, 2nd sentence); and the seller's liability for personal injury or death by the goods (Art. 5).

893 Moreover, it is worth noting that, although the Convention does not mention it while the ensuing Explanatory Notes (s. below §897) remain silent about it, authoritative commentators[510] consider that the CISG does not apply to *immovables* either, i.e., that "goods" are to be understood as movables.

894 Last but not least, the Convention enables the parties to exclude it altogether, as mentioned above (s. §884), but also to *derogate*[511] from its provisions or

---

508 S. above note 503.

509 The Convention only applies to trading, i.e., commercial sales, not to *consumer sales* (Art. 2§1). Besides, the Swiss Federal Law on Private International Law (LDIP) expressly excludes the application of the CISG to consumer sales (LDIP Art. 118§2 and 120), while LDIP Art. 120 expressly regulates the law applicable to consumer sales. S. also above note 495.

510 S., for example, INGEBORG SCHWENZER/ULRICH G. SCHLECHTRIEM, Commentary on the UN Convention on the International Sale of Goods (CISG), 5th ed., Oxford University Press, Oxford 2022., *ad* Art. 2.

511 The Convention contains a complicated set of provisions (Art. 12 and 96) permitting the contracting States to subject the validity of contracts of sale to the *written form*. To do so, they must issue a formal declaration. It suffices that one of the two States where

vary from them (Art. 6); like exclusion, derogations or variations must be explicit or implicit, but clear nevertheless (s. above §888; s. also note 507). Moreover, as also noted, certain member-States, including China, have made reservations (s. above §882).

The CISG is by no means inferior to Chinese law governing the contract of sale; it is comparable in many respects and more elaborate in some, but also more limited in scope. However, the parties to a sale contract should keep in mind that the CISG is primarily intended, and designed indeed, for the international trade of large amounts of goods transported by sea, road or air. It may prove unnecessarily complex, or even outright inadequate, for small or isolated transactions. Moreover, some features, including some implying significant legal consequences, differ from one system to another. 895

Therefore, in order to avoid to unintentionally find themselves grappling with the intricacies of the CISG, parties to a contract of sale with China would be well advised to carefully consider its application to their transaction and to draft an explicit *applicable law clause* to the effect of unambiguously provide either for its application or its exclusion; in the latter case, for the applicable national law; in case of derogation or variation, for a clear reference to the provisions of the Convention the parties intend to derogate to or vary from, and for explicit contractual provisions replacing them; and in any case, for their choice of national law for matters excluded from the scope of the Convention (s. above §892). 896

Because this book focuses on Chinese law, we will not extensively comment the CISG, which has been amply commented in specialized literature anyway, to which we refer the reader[512]. Notably, UNCITRAL makes available numerous *resources*, including the *Explanatory Notes* of its Secretariat immediately following the text of the Convention proper, and other publications[513]. Nor will 897

---

the contractual parties have their place of business has made such a declaration. If so, the contractual parties may *not* derogate, i.e., they may not agree that a form other than the written form is valid.

512 S., for example, SCHWENZER/SCHLECHTRIEM (s. above note 510).

513 Among other things, the CISG is complemented by the *Convention on the Limitation Period in the International Sale of Goods* dealing with a complex and critical area of sales law, which is subject to significantly different treatment in the various legal systems. In 2020, UNCITRAL approved the publication of a *Legal Guide to Uniform Instruments in the Area of International Commercial Contracts* (with a focus on sales) jointly prepared with the Hague Conference on Private International Law and with UNIDROIT, which provides an overview of uniform contract law texts and illustrates their relationship. These resources are available on UNCITRAL's website, https://uncitral.un.org.

we systematically compare it to the Chinese law regime of the contract of law. We will, however, selectively highlight significant differences.

III. Seller's Obligations

898 The seller's obligations mainly consist in *transferring the property* of the sold asset, and *delivering* it to the buyer. While these two notions may coincide in time or in place (or both), they must not and may not. Both are developed below.

A. Transfer of Property

899 The *seller's obligations*, i.e., which as mentioned focus on the delivery and property transfer of the goods, are mainly governed by Art. 597 ff., specifically Art. 598[514]. However, this provision focuses on the seller's obligation: it only states that the seller has the obligation of *delivering* the goods and *transferring* their property right; it falls short from stating the cause or conditions enabling the legal transfer of such right. Indeed, that fundamental tenet is not contained in the law of the contract of sale, but in *property law*, i.e., at the end of the first chapter on general provisions and the beginning of the second chapter on the creation, alteration, transfer and extinction of property rights of the Second Book on real rights of the Chinese Civil Code. Thus, it is Art. 208, 2nd sentence that states that the (creation and) transfer of the property of *movables* occurs with the *delivery* (s. above §§384 and 385). In contrast, the first sentence of the same article (Art. 208, 1st sentence) states that the (creation, alteration, extinction and) transfer of the property of *immovables* shall be registered, and that such (creation, alteration, extinction and) transfer shall only become valid upon *registration* (Art. 209§1; s. above §378).

900 *Swiss law* provides for equivalent solutions, both for movables (CC Art. 741§1) and immovables (CC Art. 656). The method of transfer of the property of movables results from Roman law, where it is known as *traditio*. It is further important to note that the *Vienna Convention* (CISG), if applicable (s. above Chap. 5 §29.II, The Vienna Convention (CISG)), expressly leaves this matter to the applicable national law (CISG Art. 4, Litt. b): indeed, the CISG does not deal with the transfer of property rights. Nor does it with immovables (s. above §893). In case of international transaction, if the parties disagree on the

[514] Whenever IPR are attached to the goods sold, they will only be sold together with such goods if the parties expressly agreed to or if the law provides for it (Art. 600).

applicable law, it is determined by the private international law of the law on conflicts of laws of the jurisdiction where the court or arbitration tribunal before which the dispute has been filed sits.

As far as *immovables* are concerned, the outcome is relatively straightforward, 901
since there is an universal consensus that the law applicable to the transfer of property is that of the immovable's location (Lat.: *locus rei sitae*)[515], although certain aspects of the transaction which may escape the scope of property law or real rights may conceivably be governed by another national law[516] (for example, the agency, intermediation, or brokerage contract, or the IPR[517] related to the sale of an immovable). Therefore, the sale proper of an immovable (e.g., a plant or an office building) located in China to a foreign investor would inevitably be governed by Chinese law.

That outcome may differ as far as *movables*, which are the focus of this chapter, 902
are concerned, however. Indeed, if the CISG applies within its scope, it will, as noted, not apply to property transfer, which will, therefore, be left to *international private law*. Unless the parties have chosen the law applicable to matters not governed by the CISG or subsequently agreed upon it, they may have to face unpredicted results. Indeed, even though most other national laws provide, like Chinese law, that property rights are transferred with the delivery, the modalities of such transfer vary, sometimes significantly, from one national law to another, thus potentially leaving one or the two parties grappling with a law it may not be familiar with (s. above §§895 and 896).

Both Chinese[518] and Swiss private international law affirm the principle by 903
which the law of the country with which the legal relationship has the *closest connection* applies. For contracts, that closest connection is deemed to exist with the *characteristic performance* of the contract at stake, i.e., with the country of the usual business location of the party which provides such performance. While Chinese law falls short from defining what that characteristic performance may be as far as a contract of sale is specifically concerned, Swiss law does specify that it is that of the *seller*[519] (PRC Law on the Choice of Law for Foreign-related Civil Relationships, Art. 6 and 41, 2nd sentence; LDIP

---

515 S. Law on the Choice of Law for Foreign-related Civil Relationships, Art. 36. S. also Swiss Federal Law on International Private Law, Art. 99§1.

516 The possibility that different aspects of an international legal relationship may be governed by different national laws is known in international private law as the doctrine of *dépeçage* and is universally accepted.

517 If Chinese law is applicable, cf. above note 514.

518 S. above note 356.

519 To be accurate, LDIP Art. 117§3, Litt. a refers to the performance of the transferor (Fr.: "l'aliénateur"; Ger.: "der Veräusserer"), thus pointing at the seller, whose obligation is to transfer the property.

Art. 117§§ 1, 2 and 3, Litt. a). Yet under the jurisprudence of Chinese courts, and even though that analysis is required in each case, it is now well established that the same generally applies under Chinese law[520].

904 However, there might be cases which, however unusual, do occasionally occur in practice, where the characteristic performance may be provided by the *buyer*. Such is the case, for example, when the buyer is required to provide essential material for the seller's performance[521]. While in practice the law of the seller generally prevails, the applicable law must always be determined on a case-by-case basis.

905 To summarize, if the CISG applies to a contract of sale between a Chinese and a foreign party (which will almost always be the case, unless the parties unambiguously excluded it; s. above §§884 and 888) and the parties have not chosen the law applicable to those matters falling out of the Convention's scope, including the property transfer, the law of the seller's place generally applies to such transfer, provided it passes the characteristic performance test, but that of the buyer may if the latter delivered such performance, subject to the national private international law applying. It is, therefore, yet another time, in the parties best interest to carefully consider the applicable law before signing the contract, to choose it after mutual agreement, to mention it in a clearly and comprehensively drafted applicable law clause, and to insert it in the contract (s. above §896). If Chinese law applies, as explained (Chinese Civil Code

520 S., for example, Shenzhen Qianhai Cooperation Zone People's Court (2015) Shen Qian Fa Foreign-related First Instance Case No. 12 深圳前海合作区人民法院（2015）沈前发涉外初字第 12 号 shēnzhèn qián hǎi hézuò qū rénmín fǎyuàn (2015) shěnqiánfā shèwài chū zì dì 12 hào, where the court held: "the seller's fulfillment of its obligation of delivering goods and transferring ownership most embodies the characteristics of the goods sales contract"; and Intermediate People's Court of Jinhua City, Zhejiang Province (2016) Zhe 07 Min Zhong 5602 浙江省金华市中级人民法院（2016）浙 07 民中 5602 号 zhèjiāng shěng jīnhuá shì zhōngjí rénmín fǎyuàn (2016) zhè 07 mín zhōng 5602 hào, which ruled that the seller's habitual residence governs due to its characteristic role. While there is no dedicated Judicial Interpretation of the SPC that explicitly defines the "characteristic performance" for sale as the seller's, namely, in the 2022 Provisions of the Supreme People's Court on Several Issues Concerning Jurisdiction in Foreign-Related Civil and Commercial Cases, the SPC responses and cases applying the closest connection analysis generally endorse this conclusion.

521 The CISG Advisory Council gives the example where the buyer provides printing films to the seller who prints and delivers books (CISG Advisory Council Opinion No. 4: Contracts for the Sale of Goods to Be Manufactured or Produced and Mixed Contracts (Article 3 CISG), adopted on 24 October 2004). In Swiss law, that would fall under Litt. b of LDIP Art. 117§3, which attributes the characteristic performance to the party conferring the use of a right. That said, the choice of that example is surprising, since such a case may fall out of the scope of the CSIG anyway (s. Art. 3§1 and above §892).

Art. 208, 2nd sentence; s. above §899), the property is generally transferred with the delivery, subject to limited exceptions which we will outline below.

If the seller fails to transfer the property because it did not have it at its disposal before the sale, the buyer has the right to *revoke* the contract and to claim damage interests to the seller for breach of contract (Art. 597§1). The position of this provision on top of seller's obligations underlines its prominence. The law reserves other laws or regulations prohibiting such transfer (*ibid.*, § 2). *Third party claims* are subject to a specific regime to which we refer the reader (Art. 612 to 614). 906

B. Delivery

The regime applying to the *delivery* governs the method of delivery, its time, place and the passing of the risks resulting thereof. The *method* of delivery can be either direct or immediate (e.g., the seller's ship consignment is unloaded onto the buyer's trucks) or indirect, mediate or deferred (e.g., the seller unloads the consignment onto the pier and the buyer is given access to it the day after). In the latter case, it is performed by the remittance of *documents* enabling the buyer to both receive such delivery and be transferred the corresponding property rights (Art. 599). Such documents may be complemented by any other delivery means such as a key, etc. (*ibid.*) They may either be agreed by the parties before the delivery, possibly already in the contract, or follow trade practice or usages (*ibid.*) 907

The seller has to deliver within the *time* limit and at the *place* pre-agreed between the parties (Art. 601, 1st sentence and 603§1). It may deliver in advance (Art. 601, 2nd sentence). If such time or place is unclear, the parties shall determine such time according to the rules of contractual supplement and interpretation of Art. 510 and 511, and such place according to Art. 510 (s. above §577 and 618ff.) If the place cannot be so determined, the law further distinguishes between whether the goods need to be transported or not: in the first case, the seller shall deliver it to the first transporter available; if they need not, the law makes yet another distinction: if the parties were aware of the location of the goods at the time of concluding the contract, the seller must deliver them at that place (Art. 603§2, item 1); if they did not yet know, the seller may deliver them at its own place of business at the time of concluding (*ibid.*, item 2). 908

As extensively outlined (s. above Chap. 5 §29.III.A, Transfer of Property), in Chinese law, the delivery results in the simultaneous transfer of the corresponding *property rights*. The same applies in Swiss law. The CISG, if it applies, does not rule the effects of delivery on property rights: it leaves them to the national law applicable. Be that as it may, one may not take for granted that 909 delivery systematically or automatically causes such transfer. Particular cases providing for another regime may apply.

910 That is typically the case of *title retention*, i.e., conditional sale contracts subjecting the transfer of ownership to payment, even though the goods were delivered (Art. 641§1)[522]. Title retention is regulated at the end of Chapter 8 on the contract of sale (Art. 641 to 643).

911 Title retention may be opposed to *bona fide* third parties, but only if it was *registered*[523] (Art. 641§2). This rule is consistent with the general regime of real rights governing the transfer of property of movable assets (s. above §§437 and 438). The authority responsible for this registration is the People's Bank of China (PBOC), which operates the CCRC Movables Financing Registry System[524] 中国人民银行征信中心动产融资统一登记系统 zhōngguó rénmíng yínháng zhēng xìn zhōngxīn dòngchǎn róngzī tǒngyī dēngjì xìtǒng. Registration in this unified registry establishes the seller's title retention rights as a security interest effective against third parties, providing legal certainty and priority in case of disputes or insolvency.

912 The seller may retain the ownership or take back the goods before their transfer if the buyer fails to pay, to fulfill any other specific provision, or disposes of the goods, namely but not only, by selling or pledging them (Art. 642§2). The seller must suffer damage. The parties may agree otherwise. The seller is mandated by law to attempt to settle the matter amicably; if it fails, it is then entitled to apply for enforcement of its title (*ibid.*, § 3). The law refers to "the realization procedure for security interests" without mentioning the topical provisions, which are contained in Title 2 on security interest in property of Chapter 3 on the protection of the property right of the Second Book on property rights of the Chinese Civil Code (Art. 386 ff.; s. above Chap. 3 §17.IV, Security in Property).

913 The seller must further deliver conform goods, i.e., conforming to the *quality* pre-agreed between the parties (Art. 615). Quality extends to packaging (Art. 619). If either is unclear, the parties should reach a supplemental agreement, as prescribed by Art. 510 (Art. 616 and 619, 2nd sentence). If they fail, quality is to be determined according to the principle of reliance (Art. 616 *in*

[522] Title retention (Fr.: "réserve de propriété"; Ger.: "Eigentumsvorbehalt") is foreseen, in Swiss law, by CO Art. 715§1. The related deed must be registered with the local bankruptcy office of the buyer's domicile in order to be valid (*ibid.*, 2nd sentence).

[523] This conforms with the principle known in Chinese law as 登记对抗主义 dēngjì duìkàng zhǔyì, i.e., "notice by registration" (s. above note 281).

[524] The full name of this register in English is "Unified Registration System for Movable Property Financing of the Credit Reference Center of the People's Bank of China".

fine and 511, item 1[525]). *Packaging* must be adequate (Art. 619, 2nd sentence)[526], i.e., it should conform with usage and, in any event, protect the goods, be both economical and ecological (*ibid., in fine*).

Methods of delivery and their consequences on the passing of the risks are extensively detailed in the *Incoterms*[527], which the parties may, and generally do, refer to for all matters such standard terms regulate. These matters typically include delivery, passing of the risks, insurances and other matters. They are to be considered as a set of contractual provisions akin to a special law superseding or derogating to the applicable (general) law, be it the CISG, Chinese or any other law the parties may have elected. The insertion of Incoterms in a contract of sale is strongly advisable in trade as their clarity, specificity, abundant related know-how and global acknowledgement as standards remove most of the risk resulting from the generic and sometimes hermetic formulation of the CISG or of national laws, or of unclear or lacunary contractual drafting. 914

IV. Buyer's Obligations

As mentioned in the introduction to this chapter, the buyer's obligations consist mainly, although not only, in that of *paying for* the goods, as well as *inspecting* them upon delivery and *notifying* the seller of any defect. They are detailed as follows. 915

A. *Payment*

The buyer's primary obligation is to *pay the price* of the goods sold (cf. Art. 595; s. above §865). It shall do so according to the amount, method, place and time agreed (Art. 626 to 628). If either is unclear, like for the goods' quality (s. above §913), the parties should clarify as prescribed by Art. 510; if they fail, 916

---

525 Art. 511, item 1 directs to a cascade of standards, from mandatory-, then recommended-, national-, then industry-, last common or special standards.

526 On the principle of reliance, s. above §228. On Art. 510 and 511 and contractual interpretation in general, s. above Chap. 4 §23.II, Contractual Interpretation.

527 Incoterms are a set of eleven globally recognized rules, published by the International Chamber of Commerce (ICC), that clearly define and standardizes the responsibilities, costs, and risks between a seller and a buyer in a contract for the sale of goods, particularly in international trade. They clarify tasks such as delivery location, transportation arrangements, insurance, and customs clearance, preventing misunderstandings and ensuring smoother transactions. The current version was issued in 2020, though earlier editions are still valid if clearly referred to by the parties.

the price and time shall be determined under Art. 511, items 2 and 5[528], and the place under Art. 627, 2nd sentence[529].

917 For reasons which can be explained both by the emphasis the legislator and trade practice put on inspection and the fact that, in commercial trade, goods are typically paid in the form of LC after the inspection agent has confirmed the conformity of the goods, even though payment is the buyer's primary obligation, it is, in the Chinese Civil Code, located after the inspection one. However, one may not deduce from that structure that the buyer's obligation to pay is subject to a successful inspection; both are independent from each other.

918 Payment by *installments* is governed by Art. 634.

B. Inspection and notification

919 Beyond payment, the buyer's next main obligation is that of inspection of the goods and of notification to the seller of any defect thus discovered. Such obligation is relative, however: it is a mere *incumbency*: the buyer is free from abstaining to fulfill it entirely. However, if it does, or if it does not regularly fulfill it, it will deprive itself of the warranty for defects in case such defects are subsequently discovered or late notification.

920 On the face of it, the law distinguishes the *time* within which the buyer should *inspect* the goods (Art. 620) from that within which it should *notify* the seller of any defect revealed by such inspection (Art. 621). As will be outlined below, there is a subtle difference between the two. The law further distinguishes between whether the time of inspection had been pre-agreed or not.

921 In both cases, the buyer must inspect the goods *upon receipt* (Art. 620), which means that, in principle, it does not have to inspect them *before* receipt, namely, upon conclusion of the contract, in particular if the goods are to be transported (s. below §935).

922 Now, if the time of inspection has been *agreed* upon, the buyer must both inspect the goods (Art. 620, 2nd phrase) and notify the seller of any defect (Art. 621§1, 1st sentence) within such term. If, however, such term has *not* been

---

528 Art. 511, item 2 prescribes alternatively market-, government-set or government-guided prices. Item 5 generally prescribes a default method of performance conducive to the realization of the contract's purpose. On Art. 510 and 511 and contractual interpretation in general, s. above Chap. 4 §23.II, Contractual Interpretation.

529 Art. 627, 2nd sentence, prescribes the seller's place of business or, if delivery was agreed as a precondition for payment, the place of delivery of the goods or related documents.

agreed upon, the buyer should both inspect (Art. 620 *in fine*) and notify (Art. 621§2, 1st sentence) the seller "*timely*"[530].

The law does not define what "timely" should be. It is further somewhat misleading inasmuch as it does set a time limit of *two years* from *delivery* beyond which, absent any notification, the goods are deemed not to be defective (Art. 621 § 2, 2nd sentence). However, it must be stressed that the two-year limitation is an *absolute* limitation subject to a relative limitation within a "reasonable time" after the buyer discovered or should have discovered the defect. 923

Several additional comments are necessary for correctly qualifying the latter requirement: *first*, although the law does not specify it, the test which applies to the question of whether the buyer should have discovered the defect and when consists in asking whether the buyer used *reasonable caution*, i.e., the caution commanded by the circumstances, which itself supposes that the buyer timely used *adequate* skills for inspecting the goods, depending on their nature[531]. 924

Second, if the buyer is *indolent* in inspecting or notifying, i.e., if it inspected or notified later than what it ought to have, i.e., could and should have, the consequence of such indolence is not, provided the buyer did notify the seller within the two-year time limitation from delivery, to deprive the buyer from the warranty for defects, but to entitle the seller to *reduce* any indemnity for defects if the buyer's indolence aggravated the damage. This consequence does not result from the regime of the contract of sale[532], but from the general regime of contractual liability to which the regime of the contract of sale refers (Art. 617; s. below §963), which imposes the aggrieved party a duty of mitigation (Art. 591§1 *in fine*; s. above §836). The latter requirement also applies in case the inspection time was agreed upon (Art. 621§3), i.e., the buyer cannot wait until the last minute of the period of time agreed for the inspection to inspect and notify. 925

Third, the legislator actually intended the two-year limit as a maximum, absolute limit for hidden defects, i.e., defects which could not be discovered by using reasonable caution, but which only unintentionally revealed themselves 926

530 Art. 620 in fine uses the expression 及时 jíshí, "timely" while Art. 621§2, 1st sentence uses the expression 合理期限内 hélǐ qíxiàn nèi, "within a reasonable period". We do not see any material difference between the two.

531 Typically, in commercial trade, buyers use inspection, conformity and testing companies with specialized skills and equipment for such inspections. Third-party entrusted inspection is specifically addressed by Art. 624 (s. below §933).

532 Unlike the CISG, which contains a specific provision to that effect (Art. 77; s. below §969).

subsequently or after enhanced inspection exceeding the reasonable caution threshold.

927 *Fourth*, the time limitation for defect notification must not be confused with the limitation of the *action* invoking the *warranty* for defects, which is of four years[533] from the cause of action (Art. 594; s. below §964 and 965). Time limitations are extensively discussed below (s. Chap. 5 §29.VII.A, Time Limitations).

928 To conclude at this stage, and *fifth*, any buyer would be well advised in any case to inspect the goods *and* notify any defect *as soon as possible*, *irrespective* of whether a period of time has been agreed to that effect or not. As we will see, this advice is also justified considering the different and potentially misleading formulations existing between Chinese law, the CSIG and other national regimes as far as, among other things, inspection and notification time is concerned.

929 These basic rules are complemented with several *secondary rules*, which are the following. The defect can relate both to the quality and the *quantity* of the goods (Art. 621§1 and 2)[534]. In other words, if a seller delivers 90% of goods of an otherwise impeccable quality, the 10% shortcoming qualify as a defect entitling the seller to claim the warranty for defects, nor merely to the remedies generally available for ordinary contractual nonperformance (s. above Chap. 4 §27, Liability for Breach of Contract).

930 If the inspection time was agreed upon but proves *too short* considering the nature of the goods and trade practice, such limit only applies to superficial defects (Art. 622§2). Although the law does not elaborate, it implies that the "timely" requirement outlined above (s. §§923ff.) applies to defects other than superficial needing additional inspection time.

931 If the seller offered the buyer a *quality assurance or guarantee* on the goods, two consequences may result thereof: first, if such assurance is longer than the two-year limit of Art. 621§2, it shall extend that limit up to the assurance's term

---

[533] Unlike Swiss law, where both limitations are of two years (CO Art. 210§1). For a comprehensive discussion, s. below Chap. 5 §29.VII.A, Time Limitations.

[534] The same applies under the CISG (Art. 51§1). The notion of defect implies that the delivery effectively occurred, even though the goods may be imperfect. In contrast, a 10% delivery would arguably not qualify as a defect, but as mere nonperformance. So would the delivery of goods whose quality is so inconsistent with the agreed one that they actually amount to something else (e.g., the delivery of an electric car instead of a petrol-powered car; such "other thing" being known in Roman law as *aliud*). The eligibility of either regime is to be assessed on a case-by-case basis, keeping in mind that the sales regime refers to that of general contractual liability anyway (s. below §963). About short deliveries, s. also below §961.

(*ibid.*, *in fine*). Second, if, on the contrary, it is shorter than that prescribed by the law, the latter shall prevail (Art. 622§2).

If the parties did not pre-agree the inspection time but the *delivery documents* signed by the buyer specify the goods quality, the latter will be deemed to have inspected the goods and found no quantity or superficial quality defects, unless there is incontestable evidence of such defects (Art. 623). This rule also implies that it does not apply to serious quality defects. 932

Finally, if the seller and the buyer have agreed on *inspection standards* but the buyer's inspection agent disagrees with the seller about them, the standards agreed between the seller and the buyer apply (Art. 624). 933

The law does not qualify the *form* or *content* of the notification; it only requires the buyer to notify "any inconformity". Such form and content can, therefore, be assumed to be subject to reasonableness. 934

Comparatively, the *Vienna Convention* (CISG), although similar to Chinese law, is more explicit than the latter as it requires the buyer to inspect the goods "within as short a period as is practicable in the circumstances" (CISG Art. 38§1) or, in other words, *as soon as possible*. This rule is moderated in case of *transportation*, where inspection is deferred until *arrival* (*ibid.*, §§ 2 and 3); the same rule may apply in case the buyer *redirects* the goods with the seller's knowledge (*ibid.*, § 33). Likewise, the buyer must give notice "within a reasonable time" (CISG Art. 39§1). Hidden defects are subject to the absolute time limit of *two years* from *delivery* (CISG Art. 39§2)[535] reproduced in Chinese law (s. above §923), unless the seller offered a longer guarantee (CISG Art. 39§2, *in fine*). The Convention further qualifies the *content* such notification which must specify the *nature* of the lack of conformity (*ibid.*) While as noted in the preceding paragraph Chinese law only requires the buyer to notify "any inconformity", we see no reason to assume that the latter requirement is lower than the former, however. 935

In turn, *Swiss law* also provides for a comparable rule as it mandates the buyer to inspect the condition of the purchased object "*as soon as feasible* in the normal course of business" (CO Art. 201§1, 1st sentence). If it discovers a defect, it must notify the seller "without delay" (*ibid.*, 2nd sentence). Hidden defects are subject the same time limit as the CISG and Chinese law (CO Art. 201§3 and 210§1; s. above §923 and preceding paragraph). Swiss courts have issued an abundant case law where notification time qualifying the buyer for the 936

535 The CISG does not apply to the limitation of *action*, which is exclusively governed by the law of its contracting States and is, in China, of four years (s. below §964). For a comprehensive discussion, s. below Chap. 5 §29.VII.A, Time Limitations.

warranty for defects have been varying from a few days to several months, depending on the nature of the goods. The notification can take any form[536].

V. Passing of the Risks

937 Two special issues, which have been repeatedly mentioned above, are of particular importance in the contract of sale: the *passing of the risks* and the *warranty for defects* (s. above §938). Because they relate to the rights and obligations of both the seller and the buyer, we are treating them separately.

938 As stressed above, the passing of the risks is a prominent feature of the contract of sale. Its regime determines beyond which point the risk of liability for damage or destruction of the goods passes from the seller to the buyer. As equally mentioned, that point of time or circumstance does not necessarily coincides with the delivery or the transfer of property.

939 Under Chinese law, the basic rule is that such passing occurs upon *delivery* (Art. 604). However, the law may prescribe, or the parties may agree otherwise (*ibid., in fine*).

940 This primary rule is declined in several secondary rules, depending on the circumstances. Thus, in accordance with global trade standards, namely, the CISG (s. below §950), Chinese law distinguishes sales involving *transportation* (A.K.A. carriage or shipping) from those not involving it. In the first case (sales involving transportation), it further distinguishes two more subcases depending on the *time of conclusion*, i.e., those where transportation was agreed before or at the time of conclusion of the contract of sale (second case), from sales occurring after transportation has departed, i.e., during transportation (A.K.A. "in transit" or "*en route*"; third case).

941 The *first case* (sales not involving transportation) is subdivided into two subcases: it distinguishes the buyer's from the seller's default. Thus, if the *seller*, by its own fault, *fails* to deliver at the pre-agreed time and place (including as per Art. 603§2, item 2; s. above §908), it shall be liable from *the time it should have delivered* (Art. 605). Conversely, if the *buyer* fails to take over the goods[537] although they were regularly delivered by the seller at the pre-agreed time and place, the buyer shall be liable from the *pre-agreed time* of delivery (Art. 608).

---

536 ATF101 II 83 = JT 1975 I 322.

537 Under the general provisions of contract law, the creditor's failure to accept the debtor's performance entitles the latter to *deposit* the subject-matter of the contract (s. above Chap. 4 §26.VIII, Deposit, in particular §783).

In the *second case* (sales involving transportation at the conclusion), the law, mirroring Art. 603§2 (s. above §908), also distinguishes two sub-cases, depending on whether the *place of delivery* had been agreed upon or not. If the place of delivery has been *agreed* upon, the risks pass upon *delivery at that place* (Art. 607§1). If the place of delivery was *not agreed* upon, the risks pass upon *delivery to the first*[538] *carrier* (*ibid.*, § 2). 942

Finally, in the *third case* (sales in transit), the risks pass upon the *conclusion* of the contract of sale (Art. 606). As stressed below, this regime *differs* from the CISG (s. §950). 943

In that respect, it is of utmost importance to appreciate, considering the relative volatility of the applicable law discussed above, that other laws may provide for different regimes whose application may result in different outcomes whose consequences may, depending on the circumstances, dramatically differ from one regime to another. 944

The *Vienna Convention* (CISG) which, unlike for the transfer of property rights, does apply to the passing of the risks, contains a complex regime allowing for multiple delivery methods and some differences with Chinese law. Although a systematic commentary of the CISG exceeds the scope of this book, because, if the parties did not exclude it, the CISG applies to Sino-foreign sales if the foreign party's place of business is located in a CISG member-State, and because the significance of the passing of the risk and the differences such regimes present, we believe it appropriate to elaborate. 945

The passing of the risks under the CISG relies on Art. 67 to 69, which like Chinese law distinguish several situations. First, the regime distinguishes sales involving *transportation* (or carriage or shipment, which are equivalent expressions; Art. 67 and 68; first and second cases) from those not involving it (Art. 69; third case). Second, among those sales involving carriage, it distinguishes sales concluded *before* such carriage (Art. 67; first case) from those concluded while the goods were in *transit*, i.e., while such carriage was already under way (Art. 68; second case), a common situation in trade. Because the CISG focuses on shipping, unlike in Chinese law, the regimes involving transportation precede those not involving it. 946

In the *first case*, when the goods were sold *before transportation*, the risks pass to the buyer upon *delivery to the first carrier*. If a *specific delivery location* was agreed, they only pass when the goods are delivered to that place (Art. 67§1). 947

[538] The law distinguishes the "first" carrier from subsequent carriers in case of multimodal transport, i.e., of chain of successive carriers, frequent in freight transport.

Moreover, they only pass when the goods have been *identified* to the attention of the buyer (*ibid.*, § 2).

948 In the *second case*, where the goods were sold in *transit*, the risks pass at the time of the *conclusion* of the contract; however, if certain "circumstances" (s. below §951) justify it, they may pass at the time of their *delivery to the carrier* (Art. 68). It is worth noting that the latter exception is not provided by Chinese law.

949 Finally, in the *third case*, when sales do not involve transportation, the risks pass upon *taking over* the goods by the buyer. However, if the buyer fails to do so, such passing retroacts to the time when the goods were placed at its *disposal*, provided they were *properly placed* (Art. 69). Unlike Chinese law which clearly separate them in two provisions (Chinese Civil Code Art. 605 and 608; s. above §941), the CISG conflates both the seller and the buyer's fault in the same provision.

950 As compared to the CISG, Chinese law largely embodies similar principles, but with some divergences. The most significant of such discrepancies is that, in case of sales in *transit*, the CISG exceptionally provides for the passing of the risks upon *delivery* instead of upon conclusion the contract of sale, (CISG, Art. 68; s. above §948), while Chinese law only prescribes that passing occurs upon *conclusion* (Chinese Civil Code Art. 606; s. above §943) while not providing for such exception.

951 Examples of *circumstances* under CISG Art. 68, where risks pass to the buyer from the time goods were handed over to the carrier who issued the carriage documents, include cases where trade customs or contract terms indicate such intent, such as in standard Incoterms[539] CIF or C&F contracts[540]; where the contract or commercial practice is based on such risk allocation[541]; or where the handover to the carrier and the issuance of the relevant documents signal that the seller has completed its obligations and that control has passed to the buyer. It is important to note that such cases are frequent in shipping, which is why the discrepancy existing between Chinese law and the CISG in that regard must be carefully considered.

---

539 S. above note 527.

540 Under a Cost, Insurance and Freight (CIF) or Cost and Freight (C&F) sale, the contract usually obliges the seller to ship goods, obtain carriage documents, and transfer these documents to the buyer, who then assumes risks from the moment the goods were handed to the carrier.

541 Such risk allocation, i.e., moving the passing of the risks from conclusion to delivery, is known as "retroactive allocation" despite delivery generally occurs after conclusion. In that context, "retroactive" abstractly refers to the risks' apportionment, not to the sequence of conclusion and delivery.

Generally speaking, the CISG is more detailed than Chinese law; namely, it provides specifically for shipping, which Chinese law of the contract of sale does not[542]. In contrast, a regime such as CISG's passing of the risk may prove overcomplex and inadequate indeed for small or isolated sales (s. above §895), especially if they do not involve shipping. Moreover, and somewhat paradoxically, CISG's scope excludes its application to certain legal issues yet critical for sales, notably property transfer, which limited scope may also plea in favor of the Convention's exclusion to the effect of avoiding *dépeçage*[543], unless its application is justified by the nature of the transaction. 952

Other national laws may also differ from either Chinese law or the CISG. Thus, *Swiss law* provides for a *radically different* rule: under it, the risks pass upon *conclusion of the contract* (CO Art. 185§1)[544]. Therefore, in a Sino-Swiss contract of sale, if the parties exclude the application of the CISG, they should take utmost care in determining the applicable law in view of that dramatic discrepancy between Chinese and Swiss law. Swiss law also contains special regimes for cases such as those described above; however, because Swiss law is not the focus of this book, we refer the reader to specialized literature in those respects. 953

The passing regime is complemented, both in Chinese law and in the CISG, by several *secondary liability rules*. Thus, under Chinese law, the seller's failure to transfer the documents and other means for the transfer of the goods does not impact on the passing of the risks (Art. 599 and 609; s. above §907). If the buyer terminates the contract because the goods are defective (s. below §962), the risks remain with the seller (Art. 610). 954

Under the CISG, the buyer does not have to pay the price if the goods have been damaged or lost after the passing but by fault of the seller (Art. 66). In case of transit, the risks do not pass if the buyer knew or had to know that the goods were damaged or lost (Art. 68 *in fine*). In case of sale not involving transportation, in addition to assuming the risks, the buyer is liable for breach of contract if it does not take over the goods regularly delivered (Art. 69§1 *in fine*). 955

Finally, both in Chinese law and under the CISG, the passing of the risks to the buyer do not preclude it to invoke the seller's *liability for breach of contract* 956

542 S., however, the regime of the *contract of transportation*, namely, of *freight*, which contains its own liability regime and is mainly governed by the Chinese Civil Code (s. below Chap. 5 §44.III, Freight Transportation) and the Chinese Maritime Code (s. below §1400 and note 667). China has not signed the Hague-Visby Rules (s. below note 669).

543 S. above note 516.

544 Swiss law reserves special circumstances or other laws (CO Art. 185§1 *in fine*). If goods are generic, they must have been individualized; if they have to be shipped, the seller must have entrusted them with the carrier (*ibid.*, § 2).

(Chinese Civil Code Art. 611 and CISG Art. 70; s. above Chap. 4 §27, Liability for Breach of Contract). Moreover, shipping under the CISG may overlap, to some extent, with the typical *contract of (freight) transportation* under the Chinese Civil Code and the Chinese Maritime Code, both of which contain specific liability regimes (s. above note 542).

957 That said, it is important to note that the fact that one of these provisions may be present in one regime but not the other does not necessarily imply that the same legal consequence does not occur in the other: while certain liability cases are definitely specific to one regime and not available in the other, other cases, however not explicitly mentioned in a specific provision, may nevertheless be indirectly construed by reference to other general provisions. In other words, the complexity of the relationship between Chinese law and the CISG calls once again for caution in the election of the applicable law (s. above §905).

958 The passing of the risk is typically regulated by the *Incoterms*, whose reference is both widespread and recommended to the effect of preventing related disputes (s. above §914).

VI. Warranty for Defects

959 The main risk faced by the buyer, other than the seller's failure to deliver, damage to the goods or their loss, is that, however regularly delivered, the goods are defective. While the delivery default and, assuming the risks had not yet passed, damage to or loss of the goods are primarily covered by general contractual liability, liability for defective goods is governed by a regime specific to the contract of sale generally known as the warranty for defects[545] and calling for specific remedies which will be outlined below.

960 The seller's warranty is mirrored by certain duties imposed to the *buyer* which the latter must rigorously fulfill in order not to be deprived from its right to the warranty for defects, namely, to inspect the goods and notify any defect. Such duties have been be outlined under the buyer's obligations section of this chapter (s. above Chap. 5 §29.IV.B, Inspection).

961 Conceivably, irrespective of Chinese law, the damage suffered by the buyer of defective goods can be compensated by an extended range of *remedies*. The choice of such remedy will depend on a cascade of choices. In the first place, the buyer may choose to insist on *performance*, provided it is possible, or not. If performance is still possible, depending on the nature of the defects and on whether the defects bears on the goods' quality or quantity, the buyer may

---

545 On the terminology related to "warranty" and "defect", s. above note 496.

further choose either, in the first case, to request the seller to *repair* or *replace* the goods or, in the second, to *complement* the delivery by delivering the shortcoming[546].

If, alternatively, the buyer elects to claim for an *economic compensation* instead of performance, another choice opens: it may choose to *maintain* the contract or not. If it maintains it, the buyer may claim a *price reduction*; if it decides not to maintain the contract, the buyer may *terminate* it. Such choices will determine the nature and extent of the damage interest the buyer will be entitled to claim, as well as its reciprocal duties towards the seller. 962

Somehow surprisingly, unlike the CISG, Swiss law and other foreign laws, 963 Chinese law does not provide for a specific regime for the warranty for defects; it refers to the *general regime of contractual liability*. Thus, Art. 617 of the Chinese Civil Code merely states that "if the subject matter delivered by the seller fails to meet quality requirements, the buyer may request that the seller bears the liability for breach of contract pursuant to the provisions in Art. 582 to 584". Therefore, we refer to that regime, which have extensively discussed above (s. Chap. 4 §27, Liability for Breach of Contract). It should be noted, in that regard, that Chinese law is remarkable in that it strongly promotes settlement, while giving the parties freedom to choose any of the solutions described above[547] and the tools for favoring any such settlement over a dispute eventually resulting in damage interest ordered by a court or arbitration.

The *limitation of action* applying to the claim for warranty for defects[548] is of 964 *four years* from the *discovery* of the defect or from when the buyer ought to have discovered it (Art. 594; s. below §982. This limitation is not to be confused with the limitation for *notifying* any such defect, which as noted is of *two years* from delivery (Art. 621§2, 2nd sentence; s. above §§923ff.) Therefore, the buyer should be aware that, even if it notified within the two-year limitation, but was indolent in inspecting and notifying, i.e., if it inspected or notified later than what it ought to have, i.e., could and should have[549], the four years limitation for filing may start *earlier* than from the notification, or even the discovery.

---

546 About shortcomings qualifying as default, s. above §928.

547 Tellingly, Art. 582, which describes such remedies, uses the conjunction 或者 huòzhě, "or", which is typically used for expressing non-exhaustive enumerations.

548 About the CISG, s. above note 535.

549 As explained, the consequence of such indolence is not, provided the buyer did notify the seller within the two-year time limitation from delivery, to deprive the buyer from the warranty for defects, but to entitle the seller to reduce any indemnity for defects if the buyer's indolence aggravated the damage (s. above §925).

965 The parties to a Sino-foreign contract of sale governed by *Swiss law* where the CISG has been excluded, or by the CISG and, for any matter out of the Convention's scope, by Swiss law[550], or because, whether the CISG applies or not, the parties did not elect Swiss law, but private international law points at Swiss law as the law applying to such out-of-scope matters (if the CISG applies) or as the applicable law (if the CISG does not apply), must be aware that, in a stark departure from Chinese law, the limitation of action for the warranty for defects is, under Swiss law, of *two years* from the timely discovery of the defect (CO Art. 210§1), not of four years. Those limitations are discussed extensively below (s. below Chap. 5 §29.VII.A, Time Limitations).

966 Comparatively, although the *Vienna Convention* (CISG) does not expressly name the warranty for defects, it contains a regime applying to remedies for "breach of contract by the seller" which includes, but is not limited to, the warranty for defects (CISG Art. 45 ff.) That regime, which is much more detailed than its counterpart in Chinese law, provides both for the *rights* which the buyer may exercise and the *damages* it may claim as a result thereof (CISG Art. 45§1).

967 Such *rights* (CISG Art. 46 to 52) cover the whole range of remedies outlined above (s. §§961ff.) including *performance* (CISG Art. 46§1), namely, in the form of replacement or *substitution* (*ibid.*, § 2), or of *repair* (*ibid.*, § 3). In addition, the buyer may offer the seller a *time extension* to enable it to perform (Art. 47§1) or *remedy itself* the defects in lieu of the seller (CISG Art. 48§1). Alternatively, as equally mentioned (s. above §961), the buyer may renounce performance, "avoid", which is the Convention's language for expressing *revocation*[551], the contract (Art. 49) and request a *price reduction* (Art. 50).

968 Irrespective of the remedy the buyer may choose, it will be entitled, in addition, to claim compensation from the seller for any *damage* it may have suffered because of the defect. Like in Chinese law (however implicitly; Chinese Civil Code Art. 584; s. above §810), the Convention explicitly entitles the buyer not

550 S. above note 535.

551 The French version of the CISG uses the verb "résoudre", which is confusing since that latter verb is understood, in Swiss law, as meaning rescission, i.e., *ex tunc*, from the conclusion, as if the contract had never existed, not *ex nunc*, from the termination, which is expressed by "résiliation". Yet in the Convention, "résoudre" is to be understood as resulting in a termination *ex nunc*, i.e., as "résiliation" (s. above note 441). The German version of the CISG does not give rise to the same misunderstanding since it uses the verb "aufheben" while rescission is expressed, in German, by "auflösen" and termination by "zurücktretten". That said, however confusing, "résoudre" is occasionally used, in French speaking jurisdictions other than Switzerland, for expressing termination. On the related terminology in Chinese, English, French and German, s. above §§239ff.

only to the *damnum emergens* or any loss, but also to any *lucrum cessans* or loss of profit (CISG Art. 74), where the latter must be contained within the seller's reasonable expectations, however (*ibid.*, 2nd sentence).

These basic principles are complemented by secondary rules: first, if the buyer has purchased *replacement goods*, it is entitled to any difference exceeding the price agreed with the defaulting seller (Art. 75). In that respect, the law accurately qualifies, for the purpose of damage calculation, the *time of the price* of the replacement goods (Art. 76). Second, however entitled to the warranty for defects, the buyer is subject to a *duty of mitigation* at all times; a disregard of such duty resulting in an increase of damage gives the seller the right to apply a proportional reduction to any compensation the buyer may be otherwise entitled to (Art. 77). The Chinese regime of contractual liability imposes the same duty (Art. 591§1 *in fine*; s. above §836). 969

The Convention does not apply to the *limitation of action* for warranty for defects, which is governed by the law of the contracting States and is, in China, as mentioned, of four years (Art. 594), and of two in Switzerland (CO Art. 210§1), even if the Convention applies. Once again, those limitations are discussed extensively below (s. below Chap. 5 §29.VII.A, Time Limitations). 970

Swiss law compares in the first place to the regimes described above in that, unlike Chinese law and the CISG, it does expressly provide for a warranty for defects regime which it names as such. The *principle* of the warranty rests on CO Art. 197§1, which defines a defect as anything that would "materially or legally negate or substantially reduce the value of the object or its fitness for the designated purpose". The seller is liable even though it may have been unaware of the defect (*ibid.*, § 2)[552]. 971

The related *remedies* are outlined at CO Art. 205 to 210. Again, while structured differently, they compare to those available in Chinese law and the CISG. Swiss law provides for three options: termination, price reduction or replacement. In the first option, it elaborates in case the goods were lost. 972

As far as the *two first options* are concerned, as noted, the buyer may choose between *revoking*[553] or claiming a *price reduction*[554] (CO Art. 205§1). There 973

[552] The Swiss warranty regime in case of sale of *immovable* has recently been profoundly revised; the new regime applies as of 1 January 2026. The revision does not impact the sale of movables. It also applies to warranty under the contract for work. For a summary description, s. below note 614.

[553] This remedy is known, in French, as "action rédhibitoire", from the same remedy in Roman law, *actio redhibitoria* (where *redhibere* means "to return"), and in Swiss legal German as "Wandelungsklage". Swiss law recurrently refers to these expressions.

[554] This remedy was known, in Roman law, as *actio quanto minoris*. Western legal literature frequently refers to this expression.

are two exceptions to this rule however: first, even if the buyer chooses to terminate, the judge may order a price reduction if he considers that termination is unjustified (*ibid.*, § 2). Second, if the price reduction equates to the sale price, the buyer may only terminate (*ibid.*, § 3), which implies that it must return the goods, while the seller must refund the buyer.

974 Termination is subject to additional rules if the goods have been *lost*. If so, the buyer may terminate anyway (CO Art. 207§1) and has only to return whatever has not been lost, if anything (*ibid.*, § 2). However, if the goods were lost because of the buyer, or if it alienated the goods, it can only claim a price reduction (*ibid.*, § 3).

975 As to the *third option*, if the goods are *commodities*, the buyer may claim their *replacement* (CO Art. 206§1). The seller can also spontaneously replace them and indemnify the buyer from any supplemental damage, provided the seller does so at once and the goods were not shipped from elsewhere (*ibid.*, § 2).

976 It is important to note that, in departure from Chinese law and the CISG (Chinese Civil Code Art. 582; CISG Art. 46§3; s. above §§963, 812 and 928), Swiss law does *not* entitle the buyer to request the seller to *repair* the defects; in other words, the seller has no such obligation and the courts may not order such remedy[555].

977 It is further worth noting that, while Chinese law does not provide for a specific regime for the warranty for defects and relies instead on the general contractual liability regime; s. above §963), under Swiss law, the *general contractual liability* regime of CO Art. 97 ff. (s. above §§841ff.) remains available, either alone or *in addition* to the warranty for defects, i.e., specifically, to the claim for price reduction[556].

978 In case of termination, the buyer must return the goods (any profit included) while the seller must refund the price (with interest; CO Art. 208§1 and 2, 1st and 2nd phrases). In addition, the law expressly compels the seller, even not faulty, to indemnify the buyer's legal and other (direct) costs (CO Art. 208§2, 3rd phrase ff.) while the faulty seller is also liable for other damages (*ibid.*, § 3). In other words, Swiss law subjects the seller of defective goods to an *objective* liability for *direct* costs, i.e., *damnum emergens*, and to liability for *fault* for *indirect* costs, including *lucrum cessans* or loss of profit[557].

979 To recapitulate at this stage, one must stress that, while Chinese law, the CISG and Swiss law roughly provide for comparable rights and remedies following

---

555 ATF 95 II 119 = JT 1970 I 238.

556 ATF 133 III 335 = JT 2010 I 223.

557 ATF 79 II 376; ATF 133 III 257 = SJ 2007 I 461.

the delivery of defective goods[558], subtle differences abound, be them related to the structure of the law, the conditions to which the exercise of such rights are subjects, the definition and terminology of notions such as defect, the remedies available, the extent of the seller's liability and particular provisions which may be contained in one law but not the other, to name a few. Therefore, as noted, foreign traders are advised once again (s. above §896) to use caution in carefully selecting the applicable law to Sino-foreign contracts of sale and thoroughly understand the scope of such selection. Finally, the reader is cautioned once again that this chapter does not ambition to propose a comprehensive comparative study of Chinese law, Swiss law and the CISG, which would exceed the scope of this book; it only aims at highlighting selected prominent features.

VII. Other Issues

Time limitations are both of the essence and especially complex in the regime of the contract of sale; therefore, although we mentioned them above, we believe it useful to recapitulate them below. The Code further regulates particular cases of termination, special sales, and other ancillary matters, which we briefly mention thereafter. 980

A. Time Limitations

Among other noteworthy provisions, the *time limitations*[559] applying to the contract of sale are certainly worth some developments to the effect of preventing misunderstandings and, potentially, damageable and irremediable consequences which a party may suffer as a result thereof. One should start by recalling[560] that the *ordinary* regime of limitation of *action* in *contractual* disputes is, under Chinese law, of *three years* (Art. 188§1). In that first respect, the Swiss trader to a contract other than a contract of sale and governed by Chinese law should be warned not to be caught short since, under *Swiss law*, the default limitation of action in contractual disputes is of *ten years* (CO Art. 127). 981

558 About the sale of *immovables* under Swiss law, s. above note 552.

559 On limitation of actions in general, s. above Chap. 2 §13, Limitation of Action. This section also discusses time limitations other than for actions, however.

560 All these notions have been visited in the preceding sections of this chapter, to which we refer for a detailed discussion; the corresponding paragraphs will not be referred to in this summary.

982 The three-year rule in Chinese law suffers some *exceptions* however, one of which applies to the contract of sale, whose limitation of action is extended to *four years* (Art. 594). However, one should pay further attention to the fact that the provision setting that limit is not located in the chapter of the Chinese Civil Code governing the contract of sale, but that it immediately *precedes* it, as the last provision of Chapter 8 on contractual liability of the Third Book on contract law.

983 That said, it should be emphasized that this limit applies to the *filing* of an action or claim by one party to a contract of sale against the other before a court or an arbitration tribunal, and that it runs from the time the filing party became or ought to be aware of the cause of action (Art. 188§2; s. above §348).

984 Such limitation of action shall not be confused with the limit for *notifying any defect*, where such notification is a necessary precondition for invoking the *warranty for defects*, to which the limitation of action does not apply; the absolute limitation for such notification is of *two years* from *delivery* (Art. 621§2, 2nd sentence). Notifying a defect or invoking the warranty does not equate to filing, before a court or an arbitration tribunal, a claim relying on the warranty: as implied by the preceding paragraph, such filing may occur later, i.e., up to four years from the cause of action.

985 In contrast, if the buyer misses the two-year limitation for notifying any defect, it shall be *barred* from filing a claim relying on the warranty, even if that claim is filed within four years from the timely discovery of the defect. The two-year limit for defect notification applies both under the CISG and Chinese law, as well as under Swiss law.

986 Said dire consequence suffers two exceptions, however. First, the two-years limit for defect notification may be *extended* if the seller has offered a longer *guarantee* or assurance (provided always the discovery is timely, where such extension is intended, in practice, for hidden defect). Even though the law only implies it, it may not be shortened. Second, it does not apply if the *seller was aware* of the defect (Art. 621§3).

987 Other than setting a limitation, the CISG, Chinese and Swiss law do not specify when the buyer should inspect and notify, but require, however by expressing this requirement with different formulations, such inspection and notification to take place *as soon as possible*; the limitation of two years, which applies in the CISG and, in compliance with the latter, Chinese and Swiss law, is an *absolute* or maximum limit primarily intended for *hidden defects*. unless the nature of the goods justifies a late inspection and notification.

988 If the buyer inspects or notifies unjustifiably later than possible and the goods are (further) damaged, the seller will be entitled to reduce its indemnity. Such consequence is justified by the general *duty of mitigation*. Therefore, whether

the parties agreed on the time of inspection and notification, as well as whether the seller offered an extended guarantee are, from that point of view, indifferent. The limit for inspection does not necessarily coincide with that for notification.

In other words, the limits for inspecting, notifying and filing may coincide, but do not necessarily do, and often do not. The buyer should inspect and notify as soon as possible but, in any case, not later (typically in case of hidden defect) than two years from delivery, unless the seller has offered a longer guarantee, and file not later than four years from the timely discovery of the defect. 989

Claims relying on *other causes* than the warranty for defect, including related to a contract of sale, must be filed by either party not later than *four years* after they became aware of their cause. Chapter 9 on limitation of actions of the First Book of the Chinese Civil Code on general provisions applies to any limitation matters not specifically regulated in the regime of the contract of sale or by Art. 594. 990

It is reminded that the CISG does not apply to the limitation of action, for which it does not provide, and which is left to the law of the contracting States. 991

While under *Swiss law* the ordinary time limitation of *action* for contractual liability is of *ten years* (CO Art. 127), i.e., much longer than in China where it is of three, it is dramatically reduced to *two years* in case of warranty for defects (CO Art. 210§1), i.e., it is shorter than in China where is it of four years. Comparatively, the time limitation for *notifying* any defect is, in Swiss law, of *two years* (CO Art. 197§1) like in China. In other words, under Swiss law, the limitation for notifying and for filing are both of two years. 992

Caution applies in these latter respects yet another time: indeed, the *dies a quo* for each notification is not the same. The limitation for notifying starts from *delivery*; that of action from the *timely discovery* of the defect. Therefore, in practice, most of the time, they will not expire simultaneously.

To summarize, the general limitation for contractual liability other than the warranty for defects under the contract of sale is of three years under Chinese law but of ten years under Swiss law; the limitation for notifying a defect and invoking the warranty for defects under a contract of sale is of two years both under Chinese and Swiss law; the limitation of action for warranty for defect is of four years in China but two years in Switzerland. Other than that, roughly speaking, the same principles apply, notably, the buyer's duty of mitigation. 993

Swiss law may apply because it was elected by the parties and the CISG excluded, or because, even though the CISG applies, the parties have elected Swiss law for any matter not covered by the Convention, or because they have not done so, but private international law points at Swiss law for any such 994 matter, since the Convention does not apply to the limitation of action. Therefore, and once again, if only for the limitation of action, parties to a Sino-Swiss contract of sale in particular are strongly advised to pay close attention to the law applicable to their contract[561].

B. Other Provisions

995 The Code further addresses various matters related to particular[562] cases of *revocation* of the contract of sale and their modalities, namely, consecutive to defects, sales in *batches* and payments by *installments* (Art. 631 to 634); it also provides for specific regimes applying to sales by *samples* (Art. 635 and 636); by *trial* (Art. 637 to 639); by *tender*[563] (Art. 644) and by *auction*[564] (Art. 645). Isolated provisions apply to goods having a "useful life", i.e., a limited time during which they can be used (such as, e.g., industrial batteries, etc.; Art. 625); excess delivery (Art. 629) and fruits produced by the goods (Art. 630).

§30. Mandate

996 The Chinese Civil Code defines the mandate (委托合同 wěituō hétóng; Chap. 23; Art. 919 ff.) as "a contract whereby the principal and the agent agree that the latter shall handle the affairs of the former" (Art. 919). The principal may thus entrust the agent with one, several or all affairs (Art. 920). As such, the mandate's all-encompassing scope permeates every aspect of business life, although the parties to a contract of mandate may not even be aware of it; its importance may not be understated.

997 The mandate can take the form of three typical contracts: the general regime, which is governed by Chapter 23 (Art. 919 ff.) of Title Two on typical contracts of the Third Book on contract law of the Chinese Civil Code, is complemented by two special forms, *brokerage* (*ibid.*, Chap. 25, Art. 951 ff.) and *intermediation*, (*ibid.*, Chap. 26, Art. 961 ff.), both of which complement the general

561 S. above §896.

562 Ordinary termination is governed by the general regime of contractual termination, s. above Chap. 4 §26, Termination.

563 On the notion of tender, s. above note 296.

564 On the notion of auction, s. preceding note.

regime, but expressly refer to the latter whenever they are silent[565]. Brokerage and intermediation will be addressed immediately after the general regime.

The contract of mandate, also simply referred to as mandate, is occasionally translated into English as contract of *entrustment*. It corresponds to "le mandat" in French and "der Auftrag" in German (CO Art. 394 ff.) The party which grants the mandate and receives the corresponding service is known as the mandator or *principal*; the party which takes over the mandate and delivers the corresponding services as mandatary or *agent*. As outlined below, "principal" and "agent" are generic expressions and are not dedicated to the mandate specifically however, thus being a potential source of confusion with neighboring legal institutions in Chinese and other laws. 998

We already addressed certain *terminology* issues about agency (s. above Chap. 2 §11.II, Distinctions and Translation Issues). They will be complemented at the end of the chapter on the contract of intermediation (s. below §§1055ff.) 999

Traditionally, and in Swiss law, the mandate is best described or understood as being the basis of a larger group of contracts known as contracts of *services* (as contrasted, mainly, with contracts of alienation, typically the contract of sale), specifically of a subgroup, within that group, of such contracts known as contracts (or obligations) said "of *best efforts*" or "*-endeavors*" (Fr. "de moyens"; Ger.: "auf Mittel" or "zur Leistung der Mittel"), as contrasted, within the same group of contracts of services, with the subgroup of contracts (or obligations) said "of *result*" (Fr.: "de résultat"; Ger.: "auf Erfolg" or "Erfolgspflicht" or "Leistungserfolg") to which belongs, typically, the contract for work (s. below Chap. 5 §38, Contract for Work) from which, for that reason alone, the mandate fundamentally differs, although that distinction is not always well understood, sometimes with serious legal consequences. 1000

As the names of these subgroups suggest, in order to perform, the debtor of an obligation of result must deliver the result which has been contractually defined and agreed upon with the creditor, while the debtor of an obligation of best efforts must only use its best endeavors to reach that result: it does not have the obligation to deliver it, and cannot be held as liable for not having performed if it does not. A good example is that of the architect compared to the contractor: the former is typically bound by a mandate to use his best endeavors; the latter, which is bound by a contract for work, must deliver, for example, a house, which is the result accurately defined and agreed with the principal. Best efforts are often tallied against *professional standards*, for example, a diploma, 1001

565 One could also consider that the contract of *property services* (Chap. 24, Art. 937 ff.) is a special form of mandate, although it does not expressly refer to the mandate. We will not cover it in this book.

a business license, minimum quality requirements, best practices, etc. Chinese law follows these distinctions.

1002 Likewise, the mandate ought not to be confused with the contract of *employment* (s. below Chap. 6 , Employment): indeed, under the latter contract, the employee, unlike the mandatary, is *subordinated* to the employer. The mandatary is not subordinated to the mandator: while it must follow the latter's instructions, the former acts *independently* and is solely liable for its performance.

1003 Another distinction must be signaled between the mandate and *representation.* While arguably less radical, that distinction is no less problematic because of the finer line distinguishing these two notions, whose overlapping is extensive. Representation is also known as *agency* and is mainly governed, in Chinese law, by Art. 161 ff. of the Chinese Civil Code, but not only: other sets of provisions, some general, some specific, which are scattered around the law, apply. It is known in Swiss law as "représentation" in French and "Vertretung" in German and governed by Art. 32 ff. of the Swiss Code of Obligations. Agency has already been extensively outlined with the general part of the Chinese Civil Code, to which we refer (s. above Chap. 2 §8.III.C, Legal Representative and Chap. 2 §11, Agency), but whose main features we recall below in the context of the mandate.

1004 As its name makes clear, the regime of representation governs the effects resulting from the representation, by one party, the representative, A.K.A. the agent, of another, the represented, A.K.A. the principal, towards a third party. As such, it is not, strictly speaking, a contract; it is best defined as a legal relationship of contractual nature superposing over a contract; while it can complement virtually any contract, its scope is limited to those features of the underlying contractual relationship which relate to representation within the performance of that contract.

1005 The frequent confusion between mandate and representation stems from the fact that, most of the time, the mandate implies, not to say that its subject matter often chiefly consists in, representation: that is typically the case of an attorney-at-law representing his client before a court. A mandate does not necessarily imply a power of representation, which would enable the representative to legally commit on behalf of the represented towards a third party, namely but not only, to conclude a contract, however. Conversely, in an agency relationship, a representative is inherently empowered for performing some kind of service; however, as noted, the agency regime is limited to the legal effects of representation, of the principal by the agent towards the third party, on the principal and the third party; it is not otherwise concerned with the performance of the agent's mandate. These distinctions may blur, however. They also apply in Chinese law. As a matter of fact, the mandate regime under the Chinese Civil

Code, as well as other typical contracts, also addresses certain aspects of representation. We will signal them and clarify their relationship with the general regime of agency as appropriate.

Finally, as noted (s. above §997), the institution of mandate, generally speaking, is characterized by several sub- or *specialized mandates*. 1006

The mandatary's main obligation is to perform the task it has been entrusted with by the principal (Art. 919 and 922, 1st sentence) and to do so *personally* (Art. 923§1, 1st sentence), with some alleviations which will be mentioned below. That said, one ought to stress once again (s. above §1000) that the mandatary's overarching obligation is that of *best endeavors* or of *diligence*. Although not specifically defined by the law, such obligation, which is frequently referred to in other contracts or about other obligations, is the yardstick of the notion. It merges with the principal's best interests. The duty of diligence is complemented or nuanced by that of *fidelity*: while diligence confounds with the agent's best efforts, fidelity focuses on respecting the principal's will or intent, which it expressed through its instructions (Art. 922, 1st sentence) or can be presumed (Art. 922, 3rd sentence; s. below §1010). Diligence and fidelity blur and overlap however[566]. 1007

The mandate regime is mostly concerned with the parties' mutual obligations, delegation to a sub-agent, relationships with third parties, liabilities and termination. Thus, the *principal* must pay the agent's agreed *fees* after the latter has performed (Art. 928§1). It must do so even if the agent has not, or imperfectly performed without its fault (*ibid.*, § 2). However, the parties may agree otherwise (*ibid.*, *in fine*). Yet it must be stressed once again at this stage that, in principle, the agent has a duty of best efforts, not of success or result. Thus, a client may not refuse to pay his lawyer's fee because he lost a trial, provided the lawyer used his best endeavors[567] and did not commit a serious professional 1008

566 The duty of diligence and fidelity is expressed, in Swiss law, by CO Art. 398§1, which states that "the mandatary is responsible for a good and faithful performance of the affairs it was entrusted with", where "good" stands for the duty of diligence and "faithful" for that of fidelity. Those notions have produced an abundant body of doctrine and jurisprudence, which may also inspire the interpretation of Chinese law.

567 The *pactum de quota litis*, which entitles the attorney-at-law to a fee corresponding to a percentage of the trial's proceeds, therefore down to none if the case was lost, is strictly prohibited in most jurisdictions, namely, civil law jurisdictions, like China and Switzerland, where it is seen as threatening the attorney's independence. Somewhat paradoxically it is admitted and widely practiced in other jurisdictions however, generally in common law ones, notably in the U.S. Contingency fees, by which the attorney may be entitled to a pre-agreed bonus on top of his fees, are admitted both in China and in Switzerland, within certain limits, however.

fault, such as missing a statute of limitation. The same would apply to a doctor whose treatment fails to cure his patient[568].

1009 Besides, as a rule, the principal must prepay the agent's *expenses* for handling the former's affairs. In spite of the imperative form of that provision, the law also provides for the case in which the principal did not, and the agent paid for them instead, namely, in case of unexpected or underestimated expenses, but also because the agent renounces asking for such prepayment, or the principal is reluctant or refuses to. If so, the principal must reimburse the agent with interests (Art. 921).

1010 On its part, as it implements its general duties of diligence and fidelity outlined above (s. §1007), the *agent* must follow the principal's *instructions* (Art. 922, 1st sentence). Should these instructions prove inadequate or insufficient and need to be modified or complemented, the agent must obtain the principal's prior approval (*ibid.*, 2nd sentence). If the agent cannot reach out to the principal while the matter is urgent, the agent must handle the matter in the principal's best interest (s. above §1007[569]) and report to the latter as soon as possible (*ibid.*, 3rd sentence).

1011 Moreover, the agent must regularly *report* to the principal, whenever the latter asks, the performance of its mandate, and do so in any case at the end of the mandate (Art. 924). It must also *turn over* to the principal any property acquired on its behalf in the course of the mandate (Art. 927).

1012 While in principle the agent must perform personally (Art. 923, 1st sentence), it may, subject to the principal's *consent, delegate* part of or the whole mandate to a third party (*ibid.*, 2nd sentence), known as the sub-agent or sub-mandatary. Such authorization or, on the contrary, prohibition, is typically, and should be, mentioned in the contract of mandate or the agent's POA (cf. Art. 165 and above §287). The principal's consent may not be presumed, but if the latter did not consent in advance, it may ratify the delegation, i.e., approve it *a posteriori* (cf. *ibid.*, 3rd sentence, 1st phrase).

1013 If, however, the agent failed to obtain such consent, it shall be *liable* towards the principal for any damage caused by the sub-agent (Art. 923, 4th sentence, 1st phrase). The agent may free itself from such liability however, if it proves that, faced with an emergency, it so sub-mandated the sub-agent in the

---

568 In that respect, the extensive disclaimers patients are now typically asked to sign everywhere before a surgery or treatment, which reflect U.S. civil liability law, disregard, in jurisdictions like China and Switzerland, that such disclaimer are unnecessary if the medical personnel was diligent, and ineffective if it committed a serious professional fault.

569 This regime is consistent with that of *negotiorum gestio* (Art. 169§3 and 979 ff.; s. above §300).

principal's best interests (*ibid.*, 2nd phrase; s. also above note 569). The mandate's sub-agency regime is consistent with the general one (s. above §§297 and 299).

The principal has the right to instruct the sub-agent *directly*. It is to be noted that, in case the principal had not approved such delegation in advance, its direct instructions would amount to a ratification. If the principal instructs the sub-agent directly, the (main) agent will only be liable for the care it may have failed to take in *selecting* and *instructing* the sub-agent (inasmuch as those instructions were not superseded by the principal's direct instructions; Art. 923, 3rd sentence, 3rd phrase). While the law only mentions those two duties, they are usually complemented, in doctrine, by that of *supervising* the sub-agent (Lat.: *cura in eligendo, instruendo et custodiendo*). The mandate regime is, in that respect also, consistent with the general regime of agency (cf. Art. 169§2 and above §299). 1014

Direct instructions from the principal to the sub-agent is to be distinguished from *parallel mandates*, i.e., the situation in which the principal were to instruct another agent (which the law designates as "third party") beside the initial agent to handle the same affair (Art. 931). To do so, the principal needs the agent's *consent*, which is the opposite of sub-agency where the agent needs the principal's consent. Even if the principal did obtain the initial agent's consent, it shall be liable for any loss the initial agent suffers because of the other agent. If, on the contrary, the principal failed to obtain the initial agent's consent, such failure will amount to a breach of the initial mandate and expose the principal to additional liability for breach of contract towards the initial agent. 1015

Whenever the agent enters into a contract with a *third party* in its own name but within the scope of its mandate while the third party is aware of the relationship between the principal and the agent, the contract shall bind the principal to the third party (Art. 925). However, the contract shall bind the agent, not the principal, to the third party if there is conclusive evidence to that effect (*ibid., in fine*). While the law falls short of being specific, such would be the case if the third party was not or ought not to be aware of the relationship between the principal and the agent. Inasmuch, the regime of Art. 925 is perfectly consistent with that of the general regime of agency (Art. 171§1 and 172; s. above §§290ff.; s. also Art. 504 which mirrors those principles in contract law; s. above §608). 1016

In some cases, however, it may be the principal's express, and perfectly legitimate indeed, *intent* that the agent does not disclose, to the third party, the relationship between the principal and the agent, and that the agent concludes a contract in its own name with the third party. In such case, whenever the *third party*, while not being aware of such relationship, prevents the agent to perform to the principal's benefit, the law mandates the agent to inform the principal 1017 accordingly, and grants the principal the right to be *subrogated* in the agent's rights towards the third party (Art. 926§1)[570]. If so, the third party may use the agent's defenses against the principal (*ibid.*, § 3, 1st sentence). However, that right of subrogation is subject to the third party's right of *objection* that, had it been aware of the relationship between the agent and the principal, it had not concluded such contract with the agent (*ibid., in fine*)[571].

1018 If, on the contrary, in the same circumstances, *mutatis mutandis*, the *principal* prevents the agent from performing towards the third party, then the agent is mandated by law to disclose the principal to the third party[572]. The law then grants the latter the *choice* to act against either the agent or the principal, while in the latter case it shall be subrogated in the rights of the agent towards the principal (Art. 926§2). This choice is final (*ibid., in fine*). If so, the principal may use against the third party both its own defenses against the agent and the agent's defenses against the third party (*ibid.*, § 3, 2nd sentence).

1019 Other than the cases mentioned above, the mandate's regime further contemplates several cases of *liability*. Thus, the *agent* is liable towards the principal for any damage it caused the latter, under two cumulative conditions: if it committed a *fault*, and provided it was *remunerated* (Art. 929§1, 1st sentence). Such fault includes *excess power* (*ibid.*, § 2), which is consistent with the general regime of agency (Art. 164§2; s. above §298). In case of *gratuitous* mandate however, an additional or qualified condition applies: it shall be liable only in case of willful misconduct or gross negligence (*ibid.*, § 1, 2nd sentence). Agents *jointly* handing an affair are liable jointly and severally (Art. 932). Conversely, if the agent suffers a loss without its fault in the performance of the mandate, the *principal* shall be liable towards it (Art. 930).

1020 Either party may *revoke* the contract anytime (Art. 933, 1st sentence). Besides, the law does not require any cause; therefore, *a contrario*, they may do so *without a cause*. It is important to note that, although this provision does not express its *imperative* nature, there is a consensus in Chinese doctrine and jurisprudence that this right cannot be contractually suppressed, rendered more difficult or renounced: either would be regarded as *null* and void and, consequently,

570 For example, the principal instructs the agent to act as proxy and to buy shares in a company which fails to issue the shares after payment.

571 For example, in the example above, the principal turns out to be a competitor of the third party.

572 For example, in the first example above (s. note 570), the principal fails to pay the shares.

unenforceable[573]. This interpretation conforms with the general tendency in civil law systems; it is also very strict in Swiss law[574].

If the revocation damages the other party, the law distinguishes between whether the mandate was onerous or gratuitous. In the first case (onerous mandate), the terminating party is liable for any loss plus positive interests, i.e., interests the other party had earned if the mandate had been performed (*ibid.*, 3rd sentence). Even though the law is not specific in that regard, any such loss may include both *damnum emergens* and *lucrum cessans* (s. above §810). 1021

In the second case (gratuitous mandate), the terminating party is also liable for such loss, but only if the revocation occurred at an *inappropriate time*; moreover, it is not liable for interest (Art. 933, 2nd sentence). However, in either case, the terminating party is not liable if it terminated without its fault (*ibid.*, 2nd sentence, 2nd phrase). 1022

The mandate is *terminated* in case of death, incapacitation, dissolution or bankruptcy of either party (Art. 934). Yet termination may not occur in two cases: if the parties agreed otherwise, or if the time is *inappropriate* considering the nature of the affair entrusted (*ibid.*), namely, if it impairs the interests of the principal (cf. Art. 935, 1st sentence *in fine* and 936, 2nd sentence). If the principal is so incapacitated, the agent must continue to handle its affairs until the principal's successors take over; conversely, if the agent is, its successors shall notify the principal and take over until the latter does (Art. 935 and 936). 1023

Even though the law falls short from mentioning it, in case of termination at an inappropriate time, i.e., if the agent, its successors or the principal's successor neglect to take care of the principal's interests, they shall be liable towards the principal, i.e., the agent shall be liable under the mandate's regime (Art. 929§1; s. above §1019), and the others either under the regime of liability for illicit acts (s. above Chap. 8 , Liability for Illicit Acts ("Torts")), or under that of contractual liability if they were contractually bound to the principal (s. above Chap. 4 §27, Liability for Breach of Contract). 1024

It is worth noting that, comparatively, Chinese law is more protective of the parties than Swiss law. In Swiss law, the parties may revoke the mandate anytime (CO Art. 404§1), save if such time is inappropriate: if they do, they may be liable towards each other (*ibid.*, § 2). However, if the time is not 1025

573 S. Notice of the Supreme People's Court on Issuing the Provisions on Case Guidance of 26 November 2010 *ad* Chinese Civil Code Art. 933.

574 ATF 115 II 464; ATF 117 II 466 = JT 199 II 1387. About the prohibition of damage interest, liquidated damages, penal clauses, etc. as deterrents hence indirect hindrances, s. below §1025 and note 576.

inappropriate, neither party is entitled to any compensation[575]: Swiss jurisprudence is very restrictive in this respect[576]. In contrast, in Chinese law, both parties are entitled to damages, even in case of timely revocation (Chinese Civil Code, Art. 933; s. above §§1020 and 1022).

1026 As to the liability of the mandatary as "contractor" damaging a third party, which may, potentially, be a special case of *liability of certain authors for illicit acts*, specifically, of "workers" (within that special regime), it is covered by Art. 1193 (s. below §1682), to which we refer.

§31. Brokerage

1027 Brokerage (行纪合同 xíng jì hétóng; Chap. 25 of the Chinese Civil Code, Art. 951 ff.) is a special form of mandate, where the latter is the *lex generalis* and the former a *lex specialis*. It is defined as a contract whereby the broker, who is the mandatary, in its own name, engages in trade activities for the client or mandator, while the latter remunerates the former for such services (Art. 951).

1028 Brokerage is best described by distinguishing it, at this early stage, from *intermediation* (Chap. 26, Art. 961 ff.; s. below Chap. 5 §32, Intermediation), which is the other special form of mandate among the typical contracts, by which the latter is defined as a contract whereby the intermediary, who is the mandatary, introduces the client or mandator an opportunity for entering into a contract, or provides it with intermediary services for the conclusion of the same, while the client remunerates the intermediary for such services (Art. 961). A broker typically conducts a large number of transactions (e.g., a grain or oil trader), while the intermediary usually intervenes for one or a few isolated business opportunities (e.g., a real estate agent).

1029 The other fundamental difference between brokerage and intermediation is that, as mentioned in the first provision of the chapter, the broker concludes in its *own name* (Art. 951), while the intermediary's role is limited to either introduce business opportunities to the client either without assisting it to conclude, or can extend to assisting it to conclude. It does not, however, consist in *representing* the client, a fortiori concluding in the latter's name (compare Art. 961, which does not mention either, with Art. 951, which is explicit in this regard), but may, if the client so empowers the intermediary (s. below §1048 and

---

575 Swiss law provides for the same solutions as Chinese law in case of *termination* (as opposed to revocation) however (CO Art. 405 and 406).

576 S. ATF 104 II 108 = JT 1980 I 77, with some alleviations: s. ATF 103 II 129 = JT 1978 I 150; s. also ATF 140 III 200 = JT 2014 II 401 confirming prior jurisprudence.

note 578). In any event, the intermediary, unlike the broker, never acts in its own name.

As a consequence of acting in its own name, the broker entering into a contract with a *third party* enjoys the rights and obligations resulting from such contract *directly* (Art. 958§1). Likewise, if the third party's default causes losses to the client, the broker shall be *liable* for it (ibid., § 2). 1030

The fact that the broker acts in its own name does not imply that it may do so freely: like in the mandate (s. above §§1007 and 1010), the broker must follow the client's *instructions*. Thus, the broker may not buy at a *price* higher or sell at a price lower than the price set by the client without obtaining the latter's consent (Art. 955§1, 1st sentence). The law even stresses this provision by providing for any "special" instructions which the client may have given the broker (*ibid.*, § 3), by which one may understand any instructions other than setting the price (e.g., about the subject-matter commodities' specifications). If the broker infringes such instructions, the client is bound anyway, but the broker is liable towards the client for compensating for any damage resulting therefrom (*ibid.*, § 2). 1031

There is, however, a fine line to draw between the general rule of Art. 951 and the relative exemption provided by Art. 956: under the latter provision, whose drafting is not limpid, where the broker is to sell or purchase a commodity whose price is fixed by the market, the commission agent "may act as the buyer or seller itself", unless the principal has indicated otherwise. The difference with Art. 951 is not obvious, since under the latter provision the broker acts under its own name anyway: therefore, one may fail to see, *prima facie*, what the difference between the broker acting as a buyer or seller and acting in its own name may be. What Art. 956 purports at conveying is that Art. 951 implies that the client has given *specific* instructions to the broker ("buy 100 tons of cement at the price of USD60.00 per metric ton FOB Shanghai") while, in contrast, where the subject-matter of the brokerage is *market-priced commodities* where the client has given *generic* instructions to the broker ("buy 100 tons of cement FOB Shanghai"), Art. 956 enables the broker to act freely ("as a buyer or a seller itself") in the client's *best interest*, which is equated to the broker's hypothetical ("as") self-interest. The standard to which the broker is subject is thus that of the mandatary's general duty of diligence (s. above §1007). 1032

This exemption is only given, however, unless the client has instructed the broker to the contrary ("...subject to the preliminary approval of our Chief Procurement Officer"). The law does not request express instructions to the contrary; it is enough that the client has "indicated otherwise", where one may suppose that a court may prove quite liberal in acknowledging such contrary intent (Art. 956 *in fine*). The nuance brought by Art. 956 to Art. 951 is intended 1033 to find a compromise between the protection of both parties on one hand, and the reality of dynamic markets on the other.

1034 In those regards, the broker must keep with due care any *assets* entrusted by the client to the effect of the brokerage contract's performance (Art. 953). Most of the time, such assets are in the form of financial assets (e.g., a credit line) or commodities (e.g., oil)[577]. If such assets are perishable (e.g., grain), subject to deterioration (e.g., falling stocks) or deteriorated (e.g., rotten grain), the broker may, with the client's consent or without it if the client cannot be reached, dispose of them, in the client's best interest however (Art. 954). This duty is also to be related to the mandatary's general duty of diligence (s. above §1007).

1035 Where the client fails, without justification, to take *delivery* of an item purchased by the broker or which the broker failed to sell, the latter may, after having urged the client, *deposit* and sell it according to the law (Art. 957). This faculty is nothing else but a special case of the eponymous remedy provided by the general part of contract law in case of nonperformance (s. above Chap. 4 §26.VIII, Deposit).

1036 Once the broker has performed, the client must pay the agreed *fees* (Art. 959§1, 1st sentence). It is to be noted that, if the client defaults, the law expressly confers on the broker a *lien* on any assets entrusted by the client (*ibid.*, 2nd sentence), unless the parties agreed otherwise (*ibid.*, *in fine*).

1037 If the broker sold *above* the price agreed, its fee "may" be increased, which implies that such increase shall have been contractually pre-agreed. However, if it was not, or if the contract is unclear, the law refers to the mechanism provided by Art. 510 (s. above §618). Yet at this point, the law gives a slight advantage to the client by ruling that if, despite the parties subjected themselves to Art. 510, they failed to reach an agreement or the fees increase cannot be determined, the related benefits shall belong to the client (*ibid.*, § 2, 2nd sentence). Besides, if the broker bought or sold *at market price* under Art. 956§1 (s. above §1032), it is also entitled to a fee.

1038 Finally, and in contrast with the mandatary, the broker bears its *expenses* itself, unless the parties agreed otherwise (Art. 952; s. above §1009).

1039 Lastly, as stressed above, the general regime of the mandate applies to any matter not specifically provided for by that of brokerage (Art. 960).

1040 *Terminology* issues are addressed at the end of the chapter on the contract of intermediation (s. below §§1055ff.)

---

577 The subject-matter of a brokerage contract can also consist in services however (e.g., shipping brokerage).

§32. Intermediation

Like brokerage, the intermediation (A.K.A., although somewhat improperly, "intermediary") contract (中介合同 zhōngjiè hétóng; Chap. 26 of the Chinese Civil Code, Art. 961 ff.) is also a special form of mandate, where the latter is the *lex generalis* and the former a *lex specialis*. It is defined as a contract whereby the intermediary, who is the mandatary, introduces the client or mandator an opportunity for entering into a contract, or provides such client with intermediary services for the conclusion of the same, while the client remunerates the intermediary for such services (Art. 961). 1041

As noted in the preceding chapter, the intermediary usually intervenes for a few isolated business opportunities (e.g., a real estate agent), while a broker typically conducts a large number of transactions (e.g., a grain or oil trader). 1042

The contract of intermediation may, therefore, take two forms, depending of the intermediary's involvement degree: where it is less involved, the intermediary simply *introduces* a business opportunity to the client; where it is more involved, the intermediary *assists* the client in concluding the contract eventually resulting from such opportunity (Art. 961). However, as explained about the brokerage contract and unlike under the latter, in neither case does it *conclude* in its own name on behalf of the client (s. above §1130). 1043

Chapter 26 is very concise. Other than those obligations resulting from the contract of intermediation definition, the law really only mentions one additional obligation of the *intermediary*, its duty of *truth*, which is expressed both positively and negatively: positively, the intermediary must truthfully report to the client; negatively, it may not conceal material facts or provide false information, where either may result in damaging the client's interests (Art. 962§1). If so, the intermediary shall be liable towards its client (*ibid.* § 2 *in fine*). The duty of truth aligns with the general duty of diligence of the mandatary (s. above §1007). 1044

The *client's* main obligation is to pay the intermediary's *fees*, which are the focus of Chapter 26. The law is not entirely clear in that regard, insofar as it distinguishes between two situations: whether the intermediary merely "facilitated" the conclusion of the "proposed" contract (Art. 963§1, 1st sentence) or did so by "providing intermediary services in connection with the conclusion of the contract" (*ibid.*, 3rd sentence). The first of these two situations (facilitation) does not, therefore, literally match the first contemplated by Art. 961, 1st sentence, i.e., where the intermediary "introduces" (or "presents") a business opportunity to the client. Besides, while the second situation (provision of services) is contemplated both by Art. 961 and 963 and better match *prima facie*, the formulation used in each provision differs, also leaving some room for 1045 uncertainty. The distinction is not mundane, since it results in fundamentally different remuneration modes.

1046 In that respect, the law further distinguishes the debtor of the fees from their amount. As far as the *debtor* of the fees is concerned, in the first case (facilitation; Art. 963§1, 1st sentence), the client is liable for them, while in the second case (services), both parties are. As far as the *amount* of the fees is concerned, they are to be paid either as pre-agreed or, if they were not, such amount is to be determined pursuant to Art. 510 (s. above §618).

1047 Several *interpretation* issues may be raised with regard to the fees. *First*, as mentioned, the first situation described by Art. 963 ("facilitation") does not match the first mentioned by Art. 961 ("introduction"). Moreover, it is not clear whereat the mere facilitation or introduction ends, and wherefrom services start; namely, it is not obvious that the first option of Art. 963, "facilitation", necessarily matches the first option of Art. 961, "presentation", and that the second option of Art. 963 matches the second option of Art. 961 despite both mention "services". Indeed, services can also consist in presenting a business opportunity and facilitate the potential conclusion of a contract; these notions overlap. *Second*, whether the provision of such services implies that the intermediary has necessarily, before providing such services, introduced the business opportunity at stake, is equally unclear.

1048 *Third*, the extent of such services, namely, whether, eventually, the client will conclude the contract itself, or be *represented* by the intermediary[578], is not specified by the law, although it alludes to it (s. Art. 965 mentioning the client concluding the proposed contract "directly", thus implying that it could have concluded it indirectly, by being represented by the intermediary). Therefore, nothing prevents the intermediary to be, in addition or within the contract of intermediation, empowered to represent the client up to concluding the proposed contract as its representative. If so, the *representation* relationship, which complement that of intermediation, were governed by the general regime of *agency* (s. above Chap. 2 §11, Agency), thus resulting in an *hybrid* contract.

1049 *Fourth* and last, the fees' amount regime (Art. 963, 2nd sentence) is mentioned, in Art. 963, in-between the mention of facilitation (*ibid.*, 1st sentence) and that of services (*ibid.*, 3rd sentence), thus speculatively suggesting that it may only apply to facilitation, but not to services. Beyond such structural or drafting

---

578 Representation is not to be confounded with the fact of acting in one's own name. A broker acts and conclude in its own name, not in that of its client, which it does not represent towards third parties, even though it covertly acts on its client's behalf; comparatively, the intermediary overtly acts in the name of its client, which it represents. Moreover, nothing prevents the client to empower its intermediary, in addition, to conclude it its (the client's) name. S. also above, §1029, and below, §1063 and note 580.

issues, we believe that that regime applies both to facilitation and services however.

The answers to these questions matter since, as outlined above, they result, legally, in halving or doubling, from the client's perspective, the intermediary's fees, depending on whether the counterparty will have to bear them with the client or not (s. next-to-last paragraph). Yet these ambiguities did not escape Chinese courts, which clarified them in the *Interpretation of the Supreme People's Court* on Several Issues Concerning the Application of the General Provisions of the Contract Law of the Civil Code of the People's Republic of China of 4 December 2023. That said, given the infinite forms intermediation may take, practically, we can only advise the parties, especially the intermediary, to carefully define their rights and obligations, in particular representation, as the case may be, and the intermediary's fees, in the contract of intermediation. 1050

The fees are due even in case of *limited* involvement, i.e., if the intermediary only introduces but does not assist the client in concluding the contract, or does assist the client but not up to the conclusion which the latter shall perform itself or "directly" (Art. 965; s. also above, §1047 *in fine*). 1051

If, however, the intermediary *fails* to facilitate the eventual conclusion of the contract, it shall not be entitled to its fees (Art. 964). The same applies if the intermediary infringed its duty of *truth* (Art. 962§2; s. above §1044). 1052

Like the broker (s. above §1038), the intermediary shall, in principle, bear its own *expenses* (Art. 963§2). However, the parties may pre-agree, in the contract of intermediation, that the client shall reimburse the intermediary's fees in case of failure (Art. 964 *in fine*). 1053

Lastly, as for brokerage, the general regime of the mandate applies to any matter not specifically provided for by that of intermediation (Art. 966). 1054

As already outlined about agency (s. above Chap. 2 §11.II, Distinctions and Translation Issues), the *terminology* resulting from the translation, from Chinese in English, French and German of the contract of mandate, the brokerage contract, the intermediation contract and, once again, agency, is the source of countless misunderstandings. Moreover, as far as Swiss law is concerned, *equivalences* between those contracts in both jurisdictions is not obvious. We will do our best to untangle them below. 1055

As already noted, the contract of mandate is also expressed, in English, namely, in some translations of the Chinese Civil Code, as contract of "entrustment". Their parties are designated as, on one side, the "mandator" or the "principal", and on the other the "mandatary" or the "agent". 1056

"Principal" and "agent" are also used for the parties to a relationship of agency governed by Art. 61, 62 and 161 ff. of the Chinese Civil Code, but also by all 1057 special laws providing for such relationship, such as the Company Law (Art. 10 and 11; s. below §§1774ff.) and others. We equally mentioned that agency is also known as "representation", where the parties are the "represented" or principal and the "representative" or agent.

1058 Comparatively, for agency in general, *Swiss law* only uses represented and representative (Fr.: "le représenté" and "le représentant"; Ger.: "der Vertretene" and "der Vertreter") instead; agent (Fr.: "agent"; Ger.: "Agent") is only used for *brokerage*, as mentioned below. Principal (Fr. "le maître"; Ger. "der Geschäftsführer") is not used in the extended context of mandate, but for the *contract for work*. Mandator and mandatary (Fr.: "le mandant" and "le mandataire"; Ger. "der Vollmachtgeber" and "der Beauftragte") may also be used for designating the parties to special mandates, such as the brokerage and the *intermediation* contracts.

1059 *Brokerage* is also translated as "commission agent contract", where the latter translation is the source of further confusion. Indeed, while brokerage contains elements of agency, it corresponds to a distinct notion altogether.

1060 Moreover, as far as *Swiss law* is concerned, confusion is aggravated by the fact that it is not only difficult to relate Chinese contracts to Swiss ones; the translation of their names in English only aggravates such ambiguities. Thus, as already mentioned about agency, it is worth recalling at this stage that brokerage, or commission agent contract, is best matched with "le contract d'agence" in French and "der Agenturvertrag" in German (CO Art. 418a ff.); however, the contrat d'agence does not correspond to agency or representation, which as explained is expressed in French by "la représentation" and German by "die Vertretung" (CO Art. 32 ff.)

1061 The contract of *intermediation* is equally misleading. Indeed, there is no encompassing equivalence in *Swiss law*; instead, the contract of intermediation in Chinese law is best matched with two contracts in Swiss law: "le contrat de courtage" and "la commission" in French or "der Mäklervertrag" and "die Kommission" in German (CO Art. 412 ff. and 425 ff.) Thus, the "contrat de courtage" or "Mäklervertrag" can be compared to the *first option* of the Chinese contract of intermediation, where the intermediary introduces a business opportunity to the client, but does not conclude the proposed contract on the client's behalf. In contrast, the "commission" or "Kommission" compares to the *second option* of the Chinese contract of intermediation, where the intermediary provides its service for assisting the client in concluding the proposed contract and, if so empowered, concludes it in the client's behalf, as its representative however, not, unlike the broker, in its own name. Therefore, "la commission" in Swiss law does not equate to the commission agent contract or brokerage in Chinese law, but the second option of the contract of intermediation[579].

Thus, the distinctive features of the contracts of brokerage and intermediation in Chinese law, and the "contrat d'agence" or "Agenturvertrage" , the "contrat de courtage" or "Mäklervertrag" and the "commission" or "Kommission" in Swiss law can be summarized as follows: brokerage corresponds to the "contrat d'agence" or "Agenturvertrag", while intermediation corresponds to both the "contrat de courtage" or "Mäklervertrag" and the "commission" or "Kommission", depending on whether, for the first, the intermediary only introduces the business opportunity to the client or, for the second, eventually assists the conclusion of the proposed contract, which it possibly concludes, if empowered as representative of the client. 1062

Such equivalences face further uncertainty where the intermediary does not only introduce a business opportunity, but also provides services for facilitating the conclusion of the proposed contract without, however, going as far as concluding it on behalf of the client, as its representative, i.e., not in the intermediary's own name. The question which then arises is whether such relationship qualifies as "contrat de courtage" ("Mäklervertrag") or "commission" ("Kommission"). Like for brokerage in Chinese law, the "contrat de courtage" ("Mäklervertrag") regime in Swiss law does not provide for representation but does not exclude it either; the jurisprudence even expressly acknowledged it[580]. Therefore, in such case, the "contrat de courtage" ("Mäklervertrag") ought to be complemented with the general regime of agency or representation, thus resulting in a *hybrid* contract (*ibid.*) 1063

§33. Loan

The contract of loan (A.K.A. "of loan of money"; 借款合同 jièkuǎn hétóng; Chap. 12 of the Chinese Civil Code, Art. 667 ff.) is the first of a group of four contracts for *financial services* including, other than the loan, the contract of *suretyship* (or "of guarantee"; Chap. 13, Art. 681 ff.; s. below Chap. 5 §34, Suretyship), of *financial leasing* (Chap. 14, Art. 703 ff.; s. below Chap. 5 §36, 1064

579 The intermediary *introducing* an opportunity is further known in Swiss law as "l'agent indicateur" or "der Hinweisagent"; that *assisting* as "l'agent négociateur" or "der Verhandlungsagent".

580 S. BLAISE CARRON/SABRINA GAURON-CARLIN, CC & CO annotés, Helbing Lichtenhahn, 12th ed., 2024, p. 400, notes ad CO Art. 412 citing ATF 139 II 217, ATF 49 II 230 and ATF 90 II 92 = JT 1965 I 137.

Financial Leasing) and of *factoring* (Chap. 15, Art. 761 ff.; s. below Chap. 5 §37, Factoring).

1065 The contract of loan is a contract whereby the borrower obtains a loan from the lender and repays the loan together with interest thereon when the loan becomes due (Art. 667). From a terminological perspective, it should be noted that 借款 jièkuǎn, the loan, can be used, like in English, both in the perspective of the lender and that of the borrower. However, as already noted[581], unlike in Chinese and in English, French distinguishes the loan from the perspective of the lender, where is it known as "prêt", from that of the borrower, known as "emprunt"[582]. German does not: like in English, both are known as "Darlehen"[583].

1066 Although the law only implies it, the subject-matter of the loan is *money*. The loan of another movable (or immovable) against consideration, typically, a rental fee, is governed by the contract of *lease* (Art. 703 ff.; s. below Chap. 5 §35, Lease).

1067 *Financial leasing*, which ought not to be confused with the lease, whereby the lessor purchases the leased item from the seller and makes it available to the lessee against a rent, and can, accordingly, be described as a form of loan, is governed by a separate regime (Chap. 15; Art. 735 ff.) which will be covered in the next chapter (s. below Chap. 5 §36, Financial Leasing).

1068 It must further be stressed that *securities* are not governed by the regime of the contract of loan but by three separate regimes: *contractual* securities (i.e., governed by contract law, as opposed to real securities governed by real rights, although the latter evidently entail contractual obligations) are governed both by, *first*, certain provisions of Title One on general rules of the Third Book on contract law and, *second*, Chapter 13 on the contract of *suretyship* (Art. 681 ff.) of Title Two on typical contracts, which will be outlined in the next chapter.

In contrast, *real* securities are governed, *third*, by an entirely separate part of the Code, i.e., by Title Four on security in property (Art. 386 ff.) of the Second Book on real rights. That latter regime, which applies both to movable and immovable securities, emphasizes, but is not limited to, mortgage, and also governs pledges and lien, has been comprehensively outlined in this book (s. above Chap. 3 §17.IV, Security in Property).

1069 In that latter respect, *bonds*, i.e., loans borrowed by corporations against shares, although Art. 667 ff. of the Chinese Civil Code remain applicable as *lex generalis*, are primarily governed by the Securities Law, the Company Law and

581 Cf. above note 308. S. also below note 585.
582 S., for example, CO Art. 1156 ff.
583 S. also below §§1070 and 1071.

administrative regulations issued by CSRC, such as the Measures for the Issue and Trading of Corporate Bonds. The general regime of corporate bonds will be addressed below (s. Chap. § 14.IV.G, Corporate Bonds).

Comparatively, *Swiss law* is replete with terminological ambiguities. It distinguishes the loan (Fr.: "le prêt"; Ger.: "die Leihe"), which in the Chinese Civil Code is governed by Chap. 12, i.e., against *interest*, from the *free* loan: the latter is known, in Swiss law, by the inexplicit expression of "prêt à usage" in French and "die Gebrauchleihe" in German (CO Art. 305 ff.), literally "loan for use", while the loan against interest is designated by the equally deceiving expression of "prêt de consommation" (CO Art. 312 ff.) in French even though, unlike its name suggest, it is not intended for *consumer credit*[584]. German is, in this latter respect, straightforward however, as it names the latter "(das) Darlehen", which in German unequivocally refers to the loan against interest[585]. Finally, *bonds*, which are designated in French by the equally ambiguous expression of "emprunts par obligations" and in German by "Anleihensobligationen" (CO 1157), are also regulated by the Swiss Code of Obligations, but by an entirely separate regime. 1070

To summarize, the contract of loan as per Art. 667 ff. of the Chinese Civil Code is a general regime applying to financial loans against interest; it does not cover securities or collaterals; it corresponds, in Swiss law, to "le prêt de consommation" or "das Darlehen", as per CO Art. 312 ff. There is no equivalent, in Chinese law, of the "prêt à usage" or "Gebrauchleihe", i.e., the free loan, although the Chinese Civil Code does allude to it (s. below §1086). 1071

Chapter 12 is very concise; it only contains basic provisions. It applies to both commercial loans, i.e., to enterprises, and private loans, to individuals (cf. Art. 668§1). Although as noted above it focuses on loans against interest, it also briefly addresses free loans (s. below §§1086 and 1087). 1072

In principle, the contract of loan must be made in *writing* (Art. 668, 1st phrase), except between individuals, if they so agree (*ibid.*, 2nd phrase). While Art. 679 seems to contradict the latter provision by prescribing that such parties must establish the contract latest at the time of disbursing, it does not: Art. 679 1073

584 Consumer credit, which purports at protecting small borrowers, is governed, in Swiss law, by a separate law, the Federal Law on Consumer Credit. It is also strongly regulated in EU law. It is not in Chinese law, where it is protected both by the Chinese Civil Code and con-sumer rights ; the latter are not covered in this book.

585 The structure and naming in German of the titles of this chapter of the Swiss Code of Obligations is also unfortunate, as it places both the free loan and the loan against interest under the title of "die Leihe", while it is widely considered that, in German, "die Leihe", as opposed to "das Darlehen", exclusively refers to the free loan.

focuses on the *time* of such agreement, which can still be entered into orally. Of course, if so, the burden of proof will be on the lender.

1074 The *contents* of the contract typically include the type, currency, purpose, principal amount, interest rate, term, method of repayment, etc. of the loan; however, that enumeration is not exhaustive (Art. 668§2).

1075 The main obligation of the *lender* is, evidently, to *disburse* the loan (Art. 671 *a contrario*). If it fails to, fully and timely as pre-agreed, it shall be liable for any damage caused to the borrower as a result (Art. 671).

1076 *Usury rates* are prohibited (Art. 680). This provision refers to the topical administrative regulations. The relevant benchmark rates are published periodically by financial regulatory authorities, i.e., in the first place, the PBOC; judicial interpretations clarify the application of these rates in civil litigation for loan disputes. The maximum lawful interest rate for loans is generally considered to be four times the benchmark (loan prime rate or LPR[586], or an agreed base rate), above which the interest is regarded as usurious and invalid. Consequently, in compliance with Art. 680 of the Chinese Civil Code, interest charged above this limit may be void, and lenders may only recover principal and lawful interest up to the prescribed cap.

1077 The *borrower's* obligations are to truthfully inform the lender about its creditworthiness (Art. 669), draw down the loan Art. 671§2), use it as agreed (Art. 673, 1st phrase), pay interest (Art. 674, 1st phrase) and reimburse it (Art. 675, 1st phrase).

1078 To that effect, the lender has the right to supervise and inspect the *use* of the loan, and the borrower has the obligation to provide the lender with financial and accounting reports, and related information (Art. 672). If the borrower redirects the loan and uses it for purposes other than that agreed, the lender has the right to withhold its disbursement, recall the loan ahead of schedule or revoke the loan contract (Art. 673).

1079 If the borrower fails to *draw down* the loan or does so *belatedly*, it must pay interest as if it had performed timely (Art. 671§2). If it *repays* the loan belatedly, it shall pay the overdue interest according to the contract or the relevant administrative regulations (Art. 676; s. next paragraph). If, on the contrary, it repays the loan *in advance*, it shall only pay interest until reimbursement, unless the parties agreed otherwise (Art. 677).

1080 However surprising that may be, the Chinese Civil Code does not explicitly regulate the legal consequences, namely, the rate, of late or *overdue interest*

586 The LPR was, as announced on 20 November 2025, by the authorized National Interbank Lending Centre under the PBOC, of 3.00%.

payment[587]. That being so, they arise from general principles of contract law and judicial interpretations. As a result, the following principles, resulting from judicial practice and legal commentaries, can be summarized as follows:

If a borrower is late in paying interest, the creditor may charge default overdue interest. Such interest is usually calculated on the basis of the PBOC's benchmark loan rate, increased by an additional percentage (typically 30% to 50% above the one-year LPR[588]). 1081

The SPC issued guidelines[589] clarifying how to calculate overdue interest and recognizing such claims in contract disputes, especially in cross-border or foreign currency cases[590]. Late interest rates applied by courts on overdue loans commonly correspond to about four times the benchmark interest rate or LPR, if the contract does not provide for liquidated damages[591]. Litigation and debt collection related to late interest follow civil procedure regulations. 1082

It is interesting to note that the late interest rates applied by courts for overdue loans represent the maximum possible below usuary rates (s. above §1076), namely, that it is considerably higher[592] than the general legal rate for overdue debts under Swiss law, which is of five percent (CO Art. 73§1; s. below §1675), while there is, in Switzerland, no practice comparable to the Chinese one for overdue loans interests. 1083

The borrower must *reimburse* the loan timely (Art. 675, 1st phrase); however, the parties may agree to extend it (Art. 678). 1084

The law provides for various settlement mechanisms in case certain conditions of the loan are missing or unclear. If the *interest payment time* has not been agreed upon or is unclear, the parties should determine it under Art. 510 (s. above §811); if they fail, the law prescribes three solutions, depending on the 1085

---

587 Although those two expressions blur or overlap, "late interest" and "overdue interest" apply both to the late payment of interest and to interest due because of the late reimbursement of the loan.

588 S. above note 586.

589 S. Interpretation of the Supreme People's Court on Several Issues concerning the Application of Law to the Calculation of Interest on Debt for the Period of Deferred Performance in the Enforcement Procedure, Interpretation No. 8 [2014] of the Supreme People's Court issued on 7 July 2014 and effective as of 1 August 2014.

590 S. the recent Official Reply of the Supreme People's Court Regarding the Basis of Calculation for the Interest on Overdue Payments in a Foreign Currency or Hong Kong, Macao, or Taiwan Currency, Interpretation No. 2 [2025] of the Supreme People's Court issued on 12 February 2025 and effective as of 13 February 2025.

591 About such clauses, namely, the conditions to which they are subject, s. above Chap. 4 §27.III.A, Liquidated Damages. For loans, under the same guidelines, they may not exceed the rate of 24%.

592 The LPR was, in November 2025, at 3%; at four times it would reach 12%.

duration of the loan: if it is shorter than one year, interest shall be paid together with the principal; if longer, at the end of each yearly term; if the remaining term is less than one year, with the principal (Art. 674, 2nd sentence).

1086 It must be emphasized at this stage that the mechanism of Art. 674, 2nd sentence applies to the interest payment time, not *rate*. If such rate was not contractually pre-agreed, the loan is deemed by law to be interest-*free* (Art. 680§2). Nevertheless, the law provides that, if the parties failed to agree *a posteriori*, the interest shall be determined according to local usages, the parties' agreed method if there was one, trade usages, market interest rates and other relevant factors (*ibid*., § 3). Therefore, beyond the apparent contradiction between the second and the third paragraph of Art. 680, the law suggests that its paragraph two poses a presumption, while giving the borrower a chance to prove and apply the interest rate even though it was not agreed. In other words, one can reasonably anticipate that the court will use its discretion and rule in equity to that effect[593].

1087 Likewise, if the *loan reimbursement time* is missing or unclear, the parties shall attempt to settle under Art. 510 (s. above §618); if they fail to, the borrower may reimburse *anytime*; however, the law expressly provides that the lender may urge the borrower to reimburse within a "reasonable" time (Art. 675), which implies that, if the lender considers that such time is not reasonable, it is entitled to file at court which shall use its discretion to rule on such reasonableness after having considered the circumstances. This understanding is confirmed by comparing the second paragraph of Art. 680 to the end of its third paragraph, where the drafting style of the former is liberal, as compared to the latter which is mandatory by affirming that loan contracts between individuals not mentioning an interest rate are "to be treated" as interest-free.

§34. Suretyship

I. Introduction

1088 A contract of suretyship (A.K.A. "of guarantee" or "of guaranty"; 保证合同 bǎozhèng[594] hétóng; Chap. 13 of the Chinese Civil Code, Art. 681 to 702) is a

[593] CO Art. 73§1 also refers to trade usages (s. below note 769).

[594] U.S. legal terminology uses "guaranty" instead of "guarantee", i.e., in the narrower sense of third-party promise to pay in case of the debtor's default, while "guarantee" has a broader meaning in the sense of "assurance" and is also used as a verb. Chinese legal terminology also marks this difference by using 担保 dānbǎo lato sensu and 保证 bǎozhèng stricto sensu, where it uses the latter for the contract of suretyship; however,

contract pursuant to which a third party, the surety, and a creditor agree that the surety shall perform the obligation or bear liability when the debtor fails to perform its obligation, or when the circumstances stipulated by the parties concerned occur, in order to guarantee the enforcement of the creditor's rights (Art. 681).

The differences between neighboring but distinct institutions involving *third parties* performing instead of the defaulting debtor have been discussed above about Art. 523 (s. above §§646 and 647), Art. 552 (s. above §§700 to 705) and Art. 581 (s. above §803). These differences are numerous, subtle and complex; they should be paid close attention to for the sake of preventing confusion. Because of their importance, we will briefly recall them below, while referring to the paragraph mentioned above or in the next for further discussion. 1089

Thus, Art. 523 applies to the case in which the debtor and a third party have agreed that the latter would perform instead of the former. Art. 524 addresses the case in which a third party has a legitimate interest in performing in place of the debtor. Art. 535 to 537 apply to subrogation, by which the creditor is entitled to substitute itself to the debtor for performing the latter's obligation when the debtor relies on the performance of a third party for performing towards the creditor (s. above §§682ff.) Art. 552 addresses the transfer or assignment of the debtor's liabilities to a third party to the extent that the latter commits to being jointly and severally liable together with the debtor towards the creditor (s. above §700). Finally, Art. 581 entitles the creditor to apply at court for a third party to perform in lieu of the debtor in case of the latter's subjective impossibility (s. above §803). 1090

Moreover, while the institutions enumerated in the preceding paragraph focus on general provisions related to third party performance or guarantees, Chinese law provides for other forms of guarantees in the form of *securities*, often specialized (such as, e.g., the mortgage), and dedicates a whole chapter to securities in the Second Book on real law of the Chinese Civil Code (s. above Chap. 3 §17.IV, Security in Property). 1091

While a comprehensive comparison between the numerous types of institutions mentioned in the preceding paragraphs would exceed the scope of this book, the following comments deserve to be emitted, however. Thus, the fact that the contract of suretyship is a typical contract does not fundamentally distinguishes it from those neighboring institution, which are equally of a contractual nature, but located in the general provisions of contract law instead of in that on typical 1092

---

the title of the former guarantee law, which was replaced in part by the contract of suretyship in the Chinese Civil Code (s. above §99), referred to 担保 dānbǎo since it also covered other types of guarantees such as mortgage, pledge, lien and deposit. In this book, for the sake of simplicity, we will use "guarantee" in all cases.

contracts; its regime is only more detailed, hence arguably more adequate for a separate transaction focusing on such guarantee in parallel to the transaction it guarantees, but to which it remains, as expressly provided by the law (Art. 682§1, 1st sentence), *ancillary*, like those other institutions.

1093 Besides, as compared to, in particular, Art. 523 and 552, one ought to note that the *parties* which *conclude* the contract providing for such guarantee (by which the third party will stand for the obligation of the debtor towards the creditor) are, setting aside other differences, different in each case: thus, the agreement is made, in the case of Art. 523, between the debtor and the creditor; in the case of Art. 552, between the debtor and the third party; and in the case of the contract of suretyship, between the third party and the creditor.

1094 As mentioned elsewhere (s. above §705), the suretyship contract can be compared, in Swiss law[595], to the "contract of surety" (as translated in the semi-official translation in English of the Swiss Code of Obligations; Fr.: "le cautionnement"; Ger.: "die Bürgschaft"; CO Art. 492 ff.) whose regime can be said to be, comparatively, more elaborate however.

1095 That said, the literal translation of "surety", i.e., "sûretés" in French and "Sicherheiten" in German, is used generically throughout the Swiss Civil Code, including about the contract of surety (cf. CO Art. 506), to indicate any kind of securities (s., e.g., CO Art. 257e, 523 or 653k) and does not, therefore, exclusively relate to the contract of surety or suretyship.

II. General Provisions

1096 Chapter 13 is divided into two sections: general provisions and liability. The *general provisions* (Art. 681 to 690), beyond defining the suretyship contract (Art. 681; s. above §1088) consistently with the ancillary nature of the suretyship (Art. 682§1, 1st sentence; s. above §1092), provide for the *nullity* of the suretyship if the principal contract is, unless the law provides otherwise (*ibid.*, 2nd sentence).

1097 Neither the Chinese State, i.e., its legal persons entities, nor non-profit legal persons and non-legal persons may be *parties* to a suretyship contract (Art. 683).

---

[595] In Swiss law, the distinctions between CO Art. 111, the contract of surety and other types of guarantees are no less confusing than in Chinese law and have given rise to an abundant jurisprudence: s., for example, Commentaire romand/CO I *ad* CO Art. 111, No. 19 ff.

Although its drafting only implies it, the law mandates the *conclusion* of the suretyship contract in written form, either separately from the principal contract, or within the latter (Art. 685§1). It is further to be noted that the law facilitates the conclusion of the suretyship contract by providing that, once unilaterally presented with a written assurance from the third party offering to act as surety, the mere reception, by the creditor, of such assurance is deemed to result in the suretyship contract's conclusion if the latter abstained from raising objections (*ibid.*, § 2). In other words, the creditor's conclusive conduct shall amount to its silent acceptance. 1098

The suretyship contract *contents* shall include the kind and amount of the principal creditor's rights guaranteed, the time limit for the debtor to perform the obligation, as well as the form, scope and term of suretyship (Art. 684); this list is not exhaustive. 1099

The law provides for two *forms* of suretyships: general (or ordinary) suretyship, and joint and several liability suretyship (Art. 686§1). If there is a doubt about the form on which the parties agreed, general suretyship shall apply by default (*ibid.*, § 2). *General suretyship* provides that the surety shall assume suretyship liability when the debtor fails to perform the obligation (Art. 687§1), while *joint and several suretyship* provides that both the surety and the debtor are jointly and severally liable in such case (Art. 688§1). 1100

One ought to stress at this stage that, under general suretyship, generally speaking, the surety is only a *last recourse*: indeed, the surety has, in principle, the right to *refuse* to assume its liability unless the dispute over the principal contract has not only been tried or arbitrated, but also after enforcement failed[596]. Therefore, in practice, such outcome can take years and prove very costly, especially before courts, until a final, non-appealable ruling is issued[597], let alone being unpredictable. 1101

However, the law provides for some *exceptions* under which the surety may not refuse to undertake liability: when the whereabouts of the debtor are unknown and no assets are available for enforcement; when the debtor is bankrupt, i.e., the court has accepted the bankruptcy application; when the creditor proves that the debtor's assets are insufficient or the debtor lost capacity for fulfilling its obligations; and when the surety has waived in writing its rights of refusal (Art. 687§2). 1102

---

596 S. also Art. 701 and 702 which provide for additional cases of refusal (§1188).

597 Indeed, as compared to courts, arbitration tribunals generally issue a final award, i.e., which cannot be appealed, while court ruling are generally subject to at least two levels of appeal.

1103 In contrast, the regime of *joint and several liability* is more *liberal* towards the creditor since the debtor's failure to perform suffices to entitle the creditor to request the surety to assume liability (Art. 688§2). This provision does not require the debtor's rights to be unenforceable. In other words, the joint and several suretyship regime does not give the surety the right of refusal provided by Art. 687§2 in case of general suretyship; therefore, the exceptions to such right provided by that provision are equally irrelevant. Moreover, the parties may, in the joint and several liability suretyship contract, provide for *other circumstances* than the debtor's default to perform (*ibid.*), while general suretyship is limited to such default which, in addition, as noted, must result in unenforceability.

1104 Although not a typical form such as the general and the joint and several liability suretyship, the law provides for another or complementary specific form of surety in case of *continuous* obligations: in such case, the parties may agree on a *maximum* surety amount and the maximum period of time to which such surety should apply in case of nonperformance of the debtor. This type of contract is typically used in case of *revolving credit*[598], where the creditor needs assurance covering several transactions over a designated period, and the surety offers a capped liability rather than an unlimited one[599].

1105 In either case (general or joint and several suretyship), the surety may require the debtor to provide a counter-guaranty or *security* (Art. 689). Inasmuch, such counter-guarantee may also, depending on its nature, be governed by the Fourth Title on securities (Art. 386 ff.) of the Second Book on real rights of the Chinese Civil Code (s. above Chap. 3 §17.IV, Security in Property). The law expressly refers to the mortgage[600] regime about the maximum amount surety provided by Art. 690§1 (*ibid.*, § 2).

III. Liability

1106 The second title of Chapter 13 (Art. 691 to 702) provides for a detailed liability regime concerned with the scope of such liability, its duration, the interruption of the time limit for claiming the surety, changes to the suretyship contract, its assignment, the surety's duties, its recourse against the debtor and its right of refusal.

---

598 S. above §§528 and 529.

599 For example, a supplier extends a credit line to a wholesale buyer, while the buyer regularly purchases goods over time and payment obligations arise successively.

600 S. above note 598.

The scope of the suretyship extends to the principal creditor's rights and the interest thereon, liquidated damages, compensation for damage and expenses for enforcing the creditor's rights. The parties may agree otherwise however (Art. 691). In addition, the first section of the chapter provides for the liability of either party, be it the creditor, the debtor or the surety, in case of *nullity* of the suretyship contract (Art. 682§2), namely in case of nullity of the principal contract, although the law does not explicitly rule out other possibilities (s. *ibid.*, § 1 and above, §1096). 1107

The suretyship is limited to the *duration* agreed upon between the parties (Art. 692§2, 1st phrase). During that period, it shall neither be suspended, nor interrupted, nor extended (*ibid.*, § 1). Moreover, that period must be longer than the time limit for the performance of the principal obligation; if it is shorter or even equal, it is deemed to be null (ibid., 2nd phrase). The law falls short from specifying a minimum duration over the time limit for performance; however, it sets a default duration in case the parties omitted or failed to clearly specify it, which is of six months (*ibid.*, 2nd sentence), and a default *dies a quo*, which shall be the expiration of the grace period starting from the creditor's request within which the debtor shall perform (*ibid.*, § 3). One may further speculate about the validity of such time period if the parties did specify it but set it shorter than six months: in such case, one may only suppose that a court, in its discretion, may consider such duration, however agreed between the parties, as null, although that would depend on the circumstances. 1108

Under both forms of suretyship, if the debtor fails to perform, the creditor faces two forms of time *limitations*. *First*, it must file against it within the suretyship validity period; if it fails to, the surety shall be freed from its liability (Art. 693). *Second*, even though the creditor may have filed during the period of validity of the suretyship, the latter is subject to the ordinary limitation of action or extinctive prescription of three years of Art. 188§1 (s. above §340ff. and, in general, Chap. 2 §13, Limitation of Action), which implies that, if the surety has refused to pay, in case of general suretyship, or if the creditor neglected to timely request the surety to undertake liability, in case of joint and several liability suretyship, the creditor shall be barred from acting against the surety. The regime of suretyship also clarifies the *dies a quo* of such limitation: it starts from the surety refusal in the first case (Art. 694§1), and from the creditor request to the surety in the second (*ibid.*, § 2). 1109

The parties to the principal contract, i.e., the creditor and the debtor, are free to modify it without the agreement of- or even consulting with the surety; however, if such *modifications* result in potentially increasing the surety's liability, the latter's obligation shall extend beyond its original commitment. If, on the contrary, the result in a reduction, the surety shall only be liable up to the reduced amount (Art. 695§1). The law further singles out the time limit for the 1110 performance of the principal contract which the creditor and the debtor may not change either way without the surety's agreement (*ibid.*, § 2).

1111 The regime of suretyship allows the principal contract's *assignment*, in whole or in part, to a third party, but protects the surety. As it does so, the law distinguishes between whether the creditor assigns or allows the debtor to, whether the surety agreed or not, whether, as a consequence, the surety shall be bound by the assignment or not, or whether it shall be freed from its suretyship liability or not. Thus, as long as the contract of suretyship does not prohibit it, the creditor is free to assign all or part of its rights towards the debtor; however, it shall not do so without the surety's agreement, and if it circumvents the surety, such assignment shall be ineffective on the latter (Art. 696§1). If, in contrast, the contract of suretyship does prohibit the creditor to assign but the latter does so anyway, the surety shall be automatically freed (*ibid.*, § 2). Alternatively, if the creditor allows the debtor to assign while it was not agreed between the surety and the creditor, the consequences are harsher: the surety shall not only not be bound by the assignment; it shall be freed from its suretyship liability, even if such assignment was not expressly prohibited by the contract of suretyship (Art. 697§1).

1112 If, instead of the debtor's obligation being assigned to a third party, a third party *joins* the debtor in assuming the latter's obligation, the suretyship liability shall not be affected (Art. 697§1).

1113 If, after the debtor defaults, the surety under general suretyship provides the creditor with true information about the debtor's enforceable assets, but the creditor, deliberately or by negligence, fails to enforce them, the suretyship shall be reduced accordingly (Art. 698). This is consistent with the general *duty of mitigation* mandated by the general regime of liability (Art. 591§1 *in fine*; s. above §836).

1114 In case of co- or *multiple* suretyship, each surety is liable proportionally to its share. If such shares have not been defined, the creditor is free to request each surety to undertake liability within the whole scope of its suretyship (Art. 699).

1115 The surety having undertaken its liability towards the creditor is entitled with a right of *recourse* against the debtor. As it does so, it shall be vested with the rights the creditor had against the debtor (Art. 700), subject to one limitation however, which is that, by doing so, the surety may not harm the creditor (*ibid., in fine*).

1116 If the debtor had a *defense* against the creditor which the debtor does or did not use, the surety has the right to invoke such defense against the creditor (Art. 701) and, arguably, since the law keeps silent about it, to refuse to undertake liability or, possibly, if it has already done so, to claim compensation from the creditor. Namely, if the debtor can invoke compensation or is entitled to revoke the principal contract, the surety may refuse to undertake liability towards the creditor (Art. 702). Inasmuch one may consider Art. 702 as a particular case of the general rule of Art. 701. Likewise, Art. 702 complements the refusal cases listed at Art. 687§2 (s. above §1101), while also making it available to joint and several liability suretyship.

§35. Lease

The lease, or contract of lease (租赁合同 zūlìn hétóng; Chap. 14 of the Chinese Civil Code, Art. 703 to 734), is a contract by which the lessor makes available the leased item to the lessor against a rent (Art. 703). Frequently, the lessor is also merely referred to as the principal and the lessee specifically as the "tenant". The lease is known in Swiss law, in French, as "le bail à loyer" and, in German, as "die Miete" (CO Art. 253 ff.)[601] 1117

Although the lease is often but, in our opinion, inaccurately translated as "leasing", it is not to be confused with the contract of *financial leasing* (融资租赁合同 róngzī zūlìn hétóng; Chap. 15, Art. 735 to 760) dealt with by the Chinese Civil Code in the chapter following that on the lease. It does not help that, both in French and in German, the contract of financial leasing is not translated but merely known as "leasing", without the qualifier of "financial"; "leasing" alone is never understood, in French- or German-speaking jurisdictions, as meaning "lease", but always "financial leasing". The most typical examples of lease and financial leasing are the rental of an apartment for the first, and the financial leasing for the purchase of a car for the second. The Chinese Civil Code has inserted the lease before financial leasing and, therefore, among the typical financial contracts which are the loan, suretyship and factoring, even though it is not a financial contract; it is justifiable by the fact that the lease and financial leasing share some common features. 1118

Although the contract of lease may be used both for movables and *immovables*, in China, as far as immovables are concerned, a fundamental distinction needs to be made between the lease and the *usufruct* of a plot of land. Indeed, as extensively discussed in the real rights chapter of this book (s. above Chap. 3 §17, Usufruct), the *land* is, in China, the exclusive property of the State, which makes it available to private use in the form of usufruct. While the law defines various forms of usufruct (s. above §453), specifically, foreign investors may 1119

601 The Swiss Code of Obligations also contains, within its Title Six on the lease, a chapter on the protection against abusive rents (CO Art. 269 ff.) and a separate title dedicated to the farm lease (Fr.: "le bail à ferme"; Ger. "die Pacht"; CO Art. 275 ff.), neither of which this book will cover. Generally speaking, it can be said that Swiss lease law is more detailed, regulated and protective of lessees than Chinese law may be.

be concerned above all by the *construction usufruct* (s. above Chap. 3 §17.III.B, The Construction Usufruct in Chinese Law) which the State, typically represented by the local authorities, may grant for the construction of a plant, a warehouse, office premises, etc.

1120 Comparatively, the rental of a warehouse, etc. will be governed by a contract of lease, which may either be combined with a usufruct, in which case the usufructuary and the lessor are reunited in the same party, or separate, where the usufructuary is also the owner of the warehouse, etc. which it rents out to the lessor while remaining the usufructuary. The differences between the lease and usufruct, which is subtle, has been discussed above (s. §465). The construction usufruct may be granted in the form of *assignment*, *allocation* or other forms (Art. 347§1), which present some similarities with the lease, but as reminded are governed by a separate regime.

1121 The typical *contents* of a lease include the name of the parties, the quantity, purpose and term of the lease, the rent, the lease's time limit, the method of payment, the maintenance of the leased item, etc. (Art. 704). Leases exceeding six months must be made in *writing* (Art. 707, 1st sentence).

1122 The law provides for a number of *presumptions* in case the contract of lease is unclear and the parties failed to clarify it or to agree under Art. 510 (s. above §229). Thus, if the leased item's use, the payment term or the lease duration is not clear and cannot be determined, the leased item is to be used consistently with its nature (Art. 709, 2nd sentence); the rent is to be paid at the end of the term if it or its remainder is of less than one year and at the end of the year if the term is more than one year (Art. 720, 2nd sentence); and its duration shall be deemed to be flexible (Art. 730, 1st and 2nd phrase).

1123 The law requires the lease to be limited in *duration* or term and sets a maximum of 20 years beyond which the lease is deemed to be invalid (Art. 705§1). However, the law expressly provides for the lease's renewal for another term of maximum 20 years (*ibid.*, § 2). If the contract was not made in writing and its term cannot be determined, the lease duration is deemed to be flexible (Art. 707, 2nd sentence). Although the law is silent about it, one may infer from the prohibition of Art. 705§1 that such omission may not be used to circumvent the 20-year maximum duration and that a lease term, however flexible, may not it in any event. It should also be noted, in that respect, that, comparatively, the *construction usufruct* is granted for much longer periods ranging, depending on its nature, from 40 to 70 years (s. above §492).

1124 The law suggests that the lease belongs to those contracts which must undergo *registration* with the competent authorities (Art. 706). The drafting of this provision is misleading, however. Indeed, leases effectively do not need, as such, to be registered, unlike, for example, pledges (s. above §1847). However, leases combined with another transaction which requires registration, such as, for example, a real estate lease involving a pledge (s. above §§438 and 536), may be indirectly subject to registration. Be that as it may, the law makes clear that the failure of such registration does not impact on the validity of the lease (Art. 706), although it may amount to an administrative offence, subject to administrative penalties.

The *lessor*'s main obligations are to make the leased item available to the lessee, and to maintain it for its contractual purpose over the duration of the lease (Art. 708; the duty of maintenance is reiterated at Art. 712). The parties may agree otherwise about *maintenance* however (Art. 712 *in fine*). If the lessor neglects to maintain the leased item despite the lessee asked it timely to do so (Art. 713§1, 1st sentence), the lessee may take care of it and the lessor shall bear the costs (*ibid.*, § 1, 2nd sentence), provided the lessee kept it properly (Art. 714) and did not damage it (Art. 713§2). If such neglect results in reducing the leased item's use, the rent shall be reduced or the term extended accordingly (*ibid.*, *in fine*). In any event, the lessee is not liable for regular *wear and tear*, provided it used the leased item consistently to its agreed purpose or nature (Art. 710). 1125

In contrast, the *lessee*'s main obligations are to keep the leased item properly (Art. 714), use it as agreed (Art. 709, 1st sentence) and to pay the agreed rent timely (Art. 720, 1st sentence). 1126

The lessee has the right to *improve* the leased item, but with the lessor's agreement (Art. 715§1). If not, the lessor has the right to request the lessee to restore the leased item to its original state (*ibid.*, § 2). 1127

Likewise, the lessee may *sub-rent* the leased item, provided the lessor agrees (however (Art. 716§1, 1st sentence). If so, the main lease contract remains valid (*ibid.*, 2nd sentence, 1st phrase). The sub-lease term may not be longer than that of the main contract; if it is, the excess period shall not bind the lessor unless the main lessor and lessee so agreed (Art. 717). Any proceeds from the leased item belong to the lessee (Art. 720). 1128

If the main lessee defaults on the rent payment, the sub-lessee may pay the main lessor on the main lessee's behalf, offset such payment against its due rent to the main lessee and require the latter to reimburse any excess payment, namely, liquidated damages (Art. 719). The law subjects the sub-lessee's right to pay the main lessor directly to the validity of the sub-lease (*ibid.*, § 1 *in fine*); however, we believe that, by accepting such payment, the main lessor would effectively, by contractually conclusive act, retroactively validate the sub-lease. 1129

Sub-rental without the lessor's consent is a cause of *revocation* (*ibid.*, § 2). Although the law does not specify it, one may infer that such revocation may be 1130 with immediate effect, namely, not for the contractual term or subject to a contractual advance notice, if any, although a motivated notice is advisable for proof purposes. Notwithstanding the foregoing, if the lessor knew or ought to know about it, but did not raise any objection within six months, it shall be bound anyway (Art. 718).

1131 The lessor is free to *sell* the leased item anytime to a third party but, if so, the law grants the lessee a right of first refusal or *preemption*[602] under the same conditions; such right is, however, subject itself to a preferable right in favor of any co-owner of the lessor or of a "close relative"[603] (Art. 726§1). The lessor must notify the lessee accordingly prior to the sale and the latter has 15 (five in case of auction; Art. 727) days to accept or be deemed to have declined (*ibid.*, § 2). A change of ownership (whether voluntary or resulting from such dispute) has no impact on the validity of the lease contract (Art. 725).

1132 In addition to the cases already mentioned above, the lessee is entitled to request a *reduction* or even a *waiver* of the rent, or an extension of the term, which the law implies should be for free, in the following circumstances: if the lessee took over the leased item's maintenance because of the lessor's neglect (Art. 713§1 *in fine*; s. above §1125); if the lessee cannot use or profit from the leased item because of a third party claim (Art. 723§1; this cause requires the lessee to promptly notify the lessor of any such claim; *ibid.*, § 2); and if the leased item is damaged without the lessees' fault (Art. 729). Although the law does not systematically mention the waiver and the extension in all the cases aforementioned (compare Art. 713§1 *in fine*, 723§1 and 729), we believe that these alternatives should be available in all of them, keeping in mind that, even if the law does not mandate them, the parties may settle consensually on any of them anyway.

1133 Moreover, other than the cases of reduction mentioned in the preceding paragraph, the parties bear liability towards each other and are entitled to *compensation* in the following circumstances: the *lessee* is liable towards the lessor, namely, in case of damage to the leased item in case of improper use (Art. 711

---

602 It has been argued that there may be slight differences between the right of first refusal and that of preemption. While that may prove true in certain jurisdictions, it is hardly relevant for our purpose and we will, therefore, not elaborate. Be that as it may, the corresponding right in Chinese, 优先购买的权利 yōuxiān gòumǎi de quánlì, which literally translates as "priority purchase right", is commonly translated as right of first refusal in English and "droit de préemption" in French (or "Vorkaufrecht" in German, which is the literal translation of preemption right), thus confirming the proximity of these two notions.

603 A close relative is defined as a person's spouse, parents, children, siblings, maternal and paternal grandparents, as well as maternal and paternal grandchildren (Art. 1045§2).

in fine; although the law mentions that the lessor may both revoke the contract and claim damages, one may assume that it may do either), improper safekeeping (Art. 714); unauthorized transformation (Art. 715§2 *in fine*); and damage caused by the sub-lessee (Art. 716 *in fine*). In contrast, the *lessor* is namely liable towards the lessee if it failed to notify the sale of the leased item, thus preventing the lessee from exercising its preemption right, thereby causing it damage (Art. 728, 1st sentence *in fine*). In contrast, as noted, the lessee is not liable for regular wear and tear, provided it used the leased item consistently with its agreed purpose or nature (Art. 710; s. above §1125).

The two enumerations above are not exhaustive however; arguably, under the general regime of contract law, namely, contractual liability, if the preliminary settlement attempt generally required by the law under Art. 510 fails, the lessee is also entitled to request a reduction of the rent, an extension of its term or another kind of indemnity as compensation for the lessor's nonperformance in other circumstances (Art. 582; s. above §§811 and 812). 1134

The contact of lease may be revoked in the following circumstances: by the *lessor*, in case of improper use of the leased item (Art. 711 *in fine*; s. above §1133); of unapproved sub-lease (Art. 716§2; s. above §1128); of persistent late payment (Art. 722 *in fine*); and of judicial seizure, dispute on the ownership of the leased item, or the use of the lease results in a violation of the law (Art. 724). 1135

In case of *death* of the lessee, its co-users are entitled to take over the lease contract at the same conditions (Art. 732). The law does not require them to be co-lessees before the lessee's death, it suffices that they were co-users. Art. 732 only mentions the case of the lessee's death; however, we submit that the same rule may apply in case the lessee was an enterprise whose legal existence came to an end because, for example, it was bankrupt. 1136

The contract of lease can be revoked by the *lessee* in case of damage to the leased item resulting in the impossibility to use it as agreed (Art. 729, 2nd sentence); and if the leased item endangers the lessee's safety or health; this cause is eligible even if the lessee was clearly aware of such dangers when entering the contract of lease (Art. 731). 1137

Finally, *either party* may revoke the lease contract of undetermined duration anytime (Art. 730). It should be remarked that, unlike in most western jurisdictions where the lease is strongly regulated, the regime of the contract of lease does not require any advance notice and, as a matter of fact, any formal notice from the lessee. In contrast, it does require an advance notice for the lessor but only requires it to be tended with a "reasonable" advance; moreover, it does not prescribe any form for such notice (*ibid.*, *in fine*). 1138

1139 In case of *termination*, i.e., expiry of the lease term, if the lessee continues in effect to lease the leased item and the lessor does not raise any objection, the contract of lease shall be deemed to continue; however, it shall transform into a flexible lease, i.e., a lease of undetermined duration (Art. 734§1), which is consistent with Art. 730 (s. above §1122). Moreover, if, at the term's expiry, the lessor offers to lease to a third party, the original lessee enjoys a right of first refusal (s. above §1131) under the same conditions (*ibid.*, § 2).

1140 At the end of the lease, the lessee must return the leased item in a state consistent with its regular use (Art. 733), being recalled that it shall not be liable for wear and tear (Art. 710; s. above §§1125 and 1133).

§36. Financial Leasing

1141 A financial leasing contract (融资租赁合同 róngzī zūlìn hétóng; Chap. 15 of the Chinese Civil Code, Art. 735 to 760) is a contract whereby the lessor purchases the leased item chosen by the lessee from a vendor equally chosen by the lessee and makes it available to the latter against a rent. In other words, the lessor retains ownership of the leased item, while the lessee is granted the right to possess said item and is, therefore, entitled to use it.

1142 The financial leasing should not be confused with the *lease* (Art. 703 ff.; s. above Chap. 5 §35, Lease), especially since the latter is occasionally and inaccurately translated as "leasing". Besides, the financial leasing is translated neither in French nor in German, where it is merely known under its name in English as "leasing" (i.e., Fr.: "contrat de leasing"; Ger.: "Leasingvertrag"[604]), without the qualifier of "financial", however: indeed, "leasing" alone is never understood, in French- or German-speaking jurisdictions, as meaning "lease". As mentioned in the preceding chapter, a lease, or rental agreement, is a contract whereby the lessor makes the leased item available to the lessee for use against a rent (Art. 703). The most typical examples of financial leasing, as compared to the lease, are the financial leasing for the purchase of a car for the first, and the rental of an apartment for the second. Yet financial leasing is commonly used for much larger financial operations such as, for example, the financial leasing of a machine-tool. It can, therefore, be described as a sort of *hybrid* contract between the lease and the *loan*. While the lessor purchases the item to be leased under a *contract of sale*, the latter is hardly, but exceptionally (s. below §1167), concerned with the rela-tionship between the lessor and the lessee.

---

[604] Cf. Swiss Federal Law on Consumer Credit (s. above note 584), Art. 11.

Swiss law regulates the financial leasing contract to a limited extend only. The Federal Law on Consumer Credit (LCC)[605] applies to financial leasing contracts on *movable* goods that are for the lessee's *private* use and provide for an increase of the installments in case of early termination; such contracts qualify, in Swiss law, as "consumer credit" contract (LCC Art. 1§2, *Litt.* a and Art. 11). Comparatively, the Chinese Civil Code, being recent and having embraced modern trends, including the financial leasing contract which it comprehensively regulates is, therefore, more adequate in that respect than Swiss law. 1143

In *international law*, the financial leasing is regulated, in its member States, which do not count China[606], by the UNIDROIT Convention on International Financial Leasing made in Ottawa in 1988. Nevertheless, although China has not joined it, the Ottawa Convention did influence the Chinese regime of the financial leasing contract (s., e.g., below §1149), with which is it generally compatible. 1144

The *contents* of a contract for financial leasing shall generally include the name of the parties, the quantity, specifications, technical performance and inspection methods of the leased item, the lease term, composition of the rent, time limit, method and currency for payment of the rent, and the ownership of the leased item upon expiry of the lease term; this enumeration is not exhaustive (Art. 736§1). While lease contracts must only be concluded in writing if their term exceeds six months (Art. 671; s. above §1121), contracts for financial leasing must be concluded in *writing* in any case (Art. 736§2). 1145

The law provides that a financial leasing contract concluded by the parties concerned by falsifying a leased item shall be *null and void* (Art. 737). The legislative intent behind this rule, which is prominently enunciated in the third article of the chapter, is to deter sham or *false financial leases*, i.e., to prevent abuse of financial leasing as a form of disguised or fraudulent financing. Indeed, before the Chinese Civil Code, the Chinese authorities had observed frequent instances where parties fabricated a leased item or misrepresented ownership to the effect of transferring funds, evade tax, or obtain credit without actual physical goods. Such false leases undermined both contractual certainty and financial supervision. 1146

Specifically, the rule serves several purposes, including the four following: *first*, it prevents false leases, where no actual property is delivered, including circular leases, where the same asset is repeatedly leased on paper to fabricate financial transactions. The nullity sanction ensures such sham contracts have no legal effect. 1147

605 S. above note 584.

606 Switzerland did not sign it either.

1148 *Second*, Art. 737 purports at protecting property rights and creditors: indeed, since in financial leasing the lessor owns the asset while possession is with the lessee, falsified ownership records could prejudice *creditors*, such as *bona fide* buyers or secured rights beneficiaries. Thus, Art. 737 protects transactional security by invalidating false ownership claims before they can take effect.

1149 *Third*, it preserves the authenticity of asset-based financing. Indeed, the financial leasing contract is a *sui generis* financing instrument tied to the real asset's existence and transfer. By declaring nullity where falsification occurs, the Chinese Civil Code reinforces the *principle of substance over form* in financial transactions, ensuring that leasing retains its economic function as real assets financing, not as disguised loans. This purpose is consistent with the UNIDROIT Convention mentioned above (s. §1144), which arguably influenced it, although China is not a member State.

1150 Last and *fourth*, Art. 737 aims at protecting financial markets order and regulatory supervision: in effect, falsified leases have historically been used to inflate assets value, evade financial regulations or both. By prescribing nullity, this provision strengthens financial regulation.

1151 The consequences of the financial leasing contract's nullity shall not be confused with those resulting from *invalidity* (in the sense of annulment): the first occurs *ex tunc*, the latter *ex nunc* (s. above Chap. 2 §10.IV, Validity of Juristic Acts). *Nullity* may result from a claim of either party to the purported financial leasing contract for unjust enrichment (enrichment *sine causa* or without a cause; Art. 985 ff.; s. below Chap. 7 §55, Unjust Enrichment), liability for illicit act (s. above Chap. 8 , Liability for Illicit Acts ("Torts")), or both, as the case may be. In contrast, the consequences of invalidity in the sense of *annulment*, which generally results from revocation or termination, is governed by Art. 760, which is the last provision of the chapter. It will be addressed further down (s. below §1172).

1152 The law further prescribes that, if a *business license* (s. below §1824) is required for the "operation or use of a leased item", the lessor's failure to obtain it shall not affect the validity of the financial leasing contract (Art. 738). The drafting of this provision is potentially misleading, however. Indeed, it arguably suggests that the contract of financial leasing belongs to those contracts which must undergo *registration* with the competent authorities (Art. 706). However, the financial leasing contract does not need, as such, to be registered. Yet financial leases involving another transaction where the latter requires registration may be *indirectly* subject to registration. Such registration may be constitutive, such as in the case of a leasing financing the creation of a building, or declarative, such as, in the same case, that of a mortgage or pledge (s. above §§437 and 438). Besides, it may be *mandatory*, as in the case of the registration of a leased car, or *voluntary*, as in that, once again, of a pledge (*ibid.*) Moreover, the *leasing company*, which is regulated as non-bank financial entity, must be properly registered and licensed accordingly[607]. Be that as it may, the law makes clear that the failure of such registration does not impact on the validity of the financial leasing contract (Art. 736), although it may amount to an administrative offence subject to administrative penalties.

Although not adjacent to Art. 736, Art. 745 complements the former by providing that the ownership of the leased item enjoyed by the lessor shall not prevail over a *bona fide third party* "without registration"[608]. In other words, the lessor is protected against good faith third party claims only if it, the lessor, has registered its property right over the leased item (s. above §438 *in fine* and note 281). 1153

The *lessor's* main obligations consists in the *delivery* of the leased asset (Art. 739) and guaranteeing the lessee the *possession* of the leased item (Art. 748§1). 1154

Once the vendor has delivered the leased item to the lessee, a distinctive feature of the financial lease is that the lessee is *vested* with the right of a buyer (*ibid.*, *in fine*). Thus, the lessee may *refuse* to accept delivery in case of serious *inconformity* (Art. 740§1, item 1). The lessee may also oppose such refusal in case of any other inconformity, even if the latter is not serious, after the vendor has been summoned by either the lessee or the lessor to deliver within a reasonable time, but still fails to deliver the leased asset timely and in conformity with the financial leasing agreement (*ibid.*, item 2). In either case, the lessee must timely *notify* the lessor of such refusal (*ibid.*, § 2). 1155

The lessor may not *modify* the leased item or any provision of the financial leasing contract related to the lessee without the latter's approval (Art. 744). 1156

The *lessee's* main obligations are to pay the *rent* or leasing fee (Art. 752, 1st sentence), and to properly *keep, use and maintain* the leased item (Art. 750§§ 1 and 2). 1157

The *rent* is generally agreed between the parties. In the exceptional case where it may not have, it shall be determined according to the substantial part of the cost of purchasing the leased item or of its whole cost, augmented by a reasonable profit for the lessor (Art. 746). 1158

---

607 The related requirements, whose details exceed the scope of this book, vary between domestic- and foreign-invested companies. Domestic financial leasing companies are mainly regulated by the National Financial Regulatory Administration (NFRA); foreign ones by MOFCOM.

608 Although the syntax of this provision is ambiguous, "without registration" relates to the *lessor's* right, not the third party's.

1159 As far as *maintenance* is concerned, the financial leasing contract slightly differ from the lease contract since, under the latter, the lessor, not the lessee is, in principle, responsible for it; under the lease, the lessee is only responsible for keeping and using the leased item properly (s. above §§1125 and 1126).

1160 The law specifically provides for each of the three parties' *liability* in various circumstances. Thus, the three parties may agree that, in case of default under the contract of sale, the *vendor* may be liable towards the lessee directly, while the lessor is required to assist the latter (Art. 741). The lessee's claim towards the vendor does not dispense the former to pay the rent to the lessor (Art. 742, 1st sentence) however.

1161 The *lessor* is liable towards the lessee if it fails to guarantee the leased item *possession* and use (s. above §1154), and if it fails to provide *assistance* to the lessee's right to claim against the vendor. In the *first case* (possession deprivation), the lessee has the right to claim compensation from the lessor if the latter takes back the leased item without justification, interferes with the lessee's right, causes a third party to do so, or other "improper" circumstances (Art. 748§2). Because the debtor's fault is not a condition of contractual liability (s. above §§794ff.), one may infer from the last cause that the lessor shall be, in principle, liable, unless the law provides that the lessee is (s. below §§1165 and 1166), or in case of qualified impossibility (s. above §§802ff.)

1162 In the *second case* (assistance failure), the lessor shall be liable if it prevents or impairs the lessee's right to claim against the vendor because the lessor failed to inform the lessee that the leased item was defective despite the lessor ought to know about it (Art. 743, item 1); if it fails to assist the lessee against the vendor (*ibid.*, item 2); or if it fails to exercise its rights against the vendor directly, thus damaging the lessee's interests (*ibid.*, § 2). The law requires the lessor to act energetically; it expressly holds the "indolent" lessor liable (*ibid.*)

1163 In principle, the lessor is not liable towards the lessee if the leased item does not conform with the lessee's selection, or is otherwise defective (Art. 747, 1st and 2nd phrase). In such case, as mentioned above, it is up to the lessee to exercise its right to refuse the leased item's delivery (Art. 740§1, item 1; s. above §1155). If, however, the lessee is dependent on the lessor's expertise for the *selection* of the leased item, or if the lessor interferes with such selection, the lessor shall be liable (Art. 747 *in fine*) and the lessee entitled to a rent reduction or waiver (Art. 742, 2nd sentence). In other words, even though the law only implies it, in certain circumstances, depending of the nature of the leased item and of its implied qualities or of the defects at stake[609], the lessor may also

[609] For example, equipment, machines or IT systems proving being technically unsuitable for their intended purpose, not compliant with safety regulations, resulting in operational losses because of insufficient capacity, etc.

be held liable for having failed its duty of *diligence* in advising the lessee, which compares with that of the mandatary (s. above §1007).

The lessor is not liable either if, during the lease, the leased item causes any damage to a *third party* (Art. 750§2). Indeed, as mentioned, the lessee is responsible for the proper use and maintenance of the leased item (*ibid.*, § 1; s. above §§1157 and 1159). 1164

In contrast, the *lessee* is liable towards the lessor for any damage to, or for the loss[610] of the leased item during the lease, and the item cannot be returned at the end of the lease while the parties had agreed that the lessor would retain the item's ownership (Art. 758§2; this consequence is also implied by Art. 756; s. next paragraph; about ownership, s. below §1155). Besides, the lessor has the right to request the lessee to keep paying the rent, unless the parties agreed or the law prescribes otherwise (Art. 751). Although the law does not specify it, one may infer that the lessor has the right to claim the rent until the end of the term agreed in the financial leasing agreement. 1165

The lessee is also liable towards the lessor if the *contract of financial leasing* (as opposed to the contract of sale, s. next paragraph) ends because it was terminated, revoked or nullified, except if the lessor caused such end (Art. 756). 1166

If the contract of financial leasing ends as a consequence of the end of the *contract of sale* (s. above §1142 *in fine*)of the leased item, because the latter was terminated, revoked or nullified, the lessee is liable towards the lessor if the lessee selected the leased item (Art. 755§1), except if the lessor has been compensated (*ibid.*, § 2) or caused the end of the contract of sale (*ibid.*, § 1). Although the law does not specify, about the first exemption (compensation), by whom the lessor should have been compensated, one may reasonably infer that it implies that the lessor was not compensated by the lessee, and that it was compensated by the vendor, although such compensation by a third party (e.g., the insurer of either party) is conceivable. The law provides for additional cases of liability for either party at the end of the lease; they are outlined below (s. §§1172 and 1173). 1167

The contract of financial leasing can be *revoked* in various circumstances. Thus, the *lessor* may revoke it if the lessee defaults on the rent, despite having been urged to pay within a reasonable time (Art. 752); if so, the lessor may take back the leased item (*ibid.*, *in fine*). Likewise, the lessor is entitled to revoke if 1168

610 The law assimilates *mixing or attaching* the leased item to another item to its damage or loss (Art. 758§2).

the lessee *disposes* of the leased item without its consent in any way, whether by transferring it[611], using it as security, investing it, etc. (Art. 753).

1169 Moreover, *either party* can revoke the financial leasing contract if the contract of *sale* of the leased item ends, whether is was terminated, revoked or nullified, and the lessor and the vendor fail to enter a new contract; where the leased item is *damaged or lost* without any party's fault and cannot be repaired or replaced; and where the leased item cannot be *used* because of the seller (Art. 754).

1170 At the end of the financial leasing, the parties may agree on the *ownership* of the leased item (Art. 757, 1st sentence), which may either remain with the lessor (s. above §1141), or be transferred to the lessee. In either case, the law provides for a sophisticated regime, depending on several factors: whether the parties agreed or not; whether the contract of financial leasing reached its term, or was revoked before it did; and whether the lessee cannot pay, or the leased item was damaged or lost.

1171 If the lease *reaches its term* and the parties have not agreed on the leased item ownership, the law poses two presumptions, depending on whether they have agreed that the lessee shall only be required to pay to the lessor a nominal price upon expiry of the lease, or not. If they have, the *lessee* shall be vested with the ownership after payment (Art. 759); if not, and the parties failed to agree under Art. 510 (s. above §618), ownership is deemed to remain with the *lessor* (Art. 757 *in fine*).

1172 If the lease is revoked or nullified[612], i.e., *does not reach its term*, and the parties have no agreement, the *lessor* shall, in principle, retain ownership; however, the *lessee* may be transferred it if either the lessor caused such invalidity, or does not insist on the return of the leased item; or the use of the leased item will be significantly reduced after its return; in any case, the lessee shall compensate the lessor (Art. 760).

1173 If, finally, in either case (whether the lease reached its term or not), the parties had agreed that, at the end of the lease, the lessee would own the leased item, but *cannot pay* its agreed residual value or the outgoing balance of the rent, the *lessor* has the right to take back the leased item anyway. If, however, its value exceeds the lessee's debt, the lessor shall reimburse the excess to the lessee (Art. 758§1). Alternatively, if, on the contrary, the parties had agreed that the lessor would retain ownership, but the leased item is *damaged or lost*, the *lessor* is also entitled to compensation (*ibid.*, § 2).

---

611 Although the law does not specify it, this case can only refer to the transfer of the leased item's possession, not of its property, since during the lease its proprietor is the lessor.

612 S., namely, above §§1146ff. Although Art. 727 provides for a case of nullity specific to the financial leasing contract, nullity can stem from other causes.

§37. Factoring

1174 A factoring contract (保理合同 bǎo lǐ hétóng; Chap. 16 of the Chinese Civil Code, Art. 761 to 769) is a contract under which a creditor of due or future account receivable assigns them to a service provider known as "factor", which provides for the accommodation of funds, the management or the collection of account receivable, of guarantee of payment by the debtor of account receivable, and for related services (Art. 761). The characteristic feature of this contract is the claim's *assignment*, which results in substituting the factor for the original creditor.

1175 The factoring contract translates as "contrat d'affacturage" in French; is it usually not translated in German and known, therefore, most of the time under its English name as "Factoringvertrag", although it is occasionally translated as "Forderungskaufvertrag", literally "contract of claims purchase". In any event, there is no specific legal basis governing such contract in *Swiss law*, where it is merely considered as a *sui generis* contract for the provision of services governed by its contractual terms and, depending on its features, absent a clear contractual regulation, by the regime applying to the assignment of claims (CO Art. 164 to 174), to the loan (CO Art. 305 ff.), the mandate (CO Art. 394 ff.) and the contract of sale (CO Art. 184 ff.)[613]

1176 Reflecting the above, and even though it is, in the Chinese Civil Code, unlike in Swiss law, a typical contract, the factoring contract is governed, in Chinese law, by the relevant provisions pertaining to the regime of *assignment of contracts*, contained in Chapter 6 (Art. 543 to 556; s. above Chap. 4 §25, Modification and Transfer) of the First Title on general provision of the Third Book on contract law of the Code, whenever the regime of the factoring contract is silent or unclear (Art. 769). Depending on the features of the factoring contract at stake, this reference does not exclude the application of other regimes of Chinese law, such as those mentioned in the preceding paragraph about Swiss law.

1177 The *contents* of the factoring contract generally include the description of the services, their scope and terms, information on the contractual relationships underlying the transactions having resulted in accounts receivable, information on the latter, the factor's remuneration and the method of its payment (Art. 762§1). A factoring contract shall be in *written* form (*ibid.*, § 2).

1178 In order to be able to operate legally, factoring companies are mandated to *register* such assignments or claims on the Uniform Registration Platform for Security Interests over Movable Assets and Rights (s. above §536), in compliance

---

613 Factoring is widely used, in Switzerland, in the healthcare industry.

with the general registration system outlined in the real rights chapter of this book (s. §§437 and 438).

1179 Like for the contract of financial leasing (s. above §1146), the Chinese legislator addresses *fraud* from the outset by providing that, if the creditor and the debtor of account receivable enter into a factoring contract with the factor by using falsified account receivable to the effect of obtaining undue advantages from the factor (e.g., a loan), the debtor may not invoke the non-existence of the account receivable as defense against the factor, unless the factor is clearly aware of the falsification (Art. 763).

1180 Typically, under a factoring arrangement, the creditor sends its invoice to its debtor and asks it to pay it to the factor. The law expressly provides that the creditor should give *notice* to the debtor that it assigned the corresponding claim to the factor and pass the latter's detail to the former (Art. 764). After the assignment notice, the creditor and the debtor may not, without justification, *modify* the underlying contract anymore, if such modification results in an adverse effect on the factor; if so, such modification or impact shall be ineffective (Art. 765).

1181 The law, reflecting practice, distinguishes between *two sub-types* of factoring contracts: *recourse* and *non-recourse* factoring. The difference between recourse factoring and non-recourse factoring lies in who bears the risk if the customer fails to pay the invoice. In essence and as described below, recourse factoring offers cheaper financing but greater risks for the seller, while non-recourse factoring provides greater security at a higher cost.

1182 Under *recourse* factoring, the *seller* remains liable for unpaid invoices. If the debtor does not pay, the creditor must buy back the invoice from the factor or replace it with the latter with another collectible one. In practice, other typical features include lower factoring fees and higher advance rates (given that the factor bears less risk); easier requirements imposed by the factor on the debtors' creditworthiness for accepting the assignment of their debts (since the factor's exposure is lower); and, frequently, a personal guarantee or minimum volume commitment from the creditor.

1183 In contrast, *non-recourse* factoring consists in the *factor*, instead of the creditor, assuming the risk of default. Other than that, given the higher risk, typical features include higher fees, lower advance rates, stricter creditworthiness requirements, and better protection of the creditor. However, the factoring contract's scope is usually limited to the most serious risks, for example, the debtor's insolvency, while disputes with the debtor related to performance may be contractually excluded.

1184 Under the factoring contract regime of the Chinese Civil Code, in case of recourse factoring and default of the debtor, the factor is entitled not only to the refund of the claim by the creditor, but also to interest (Art. 766, 1st sentence). However, the factor may claim against the debtor directly; if it does so, it shall be vested with the creditor's rights (*ibid.*, 2nd sentence). Eventually, and in any event, the factor must refund any positive balance on the creditor's account to the latter (*ibid., in fine*). In case of non- recourse factoring, the debtor is also vested with the creditor's rights towards the debtor, but may not, as explained, require the creditor to refund the claim (Art. 767).

The law expressly permits *multiple* factoring, i.e., the creditor to conclude sev- 1185
eral factoring contracts with several factors for the same claims. If so, it sets a priority order, depending on the circumstances: factors having *registered* (s. above §1178) the claim enjoy priority over factors not having registered, and factors having registered first have priority on those having registered subsequently; if they have not registered, the factor whose *notice* (s. above §1079) of assignment first reached the debtor shall enjoy priority; if they have neither registered nor notified, they shall have a claim on the account receivable proportionally to the amount of financing they extended to the creditor or to the fees they charged (Art. 768).

§38. Contract for Work

A contract for work (承揽合同 chénglǎn hétóng; Chap. 17 of the Chinese Civil 1186
Code, Art. 770 to 788) is a contract whereby the contractor, following the requirements of the client, completes the agreed work and delivers its results, which the client remunerates (Art. 770§1).

The contract for work is to be distinguished from the *contract for technical* 1187
services which is a sub-type of technology contract (s. below Chap. 5 §40, Technology) defined as a contract whereby one party solves a particular technical problem for the other party by utilizing its technical knowledge while, as expressly specified by the law, being neither a contract of work, nor a contract for construction projects (Art. 878§2; s. below Chap. 5 §40.V, Technical Consulting Contracts and Technical Services Contracts; for contracts for construction projects, s. below §1190).

Terminology issues need to be addressed from the outset, since alternative 1188
translations, which abound, add to the confusion. To start with, the contract for work is also translated, in English, as contract *of* work, which is especially confusing for French and German speakers, since contract of work literally translates, in French, as "contrat de travail" and in German as "Arbeitsvertrag", which means *labor* or *employment contract* (s. below §1430), not contract for work: the latter translates as "le contrat d'entreprise" and "der Werkvertrag"

(CO Art. 363 ff.), while "work" translates, in this context, as "l'ouvrage" and "das Werk". That is also true of most other continental European languages.

1189 The contract for work is also alternatively translated as contract for *works*, as well as by the expression of contract *for services* or simply "service contract", which may be better suited for intellectual subject-matters (e.g., the design of a software), while "works" naturally suggests construction or craftmanship; however, the latter translation is, in turn, not to be confused from the generic expression of contracts *of* services, which cover all contracts offering services (e.g., the mandate; Art. 919 ff.; s. above Chap. 5 §30, Mandate), not only the contract for work. "Works" in plural is generally favored for public procurement and construction, where the expression "contract for work *and material*" is also often used.

1190 Yet in Chinese law, the contract for work whose subject-matter is *construction* is governed by another, dedicated, eponymous typical contract which is the *construction project contract* (Art. 788 ff.; s. below Chap. 5 §39, Construction). The latter is a special contract for work (as, comparatively, brokerage or intermediation are special mandates), which immediately follows the latter and will be covered in the next chapter.

1191 As mentioned about the contract of mandate (s. above §§1000 and 1001), the contract for work is best defined by comparison to the former, where the mandate is qualified of contract (or obligation) said "of *best efforts*" (Fr. "de moyens"; Ger.: "auf Mittel" or "zur Leistung der Mittel"), as contrasted with contracts (or obligations) said "of *result*" (Fr.: "de résultat"; Ger.: "auf Erfolg" or "Erfolgspflicht" or "Leistungserfolg") to which belongs, typically, the contract for work. Thus, for example, in a construction project, the architect is bound to the principal by a mandate or an obligation of best efforts, while the general contractor by a contract or an obligation of result. The obligation of result is expressly mentioned in the first article of Chapter 17 (Art. 770§1).

1192 A *work* can be anything. The law mentions processing, on-order manufacturing, repairing, duplicating, testing and inspecting as examples but makes clear that the list is not exhaustive (Art. 770§2).

1193 The *contents* of a contract for work shall generally include such clauses as the subject matter, quantity and quality of the contracted work, remuneration, the method of performing the work, supply of materials, the time of performance, standards and methods of inspection, etc. (Art. 771).

1194 The contract for work's regime is otherwise concerned by both parties' typical performance, supplies, specifications, delivery, preservation and confidentiality; it also contains special provisions complementing the general contractual regime of liability and termination.

As outlined, the main obligation of the *contractor* is to deliver the result, which is the work ordered by the client (Art. 770§1 and 780, 1st sentence). The contractor must complete the work with its *own* equipment, technology and labor forces (Art. 772); the parties may agree otherwise however (*ibid., in fine*). 1195

As it does so, it must strictly follow the client's instructions, which in the case of a contract for works typically take the form of *specifications*, such as drawings or technical norms (cf. Art. 776, 1st sentence), which in turn define the client's *quality* requirements; if they are not met, such noncompliance shall amount to nonperformance, and the contractor shall be liable towards the client for meeting them or compensation (Art. 781). 1196

If, in the course of the work, the contractor finds that these instructions or *specifications* are "unreasonable", by which one may understand unclear or inadequate, it must timely notify the client (Art. 776, 1st sentence), so that the latter can adjust them accordingly. 1197

The contractor must complete the work with its own *equipment, technology and labor* forces (Art. 772); the parties may agree otherwise however (*ibid., in fine*); however, the *materials* may be provided either by the contractor or by the client. If the materials are provided by the *contractor*, its duties are to select such materials, to use them according to the client's instructions, and to accept that the client inspects them as prescribed by Art. 779 (s. next paragraph). Even though the law falls short of specifying it, the duty to select such materials implies that it must be proper; improper materials would amount to a breach of contract. If, however, the materials are provided by the *client*, the contractor's duty is to promptly inspect them, notify the client of any defect and request it to remedy such defects by replacing the materials, complement them or else, as the case may be (Art. 775§1), and to properly *keep* them (Art. 784). The contractor may not make changes to the agreed materials without the client's approval, however, or change any of them if they are in good condition (*ibid.*, § 2). 1198

During performance, the contractor must accept and, therefore, may not obstruct the client's *supervision and inspections* (Art. 779). 1199

Once the work is completed, the contractor must deliver it to the client. Upon *delivery*, the contractor must provide the client with the necessary technical data and proofs of quality (Art. 780§1). However, if the client fails to pay, the law grants the contractor either a *lien* on the work, or the right to refuse delivery until payment (Art. 783). 1200

During and after delivery, the contractor shall maintain *confidentiality* in accordance with the requirements of the client; namely, it may not retain replicas (models or scale models) or technical data, unless the client expressly grants it permission to do so (Art. 785). 1201

1202 If the work cannot be performed because the client failed to *assist*, the contractor may urge the client to assist within a reasonable time. If the client persists in failing anyway, the contractor may *revoke* the contract (Art. 778 *in fine*).

1203 The law provides for the contractor to subcontract the work to a *third party* under certain conditions. It distinguishes main work from ancillary work. The difference is that the contractor may freely subcontract *ancillary* work (Art. 772§2) but may only subcontract *main* work with the client's approval (*ibid.*, § 1); if it neglected to obtain it, the client may revoke the contract (Art. 772§2 *in fine*). In both cases, the contractor remains accountable for the subcontractor's performance. Subcontracting ought not to be confused by *co-contracting*, which calls for a joint and several liability regime (Art. 786; s. below; §1211).

1204 In contrast and as implied above, the first obligation of the *client* consists in instructing the contractor, namely, by providing it with the necessary *specifications* (Art. 771 and 776). If the parties so agreed, the client must also provide the materials (Art. 774). The client may *modify* such instructions or specifications, but at its own costs (Art. 777). In particular, even though the law only implies it, if the contractor notifies the client that its instructions or specifications are unclear or inadequate, the latter must promptly *adjust* them (Art. 776). Generally speaking, the contractor is under the obligation to *assist* the contractor if the latter demands it (Art. 778, 1st sentence).

1205 The client has not only the right to supervise and inspect during the work performance (Art. 779; s. above §1199), it has, upon *delivery*, the obligation to *inspect* the work results and either to *accept* it (Art. 780, 2nd sentence; s. next paragraph), or to *reject* it (Art. 781; s. below §1208).

1206 Provided the work is *compliant*, the client must pay the contractor's *remuneration* (Art. 782, 1st sentence). Even though the law does not specify it, such remuneration, or at least the method by which it should be calculated, is usually pre-agreed (cf. Art. 771). It must do so within the pre-agreed *time* limit (Art. 782, 1st sentence). If the time limit has not been pre-agreed or is unclear, the parties shall determine it by mutual agreement under Art. 510 (*ibid.*, 2nd sentence; about Art. 510, s. above §618). If the parties failed to determine it or to agree under Art. 510, the client shall pay upon delivery (Art. 782, 2nd sentence). The time of delivery is of the essence in works projects backed by very large loans such as construction projects, where every day of delay typically carries heavy additional costs and late interest.

1207 If, however, the work has only been *partly* delivered, the client shall only pay that part of the price corresponding to the delivery (Art. 782, 3rd sentence).

1208 In addition to the general regime of contractual liability (s. above Chap. 4 §27, Liability for Breach of Contract), the regime of the contract for work provides for several specific *liabilities*, some of which have been briefly mentioned above, and which we recapitulate below.

First and foremost, if the work is *defective*, i.e., does not meet the specifications underlying the client's quality requirements, the client has the right to request the contractor to assume liability for breach of contract and may choose to request it to do so in the form of repairs[614], rework, remuneration reduction, compensation for loss, etc., provided however, as expressly requested by the law, that such choice is reasonable (Art. 781). 1209

If the contractor notifies the client that the *instructions or specifications* are *inadequate,* but the client does not react timely or because, even though it did react timely, in either case, such instructions or specifications resulted in damaging the contractor anyway, the client shall be liable for it (Art. 776). In contrast however, even though the law falls short from mentioning it, under the general regime of contractual liability, the client shall not be liable for any damage caused to the contractor, and the latter shall be liable for any damage caused to the client if the contractor did not notify the client timely; therefore, it is safe to understand "timely" as "as soon as possible". Besides, the use of the verb "notify" instead of "inform" suggests that such notification should be formal enough, so that either party can rely on it as a proof. 1210

Likewise, if the contractor *modifies* such instructions or specifications during performance of the work and, as a result, causes a loss to the contractor, the client shall be liable for it (Art. 777). If the contractor damages the materials provided by the client because of improper *safekeeping*, the contractor shall be liable for it (Art. 784). *Co-contractors* bear joint and several liability (Art. 786); the parties may agree otherwise, however. Co-contracting ought not to be confused with *subcontracting* which calls for a specific liability regime (Art. 772; s. above §1203). Finally, the client shall also be liable towards the contractor in case of untimely and damageable *revocation* (Art. 787), as outlined in the next paragraph. 1211

Like the liability regime, the general contractual termination or revocation regime is complemented by a few provisions specific to the contract for work. Thus, generally speaking, the client may *revoke* the contract for work anytime before completion of the work, provided such revocation does not damage the contractor; if so, the client shall be liable to compensate for it (Art. 787). 1212

[614] The Swiss warranty regime in case of sale of *immovable* has recently been profoundly revised; the new regime applies as of 1 January 2026 (s. above note 552). The revision provides, notably, for the client's imperative right to free repairs (CO Art. 368§2*bis*); and fixes the (formerly "immediate") notice limitation to 60 days (CO Art. 367§1*bis*). The same solution applies in Chinese law under the construction project contract (s. below §1234).

Besides, as noted above, the client has the right to revoke the contract if the contractor *subcontracted* without the client's approval (Art. 772§2 *in fine*; s. above §1203). In contrast, the contractor has the right to revoke if, despite it urged the client to assist and set it a time limit, the latter still failed to (Art. 778 *in fine*).

1213 Lastly, the case in which the contractor damages a third party is a special case of *liability of certain authors for illicit acts*, specifically, of "workers" (within that special regime), covered by Art. 1193 (s. below §1682), to which we refer.

§39. Construction

1214 As its name makes plain, a construction project contract (建设工程合同 jiànshè gōngchéng hétóng; Chinese Civil Code, Chap. 18, Art. 788 to 808) is dedicated to construction projects; it also applies to engineering survey and design (Art. 788§2). As such, it is a sub-type of *contract for work* (Art. 770 ff.; s. above Chap. 5 §38, Contract for Work). The regime of the contract for work applies as *lex generalis* whenever the construction project contract regime, as *lex specialis*, is silent (Art. 808). The law defines it as a contract whereby the contractor carries out the construction of a project, and the principal party pays the price (Art. 788§1). The principal is designated, in the law, as the party awarding the contract or the "contract-awarding party", since such contract are generally awarded at the outcome of a tendering process.

1215 The construction project contract does not fundamentally differ from the contract for work; it is only more detailed and adapted to typical construction-related legal issues. These issues include, namely, tendering and bidding, multiple contracts, public works, supervision, inspection and acceptance, concealed works, suspension, alteration or assignment of the project, and liability issues specifically resulting from the default of either party in the course of a construction project.

1216 The SPC has, among other things, issued a *judicial interpretation*, namely, Interpretation (I) on Issues Concerning the Application of the Law in the Trial of Cases Involving Disputes over Construction Contracts for Construction Projects of 29 December 2020, which clarifies certain provisions of Chapter 18 of the Chinese Civil Code on construction contracts.

1217 Furthermore, construction projects are also subject, in China, to *secondary legislation* including, notably, the Construction Law, the Tendering and Bidding Law, and administrative regulations such as the Regulations on the Quality Management of Construction Projects, the Regulations on the Administration of Work Safety in Construction Projects and the Regulations on the Administration of Survey and Design of Construction Projects.

There is no specific construction contract in *Swiss law*. Construction projects are governed by default by the regime of the contract for work (Fr.: "contrat d'entreprise"; Ger. : "Werkvertrag"; CO Art. 363 ff.) In practice, the contracts governing construction projects located in Switzerland are generally *sui generis* contracts formed by a basic contract for work complemented by a set of rules designed by the Swiss Society of Engineers & Architects known as *SIA norms* (where SIA stands for "Société suisse des architectes et ingénieurs" in French); such norms overwhelmingly outweigh the contract for work regime contained in the Swiss Code of Obligations. The SIA norms are extremely complex and specifically intended for professionals; they focus on clarifying the notions of measurable work in the many situations typically encountered in such projects; they are widely accepted; Swiss courts are familiar with them. Unlike the Swiss Code of Obligations, they are not suitable for non-professionals, for which they may prove hermetic, however; Swiss courts have occasionally declared them unapplicable for being unclear. 1218

The Chinese Civil Code's description of the *contents* of a construction contract is detailed: they shall generally include such clauses as the project scope, period for construction, time of commencement and completion of intermediary deliveries, project quality and costs, delivery time of technical documents, responsibilities for the supply of materials and equipment, payments and accounts settlement, final delivery, inspection and acceptance upon project completion, scope and period of quality warranty, and mutual cooperation; this enumeration is not limitative (Art. 795). The contents of an *engineering survey or design* contract (s. below §1223) shall generally contain such clauses as the time limit for submission of relevant basic data and budget estimates, quality requirements, costs, other cooperation conditions, etc. (Art. 794). A construction project, engineering survey or design contract must be concluded in *writing* (Art. 789). 1219

However, in China, like in the global construction industry, the parties also use *model contracts* not only issued by the Chinese government[615], but also internationally accepted model contracts; both are widely used for both domestic 1220

---

615 These model contracts include standard tender documents published by the National Development and Reform Commission (NRDC) and other ministries (e.g., the Standard Construction Tender Documents), as well as special types of documents, such as the Highway Project Standard Construction Tender Documents; model contracts jointly published by the Ministry of Housing & Urban-Rural Development and SAMR, such as the Model Construction Contract for Construction Project (GF-2017-0201); the Model General Contracting Contract for Construction Project (GF-2020-0216); and the Model Subcontract.

and overseas projects. International contract models are almost systematically the model contracts of the International Federation of Consulting Engineers (FIDIC); they are typically used in foreign-invested domestic projects in China, and in Chinese contractor projects overseas.

1221 Construction projects are generally subject to *tendering*. Whenever so, the process, i.e., tendering and bidding[616], must be fair, open and impartial (Art. 790). This provisions expressly refers to the relevant laws; such laws are, mainly, the Tendering and Bidding Law (2017 Amendment) and its implementation regulations, the Construction Law and, as the case may be, sector-specific regulations on bidding and tendering; these laws and regulations collectively ensure the principles of openness, fairness, and impartiality in construction projects bidding in China. Tendering will not be covered in this book; readers are invited to consult specialized literature on this topic.

1222 Contracts for key *public* construction projects are subject to specific procedures; the related investment plans, feasibility study reports and other documents must be approved by the authorities (Art. 792)[617].

1223 The principal, after having awarded the contract, may, and usually does, enter into a construction project contract with a *general contractor*, and may also enter into separate or *ancillary contracts* for engineering survey, design and construction with an engineering survey, design and construction contractor respectively (Art. 791, 1st sentence). However, the principal may not *split* one construction project that could be completed by one contractor into several parts, and conclude separate contracts with multiple contractors (*ibid.*, 2nd sentence). The legislator's intent behind this restriction is to promote the principle of general contracting (总承包 zǒng chéngbāo), by encouraging unified management and responsibility by a single contractor for the entire project to ensure consistency, quality, and efficiency in construction, thus preventing coordination difficulties, increased risks, and potential disputes. This legislative approach is aligned with the Construction Law (Construction Law, Art. 24§1), which encourages general contracting to optimize project management, control costs, and improve the overall project delivery; it also protects the rights of contractors by preventing the division of projects into smaller parts that could undermine contractors' capacity and interests. This unified contracting reflects a broader legal policy to maintain order, fairness, and accountability in construction activities.

---

[616] On the notions of tendering and bidding, s. above note 296.

[617] Other than the Construction Law, the related requirements are mainly issued by the State Council and sector-specific authorities, such as the National Development and Reform Commission (NDRC) and the Ministry of Housing & Urban-Rural Development (MOHURD).

Among ancillary contracts, the law also provides for contracts on entrusted *supervision* (Art. 796, 1st sentence), which is generally performed by specialized professionals, whose rights and obligations are governed by the regime of *mandate* (Art. 919 ff.; s. above Chap. 5 §30, Mandate) as well as other relevant laws and administrative regulations (Art. 796, 2nd sentence). The supervisor's rights and obligations extend, beyond the supervision of the construction project performance, to its *inspection and acceptance*, which will be detailed further down (s. §§1227ff.) 1224

The general contractor or the engineering survey, design or construction contractor may, subject to the consent of the principal, *subcontract* a third party with the completion of parts of its contracted work. If so, the subcontractor bears joint and several liability together with the general contractor or the engineering survey, design or construction contractor towards the principal for the nonperformance of the subcontracted work (Art. 791§2, 1st sentence). 1225

Subcontracting is subject to certain *restrictions*. First, a contractor may not subcontract the entirety of the construction project to a third party (Art. 791§2, 3rd sentence, 1st phrase), which would effectively result in *assigning* it in the guise of subcontracting. Second, subcontracting may not be used as a way to disguise the *splitting* of the project, thus circumventing the prohibition of Art. 791§1, 2nd sentence (Art. 791§2 *in fine*; s. above §1223). Third, subcontracting is subject to *professional qualifications* requirements. This requirement is double: a contractor may not subcontract if the subcontractor is not adequately qualified (*ibid.*, § 3, 1st sentence). Fourth, a subcontractor may not, in turn, *subcontract* its own subcontracted work (*ibid.*, 2nd sentence). Finally and fifth, the subcontracting contractor must retain and perform on its own[618] the main works of the construction project contract it was awarded (*ibid.*, 3rd sentence). 1226

The law mandates that a construction project can only be used by the principal after it has been *delivered* by the contractor; such delivery is itself subject to the principal's *acceptance*; in turn, such acceptance is subject to the outcome of the project's *inspection* (Art. 799§2). As noted, while *supervision* is a continuous and relatively informal[619] process throughout the project's performance, inspections are punctual[620] and formal, meaning that they follow a predefined protocol and are formally recorded; the final inspection is generally preceded by several *intermediary* inspections, where the continuation of the 1227

618 This requirement is the equivalent, for a construction company, of the *intuitu personae* requirement of certain obligations (s. above §§645 and 686).

619 Supervision is usually recorded in the form of *progress reports*, which do not carry out the same formal weight as inspection reports though.

620 Formal inspections are usually conducted at the end of each pre-agreed construction project stages known as *milestones*.

project is subject to the intermediary acceptance of each intermediary inspection. Although the law only alludes to it, after delivery, the use of the construction project is still subject to the competent authorities' approval[621].

1228 In the course of the construction project performance, the supervisor may, informally or formally, inspect the progress and quality of the works at any time, but it shall not disturb their normal operation (Art. 797). If, at a certain stage of the works, the construction project plans for the *concealment* of part of the project (such as the pouring of a concrete slab that would encase underlying pipes), prior to such concealment, the contractor must notify the supervisor and invite it to inspect the works before concealment.

1229 After a construction project is completed, the principal shall promptly conduct the *final* inspection, which shall be conducted on the basis of the construction plans and description, as well as the criteria for inspection and acceptance, namely, the standards for quality inspection of construction projects promulgated by the State (Art. 799§1, 1st sentence; about standards, s. next paragraph). After the project has passed the final inspection and has been accepted by the principal[622], the latter shall *pay* the contractor the agreed price and *take over* the construction project (Art. 799§1, 2nd sentence).

1230 China promotes well-established construction *standards* that are nationally recognized and broadly applied across the industry. These standards are embodied in building codes, quality control protocols, and inspection processes mandated by government agencies such as the Ministry of Housing & Urban-Rural Development (MOHURD). The construction inspection system covers medium to large-scale projects, especially in urban areas, and mandates inspections at different stages to ensure compliance with design, safety, materials, and workmanship requirements. Specific standards (designated as JG standards or construction industry standards[623]) govern design, materials, methods, safety, environmental impact, and quality control inspection protocols. Internationally, besides FIDIC (s. above §1220), other international standards include various ISO standards, European Norms (EN), and Global Construction

621 Such use is also subject to the authorities' approval following the principal's final acceptance of the construction project. This approval is governed by the Construction Law and its implementing regulations.

622 Chinese law conflates the notions of inspection and acceptance by using the expression of 进行验收 jìnxíng yànshōu which literally translates as "acceptance inspection" but is usually expressed in English by "final inspection" or "final acceptance".

623 These standards are named 建筑行业标准 jiànzhú hángyè biāozhǔn, which translate as construction industry standards. The abbreviation "JG" refers specifically to 建筑工程 jiànzhú gōngchéng, i.e., building and construction engineering.

Measurement Standards (GCMS) issued by institutions like the Royal Institute of Chartered Surveyors' (RICS).

Because nonperformance in construction project contracts often results in very substantial loss, the law provides for a detailed *liability* regime covering most of the numerous failures typically occurring in such projects. Specifically, it addresses the liability of either the principal, the contractor or the subcontractor resulting from delays, quality issues, personal injuries, material damages, shortages, suspension, alterations, conformity, payment default, invalidity, and related causes. 1231

Thus, if, prior to *concealment* works (s. above §1228), the principal or the supervisor fail to timely inspect the works despite they were notified by the contractor, the latter may postpone the project accordingly and claim for compensation for any damage resulting thereof, such as workers' idleness, etc. (Art. 798, 2nd sentence). 1232

Where loss is caused to the principal because the construction project is delayed due to the failure of the engineering survey or design party to conform to the agreed quality requirements or to submit the *survey report* or the *design plans*, etc. timely, the law places the surveyor or the designer before a choice: they shall either perfect such report, plans, etc., or reduce or waive their fees; in either case, they are liable for any loss suffered by the principal as a result (Art. 800). In other words, even if they perfect their work eventually, they may have to, in addition, reduce, up to waive their fees as compensation for any damage resulting from their delay, while in both cases, if such waiver does not suffice to cover such loss, they may be required to pay additional compensation on top of their fees. 1233

If the quality of a construction project fails to meet the pre-agreed requirements because of the contractor, the principal has the right to demand repairs, rework or reconstruction free of charge by the contractor[624], and that the latter complies within a reasonable period of time. If the construction project is delivered beyond the deadline initially agreed because of such repairs, etc., the contractor shall be liable for breach of contract (Art. 801), i.e., for any damage suffered by the principal despite such repairs, etc. 1234

The law *extends* the contractor liability for personal injuries or property loss it caused if they occurred within a "reasonable period of the construction project's use" (Art. 802). The reference of this provision to the construction project's "use" implies that it applies *after* its delivery and acceptance. In other words, the principal's acceptance does not immediately frees the contractor from its liability; as such, this regime compares to that of the guarantee for 1235

624 The same solution applies in Swiss law (s. above note 614).

defects under the contract of sale, by which the buyer enjoys some time after delivery for signaling any defect after inspection of the goods, namely, hidden defects, for which the seller shall be liable. The construction project contract regime is less specific than that of the contract of sale in this regard, since the former, unlike the latter (s. above Chap. 5 §29.VI, Warranty for Defects and Chap. 5 §29.VII.A, Time Limitations), does not fix any *time limitation* for notifying defects or for filing at court (or an arbitration claim) [625]. Namely, the former regime does not define the notion of "reasonable time" used in Art. 801.

1236 That said, Art. 801 calls for several noteworthy comments. Practice, namely, the jurisprudence of Chinese courts, has clarified that, as far as property damages are concerned, this provision implicitly addresses *hidden defects*. Moreover, Art. 801 is considered as being *mandatory*, i.e., the parties cannot, in principle, derogate from it by freeing the contractor from any liability immediately upon acceptance of the construction project by the principal. However, at the same time, the contractor cannot be held liable for construction defects, however hidden, indefinitely. Yet by not setting any time limitations for notifying such defects, the law leaves it to the courts (or arbitration tribunals, which are often preferred in construction disputes; s. below §1251) to decide what such "reasonable" time should be. This implies that the parties may, in fact, pre-agree, in the construction contract, such time limitation for *property damages*, and often do; such provisions will not be automatically regarded as invalid. However, they will be unenforceable if the court or arbitration tribunal assesses it, in its discretion, as unreasonable. In contrast, any such provision applying to *personal injury* is generally regarded as *invalid.*

1237 Chinese domestic *standard* construction contracts (s. above §1230) generally provide for such time limitation. The period typically starts from the date of completion or final acceptance certificate, usually lasting about one year. In international construction projects, namely, under FIDIC standard construction contract (*ibid.*), the latter provides for a specific period known as the Defects Notification Period (DNP). That period is usually stated in the contract's appendices; it commonly lasts at least one year from completion or taking over of the works, but the exact duration is contractually agreed. However self-evident, it should be stressed once again that these limitations are not statutory but *contractual* and remain subject to reasonableness under Art. 801 of the Chinese Civil Code, however.

1238 Comparatively, *Swiss law* sets a time limitation, for immovable defects resulting from a construction project, to five years (CO Art. 271§2). This limitation also applies if the defect results from a movable integrated into the damaged immovable (*ibid.*, § 1, 2nd sentence). Defects to movables are subject to a

[625] Unlike Swiss law, s. below §1238.

limitation of two years (*ibid.*, § 1, 1st sentence). Like in Chinese law, the parties may shorten these limitations within reasonableness, i.e., provided the principal's rights are not unfairly impaired[626]. The *dies a quo* is that of the effective takeover; the parties may not change it contractually[627]. After the time limitation has expired, the guarantee right lapses[628]. Personal injuries are governed by the civil liability regime and subject to a three-year limitation from the knowledge of the damage and an absolute limitation of 20 years[629] (CO Art. 60§2). Finally, one also ought to note that the Swiss warranty regime in case of *sale of immovable* has recently been revised and fixes, among other things, the (formerly "immediate") notice limitation to 60 days[630].

If the principal fails to make available raw *materials, equipment, sites, funds* 1239
or technical data as and when agreed, the contractor may, like for late inspection in case of concealment works (s. above §1232), extend the period of construction accordingly, and shall be entitled to request compensation for losses caused by work suspension, workers' forced idleness, etc. (Art. 803).

If the construction of a project is *ended or suspended* due to reasons attributable 1240
to the principal, the latter must take measures to prevent or mitigate the loss it so provoked, and compensate the contractor for any loss and actual expenses resulting thereof such as workers' forced idleness, re-transportation, relocation of machinery equipment, overstocking of materials and structural components, etc. (Art. 804).

In case the principal *alters its plans, provides inaccurate materials or fails to* 1241
make available the necessary working conditions as scheduled for engineering surveying or designing, resulting in the rework or suspension of such assignments, the principal must increase said contractors' fees according to the actual volume of work undertaken by them (Art. 805).

The law further provides for special liability regimes for two special cases: in- 1242
validity, and payment default. The reason why it provides specially for *invalidity* is that, if a construction project is found to be invalid after it has started, let alone after it has been completed, the consequences resulting thereof on the parties' liabilities and the aggrieved parties (workers, subcontractors, investors, lenders, etc.) can be disastrous, while the regime of unjust enrichment, which is very concise (s. below Chap. 7 §55, Unjust Enrichment), is arguably

626 ATF 108 II 194 = JT 1983 I 119.

627 ATF 118 II 42 = JT 1993 I 300.

628 ATF 130 III 362.

629 Such extraordinary long limitation was introduced, namely, in the wake of personal injuries suffered by workers because of asbestos several years after the works.

630 S. above note 614.

insufficiently detailed, therefore inadequate to address them. To that effect, the law contemplates different situations.

1243 Thus, if a project construction contract is found invalid after it has been *accepted*, the law prescribes that the contractor is nevertheless entitled to be compensated *as if* the contract had been valid (Art. 793§1). If, on the contrary, the project *fails* to pass the final inspection, the solution depends on whether the project can be *repaired* successfully or not (*ibid.*, § 2). If it *can* and, as a result, eventually passes the final inspection, the contractor is entitled to the agreed price even though the contract is invalid, but must bear the repair costs (*ibid.*, 1st item); if it *cannot* be repaired, the contractor is not entitled to any payment (*ibid.*, 2nd item).

1244 However, in either case, the principal shall be liable towards the contractor for any loss resulting from the contract's invalidity to the extent the principal has caused it (*ibid.*, § 3); the law implies that if both parties are at fault, their *mutual* liabilities shall be apportioned proportionally to their fault, which accords with both the general regime of contractual liability (Art. 592; s. above §837) and, to the extent the contract is found invalid, with that of liability for illicit acts (Art. 1173; s. below §1651).

1245 Likewise, and for similar reasons, the construction contract regime provides for detailed solutions in case of *default payment* from the principal to the contractor. Thus, in such case, the contractor shall urge the contract-awarding party to effect the payment within a reasonable period of time; if the principal persists in defaulting, the contractor may negotiate with the latter to the effect of converting the project into monies; alternatively, it has the right to apply to the competent court for auctioning of the project, unless it cannot, by nature, be converted or auctioned off. Payments for the project (to workers, subcontractors, lenders, etc.) shall be made on a priority basis from the proceeds of such conversion or auction (Art. 807).

1246 The general regime of *contractual liability* (s. above Chap. 4 §27, Liability for Breach of Contract) applies as *lex generalis* to any matter be covered by the special liability cases contained in the construction project contract regime; as noted above (s. §1244), so does, to the extent the contract were to be found invalid, or if the liability case at stake is not contractual (namely, in case of damage to a third party, s. next paragraph), the regime of *liability for illicit acts* (s. below Chap. 8, Liability for Illicit Acts ("Torts").

1247 Finally, it should not be forgotten that, in case of damage to a third party, while the contractor may, as mentioned in the preceding paragraph) be liable under the general regime for liability for illicit acts, the master may, in certain circumstances, also be liable (or be liable in the stead of the contractor) towards such third party or the contractor under the special regime of *liability of certain authors for illicit acts*, covered by Art. 1193 (s. below §1682) and to which we refer.

Finally, the law also provides for two special cases of *revocation* of the construction project contract, one to the benefit of the principal, the other of the contractor. First, the *principal* may revoke the contract if the contractor *assigns* the entire construction project or illegally subcontracts it (Art. 806§1), as prohibited by Art. 791§2 (s. above §1226). 1248

Second, the *contractor* may revoke the contract if the principal provides the main building materials, building components and fittings as well as equipment which prove not being in *conformity* with the mandatory standards, or fails to abide by its obligation to assist the contractor[631], making it impossible for the latter to undertake construction, and persistently fails even after having been urged by the contractor to do so within a reasonable period of time. 1249

In case of revocation, if the project construction already completed meets the pre-agreed quality requirements, the principal must *pay* the corresponding pre-agreed price; if the project, however completed, does not meet the pre-agreed quality requirements, the regime applying for the *settlement* of the parties' mutual claims in case of invalidity of the construction project contract shall apply (Art. 808§2 and 793; s. above §§1242 and 1243). 1250

Given the prominence of Chinese construction in global infrastructure projects, *international dispute resolution*, namely, in cases between a foreign principal and a Chinese contractor about a project located in the principal's country, both the applicable law and the forum should be carefully considered. If the law of the host country is not mandatory, the Sino-foreign parties often choose a neutral law[632]; however, the Chinese party may impose Chinese law, even if the project is located abroad, if it enjoys superior bargaining power. Besides, for projects abroad, while arbitration before a neutral institution[633] is generally preferred over litigation, the host country courts competence may be mandatory; alternatively, the host country may impose a local arbitration institution; alternatively, as for the applicable law, the Chinese contractor may impose a Chinese arbitration institution[634]. In any case, if Chinese law applies, the SPC 1251

---

631 Such obligation of assistance is set by the regime of the contract for work (Art. 778, 1st sentence, applicable by the reference of Art. 808; s. above §§1202, 1204 and 1212).

632 For example, English law or Swiss law, which are often selected.

633 For example, the International Chamber of Commerce (ICC), the London Court of Arbitration (LCIA), or the Swiss Rules, which are often selected.

634 There are numerous arbitration institutions in China. Those most often selected for large projects include the China International Economic and Trade Arbitration Commission (CIETAC); alternatively, the Hong Kong Court of Arbitration (HKIAC) which, while

Interpretation mentioned above (s. §1216) may be relied on, namely, in arbitration.

§40. Technology

I. Introduction

1252 The chapter of the Chinese Civil Code on technology contracts (技术合同 jìshù hétóng; Chap. 20 of the Chinese Civil Code; Art. 843 to 887) actually covers several *sub-types* of technology contracts, in three groups: the first group is formed of technology development contracts (Section 2; Art. 851 to 861) which include themselves three sub-types: the contract on entrusted development, the contract on cooperative development, and contracts on industrial application of technological achievements (where the latter can combine with either of the two first); the second group is formed of two sub-types: technology transfer contracts and technology license contracts (Section 3, Art. 862 to 877); so is the third group, which is formed of technical consulting contracts and technical services contracts (Section 4; Art. 878 to 887). The law even mentions two more sub-types, technology intermediation service contracts and technical training contracts, which the Chinese Civil Code does not regulate however (Art. 887; s. below §§1331 to 1333).

1253 The special regimes governing all those sub-types are complemented by general provisions forming the first section (Art. 843 to 850), which apply to all of them. The liberal drafting of the technology contract regime and of its sub-regimes thus allows technological contracts to take multiple forms. As a result, they frequently qualify as contracts *sui generis* which, while their technological features are governed by the technological contracts regime, may also be governed, in parallel, by other regimes, laws and regulations as far as the other features with which they mix are concerned, such as, for example, the mandate which may govern the non-technological features of technology-related services.

1254 Technology contracts have been regulated in China since as early as 1987, at a time where technology was only a fraction of what it has become ever since, with the promulgation of the former Law on Technology Contracts (中華人民共和國技術合同法 zhōnghuá rénmín gònghéguó jìshù hétóng fǎ), repelled in 1999 by the Contract Law, which in turn the Chinese Civil Code effectively replaced as of 2020. Given the importance technology business transactions

belonging to a jurisdiction separate from Mainland China, as SAR, pertains to Greater China, is also frequently favored.

have gained ever since, the Chinese legislator can be said to have used astonishing foresight, and Chinese law to be remarkably progressive.

It is worth noting that there is no equivalent, in *Swiss law*, namely, in the Swiss Code of Obligations, to Chapter 20 of the Chinese Civil Code: technology contracts are not regulated as such in Swiss law, which regards them as mixed contracts *sui generis* whose features may be governed by various regimes, depending of their nature. These regimes may include the contract for work (CO Art. 363 ff.; e.g., software development); the mandate (CO Art. 394 ff.; e.g.: research, consulting, support); the contract of sale (CO Art. 184 ff.; e.g.: technology transfer; IT sale involving physical goods); licensing, which is not specifically regulated as a typical contract either, but usually by analogy to the contract of lease of immaterial (or intellectual property) rights (CO Art. 253 ff.), or the mandate for services. Comparatively, Chinese law provides, therefore, welcome clarity. 1255

Thus, certain aspects typical of technology contracts, such as the duty of confidentiality or noncompete clauses, may be governed, if the technology contract is silent, unclear, inadequate or lacunary in that particular respect, either by the general provisions of contract law (s. above Chap. 4 , General Provisions of Contract Law), other typical contracts such as those mentioned in the preceding paragraph, or *other laws*, as the case may be. 1256

In particular, the protection of *intellectual property rights*, which are inevitably involved in a technology contract, is not, at least in the first place, provided by the technology contracts regime, but by intellectual property law, i.e., primarily, the Trade Mark Law, the Patent Law, the Copyright Law, related secondary legislation, and the topical international treaties and systems. Patent law (and, arguably, copyrights) is expressly acknowledged by the technological contracts regime as a *lex specialis* prevailing over the latter (Art. 877; s. below §1314). Intellectual property is not covered in this book; the reader is invited to consult specialized literature or seek professional advice. 1257

Although the *Vienna Convention* (s. above Chap. 5 §29.II, The Vienna Convention (CISG)), which was issued in 1980, traditionally applies to the sale of physical goods and fails to mention immaterial goods such as software, etc., it does not exclude them (like, e.g., financial instruments, which are expressly excluded) either. Meanwhile, the understanding of CISG's scope has expanded to take technological developments into account. As a result, courts or arbitral tribunals now often consider software and other digital goods as capable of fitting within the broad notion of "goods" under the CISG, provided that the transaction's features are closer to a sale than a license or a service agreement. Therefore, the provisions related to the sale of a technology contained in a contract between a Chinese and a foreign party, where the latter belongs to a jurisdiction which is also a member-State of the CISG, such as Switzerland, shall 1258 be governed by the CISG, thus superseding Chinese (or any other law chosen by the parties, or pointed at by international private law, unless they explicitly excluded the CISG[635]) to that extent, the rest of the contract being governed by Chinese law or the law chosen by the parties[636].

1259 As far as technology contracts between a Swiss and a Chinese party are concerned, because technology-related *services*, in one or the other of the many forms of technology contracts (s. above §1252), often are partly if not the only subject-matter of technology contracts[637], one ought to recall that the *Sino-Swiss FTA* purports at facilitating the provision of services and fostering the protection of IPR between both countries (s. above §§876ff.)

1260 Technology contracts are also concerned with the regulations governing the *import and export of technology*, which is equally to be considered as a *lex specialis* (Art. 877; s. below §§1314 to 1315).

1261 Generally speaking, technology contracts may have gained in relevance ever since the two laws on *joint-ventures* have been repelled by the Chinese Civil Code (s. below Chap. 9 §66, Joint-ventures). Indeed, the Chinese law of JVs, whose inception occurred since as early as 1979, even before that of the first technology law in 1987, emphasized technology exchange from the outset (s. both the former EJV and the CJV laws, Art. 1; s. also EJV Law, Art. 5§2 and CJV Law, Art. 4 and 8); typically, technology-related agreement provisions used to be incorporated in the partnership agreement underpinning the JV, rather than in a separate, specific technology contract. Now that JVs must take the form of a limited liability company, a shareholding company or a partnership enterprise or contract, and that the latter regimes do not provide for technology-related contractual provisions, the regime applying to the latter is necessarily governed by Chapter 20 of the Third Book of the Chinese Civil Code on technology contracts.

1262 Should technology-related provisions be contained in the JV *partnership agreement* (s. below Chap. 5 §41, Partnership and Chap. 9 §66, Joint-ventures) anyway, the technology contracts regime, as *lex specialis*, would still apply to those provisions of the partnership agreement falling within the scope of the technology contracts regime, or whenever the partnership agreement may be silent, unclear, inadequate or lacunary about such issues.

---

635 S. above §921.

636 S. above §896.

637 In particular, trade between China and Switzerland for the sale of machine-tools, etc., represents a sizable share of their trade and imply related services.

II. General Provisions

The general provisions section of the technology contracts regime is concerned by the generic definition of the technology contract, its contents, payments, service inventions, and nullity. 1263

According to the law's generic *definition*, a technology contract purports at defining the parties' rights and obligations related to technology development, transfer, licensing, consulting or services (Art. 843) to the effect of protecting IPR, advancing science and technology, and promoting the research and development, transformation, application and popularization of scientific and technological achievements (Art. 844). 1264

It should be noted from the outset that the *notion* of "technology" itself is an *undefined* one; namely, it can barely be inferred from the definition of the technology contract (s. preceding paragraph) as loosely relating to IPR and scientific "achievements". 1265

Yet it is not to be confounded to that of *intellectual property rights*, to which, as mentioned, it relates, but does not identify. Likewise, the law's reference to IPR should not be understood in the narrow sense of *patents*. On the contrary, the rest of the definition of the technology contract supports a wide-encompassing notion, including technological achievements which may also be protected by other IPR, namely, *copyrights*, or may not, either because they have not yet been patented, or because, however corresponding to the notion of technological achievements *lato sensu*, they may not qualify as IPR *stricto sensu* and are, therefore, neither patentable, nor protected by copyrights, such as *know-how*, or commercial, trade or business *secrets*[638]. 1266

With respect to *patents*, one should further note that the regime of technology contracts under the Chinese Civil Code uses the expression "technological achievement", while the Patent Law that of "invention". Under the Patent Law, the notion of invention has two meanings: inventions *lato sensu* under the latter law include inventions *stricto sensu*, utility models and designs (Patent Law, Art. 2§1). In turn, inventions *stricto sensu* are defined as "new technical solutions proposed for a product, a process or the improvement thereof." (*ibid.*, § 2). As such, inventions may overlap with technological achievements and fit well as the possible subject-matter of a technology contract as per the latter's definition (s. above §1264); yet neither the notion of invention, nor that of patent, keeping in mind that not every invention is patentable, are substitutes for that of technological achievement. 1267

---

638 S. below §§1493ff.

1268 Notably, among other IPR, *software* qualifies as work (in the sense of copyrights subject-matter) and, even though it may be patentable if it meets specific conditions, is typically protected by *copyrights*[639](Copyrights Law, Art. 3, item 8), to which the technology contracts regime expressly refers (cf. Art. 876; s. below §1313); it is also commonly the subject-matter of technological contracts.

1269 In contrast, conceivably, a *trademark* can hardly amount to a technological achievement; they are typically the subject-matter of *licensing* agreements, not of technological contracts: even though technological contracts can also bear on licensing, their subject-matter is technology, not trademark, however related to that technology; yet nothing would prevent a technology licensing contract to provide, in addition to the licensing of the technology at stake, that of the related trademark in the form of an ancillary provision.

1270 *Other IPR* extend, notably, to *sui generis* IPR, among which it is worth mentioning the *layout designs of integrated circuits*[640] and *new varieties of plants*[641] (cf. Art. 876), the rights to which are protected, in Chinese laws, by dedicated laws.

1271 Arguably, not any *know-how* is capable of being the subject-matter of a technology contract: the law systematically refers to *technical* know-how (cf. Art. 862§1 and 2; s. below §1313). That notion is undefined and flexible, however.

1272 Likewise, even though the notion of "technology" is of particular significance with respect to its *import or export*, which are discussed below (s. §1317), it is defined neither in the Regulations on the Administration of Import and Export of Technologies (s. above §1315), nor in the Foreign Trade Law (2022 Amendment)[642], to which the former refers as to which technologies are restricted or prohibited from import or export.

1273 To conclude at this stage, "technology" is an undefined notion which has to be circumscribed by reference to the various legal provisions, pertaining to the regime of the technology contract or to other laws, applying it. One may reasonably suppose that it was the legislator's deliberate intent to preserve enough

---

639 A work qualifying for copyrights is automatically protected by copyright law from its inception; such protection is not subject to being granted after a successful application process like for patents.

640 The layout designs of integrated circuits are mainly governed by the Regulations on the Protection of Integrated Circuit Layout Design of 2 April 2001.

641 New varieties of plants are mainly governed by the Regulation on the Protection of New Plant Varieties (2025 Revision) and the Seed Law (2021 Amendment).

642 S. above note 650.

flexibility to accommodate the constant and swift evolution of this multi-faceted notion.

The law's description of the *contents* of a generic technology contract is unusually detailed: it includes the name of the project, the contents, scope and requirements of the subject matter, the plan, location and manner of performance, the confidentiality of the technical information and materials, the ownership of the technological achievements resulting thereof, the methods for proceeds distribution, the criteria and methods of inspection and acceptance, and the definitions of the related technical terms and terminology; this enumeration is not exhaustive[643] (Art. 845§1). It is complemented by a list of *documents* which are usually appended to the contract and may include background technical materials, feasibility studies and technical evaluation reports, project task paper and plans, technical standards, technical specifications, original design and process documents, as well as other technical documents relevant to the performance of the contract; the parties may agree that they shall constitute integral parts of the contract (*ibid.*, § 2) and would be well advised to do so for the sake of preventing or minimizing misunderstandings on the contract's subject-matter. 1274

Although not comprehensively protected by the technology contracts regime, the law requires *patents* to be expressly mentioned in the contract, which must state the name of the invention, of its applicant, patentee, the date of the application, its number, the patent number and the validity period of the patent (Art. 845§3). 1275

The technology contracts regime pays particular attention to the methods of *payment* which the parties may have agreed upon for prices, fees or royalties (Art. 846§1, 1st sentence). The law identifies four such methods: lump-sum payment based on a unique calculation; payment by installments based on a unique calculation; royalties payment (which is, by definition, a periodic payment, as opposed to a unique payment); or royalties payment augmented by the advance payment of an initial fee (*ibid.*, 2nd sentence). 1276

The law further details the payment modalities of *royalties* (or licensing fees), which may be calculated as a percentage. The law's description of the basis on which such percentage should be calculated is complicated: it may be calculated either on the product price; on the increase of the product's value after exploitation of the patent or of the licensed know-how[644]; on the profit resulting from such exploitation; or on product sales (Art. 846§2, 1st sentence). The royalty rate may be fixed or variable, i.e., subject to an annual increase or decrease (*ibid.*, 2nd sentence). The parties may also agree on the inspection of the 1277

643 S., for example, below §§1300 and 1302.

644 S. below Chap. 5 §40.IV, Technology Transfer Contracts and Technology License Contracts.

relevant accounting (*ibid.*, § 3). Finally, the parties are free to agree on any other method (*ibid.*, § 2, 1st sentence *in fine*).

1278 The drafting of this provision implies that the various methods are not mandatory, and that the concern of the legislator is to provide the parties with guidance to the effect of achieving a degree of clarity and uniformity in the drafting of technology contracts, thus reducing the risk of disputes and increasing legal certainty.

1279 The technology contract regime of the Chinese Civil Code is further concerned by technological achievements completed by an *employee*[645]. This notion recoups that of *service inventions* which are, in turn, regulated by the *Patent Law*. Even though the former uses the expression of "technological achievement" and the latter that of "invention", it can be assumed that the two notions, however not identical, *coincide* to the effect of the service inventions regime under the technology contracts one (cf. above, §1267).

1280 While in *Swiss law*, the regime of such inventions is governed by *labor* law, i.e., by Title Ten on the labor contract of the Swiss Code of Obligations (CO Art. 332 ff.), in Chinese law, it is governed, as noted, by both the technology contracts regime of the Chinese Civil Code, and that of service inventions under the Patent Law (Art. 6, 7 and 15)[646]; it is not, unlike Swiss law, governed by the Chinese Labor Contract Law.

1281 As noted, a *service technological achievement* as defined under the technological contract regime is a technological achievement completed by an employee. It can have been achieved either while performing the work the employee was assigned to or, if not during such work, by using the material, equipment, etc. made available by his employer (Art. 847§2). This definition is consistent with that of the service invention contained in the Patent Law (Art. 6§1, 1st sentence) addressed in the next paragraph. The technological contract regime uses neither the expression of "service technological achievement", nor that of "service invention" however; these notions have to be inferred from the substance of the law.

1282 Art. 847§1, 1st sentence of the Chinese Civil Code provides that if the employer has the right to dispose of the technological achievement, it has that of concluding a technological contract bearing on such achievement. In turn,

---

645 If the party having completed a technological achievement is not an employee, but the researcher-developer party to a contract of technological development, s. below §§1305ff. The same applies to the consultant party to a technological consulting contract, s. below §1341.

646 In contrast, the Swiss Federal Patent Law does not specifically regulate service inventions; only the Swiss Code of Obligations does (Art. 332).

Art. 6§1 of the Patent Law prescribes that the right to register the employee's invention belongs to its employer, which becomes the patentee after it has successfully registered. One may, therefore, safely *conflate* the notions of technological achievement and invention, and infer from the combination of those two provisions that the right to dispose of a technological achievement completed by an employee belongs to the employer, which may register it and conclude (whether is has registered such invention or not) a technology contract whose subject-matter may be that achievement, namely, the corresponding patent or, absent such registration, the right to patent it, but may also be any other right of disposition resulting thereof.

If, however, such technology contract consists in transferring the invention, the employee who has invented it enjoys, by law, a right to first refusal or of *preemption*[647] under the same conditions (Art. 847§1, 2nd sentence). 1283

In addition to the abovementioned right of preemption, the employee enjoys, also by law, the right that his *name* be mentioned on all documents related to his invention or technological achievement (Chinese Civil Code, Art. 849 and Patent Law, Art. 16§1). This provision is complemented by the Patent Law which requires the employer, in addition, to *reward* the inventor employee for its service invention (Patent Law, Art. 15§1) in the form of property rights (i.e., not only IPR), incentives such as equity, options, dividends, etc. to the effect that they enjoy a reasonable share of the benefits resulting from their invention (*ibid.*, § 2). 1284

In contrast, the inventor of a *non-service* technological achievement, i.e., however he may be an employee, of an invention unrelated with the performance of his work and without his employer's material, equipment, etc., is entitled to dispose of it and may conclude a technology contract to that effect (Chinese Civil Code, Art. 848 and Patent Law, Art. 6§2). 1285

In case of service invention where the employee used the employer's material, equipment, etc., the parties may agree that the employee shall have the right to patent any invention (Patent Law, Art. 6§3). However, this *waiver* cannot apply to the case where the employee has made an invention while performing his work: Art. 6§1 is mandatory to that extent. 1286

Given the relative complexity of the service regime, it is common, and advisable indeed, to anticipate service technological achievements or inventions in labor or technology contracts (typically, in research & development agreements) and to stipulate, in a dedicated *clause*, the allocation and disposal of rights in unpatented service inventions. It is equally advisable to extend the scope of labor or technological contracts to the ownership of non-patentable 1287

---

647 S. above note 602.

service technological achievements or inventions such as know-how or other non-patentable, yet commercially valuable technological achievements (s. above §1266 and note 638). Whenever so, mandatory provisions of the law may not be derogated from (s., namely, below §1286).

1288 Finally, the law provides for the *nullity* (无效 wúxiào; s. above §§241ff.) of any technology contract that constitutes an illegal monopoly of technology or infringes upon the technological achievements of others (Art. 850).

1289 The first prohibition (*monopoly*) is consistent with the Anti-Monopoly Law (AML), which prohibits monopolistic conducts consisting in, among other things, "utilizing data and algorithm, technology, capital advantage, or platform rules" (AML, Art. 9) as well as "an agreement to restrict the purchase of new technology or new equipment or restrict the development of new technology or new products" (AML, Art. 17, item 4); that prohibition may be mitigated for "technological improvement or research and development of new products" (AML, Art. 20§1, item 1 and § 2) however. Yet while the Anti-Monopoly Law provides for a vast array of sanctions which may, for serious cases, be extremely severe (AML, Art. 56), and for civil liability (AML, Art. 60), it does not provide for the nullity of such contracts. Therefore, comparatively, it can be said that Art. 850 of the Chinese Civil Code goes even farther; notably, it should be reminded that, as a consequence of nullity, the right holder would be not only deprived of any right to the sale price or licensing fees under such contract, but also liable for unjust enrichment (s. above §1151). Lastly, the parties to the infringing contract may be liable towards the third-party, namely, under patent law.

1290 All restrictions on competition do not amount to monopoly, which is the extreme form of any such restriction. Restrictions not amounting to a monopoly are merely prohibited if the scope of the technology transfer or licensing contract amounts to such restriction (Art. 864 *in fine*; s. below §1319), which implies that they would be unenforceable, not null and void, unless such restriction amounts to a monopoly.

1291 The second prohibition (*third party technology*) is more questionable. First, it literally suggests that a technology contract were null and void if it were to infringe the technological achievements of others, even if the latter were not patented and, in the extreme, even if the technology of the "infringing" technology contract were patented, which is obviously incompatible with patent law. We feel confident by affirming that, in the first case (neither party's technology patented), absent another qualification, such as a violation of the Anti-unfair Competition Law (e.g., infringement of a third party's trade secret, Anti-unfair Competition Law, Art. 10), and in any event in the second (infringing technology patented; infringed technology not patented), such nullity could not be successfully invoked.

Second, certain technological achievements, however acknowledged by the technological contract and other legal regimes (such as the Anti-unfair Competition Law mentioned in the preceding paragraph), do not qualify for patenting, such as *know-how* (s. above §1266 and note 638) and enjoy, as such, a lesser protection, such as to their priority, definition or scope, which also questions the applicability of this provision. 1292

And third, even if nullity could be successfully invoked, namely, because the third party technology were patented while that of the infringing technology contract were not, or because, even though the latter were patented, because the first patent would take precedence over the second, *partial nullity*, i.e., nullity limited to those parts of the technology contract infringing upon the third party technology, could apply, in accordance with Art. 156 (s. above §258), rather than the automatic nullity of the whole contract, as the somewhat rough drafting of Art. 850 suggests. 1293

In any event, Art. 850 should be understood as a *caveat*: both the risks of technological monopoly and of third-party rights, namely, of patent infringement, should be carefully assessed to the effect of preventing the serious consequences that may result from nullity, however partial. 1294

III. Technology Development Contracts

A technology (or technological) development contract (技术开发合同 jìshù kāifā hétóng; Art. 851 to 861) purports at the *research and development* (R&D) of any new technology, product, process, variety or material, as well as of any related "system" (Art. 851§1). What a "system" exactly should be is unclear; it seems that this expression is actually intended to expand the scope of any technology development contract to areas surrounding its specific subject matter. 1295

Technology development contracts include two *sub-types* which are the contract on *entrusted* (A.K.A. "commissioned") development (委托开发合同 wěituō kāifā hétóng) and the contract on *cooperative* development (合作开发合同 hézuò kāifā hétóng; *ibid.*, § 2). Its regime even applies to a third sub-type which are contracts whose subject-matter is the practical value, for *industrial application*, of any technological achievement, which are also governed by the provisions of the technological development contract (*ibid.*, § 3). The technology development contract for industrial applications can be either an entrusted or a cooperative technology development contract and can, therefore, be considered as being itself a sub-type of either. 1296

The *parties* to a technology development contract are designated by the law as the "researcher-developer" (which is the principal) and the "client". The law 1297 does not specify the *contents* of a technology development contract beyond mandating its *written* form (Art. 851 §3). Therefore, the parties shall refer to the contents listed in the general provisions of technology contracts (Art. 845; s. above §1274).

1298 Entrusted development contracts are specifically governed by Art. 852, 853, 859 and 861, last phrase; cooperative development contracts by Art. 855, 856 and 860. The other provisions of the regime of technological development contract which are, other than Art. 851 mentioned above, Art. 857, 858 and 861 (except the last phrase), apply to either sub-type. Rather than giving each of the entrusted and the cooperative development contract a unique definition, the law defines them by defining their parties' rights and obligations. The technological development contract for industrial application is not defined beyond Art. 851 §4; nor is it specifically addressed throughout the technological development contract regime.

1299 Other than the technological development contract definition, and termination which will be addressed at the end of this section, the only two provisions applying irrespectively of the technological development contract sub-type are about *disagreements* between the parties about technical difficulties (Art. 858) and other issues (Art. 861), for which the law provides guidance.

1300 Such difficulties are qualified as technical, insurmountable, and resulting in the partial or complete failure on the R&D project (*ibid.*, § 1, 1st and 2nd phrase). The consequences of the occurrence of such risks should be, in principle, pre-agreed by the parties (*ibid.*, 1st sentence *in fine*), although this item is not included in the list of contents provided by the law in the general provisions of technological development contract (Art. 845§1; s. above §1274). If they have not, they should attempt to under Art. 510 (s. above §618); if they fail, they should "reasonably" share the consequences resulting from the risk (Art. 858§1 *in fine*).

1301 When either party becomes aware or ought to be aware of any circumstance that may cause the failure of the R&D project, it has a duty to promptly *notify* the other party and to take damage mitigation measures, in accordance with the general principles of contractual liability (s. above Chap. 4 §27.IV, Mitigation and Exoneration.) If it fails to, thus aggravating the damage, it shall be liable for it (Art. 858§2).

1302 The same mechanism applies to disagreements related to *other issues* including the rights to use and transfer and the methods to distribute proceeds of the technical know-how (s. above §1265) achieved through entrusted development or cooperative development (Art. 861, 1st sentence). Unless they have been agreed upon and if the parties fail to settle under Art. 510, *both* parties are entitled to use and transfer that know-how before the related technology is patented (*ibid.*, 2nd sentence). However, in such case, the researcher-developer under *entrusted* development may not transfer the R&D achievement to a third party before its delivery to the client (*ibid.*, *in fine*).

As far as rights and obligations applying specifically to one sub-type of tech- 1303
nological development contract or the other, the obligations of the researcher-developer of an *entrusted* development contract (in addition to the obligation mentioned at the end of the preceding paragraph) consist in working out and implement R&D plans as pre-agreed, rationally use R&D expenses, complete R&D work as scheduled, deliver R&D achievements, and provide relevant technical materials and necessary technical guidance to help the client master the R&D achievements (Art. 853). Reciprocally, the client of an entrusted development contract shall pay R&D expenses and fees as pre-agreed, provide technical materials, raise requests on R&D, complete all cooperative work and accept R&D achievements (Art. 852).

In contrast, the obligations of the parties to a contract on *cooperative* develop- 1304
ment consist in making investments as pre-agreed, including investment in the form of technology, participating in R&D work according to the division of labor, and cooperating and coordinating with each other during R&D (Art. 855).

Beyond the general rights and obligations of the parties to either sub-type of 1305
technological development contract, the law is concerned with *patents*. The right to apply for a patent under a contract on *entrusted* development thus belongs to the *researcher-developer*[648], unless the parties agreed otherwise (Art. 859§1, 1st sentence).

Comparatively, because of its nature, the patent regime applying to contract on 1306
cooperative development is more elaborate: the right to apply for a patent belongs to both parties *jointly* (Art. 860§1, 1st sentence). If one party assigns its right to a third party, the other party enjoys a right of first refusal or *preemption*[649], unless the parties agreed otherwise (ibid., 2nd sentence).

From the structure of Art. 860§1, one may notice that the law only allows the 1307
parties to vary from it about the right of first refusal, not about the joint right to apply for a patent. However, the *waiver* to the latter is expressly foreseen by the next sub-section: thus, if one party waives its joint right to patent, the other party has the right to apply for the patent (*ibid.*, § 2). If there is more than one

---

648 That situation is not to be confounded with that where the researcher-developer were an *employee*, i.e., under a labor contract, not the party to the technological contract, in which case its employer were entitled to the right to patent (s. above §§1279ff.)

649 S. above note 602.

counterparty, the other parties have the right to apply, individually or jointly (*ibid.*) The parties may agree otherwise (*ibid., in fine*).

1308 The waiver must be *express*; the mere fact of abstaining from applying may not be interpreted as a waiver by conduct implying consent: indeed, the law expressly provides that if a party to a cooperative contract does not agree to apply for a patent, the other party does not have the right to (*ibid.*, § 3). Although this provision falls short from adding that the parties may agree otherwise (i.e., that one party may waive its right to disagree), given Art. 860§2 expressly providing that one party may waive its joint right to patent, that apparent omission in Art. 860§3 does not seems to contradict Art. 860§2 by implicitly preventing such waiver.

1309 Moreover, the right of the other parties to patent instead of the waiving party is limited: indeed, in such case, the law entitles the waiving party to exploit the patent *free of charge*, even if it was applied for by, and granted to, a counterparty or counterparties (Art. 860§2 *in fine*).

1310 In both sub-types of technological development contract, whether entrusted (Art. 854) or cooperative (Art. 856), the parties are *liable* for breach of contract if its breach causes the standstill, delay or failure of the R&D project. Liability of either party for untimely notification in case of technical difficulties has been mentioned above (Art. 858§2; s. §1301).

1311 Finally, where the technology which is the subject matter of a technology development contract has been made *public* by others, rendering the performance of said contract meaningless, the parties concerned may *revoke* the contract (Art. 857).

IV. Technology Transfer Contracts and Technology License Contracts

1312 Section 3 of Chapter 20 on technology contracts governs both technology *transfer* (技术转让合同 jìshù zhuănràng hétóng) and technology *license* (技术许可合同 jìshù xŭkě hétóng) contracts. As their names make clear, the first purports at the *assignment*, by the owner of a technology, to a third party, of the rights relating to a patent, patent application, or technical know-how (Art. 862§1), while the second at their *licensing* for exploitation or use of such rights (*ibid.*, § 2). Technology *transfer* contracts may consist, among others, in contracts on patent assignment, on the assignment of patent application rights, and on that of technical know-how (Art. 863§1). Technology *license* contracts may consist, for their part, in contracts on the licensing of a patent exploitation or of technical know-how (*ibid.*, § 2). Both subtypes may also apply to the exclusive rights of integrated circuits layout designs, to the rights related to new varieties of plants, to computer *software copyrights* and to other IPR (Art. 876). As their drafting implies, these lists are exemplative.

As the enumeration above implies, technology transfer and technology licensing contracts are not limited to patents or patent application rights, but extends to other IPR, namely, *software copyrights*, and to *know-how*, which cannot be patented or have not yet been (s. above §1265). 1313

The transfer and licensing of technology contracts regime is, as the case may be, superseded by *patent law* as well as by the regulations governing the *import and export of technology*; both of them are, therefore, to be regarded as *lex specialis* (Art. 877). While Art. 877 only mentions patent law, one may reasonably consider that the same stands true for *copyrights law*, since copyrights are expressly mentioned at Art. 876. 1314

The *export* of technology out of China in particular is a sensitive issue given the strategic stakes it underpins; it is, therefore, subject to a strict supervision regime mainly governed by the Regulations on the Administration of Import and Export of Technologies (2020 Revision)[650]. In case of import or export, technology contracts may require registration, depending on their classification. Technologies are categorized as prohibited, restricted, or freely transferable under a catalogue maintained by the Ministry of Commerce (MOFCOM). Restricted technologies transfer or licensing contracts require government approval prior to import or export, while contracts related to free technologies must be registered within 60 days of signing them; such registration is also required for customs, tax, and foreign exchange clearance. Other administrative provisions may apply to sensitive fields (e.g., encryption, national security technologies, rare earths, and other strategic sectors). 1315

While this book will not cover these regulations in detail, the Chinese and the foreign parties to any such contracts are advised to carefully consider their implications. These regulations also apply to the *import* of technologies into China; however, imports may be less closely scrutinized than exports. Technology contracts as such, namely, domestic technology transfer or licensing contracts, are not required to be registered, although any such contract with a Chinese but foreign-invested company may. 1316

---

650 The Regulations of the People's Republic of China on the Administration of Import and Export of Technologies (2020 Revision) have been themselves promulgated under the Foreign Trade Law (2022 Amendment), which applies to the protection of foreign-trade-related intellectual property related to the import and export of goods, technology and services (Art. 2).

1317 As noted, it is worth recalling, in this regard, that the *notion* of "technology" is not only not confined to patents or copyrights, as noted above (s. §§1265 and 1313), it is not even defined, neither in the Chinese Civil Code, nor in the Regulations on the Administration of Import and Export of Technologies (s. above §1315), nor in the Foreign Trade Law (2022 Amendment) (s. above note 650) to which the former refers as to which technologies are restricted or prohibited from *import or export* (Regulations on the Administration of Import and Export of Technologies, Art. 7 and 28): the latter only circumscribes it by listing the reasons why it were "necessary" to restrict or prohibit the import or export of such technology (Foreign Trade Law, Art. 19). This approach suggests that the legislator intends to preserve its discretion to decide what amounts to "technology" and other related undefined notions such as "know-how" and may, as such, be subject to restrictions or prohibitions.

1318 The definitions of both a technology transfer or licensing contract pose as a primary condition that the patent *exists* and be *specific*; in other words, neither contract can bear on a prospective or unidentified patent (*ibid.*)

1319 The law does not define the contents of a technology transfer or license contract. It simply mandates its *written* form (Art. 863§3). However, it provides that *ancillary* agreements providing for special equipment and raw materials for the exploitation of the technology, or for relevant technical consultation and services, are deemed to form an integral part of the contract (*ibid.*, § 3). Such agreements may also bear on the *scope* within which the patent is exploited or the technical know-how used (Art. 864).

1320 Said agreements on the scope of any such contracts must not result in restricting technological *competition* and technological development, being reminded that technological contracts resulting in a technological monopoly, which is the extreme form of competition restriction, are null and void (Art. 850; s. above §§1289ff.) Inasmuch, the law silently refers to the Anti-monopoly Law, which potentially prohibits any form of restriction of the competition (AML, Art. 2 *in fine*).

1321 The provisions forming the regime of the technology transfer and of the technology licensing contracts are divided into three groups: some only apply to patents (Art. 865 to 867); some only to know-how (Art. 868 to 871); the liability regime applies to both (Art. 872 to 875).

1322 As far as *patents* are concerned, the law regulates licensing (as opposed to transfer), validity and the parties' mutual rights and obligations. Thus, a technology licensing contract is only *valid* if, and as long as, the patent which underpins it is valid itself (Art. 865). As such, this provision implies that the licensor must, at the conclusion of and during the contract, simultaneously be the patentee of the licensed rights (Art. 870; s. below §1324). The patent may become invalid because its validity period expires or because it was invalidated before (*ibid.*), for example, by another patentee enjoying a preferrable right. The consequences of such invalidity would therefore occur *ex nunc*, while if the licensor had not been the patentee at the time of conclusion, they would arguably occur *ex tunc* (on those notions, s. above Chap. 2 §10.IV, Validity of Juristic Acts).

Regarding the parties to a technology patent licensing contract mutual *rights* 1323 *and obligations*, the *licensor* to a patent exploitation licensing contract shall, as pre-agreed, license the licensee to exploit the relevant patent, deliver technical materials related to patent exploitation, and provide necessary technical guidance (Art. 866). In counterpart, the *licensee* shall exploit said patent as pre-agreed, refrain from licensing a third party who is not included under contractual agreements to exploit the patent and pay royalties as pre-agreed (Art. 867). This latter provision also implies that the licensee has the right to *sub-license* with the licensor agreement.

As far as *technical know-how* is concerned (s. above §1265 and 1313), the re- 1324 lated regime applies both to transfer and licensing. The parties' mutual rights and obligations consist, for the *transferor* and the *licensor*, in providing technical materials, technical guidance, guaranteeing the utility and reliability of the technology and respecting confidentiality (Art. 868§1). They must also ensure that they are the legitimate owners of the technology provided and that it is complete, errorless, effective and capable of attaining the pre-agreed objectives (Art. 870). In turn, the *transferee* and the *licensee* shall use the technology, pay the fees or royalties, and respect confidentiality (Art. 869). They further shall, in accordance with the pre-agreed scope and period of time, fulfill their confidentiality obligations in respect of those parts of the technology that have not yet been made public (Art. 871).

As noted above, beyond provisions applying specifically to either patents or 1325 know-how, the *liability* regime of technology transfer and technology licensing contracts applies to *both* patents and know-how, while distinguishing between the same three groups: the licensor or transferor; the licensee or transferee, and both parties.

Thus, the *licensor* who fails to license- or the *transferor* to transfer the technol- 1326 ogy as agreed is liable towards the licensee or the transferee; in particular, it shall reimburse the royalties or fees (Art. 872§1, 1st sentence). In contrast, the *licensee* who fails to pay the royalties- or the *transferee* who fails to pay the fees is liable towards the licensor or transferor (Art. 873§1, 1st sentence).

Either party who exploits the patent or uses the know-how beyond the agreed 1327 scope, or allows a third party to exploit the patent or use the know-how without the other party's authorization, as well as the party which breaches confidentiality, is liable towards the other party; in particular, they shall cease to do so (Art. 872§1, 2nd sentence and Art. 873§1, 2nd sentence).

1328 That liability regime is complemented by two provisions: the duty of *confidentiality*, which is prescribed for both parties (Art. 868§1, 869 and 871), may not prevent the licensor (of a technology which, although being patentable, is not yet patented) to apply for the patent, unless the parties agreed otherwise (Art. 868§2)[651].

1329 Besides, where the exploitation of a patent or use of technical know-how by the licensee or the transferee infringes upon the legitimate rights and interests of *third parties*, the liability resulting thereof shall be borne by the *licensor* or the *transferor*, unless otherwise agreed upon by the parties concerned. Moreover, it shall be reminded that, according to the general provisions on technology contracts, any such contracts are deemed to be *null and void* (Art. 850); we have suggested to relativize this consequence however (s. above §§1291ff.)

V. Technical Consulting Contracts and Technical Services Contracts

1330 Section 4 of Chapter 20 on technological contracts (Art. 878 to 887) governs, as its title suggests, two sub-types of technological contracts: technical (rather than "technology-" or "technological-" as it should literally translate) consulting contracts and technical services contracts. A technical *consulting* contract (技术咨询合同 jìshù zīxún hétóng) is defined by the law as a contract by which a party with technical knowledge provides the other party with feasibility studies, technical forecasts, specialized technical investigations, or analysis and evaluation reports, among others, in respect of a particular technical project (Art. 878§1). In contrast, a technical *services* contract (技术服务合同 jìshù fúwù hétóng) is a contract whereby one party solves a particular technical problem for the other party by utilizing its technical knowledge, while being neither a contract of work (Art. 770 ff.; s. above Chap. 5 §38, Contract for Work) nor a contract for construction projects (Art. 788 ff.; s. above Chap. 5 §39, Construction; the contract for technical services is defined at Art. 878§2).

1331 The law also mentions, at the end of the chapter on technical consulting contracts and technical services contracts, technology *intermediation* contracts and technical *training* contracts (Art. 887). It does not regulate them however but merely prescribes that any special law or administrative regulations that may

[651] Confidentiality duties related to employment are discussed below about the latter's contract (s. §§1493ff.)

govern them, "if any", shall prevail. As a matter of fact, to our best knowledge, we are not aware, to this day, of any law or administrative regulation dedicated to technology intermediation contracts and technical training contracts. It seems, therefore, that the Chinese legislator's concern was merely to reserve any future specific regulation of technology intermediation contracts and technical training contracts.

Instead, the intermediation contract (Art. 961 ff.; s. above Chap. 5 §32, Intermediation) regime may apply to the *technology intermediation contract* (技术中介合同 jìshù zhōngjiè hétóng) whenever intermediation issues are at stake and the regime of the technical consulting or services contract is silent. It is to be further noted that, unlike certain inaccurate translations suggest and given the ambiguity of the related terminology (s. above §§997, 1028, 1029, 1055 and 1059ff.), Art. 887, while mentioning the technology intermediation contract, specifically refers to "intermediation" as in the intermediation contract of Art. 961 ff., not to "brokerage" as in the brokerage contract (行纪合同 xíng jì hétóng) of Art. 951 ff. (s. above Chap. 5 §31, Brokerage). However, nothing would prevent (s. above §1253) the conclusion of a technology brokerage contract, in which case brokerage would naturally be governed, to that extent, by the brokerage, not intermediation, contract regime. In either case, the parties are advised to carefully analyze the contract's characteristics and to specifically mention the legal regime to which the contract is subject. 1332

Likewise, the services provided in the form of training under a *technical training contract* (技术培训合同 jìshù péixùn hétóng) may be governed by the regime of mandate (Art. 919 ff.; s. above Chap. 5 §30, Mandate). Moreover, training being, in China, regarded as a political issue and, as such, strictly regulated, it must, in general, comply with the applicable regulations, namely, the Vocational Education Law (2022 Revision) and the related secondary legislation. 1333

Technical consulting contracts are specifically governed by Art. 879 to 881); technical services contracts by Art. 882 to 884; Art. 885 and 886 apply to both. 1334

As far as the parties' *rights and obligations* under the technical *consulting* contract are concerned, the *client* shall, as agreed, describe the issue for which it seeks consulting, provide background technical information and relevant technical materials, accept the consultant's work result (e.g., a report, etc.) issued by the consultant and pay its remuneration (Art. 879). In turn, the *consultant* shall complete the consulting report or solve the relevant issues within the agreed time limit and ensure that the consulting report submitted meet the requirements agreed upon (Art. 880). 1335

The parties' *liabilities* are governed by the two next articles: thus, the *client* shall be liable if it affects the progress or the quality of the consultant's work 1336 by failing to provide the necessary materials and data as agreed, to accept or to timely accept the work results. If so, the client shall not be entitled to recover the remuneration already paid, while still having the obligation to pay the remuneration not yet paid (Art. 881§1).

1337 Moreover, any damage resulting from a decision made by the client pursuant to the consulting report and opinions given by the consultant in accordance with the pre-agreed requirements shall be borne by the client, unless otherwise agreed upon by the parties concerned (Art. 881§3). Unlike this provision suggests *prima facie*, it does not necessarily exonerate the consultant's liability, namely, in case such damage results from erroneous advice provided by the latter. Indeed, the contract of consulting is fundamentally a mandate. As such, the consultant, who is the mandatee, has, to an extent, the right to be wrong, provided it used its best endeavors, such as a medical doctor failing to cure its patient or a lawyer failing to win a case despite they did their best. However, the mandatee or consultant's liability could be engaged anyway if it failed to use such best endeavors, which may typically occur if the consultant fails to comply with professional standards (such as an engineer making a calculation error) or disregard the client's instructions (such as an engineer ignoring the data provided by the client). In addition, such negligence is generally required to be relatively serious. However, in accordance with Art. 881§3, an engineer shall not be liable if, for example, it predicts a risk to be low, that the client decides to proceed with the project anyway, and that that risk occurs. One may further refer, on that issue, to the liability of the mandatee generally, which has been discussed about the mandate (s. above §§1007, 1010 and 1019).

1338 Conversely, the *consultant* shall be liable towards the client if it fails to submit a consulting report as scheduled or submits a consulting report that is not in compliance with the pre-agreed requirements. If so, the compensation it owes the client may take the form of a waiver or reduction of its remuneration (Art. 881§2). The consultant's liability resulting from the client's decision pursuant to the former's advice has been discussed in the preceding paragraph.

1339 The mutual rights and obligations of the parties to a technical *services* agreement consist, for the *client*, in making available working conditions, cooperating with the consultant, accepting the work results and paying its remuneration (Art. 882). The *consultant* shall render the agreed services, solve technical problems, guarantee the quality of its work and share the knowledge it uses for solving technical problems (Art. 883). Beyond its generical drafting, one may gather that the law does evidently not purport at compelling the consultant party to a technical services agreement to share commercial or technical secrets, however.

1340 The *liability* of the *client* party to a technical services contract compares in every respect to that under a technical consulting contract (Art. 884§1; s. above

§1336). So does that of the service provider, if it fails to provide the agreed services (*ibid.*, § 2; s. above §1338).

The remaining provisions common to both the technical consulting and services contracts are concerned with inventions and expenses. Technological achievements, i.e., in the patent law terminology, *inventions* (s. above §1279), completed by the consultant in the course of either contract's performance belong to the *consultant* (Art. 885, 1st sentence); those completed by the client pursuant to the consultant's work result belong to the *client* (*ibid.*, 2nd sentence). However, the parties may agree otherwise (*ibid.*, *in fine*)[652]. 1341

Finally, *expenses* related to the performance of either contract are borne by the *consultant*, unless the parties agreed otherwise (Art. 886). 1342

§41. Partnership Contract

A partnership contract (合伙合同 héhuǒ hétóng; Chap. 27 of the Chinese Civil Code, Art. 967 to 978) is defined as an agreement on sharing of benefits and risks concluded by two or more partners for purpose of their common undertakings. It should be noted that the partnership contract is, as a typical contract, one of the few new additions to the Chinese Civil Code: it was neither a typical contract under the former Contract Law, nor regulated as such, i.e., separately from the partnership enterprise mentioned in the following paragraph, which only incidentally mentioned it. 1343

The partnership contract can only be soundly explained together with the partnership *enterprise* (合伙企业 héhuǒ qǐyè) which, as its name suggests, is not a contract, but a company (in the common sense, not to the narrow one given by the Company Law) or a corporate form. The partnership enterprise is governed neither by the Chinese Civil Code, nor by the Company Law (which only applies to the limited liability company and to the shareholding company, consistently with the narrow definition it gives of a "company"), but by a dedicated law, the Partnership Enterprise Law (s. below Chap. 9 §65, The Partnership Enterprise). 1344

It adds to the confusion that the partnership enterprise regime also refers to the partnership contract regime; however, it only does so implicitly. Moreover, it does not refer to it as partnership contract (合伙合同 héhuǒ hétóng), but as partnership *agreement* (合伙协议 héhuǒ xiéyì[653]; cf. Partnership Enterprise 1345

[652] S., *mutatis mutandis*, above note 648.

[653] It does not help that, while 合同 hétóng generally translates, in English, as "contract", both 协议 xiéyì and 合同 hétóng may be translated as "agreement"; it would be

Law, Art. 14, item 2); yet both refer, if not to the same legal institution, to the same legal notion, which is governed by Chapter 27 of the Chinese Civil Code on the partnership contract as *lex generalis* whenever contractual issues related to the partnership agreement are at stake and the Partnership Enterprise Law, as *lex specialis*, is silent.

1346 The main difference between the partnership contract and the partnership enterprise is that the partnership enterprise enjoys *legal personality*; the partnership contract does not. Therefore, unlike the partnership enterprise (s. below §2220), a partnership contract needs not to, and cannot indeed, as companies do, be registered with the authority, i.e., with the equivalent, in China, of the register of commerce or of companies.

1347 Despite this fundamental difference, it can be said that the partnership contract is suited for smaller business ventures than the partnership enterprise, as the limited liability company compared to the shareholding company (s. below §2209). Another distinction can be made between the personal nature of the two first, and the capital-based one of the two last (s. below §1752). Be that as it may, the partnership contract can be said to be the smallest legal form of business venture among the four. As such, it is suited for partners whose venture is too small for justifying a corporate organization, while contract law suffices to give them an adequate legal framework for defining their mutual rights and obligations. Namely, while both the partnership contract and the partnership enterprise provide for a minimum of two partners and no maximum (with some exceptions for the limited liability partnership enterprise, s. below §2279), a larger number of partners generally justifies the enterprise rather than the contractual form.

1348 Even though the law does not mention it, there is a consensus about the silent requirement that the parties to a partnership contract must be individuals or *natural persons* and that *legal persons* may not[654]: judicial interpretations and commentaries emphasize the former[655], excluding legal entities to avoid conflicts with corporate structures. Namely, legal persons lack the personal liability suited for such partnerships, which operate under unlimited partner

incorrect to translate 协议 xiéyì as contract, however. 协议 xiéyì usually refers to any type of agreement reached between parties, whether oral or written, and does not necessarily create legally enforceable obligations. 合同 hétóng specifically means "contract" in the legal sense; it denotes a formal, legally binding document that creates enforceable rights and obligations for the parties involved.

654 Comparatively, this restriction does not apply in Swiss law (s. below §1354).

655 S. also Art. 977, which provides that the contractual partnership dissolve upon a partner's death or incapacity, underscoring its personal nature and unsuitability for legal persons with perpetual succession (s. below §1362).

responsibility rather than limited liability. Partnerships involving legal persons fall under the Partnership Enterprise Law, not the partnership contracts.

Another difference between the partnership contract and the partnership enterprise noteworthy for foreign investors is that, unlike a foreign-invested partnership enterprise, a partnership contract between a foreign and a Chinese party is, in principle, not subject to the registration and approval requirements applying to *foreign investment* (s. above §46). 1349

Indeed, the FIL, which mandates such registration and subjects any such investment to approval, defines "foreign investment" as investment activities carried out directly or indirectly by foreign investors, i.e., foreign natural persons, foreign enterprises or other foreign organizations (FIL, Art. 2). However, while the two first items of this provision specifically refer to enterprises, the two last mention "foreign investors, independently or jointly with other investors, invest in a new project in China" and "investment through other legal means", thus leaving ample room for interpretation to the authorities (s. above §§6 to 8). 1350

Therefore, should a partnership contract purporting at circumventing such requirements come to the knowledge of the authorities, or should they deem that, however unintentionally, such contract effectively amounts to such circumvention, its parties may expose themselves to the consequences, namely, in the form of administrative sanctions, resulting from an infringement of the FIL, and could be required to adopt a corporate form subject to registration, records filing and review under the FIL (s. above Chap. 1 §5, Management). This warning should be particularly heeded where the subject-matter of the partnership contract neighbors, and in any event falls within, any of the restricted or prohibited activities of the Negative List. 1351

Ever since the *joint-ventures* laws, i.e., the Equity Joint-venture Law and the Contractual (or Cooperative) Joint-venture Law have been abolished as of 1 January 2025 (s. above §§30 to 32), whenever an old JV has transformed into a limited liability company or a shareholding company, the partnership contract has become, silently but effectively, a substitute of the old JVs laws by governing the partnership agreement underpinning the parties' intent to form and operate a JV within the JV's new corporate form, be it a limited liability company or a shareholding company. This transformation is discussed extensively below under the chapter of this book dedicated to JVs, to which we refer (s. Chap. 9 §66, Joint-ventures, in particular §§2340, 2342, 2347 and 2351). 1352

Partnership contracts may also be mentioned in relation to *variable interests entities*, to the effect of structuring the overarching partnership relationship 1353 between the VIE partners[656] (s. below §2397). We refer to the topical chapter of this book for further discussion (s. below Chap. 9 §68, Variable Interests Entities).

1354 In *Swiss law*, the partnership contract corresponds to the "société simple" in French and the "einfache Gesellschaft" in German (CO Art. 530 ff.) Like in Chinese law, the "société simple" is not a company, but a contract (s. below §1755). Its regime is similar in most respects to that of its Chinese counterpart; however, the Swiss regime differs insofar as, unlike in Chinese law (s. above §1348), legal persons can be a party to a "société simple". For the sake of preventing confusion, it is worth recalling that, in contrast, the Chinese partnership *enterprise*, i.e., the first of its two its two sub-forms, the *general partnership*, corresponds, in Swiss law, to the "société en nom collectif" in French and to the "Kollektivgesellschaft" in German (CO Art. 552 ff.); its other sub-form, the *limited liability partnership*, corresponds to the "société en commandite" in French and to the "Kommanditgesellschaft" in German (CO Art. 594 ff.; s. below §1754).

1355 Unlike with other contracts, the law does not explicitly mandate or even describe the *contents* of a partnership contract, thus leaving the partners free to define it. If its *term* is not defined and the parties fail to agree under Art. 510 (s. above §618), it shall be deemed to be unlimited (Art. 976).

1356 While not being a company and, *a fortiori*, a capital-based company, the common undertaking mentioned in the partnership's contract definition (Art. 967 *in fine*) primarily consists in a common *capital*[657], to which each partner must timely contribute as agreed (Art. 968). Such contributions, as well as any profit generated by or assets derived from the partnership contract performance or affairs, are the partnership's *property* (Art. 969§1). A partner may not *assign* part or all of its share to a third party without the unanimous consent of its partners; it is free to do so to another partner though (Art. 974).

1357 *Decisions* within the partnership are subject to the unanimous consent of the partners, unless they agreed otherwise (Art. 970§1). The partners shall conduct the partnership's affairs jointly (*ibid.*, § 2, 1st sentence); the law provides, although implicitly, that one of them may be designated as *managing partner* (*ibid.*, § 3).

1358 The partnership contract may provide, or the partners may decide the *delegation* of certain affairs to one or several of them, while the other ones shall not

[656] Keeping in mind, however, that the parties to a contractual partnership cannot be legal persons (s. above §1348).

[657] The Swiss regime of contractual partnership is more liberal in that respect since partners can contribute financially, but also by receivable, in kind or by their work (CO Art. 531§1). Art. 968 of the Chinese Civil Code does not provide for those alternatives.

interfere but retain the right to supervise their performance (Art. 970, 2nd sentence), and the managing partner is vested with that of objecting and suspending the performance of affairs performed by other partners (*ibid.*, § 3).

In principle, unless the partnership contract expressly provides for it, the partners are not entitled to any *remuneration* for the execution of the partnership's affairs (Art. 971); instead, they are to a share of the partnership's *profit*, while simultaneously having to bear their shares of its *loss* (Art. 972, 1st phrase). Such *distribution* is made according to the partnership contract (*ibid.*); if the contract is silent or unclear, the parties shall consult and agree; if they fail to, profit and losses are to be shared *pro rata* to each partner's capital contribution; if such contributions cannot be determined (e.g., in case of contribution in kind), they shall be shared equally (*ibid.*, 2nd phrase ff.) 1359

Unlike for other contracts, or for the partnership contract's term (Art. 976; s. above §1355), the law does not expressly refers to the methods of *supplement*, interpretation and settlement provided by the Chinese Civil Code in case a contract is unclear or lacunary; yet such methods, especially Art. 510, may apply (s. above §618 and Chap. 4 §23.II, Contractual Interpretation). 1360

A prominent feature of partnership, whether contractual or the partnership enterprise[658], is that partners bear *joint and several liability* for the debts of the partnership. The creditor of a partner (as opposed to of the partnership) shall not be allowed to exercise, by subrogation, the rights of that partner towards the partnership contract, with one exception however: the right of that partner to request the *distribution* of profit (Art. 975; that share of profit is to be understood as net, after that partner has borne its share of losses). Besides, if a partner pays off the debts of the partnership in excess of the share of the debts that it is required to assume, it has the right to recover such *excess* payment from the other partners (Art. 973). 1361

Various circumstances lead to the partnership contract's *end.* In principle, a partnership contract with a fixed term ends at its expiry (Art. 976§2 by implication); if there is no such term[659], a partner may terminate it anytime (Art. 976§2); in both cases, it ends in case a partner dies (Art. 977), consistently with the overarching personal nature of the partnership. 1362

These rules are subject to the following *reservations* however: if, after its term has expired, a partnership effectively continues without any partner objecting, it shall keep existing and transform into an unlimited term partnership contract (Art. 976§2). If there is no such term, the terminating partner must notify its 1363

---

658 With some exception for the latter, s. below Chap. 9 §65.III, Specialized General Partnership and Chap. 9 §65.IV, Limited Liability Partnership.

659 S., however, above §1355.

partners reasonably in advance considering the nature of the partnership's business (Art. 976§3 *in fine*), which means that such notice shall not damage the partnership, provided the other partners are not at fault themselves. The same reservation applies in case a partner dies (Art. 977 *in fine*); moreover, in the latter case, the partnership contract may provide otherwise (*ibid.*, 2nd phrase); it may be noted that the law does not provide so for the other cases of termination.

1364 Once the partnership ends, the partner may request the *division* of the partnership's assets; however, he may not do so before it does (Art. 969§2).

§42. Deposit

1365 A contract of deposit (A.K.A. of safekeeping or custody; 保管合同 bǎoguǎn hétóng; Chap. 21 of the Chinese Civil Code, Art. 888 to 903) is defined as a contract whereby the depositary keeps the item delivered by the depositor, then returns it (Art. 888). It is known, in Swiss law, as "le dépôt" in French and "der Hinterlegungsvertrag" in German (CO Art. 472 ff.)

1366 While the contract of deposit may apply to both physical and financial assets, it is, in practice, primarily used for the former. Where it is used for the custody of financial assets, namely, on *bank accounts* which, as such, bear an economic significance far greater than the deposit of physical assets, banking contracts are predominantly governed by secondary or special laws, which we will be briefly outline below (s. §§1378 and 1379).

1367 The contract of deposit is closely related to the contract of *warehousing* (Art. 904 ff.): the latter refers to the former for any matter it does not cover (Art. 918). A warehousing contract shall refer to a contract whereby the depositary stores the items handed over by the depositor for warehousing and the depositor pays warehousing fees (Art. 904). In other words, under a warehousing contract, the depositary does not only keep the goods safe; it also stores them[660]. Where the contract of deposit focuses on safekeeping, that of warehousing emphasizes storage. In other words, related to each other, the contract of warehousing is a *lex specialis* and that of deposit a *lex generalis*.

---

660 If, for example, the depositor agrees with the depositary that the latter shall keep safe a consignment of coal, whether the contract qualifies as deposit or warehousing will depend on whether the premises on which the coal is deposited are owned or rented by the depositor or the depositary: in the first case, it will be a contract of deposit; in the second, of warehousing.

Both contracts give rise to certain issues as far as the *terminology* applying to the parties is concerned: they are discussed below, in the next chapter on the contract of warehousing (s. §1382). 1368

The contract of deposit is also typically related to the general regime of *contractual performance* as both a performance guarantee, and as alternative mode of performance in case the creditor refuses to accept the debtor's regular performance; both those regimes are contained in the general part of contract law governed by Title One of the Third Book of the Chinese Civil Code (s. above, for the former, Chap. 4 §27.III.B, Deposit, and for the latter, Chap. 4 §26.VIII, Deposit). 1369

Deposit is *implicit* whenever it is usual. The law gives, as examples, small transactions such as deposit related to shopping, dining, accommodation, etc. (Art. 808§2). However, deposit is also used for sizable transactions, typically, the deposit of large amounts of commodities, which require costly safekeeping measures such as for frozen food, grain, oil, etc. Therefore, and conversely, it can be assumed that an *explicit* agreement between the parties is needed for any other situation but the most mundane. The law does not require a written agreement, however. In any event, the contract, even oral, should be concluded upon the deposit of the item. The law provides that the parties may agree otherwise (Art. 890), which, somewhat paradoxically, implies that, one way or the other, they have to agree at the time of the deposit. 1370

The depositary is not entitled to any *fees*, unless the parties have pre-agreed or agree under Art. 510 (Art. 899; about Art. 510, s. above §618). Where fees have been agreed upon, the depositor shall pay them to the depositary at the agreed time (Art. 902§1); if such time has not been agreed and could not under Art. 510, the fees shall be paid upon collection of the item (*ibid.*, § 2 and s. below, §1377). In case of default, the depositary has the right to hold a *lien* on the item, unless the parties agreed otherwise (Art. 903). 1371

The depository's main obligation is to properly *keep* the item deposited (Art. 892§1) at the *place* and as (i.e., according to the "method"[661], as expressed in the Chinese original text) agreed between the parties (*ibid.*, § 2, 1st sentence). Such place and method may not be changed without the depositor's consent, except in case of urgency (*ibid.*, 2nd sentence). Namely, the depositary may neither transfer the items to a third-party depositary (Art. 894§1), nor use such item or allow a third-party to use it (Art. 895) without such consent. The depositary must issue a *certificate of deposit* to the depositor, unless trade practice provides otherwise (Art. 891). 1372

---

661 Such "methods" may consist, for example, in preserving food at a certain temperature, ventilating grain or oil regularly, etc.

1373 If the item is defective or requires, by nature, *special safekeeping measures* as those mentioned above (s. §1370 and note 660), the depositor must inform the depositary accordingly; if it fails to, the depositary shall not be liable in case of damage while the depositor may, unless the depositary know or ought to know and did not take any measures (Art. 893).

1374 Unless they are supported by judicial preservation or enforcement, the depositary is compelled by law to ignore *third-party claims* on the deposited items, promptly notify the depositor and return them to the latter only (Art. 896).

1375 In case of *damage* to the deposited item, the depositary shall be liable even if it was not at fault, in accordance with the general regime of contractual liability (s. above §794); however, if safekeeping was provided for free, it shall only be liable if it was at fault, according to the general regime of civil liability (s. above §§1641 and 1644); such fault may consist in intention or negligence; however, the law has risen the threshold of negligence, which must be gross (Art. 897).

1376 A special regime applies in case of deposit of *financial items* such as currencies or negotiable securities, the purpose of which is to prevent disputes about the valuation of such items and protect the depositary. In such case, the depositor must make a *declaration* to the depositary describing such items; in practice, the depositary shall then inspect them and, after having stated that they correspond to the description, seal them and countersign the depositor's declaration, thus providing the latter with proof of the deposit. If the parties have proceeded accordingly, in case of damage, the depositary is liable towards the depositor to compensate for the value declared (cf. Art. 901 and next paragraph *in fine*); in contrast, absent such a declaration, the depositary is only liable towards the depositor as if the financial items were ordinary items (Art. 898). In other words, absent such declaration, a deposit of cash pursuant to a burglary or a fire would, in practice, be worth the price of paper and not be compensated. This regime is typical of safe deposits into banks or hotels; however, as noted above (s. §1366) and outlined below (s. §§1378 and 1379), financial deposits in banks are systematically superseded by specific contracts governed by banking law rather than the contract of deposit as per the Chinese Civil Code.

1377 The depositor may *collect* the deposited item anytime; likewise, the depositary may ask the depositor to do so anytime, provided the period of safekeeping has not been or is not clearly agreed upon. If it has, the depositary may not do so ahead of schedule, unless it has a special reason (Art. 899), which the law does not define however. In either case, or at the *end* of the period, the depositary shall return the item together with its *fructi*, if any (Art. 900); *fungible* items may be replaced by items of the same kind, quality and quantity, i.e., as pre-agreed; and *currencies* must be returned in the same currencies and amount (Art. 901).

As mentioned at the beginning of this chapter, deposit contracts relating to *bank accounts* (such as savings-, demand-, or term deposit accounts with a bank) are governed by separate banking regulations and not solely by the Chinese Civil Code. These are mainly subject to the Law on Commercial Banks, which regulates the conduct of banks, including operations and protection of deposits; rules and policies issued by PBOC and the China Banking & Insurance Regulatory Commission (CBIRC), which address detailed regulatory requirements, compliance, account opening, and deposit protections; and specific contractual terms and conditions provided by each bank, tailored according to regulatory requirements, which apply to deposit accounts and the rights and obligations of the bank and the depositor. Deposit contracts with banks are recognized as *financial contracts* subject to regulatory oversight, liquidity requirements, and *consumer protection* laws. 1378

It is further worth noting that the opening, management, and settlement of bank deposit accounts are typically subject to separate procedural and documentary requirements, including verification of identity, legal corporate status, and compliance with central bank rules. Deposit protection (such as insurance and compensation mechanisms in case of bank insolvency) arises from banking-specific laws rather than the general contractual liability regime under the Chinese Civil Code. This book does not cover banking law; readers are invited to seek specialized advice. 1379

§43. Warehousing

The warehousing contract (仓储合同 cāngchú hétóng, Chap. 22 of the Chinese Civil Code, Art. 904 to 918) is defined as a contract whereby the depositary stores the items handed over by the depositor for warehousing, and the depositor pays warehousing fees (Art. 904). 1380

Under a warehousing contract, the depositary does not only keep the goods safe; it also *stores* them[662]. As noted about the contract of deposit, the contract of warehousing is a development of the former: that is more visible in the structure of *Swiss law*, where the contract of warehousing (Fr.: "le contrat d'entrepôt"; Ger.: "der Lägergeschäft"; CO Art. 482 ff.) is a *sub-type* of the contract of deposit (CO Art. 472 ff.) included in the chapter of the Swiss Code of Obligations dedicated to the latter rather than governed by a separate chapter. Yet although the contract of warehousing is, in Chinese law, a typical contract on its own, the contract of warehousing regime refers to that of the contract of deposit for any matter it does not cover (Art. 918). In other words, as 1381

[662] For an example, s. above note 660.

mentioned, related to each other, the contract of warehousing is a *lex specialis* and that of deposit a *lex generalis*.

1382 The *terminology* related to the *parties* deserves being clarified. Thus, in English, the parties to a contract of deposit or to a contract of warehousing are designated as "the depositor" and "the depositary" (i.e., the latter being the warehouse operator) in both cases; however, in Chinese, they are differentiated: for the contract of deposit, the Code uses 出质人 chū zhì rén for the depositor (the party delivering the property) and 受质人 shòu zhì rén for the depositary (the party receiving and safeguarding it). These terms emphasize the act of delivery and receipt for safekeeping, typically in a non-commercial context. In contrast, for the contract of warehousing, the Code uses 存货人 cún huò rén for the depositor and 仓储人 cāng chǔ rén for the depositary or warehouse operator. These reflect the commercial nature of storage, where 存货人 cún huò rén meaning "person storing goods" and 仓储人 cāng chǔ rén "warehousing person." Comparatively, *Swiss law* is also confusing: it does the same as Chinese law in legal German by using "der Hinterleger" and "der Aufbewahrer" for the depositor and the depositary under the contract of deposit, and "der Einlagerer" and "der Lagerhalter" for the contract of warehousing. However, Swiss legal French uses "le déposant" for the depositor under both contracts, while for depositary it distinguishes "le dépositaire" under the contract of deposit from "l'entrepositaire" for the warehouse operator.

1383 Like the contract of deposit, the contract of warehousing is also related to the general regime of *contractual performance* as both a performance guarantee, and as alternative mode of performance in case the creditor refuses to accept the debtor's regular performance. Indeed, in most cases where the subject-matter of the transaction is *goods* (typically, commodities such as oil, coal, grain, etc., but also, conceivably, vehicles, machines, etc.), warehousing, not only deposit, will be needed. Both those regimes are contained in the general part of contract law governed by Title One of the Third Book of the Chinese Civil Code (s. above, for the former, Chap. 4 §27.III.B, Deposit, and for the latter, Chap. 4 §26.VIII, Deposit).

1384 The law does not explicitly mandate that a warehousing contract needs not being concluded in *writing*; it only requires the parties to be in agreement (Art. 905); the contract of deposit regime, which applies by default, does not either (s. above §1370). However, in practice, other than for small, private transactions, as a mere matter of proof, it always is, as it should. Anyway, because the law mandates the depositary to issue a *warehousing receipt* anyway (Art. 908 ff.; s. below §1388), one can hardly conceive how, but for the smallest transactions (e.g., parking a bicycle in a paying enclosed rack), the parties could not conclude a warehousing contract in writing; even absent it, the warehousing receipt, however unilateral, because of its detailed content, which is mandated by law (*ibid.* and s. below §1389), would prove such contract's existence.

If the deposited goods are *hazardous* such as inflammable, explosive, toxic, corrosive or radioactive[663], or if they are perishable[664], the depositor must not only inform the depositary accordingly but also provide it with the relevant "materials" (Art. 906§1). The law does not define what such "materials" should be but, conceivably, it can consist in documents, data, protocols, training, equipment such as measuring equipment, etc. necessary for safely keeping such hazardous items. Hazardous goods are further subject to certain special liability regimes for illicit acts (s. below §1394). 1385

If the depositor fails to inform or provide the depositary accordingly, the latter may refuse to accept the items for warehousing and may take appropriate measures to prevent any damage at the expenses of the depositor (Art. 960§2). However, the law imposes depositaries operating warehouses storing hazardous items such as inflammable, explosive, toxic, corrosive or radioactive to have corresponding warehousing conditions (*ibid.*, § 3). 1386

The depositary must *inspect* the items to be warehoused before accepting them; if it finds any inconsistency with their contractual description, it must immediately notify the depositor (Art. 907§1). While the law falls short of mentioning it, but as implied *a contrario* by the next subsection of this provision, if the depositor fails to amend the items' contractual description accordingly, the depositary should reject them. Indeed, if it neglects to, and the items are subsequently found not to be in conformity with their contractual description in terms of varieties, quantity or quality, the depositary shall be liable for compensation (*ibid.*, § 2). The depositary liability is further outlined at the end of this chapter (s. below §1393). 1387

Upon acceptance, the depositary must issue the depositor with proof of deposit in the form of a *warehousing receipt* (Art. 908), which it shall sign or seal (Art. 909, 1st sentence); it is the proof for collecting a warehoused item (Art. 910, 1st sentence) and legitimating its holder to examine the items or take samples (Art. 911). The warehouse receipt is also a *negotiable instrument*: when endorsed by the depositor or the holder of the receipt while such endorsement is, in turn, signed or sealed by the depositary, the right to collect the relevant stored item may be transferred (*ibid.*, 2nd sentence). 1388

---

663 About the classification of hazardous goods, s. below §1413.

664 Typical examples include: oil or chemical tanks emitting taxic or inflammable gases, grain silos subject to spontaneous combustion induced by fermentation, pollutant industrial waste dumps, etc.

1389 The law mandates and abundantly details the warehouse receipt's *contents*, which shall include: the name and domicile of the depositor; the variety, quantity, quality, package, number of pieces and marks of the item handed over for warehousing; the standards for wear and tear of the item handed over for warehousing; the latter's site; its term; its fees; the insured amount, period of insurance and name of the insurer if insurance has been purchased for the items; the name of the issuer of the warehouse receipt; and the place and date of its issuance (Art. 909). However unilateral, in practice, these requirements almost amount to mandating the warehousing contract to be concluded in *writing* (s. above §1384).

1390 The depositor or holder of the warehousing receipt shall *collect* the item at the end of the warehousing period (Art. 915, 1st sentence). If it does so belatedly, it shall bear the additional warehousing fees (*ibid.*, 2nd sentence, 1st phrase); however, if it does so in advance, it shall not be entitled to a reimbursement of the unused warehousing fees (*ibid.*, 2nd phrase). If such period has not, or not clearly, been agreed upon, the depositor of holder may do so anytime (Art. 914, 1st sentence). Conversely, the depositary may ask the depositor or holder to do so anytime too, provided it does so with a reasonable advance notice (*ibid.*, 2nd sentence).

1391 If the depositor or the holder of the warehousing receipt fails to collect the item upon expiry of the period of warehousing, the depositary may urge the depositor or holder to collect it within a reasonable period of time; if it still fails to do so, the depositary may dispose of and *vacate*[665] the item, including by selling or auctioning it and keeping the profit resulting thereof (Art. 916): because the law provides the depositary with a legal basis to that effect, such disposal shall not amount to breach of contract or unjust enrichment. This provision is consistent with, and should not be confused with, deposit as a mode of *alternative performance* (s. above Chap. 4 §26.VIII, Deposit).

1392 The depositary must promptly notify the depositor or the holder of the warehouse receipt if it finds that a stored item *deteriorates* or is otherwise damaged (Art. 912). If such deterioration or damage endanger the safety or operation of the warehouse, the depositor must urge the depositor or holder to take the necessary measures (Art. 913, 1st sentence). In case of emergency, the depositary may take necessary measures on its own, provided it notifies the depositor or holder accordingly as soon as possible; the law acknowledges that, in such case, that notification may only be possible after such measures have been taken (*ibid.*, 2nd sentence). Again, these provisions are consistent with the general

---

[665] Art. 916 uses the verb 提存 tícún which, actually, literally translates as "deposit", but should be understood, in this particular context, in the sense of "vacate" or "dispose of".

duty of mitigation under the general regime of contractual liability (s. above Chap. 4 §27.IV, Mitigation and Exoneration).

If a warehoused item is damaged or destroyed due to improper warehousing under the depositary's watch, it shall be *liable* for compensation (Art. 917, 1st sentence). Such impropriety includes the depositary's failure to notify the depositor or holder in accordance with the preceding paragraph. The depositary liability implies that the item has been carefully inspected and described in the warehousing contract (s. above §1387) and on the warehousing receipt (s. above §§1388 and 1389). It is further subject to specific *exemptions*: if a warehoused item deteriorates or is damaged because of its nature or inadequate packaging while neither corresponds to their contractual description[666], or because its conservation period has expired, the depositary shall be exempted (*ibid.*, 2nd sentence). 1393

Finally, in case of damage caused by *hazardous* goods, one ought to recall that the warehousing contract liability regime is complemented by that of Chapter 8 on extreme hazards or "high-risks" liability (Art. 1236 ff.) of the Seventh Book on liability for illicit acts of the Chinese Civil Code (s. above Chap. 8 §62, Extreme Hazards Liability) as well as, as the case may be, that of Chapter 7 on liability for environmental pollution and ecological damage (Art. 1229 ff.; s. above Chap. 8 §61, Liability for Environmental Pollution and Ecological Damage). Both regimes are to be considered as *leges speciales* to the liability regime under the warehousing contract. 1394

§44. Transportation

I. Introduction

A contract of transportation (运输合同 yùnshū hétóng; Chap. 19 of the Chinese Civil Code, Art. 809 to 842) is a contract by which the carrier transports passengers or goods from one place to the agreed destination, and the passengers, the consignor or the consignee pays a fare or the freight (Art. 809). The "consignor" is the party that sends the goods; the "carrier" that which transport them or passengers; the "consignee" that which receives the goods; the "fare" is the price passengers pay to the carrier for the transport; the "freight" is the price the consignor or the consignee pays to the carrier for transporting goods. 1395

Transportation is an immense topic embracing multiple modes (passengers, goods, by road, sea, air and rail, etc.) with innumerable legal implications 1396

666 This provision is also to be understood as a being intended to indirectly fight fraud.

(contractual, tax, customs, traffic, post mail, environment, etc.) both domestically and internationally, most of which vastly exceed the scope of this book. Yet given the formidable volume of import from- and export to China, and despite the prevalence, in certain cases, as briefly outlined below, of other laws and treaties, the contract of transportation under the Chinese Civil Code, which remains the overarching law governing the basic relationship at stake, cannot be ignored.

1397 The main Chinese laws and international treaties governing transportation of passengers or goods by road, sea or air are the following; this enumeration is only intended to provide general indications; it is neither comprehensive nor exhaustive; readers needing actual advice are invited to seek specialized counselling.

1398 In *Chinese law*, transport by *road* of passengers and goods are mainly governed, domestically, by the Law on Road Traffic Safety (2021 Amendment); transport by *sea* by the Maritime Code and the Regulations on International Ocean Shipping[667]; transport by *air* by the Civil Aviation Law; transport by rail by the Railways Law, as well as secondary or related laws and their implementing regulations.

1399 In *international law* (irrespective of whether these treaties apply to China or not), transport by *road* of passengers and goods are mainly governed by the Convention on the Contract for the International Carriage of Goods by Road (1956), known as CMR or CMR 1956; transport by *air* by the Warsaw Convention (1929) and the Montreal Convention (1999)[668]; transport by *sea* by the Hague-Visby Rules (1924, 1968 and 1979[669]); and transport by *rail* by the Convention Concerning International Carriage by Rail (COTIF 1999).

---

667 The Maritime Code regulates substantive maritime commercial law and claims relating to ships and shipping, while the Regulations on International Ocean Shipping govern administrative, operational, and safety standards for ships engaged in international ocean shipping under Chinese jurisdiction or coastal control. The former is broader in legal scope, the latter more specific to the regulation of shipping operations and compliance.

668 The Montreal Convention, signed in 1999, replaced the Warsaw Convention system in countries ratifying it, which include China and Switzerland. Presently, the Montreal Convention has already almost entirely superseded the Warsaw Convention.

669 The original Rules, then known as the Hague Rules, were amended twice by the First Protocol of 23 February 1968, after which they were renamed Hague-Visby Rules, and the Second Protocol of 21 December 1979. The Hamburg Rules of 31 March 1978 were intended to replace them but failed to; neither China nor Switzerland signed it. The Hamburg Rules should be replaced by the Rotterdam Rules of 23 September 2009 which have not yet entered into force; while Switzerland signed them, China has not.

China is a member-State to the Warsaw and the Montreal Conventions, but neither of the CMR, nor of the Hague-Visby Rules, nor of COTIF. Given the formidable volume of Chinese shipping, it is noteworthy that China did not sign the Hague-Visby Rules; instead, China primarily regulates maritime transport through its domestic law, i.e., the Chinese Maritime Code, which incorporates principles similar to those in the Hague and Hague-Visby Rules. China is, however, member of the UN TIR Convention (1975) on the international transport of goods under TIR Carnets, which facilitate cross-border trucking and freight transport along routes such as the projected New Silk Road. 1400

Comparatively, in Swiss law, transportation of goods is governed by the eponymous contract of transportation (Fr.: "le contrat de transport"; Ger.: "der Frachtvertrag"; CO Art. 440 ff.) which only applies to goods, not to persons, however. Swiss law does not provide for a nominate contract applying to the latter. In Swiss law, the consignor is known as "l'expéditeur" in French and "der Absender" in German; the carrier under the obsolete name of "le voiturier" (the coach operator) in French and, more straightforwardly, "der Frachtführer" in German; the consignee as "le destinataire" in French and "der Empfänger" in German. The contract of transportation is subject to the regime of the mandate (CO Art. 394 ff.) for any matter about which its own regime is silent (CO Art. 440§2). Because they only apply to goods, contracts for the transport of persons and multimodal contract are, therefore, *sui generis* contract[670]. 1401

Like in China, transportation is also indirectly governed, in Switzerland, by a multitude of other laws and regulations, which, for the reason mentioned above[671], we shall not outline here, and international treaties. In this later respect, as noted, while Switzerland is a member-State of all the treaties referred to above, China is a member neither of CMR, nor of the Hague-Visby Rules, nor of COTIF; therefore, a Swiss party to a contract of transportation by *road, sea* or *rail* with a Chinese party would not be able to invoke any of these. 1402

While the fact that China has not signed many of these conventions hardly has any practical implications on road or train transportation given the quasi non-existence of transportation of passengers or goods by *road* (and because both countries being members of the TIR Convention anyway) or *rail* between China and Switzerland[672], it has more serious implications for transportation by *sea*, being recalled that Switzerland itself operates a substantial maritime 1403

670 S., for example, Tercier, No. 4640. In Switzerland, companies transporting persons typically operate under a concession granted by the State.

671 S., namely, RS 74, 63, .74 and .63; this reference is not exhaustive.

672 The completion, if ever, of the New Silk Road may potentially alter this assessment in the future, however.

fleet[673]. In either case, the contract will be governed by the law chosen by the parties; in practice, the law of choice in contracts of transportation by sea is, most of the time, English law; transportation contracts not governed by an international treaty generally provide for disputes resolution by arbitration in a neutral forum.

1404 In contrast, a Chinese and a Swiss party are governed, for transport by *air*, by the Montreal Convention which, according to the principle *pacta sunt servanda*, supersedes national laws, be they Chinese law, Swiss law or another national law chosen by the parties. The Montreal Convention provides for an embedded disputes resolution mechanism.

1405 The transportation contract regime is divided into four sections corresponding to the three *sub-types* of contract regimes applying to passengers, goods, or both, the latter being known in the industry as *multimodal* contracts, while the remaining section contains general provisions governing all of them.

II. General Provisions

1406 Among the general provisions forming the first section (Art. 809 to 813), beyond the transportation contract generic definition, the law asserts the semi-public nature of transportation contracts by mandating that carriers, however private, operating *public* transportation services are obligated to transport passengers and goods, subject to reasonableness (Art. 810).

1407 The *general duties* of *carriers* consist of safely transporting passengers and goods, to the agreed destination, within the agreed or a reasonable time (Art. 811), and via the agreed or usual routes (Art. 812).

1408 The main duty of *passengers* is to pay the fare and that of *consignors or consignees* to pay the freight (Art. 813, 1st sentence). If the carrier fails to follow the agreed or usual route, thus increasing the fare or freight, the passenger, consignor or consignee may refuse to pay the increased portion of the fare or freight (*ibid.*, 2nd sentence).

---

673 As of 2025, Switzerland's commercial maritime fleet ranked 9th or as much as approximately 30% of China's, which ranks as the largest; its size in the global trade is, therefore, notable.

III. Freight Transportation

The *passenger* transportation contract (客运合同 kèyùn hétóng) is governed by Section 2 (Art. 814 to 824) of Chapter 19 on transportation contracts of the Chinese Civil Code. Its regime is hardly relevant for foreign operators however: indeed, as noted, passenger transportation by road, sea or train is unrealistic as far as foreign operators are concerned. As for air transportation, domestic flights are barred to foreign airlines, while international flight entering or exiting China are governed by international law, as mentioned above (s. §§1399ff.) Therefore, this chapter of this book will focus on freight transportation instead; if needed, we refer the reader, for passenger transportation, to Art. 814 to 824, which are straightforward. 1409

The *freight* (or cargo) transportation contract (货运合同 huòyùn hétóng) is governed by Section 3 (Art. 825 to 837) of the same chapter. The related regime is concerned with the specific rights and obligations of the three parties involved, i.e., the consignor, the carrier and the consignee, and their liabilities, before departure, en route and upon arrival. 1410

Before departure, the *consignor* has the obligation to declare the goods, provide the carrier with all the documentation necessary for the related formalities, and to properly package them, especially if the goods are hazardous. Its *declaration* obligations bear on the name of the consignee or of the consignee by order[674], as well as the name, nature, weight and quantity of the goods, the place of delivery, etc. (Art. 825§1). The *formalities* mentioned above may consist in examination, approval, inspection, etc. which shall be completed by the consignor (Art. 826). 1411

Packaging should be pre-agreed and, if so, conform with the contract; if it has not been pre-agreed, the law refers to Art. 619 which governs packaging under a contract of sale (Art. 827§1; s. above §913). 1412

The consignment of *hazardous* goods, which the law defines as inflammable, explosive, toxic, corrosive or radioactive, subjects the consignor to additional obligations under the special regulations applicable. Namely, it shall properly package them, affix warning signs and labels, and provide the carrier with written documents containing the name, nature and precautions relevant to such items (Art. 828§1). The transportation of hazardous items is governed by a maze of regulations depending on their mode of transportation, by road, sea, 1413

674 A "consignee by order" refers to a consignee who is designated "by order" of the consignor on the bill of lading. This term indicates that the goods are consigned not directly to a named consignee, but rather to whoever presents a properly endorsed bill of lading, allowing for claiming the delivery of the goods. A similar faculty is provided by the warehousing contract for the endorsement of the warehousing receipt (s. above §1388).

air or rail, both in Chinese and international law, whose enumeration would exceed the scope of this book. However, one may point out that, in China, the classification of hazardous goods is uniformized under two norms, the List of Dangerous Goods (GB 12268-2025) and the Classification and Code of Dangerous Goods (GB 6944-2025)[675]. These national standards define the classification, categorization, packaging requirements, and handling rules for hazardous goods during transportation, storage, and distribution. Recently updated, they align with the 23rd UN Model Regulations on the Transport of Dangerous Goods (2023).

1414 Besides, like for the contract of warehousing (s. above §1394), in case of damage caused by hazardous goods, the special regimes outlined in the preceding paragraph may be complemented by that of Chapter 8 on extreme hazards or "high-risks" *liability* (Art. 1236 ff.) of the Seventh Book on liability for illicit acts of the Chinese Civil Code (s. above Chap. 8 §62, Extreme Hazards Liability) as well as, as the case may be, that of Chapter 7 on liability for environmental pollution and ecological damage (Art. 1229 ff.; s. above Chap. 8 §61, Liability for Environmental Pollution and Ecological Damage). How these regimes relate to each other, namely, which of them would have to be regarded as a *lex specialis* to the other would have to be assessed in the light of the treaties, laws and regulations coming into play.

1415 If the consignor fails either to comply with the necessary formalities, provide the carrier with the relevant documents, properly package the goods or comply with the related additional requirements in case they are dangerous, the carrier has the right to *refuse* to transport the goods (Art. 827§2 and 828§2). In addition, in case of dangerous goods, the carrier has the right (and, even though the law does not expressly formulate it as such, under the general duty of mitigation[676], the obligation) to take the necessary measures for preventing the potential damage that may result from improper packaging or from related improper preventive measures, while the consignor shall bear the costs resulting therefrom (Art. 828§2 *in fine*).

1416 *During* transportation, i.e., before delivery, the consignor has the right to require some *changes* to the initial agreement by asking the carrier to suspend transportation, return the goods, change the place of destination or deliver the

---

[675] The Classification and Code of Dangerous Goods specify the classification, hazard categories, packaging groups, naming and coding rules for dangerous goods.

[676] In the context of transportation of hazardous goods, the general duty of mitigation pertains both the regime of contractual liability (s. above §836) and that for illicit acts (s. above §1651); where hazardous goods are concerned, it may be complemented or superseded by the special law or regulations applying to the transportation of such goods, as the case may be.

goods to another consignee. If so, the consignor must compensate the carrier for any damage resulting thereof (Art. 829) such as re-routing, storage, etc.

Upon *arrival*, the carrier shall promptly *notify* the consignee, provided the carrier has been informed by the consignor who the consignee is, i.e., in case the consignee has been identified and is not a consignee by order[677]. Upon notification, the consignee shall take *delivery* of the goods. Both parties must act promptly (Art. 830, 1st sentence). If the consignee takes over the goods belatedly, i.e., after the pre-agreed time limit for doing so, it must pay the carrier the costs resulting from such delay, for example, storage, etc. (*ibid*., 2nd sentence). 1417

Upon delivery, the consignee must *inspect* the goods within the pre-agreed time limit. If such limit has not been or is not clearly agreed upon, and still cannot be determined pursuant to Art. 510 (s. above §§618ff.), the consignee shall inspect the goods within a "reasonable" period of time (Art. 831§1). It is noteworthy that the consignee's *silence* after delivery shall be deemed to amount to *acceptance* (*ibid*., § 2). 1418

The *carrier* is, in principle, *liable* for any damage to the goods or their destruction, subject to several *exceptions* if the damage or destruction was caused by force majeure[678] (s. above §327), the natural properties of the goods themselves, reasonable wear and tear, or by the fault of the consignor or the consignee (Art. 832). Such fault may consist in but is not limited to omitting to comply with the duties described above. In contrast, if the goods are destroyed because of force majeure, the carrier is not entitled to the freight if they have perished *before* delivery, whereas the consignee is not entitled to a reimbursement of such freight having perished *after* delivery (Art. 835, 1st sentence). Laws providing otherwise are reserved (*ibid*., *in fine*). 1419

Commercial freight contracts, which usually relate to large amounts of goods whose economic value is substantial, generally provide for *liquidated damages* (Art. 585; s. above Chap. 4 §27.III.A, Liquidated Damages) to the effect of preventing disputes about the *quantum* of the damage (Art. 833, 1st sentence). If such amount has not been or is not clearly agreed upon, and still cannot be determined pursuant to Art. 510 (s. above §§618ff.), it shall be calculated at the *market price* of the goods in the place of delivery when the goods are delivered or ought to be delivered (Art. 833, 2nd sentence); this regime accords with that provided by the general regime of contractual liability (Art. 1184; s. above §1661). The law further reserves the provisions of other applicable laws and administrative regulations on calculation methods and the upper limit of compensation that shall apply. 1420

677 S. above note 674.

678 The archetypical and most frequent case of force majeure is shipwreck.

1421 If *two or more carriers* provide combined transportation over several sections of the transportation route, the carrier who concludes the contract with the consignor is responsible for the entire operation; in case of damage, the latter is jointly and severally liable with the carrier in charge of the section where the damage occurred. The transportation mode must be the same, be it by road, sea, air or railways (Art. 834).

1422 Finally, if the consignor or the consignee fails to pay the freight, storages fees or related costs, the carrier has the right to exercise a *lien* on the goods transported, unless the parties agreed otherwise (Art. 836). If the consignee is unknown or the consignee refuses to take delivery of the goods without justifiable reasons, the carrier may *dispose* of the goods in accordance with the law. In both respects, these solutions compare with those provided for the contracts of deposit (Art. 903; s. above §1371) and of warehousing (Art. 916; s. above §1391).

IV. Multimodal Transportation

1423 "Multimodal" refers to transportation combining different modes, i.e., road, sea, air or railways. The multimodal transportation contract (多式联运合同 duō shì liányùn hétóng) is governed by a relatively short Section 4 (Art. 838 to 842) of Chapter 19 on transportation contracts; it complements the three other subtypes of contracts described above. The related regime is mostly concerned by liabilities of the various parties which can be numerous, since they typically include the consignor, the multimodal operator, multiple carriers, the consignee and possibly transferees of either the consignor or the consignee's multimodal transportation documents.

1424 The basic principle is that the operator of multimodal transportation is responsible for providing the transportation or organizing it; as such, it enjoys the rights and assumes the obligations of a carrier throughout the *entire* transportation (Art. 838).

1425 The multimodal operator has the right to agree, with *multiple carriers*, to each section of, or mode along the transportation route, on their respective responsibilities; however, such agreements may not diminish the obligations of the multimodal operator as mandated by Art. 838 (Art. 839).

1426 The multimodal operator shall, upon receipt of the goods, issue the *multimodal transportation documents* which may, upon request of the consignor, be *transferable* or not (Art. 840). If the consignor causes damage to the multimodal operator by the former's fault at the time of consigning the goods, the consignor shall still be liable towards the operator, even if it had already transferred the multimodal transportation documents (Art. 841).

Finally, if goods are damaged or destroyed on a particular section, the laws regulating the transport mode of that particular section shall apply to the regime of liability, in particular to the extent of the multimodal operator's liability (Art. 842, 1st sentence). If that section cannot be ascertained, the multimodal operator shall be liable (2nd sentence). 1427

Chap. 6 Employment

§45. Introduction

The contract of employment (or labor contract) is obviously of primary importance to foreign investors, for at least two reasons: first, a foreign investor will necessarily have to rely on local (domestic or expatriate) employees. Second, and even though that is frequently ignored, not to say deliberately so, the contract of employment of expatriate workers in China is mandatorily governed by Chinese law; it may not be subjected to foreign law, typically to the law of the foreign employer, as often seen in practice nevertheless, however illegal under Chinese law (s. below §§1438ff.) 1428

Somewhat surprisingly, the Labor Contract Law, which otherwise governs it, does not provide a general *definition* of the contract of employment. However obvious that may be, the contract of employment can be defined, as, for example, in Swiss law, a contract by which the employee undertakes to work in the service of the employer for a limited or unlimited period and the employer undertakes to pay him a salary based on the amount of time he works or the tasks he performs (CO Art. 319§1). 1429

Terminology wise, the contract of employment or labor contract calls for some comments. It is expressed, in Chinese, by 劳动合同 láodòng hétóng, where 劳动 láodòng stands for work or labor; 劳动 láodòng does not stand alone for "employment" however. Yet it translates, in English, either as contract of employment, or as labor contract, that are equivalent expressions, and which we will use indifferently in the chapter. In contrast, in other European languages, whether pertaining to the Latin or the Anglo-Saxon group, it is not known as contract of employment but as labor contract or, literally, contract *of work* (Fr.: "contract de travail"; Ger.: "Arbeitsvertrag"). Again, however evident that may be for native English speakers, it is, therefore, not to be confused with the contract *for work*[679], which is an entirely different contract (Chinese Civil Code, Art. 770 ff.; s. above Chap. 5 §38, Contract for Work) translating in French as "contrat d'entreprise" and in German as "Werkvertrag". Moreover, in the later expression, the word qualifying such contract, "Werk", which is the subject-matter of the contract for work, is yet another false friend of "work", which where the later can be, by name if not in substance, the subject-matter of both the labor contract and of the contract for work. 1430

The purpose of labor law is to strike a balance between the interests of workers and employers. From that perspective, Chinese offers its workers comprehensive 1431

679 For alternative translations, s. above §§1188 and 1189.

protection; in some respects, it can be said to be more protective than some foreign jurisdictions. From that perspective, the following general comments may be of special interest to *foreign employers*: first, some foreign employers have complained that the authorities, concerned by deterring the repetition of historical precedents by which Chinese workers were abused by foreigners with impunity, are allegedly stricter with foreign-invested employers than with Chinese ones. Second, in contrast, Chinese parties in general, Chinese workers being no exception, are, because of the emphasis society puts on consensus, more reluctant than their western peers to engage into litigation, or, generally, any kind of dispute; therefore, many renounce their rights, however legitimate, by fear of retribution; nevertheless, they often prove being more daring with foreign employers, who may be more pliant than their domestic counterparts. Third, because Chinese labor law provides for comprehensive and, compared to some foreign jurisdictions, generous overtime compensation and severance packages, and because the cost of labor in China has steadily increased and is not cheap anymore as it used to be until the beginning of the 21st century, the economic consequences of noncompliance or of a layoff, even legal, are significant, so that foreign employers may want to consider them not only when they face them, but to anticipate them.

1432 The contract of employment is the only typical contract not governed by the Chinese Civil Code; it is governed by a separate law (s. above §557). It was already so under the former regime of the Contract Law (s. above §551). As it reformed Chinese civil law, the legislator elected to maintain this segregation. By doing so, Chinese law follows the French tradition where labor law, including the contract of employment, is primarily governed by the Code du travail (labor code), which is separate from the French Civil Code, while Swiss law adheres to the German tradition by which the contract of employment is contained in the Code of Obligations, which is itself part of the Civil Code[680].

1433 The contract of employment is thus primarily governed, in Chinese law, by the *Labor Contract Law* (2012 Amendment), which has been effective as of 1 July 2013. The 2012 Amendment amends the Labor Law of 2007, which replaced itself the obsolete law of 1994, modified specific sections of the 2007 law, mainly in response to abuses of labor dispatching and ambiguities in the original law. After 2013, the Labor Law was also influenced, as of 2017, by the adoption of the General Rules of the Civil Law (effective as of 1 October 2017) which impacted certain aspects of labor law and the contract of employment, before the General Rules were superseded, in 2020, by the Chinese Civil Code, which comprehensively regulates contract law, among other things.

---

680 S. above note 89.

Other than the contract of employment strictly speaking, labor law relies on a vast array of secondary laws and administrative regulations, which exceed the scope of this book which will, therefore, not cover them. For matters of general contractual law, the Chinese Civil Code applies. 1434

The Labor Contract Law is complemented by the *Labor Law* (2018 Amendment), with which it ought not to be confused. The Labor Law, which was initially enacted in 1994, was amended twice, in 2009, then 2018; the 2018 Amendment is effective as of 29 December 2018. It sets an overarching framework for labor law that includes but is not limited to the contract of employment whose regime, primarily governed by the Labor Contract Law, the Labor Law does not alter, but reiterates, while being more detailed[681]. The Labor Law relates to the Labor Contract Law as a general law and the latter to the former as a special one. Provisions of a contract of employment countering the Labor Law result in their invalidity. This chapter focuses on the Labor Contract Law, but selected features of the Labor Law will be signaled as appropriate. 1435

On 31 July 2025, the SPC released the *Judicial Interpretation*[682] *II* ("Interpretation II") on the Application of Law in Labor Dispute Cases, along with a set of illustrative cases. Both have taken effect on 1 September 2025. Interpretation II harmonizes judicial practices and consolidates four prior labor dispute guidelines which it supersedes. 1436

The issues addressed by the Judicial Interpretation II include employer liability in outsourcing and subcontracting arrangements; the determination of labor relationships in mixed employments; exemptions to double-wage compensation for failure to enter a written labor contract; eligibility for the enforcement of non-compete contractual clauses; liability for failure to pay social insurance contributions; and defenses related to arbitration time limitation raised during litigations, among others. Both Interpretations will be addressed as appropriate throughout the presentation of the Labor Contract Law. 1437

As hinted above, it is worth stressing that the contract of employment of *expatriate employees* employed in China by an FIE is governed by *Chinese law*. The parties, even if both the employee and the foreign investor or parent company are foreign, and often of the same nationality, are not free to elect the law of their home jurisdiction or another foreign law to escape Chinese law. Indeed, Chinese international private law, i.e., the Law on Choice of Law for Foreign- 1438

681 The Labor Law complements certain chapters already contained in the Labor Contract Law including the labor contract, supervision, inspection, and liabilities; it also contains additional chapters such as promotion of employment, workings hours, rest and leaves, wages, labor safety and sanitation, special protection for female and juvenile workers, training, social insurance and welfare, and labor disputes.

682 On judicial interpretations generally, s. above §102.

related Civil Relationships, makes clear that the labor contract shall be governed by the law of the *workplace* of the laborer (Art. 43, 1st sentence). This provision further clarifies that, were it is difficult to determine the workplace, the law of the place of the employer's principal office shall apply (*ibid.*, 2nd sentence), while dispatch services shall be governed by the law of the place "of dispatch" (*ibid.*, 3rd sentence), which is that of the dispatch agency. Although Chinese law, including Chinese private international law, embraces freedom of choice of law (Law on Choice of Law for Foreign-related Civil Relationships Art. 3; s. above §554), Art. 43 is *mandatory* (*ibid.*, Art. 4). This issue is further discussed below (s. §1446).

1439 It results thereof that, in the typical case of an expatriate worker formally employed by an FIE registered in China and working in China, Chinese law shall apply to the contract of employment. In other words, a French-invested enterprise employer in China and its French employee working in China may not subject the latter's contract of employment to French law. Likewise, they would not be free to choose the related forum, i.e., to subject any dispute between them to a French court or to foreign arbitration. If they do, such choice shall be dismissed as ineffective by a Chinese court or labor arbitration tribunal, and may, not to say should also be so by a foreign court or a foreign arbitration tribunal[683]. Indeed, as a consequence of the mandatory application of Chinese law, only Chinese jurisdictions are competent[684]. Foreign workers need not being overly concerned since recently Interpretation II has expressly confirmed that the protections of Chinese labor law also apply to them (Interpretation II, Art. 4).

683 S. below note 684 however.

684 In 2025, a Swiss court tried a dispute between a French employee and his Swiss employer. The employee had been working permanently in China for several years as chief representative of a French FIE registered in China, formally under a contract of employment subject to Chinese law which had been filed with the Chinese authorities but that the parties had otherwise ignored. He was simultaneously bound by a contract of employment with the Swiss company, a subsidiary of the French investor. That contract was not a secondment contract but a comprehensive contract of employment. The parties had elected Swiss law and the competence of Swiss courts. Both parties considered that contract as the only one applicable. Although both the choice of law and forum were illegal under Chinese law, and even though the Swiss court should have, under Swiss international private law, applied Chinese law (LDIP Art. 121§1) and, consequently, declined its competence (LDIP Art. 115 *a contrario* and 13), it silently admitted its competence because neither party objected (LDIP Art. 6, 1st phrase) and applied Swiss law as chosen law, under which it ruled, thus simultaneously disregarding the statutory nature of Chinese law. However flawed, neither party appealed the ruling. (The case is not published.)

It is to be noted that the foregoing also applies to *foreign branches* (s. below Chap. 9 §64.XI, Branches of Foreign Companies) and *representative offices* (s. below Chap. 9 §67, Representative Offices) despite, since neither enjoy legal personality, their foreign representatives must be hired by the foreign parent (s. below §§2184, 2376 and 2184). Therefore, their labor contract must be subject to Chinese law, even though the employer is not an entity registered in China. However, in practice, such contract is generally doubled by a *contract of secondment* governed by the law of the employer which clarifies the relationship between both contracts and offers the possibility to subject to their home law certain aspects of their contractual relationship not mandatorily governed by Chinese law (e.g., adhesion to a home pension fund)[685]. That said, this complicated relationship is often misunderstood by the parties, thus giving rise to unnecessarily complex disputes. So is *temp employment*, addressed in the next paragraph, which is, under Chinese law, mandatory for the local workers of such foreign branches and representative offices. 1440

As already mentioned, in practice, the foreign parties to a relationship of employment in China often deliberately sign two contracts, i.e., the first, which is purely formal, under Chinese law, which they file with the Chinese authorities for satisfying the requirements of Chinese law but otherwise ignore, and the second, which they consider as material, under their home law which they voluntarily apply, while in case of dispute the home court often disregards both the statutory nature of Chinese law with respect to the applicable law and the forum applicable to employment in China and international private law[686]. This strategy may result in unexpected, and unwanted indeed, results, however. 1441

As outlined about the representative office (whose temp work regime also applies *mutatis mutandis* to foreign branches; s. below §§2376 and 2184), because they are deprived of legal personality, foreign branches and representative offices may not employ local workers directly; they must do so through a specifically licensed agency, with which such workers will enter a contract of employment while the agency will make such workers available to the branch or the representative office under a *contract of services*. As noted, that relationship is known as *dispatching* (often but ill-named “temp work”, s. below §1579) and governed by a dedicated section of the Labor Law. There is no contractual relationship between the branch or the representative office on one hand, and the worker on the other; nonperformance by the worker (which may, among other things, consist in the inobservance of internal regulations such as a staff handbook, code of conduct, etc. that do not amount to a contract between the worker and the branch or representative office however) will result in a 1442

685 S. preceding note, however.

686 *Ibid.*

breach of both the contract of services, thus rendering the agent liable towards the branch or representative office, and of his contract of employment with the agent, which will render the worker liable towards the agent. Therefore, while the contract of services with the agent is of primary concern to the branch or representative office, the contract of employment in particular, and labor law more generally, are, comparatively, of indirect concern to them. Dispatching is elaborated further down in this chapter (s. below Chap. 6 §50.II, Labor Dispatch).

1443 As far as *bilateral labor relations* between China and *Switzerland* are concerned, the *Sino-Swiss FTA* purports, among other things, at the facilitation of services (s. above note 498). China and Switzerland have also signed an *Agreement on Social Security* on 30 September 2015 effective 19 June 2017.

1444 The Labor Contract Law, which contains almost a hundred articles, is divided in eight sections, three of which cover the labor contract's conclusion, performance and termination (Chap. 2 to 4). Chapter 5 contains three special types of contracts which are the collective contract, labor dispatch and part-time work. Two more chapters apply to administrative compliance (Chap. 6) and liabilities (Chap. 7). The law is complemented at the beginning and the end by general (Chap. 1) and supplemental (Chap. 8) provisions.

§46. General Provisions

1445 As mentioned, the law applies to enterprises, individual employers and other organizations "in China" establishing a "labor relationship" with workers (Art. 2§1). This formulation encompasses all *employers* (designated in the law as 用人单位 yòngrén dānwèi, which literally translates as "employing units"[687]), including public entities (*ibid.*, § 2). The notion of *labor relationship* is equally extended and may consist in concluding, performing, modifying, revoking or terminating a contract of employment (Art. 2§1 *in fine* and 2 *in fine*).

1446 Although from the syntax of the original Chinese version of Art. 2§1, the reference to the *Chinese territory* relates to the employers, under Chinese international private law, Chinese labor law applies to any work performed in China (s. above §1438). Indeed, as mentioned, Chinese international private law, i.e., the Law on Choice of Law for Foreign-related Civil Relationships, makes clear that the labor contract shall be governed by the *law of the workplace of the laborer* (Art. 43, 1st sentence). This provision further clarifies that, were it is difficult to determine the workplace, the *law of the place of the employer's*

687 "Employing unit" pertains to the socialist administrative vocabulary; in the context of the contract of employment, its meaning does not differ from that of employer.

principal office shall apply (*ibid.*, 2nd sentence), while dispatch services shall be governed by the law of the place of dispatch (*ibid.*, 3rd sentence). In case of work in China or, in case of doubt, for an enterprise in China, both point at Chinese law. Art. 43 is mandatory (*ibid.*, Art. 4).

Likewise, as also noted, Chinese law does not only apply to employer enterprises registered in China, but also to the *foreign parents* of branches and representative offices in China employing foreign representatives directly (s. above §§1440 to 1442). 1447

The law firmly rests the labor contract on core *principles* which are lawfulness, fairness, equality, voluntariness, consensus through consultation, and good faith (Art. 3§1). However obvious, it stresses the binding nature of the labor contract (*ibid.*, § 2). This reminder is to be understood in a general context in which Chinese workers were routinely abused absent labor contracts, or because the latter were ignored[688]. Furthermore, Chapter 1 of the law strongly emphasizes *alternative dispute resolution* (ADR), namely, settlement over litigation (Art. 3 to 6), which is a distinctive feature of Chinese labor law, and which we elaborate below. 1448

Thus, Chinese labor ADR rests on two levels: at the *lower level*, on an institutionalized *tripartite mechanism* gathering employers, workers represented by their labor union and the local competent authority for labor relationships (Art. 5); at the *upper level*, on *multi-tier dispute resolution* combining institutional mediation, institutional arbitration and, eventually, litigation, where litigation is, both by law and in practice, the last resort. As a result, compared to some foreign jurisdictions where litigation is the norm rather than the exception, the vast majority of labor disputes in China are settled amicably instead of before courts. Labor dispute resolution is detailed in the Labor Law (Chap. 10). 1449

At the lower level, the *first step* of such multi-tier system is to anticipate disputes by promoting *consultation*. Thus, the law encourages, if not mandates, employers to *inform* and *consult* with their workers when formulating or modifying *internal rules or regulations* or making *decisions* applying to their labor relationship (Art. 4§2 and 4). Such rules, etc. may bear on but are not limited to matters such as remuneration, working hours, rest and vacation, occupational safety and health, insurance and welfare, training, labor discipline and labor quota control (*ibid.*, § 2). They must uphold basic *principles* including lawfulness, fairness, equality, voluntariness, consensus through consultation, and good faith (Art. 3§1). 1450

---

688 Although labor policies succeeded in fighting this issue to a significant extent, it still persists today (s. below §1482 and 1483).

1451 Such consultations are to take place during general meetings gathering all the employees, or meetings in smaller committees between the employer and workers' representatives (Art. 4§2 and 6§2 *in fine*; s. next paragraph). The workers are represented by labor unions (s. next paragraph) or elected representatives (Art. 4§2). The law places employers and workers on equal footing (*ibid., in fine*).

1452 *Labor unions* are promoted by the law and the authorities. They are mandatory for enterprises with 25 employees or more (Trade Union Law, Art. 10) and encouraged for less. They are primarily governed by the Trade Union Law, while their role is acknowledged, both in the Labor Law and the Labor Contract Law, both generally (Labor Law Art. 7 and 88; Labor Contract Law Art. 5, 6, 56, 73§3 and 78) and in specific cases (Labor Law Art. 27, 30, 33§2, 41, 80§1 and 81; Labor Contract Law Art. 4§§ 2 and 3, 41§1, 43, 51§2, 53 and 64). They are tasked with establishing a "collective consultation mechanism" gathering both the employer and the employees to the effect of facilitating the settlement of disputes (Art. 6, 2nd phrase). These mechanisms are typically internal to each enterprise. They also have the right to denounce violations to the authorities (Art. 78)[689].

1453 Labor unions typically rely on *collective contracts* (s. below Chap. 6 §50.I, Collective Contracts), which aim at harmonizing labor contracts in certain trades to the effect of containing the negotiation of individual labor contracts within boundaries ensuring minimum workers' protection, as well as preventing disputes and facilitating their settlement by offering a set of regulations and good practices to which the parties may refer (s. below §1521 as well as Art. 56 and §1577).

1454 The *second step* of such multi-tiers dispute resolution system is that, if the workers were not or not properly informed, if no consultation took place or if the employer did not take it into account, where the workers disagreed with the implementation of such rule, etc., they enjoy a *right of reconsideration* or of *remediation*, conferring them the right to ask the employer to consult, and to change it (Art. 4§3). The matter to which such rule, etc. applies must have a certain "importance" however (*ibid.*) "Important" is defined as impacting on workers "directly" their "immediate interests" (Art. 4§2, 3rd phrase). The law also encourages *renegotiation* for matters not specified in the contract of employment (Art. 18, 1st sentence; s. below §1472).

1455 Beyond these reservations, it is generally acknowledged that workers enjoy a wide *right of participation* consisting, as outlined, in the right to be informed,

---

689 In this latter respect, the foreign employer should be warned that denunciation is more embedded, and frequent indeed, in Chinese culture, where it is regarded as a civic act, than it may in the western culture.

consulted, to ask for changes, and to have their opinion taken into account[690]. That is not to say that these rights are systematically respected; violations still frequently occur[691]. Yet the authorities are generally firm at enforcing them. Some western employers complain that, although they consider having a higher awareness of those rights, they are subject to closer scrutiny than some of their domestic peers.

The *third step* is taken if the employer refuses to reconsider or remediate, where 1456
those rules and regulations have a direct bearing on the immediate interests of workers and are in contravention with the law and the relevant regulations, the workers (Art. 77) and the labor unions (Art. 78 and s. above §1452 *in fine*) have the right to *denounce* such violations to the competent labor authority[692], which will order the employer to rectify and give it a warning (Art. 80, 1st sentence). Moreover, the employer shall be liable for compensation for any damage caused to its workers (*ibid.*, 2nd sentence).

At the *upper level*, the next steps are governed by the regime of *multi-tier dis-* 1457
pute resolution contained in the Labor Law (Art. 77 ff.), which provides for three stages. They deserve some elaboration in the context of the Labor Contract Law since the latter constantly refers to dispute resolution. These steps are mediation, arbitration and litigation[693] (Labor Law, Art. 77§1).

Before describing these further steps, one should note that *negotiation*, which 1458
is mentioned at the end of Art. 77§1 of the Labor Law providing for the upper level mechanism, is not an additional intermediary step; it is nothing else but a reference to the lower level mechanism described above (s. §1451ff.), even if,

---

[690] Such rights expressly include that of *criticizing* and, in certain cases, that of exposing and charging the employer without fear of retribution (s. below §1520). Unlike in western societies, criticizing the authority is traditionally frown upon in Chinese society, which explains the special protection so provided.

[691] S. above note 688.

[692] S. above note 689.

[693] *Mediation* is a voluntary, informal process or ADR method by which a neutral third party, the mediator, helps the parties to settle; he only issues non-binding, i.e., non-enforceable recommendations. *Arbitration* is a formal process or ADR method by which a neutral arbitrator (or panel of three) operates like a court and issues an enforceable decision or award, which may be final or not; it is more formal than mediation, but less formal than litigation, and potentially faster, more flexible and less costly than the latter. *Litigation* refers to the formal court or judiciary processes at the outcome of which a judge or tribunal or court issues an enforceable judgment or ruling, which can typically be appealed; compared to ADR, it is the most formal, and often the slowest and most costly dispute resolution method. In certain cases, like for labor dispute resolution in China, mediation and arbitration, which are usually private, can be *institutional*, i.e., promoted and regulated by the State.

by mentioning "negotiation", Art. 77§1 in fine of the Labor Law does expressly refer to the Labor Contract Law.

1459 Thus, in case those negotiations, i.e., the lower-level mechanism, failed, the *fourth step* provided by the Labor Law further entitles the worker to apply for *mediation* before the mediation committee, which is supposed to be available in every enterprise[694].

1460 If mediation fails too, the parties may take a *fifth step* and apply for *arbitration*; they may also do so directly instead of mediation (Labor Law, Art. 79, 2nd and 3rd sentence and Art. 83; time limits applying to arbitration have been recently clarified by Interpretation II, Art. 20 and 21). Such committees are set up by the local labor authority; they are composed of representatives of the labor union and the employer as co-chairs and chaired by a local labor official. Mediation and arbitration committees are formed of representatives of the labor union, of the employer and of the local labor authority. The first is chaired by the representative of the labor union; the second by the labor official (Labor Law, Art. 80 and 81).

1461 Finally, in a *sixth and last step*, the arbitral sentence can be *appealed* by either party before the competent court (Art. 79 *in fine* and 83) which, in other words, elevates the dispute to the *litigation* or *judiciary* (as opposed to ADR) stage. Unlike the mediation and arbitration committees which are specialized labor institutions, there are no specialized labor courts in China; civil courts are competent.

1462 The sequence described above is flexible however; it is not subject to the rigid principle of *exhaustion of remedies* preventing the claimant to resort to one remedy before it has exhausted the remedy at the inferior level in the judicial hierarchy of remedies: both the Labor Contract Law and the Labor Law clearly focus of pragmatism to the effect of favoring settlement (s. Labor Contract Law, Art. 3 to 6 and above §1448, as well as Labor Law, Art. 78). Namely,

---

[694] In practice, if an enterprise (typically small or medium enterprises) does not have such committee, mediation may still be conducted through several alternative organizations. These include people's mediation institutions established at the grass-roots level (such as township- or neighborhood-level organizations), external mediation committees set up by the local labor authority, or organizations specifically designated for labor dispute mediation by the relevant government office. The trade union may act as a mediator only if it is involved in these organizations or as a representative within a mediation committee, but it is not automatically responsible for mediation if no internal committee exists. Some local authorities may also maintain panels or rosters of external labor mediators who are approved to conduct mediation in labor disputes, providing parties with additional options for mediation outside the enterprise.

mediation can intervene at every step of the arbitration or before the court (Labor Law, Art. 77§2).

§47. Formation

Chinese labor law is designed for offering extended protection to workers irrespective of whether a formal contract was concluded or not. Namely, it contains strong deterrents to discourage employers from not entering into such contract formally in an attempt to escape their obligations or weaken workers' protection. Besides, it strongly promotes open-ended contracts by rendering them mandatory after a limited number of extensions of a fixed-term contract or absent a written contract, and by mandating the employer to either extend the latter or pay severance at its term. 1463

Thus, a contractual labor relationship is deemed by law to have *formed* as of the date the employer effectively employs the worker (Art. 7), i.e., irrespective of whether a contract has been concluded or not (cf. Art. 3§2, 1st sentence). Moreover, Interpretation II has established the "penetration" principle (s. below §1606) to identify the *actual employer* in case of subcontracting, outsourcing, or affiliated employment cases, even absent a written contract (Interpretation II, Art. 1 and 3). 1464

While the contract itself becomes effective once it has been signed (or, for the enterprise, sealed) by both parties (Art. 16), it does not change anything to the fact that, if the contract was established *after* the work started, its contractual effects shall be deemed to *retroact* to such start; should the contract mention that it is valid from its date while work effectively started earlier, such date would be legally invalid; only the *effective* start date is valid. If the contract was concluded *before* work started, the contract will be valid from the date of its conclusion, but the work will be deemed to have begun from its start anyway, not from the date of the contract (Art. 10§2). 1465

Before the contract is concluded or the work starts, the employer has a *duty of information* towards the (future) worker. Such information must be truthful and comprehensive. It must include, among other things, a description of the work and its conditions, its place, occupational hazards, work safety and remuneration (Art. 8, 1st sentence). Such duty is matched by the worker's *right of information* related to the contract of employment, at least when such information is basic, and directly related to the work (*ibid.*, 2nd sentence). 1466

Upon recruiting the worker, the employer is also under a *prohibition to coerce* him by retaining the latter's identity card or other certificates, requiring a guarantee, or collecting and retaining money or other assets (Art. 9). The law 1467 expressly rules out any pretext (*ibid., in fine*). Violations result in administrative penalties (Art. 84). Although it does not mention it, such prohibition purports at preventing employers to pressure their employees to waive their rights.

1468 The conclusion of a contract of employment in *written form* is mandatory (Art. 10§1). The omission of such form has rather serious detrimental consequences for the employer. If the written contract is not immediately established from the start of employment (Art. 7; s. above §1463), the law grants the employer a *grace period* of one month to comply (Art. 10§2). If the employer misses the grace period for *less than a year*, it shall pay the worker *double wage* from the start (Art. 82§1). If such failure persists for *more than a year*, the parties are, in addition, deemed to have concluded an *open-ended contract*, while the employer must pay double-wage until a written contract is established (*ibid.*, §2 and Art. 14§4; s. below §1479). The remuneration shall match the rate defined in the collective contract (s. below Chap. 6 §50.I, Collective Contracts) applicable to the same trade or, absent any such collective contract or rate, the rate in the same trade according to the tenet "equal pay for equal work" (Art. 11).

1469 The contract's *contents* are detailed by the law. *Mandatory* terms shall include: the name, domicile and legal representative or general manager of the employer; the name, address and identity document number of the worker; the contract's term; the job description; the place of work; the working hours, rest and vacations; the remuneration; social insurance information; information related to working conditions and occupational hazards and protection; and any other terms required by laws and regulations (Art. 17§1). *Optional* terms may include probation period, training, confidentiality, supplementary insurance and welfare benefits (*ibid.*, § 2).

1470 The employer must *copy* the worker the contract of employment (Art. 16§2). If it has failed to, the authority may order it to comply (Art. 81, 2nd phrase).

1471 The parties have the right to *modify* the contract anytime, provided they mutually agree, make such changes in writing and each keep a copy of the amended contract (Art. 35; s. below §1513).

1472 The law provides a cascading dispute resolution mechanism or contractual supplement (for the latter, s. Chinese Civil Code, Art. 510 and 511; s. above Chap. 4 §23.II, Contractual Interpretation) for disputes resulting from working conditions *not specified or unclear* in the labor contract (Art. 18). They should first be resolved by *renegotiation* (Art. 18, 1st sentence *in fine*), which accords with the general tenet of reconsideration[695] (Art. 4§3; s. above §1454). Second, if

[695] Renegotiation tends at resulting in the reconsideration, by the employer, of the disputed provision or lack thereof.

renegotiation fails, the *collective contract* applies (Art. 18, 2nd sentence). Third, if there is no collective contract or if it is silent about *remuneration*, the principle "equal pay for equal work" shall apply (*ibid.*, 3rd sentence; cf. Art. 3 and 11 *in fine*; s. above §1468); if the collective contract is silent about *working conditions*, the relevant official regulations shall apply (*ibid.*, 4th sentence).

Besides, if the contract is *unclear or lacunary*, the law also prescribes that the authority will order the employer to rectify (Art. 81, 1st phrase). There is, therefore, some apparent overlap between Art. 18 and 81. In practice, however, the authority will only intervene in case of persistent refusal from the employer to negotiate; it will prioritize mandatory content, press the parties to negotiate, and favor settlement over coercion. 1473

Among other things, the Labor Contract Law distinguishes contracts depending on their *duration* (Art. 12), i.e., between fixed-term contracts (Art. 13), open-ended contract (Art. 14) and project-based contracts (Art. 15). 1474

Chinese law severely restricts open-ended contract to the effect of preventing employers to enter chain contracts with the aim of circumventing the protection it grants to open-ended workers, namely, against termination. To that end, in several cases it defines, the law commands the employer to transform a fixed-term contract into an open-ended one; this prescription is *mandatory*. 1475

Thus, as a result, unless the worker insists on a fixed-term contract (Art. 14§3 *in fine*), the employer must conclude an open-ended contract *after two fixed-term contracts* with the same employer, i.e., from the second renewal or the third contract (Art. 14§3, item 3). That leaves the employer with the option, not to say the dilemma, of concluding either two short fixed-term contracts with the prospect of having to conclude an open-ended contract sooner or, in contrast, two long fixed-term contracts with the perspective of being bound longer by fix terms. 1476

Either way, Chinese workers are well protected against *chain contracts*, i.e., a succession of short fixed-term contracts[696]. This prohibition, and the corresponding worker's eligibility for the protections provided by labor law, has been confirmed and reinforced recently by Interpretation II (Art. 9 to 11). However, in order to be eligible, the worker must not fall under any cases entitling the employer to *revoke* the contract in the circumstances defined by the law at 1477

696 While a mere or even successive renewals of labor contracts are not illegal *per se*, chain contracts have been declared illegal under Swiss law: unless the employer can justify such practice, they will be deemed to amount to an abuse of law (CC Art. 2§2; ATF 124 III 469 ; ATF 129 III 618 c. 6.2). On chain contracts, s. also below, §1484. On the notion of abuse of law in Swiss law, s. above note 96.

Art. 29, item 1 (referred to by Art. 39, item 5), 39 or 40§1 and 2. Revocation will be outlined below (s. below Chap. 6 §49, Termination and Revocation).

1478 Other cases, which are, given the high turnover of the Chinese labor market, less frequent, include where the worker has been consecutively working for the same employer for *ten or more years* (Art. 14§3, item 1), which would imply that he had already been bound by two fixed-term contracts of five years each on average or more[697], a rather rare occurrence in China nowadays.

1479 Moreover, it must be stressed, with respect to fixed-term and open-ended contracts, that if an employer fails to conclude a labor contract *in writing* with a worker within one year from the date when it employs the worker, it shall be *deemed* to have concluded an open-ended contract (Art. 14§4). Moreover, the employer shall suffer the same consequence than when failing to conclude a written contract upon recruitment, which is that it shall pay the worker *double wage* from the day the open-ended contract should have started (Art. 82§2; s. above §1468).

1480 Finally, although the employer is not mandated by law to extend a fixed-term contract, it is strongly incentivized to do so since, if it does not, it must pay the employee a *severance* in addition to his wage until the end of the employment. If the employer offers to extend, it must offer the same or better conditions. If the worker refuses, however, the employee is free from the obligation to pay the severance (Art. 46, item 5)[698]. Severance is outlined further down (s. §§1563ff).

1481 It results from the foregoing that the negligent or reckless employer which omits to enter a written contract with its worker shall not only suffer having to pay such worker double wage from the start and to be bound by an open-ended contract after one year; in addition, it shall be liable for any supplemental damage suffered by the employee as a result of the employer's omission, and be struck by an administrative penalty, if only a warning in case of light negligence.

1482 That said, while the double wage sanction is widely recognized and frequently cited by labor arbitration tribunals, its implementation, in practice, is said to be subject to considerable variations and ongoing adjustments through judicial interpretation, with results that can be deemed moderately efficient but not uniformly rigorous across all regions and types of employers. In practice, labor authorities and arbitration commissions do routinely grant double wage compensation to employees where employers are found in violation of the law,

---

697 Art. 14§2, item 2 provided for a transitory rule for workers already employed for several years before the law became effective and close to retirement; it is now obsolete.

698 Art. 46, item 5 does not apply to project-based contracts (s. below §1484).

especially in cases involving clear evidence and urban employment relationships; whether or the extent to which such sanctions are voluntarily followed or enforced, and act as a deterrent remains to be ascertained (s. next paragraph).

Recently however, the SPC clarified in its Judicial Interpretation II effective as of 1 September 2025 (s. below §1500) that *exemptions* to the double wage penalty may apply: for example, if the failure to sign is due to force majeure[699], employee refusal, ongoing disputes, or other statutory exemptions, thus reflecting a limited departure from automatic sanctions towards, to some extent, a fault-based application. Some local authorities and courts have been known to interpret those provisions differently, leading to inconsistencies in enforcement, especially for migrant workers or those in smaller, less regulated enterprises. Nevertheless, the law has reportedly resulted in a marked increase in the proportion of workers with written contracts, as well as improved wage payment regularity and social insurance coverage. Yet enforcement challenges persist, especially for rural migrant workers, small private enterprises, and sectors with limited regulatory oversight, where employees may not be aware of their rights or may not pursue claims effectively. Finally, as noted, foreign employers may be subject to closer scrutiny and more aggressive enforcement than some domestic ones. 1483

It should be noted at this stage that the law does not extend the protection, described above, of fixed-term contracts against *chain contracts* (s. above §1477) to *project-based* ones. However, while the law allows for some flexibility for genuine project-based contracts, Chinese courts have begun scrutinizing employers who attempt to use successive project-based contracts as a mean to avoid statutory obligations, typically when projects are artificial or the work continuous instead of being truly project-based. If courts find that the succession of project-based contracts merely masks a fixed-term or open-ended relationship, they may requalify the contract accordingly and grant the aggrieved worker an open-ended contract, thus entitling him with rights resulting from it, also retroactively. 1484

Comparable, although not identical, safeguards apply to *probation* periods to the effect of preventing employers to abuse them in an attempt to escape the protection conferred by the law to regular employees, namely, for minimum wages and in case of termination, by imposing excessively long or repeated probation periods. Thus, the probation duration is limited to one month for contracts of between three months and one year; to two months between one and three years; and six months for more than three years or open-ended 1485

[699] Although frequently (and abusively) invoked, force majeure remains an exceptional circumstance (s. above §§327, 724 and 833, and Chinese Civil Code, Art. 180, 563§1, item 1 and 590).

employment (Art. 19§1). No probation may be imposed for employment of less than three months or for project-based contracts (*ibid.*, § 3).

1486 The probation agreed upon may not be extended or repeated (Art. 19§2). The probation period must be counted in the employment duration (*ibid.*, § 4, 1st sentence). A labor contract may not only provide for a probation period; if so, such period shall be considered as a regular employment duration, not as probation (*ibid.*, *in fine*).

1487 The probation wages are also protected: they may not be lower than the lowest wage for the same work in the employer's enterprise or less than 80% of the regular wage agreed in the labor contract after the probation has ended, and than the minimum wage at the employer's location (Art. 20), whichever of those three benchmarks is the highest. Such minimum wages are published by the local authorities.

1488 Finally, a worker under probation is also specifically protected against termination (Art. 21). Termination is discussed further down in this chapter (s. Chap. 6 §49, Termination and Revocation).

1489 In case the employer fails to comply, the authority shall order it to rectify (Art. 83, 1st sentence). Moreover, the employer shall have to pay the worker the difference between his probation wage and post-probation wage for any period exceeding the maximum duration permitted by the law for probation (*ibid.*, 2nd sentence). The penalties prescribed by the law in case no written or open-ended contract was concluded (s. above Chap. 6 §47, Formation), as the case may be, also apply.

1490 Other than with the general regime applying to the formation of the labor contract, the penultimate part of Chapter 2 (Art. 22 to 25) is concerned with *specific cases*: vocational training, confidentiality, noncompete, and liquidated damages. The last provisions (Art. 26 to 28) are concerned with the labor contract's invalidity.

1491 To start with, in principle, *liquidated damages*, albeit they are expressly acknowledged by the Chinese Civil Code (Art. 176 and 585; s. above Chap. 4 §27.III.A, Liquidated Damages), i.e., contractually binding financial penalties to be paid by the employee to the employer in case the former breaches the labor contract are, in Chinese labor law, *prohibited* (Art. 25). This prohibition suffers three *exemptions* however: in case of breach of a vocational training agreement, as well as of a confidentiality- or of a noncompete clause or agreement.

1492 *Vocational training* can be specifically and separately agreed upon between the employer and the worker (Art. 22§1). Because vocational training is a supplemental cost to the employer, in such case, the vocational training agreement can expressly provide that the worker who breaches the labor contract or the vocational training agreement may have to pay the employer the penalty which may have been specified in the agreement (*ibid.*, § 2, 1st sentence). Such penalty may not exceed the cost of the worker's nonperformance (*ibid.*, 3rd sentence) and, in any case, not that of the training (*ibid.*, 2nd sentence). Finally, the employer may not carry over the training costs on the worker's subsequent wage increases (*ibid.*, § 3).

The parties may further agree on a confidentiality clause by which the worker commits towards the employer to keep certain information secret. Such information is typically related to *intellectual property* rights owned by the employer. However, when it does not qualify as intellectual property but, more generally, as information of commercial value which the employer intends to keep secret, it is encompassed by the generic expression of *business secrets*[700]. Such duty may be agreed upon either in the form of a specific clause contained in the contract of employment or in a separate agreement which complements the former. In such cases, the parties may expressly agree on liquidated damages in the event of breach (Art. 23§2 *in fine*). 1493

Employers, especially foreigners, often overlook that Chinese law does not provide for a general duty of confidentiality, especially for business secrets. The employer will not be entitled to damages unless such duty has been agreed upon contractually. IPR will only be protected by intellectual property law, provided they meet the conditions posed by the topical laws and regulations for such protection[701]. Even so, damages may prove hard to obtain and much more elusive than if agreed in the contract of employment in the form of liquidated damages. 1494

In order to be enforceable, a confidentiality clause is subject to additional conditions which, unless they are strictly complied with, shall result in such clauses to prove useless. Thus, they must carefully define such business secrets or IPR; precisely which employee in which capacity is bound; the duty's duration, namely, after the employment's end. In addition, such secrets or rights must be protected by adequate secret protection measures[702], which prove too often to 1495

700 Examples include unpatentable know-how, business strategy white papers, suppliers and clients lists, not yet registered IPR, etc. About technical know-how, s. above §1271.

701 Such conditions imply, primarily, for trademarks and patents, adequate registration; subject to the other conditions set forth by the law, the protection of copyrights is automatic, however. For detailed explanation, the reader is invited to consult specialized literature and take professional advice.

702 Example of such measures range from the most elementary like locking premises, safes, basic access control and passwords, to the most sophisticated, like extended access control (incl. segregated access, automatic access control through face recognition, blocking and alarms in case of unauthorized data export, concealed GPS tagging, etc.)

be insufficient, if existing at all. Finally, in accordance with the general principles of liability, the penalty must be commensurate with the potential or effective damage (s. above §821). It must be stressed, namely, to the attention of the foreign employer, that those conditions are not mentioned in the law but have been developed by the jurisprudence, which frequently resulted in employers overlooking them to suffer irreparable, sometimes considerable, damage. Professional advice for the drafting or revision of such confidentiality clauses or agreement before the conclusion of the related labor contract is therefore recommended.

1496 *Noncompete* clauses, or agreements[703] prohibiting an employee to compete with his employer during or after the employment are subject to specific conditions in addition to those applying to confidentiality clauses in general. They call for several comments.

1497 *First*, before outlining Art. 24§2, it should be stressed that the employer is, to an extent, protected against the competition of its employee even without a noncompete clause or agreement by Art. 39, item 4, which gives it the right to ask the worker to rectify and, if the latter refuses, to revoke the contract of employment immediately without notice. However, Art. 39, item 4 is limited to the work of an employee for a competitor; it does not apply to the employee's own business. Art. 39, item 4 is discussed in more detail with revocation (s. below §§1549ff.) In contrast, a noncompete clause or agreement as per Art. 24§2 may apply both to work for a competitor and to the worker's own business. Yet if adequately drafted, a noncompete clause or agreement provides for a more comprehensive protection than Art. 39, item 4.

1498 *Second*, a noncompete commitment can only bind *senior* managers, senior technicians, or "other employees specifically bound by a confidentiality duty" (Art. 24§1, 1st sentence). Unlike the two first categories, those "other employees" need not being senior, but to be *specifically* bound by a confidentiality duty because of their actual access to trade secrets or confidential information. However, an employee being neither senior, whether as manager or technician, nor having access to trade secrets or confidential information may not be bound by a noncompete clause.

1499 *Third*, the scope of business, geographic area and the terms of the prohibition to work for a competitor must have been *agreed* upon by the parties and must

Overall, a secret protection strategy should be designed, implemented and monitored. Experience tells that even the most elementary measures are frequently overlooked.

703 Despite such agreements are often named "noncompete and non-circumvention agreement", there is no fundamental difference between noncompete and non-circumvention, circumvention merely being one form of competition. Chinese law does not regulate circumvention separately from competition.

be *limited*, i.e., they may overreach the prohibition's purpose[704] (*ibid.*, 2nd sentence). *Fourth*, the *duration* of the prohibition may not exceed two years (*ibid.*, § 2). Even though that paragraph, unlike the preceding, does not mention it, it can be assumed that the duration must also have been agreed upon.

Last but not least, *fifth* and, once again, often unknown by foreign employers which wrongly assume that Chinese law is identical to their home law regime in that respect, an employer which binds its employee by a noncompete clause after the end of the employment must *compensate* for the loss of profit suffered thereof by the employee by continuing to remunerate him throughout the noncompete. This compensation must be paid monthly (Art. 23§2, 1st sentence). It can be described as a substitute wage. It may neither be lower than 30% of the employee's average monthly salary for the twelve months prior to the employment's end, nor than the local minimum wage. Therefore, if the latter is higher than the 30% threshold, the employer will have to pay such local minimum. These standards were established by the SPC in its Interpretation IV (2013) which is no longer valid[705], but they were upheld and developed in its Interpretation II (2025). Some local standards are higher. The parties are free to agree on a higher compensation. 1500

Where the parties have not provided for liquidated damages in the contract, the worker which caused damage to the employer by breaching a confidentiality or noncompete clause or agreement is *ad minima* liable for compensating for any such damage (Art. 90). The difference with liquidated damages is that, as explained, in such case, the parties pre-agreed amount of the compensation in case of violation, i.e., irrespective of the damage, whereas in the case of Art. 90, compensation is limited to the damage suffered which, consequently, the employer must prove, in accordance to the ordinary rules on contractual liability (s. above Chap. 4 §27, Liability for Breach of Contract). 1501

Moreover, as mentioned (s. above §1497), if the employee engages into competition and the noncompete clause or agreement is breached in the course of the employment (as opposed to after it has ended), such breach may also amount to a cause of *revocation* under the conditions posed by Art. 39, item 4 or 2, as discussed below, being noted that to hold multiple jobs is not illegal *per se* in China (s. §1549ff.) 1502

The three last provisions of Chapter 2 (Art. 26 to 28) address the labor contract's *invalidity*. Thus, a labor contract is invalid in case of either party's 1503

[704] For example, a bank employee working as senior credit manager for the Shenzhen region could not be prohibited to work in any capacity, even not related to credits, in any bank throughout China for five years: it would overreach all three limits.

[705] Interpretation IV (2013) applied to the 2007 Labor Contract Law, repelled ever since (s. above §1433).

vitiated consent[706] (Art. 26§1, item 1), if the employer disclaims its liability towards the employee or denies the latter's rights (*ibid.*, item 2)[707], or the contract violates the law or applicable administrative regulations (*ibid.*, item 3)[708]. Invalidity may be total or partial (*ibid.*, § 1); partial invalidity does not affect the remainder of the contract (Art. 27).

1504 Although revocation will be discussed in detail below (s. Chap. 6 §49, Termination and Revocation), it should also be mentioned at this stage that such invalidity also entitles the worker to "revoke" the contract (Art. 38§1, item 5). At the same time, the invalidity regime of the Labor Contract Law presents both similarities and discrepancies with the *general regime of invalidity of juristic acts* contained in the Chinese Civil Code. The relationship between both regimes calls for discussion.

1505 In the Chinese Civil Code, invalidity is subject to Art. 143 ff. (s. above Chap. 2 §10.IV, Validity of Juristic Acts). In relation to each other, the Code's regime is a *lex generalis* and the Labor Contract Law a *lex specialis*. Therefore, in accordance with the principle *lex specialis derogat leges generali*, where the Labor Contract Law provides for a specific regime, it should supersede the Chinese Civil Code; in contrast, the Code should apply where the Labor Contract Law is silent.

1506 As explained with regard to the general regime of invalidity, depending on the cause of invalidity, the Code provides either for invalidity *de jure*, or for rescission (s. above §§237ff.) Invalidity *de jure* is expressed, in Chinese, by 无效 wúxiào (cf. Art. 157); to rescind by 撤销 chèxiāo (cf. Art. 155; s. above §241). Invalidity, in the sense of Art. 143 ff. of the Code[709], has an effect *ex tunc*, as if the contract had never been concluded (Art. 155; s. above §§238 and 239). Revocation has an effect *ex nunc*, from the revocation, or from the term set by the revocation notice (Art. 563§1; s. above §§242 and 243).

706 Either party's consent is deemed to be vitiated if a party deceives or coerces the other or takes advantage of the latter's difficulties to conclude or amend a labor contract contrary to his will (Art. 26§1, item 1).

707 Interpretation II has recently clarified that the employee's renunciation to social insurances amounts to such a circumstance (Art. 19).

708 This cause is to be contrasted with the fact that the employer's internal rules and regulations may be illegal, which is a cause of revocation (Art. 38§1, item 4), not invalidity. In practice however, because the labor contract may refer to such internal rules and regulations (which are often appended to the contract), the distinction between these two causes may be blurred.

709 "Invalidity" is ambivalent and may be used whenever it has an *ex tunc* or *ex nunc* effect, s. above §249.

1507 That reminded, one may observe that Art. 26 to 28 of the Labor Contract Law mirror, even if not exactly, Art. 143 ff. of the Chinese Civil Code[710]. Yet certain differences, not to say incoherencies, should be pointed at.

1508 First, in case of vitiated intent, the Code provides for *rescission*, while the language used by the Labor Contract Law expresses invalidity *de jure*, yet both Art. 26§1 and Art. 38§1, item 5 use the word or verb 撤销 chèxiāo, to be invalid, not 无效 wúxiào, to rescind. This difference is consequential: rescission, as provided for by the Code, is subject to strict *time limits*; the right of rescission extinguishes if it is not used timely (Chinese Civil Code, Art. 152; s. above §257). Invalidity *de jure* is not subject to any such limit: such invalidity exists, and may be stated, anytime. In other words, the worker invoking Art. 26 of the Labor Contract Law is not subject to the time limits set by Art. 152 of the Chinese Civil Code.

1509 Second, Art. 38§1 of the Labor Contract Law expressly provides the employee with causes of *revocation* (解除 jiěchú; cf. Chinese Civil Code, Art. 563§1; s. above §243), while its item 5 clearly refers, as noted in the preceding paragraph, to *de jure* invalidity (无效 wúxiào). Yet strictly speaking, that drafting is, arguably, legally incoherent: indeed, and first, a revocation cannot result in invalidity *ex tunc*, such as that provided for by Art. 26 of the Labor Contract Law and Art. 155 of the Chinese Civil Code; only *ex nunc*; second, because the invalidity addressed by Art. 26 of the Labor Contract Law exists *de jure* and, therefore, dispenses with rescission, it can *a fortiori* not be subject to revocation: indeed, a contract which is deemed by law never to have existed cannot be ended, be it by revocation.

1510 Beyond these terminological issues, one may conclude that the circumstances enumerated at Art. 26 of the Labor Contract Law are causes of invalidity *ex tunc* and *de jure*. Despite the wording of Art. 38§1 and of its item 5, such invalidity is not, strictly speaking, a cause of revocation in the narrow sense given to this expression. Therefore, the inclusion of Art. 26 among the causes listed by Art. 38 should be understood as intended by the legislator to give the worker the same rights, *mutatis mutandis*, like for those genuine cases of revocation, namely, as far as financial compensation is concerned.

1511 Indeed, the extent and consequences of invalidity depend on the circumstances and shall be settled by labor arbitration or the court (Art. 26§2). If the labor contract is declared invalid by the labor arbitration tribunal or the court, but the worker has performed anyway, the employer remains obligated to pay such

[710] Art. 26§1, item 1 of the Labor Contract Code corresponds to Art. 143, item 2 and 146 to 151 of the Chinese Civil Code; Art. 27 paraphrases Art. 156; Art. 28 implements Art. 157, 3rd sentence in the context of a labor relationship.

work (Art. 28, 1st sentence[711]). If the corresponding remuneration has not been agreed upon, it shall be decided on an "equal pay for equal work" basis (*ibid.*, 2nd sentence), in accordance with Art. 11 (s. above §1468). Finally, where invalidity caused damage to one party because of the fault of the other, the latter shall be liable towards the former (Art. 86).

1512 Yet Art. 46, item 1 expressly mentions Art. 38 (all items) among the cases entitling the worker to financial compensation under Art. 47. Therefore, the compensation resulting from invalidity mentioned in preceding paragraph will be calculated by applying, *mutatis mutandis*, the severance regime following a revocation. Revocation under Art. 38 and such regime will be discussed in detail below (s. Chap. 6 §49, Termination and Revocation).

§48. Performance and modification

1513 Chapter 3 of the law on performance and modification (Art. 29 to 35), with seven articles only, is very short. Indeed, but for a few clarifications, it essentially rests on the rights and obligations agreed upon by the parties in the contract of employment (Art. 3§2, 17 and 29) while silently referring to the general regime of contract law, formerly contained, at the time the Labor Contract Law was enacted in 2012, in the 1999 Contract Law, now incorporated in Title 1 on general rules of the Third Book on contract law of the 2020 Chinese Civil Code (Art. 463 ff.; s. above Chap. 4 , General Provisions of Contract).

1514 The parties have the right to modify the contract anytime, provided they mutually agree, make such changes in writing and keep each a copy of the amended contract (Art. 35).

1515 As such, Chapter 3 is mostly concerned with protecting workers against typical *abuses* including salary payment default, underpayment, late payment, overwork, overtime, occupational hazards, retribution and corporate changes. Such protections specifically relate to performance, as their position in Chapter 3 makes clear; formation-related protections have been outlined in the preceding section; termination and revocation, as well as special forms of labor contracts, will be addressed in the next sections.

1516 The main, but, by far, not the only obligation of the employer towards the employee is to pay his *salary* (Art. 30). Its amount must correspond to the contract and the law or applicable administrative regulations (*ibid.*) It must be paid timely (*ibid.*) If the employer defaults, either because it did not pay timely, paid

[711] As noted, this provision is consistent with Art. 157, 3rd sentence of the Chinese Civil Code.

less or not at all, the worker may petition at court, which will issue the employer an order to pay (Art. 30). Alternatively, the worker may complain with the local labor authority which shall do the same and fix the employer a time limit to do so (Art. 85§1, item 1 and 2). If the latter ignores the authority's order, the authority may discretionarily increase the owed wage up to between 50 and 100% (Art. 85§1, 2nd sentence). Although the law does not specify it in case the worker applies at court, one may assume that the latter enjoys the same discretion. This provision also applies if the employer pays a wage below the local legal minimum (Art. 85§1, item 2).

While that notion, which is reminiscent to the industrial revolution era in the West, has gradually disappeared as manufacturing moved to China, Chinese labor law still strictly regulates *quotas*. Like most western labor laws, Chinese law also regulates *overtime*. "Quota" refers to the established work quantity or productivity target that an employer sets for employees within a standard work period. Quotas must comply with national and local labor regulations. They are intended to prevent employers from imposing excessive workloads on employees or force them to work overtime. 1517

Quotas regulations are mandatory. Overtime is not prohibited as such but must be contained within certain boundaries set by administrative or industry regulations which pose limit to quotas, overtime or both, and be compensated as mandated by the law. Art. 31 prohibits employers from exceeding such quotas or overtime thresholds; the prohibition expressly extends to any *disguised forms* employers may resort to, to the effect of compelling workers to exceed such quotas or overtime thresholds. 1518

As noted, overtime must be compensated according to the law; such compensation is generous. Overtime rates are not prescribed by the Labor Contract Law but by the Labor Law (Art. 44). They amount to 150% of the wage for regular overtime or longer hours; 200% for weekends or rest days if no rest can be arranged after the worker has been asked to work during his rest day or days; and 300% during national holidays[712]. 1519

Likewise, employers are not, and could not be, absolutely prohibited to expose their workers to *occupational hazards*, but they must comply with the related administrative regulations aimed at sheltering workers from such risks. If the employer instructs or orders an employee to perform some work in violation of 1520

---

712 Unlike in other countries where workers are allocated a certain number of vacation days which they are free to take at any time of their choice after agreement with their employer, in China, holidays are set nationwide, and workers generally take them over those periods. There are seven such official national public holidays, as regulated by the State Council under the Regulations on National Statutory Holidays; three of them extend over more or less one week and are known as "golden weeks".

such regulations or internal rules implementing the same, the employee has not only the *right to refuse* (Art. 32§1), but also that of *criticizing*[713] such disregard, *exposing* the employer and *charging* it before the competent authorities (*ibid.*, § 2). Such refusal is deemed not to amount to a violation of the worker's obligations (*ibid.*, § 1). While the law does not specify it, by giving the worker the right to do so, it also implies that the employee is protected against *retribution* from the employer if the former criticizes, exposes or charges the latter.

1521 Whenever such infringements violate the *collective contract*, if any, the *labor union* is expressly given by law the right to intervene (Art. 56; s. below §1577).

1522 Finally, *corporate changes* including the change of the employing enterprise's name, its legal representative, general manager, investor or investors, etc. (Art. 33), namely in case of merger, division, etc. (Art. 34, 1st phrase) may not impact on the labor relationship. Thus, the succeeding company, if any, becomes the new employer (*ibid.*, 2nd phrase).

§49. Termination and Revocation

1523 In practice, especially for foreign employers often paying higher wages and arguably more vulnerable to severance pay claims (s. above §1431), termination and revocation of the labor contract, governed by Chapter 4 of the law (Art. 36 to 50), is a focus point. As extensively outlined in this book about the validity of civil juristic acts and contractual termination (s. above Chap. 2 §10.IV, Validity of Juristic Acts, and Chap. 4 §26, Termination), "termination" (终止 zhōngzhǐ) and "revocation" (解除 jiěchú) are distinct notions, which the Labor Contract Law reflects. Both end the employment relationship, but the situations and procedures differ significantly.

1524 *Termination* refers to the ending of the labor contract resulting from its fulfillment, the occurrence of agreed conditions, or the law, such as the expiration of the contract's *term*, retirement, death, or the dissolution of the employer. Termination may occur both with fixed-term contracts, when the term is reached, and project-based contracts, when the project is completed.

1525 In contrast, *revocation* refers to the *early* dissolution of a labor contract before its agreed or legal expiry, usually by unilateral action from either the employer or the employee, but also by mutual agreement. Typical grounds include either counterparty's serious breach of contract. It also applies with *open-ended* contracts, when either party terminates (or both, by mutual agreement, terminate) for the term set by law from the termination notice.

---

[713] S. above §§1454 and 1455 as well as note 690.

Although termination can be said to be the ordinary case and revocation a special one, the title of Chapter 4 mentions and addresses revocation before termination. The distinction between 终止 zhōngzhǐ, termination and 解除 jiěchú, revocation is consistent throughout the Chinese Labor Contract Law; nevertheless, the reader should be warned that translations may not[714]. In this chapter, we will use "termination" and "revocation" as defined in the two preceding paragraphs, and address termination before revocation. 1526

The corresponding terminology used in *Swiss law* for the contract of employment (CO Art. 319 ff.) is not straightforward either. For *termination*, Swiss French legal language simply uses "fin" and "prendre fin" (end; to end), which is expressed in German by "Beendigung" and "endigen" (cf. CO Art. 334 ff.) *Revocation* is translated by "résiliation" and "résilier", or "congé" and "donner son congé" (literally: "to give one's rest") in French, and by "Kündigung" and "kündigen" in German. In addition, Swiss legal German uses "Auflösung" and "auflösen" for *immediate* revocation (generally known in legal English language as revocation "for a cause"[715]), while French does not make such distinction and uses "résiliation" and "résilier" both for ordinary revocation (which typically occurs where either party revokes an open-ended contract for the legal term; s. CO Art. 335§1) and immediate revocation (cf. CO Art. 337 ff.) 1527

Ordinary termination is governed by Art. 44. All the cases listed in this provision are cases of *passive* termination (s. above §244), i.e., occurring automatically by law. They include the contract's expiry; the worker's retirement[716]; his death; the employer's bankruptcy; its business license revocation, or when it is ordered to close down or to dissolve, or decides to dissolve; as well as, as usual, any other circumstances provided for by laws and administrative regulations. 1528

One should draw the foreign investor's attention on the fact that, in China, the *retirement* age, which is statutory, intervenes earlier than in most western 1529

714 On terminology issues, s. above Chap. 2 §10.IV, Validity of Juristic Acts.

715 However widespread, that terminology is, strictly speaking, confusing: indeed, and evidently so, termination, i.e., for the contract's term, also occurs "for a cause", be such cause contractual or legal. Yet "termination for a cause" is generally understood a referring to *immediate* termination. That said, "termination for a cause" is often used in lieu of "revocation", in order to contrast it with "termination" which, unlike revocation, generally occurs at the contract's term, not early, i.e., where there is a "cause" (s. above §1525).

716 The point of time from which retirement starts is deemed to be that when the worker starts to enjoy his legal pension (Art. 44, item 2).

countries[717]: prior to 2025, it was of 60 for men, 55 for female white-collar workers (cadres), and 50 for female blue-collar workers. As of 2025, it will be gradually raised over 15 years to 63 for men, 58 for female cadres, and 55 for female blue-collar workers. Employees may voluntarily retire up to three years early if pension contributions are met.

1530 However, the law mandates the labor contract to be *extended* despite it is expiring (Art. 44, item 1) if such expiry threatens to deprive the protection afforded by the law to the worker's health and to elderly employees. The related circumstances are precisely enumerated by the law (Art. 42). They include: potential, suspected or confirmed occupational disease or injury resulting in total or partial work incapacity (*ibid.*, items 1 and 2); ongoing treatment for non-occupational illness or injury (item 3); pregnancy or maternity (item 4); and elderly workers having been employed continuously for 15 years and being less than five years away from retirement (item 5). Other circumstances are reserved (item 6).

1531 In such cases, Art. 45, 1st sentence mandates, and effectively, although not expressly, orders the employer to extend the employment term until the related circumstances have disappeared. In case of occupational disease (Art. 42, item 1 and 2), it implies that, if such disease is potential or that investigations are under way at the time of the expiry, they must be conducted or completed (*ibid.*, item 1).

1532 If such disease or injury results in a work incapacity, total or partial, the termination must then be handled in accordance with the law and regulations governing insurance for occupational (A.K.A. "work-related") diseases (工伤保险 gōngshāng bǎoxiǎn; Art. 45, 2nd sentence). That insurance is governed by the Regulations on Work-Related Injury Insurance (2010 Revision), social insurance law, and relevant administrative regulations. The regime is mandatory. It provides medical coverage, disability compensation, and death benefits in the event of work-related injury or occupational disease. All employees[718] are covered once registered by their employer with the local social insurance bureau. Employers must pay mandatory monthly contributions as a percentage of the employee's salary, whose base is regulated locally, and industry risk level; employees do not contribute[719]. The detail of such regime exceeds the scope of this book and will, therefore, not be addressed.

717 The statutory retirement age, which varies from country to country, is typically reached, in Europe, between 65 and 67 years old. There is no statutory retirement age in the U.S.; full eligibility to age-related benefits is reached around 65 to 67.

718 Foreigners working in major cities may also be covered, subject to local regulations.

719 The same system prevails in Switzerland.

Revocation is governed by a considerably more complex regime (Art. 36 to 43). The law distinguishes three situations: mutual revocation (Art. 36), revocation by the worker (Art. 37 and 38) and revocation by the employer (Art. 39 to 43). It also distinguishes revocation for a term upon advance notice, which is only available to the employee (Art. 37), from revocation for a cause (A.K.A. termination for a cause). Such causes are divided between causes invokable by the employee (Art. 38) and the employer (Art. 39 and 40), as well as the modalities applying to the latter (Art. 41 to 43). 1533

First and foremost, a contract of employment can be revoked anytime by *consensus* (Art. 36), whether fixed-term, open-ended, project-based or during probation. The position of this provision, which is the first of the Labor Contract Law termination (lato sensu) regime, signals the emphasis placed by the legislator on consensus (s. above §1448). 1534

Second, the *employee* can revoke his contract anytime with a 30-day notice[720] (Art. 37, 1st sentence). This right is only available to the employee, not the employer. Moreover, although the law only implies it, this provision applies to *open-ended contracts*, neither to fixed-term, nor to project-based contracts. Indeed, any such revocation would infringe the agreed term, whether it is a fixed term or the project completion. As such, the worker would be liable under Art. 90, 1st phrase and *in fine*, even though he had abided by the 30-day notice. That said, the notification must be tendered in writing (Art. 37, 1st sentence). During probation, the notice is shortened to three days only (Art. 37, 2nd sentence). 1535

Third, *causes* entitling the *employee* to revoke *without notice* (Art. 38) include: the employer's failure to provide occupational protection or the agreed work conditions; to pay labor remuneration timely and in full; to pay social insurance; and illegal internal rules and regulations impairing the worker's rights and interests (Art. 38§1, items 1 to 4). Item 5, invalidity, has been extensively discussed above (s. §§1503ff.) Item 6 reserves other causes that may be provided by law. 1536

The second paragraph of Art. 38 provides for additional causes which expressly entitle the worker to revoke *immediately without notice*. These causes include *coercion*, i.e., circumstances in which an employer forces an employee to work by using violence or threat or by restraining his freedom, as well as where the 1537

[720] Under Swiss law, the notice must be given for the *end of the month* immediately following the end of the minimum legal term (cf. CO Art. 339c§1). Chinese law does not pose this additional requirement: the notice may be given for the end of the term, even if it expires in the course of the month.

employer orders or forces any employee to perform work endangering the latter's life, thus violating safety regulations (Art. 38§2).

1538 It should be noted however that, while Art. 38§2 expressly dispenses the worker from advance notice, Art. 38§1 does merely not require any, but does not expressly dispense from it. This discrepancy is to be understood as the legislator's intent to stress the worker's right to revoke immediately without notice in the extreme circumstances described by Art. 38§2. Nevertheless, no notice, whether in advance or not, is needed by law in the cases listed under Art. 38§1 either. In practice, however, workers are advised to tender a notice for facilitating the related proof administration, namely, as to the point of time the labor relationship has ended.

1539 As far as revocation by the *employer* is concerned, a notable feature of Chinese labor law is that the employer may only revoke a labor contract for a *cause*. Indeed, as noted, the option offered to the employee by Art. 37 to freely revoke an open-ended contract is not available to the employer. At this stage, it is worth stressing, namely, to the attention of foreign employers, that those causes, however available in theory, face considerable hurdles in practice and are, therefore, of limited application. Since open-ended contracts are strongly favored by the law (s. above §§1475 to 1479), most of the time, the only way effectively available to an employer to put an end to an open-ended labor relationship is by *consensus*, which implies the payment of a mutually agreed severance. Severance will be discussed in the next section (s. below §§1563ff.)

1540 Among the causes available to the employer, the law distinguishes causes entitling the employer to revoke the labor contract with advance notice (Art. 40), immediately without notice (Art. 39), and in case of mass layoff (Art. 41). Moreover, the law lists circumstances under which the employer is prohibited to revoke (Art. 42), as well as certain modalities applying to the revocation (Art. 43).

1541 The employer may revoke the labor contract with a 30-day written advance *notice*[721] in case the worker is ill, injured, incompetent or of new circumstances (Art. 40). All these causes are strictly qualified and narrowly interpreted by the labor authorities, arbitration tribunals and courts, however.

1542 The first case, *illness or injury* (Art. 40, item 1), applies to *non-occupational* illness or injury. Occupational illness or injury is governed by a separate regime under Art. 42, which we outlined above (s. §§1530 to 1532). The worker must not only be unable to resume his work; he must also prove unable to perform another work which the employer is expected to have arranged for him, taking into account his illness or injury. The incapacity must persist after the end of

---

721 S. above note 720.

the medical treatment period. The law does not mention partial incapacity. The question of whether such incapacity justifies the revocation or not is, therefore, silently left to the discretion of the court.

The second case, *incompetence* (Art. 40, item 2), is only available after the employer has either (re-)trained the employee or assigned him to another post, which should arguably be better suited to the worker's abilities. 1543

The third and last cause, *new circumstances* (Art. 40, item 3), must comply with three conditions according with the Roman law doctrine of *rebus sic stantibus*: the changes must be objective; of such magnitude since the circumstances having formed the basis of the conclusion that the work then agreed cannot be performed anymore; and the parties must have failed to reach a consensus. 1544

Alternatively, instead of giving the worker a 30-day notice, the employer may pay him an extra month's salary (Art. 40§1 *in fine*). The law implies that, in such cases, the employer immediately frees the worker from his duty to work. Besides, it should be noted that, as expressly acknowledged by Art. 46§3, the worker is entitled to the severance prescribed by Art. 47, and that such severance adds up to the extra month wage provided by Art. 40. 1545

The employer may further revoke the labor contract *immediately without notice* in the following cases: where probation fails; the worker has breached internal rules or regulations, damaged the employer or competed with it; or is under criminal investigation (Art. 39, item 1 to 4 and 6). Like for the causes available to the employee Art. 38§1, item 5; s. above §1536), this provision also mentions invalidity (Art. 39, item 5). 1546

Probation must prove the worker to be inapt for the position contemplated. The violation of the internal rules or regulations must be serious. The damage caused to the employer must be severe and caused either by serious negligence or deliberately for personal benefits. 1547

Art. 39, item 6 deserves some elaboration, namely because various translations wrongly suggest that the employer may revoke the labor contract if the employee is "under criminal investigation" or "investigated for criminal responsibility". The correct translation reads: "is *held criminally responsible*". The prevailing interpretation and administrative guidance has clarified that the employee should have been criminally *condemned*, or at least indicted[722]. A mere investigation is insufficient and revocation on that basis would be illegal. 1548

722 The latest known average conviction rate in China following indictment reached 99.975% in 2022 according to official reports from the SPC and the Supreme People's Procuratorate, which explains why revocation of the labor contract on the ground of Art. 39, item 6 of the Labor Contract Law following an indictment but before any conviction may have been tolerated in practice.

Likewise, a revocation based on an indictment may result in the employer's liability if the indictment is eventually quashed.

1549 Finally, the *noncompete* cause is subject to three conditions: the worker must work for another employer; his second employment must seriously affect his first employment; the employer must have asked him to rectify and the employee must have refused. These conditions call for the following comments: *first*, to hold multiple jobs is not illegal *per se* in China; as a matter of fact, it is very frequent. In order to be illegal under Art. 39, item 4, such competition must seriously harm the original employer.

1550 *Second*, this cause only applies if the worker is employed by another employer. It is not eligible if, however competing with his employer, he does so on his own, for example, with his own company. In the latter case, the employer would have a cause under item 2 of Art. 39, i.e., as the employee, by competing with the employer, may commit a serious breach of contract, which would qualify as a breach of internal "rules and regulations". Alternatively, it may under a noncompete clause or agreement, as signaled above (s. §1496) and in our fourth comment below.

1551 *Third*, this provision contains a mistake inasmuch as its drafting, which links the condition of serious competition to that of the refusal to rectify by using the conjunctions 或者 huòzhě, "or", instead of "and". Yet court practice has confirmed that these conditions are *cumulative*, not alternative. In other words, the competition must have seriously impacted on the original work *and* the employee must have refused to rectify after having been asked by the original employer.

1552 *Fourth* and eventually, the noncompete cause of Art. 39, item 4 may be reinforced, if so pre-agreed between the parties, by a *noncompete clause or agreement* in the sense of and under the conditions posed by Art. 23§2 and 24 (s. above §§1496 to 1501). Consistent with our first comment above, the breach of such noncompete agreement would then amount to a serious breach under Art. 39, item 2, not item 4.

1553 Whenever the employer intends to revoke a labor contract unilaterally, the law requests it to notify the *labor union* in advance (Art. 43, 1st sentence). Although this provision is not specific, practically it may only apply to revocation under Art. 40, since Art. 39 implies immediate revocation (of which the labor union should be notified too, even though it cannot, by definition, be notified in advance) and Art. 41 provides for notification to the workers and the local labor authorities 30 days in advance (s. below §1556), which in practice will inevitably imply the labor union to be involved.

1554 *Mass layoff* is governed by a special regime. Mass layoff is defined as the layoff, in the circumstances described below, of either more than 20 workers, or more than ten percent of the total of the enterprise's employees (Art. 41§1). In other words, it means that that regime may apply either when 21 or more workers are laid off or, in enterprises of 20 workers or less, when three (for enterprises employing exactly 20 workers) and as soon as more than one (for enterprises employing 19 workers or less) workers are.

The circumstances in which that regime applies include the enterprise's reorganization; serious difficulties; major internal changes; and major economic changes. The reorganization (or "revitalization") must take place under the Enterprise Bankruptcy Law[723] (Art. 41, item 1). The enterprise must meet serious difficulties in its production and management (*ibid.*, item 2). The internal changes may relate to a major technological update or adjustment of the business model; in order to qualify, this circumstance is subject to an additional condition however, which is that the employer must also have adjusted the labor contracts accordingly, but that such adjustment failed and the layoff remains necessary anyway (*ibid.*, item 3). Finally, the circumstance relating to major economic change (*ibid.*, item 4) is identical to that contemplated by Art. 40, item 3 (s. above §1544). 1555

If both the quota of laid-off employees and any of the circumstances described above qualify, several consequences apply: *first*, the employer must consult with both the employees and the local labor authority (Art. 41§1). As it does so, the employer must, but may not only, explain the situation to its employees, it must also solicit their opinion; in other words, the law requires both parties to actively engage in a discussion; a unilateral explanation by the employer shall not suffice. Moreover, the employer must submit a layoff plan to the competent authority. Finally, the employer must do both 30 days in advance of the effective layoff; thus, such consultations replace the notice which the law may require in other circumstances. 1556

Second, when carrying out the layoff, the employer must respect a certain *priority* order by giving such priority to three groups of employees: those with long fixed-term contracts; those with open-ended contracts; and those who are supporting their family alone or are supporting children or elders (Art. 41§2). The law does not set a pecking order among these three groups, however. 1557

Third, if the employer recruits again within six months from the layoff, it must notify the laid-off workers accordingly and, under equal conditions, give them preference over new recruits (Art. 41§3). 1558

Because those conditions are often perceived as excessively constraining, especially for small numbers of workers, employers, not least foreign employers, 1559

723 Such reorganization is known, in Swiss law, as "sursis concordataire" in French and "Nachlassstundung" in German (LP Art. 293).

often prefer reaching a consensus with their employee about the severance and lay them off by mutual agreement.

1560 Finally, the employer is *prohibited* to revoke a contract of employment in certain circumstances defined by the law. These circumstances have been described above (s. §§1530 to 1532). We have also mentioned that it must notify the labor union of its intent to revoke (s. above §1553).

1561 Last but not least, in case of *violation* of the termination or revocation regime, the employer which should, deliberately or by negligence, ignore the legal requirements applying to termination or revocation exposes itself to serious consequences. *First*, the worker may insist towards the employee on the continuous performance of the contract (Art. 48, 1st sentence)[724]. *Second*, the labor union has the right to demand the employer to rectify. The employer must then consider the labor union's demand and notify it in writing about the settlement of the matter (Art. 43, 2nd and 3rd sentences; s. also, generally, Art. 78 and below, §1597). *Third*, the competent labor authority may intervene (presumably upon denunciation by either the labor union or the worker), order the employer to rectify and give it a warning (Art. 80, 1st sentence). *Fourth* and mostly, in case of persisting illegal termination[725] or revocation, the employer shall pay the worker *double* the severance prescribed by Art. 47 (Art. 48 *in fine* and 87; for the severance calculation, s. below §§1566ff.)

1562 To conclude on the end of the contract of employment, it results from the above that, in Chinese labor law, *the employer may only unilaterally revoke a labor contract for a cause*. As noted, unilateral termination, subject to advance notice, is only available to the employee. Alternatively, revocation of an open-ended contract is possible anytime provided the parties mutually agree, i.e., by consensus, which systematically implies severance pay. Finally, fixed-term and project-based contract terminate, as opposed as being revoked, naturally at their term, be it the expiry of their duration or the performance of the agreed work; however, even so, in case of fixed-term contract (or project-based chain contracts), the employer may have to pay severance (s. next paragraph). If the employer refuses to pay, such refusal could conceivably result in more serious consequences, such as the suspension of its business license, etc.

---

724 If the employer accepts, Interpretation II has recently clarified that it must pay the salary, etc. between the illegal termination or revocation and the contract's continuation (Interpretation II, Art. 18).

725 Although Art. 87 expressly mentions illegal "termination" along with illegal revocation, an illegal termination is in fact a revocation. On the related terminology issues, s. above §§1523ff.

Severance pay, designated in the law by "financial compensation", is governed by Art. 46 to 48. Art. 46 lists the circumstances in which severance is owed; Art. 47 outlines its calculation; Art. 48 contains related modalities. 1563

Severance is owed in the following cases (Art. 46, items 1 to 7): in case of revocation for a cause by the employee under Art. 38; of consensus; of revocation for a term by the employer under Art. 40; of mass layoff under Art. 41; in case it does not renew a fixed-term contract terminated under Art. 44, item 1, or the employee refuses to extend it; after a project-based contract has been performed; in case of bankruptcy (Art. 44, item 4), license revocation, order to close down or to dissolve or of early dissolution (*ibid.*, item 5); and in other cases provided by the law. 1564

The foreign employer may like to note that, unlike in most western jurisdictions, severance is owed even in case of *fixed-term* contract if the employer does not offer to extend it to the same or better conditions, provided the worker does not refuse it (Art. 46, item 5). The benefit of this provision does not extend to project-based contracts however, save in case of chain contracts (s. above §1480 and 1484). 1565

The severance *calculation* is governed by Art. 47. Severance is to be understood as the financial compensation owed by the employer to the worker under Art. 46 and 47 in addition to his regular salary and benefits until the term of the contract. It combines several factors. 1566

First, the severance is calculated on a basis of *one month of wage per year of employment*. In case the contract starts or ends in the course of a civil year, the law counts a full year if the employee worked for six months or more and for half a year if less (Art. 47§1). 1567

Second, both the monthly salary and the number of years used for the calculation are *capped*; they may correspond neither to the real salary nor to the number of years if they exceed those caps. The salary cap is three times the official average local salary for the year preceding the end of the contract (Art. 47§2). That reference salary is published yearly by the local labor authorities. The law is quite accurate about which authority at which administrative level is competent for publishing that rate. The duration of the employment is capped at twelve years (*ibid.*, *in fine*). 1568

Third, the notion of monthly salary used for the calculation does not correspond to the last month's salary, but to its *average* over the twelve months preceding the contract's end (Art. 47§3). Moreover, even though the law does not 1569 expressly mention it, such "salary" includes all the related benefits, such as bonuses and other perks[726].

1570 *Fourth* and lastly, as mentioned (s. above §1560), in case of failure to conclude a written contract, to transform a fixed-term contract into an open-ended contract, or of illegal termination or revocation, the employer must pay *double* severance (Art. 82 and 87; s. above §§1468, 1479ff. and 1561).

1571 The settlement of the labor relationship is subject to strict conditions; it may neither be vague, nor drag indefinitely. Both parties must comply with certain obligations. As far as the *employer* is concerned, first, the employer must issue the employee with a certificate of termination or revocation; it must issue it upon termination or revocation (Art. 50§1) and keep a copy of it for two years (*ibid*., § 3). Second, it shall comply with the formalities applying to the employee's personal file and his social insurance account within 15 days from termination or revocation (*ibid*., § 1 *in fine*). Third and last, the severance payment must occur upon completion of the handover mentioned in the preceding step (*ibid*., § 2). On his part, the *employee* must hand over the matters related to his work as agreed between the parties (*ibid*., § 2, 1st sentence).

1572 To conclude about revocation by the employer and severance, as noted, employers, notably foreign employers, will often choose to offer their employees, and the latter will generally accept, double severance in order to settle and dispense with a challenging dispute, since such dispute would, in principle, not result in a lower severance from the point of view of the employer and a higher severance from that of the worker, let alone the related legal costs and the indefinite deferment of the end of the labor relationship and of the severance payment.

§50. Special Provisions

1573 Chapter 5 of the Labor Contract Law (Art. 51 to 72) contains three sections applying to special types of contracts: collective contract, so-called "part-time" employment and labor dispatch. It is also the place to recall that *service inventions*, i.e., inventions made by the employer in the course of its employment, are not, like in Swiss law, governed by labor law, but by the technology

---

726 In Switzerland, although the payment of the so-called "13th" (month of salary) is not mandated by law, it has become generalized. Moreover, perks regularly paid for several years (where as little as three may be considered as sufficient) may be considered as part of the basic salary and become mandatory the following years. Swiss employers often offer a 13th salary to their Chinese employees in China.

contracts regime under the Chinese Civil Code, to which we refer (s. above §§1279ff.)

I. Collective Contracts

1574 A collective contract (集体合同 jítǐ hétóng; Fr.: "convention collective"; Ger.: "Gesamtarbeitsvertrag") is a set of general contractual conditions negotiated between a labor union or employees' representatives (s. above §§ 1452 and 1453) with an employer or an industry which is imposed by law to the latter under the supervision of the local labor authorities (Art. 51 to 54). It has the advantage of standardizing such conditions, guaranteeing minimum standards, protecting employees, often incapable of negotiating individual contracts, against the abuse of the superior bargaining power usually enjoyed by the employer, providing employers with visibility and reducing labor disputes.

1575 That said, collective contracts are, in China, considered to be only moderately successful and have notable limitations in practice such as weak worker representation, limited union independence, and local government priorities. Most unions operate under the All-China Federation of Trade Unions (ACFTU) 中华全国总工会 zhōnghuá quánguó zǒng gōnghuì; however, it is often considered as lacking autonomy and acting primarily according to local governments' and enterprises' interests. Thus, in practice, collective bargaining power remains marginal; the coverage of collective contracts remains uneven, mostly applying to large and SOEs rather than private or smaller ones; the workers' participation is limited and the enforcement of collective contracts weak, especially in those areas where it should matter most, i.e., wages and disputes. Collective contracts do not appear to be more strictly enforced with foreign employers; however, western employers often have higher standards than domestic ones, while enforcement mostly depends on local policies.

1576 While collective contracts bear on work conditions in general, the law stresses that the *minimum wages* they stipulate may not be lower than the wages prescribed by the local labor authorities, and that that stipulated in the individual contract of employment may not be lower than that of the collective contract (Art. 55). As noted, the law anticipates this requirement about the individual labor contract's formation (Art. 11, 1st sentence; s. above §1468).

1577 A *breach* of the collective contract by the employer compares to the breach of an individual labor contract: if so, the labor union may demand the employer to rectify or assume liability; if consultations to that effect fail, the labor union may file for labor arbitration or litigation (Art. 56; s. also above §§1453 and 1521; s. also Art. 78 and below, §1597). While Art. 56 only mentions consultations after having mentioned the employer's liability, and only mentions labor unions, in practice, consultations will always precede any escalation of the dispute; likewise, if the workers are not represented by a labor union, they may be so by elected representatives; alternatively, since a violation of the collective contract automatically amounts to an infringement of the individual one, nothing prevents the worker to act individually. Collective contracts are subject to a specific dispute resolution process (s. Labor Law, Art. 84).

II. Labor Dispatch

1578 Simply speaking, labor dispatch (劳务派遣 láowù pàiqiǎn; Art. 57 to 67) is a tripartite contractual relationship by which an agent employs a worker whom the former places with a third party where the latter works. The law further stresses that dispatching is primarily governed by the regime applying to ordinary contracts of employment, and that the dispatching regime is only *subsidiary* (Art. 66§1). Thus, the law limits dispatching to *temporary, auxiliary and replacement* positions (Art. 66§1, 2nd sentence). This enumeration is alternative. The first (temporary) is defined as of a duration of six months or less; the second (auxiliary) as providing for ancillary or support positions to senior ones; and the third (replacement) as replacement during leaves (*ibid.*, § 2). These notions may overlap. The labor authorities may prescribe maximum quota of dispatched workers (*ibid.* § 3).

1579 Labor dispatch is plagued with *terminology* issues. Indeed, dispatch is often confused with or assimilated to "*temporary*" or "temp" work. First, "dispatch" does not equate to "temporary": while dispatched workers are often placed for a short period of time indeed, typically for a mission or a replacement, as per two of the three definitions given by the law in the preceding paragraph, temporary work can also occur through direct employment, not only through dispatch. Second, "temporary" does not equate to "part-time" either: the latter expression is to be contrasted with full-time employment; part-time employment applies where the worker works less than full time, for example, only a few hours a day or a few days a week. Thus, a temporary dispatch job may also be part-time; however, part-time may also occur through direct employment.

1580 Those notions are governed by specific regimes: *dispatch* (including *temporary*) is governed by the dedicated regime of Art. 57 ff. of the Labor Contract Law; *part-time* by that of Art. 68 ff. (s. below Chap. 6 §50.III, Part-time Employment); a temp job can be either a fixed-term or a project-based contract (s. above §1474). Once again, it is important to understand that all these regimes may combine or overlap.

1581 Overlapping is aggravated by the fact that, as far as foreign employees are concerned, dispatch applies to, and is mandatory for *foreign representative offices*

(s. below Chap. 9 §67, Representative Offices). Indeed, as outlined, foreign representative offices do not enjoy legal personality; as such, they cannot employ workers directly; only their foreign parent can; Chinese law mandates the latter to do so by hiring dispatch workers from an agency specifically licensed to that effect[727] (A.K.A. "temp agents").

Because a representative office, as its name clearly indicates, can only act as a representative, another regime, that of *representation*, is superposed to that of dispatch and, as the case may be, the neighboring regimes mentioned above. Representation is governed by Art. 61 and 62 of the Chinese Civil Code, as well as the agency regime under Art. 161 ff. of the same. While FIEs not being representative offices and domestic enterprises may also recourse to dispatching agents, this chapter will focus on foreign representative offices; unless mentioned otherwise, such comments apply *mutatis mutandis* to users of dispatched workers not being a representative office, however. 1582

Before proceeding, it is worth recalling that *foreign branches* (s. below Chap. 9 §64.XI, Branches of Foreign Companies) which are, under Chinese law, a corporate entity distinct from a foreign representative office, are not subject to the obligation of hiring employees through a licensed dispatching agent in the sense that, while a branch, like a representative office, may not employ a worker directly since both lack a legal personality, branches may do so through their foreign parent, which may employ Chinese workers directly without resorting to a Chinese licensed dispatching agent (but may be subject to other constraints; s. below §2391). 1583

Beyond terminology issues, labor dispatch faces serious, widespread and persistent *conceptual misunderstandings*. As mentioned, the following comments will focus on foreign representative offices. At the same time, the issues pointed out there should be relativized since such offices are gradually phased out, may hire foreign representatives directly and typically hire small numbers of local workers. That said, larger companies, including foreign invested, may occasionally use larger numbers of dispatch workers, for example, for a specific project necessitating a large number of workers for a short duration, and ponder whether the advantages of doing so balance the corresponding inconveniences. 1584

As far as the relationship between *the agent and the worker* is concerned, the only *contract of employment* passed in a tripartite dispatch relationship is entered between them; no such contract is passed between the foreign parent, or its representative office, and the worker. The law clearly states that the agent is 1585

727 The main of these agencies is Beijing Foreign Enterprise Human Resource Service Co. (known as FESCO). Its Shanghai counterpart is Shanghai Foreign Service (Group) Co., Ltd. (FSG).

to be the employer (Art. 58, 1st sentence). The contract, which is an ordinary, fixed-term contract for minimum two years (*ibid.*, 3rd sentence), irrespective of the duration of the placement (*ibid.*, last sentence), is to be complemented with the specifics related to the placement (*ibid.*, 2nd sentence).

1586 As far as the relationship between *the agent and the user* is concerned, the contract of service between the agent and the user may be qualified of *mandate*, i.e., for the provision of dispatch services; as such, it is governed by Art. 919 ff. of the Chinese Civil Code (although the law does not mention it), where the latter regime is the *lex generalis* and Art. 57 ff. of the Labor Contract Law, as far as the relationship between the agent and the user is concerned, the *lex specialis*. This agreement is merely designated as "agreement of labor dispatch" (Art. 59). Also, while the law only implies it by prohibiting the agent to keep the worker's salary, in practice, the user pays the worker's salary to the agent, which in turn pays the worker (Art. 60§3).

1587 As far as the relationship between *the employee and the user* is concerned, the employee is merely bound to the user by the latter's *instructions* (which the user legally issues on behalf of the foreign parent) to the former. The law provides that the agent shall inform the worker of the dispatch agreement's content (Art. 60§1). It also expressly provides that the user shall specifically instruct the worker (Art. 62§1, item 2). In practice, users also often issue *internal regulations* in the form of staff regulations or code of conduct, employee's handbook, etc. for general purposes. The law also transfers the user certain duties attributed to the employer in an ordinary labor relationship, such as compliance with occupational standards, paying overtime, bonuses and welfare benefits and providing training (*ibid., items* 1, 3 and 4).

1588 By following them, the employee is merely performing his duties towards the agent to follow the user's instructions. Thus, the *employee's inobservance of the user's instructions* amounts both to a breach of the contract of employment between the worker and the agency and, in turn, of a breach, by the agent, of its contract of service with the user. Consequently, the worker is liable for such breach towards the agent, while the latter is liable of the same towards the rep of. Those instructions can be either specific, on a day-to-day basis, or general, in the form of internal staff regulations, etc.[728]

[728] This relationship is notoriously misunderstood by some licensed dispatching agents which, in their service contract template with the service user, have been giving the latter the right to conclude a "contract of employment" with the worker. Such "contract of employment" cannot exist between the worker and the service user in a dispatching relationship: it amounts, in reality, to instructions given by the service user to the worker. As explained in the preceding paragraph, the only contract of employment which can exist is between the agent and the worker.

In that triangular relationship, fees may be exclusively charged by the agent to the user; neither the agent, nor the user may charge fees to the worker (Art. 60§3). Chain contracts (Art. 59§2 *in fine*), re- or sub-dispatching (Art. 62§2) and self- or internal dispatching (Art. 67) are prohibited. The principle "equal pay for equal work" applies between dispatched and permanent workers (Art. 63); this provision also sets detailed rules for determining the applicable rate in case of doubt or disagreement. Wages must be locally compliant (Art. 61) and regularly adjusted (Art. 62§1, item 5). 1589

Generally speaking, *dispatched workers* enjoy the *same rights* than workers hired directly by their employer; the law makes clear that they shall not be treated less well than the latter. Thus, they have the right to join labor unions, to protect their rights and to revoke their contract of employment with the agent, like under any labor contract (Art. 36 and 38). Conversely, the *user* is extended the benefit granted to the employer under a regular labor contract to revoke (Art. 39 or 40§§ 1 and 2; about revocation of the labor contract in general, s. above Chap. 6 §49, Termination and Revocation), i.e., not by allowing the user to revoke the contract of employment, to which it is not a party, itself, but to send the worker back to the agent, which may then revoke it (Art. 65§2). 1590

In practice, however, this relationship is more than often misunderstood by all parties, last but not least by the agents, which have been criticized for charging fees while in effect shifting the employer's duties on their customers' shoulder[729]. As noted in general about regular employers (s. above §1584), foreign representative offices are, therefore, advised to carefully weigh the related constraints and to clarify such relationships before engaging into dispatch. 1591

III. Part-time Employment

As already noted about dispatch (s. above §1579), part-time employment (非全日制用工 fēi quánrì zhì yònggōng; Art. 68 to 72) ought not to be confused neither with the former, nor with temporary employment; at the same time, they may overlap. While *temporary employment* is governed by the basic regime applying to labor contracts, either as fixed-term or as project-based contract, part-time employment is governed by its own regime. Both are typically subject to *dispatch*; whenever so, the two regimes combine: the basic regime, including that of fixed-term or project-based contracts, as *lex generalis*, relate to the dispatch and the part-time employment regimes as *leges speciales*. There is no clear hierarchy between the dispatch and the part-time regimes however: 1592

---

729 S. preceding note.

each are to be regarded as a *lex specialis* in its field as it relates to the other. Anyway, the part-time regime is very short, with only five articles.

1593 Part-time employment is defined as a form of employment under which remuneration is calculated by the *hour*, and the workers generally work not more than four hours per day in average, and not more than an aggregate of 24 hours per week for the same employer (Art. 68). As the adverb "generally" suggests, the threshold of four hours per day and 24 hours per week is not absolute, but relative: the concern of the legislator is to prevent abuses, as will be seen below. One may deduct from that definition that, in the context of dispatch, in order to qualify as part-time employment, the "employer" in the sense of Art. 68 is to be deemed as being the user.

1594 The part-time regime is significantly less constraining than the regular one. Thus, unlike the regular contract of employment, the part-time employment contract can be concluded *orally* (Art. 69§1). The employee is expressly permitted *multiple jobs*, i.e., to work part-time for several employers, provided the later employment does not prejudice the earlier (Art. 69§2)[730]. Besides, either party may *terminate* with notice, but anytime: in other words, while the law requests the employee to notify the employer, the former is not expected to do so in advance. Moreover, upon termination, the employer is not required to pay any severance to the employee (Art. 71).

1595 The law also grants some *protection* to the part-time worker. A part-time contract may not be subject to probation (Art. 70). The hourly remuneration may not be lower than the minimum hourly wage set by the local labor authority (Art. 72§1). The salary must be paid not later than every 15 days (*ibid.*, § 2).

1596 Generally, however, the part-time regime may not be abused for the only sake of escaping the obligation to conclude a written contract, revoke for a cause or pay severance. For example, an employer which would conclude part-time contracts while drifting away from the four hours a day, 24 hours a week threshold without sufficient justification would probably be demanded by the labor authorities to reduce the work time or to conclude a regular labor contract.

IV. Supervision and Inspection

1597 The first half of the chapter on supervision and inspection (Art. 73 to 76) of the law is directed at the labor authorities, whose competences it defines. The second half (Art. 77 to 79) grants not only employees, but also labor unions and

[730] Multiple jobs are not prohibited *per se* under the general regime of the labor contract (s. above §1549).

even "all organizations and individuals" the right to *denounce* violations of labor law to the authorities (s. above §1456). Employees have also the right to file for arbitration or at court (Art. 77 *in fine*; s. above §§1460 and 1461). As already noted, in case of violation or dispute, the law grants *labor unions* (s. above §1452) the right to intervene towards employers directly, put forward their opinion, demand rectification and, as the case may be, assist workers before labor arbitration tribunals or the courts (Art. 78). Finally, the law even encourages the general public to denounce violations and entitles them to rewards for particularly meritorious services (Art. 79)[731].

§51. Liabilities

The next-to last chapter of the law before supplementary provisions is, with 15 1598 articles, a lengthy chapter titled "legal liability" and addressing all manners of violation of the law, whether by the employer, the employee, the labor authority or a third party, and its consequences in the form of civil, administrative, criminal, as well as joint and several liability.

In most cases of violation by the *employer*, the labor authority shall ask it to 1599 *rectify* and give it a *warning*, while if the worker suffered damage, the employer shall face *civil liability* for compensating it (e.g., Art. 80). Such infringements range from illegal internal rules and regulations (Art. 80); unclear labor contracts (Art. 81); failure to copy it to the worker (*ibid.*); illegal probation period (Art. 83); to failure to issue a written termination or revocation certificate (Art. 89). More serious offenses, such as detaining the worker's papers, collect money or valuables, or retain his personal file, may result in an *administrative penalty* (Art. 84).

Failure to pay the worker's *remuneration* is subject to a strict regime providing 1600 not only for the payment of the missing portion of any such remuneration, but also for penalties in addition to the remuneration, if the latter is not paid within the time limit set by the authority. Such regime encompasses all sorts of remuneration and applies to the salary, part payment, late payment, payment below the legal minimum rate, overtime, severance (Art. 85), and payment at the probation rate after the probation was converted in regular employment (Art. 83, 2nd sentence); it even applies, *mutatis mutandis*, in case the contract was invalidated for one of the causes listed under Art. 26 (Art. 86; s. above

[731] S. above note 689.

§§1503ff.[732]) Moreover, as stressed elsewhere, certain violations entitle the worker to be paid *double wage*: they include failure to conclude a written contract (Art. 82§1); to timely convert a contract in an open-ended one (*ibid.*, § 2); and illegal termination (Art. 87).

1601 The most serious offenses incur both an administrative penalty, a *criminal investigation*, where the latter may result in a criminal conviction, and civil liability. They include violence, intimidation, freedom restrictions, hazardous work, whether forced or causing serious harm, humiliation, corporate punishments and illegally searching a worker (Art. 88).

1602 In contrast, the *worker* may be liable for compensation towards the employee in case illegal revocation (s. above §§1503ff.) or, as outlined, of breach of a noncompete clause or agreement (Art. 90; s. above §§1546 and 1549ff.)

1603 The labor *authorities* and the responsible officers may be held administratively or, as the case may be, criminally liable in case of negligence or violation of the law (Art. 95).

1604 *Third parties* include labor dispatching agents and investors. Labor dispatching is subject to a specific regime; while users are also mentioned, this provision focuses on agents (Art. 92). Besides, by pointing at "unqualified" employers and their "investors", the law actually aims at unregistered or unlicensed employers, including the foreign parents of foreign representative offices or of foreign branches, which may all face civil, administrative and criminal liability, as the case may be (Art. 93).

1605 Finally, the new employer of a worker may be *jointly and severally liable* with the worker if the latter has not revoked his contract with his former employer (Art. 91). So are the contracting and the contractor parties to a project where the contractor hires workers in violation of the law (Art. 94).

1606 Finally, it should be added that Interpretation II emphasized the "penetration" principle (透析原则 tòuxī yuánzé, which is the equivalent of the principle known in English as "piercing the corporate veil"), requiring courts to identify the *real employer* in arrangements involving subcontracting, outsourcing, or affiliated entities, thus deterring employers to evade their responsibilities (Interpretation II, Art. 1 and 3).

---

[732] This provision compels both parties to indemnify the other in case one party is liable for the invalidity it caused to the other; conceivably, it will rarely apply to the employee, which is generally the weaker party. S. also below, §1602.

§52. Supplementary Provisions

The last chapter of the Labor Contract Law on supplementary provisions contains only three articles. The first provides that the law shall apply as *lex generalis* in case of employment with a *public institution*, whose regulations apply as *lex specialis* (Art. 96). 1607

The last two articles govern the transitory regime between the 2008 law and the 2012 Amendment. Because of the time elapsed since the latter, they have practically become obsolete. 1608

Chap. 7 Quasi-contracts

§53. Introduction

As already outlined about Chapter 5 on civil rights of the First Book of the Chinese Civil Code on general provisions (s. above §173), *negotiorum gestio* (Art. 121) and unjust enrichment (Art. 122) are listed among the *sources of obligations*, along with contracts (Art. 119), liability for illicit acts (Art. 120), and the law (Art. 118§2 *in fine*). Because, absent an agreement between the parties, they do not quite amount to contracts *stricto sensu*, but create rights and obligations similar to them nevertheless, *negotiorum gestio* and unjust enrichment are known as *quasi-contracts*. The Code expressly acknowledges *creditors' rights* resulting from all those sources (Art. 118§2; s. above §174). 1609

The notion of quasi-contracts[733] (准合同 zhǔn hétóng) should not be confused with that of *noncontractual liability*. The latter encompasses all forms of liability which are not contractual, including not only quasi-contracts, but also liability for illicit acts. Moreover, while noncontractual liability is often used, in practice, for referring to liability for illicit acts, as mentioned, it does not equate to it either (s. above §316). Quasi-contracts, contractual liability, liability for illicit acts and the general principles of civil liability are all governed by different parts of the Chinese Civil Code (s. above §309). 1610

Negotiorum gestio (Fr. "gestion d'affaires", A.K.A. "gestion d'affaire sans mandat" or "gestion d'affaire pour autrui"; Ger. "Geschäftsführung ohne Auftrag"; CO Art. 419 ff.) designates the obligations resulting, for both parties, from the management of a third party's affairs without a mandate from the latter. The legal English language generally uses the Latin expression for it. *Unjust enrichment* (Fr. "enrichissement illégitime"; Ger.: "ungerechtfertigter Bereicherung"; CO Art. 62 ff.) refers to the enrichment of one party resulting from the impoverishment of the other absent a legal basis. 1611

It may not be immediately obvious why these purely legal concepts matter for business law. The reason is that they are frequently referred to as *subsidiary regimes* in other regimes which do regularly apply to business transactions as alternative source of liability or, on the contrary, as causes for exemption from such liabilities. That is the case, namely, for the general regimes of agency, 1612

733 In this book, beyond the formal notion of quasi-contract *stricto sensu* as per Art. 979 ff., we also use the expression "quasi-contracts" informally for limited or ancillary contractual features which are typically superposed onto a comprehensive contract, such as representation or agency (s. above §856), or for atypical contractual forms, such as JVs (s. above §144 and note 103).

contractual liability and liability for illicit acts. These cases will be addressed below, both for *negotiorum gestio* and unjust enrichment.

1613 Absent any special provision to the contrary, *negotiorum gestio* and unjust enrichment are both subject to the general *limitation of action* of *three years* prescribed by the Chinese Civil Code as default limitation of action for a civil claim (Art. 188§1; s. above §§340, 347 and 348). This limitation is *subjective*, i.e., it runs from when the victim became aware or ought to have become aware of the damage; the *objective* limit is of *20 years* since that right was infringed (Art. 188§2, 2nd sentence; s. above §341). It is subject to numerous accommodations and exemptions which we discussed above and to which we refer (s. above Chap. 2 §13, Limitation of Action). Comparatively, in *Swiss law*, the same (subjective-, from the damage awareness) limitation of three years applies to *negotiorum gestio* (CO Art. 60§1 and 67§1[734]) and to unjust enrichment (CO Art. 67§1); the objective (absolute) limitation is *shorter* though, i.e., of ten years (Art. 67§1 *in fine*).

§54. Negotiorum Gestio

1614 *Negotiorum gestio* 无因管理 wú yīn guǎnlǐ[735] (Chinese Civil Code, Third Book, Title Three, Chap. 28, Art. 979 to 984) is defined as a quasi-contract where a party (known as "the manager"), under no legal or contractual obligation, manages the business of a third party (known as "the beneficiary") in order to prevent damage to the latter's interests; if so, the manager has the right to ask the beneficiary to reimburse the former's necessary expenses or compensate for any damage resulting thereof (Art. 979§1).

1615 It is important to note from the outset that, if the beneficiary subsequently *ratifies* the management by approving of it, then the latter is not subject to the regime of *negotiorum gestio*, but to that of the *mandate* (Art. 919 ff.; s. above Chap. 5 §30, Mandate); such submission occurs *retroactively* to the commencement of the management (Art. 984). In other words, and as its name implies, the regime of *negotiorum gestio* is only subsidiary to that of the mandate, insofar as it only applies if and as long as the management has not been not ratified.

1616 The principle posed by Art. 979§1 is tempered by the two next provisions however. *First*, if, however, the management of the beneficiary's affairs is contrary

[734] S. above note 226.

[735] Some translations return "unjust enrichment" for 无因管理 wú yīn guǎnlǐ: this is legally incorrect; 无因管理 wú yīn guǎnlǐ means, in legal Chinese, *negotiorum gestio*. Unjust enrichment is correctly expressed, in legal Chinese, as 不当得利 bùdāng dé lì, as in the Chinese Civil Code (Art. 985 ff.)

to the "true intent" (s. below §1622) of the latter, the manager is not entitled to the rights provided by Art. 979§1, unless such intent violates the law or is contrary to public order and good morals.

Second, Art. 980 literally provides that, if the management does not fall within the circumstances specified under Art. 979, but the beneficiary benefits it anyway, it shall be, within the scope of such benefits, under the obligation to indemnify the manager as prescribed by Art. 979§1 anyway. The drafting of Art. 980 is not very clear, as acknowledged by several commentators; likewise, for this reason, its various translations struggle at expressing its plain meaning. It deserves, therefore, some developments. 1617

Art. 980 actually addresses situations that do not squarely fall within the circumstances specified in Art. 979. Specifically, it applies when the management does not qualify as lawful, as stipulated by Art. 979, but results in the beneficiary gaining some benefit anyway. This corresponds to two cases, identified in doctrine as *unlawful or improper management without mandate* 不适法无因管理 bùshì fǎ wú yīn guǎnlǐ and *quasi-management without true mandate* 不真正无因管理 bù zhēnzhèng wú yīn guǎnlǐ[736]. While the scope of Art. 980 has been debated, the consensus is that it covers management that is not legally justified under Art. 979 but, because it still confers some benefits on the beneficiary, obliges the latter to reimburse or compensate the manager within the scope of the benefit. Such liability cases thus qualify as quasi-*illicit*, as contrasted with quasi-contractual ones; nevertheless, they fall under the same regime. 1618

The manager must manage the third party's affairs in the latter's *interest* (Art. 981, 1st sentence); it shall not discontinue such management without justification if such discontinuation impacts on the beneficiary (*ibid.*, 2nd sentence). 1619

The manager must, as far and, if so, as soon as possible, *notify* the beneficiary (Art. 982, 1st sentence). Unless the management of such affairs is urgently necessary, the manager must wait for *instructions* from the beneficiary (*ibid.*, 2nd sentence). At the end of the management, it must *report* to the beneficiary (Art. 983, 1st sentence) and timely transfer it any *benefits* derived from the managed affairs (*ibid.*, 2nd sentence). 1620

---

736 The notion of quasi-management *without* true mandate (不真正无因管理 bù zhēnzhèng wú yīn guǎnlǐ) refers to a situation where a person intervenes in another's affairs but does not have the lawful or true purpose of managing affairs for the benefit of the third party. Unlike true *negotiorum gestio*, quasi-management without true mandate occurs when the manager lacks this *altruistic* intent. This includes cases where the manager mistakenly treats an affair as its own or, knowingly but without authorization, manages another's affairs as if they were its own.

1621 The *limitation of action* for *negotiorum gestio* has been mentioned in the introduction to quasi-contracts (s. above §1613).

1622 The Swiss law regime of *negotiorum gestio* (Fr.: "la gestion d'affaires sans mandat"; Ger.: "die Geschäftsführung ohne Auftrag"; CO Art. 419 ff.) is similar in most respects to Chinese law. However, it may be noted that, where Chinese law refers to the notion of "true intent" (真实意思 zhēnshí yìsi), the notion this expression means to convey would be actually be better served by "*presumed* intent" or, like in Swiss law, "interests and presumable intents" (Art. 419), since one can hardly conceive how, by definition, absent a mandate or instructions, the manager could know the beneficiary's "true" intent; moreover, although 真实 zhēnshí accurately translates as "true", 意思 yìsi, which is generally translated by "will", "intent" or "intention" has actually a vaguer connotation: it best translates as "meaning" which, combined with "true", suggests that "presumed intent" is a better translation than the more assertive combinations of "true intent", "true intention" or "true will".

1623 The regime of *negotiorum gestio* is, namely, *referred* to, explicitly or implicitly, in relation with the general regime of agency or representation (s. above §300), contractual liability (s. above §§326 and 328), contractual conclusion (s. above §593), the general regime of liability for illicit acts (s. above §§1634 and 1651) and the related special regime of liability for environmental pollution and ecological damage (s. above §1722).

1624 As the express reference to *negotiorum gestio* in the regime of liability for environmental pollution and ecological damage suggests, *negotiorum gestio* may occur, for example, in case of toxic leaks suddenly emanating or threatening to emanate from a (beneficiary) factory, plant or warehouse because of a fire, malfunction, pipe rupture, etc., thus causing or threatening to cause serious and extensive pollution, and the neighboring (managing) enterprise engages costly human resources and equipment, etc. to prevent, stop or mitigate it.

§55. Unjust Enrichment

1625 As briefly mentioned in the introduction to quasi-contracts (s. above §1611), unjust enrichment 不当得利 bùdāng dé lì[737] (Chinese Civil Code, Third Book, Title Three, Chap. 29; Art. 985 to 988) refers to the enrichment of one party resulting from the impoverishment of the other absent a legal basis. It rests on the *Roman law* concept of unjust enrichment which may occur is three cases: without a legal cause (*sine causa*); for a cause which never occurred (*causa non secuta*); and for a cause which ceased to exist (*causa finita*). It is governed

[737] About translation issues, s. above note 735.

by a similar regime in *Swiss law* (Fr. "enrichissement illégitime"; Ger.: "ungerechtfertigter Bereicherung"; CO Art. 62 ff.) Like *negotiorum gestio*, it is a *subsidiary* regime, which is frequently referred to in other regimes (s. below §1631).

The basic *principle* is that, in case of unjust enrichment, the enriched party has 1626
the obligation to return the resulting benefits to its legitimate owner (Art. 985), but that that principle is subject to three *exemptions*, including: payments made for fulfilling a moral obligation; advance payments of a debt, i.e., before it becomes due; and payments made with clear knowledge that there is no payment obligation.

While the first case is unlikely to find application in business, the second may 1627
frequently, for example, in case of payment of a *retainer*. The latter case supposes that the corresponding debt will, eventually, become due; if not, or if it only partly does, as is typical, once again, of a retainer which has only partly been used, the beneficiary must return it or the unused remainder. The third case may find application, among other things, in case of *corruption* not eventually followed by the desired effect, in which case the corruptor will not be entitled to the protection of the law; while such situation does take place in practice, its application is not limited to this example, however. A very frequent case of unjust enrichment is that of *payments made in error* to a third party which was not the originally intended beneficiary.

The *good faith* of the enriched party is protected: thus, if an enriched party does 1628
not, and is not required to, know that the acquired benefit has no legal basis while such benefit has ceased to exist, the enriched party shall not bear the obligation to return such benefit (Art. 986). However, if, on the contrary, an enriched party knows or should know that the acquired benefit has no legal basis, the party suffering loss may request the enriched party to return such benefit and to compensate for any loss (Art. 987).

Finally, if the enriched party has transferred gratuitously the benefit to a *third* 1629
party, the impoverished party has the right to ask the third party to return it, which the latter will find itself under the obligation to (Art. 988). This provision implies that the originally enriched party must be of good faith; if not, Art. 987 shall apply and the impoverished party shall have the right to ask the originally enriched one to compensate the former although the latter already transferred the benefit to the third party; the *gratuity* of the transfer vests the originally enriched party with the presumption that it was of good faith, while an onerous transfer would result in the opposing effect.

The *limitation of action* for unjust enrichment is the same as for *negotiorum* 1630
gestio (s. above §1613).

1631 As *negotiorum gestio*, the regime of unjust enrichment is namely *referred* to, explicitly or implicitly, in relation with contractual conclusion (s. above §593), judiciary deposit (s. above §783), the contract of financial leasing (s. above §1151), of construction (s. above §1289) and of warehousing (s. above §1391).

Chap. 8 Liability for Illicit Acts ("Torts")

§56. Introduction

As we have seen, in Chinese law, there are five main sources of civil liability, four of which are contained in the Chinese Civil Code: a general regime applying to all forms of liability; liability for breach of contract; quasi-contracts; liability for illicit acts; and liability stemming from laws other than the Code (s. above §309). Liability for illicit acts is treated by the Code after the law of contracts, including liability for breach of contract, and forms its last book. 1632

As noted (s. above §312), liability "for illicit acts", as it is generally known in civil law systems, which is expressed in the Chinese Civil Code by 侵权责任 qīnquán zérèn, is frequently but inaccurately translated, in English, as "torts", which incorrectly refers to the *common law* notion of liability for illicit acts. While presenting some similarities, the notion of torts also contains concepts fundamentally differing from the civil law systems' notion of liability for illicit acts[738], to which the Chinese regime best compares. 1633

It is also worth recalling that liability for illicit acts is not the only source of *noncontractual* (as opposed to contractual-) liability: quasi-contracts, i.e., unjust enrichment and *negotiorum gestio*, also are noncontractual sources of obligations or liability, but are, traditionally, given their Roman law roots, treated separately, by civil law systems, from liability for illicit acts, because they do not initially result from an illicit act[739]. 1634

The Seventh Book of the code on liability for illicit acts is an important one, with almost one hundred articles (Art. 1164 to 1258). It is remarkable, namely, as compared to Swiss law, as it addresses not only traditional forms of liability such as liability for domestic animals or for buildings, which are covered by the Swiss Civil Code, but also embraces modern forms of liability such as product liability, liability for traffic accidents, medical liability, environmental liability and high-risk liability, which are conspicuously absent from the Swiss Civil Code, despite the major challenges such risks pose in today's society. 1635

The book on liability for illicit acts contains three general and seven special chapters. Among the three general chapters, beyond the first usual one on general provisions, the second applies to damage compensation in general, while 1636

---

738 S. above note 202.

739 Liability for illicit acts can subsequently result from *negotiorum gestio* or unjust enrichment, if the author's act exceeds the boundaries of liceity under either regime however.

the third contains special liability regimes which may apply depending on who is the author of the damage.

1637 The seven chapters on special liability regimes have been evoked above and apply, in the following order, to product liability, motor vehicle accident liability, medical liability, liability for environmental pollution and ecological damage, high-risk liability, liability for domestic animals, and liability for buildings and objects.

1638 In this book, after outlining the general chapters, we will detail those special chapters which are of most relevance to foreign investors in China, namely, *product liability*, *liability for environmental pollution and ecological damage*, and *high-risk liability*.

§57. General Provisions

1639 As noted about contractual liability, although the law only implies it (s., e.g., Art. 186; s. also above §§317 and 792), it can be assumed that the general regime of civil liability contained in Chapter 8 of the First Book of the Code on general provisions (Art. 176 ff.) also applies by default to, among other liability regimes, liability for illicit acts, provided the latter is silent or not specific enough, according to the principle *lex specialis derogat leges generali* (Art. 11; s. above §117).

1640 The first article of the chapter proclaims that the book applies to liability for illicit acts[740] (Art. 1164). The principle of such liability is contained in the next article which proclaims that the author causing damage to others by infringing upon their civil rights and interests by fault shall assume liability (Art. 1165).

1641 Although it may not be obvious at first sight, Art. 1165 thus enunciates the four basic *conditions* to which liability for illicit acts is subject in most civil law jurisdictions: a *damage*, an *illicit act*, a *causality link* between such damage and such act, and a *fault* (Art. 1165). Swiss law is not different in that regard (cf. CO Art. 41§1). These conditions are enunciated neither in the general provisions of the Chinese Civil Code at Art. 60 (s. above §139), nor in those of the chapter on civil liability at Art. 176 (s. above §319).

1642 Moreover, the Chinese Civil Code falls short from expressly stating which party bears the *burden of proof*: as noted about contractual liability (s. above §797), this allocation is to be derived from the general principle set by the

[740] The reference to the illicit and noncontractual nature of the liability regulated by the Seventh Book of the Chinese Civil Code is actually implicit: Art. 1164 expressly refers to the "infringement of civil rights and interests".

Chinese law of civil procedure, namely, Art. 67 of the Law of Civil Procedure stating that a party shall bear the burden to provide evidence supporting its claims[741]. A logical corollary of this principle is that the other party bears the burden of proving the contrary.

Therefore, like in Swiss law, under the Chinese general regime of liability for illicit acts, the *victim* bears the burden to prove the author's liability, that is to say, all of its four components which, as noted, are the damage (both its existence and its extent), the illicit act having caused it, the causal link between the author, its act and the damage, and the author's fault[742]. 1643

Art. 1165 thus sets the one condition which fundamentally differentiates noncontractual from contractual liability: the author of a noncontractual damage is only liable if it was at *fault* (Art. 1165§1). Indeed, in contrast, as stressed about liability for breach of contract (s. above §794), contrary to liability for illicit acts, the fault of a contractual damage's author is presumed, while it is not for liability for illicit acts. Consequently, the *victim* of noncontractual damage bears the burden to prove that the author was at fault, while the author, not the victim, of contractual damage bears the burden to prove that it was not at fault. 1644

However, because the Seventh Book also contains special regimes of liability for illicit acts setting higher liability standards, the second paragraph of Art. 1165 provides for the *reversal* of the burden of proof where the *author* is presumed by law to be at fault (Art. 1165§2), like for liability for breach of contract. 1645

Moreover, Art. 1166 provides for *objective liability* whenever the Seventh Book (or possibly secondary legislation) has set up a special regime calling for it, i.e., where the author is deemed to be at fault, therefore liable, without any possibility to prove that it was not at fault, i.e., irrespective of whether it was faulty or not. 1646

Art. 1186, which is contained in the next chapter of the Code on damage compensation, introduces some confusion: it provides that if the damage is caused without any fault neither from the author nor from the victim, then the damage should be borne by both parties "according to the law". At first reading, that 1647

---

741 Art. 42§1 of the Swiss Code of Obligations prescribes that the victim bears the burden to prove the damage. However, because of CC Art. 8 which, like Art. 67 of the Chinese Law on Civil Procedure, poses the general principle by which a party must prove the facts from which it derives the right it claims, under Swiss law, a victim must prove all the conditions of liability for illicit act set forth by CO Art. 41, i.e., not only the damage, but also the illicit act, the causal link and the author's fault. S., for example, HENRI DESCHENAUX/PIERRE TERCIER, La responsabilité civile, 2ème éd., Staempfli, 1982, § 21 Nos 15 and 16.

742 S. above note 452.

provision seems to contradict the fundamental principle set forth by Art. 1165 by which the author is only liable if it was at fault. Therefore, a literal reading of Art. 1186 could give the impression that it runs counter Art. 1165 inasmuch as, according to the latter provision, the author would be liable for half (or part) of the damage even though it was not at fault, provided the victim was not either, which Art. 1165 assumes anyway. Therefore, in order to reconcile this apparent contradiction, one ought to consider the addition, in Art. 1186, of the phrase "according to the law", which suggests that the *non-faulty author* may be liable for half of the damage anyway if *another* law (but the Chinese Civil Code) provides for it[743].

1648 The general provisions further provide for alternative *remedies*, which Art. 1167 non-exhaustively lists as ceasing the infringement, eliminating the obstruction or the danger, "etc." As such, this provision silently refers to the general provisions on civil liability where Art. 179 further provides an equally non-exhaustive list mentioning, in addition to those reiterated by Art. 1167: removal of obstacles, return of property, restoration to original condition, repair, reworking or replacement, resumption of performance, compensation for loss, elimination of adverse effects, rehabilitation of reputation, and extension of apology (s. above §322)[744]. These remedies can be applied individually or in combination (Art. 179§3).

1649 Since this chapter does not recall it, one ought to keep in mind that the general provisions on civil liability provide that, in case the author is liable both contractually and for illicit act *concurrently*, the victim has the choice to seek redress under either regime (Art. 187; s. above §325).

1650 The rest of the chapter essentially deals with two particular aspects typical of the law of liability: joint (and several) liability and mitigation. *Joint liability* is governed by Art. 1168 to 1172, which provide both for *external* and *internal* liability, in accordance with the general principles set forth in the chapter on civil liability contained in the First Book of the Code on general provisions (Art. 177 and 178, s. above §§329 to 331).

1651 *Mitigation*[745] is addressed by Art. 1173 to 1177 by considering various circumstances which may mitigate the author's liability, or not. They include the

---

[743] On the reduction of the compensation for which the non-faulty author may be liable under Swiss law, s. below note 753 *in fine*.

[744] Art. 179 also mentions "payment for breach of contract" which evidently applies to contractual liability, not to liability for illicit acts: liquidated (A.K.A. pre-agreed) damages would not qualify as remedy for liability for illicit acts given their contractual nature. In contrast, conceivably, punitive damages may apply both in case of contractual liability and liability for illicit acts. About these notions, s. above note 206.

[745] About the duty of mitigation in case of *contractual* liability, s. above §836.

victim's fault or *mutual liability* (Art. 1173 and 1174)[746], third-party's fault (Art. 1175) and urgency (Art. 1177)[747]. While urgency mirrors the general provisions on civil liability (Art. 182 and 184, s. §322), these exonerating circumstances ought to be complemented by *force majeure* (Art. 180; s. above §327) and *negotiorum gestio* (Art. 183; s. below Chap. 7 §54, Negotiorum Gestio) which are foreseen by the general provisions on civil liability, but not recalled in the general provisions on liability for illicit acts (s. above §§326 to 328). In accordance with the general rule of proof and contrary to the damage, which the victim must prove (s. above §1644), the *author* bears the burden to prove such circumstances.

Generally speaking, the Swiss law of liability for illicit acts has produced an abundant body of doctrine and jurisprudence from which the Swiss lawyer may draw inspiration about Chinese law in that field since, while evidently not identical in every respect, both national laws fundamentally rest on comparable principles. 1652

§58. Damage Compensation

Art. 1179 provides for various rules applying to damage compensation in case of *injury, disability or death*. The case of death is further detailed in the next two articles (Art. 1180 to 1181). Psychological damage is addressed by Art. 1183[748]. Although not pertaining to liability for illicit acts, one may recall in this context that contractual clauses exempting the author from its liability in case of physical injury are invalid (Art. 506, item 1; s. above §610). 1653

Damage compensation for *property* is dealt with by two non-consecutive articles at Art. 1182 and 1184. Its principle is grounded in the First Title on general principles of the Book on real rights (Art. 238; s. above §389) and, generally, from the standpoint of civil liability, by Art. 179§1, item 8 (s. above §322), which provides for compensation as one of the remedies available to victims. Again, however not related to liability for illicit acts, one should remind that contractual clauses exempting the author from its liability in case of intentional or grossly negligent damage to property are invalid (Art. 506, item 2; s. above §610). 1654

---

[746] The same solution applies in case of contractual liability (s. Art. 592 and above §837).

[747] The Chinese Civil Code also contains a novel provision on *risky group hobbies* (Art. 1176) reflecting today's leisure society and further referring to a special regime applying to organizers (Art. 1198 to 1201).

[748] Psychological damage is referred to, in the Swiss Civil Code, by its compensation, i.e., in French, as "réparation morale" and in German as "Leistung von Genugtuung" (CO Art. 47); psychological damage itself is commonly known as "tort moral" and "immaterieller Schaden", i.e., for the latter, literally, immaterial damage.

1655 It should be reminded at this stage that, while both are quantifiable, the *damage* and its *compensation* are two distinct notions. The burden of proof of the damage existence and extent is on the victim's shoulders and has been addressed in the preceding section (s. above §1643). This section is concerned with compensation, i.e., its form and measure.

1656 Although contained in those two provisions (Art. 1182 and 1184) only[749], the regime of compensation for property loss resulting from an illicit act[750], which determines the *quantum* or amount of compensation, is of immense significance in practice, also for foreign investors in China, since it applies to the compensation of all damage resulting from illicit acts generally, including all special regimes, unless they contain special rules derogating the general regime formed by those two provisions.

1657 Art. 1182 and 1184 set forth the following principles: first, the compensation shall "relate"[751] to the *loss* suffered by the victim (Art. 1182, 1st sentence). It falls short of defining the notion of loss or damage[752], which party bears the burden of proving both its existence and its economic value, and how to determine the *quantum* of compensation however (s. next paragraph).

1658 Second, a measure of compensation can be provided by the *gains* obtained by the author, if any (Art. 1182, 1st sentence *in fine*).

1659 Third, the parties may reach an *agreement* about the amount of compensation, in accordance with the general principle set forth by Art. 176 (s. above §320). Although Art. 1182 does not expressly mandate such settlement attempt, it makes it a condition to apply at court (s. following paragraph). In practice, Chinese courts or the authorities strongly pressure the parties to reach such agreement.

---

749 As noted (s. above §1653), the article in-between, Art. 1183, is limited to psychological damage.

750 The quantum of compensation for contractual damage is governed by Art. 577 and 584 (s. above Chap. 4 §27.II, Compensation).

751 Art. 1182 uses the word 按照, ànzhào, which can be translated as "according to", "on the basis of" or "as per". It does, therefore, not go as far as prescribing that the compensation should necessarily replace the victim in the same situation as if the damage had never occurred, which is sometimes impossible.

752 Swiss law does not define the notion of damage either, s. CO Art. 41. However, Swiss jurisprudence has defined damage as an involuntary decrease of net wealth. It can take the form of a decrease of assets, an increase of liabilities, a non-increase of assets or a non-decrease of liabilities (ATF 129 III 18; ATF 133 III 462), i.e., the difference between the wealth of the victim after the damageable event, and the amount which that wealth had reached if there had been no damageable event. This reasoning is known as the *theory of difference* (ATF 132 III 359 = JT 2006 I 295; ATF 144 III 155 = JT 2018 II 287). The *loss of profit* is also a damage (ATF 90 II 417).

And fourth, if both the loss and the gains cannot be determined, and if the parties have failed to reach an agreement, then either party can apply to the *court* and ask it to determine the compensation amount[753] (Art. 1182, 2nd sentence). These two conditions (that the damage could not be determined, and that the parties failed to agree) are expressed cumulatively. 1660

Art. 1184 complements Art. 1182 by setting forth a *standard* for the calculation of the compensation amount or *valuation method* by which the *market price at the time of the damage*[754] applies; however, this provisions expressly reserves "other reasonable methods". 1661

Such "other reasonable methods" are not defined by the Code. One may recall, however, that expropriation (as well as requisition) is specially addressed by both the Code[755] and the FIL[756], both of which set the standards applying to compensation. As *lex specialis*, they prevail over the general standard set by Art. 1184 of the Code. Be that as it may, the former standards are limited to expropriation (or requisition), while both the expropriation and the general standards only set basic principles which are too vague to be of practical use. 1662

Instead, the foreign investor may find guidance in the *1992 World Bank Report and Guidelines on the Treatment of Foreign Direct Investment*[757]. That report 1663

---

753 In Swiss law, the victim bears the burden of proving the *damage* (as opposed to the compensation, s. below) and its value (CO Art. 42§1). If such value cannot be exactly established, the judge determines it in equity by considering the normal course of events and the steps taken by the person suffering damage (CO Art. 42§2). This rule must be applied restrictively (ATF 142 IV 237 = JT 2017 IV 39). CO Art. 42§2, which derogates to CO Art. 42§1, only applies if the prejudice is of such a nature that it is impossible to establish it, or if the necessary proofs lack, or if their administration cannot reasonably be requested from the claimant (ATF 84 II 6, ATF 105 II 87 = JT 1980 I 17, ATF 122 III 219 = JT 1997 I 246). The judge further determines both the form and the extent of the *compensation*, taking into account the circumstances and the gravity of the fault (CO Art. 43§1). The judge enjoys *discretion* to assess the related evidence (ATF 54 II 192). He can *reduce* the compensation in case of fault of the victim (CO Art. 44§1) or, in case the author was not at fault or lightly faulty, if the latter were to face hardship (CO Art. 44§2).

754 Swiss law does not contain any such standard. About the methods generally admitted by Swiss courts, s., for example, FRANZ WERRO/VINCENT PERRITAZ *in*: Commentaire romand/CO I *ad* Art. 42, Nos 3 to 13, and HENRI DESCHENAUX/PIERRE TERCIER, La responsabilité civile, 2nd ed., Staempfli, 1982, pp. 216 ff. On international methods applying to foreign investment, s. below §§2347ff.

755 Art. 117, s. above §172.

756 Art. 20, s. above §19.

757 The World Bank Group, Report to the Development Committee and Guidelines on the Treatment of Foreign Direct Investment *in*: Legal Framework for the Treatment of Foreign Investment, Vol. II, http://documents.worldbank.org/curated/en/

consists of two volumes. The first volume contains four studies of the major contemporary sources of legal principles governing foreign investment. Together, these studies provide a comprehensive survey of bilateral investment treaties, multilateral legal instruments, recent national investment codes and international awards related to the legal relationship between foreign investors and their host governments in recent years. The study of arbitral awards also surveys the broad array of conflicting doctrinal views on this important subject. The second volume includes the guidelines for universal standards for the legal treatment of FDI, along with a detailed report[758].

1664 The Report and the Guidelines do not only address expropriation but also apply to the *admission* and the *treatment* of foreign investment (i.e., their non-discrimination), as well as to "unilateral alterations or termination of contracts", i.e., as far as the latter is concerned, to liability for breach of contract. As such, they are designed to address the liability of the *State*[759] towards *foreign investors*, not between non-State parties.

1665 The Report and the Guidelines are not binding[760]. However, as a member of the World Bank and of the ICSID Convention[761], a Chinese court could hardly arbitrarily refuse to consider their application[762]. Moreover, the Guidelines are routinely used in international arbitration.

1666 Notwithstanding the foregoing, nothing prevents the Guidelines' *scope* to extend to contractual, or noncontractual, liability, to the liability of a non-State author, or to both, towards a foreign or a domestic investor[763], considering, among other things, that neither expropriation, nor (non-) admission, nor (mis-) treatment qualify as liability for breach of contract and are, therefore, noncontractual by nature[764]. For example, if a plant were to be destroyed by fire because of the negligence of the external service provider contracted for the

955221468766167766/Guidelines ("1992 World Bank Report" and "1992 World Bank Guidelines").

758 S. https://documents.worldbank.org/en/publication/documents-reports/documentdetail/955221468766167766/guidelines.

759 S. 1992 World Bank Report, p. 16 § 14.

760 1992 World Bank Report, p. 14 § 8.

761 On the ICSID Convention, s. above Chap. 1 §6.II, The Washington Convention. On the multilateral, bilateral and domestic guarantees for the protection of foreign investment, s. above §§400ff.

762 As put by the Report: "Thus, the guidelines, while not having a binding character as such, have a basis in existing legal instruments and may not be inconsistent with what some sources may consider to be settled international law." 1992 World Bank Report, p. 14 § 9.

763 The Report suggests that the Guidelines may apply to domestic investors, s. p. 15 § 11.

764 S. also 1992 World Bank Report, p. 15 § 12 and 13, which gives a liberal definition of foreign investment.

plant's safety against fire hazard, that would be a case of contractual, but non-State, liability of the provider, for which one of the valuation methods described in the 1992 World Bank Report could be used. Alternatively, if that plant was destroyed by an arsonist confessing that he was paid by a competitor, that would be a case of liability for illicit acts or of criminal liability of the competitor, for which the same methods could be used.

Indeed, if the applicability of the Guidelines to non-State and/or liability for illicit acts were to be challenged, the victim could submit that the methods detailed therein arguably qualify as "reasonable methods" as put by Art. 1184 of the Chinese Civil Code (s. above §1667 *in fine*). 1667

The Guidelines address a great variety of valuation *methods* including the Net Asset Value, the Asset Accumulation Method, the Replacement Value, the Intrinsic or Market Value, the Net Book Value, the Historical Book Value, the Adjusted Book Value, the Discounted Cash Flow Value, the Liquidation Value and the Market Data Comparable Value[765]. 1668

To the knowledge of the author, the Report and the Guidelines are not frequently relied upon in Chinese judicial proceedings or in the China-related commercial arbitration practice. Generally, the parties and the courts rely on expert appraisal reports, which in turn generally rely on the *Generally Accepted Accounting Principles* (GAAP) accounting standards[766] for appraising the damage. Nevertheless, such practice, however prevalent, does not preclude the use of the World Bank Report and Guidelines which, because of the variety of the methods they contain, may provide more flexibility hence more adequate methods. 1669

The parties which may agree on the amount of compensation shall also agree on the *payment method* (Art. 1187, 1st sentence). If they fail to, i.e., if compensation is ruled by a court, the compensation must be paid as a *lump sum* (*ibid.*, 2nd sentence). However, if the author faces "genuine difficulty" in paying the compensation as a lump sum, it may be authorized by the court to pay by *installments*. If so, the victim has the right to request *security* (*ibid.*, 3rd sentence). 1670

The compensation foreseen at Art. 1182 is to be distinguished from compensation for *expropriation* (Art. 243 to 245; s. above §§397ff.) where, unlike the damage contemplated by Art. 1182, expropriation is legitimate, provided it is compensated in accordance with the law. It is also to be differentiated from 1671

---

765 S. 1992 World Bank Guidelines, Guidelines IV.

766 The GAAP is the accounting standard adopted by the U.S. Securities and Exchange Commission (SEC), and is the default accounting standard used by companies based in the United States.

damage caused to *possession*, whose compensation is provided by Art. 459 to 462§1 (s. above §544ff.)

1672 Compensation is only one of the remedies available to the victim, which as detailed can resort to the numerous alternative remedies foreseen by the law, also in combination (s. above §1648).

1673 It is worth noting that the chapter contains a special provision for *intellectual property rights*: in case of infringement, the victim is entitled to claim, in addition to damage compensation, *punitive damages* (Art. 1185). It is unclear whether one should understand that punitive damages are reserved to IPR. Given the generic nature of punitive damages, we see no reason why they should[767], and rather regard this provision as an affirmation by the Chinese legislator to protect IPR[768], not an exclusion of the eligibility of other infringements.

1674 The liability of the *non-faulty author* despite the exoneration of Art. 1165 has been discussed above (Art. 1186; s. above §1647).

1675 Finally, it is noteworthy that the Chinese Civil Code does not specifically provide for *interest* that may be due on any such damage compensation. Comparatively, *Swiss law* does, on any due debt, and fixes it at *five percent per annum* (CO Art. 73§1)[769]. It remains that interest is, however in general terms, indisputably a form of damage acknowledged under the Chinese Civil Code (s. Art. 113, 577 and 585; s. above §810 as well as §§1654 and 1657). Its *rate* has been pegged by judicial interpretations (s. above notes 589 and 590) to the benchmark rate which is the *Lend Prime Rate* or LPR; it is currently of *three percent*[770]; in other words, unlike under Swiss law, the interest applied to damage compensation is *dynamic*. Moreover, Chinese courts may use their discretion to increase it up to satisfaction of the loss. *Liquidated damages* (s. above Chap. 4 §27.III.A, Liquidated Damages) providing for a higher interest are acknowledged by Chinese law, within certain limits however[771]. *Anatocism* or

767 Punitive damages are foreseen by Art. 179§2, s. above §323. However, Art. 179§2 subjects them to a specific legal basis: Art. 1185 is one such basis but does not exclude others.

768 This provision was clearly inserted to satisfy the growing frustration of the international investors' community about the weakness of the deterrents provided by Chinese law in the past.

769 Under Swiss law, the late interest rate can exceed the legal five percent if the parties so agreed, or trade usage calls for another rate; however, such usage is typically difficult to prove. CO Art. 732 is currently under revision (s. FF 2023 1335); it may align with the dynamic approach used by Chinese law. In practice, in Switzerland, unless another rate was agreed upon, the five percent legal interest is, in disputes, systematically applied.

770 S. above note 586.

771 S. above note 470.

double-interest (interest over late interest) is prohibited, both in China and Switzerland. Overdue interest for *loans* is subject to specific rules (s. above §1082).

§59. Liability of Certain Authors

Chapter 3 of the book on liability for illicit acts (Art. 1188 to 1201) contains special provisions which complement the general regime depending on who is the author of the damage. It focuses on four author's groups: individuals whose capacity is impaired; individuals acting in the course of their work; internet users and public places managers. 1676

The first group, impaired capacity, be it related to individual with no capacity, limited capacity, or temporarily deprived of consciousness or control, is covered by Art. 1188 to 1190 and 1199 to 1201. We will not discuss them in this book as this regime hardly relates to business law. 1677

I. Workers

As for the second group, the chapter further dedicates three more articles to the liability for *damage caused to third parties by individuals performing their work* (Art. 1191 to 1193). These provisions address four cases: employment, dispatch, labor services, and contracting. They further envision, within each case, several sub-cases depending on who harms whom. For each case and sub-case, the law clarifies which party is liable in the first place and, as the case may be, if that party may subsequently recoup its liability by holding another party liable in the second place. 1678

Thus, in case of *employment* (Art. 1191§1), if the employee damages a third-party, the employer is liable but may claim back from its faulty employee. 1679

In case of *dispatch* (Art. 1191§2), in case the dispatch damages a third-party, the employer using the dispatch is liable, but may claim back from the faulty dispatching employer. 1680

In case of *provision of labor services between individuals* (Art. 1192), the party using the service is liable, but may claim back from the faulty provider. This provision also envisages the cases in which the provider is harmed either by the user (Art. 1192§1 *in fine*) or by a third party (Art. 1192§2): in the first case, both parties are liable proportionally to their fault; in the second, the user is, but may claim back from the third party. 1681

1682 *Prima facie*, Art. 1193, which applies to the contractor (承揽人 chénglǎn rén) relates to the *contract for work* (as opposed to the labor contract) governed by Art. 770 ff. (s. above Chap. 5 §38, Contract for Work). However, because of its lack of specific reference to the latter, its general formulation and its location in the general provision of the Seventh Book, arguably, Art. 1193 could, conceivably, also relate to other similar contracts such as, for example, the construction project contract or the mandate. Be that as it may, in case the contractor damages a third-party, the faulty master is liable in case of *culpa in instruendo et eligendo* (s. above §1014), i.e., of faulty instructions to- or selection of the contractor. The law expressly mentions that the non-faulty master is not, however. The same applies if the contractor itself suffers damage.

1683 It is worth noting that, while the cases addressed by Art. 1191 to 1193 focus on damage caused to third-parties, hence of a noncontractual nature, thus justifying their location in the general part of the Seventh Book on liability for illicit acts, they also extend to certain cases of liability for *breach of contract* (e.g., the liability of the labor services user towards the provider, or that of the master towards the contractor): as such, the liability regimes so envisioned are of an *hybrid* nature. However, liability for breach of contract is comprehensively treated by Chapter 8 of the Third Book of the Chinese Civil Code on contracts (s. above Chap. 4 §27, Liability for Breach of Contract), and by special provisions relating to the typical contracts governed by the same book, which Art. 1191 to 1193 mostly mirror as far as liability for breach of contract is concerned.

II. Internet Users and Providers

1684 The third group of authors relates to the *internet*, thus testifying the modernity of the Chinese Civil Code in addressing what has become a major cause of damage in our era and is, for obvious historical reasons, conspicuously absent from old codes such as the Swiss Civil Code.

1685 Internet-related liability is covered by four provisions (Art. 1194 to 1197). The first and the last ground the liability of both the *user* and the internet access *provider* for damaging a third-party through the use of the internet; the last, Art. 1197, complements the principle set by the first, Art. 1194, for the provider's liability, by adding that the latter is liable for the damageable use of the internet not only by itself, but also *by a third-party*, if the provider fails to take the necessary measures for preventing such damage.

1686 This latter case of extended liability is subject to the provider's *awareness* of such damageable use; however, actual awareness is not required: the provider shall also be liable if it *should* have been aware. The Code does not further define the extent of the provider's duty of awareness.

Art. 1195 and 1196 further provide for a *notice mechanism* to the effect of addressing the alleged damage. The alleged victim may give a *notice of infringement* to the provider that it has allegedly been damaged by a third-party through the use, by the latter, of the internet (to which the provider is providing access, through the network it operates) and ask the provider to take the "necessary measures" (s. below §1691). As the alleged victim does so, it must file, with the provider, the related preliminary evidence and disclose its identity (Art. 1195§1). 1687

Upon receipt, the provider must timely forward such notice to the third-party (Art. 1195§2). "Timely" is, as often, not defined, thus left to the discretion of the authority or the court, as the case may be (s. also below §1695). In turn, upon receipt, the third-party may file counter-evidence with the provider, together with its identity and a *notice of non-infringement* (Art. 1196§3) 1688

If so, the provider must timely forward such notice and counter-evidence to the alleged victim, and inform it that it may file an administrative complaint with the authority, or file a lawsuit at court (Art. 1169§2) 1689

If the alleged victim abstains from doing so, or fails to timely notify the provider that it has, the provider shall, timely again, terminate the measures (Art. 1196§2 *in fine*). Since the law is further silent about it, one understands, by deduction, *a contrario*, that if the alleged victim does file, the provider shall maintain the measures until ordered otherwise by the authority or the court. 1690

Such *measures* are non-exhaustively defined as "deletion, blocking and unlinking" (Art. 1195§1), thus allowing the provider to take any other measures it believes fit, which one understands as being technical measures preventing or restricting the damageable use of the internet, either to the author, to the users, or to both. 1691

Art. 1195 is silent about how the provider should determine whether it should take such measures and, if so, which, other than based on such preliminary evidence and on "the type of service" (Art. 1195§2). In other words, this provision makes the provider judge of whether such measures are *prima facie* justified, and which measures adequately prevent it. As such, providers are left off with the complex task of referring to the related secondary legislation, regulations and policies in order to comply. 1692

If the *provider* fails to take such measures, fails to take them timely, or takes inadequate measures, it shall be *liable* towards the alleged victim for the damage aggravation (Art. 1195§2 *in fine*). In contrast, if the alleged *victim*'s notice was ill-founded, the latter shall be liable, both towards the provider and the alleged author, as the case may be (Art. 1195§3). Art. 1195§3 reserves other 1693 provisions of the law, thus referring generically to the abundant secondary legislation in that field.

1694 If the provider fails to take the necessary measures after it became aware or should have become aware of an infringement, it shall be *jointly and severally* liable with the author (Art. 1197). Joint and several liability is further regulated by Art. 177 and 178 in the chapter on civil liability of the First Book on the general provisions of the Code (s. above §§323 to 325).

1695 As noted above, the whole mechanism is subject to the requirement of *timeliness*, even though the Code does not set any deadline. Generally speaking, it is safe to assume that, by "timely", one is to understand "immediately" or "as soon as business allows".

1696 While *foreign investors* in China need not being concerned by the above mentioned duties imposed to internet providers since foreign operators may not provide internet access or operate internet networks in China, which are monopolized by a small number of licensed Chinese operators, they should be acutely concerned about their rights and obligations as *potential authors or victims* of damages caused through the internet.

1697 Other than that, internet-related business is heavily regulated in China, namely, when it comes to the issuance of a *domain name*, of a *business license* for online business, and to *consumer protection*. Moreover, because by nature the internet is not confined within borders, questions arise about the consequences of *transnational infringements*. These matters are not covered in this book, whose scope they exceed, however.

III. Managers of Public Places

1698 Art. 1198 applies to managers or operators of public or business places including hotels, shopping malls, banks, railway stations, airports, stadiums and places of entertainment, as well as organizers of mass activities. While railways stations, airports are out of reach of foreign investors in China, hotels and shopping malls are frequent targets of foreign investment[772]. Moreover, this enumeration is to be understood as being exemplary, rather than exhaustive.

---

772 Popular shopping, dining and entertainment districts such as Sanlitun 三里屯 in Beijing and Xintiandi 新天地 in Shanghai would probably qualify as "places of entertainment". Stadiums have been increasingly invested by large companies, also in China and by foreign investors (e.g., Nike). Both are actual or potential targets for foreign investors. While there are foreign banks in China, retail banking is restricted to them, therefore their exposure is comparatively small.

Managers are liable for damage suffered by third parties resulting from their failure to ensure the public's *security*. If a third party is liable, the managers, etc. remain liable for the portion of the damage uncovered by the third party's compensation, towards whom they may claim back their own damage after indemnification of the victims (Art. 1198§2). 1699

Among other risks, although terrorism has been contained in China so far, foreign investors should pay close attention to their liability given the rise of such acts worldwide. Substandard construction and patchy maintenance are also frequent causes of mass casualties in China. The resulting liabilities may be eventually attenuated by those of third-party contractors resulting from contracts of public security services, of work, of maintenance, etc., concluded with them by the liable manager or operator, as the case may be. They may also potentially combine with other types of liabilities, for example, extreme hazards liability[773], etc. 1700

§60. Product Liability

Chinese law already contained a wealth of laws and regulations providing for product liability at large and, generally, *consumer protection*, when the Chinese Civil Code was issued. Other than eponymous laws on product quality and consumer protection, other laws range from generic norms on unfair competition, standards for advertisers or pricing standards, to industry-specific ones such as food processing, pharmaceutical products or medical devices. Most if not all of them provide for the liability of the producer in one way or the other. Many overlap. Consumer protection (other than Chapter 4 of the Seventh Book of the Code) is not covered in this book, whose scope it exceeds, however. This chapter focuses on Art. 1202 ff. of the Code, within the regime of liability for illicit acts. 1701

By inserting a chapter on product liability in the Seventh Book of the Chinese Civil Code on liability for illicit acts, the Chinese legislator closed any loophole which the existing array of laws and regulation may not have yet filled until the Code was promulgated: as its location makes clear, Chapter 4 on product liability of the Seventh Book of the Code applies to *liability for illicit acts*, i.e., absent any contractual relationship usually existing between a producer and a consumer. Yet that relationship may not exist: Art. 1202 ff. fill that gap. As 1702

[773] In 2009 the television cultural center tower burnt because fireworks were fired from its rooftop. Under the Chinese Civil Code (which by then had not yet been enacted), this could potentially have been a combined case of manager of public place-, extreme hazard- and, if the pyrotechnician was a contractor, of master- or contractor special authors liabilities, along with the authors' contractual and delictual liabilities.

such, the Chinese legislator also uses that opportunity to reaffirm, in the Code, its commitment to one of the major society challenges which consumer protection poses nowadays, in particular in China, given the sheer size of its population.

1703 Chapter 4 is relatively short, with only six articles (Art. 1202 to 1207). Its core principle is that the *producer* or manufacturer shall be liable if its product causes damage to others due to a defect (Art. 1202).

1704 However, the producer's liability is extended to the *seller*, where both are *jointly and severally* liable, thus enabling the victim to seek compensation from either (Art. 1203§1). The producer and the seller both enjoy the right to claim back any compensation either of them may have paid to the victim from the other (Art. 1203§2). Even though this provision does not expressly refer to the general regime of joint and several liability, Art. 177 and 178 pertaining to the chapter on civil liability of the First Book on the general provisions of the Code further apply (s. above §§329 to 332).

1705 The producer and the seller also enjoy the right of claiming back any such compensation from any *third-party* having caused the defect at stake, such as the transporter or the party providing storage (Art. 1204).

1706 The chapter mentions, among the *remedies* available to the victim, ceasing and desisting from the infringement, removing the obstacle and eliminating the danger (Art. 1205). This list is not exhaustive. Therefore, the victim may also refer to the general regime of civil liability which provides, at Art. 179§1, for a wide range of remedies (s. above §322), including those mentioned as examples by Art. 1205.

1707 The producer and the seller's liability is not limited to repairing the damage a defective product may have caused: if the defect is found after the product has been put on the market, their liability extends to *containment* measures as soon as that product is found defective (Art. 1206§1). These measures include alerts, recalls and any other measure adequate to prevent the damage potentially caused by the defective goods from spreading. One may think, typically, of toxic food, cars whose air bags were found not to trigger in case of shock or, on the contrary, to spontaneously burst, e-cars whose battery was found to spontaneously take fire, etc. In such cases, the producer and the sellers have a duty to immediately alert the consumers and call back such products, generally at a considerable cost for the producer and the sellers, which they must bear (Art. 1206§2).

1708 It is worth noting that this chapter provides for an aggravation of the producer's or the seller's liability in the form of *punitive damages* (s. above §323) which the victim is entitled to claim in addition to the compensation of its damage in two cases (which may cumulate; cf. above §324): if the producer or the seller failed to take the containment measures directed by Art. 1206, or took ineffective measures, which includes untimely ones, and in case the defect caused the victim's death, or a "serious health damage".

Punitive damages are foreseen by Art. 179§2 which expressly requests that punitive damages rest on a specific legal basis however (s. above §323). Art. 1207 provides such a basis. As such, this additional remedy affirms the Chinese legislator's determination to hold accountable the producers of defective products together with any other party, namely, not only sellers, but also other liable third parties, which may cause, facilitate or aggravate the damage caused by such products. 1709

§61. Liability for Environmental Pollution and Ecological Damage

Once again, Chapter 7 of the book on liability for illicit acts on environmental damage (Art. 1229 to 1235) is a good example of the Chinese Civil Code's modernity as it reflects the evolution of society's challenges, in particular China's which, as the world's new factory, has become a major pollution emitter. Yet environmental pollution liability is mostly unmatched by older western civil codes, among which the Swiss one[774]: indeed, while most, if not all, western jurisdictions including Switzerland have developed a dense body of environmental protection-related laws and regulations, the Swiss Civil Code itself is silent about it. 1710

The first article of the chapter affirms the basic principle by which the author of environmental damage shall be liable for it (Art. 1229). The *victim* may be any third-party, be it a private civil subject or the State which, as universal owner of the land and natural resources in China[775], is interested in the first place. 1711

That being so, one should recall that the land and natural resources are already protected by *real rights* against damage in general, if not specifically against pollution. Thus, with respect to environmental liability, the State is not only concerned as victim, but also as author: the authorities must preserve the value 1712

---

774 The Swiss Civil Code does contain certain specific liability regimes which can indirectly address environmental damage, including the liability of the animals owner (CO Art. 56; potentially applying to cattle breeding-related pollution, etc.), the liability of the building's owner (CO Art. 58; potentially applying to pollution caused by the operation of a plant, etc.), and the liability of civil servants (CO 61; potentially applying to pollution resulting from the negligence of a civil servant). However, environmental liability is mostly addressed by specific secondary legislation.

775 S. above Chap. 3 §16.II, State-, Collective- and Private Property.

of State property (Art. 259§1) and are liable for its destruction (Art. 258; s. above §420).

1713 The law further protects natural resources given out in *usufruct*: they shall be used reasonably (Art. 326§1, 328 and 329; s. above §458), which implies that their natural environment shall be protected.

1714 In case of *construction usufruct*, the purpose of the use of the land (Art. 348§2, item 4) is of the essence: it must prescribe a *rationale use* of the land; any change is subject to the competent authority's approval (Art. 350). The requirement of rationale use extends, among other things, to the protection of the environment and, generally speaking, the prohibition to damage the usufruct, as well as compliance with the law (Art. 346; s. above §§476 and 477).

1715 Besides, the *general rules on contracts* mandate the parties to "avoid wasting resources, polluting the environment and destroying the ecology during performing the contract" (Art. 509§2; s. above §617).

1716 That reminded, getting back to the environmental liability of Art. 1229 ff., the latter regime, namely, Art. 1230, arguably differs from the foregoing in the sense that it seems to provide for a *hardened regime* as compared to the real law-related regimes recalled above or to the general civil liability regime.

1717 However, the drafting of Art. 1230 is ambiguous. It provides that, in case of ecological damage, "the author *shall* assume the burden to prove that it should not be liable, or that its liability could be mitigated under certain circumstances as provided for by law, or to prove that there is no causation between its conduct and the damage" (our emphasis). In this translation, "shall" corresponds to the Chinese verb 应当 yīngdāng, which is also translated as "must", "ought to" or "be supposed to", but can also be translated in the less affirmative form of "should". However, it is generally considered that 应当 yīngdāng carries the same mandatory weight as "shall" and is more affirmative than "should", i.e., the same way "shall" is more affirmative than "should"[776].

1718 Yet Art. 1230 does not say that the victim does not bear the burden to prove the liability as requested by the general regime of liability for illicit acts, i.e., the damage, the illicit act, the causation and the author's fault (s. above §§1642 and 1643). Moreover, Art. 1230 brings nothing new, since the author's burden to prove that some of these four conditions are not met, that none of them are met (s. above §1642 *in fine*), or any mitigating or exonerating circumstances, is already foreseen by the Code anyway (s. above §1651).

1719 Therefore, one may arguably conclude that, by mandating, contrary to the general regime of liability, the apparent author to prove that it is not liable, instead

[776] "Should" is generally translated as "应该" yīnggāi.

of the victim proving that the alleged author is liable, by using the verb "shall" (应当 yīngdāng) to that effect, by singling out, thus stressing, causation, although it is already one of the generic conditions of liability anyway, by prominently displaying Art. 1230 on the beginning of Chapter 7, immediately after Art. 1229 posing the principle of environmental liability, the Chinese legislator intended to provide for a *reversal of the burden of proof of causation.* Such reversal is expressly permitted by Art. 1165§2 (s. above §1645). If so, it would affirm the Chinese legislator's reinforced commitment to protect the environment.

As it does, this provision seems to create a *double presumption*, since causation breaks down into two sub-links: *first*, that the apparent author of the damage is deemed to be the actual author of the apparent cause of the damage; *second*, that the apparent cause is deemed to have actually caused the damage. Both presumptions are subject to the *proof of the contrary*, whose burden Art. 1230 places on the apparent author's shoulders. 1720

In other words, one may infer from Art. 1230 that it may be enough for the victim to merely render *plausible* that a third-party caused pollution, while the latter would bear the burden of proving that it is not liable. Of course, the general environmental liability regime is further qualified, often in considerable detail, in secondary legislation. However, until the interpretation of the Chinese Civil Code has solidified, the foreign investor operating a potentially polluting business would be well advised to be aware of the potential challenges posed by the environmental liability regime, to use enhanced caution, and to foresee adequate preventive measures. 1721

As noted, Art. 1230 permits the apparent author to invoke any of the *mitigating* or *exonerating circumstances* foreseen by Art. 1173 to 1177 by considering various circumstances which may mitigate or exonerate the apparent author's liability. They include the victim's fault (Art. 1173 and 1174), third-party's fault (Art. 1175) and emergency (or urgency; Art. 1177). Urgency mirrors the general provisions on civil liability (Art. 182 and 184; s. above §328); moreover, although they are not recalled in the general provisions on liability for illicit acts, these circumstances are complemented by force majeure (Art. 180; s. above §327) and *negotiorum gestio* (Art. 183; s. above Chap. 7 §54, Negotiorum Gestio), both of which are also foreseen by the general provisions on civil liability. The fault of a third-party is expressly addressed by Art. 1233. 1722

Likewise, *joint liability* is already governed by the general regime of liability for illicit acts (Art. 1168 to 1172; s. above §§1650) and the chapter on civil liability contained in the First Book of the Code on general provisions (Art. 177 and 178, s. above §§329 to 332). However, Art. 1231 further qualifies it by adding specific factors which may be taken into account for determining the relative liability of the co-authors, such as the type of pollutant, its 1723 concentration, its emission amount, the method used for assessing ecological damage, its scope and the degree of such damage. This list is not exhaustive.

1724 In case of *intentional damage*, Art. 1132 entitles the victim to request *punitive damages*. As recalled about product liability (s. above §1708), the latter's principle is foreseen by Art. 179§2, which expressly requests that punitive damages rest on a specific legal basis however (s. above §§323 and 324). Art. 1132 provides such a basis. As such, this additional remedy affirms once again the Chinese legislator's determination to hold polluters accountable. Even though this provisions expressly refers to voluntary damages and does not mention negligence, one may further anticipate that a Chinese court may consider *gross negligence* as akin to voluntary and, therefore, as equally justifying punitive damages.

1725 *Remedies* are addressed by Art. 1234 and 1235. They include compensation for *damnum emergens* and *lucrum cessans*, temporary or permanent; investigation, appraisal and evaluation costs (which can be considerable); cleaning and restoring; and preventing measures against expansion and reiteration (Art. 1235). In case of restoration, the authorities can set a time limit. If the author has not completed such restoration within the limit, the authorities can mandate a third party in the author's stead, at the latter's expenses (Art. 1234).

1726 In addition, the victim may claim other remedies foreseen by the Code in the general regime of civil liability (Art. 179§1; s. above §322), in the general regime of liability for illicit acts (Art. 1197; s. above §1648) and in real law (Art. 234 to 238; s. above §389).

§62. Extreme Hazards Liability

1727 Chapter 8 on extreme hazards liability (Art. 1236 to 1244) of the Seventh Book on liability for illicit acts, which the Code literally titles "high-risk" liability, is another example of the Chinese Civil Code's embrace of contemporaneous society challenges, where technology has created new risks of an unprecedented scale. Once again, most western civil codes, which were enacted before such risks became prevalent, are at loss to adequately address them, for lack of a specific regime, among which the Swiss Civil Code, and eventually did so through ulterior secondary legislation. By placing a specific regime in a paramount legal instrument like the Chinese Civil Code however, the Chinese legislator has signaled its chief concern for the containment of such risks.

1728 The *definition* of "high-risks" hazards is non-exhaustive and includes risks related to: nuclear activities; aircrafts; flammable, explosive, poisonous, highly radioactive, strongly corrosive, highly pathogenic or other high-risk materials;

high altitude, high pressure or underground excavation activities; high-speed railways; the loss or abandonment of extremely hazardous material; the illegal possession of the same; and the unauthorized entry in an extremely hazardous activity area or an extremely hazardous materials storage (Art. 1237 to 1243).

The extreme hazards liability regime provides for an *objective* liability: as compared to the general regime of liability for illicit acts, whose principle is posed by Art. 1165, Art. 1236, it mentions neither the precondition of the author's *illicit act*, nor that of its *fault*. Therefore, it suffices that the author has caused the damage by engaging in an extremely hazardous activity, even though the exercise of that activity may have been licit, and despite the author may not have committed any fault, for the author to be automatically liable. In other words, the two only conditions to be met are *damage* and the *causal link*. 1729

Objective liability is expressly permitted by Art. 1166, subject to a specific legal basis which Art. 1236 provides. Besides, however objective, the extreme hazards liability of Chapter 8 does take the (absence of) fault of the objective author into account in specific cases discussed below (s. below §§1732 to 1739), in accordance with the general regime of liability for illicit acts of Art. 1165§2 (s. above §§1641 to 1647). 1730

Each case of extreme hazards liability provides for specific mitigating or exonerating circumstances, most of which amount to a *reversal of the burden of proof.* Such circumstances are *the victim's intentional fault*, *force majeure* and a *third-party's fault*, in accordance, once again, with the general regime of liability for illicit acts (Art. 1173 and 1174; s. above §1651) and civil liability (Art. 177 and 178; s. above §§327 and 329 to 332; compare also with the similar regime provided for contractual liability; s. above §§837 to 839). 1731

Thus, the objective author may be exonerated if it can prove that *the victim has intentionally caused damage* resulting from a nuclear, aircraft, extremely hazardous material or extremely hazardous activity hazard. This provision aims at acts such as terrorism, sabotage or vandalism. 1732

Art. 1239 (extremely hazardous material) and 1240 (extremely hazardous activity) do not only provide for the exoneration of the objective author because of the victim's intentional fault but extend such exoneration to *gross negligence*. Art. 1238 (aircraft hazard) does not mention gross negligence, however; therefore, one should conclude that this omission is deliberate, and that the victim's gross negligence may not be invoked as an exonerating circumstance by aircraft operators. However, in such case, the operator would be conceivably entitled to ask for a reduction of indemnity under the general regime of liability for illicit acts (s. above §1651). 1733

The objective author may further be exonerated because of *force majeure* in case of damage resulting from nuclear, extremely hazardous material or 1734 extremely hazardous activity hazard. Specifically, in case of nuclear damage, Art. 1237 mentions a war, an armed conflict or a riot. While Art. 1239 (extremely hazardous materials) and 1240 (extremely hazardous activities) do not, one may assume that any such circumstances could be successfully invoked for those two cases too. Again, Art. 1238 (aircraft hazard) does not mention force majeure; therefore, one should conclude that this omission is deliberate and that force majeure may not be invoked as an exonerating circumstance by aircraft operators.

1735 The *fault of a third party* is taken into account in two cases: in case of loss or abandonment of extremely hazardous material (Art. 1241), and in case of illegal possession of the same (Art. 1242). In the first case, if such material has been handled by a third-party (designated by the law as "the manager"), such manager shall be liable in the stead of the owner. In the second case, the illegal possessor shall be. However, both are subject to joint liability with the owner if the latter was at fault. The notions of joint liability and fault in this context are discussed in the following paragraphs.

1736 The Code foresees *joint liability* in the same two cases: loss or abandonment (Art. 1241) and illegal possession (Art. 1242) of extremely hazardous material. In the case of Art. 1241, if such material has been handled by a manager, the latter shall be jointly liable with the owner if, as noted in the preceding paragraph, the owner was also at fault. In the case of Art. 1242, if the owner and the manager were also at fault, they shall be jointly liable with the illegal possessor. Joint liability conforms with the general regime of liability for illicit acts (Art. 1168 to 1172; s. above §1650).

1737 As mentioned, in the case of Art. 1241, the owner must have been at *fault*, whereas in that of Art. 1242, the manager must too. Art. 1242 characterizes such fault as the author having lacked to exercise a "high duty of care" or "high degree of care" (尽到高度注意义务 jǐn dào gāodù zhùyì yìwù). While Art. 1241 falls short to provide such characterization, one may assume that the standard of Art. 1242 also applies to Art. 1241 and that this notion equates to that of gross negligence[777].

1738 Likewise, Art. 1243 (unauthorized entry into an extremely hazardous area or in a storage for extremely hazardous material) exonerates the objective author if it can prove that it took sufficient safety precautions and gave sufficient warnings.

---

[777] Irrespective of the national law considered, gross negligence is traditionally distinguished from light negligence according to the following standard: gross negligence *must* not happen, while light negligence *should* not happen.

In other words, with Art. 1241, 1242 and 1243, the extreme hazards liability regime, which fundamentally creates an objective liability, reintroduces the notion of fault as a condition to the objective author's liability in case a third-party has effectively caused the damage, provided the author can prove that it was not at fault: inasmuch, because the Chinese legislator intended this regime to be harder than the ordinary one, such temperance remains subject to a *reversal of the burden of proof*, as compared to the ordinary regime of liability for illicit act under which the victim, not the author, bears the burden of proving the latter's fault (Art. 1165; s. above §§1642 and 1643). 1739

Secondary legislation may set a maximum compensation amount or *cap* for the damage caused by certain hazards. In particular, extremely hazardous activities are typically insured, whereby such insurance is required by law, and such regulation may mandate both a minimum and a maximum compensation. These caps are legal, let alone because any such insurance cover would generally rest on a mandatory legal basis; Art. 1244 expressly acknowledges it. However, according to Art. 1244, such caps, even while provided by or grounded on another law or regulation, shall be *ineffective*, and the extreme hazards liability regime of Chapter 8 shall prevail anyway in case the objective author acted intentionally or was grossly negligent. 1740

Most, if not all, of the areas listed by Chapter 8 as entailing risks qualified as "extreme" are areas in which foreign investors are frequently, and heavily indeed, invested[778]. While specific secondary legislation and regulations abound, foreign investors must be aware that the Chinese Civil Code is on top of the legal hierarchy in that respect, and that it sets a mostly objective liability regime, harder than the general one of liability for illicit act[779]. 1741

---

778 Examples include nuclear power plants, chemical plants and high-speed trains.

779 On the last chapter (not numbered) or section of the Chinese Civil Code on supplemental provisions (Art. 1259 and 1260), following its last book on liability for illicit acts and closing the Code, s. above §114.

Chap. 9 Company Law

§63. Introduction

Chinese company law mainly rests on the eponymous Company Law. Its current version is the second revision of the fourth amendment of the original 1993 law; it was issued on 29 December 2023 and is effective as of 1 July 2025. As such, it replaces the preceding version of 26 October 2018 which came into effect the same day; however, the latter remains applicable to some extent: the current law provides for a gradual replacement, which we will outline below. 1742

The Company Law governs the two main types of companies available under Chinese law, which are the *limited liability company* and the *shareholding company* (also translated as "company limited by shares", "stockholding company", "stock company" or simply as "corporation"; we will use "shareholding company" throughout this chapter). 1743

In order to regulate the other forms of companies available under Chinese law, namely, *partnerships* and *representative offices*, the Company Law is mainly complemented by the Partnership Enterprise Law of 27 August 2006 effective as of 1 June 2007, and by various regulations on foreign representative offices; the contractual partnership (which is not a form of company) is governed by the Chinese Civil Code. Abundant secondary legislation applies and will be mentioned where appropriate. 1744

The 2023 Company Law is a logical development of the major overhaul which aimed at the modernization of Chinese law, including foreign investment law, over the recent years. It is a milestone which follows the FIL issued in 2019 effective as of 2020, and the Chinese Civil Code issued in 2021 effective as of 2022. While to enhance the attractiveness of China as target for foreign investment was only one of the factors which motivated that overhaul, it was an important one, nevertheless. 1745

The most notable change brought about by the FIL is that it mandates FIEs, which had typically existed so far in the form of JVs (EJV or CJV) or of a WFOE, to transform into one of the forms made available to domestic investors by the Company Law, i.e., the limited liability company, the shareholding company, or the partnership (FIL Art. 31). 1746

As explained in the foreign investment law chapter of this book (s. above §§30 to 32), this change purported at establishing a level playing field for both foreign and domestic investors. As such, FIEs do not enjoy anymore the special status which those dedicated laws had granted them so far. Generally speaking, 1747 with some exceptions, they do not enjoy anymore the privileges once granted to foreign investors such as favorable tax treatment, etc., either.

1748 As a result, the three laws applying to FIEs until the inception of the FIL were abolished by the same as of its promulgation, i.e., on 1 January 2020 (FIL Art. 42§1). FIEs had five years, until 31 December 2024, to transform themselves. While former JVs kept being governed by the same laws, however abolished, until 31 December 2024 (FIL Art. 42§2), since 1 January 2025, they are governed by the laws applying to whichever company form into which they chose to transform themselves. Transitory issues will be discussed later in this chapter.

1749 In Chinese company law like in other areas of the law, *terminology* issues abound. To start with, "company" as used in common language in the sense of formal business organization (whatever "formal", "business" and "organization" mean) is not a notion which easily lends itself to a definition, also in Chinese law. The Chinese Company Law narrowly defines "company" (公司 gōngsī) *stricto sensu* as either the limited liability company or the shareholding company (s. below §1771); however, Chinese business organizations are by far not limited to these two types. Neither is their incorporation or registration, nor the fact that they enjoy legal personality or not, that they may have limited liability or not, that its stakeholders may be personally liable or not, that they may be for-profit or not, or that they may have their own property or not provide for clear criterions enabling to sort out business organization between companies and non-companies.

1750 Chinese law does refer to the notion of "enterprise" (企业 qǐyè) however, which covers not only the limited liability company and the shareholding company (and included, before the reform introduced by the FIL, JVs and the WFOE), but also the partnership enterprise. "Corporation", which is often used, in the English common language, interchangeably with "company", but may also specifically refer, in certain jurisdictions, to the shareholding company, does not correspond to a defined notion in Chinese law either.

1751 In this chapter, we will use indifferently "company", "corporation" or "corporate entity" in the common sense of formal business organization *lato sensu*, not necessarily as referring, in Chinese law, to the limited liability company, the shareholding company and the partnership enterprise (as well as, whenever now abrogated forms of companies may be referred to, to JVs and the WFOE), and will clarify the related terminology whenever necessary.

1752 Chinese and Swiss law share the same fundamental distinction between *capital companies* (Fr.: "sociétés de capitaux"; Ger.: "Kapitalgesellschaften") and *partnerships* (Fr. "sociétés de personnes"; Ger.: "Personengesellschaften"), whose liability is, in principle, limited to their capital for the first and personal for the second. In Chinese law, the first category includes the limited liability company and the shareholding company; the second the partnership enterprise. The representative office, which is a special form of branch, is neither.

The Chinese *limited liability company* ("Ltd.") corresponds to the "société à responsabilité limitée" ("Sàrl") in French and the "Gesellschaft mit beschränkter Haftung" ("GmbH") in German; the *shareholding company* corresponds, in Swiss law, to the "société anonyme[780]" ("S.A.") in French and the "Aktiengesellschaft" ("A.G.") in German. 1753

The Chinese *partnership enterprise* entails two sub-forms: the first, the *general partnership*, corresponds, in Swiss law, to "société en nom collectif" in French and the "Kollektivgesellschaft" in German; its other sub-form, the *limited liability partnership* (not to be confused with the limited liability *company*), corresponds to the "société en commandite" in French and to the "Kommanditgesellschaft" in German. In addition, unlike Chinese law, Swiss law provides for an alternative form of the limited liability partnership, enabling it to divide its capital in shares and to be organized like a shareholding company: the "société en commandite par actions" in French and the "Kommanditaktiengesellschaft" in German; Chinese law does not enable it. 1754

The *contractual partnership* which, although it is not a form of company, will be addressed together with the partnership enterprise given their similarity, corresponds to the "société simple" in French and the "einfache Gesellschaft" in German. 1755

Swiss law also provides for the *cooperative* (Fr.: "société coopérative"; Ger.: "Genossenschaft"), which is a corporate entity consisting of persons or enterprises aimed at promoting or safeguarding the economic interests of its members, or which is founded for charitable purposes; Chinese law provides for rural cooperatives and urban cooperatives. Cooperatives fall outside of the scope of this book and will not be discussed. 1756

Associations (Fr.: "association"; Ger.: "Verein"), which can generally be described as groups of individuals or entities united for a common non-commercial purpose, enjoy legal personality but are not companies either. Therefore, although they are known both in Chinese and Swiss law, they will not be covered in this book. So will *foundations* (Fr.: "foundation"; Ger.: "Stiftung"), also known in both jurisdictions (and often compared, in common law, to the *trust*, 1757

---

780 "Société anonyme" literally translates in English as "anonymous company" since it is free to choose its name, which enables its shareholders to remain anonymous, as opposed to partnerships, which must bear the name of their partners; unlike its Chinese, English and German equivalents, its name in French does not contain a reference to its capital or shares.

although they differ), which purport at allocating assets to the benefit of a special goal and, like associations, enjoy legal personality but are not companies.

1758 *Sole proprietorships* (Fr.: "entreprise individuelle"; Ger.: "Einzelunternehmen") are, by definition, not companies, which suppose two or more investors. While, both in China and in Switzerland[781], they can be registered, they do not enjoy a legal personality distinct from its proprietor; moreover, in China, only Chinese citizen can. Therefore, they will not be covered in this book either

1759 *Branches* (Fr.: "succursale"; Ger.: "Zweigniederlassung") will be addressed below in the subsection on the general provisions of the Company Law; so will *subsidiaries* (Fr.: "filiale"; Ger.: "Tochtergesellschaft"), although this latter concept, as a company form, is, unlike in Chinese law, somewhat alien to Swiss law. Moreover, *branches of foreign companies* are specifically governed by Chapter 13 of the Company Law (s. below Chap. 9 §64.XI, Branches of Foreign Companies).

1760 Finally, there is no obvious equivalent, in Swiss law, to the Chinese *representative office of foreign enterprise* (s. below Chap. 9 §67, Representative Offices), which can be described as a sub-type of branch of foreign companies, but with limited scope; namely, it may not earn profit, even though there are some exemptions. Chinese branches of foreign companies and representative offices of foreign enterprises do not overlap, however; they are governed by separate regimes. Both forms will be further compared at the end of the chapter of this book on representative offices (s. below §§2386ff.)

1761 We have omitted certain specialized and relatively marginal Chinese company types (s. above note 97) whenever we considered that they exceed the scope of this book. Swiss legal entities are listed at CO Art. 927. As one can see, Chinese and Swiss company law structurally differ inasmuch as Swiss company law is entirely (but for secondary law) contained, for capital companies, in the Swiss Code of Obligations and, for partnerships *lato sensu*, in the Swiss Civil Code; comparatively, as outlined, solely the contractual partnership is governed by the Chinese Civil Code; the limited liability company and the shareholding company (including State-owned companies and branches of foreign companies) are governed by the Chinese Company Law, while the partnership enterprise, the representative office and the other forms of enterprises mentioned above are governed by separate, *ad hoc* laws.

1762 This chapter will continue by extensively commenting on the Company Law, i.e., the limited liability company, the shareholding company and its general

[781] In Swiss law, only the registration of sole proprietorships is regulated; it is governed by CO Art. 931 and 945 and ORC Art. 16 to 39.

provisions. It will then address partnerships, JVs, representative offices and variable interests entities[782].

§64. The PRC Company Law

I. Introduction

The 2023 revision of the Company Law has introduced significant changes compared to the precedent 2018 version. These amendments impact on capital contributions, corporate governance, shareholder rights, company establishment, and liquidation procedures. It represents the most comprehensive overhaul of the Company Law since 2005, aimed at modernizing the legal framework, promote transparency, and facilitating business operations in China. These changes will be discussed as appropriate throughout this chapter. 1763

The 2023 Company Law is the centerpiece of Chinese company law. It entered into force as of 1 July 2024. As intended by the FIL, it is equally relevant to domestic and foreign investors. As far as the latter are concerned, it is equally relevant to FIEs which already existed before 1 January 2025, that is the cut-off date beyond which the FIL mandated all WFOE and JVs to transform into a limited liability company, a shareholding company or a partnership (s. above §32), and for those which have been or will be registered thereafter. Indeed, practice shows that the majority of pre-2025 FIEs are transforming into, and that new FIEs incorporate as, either a limited liability company or as a shareholding company; partnerships and representative offices only play a marginal role[783]. 1764

The Company Law has been continuously clarified in five *Provisions of the Supreme People's Court* on Several Issues Concerning the Implementation of the Company Law (I)-(V). The areas they cover include: the company establishment, capital contributions, types of companies, and organizational structure (Interpretation I); shareholder rights and obligations, company governance, and internal decision-making mechanisms (Interpretation II); company property and creditors protection, transactions by company officers, and company registration issues (Interpretation III); company resolutions, shareholders' information rights, profit distribution, preemptive rights, and shareholder derivative actions (Interpretation IV); and updates and clarifications based on recent legislative amendments and judicial practice, including dispute resolution, 1765

---

[782] On *private equity investment funds*, which are not a corporate form, however, s. below note 926.

[783] On the transitional period, s. also above, note 7.

shareholder litigation, and enforcement of company law provisions (Interpretation V).

1766 Finally and recently, on 30 September 2025, the SPC released a *Draft Interpretation* on Several Issues Concerning the Implementation of the Company Law for public comments. This 90-points draft purports at a comprehensive integration and revision of the existing Provisions, marking the first systematic update to China's judicial interpretations of the Company Law since their gradual issuance following the entry into force of the Company Law in 2006. Its promulgation is expected sometime in 2026.

1767 The provisions of the Company Law can be grouped into four sets: the two main sets apply to the limited liability company and to the shareholding company specifically, i.e., to their formation, their operation and the transfer of their equity. The two remaining sets contain general and special provisions applying to either type of company. We will outline general provisions first, followed by the regimes governing each type of company; special provisions will be addressed last. The Provisions and the Draft Interpretation exceed the scope of this book and will not be covered; the reader can refer to the list of topics they address (s. above §1765) in order to complement the following outline however.

II. General Provisions

1768 The general provisions in the sense intended in this chapter of the book are not limited to the chapter of the same name in the Company Law (Chapter 1, Art. 1 to 28), but extend to Chapter 2 of the law on company formation (Art. 29 to 41) as well as to Chapter 15 (Art. 265 and 266) containing supplemental provisions, all of which are of general application to both the limited liability and the shareholding company.

1769 General provisions include definitions, several provisions on liability other than those contained in Chapter 14 of the Law on liability, provisions on bylaws, the company name, domicile, business scope and legal representative, the transformation of the company from a limited liability company to a shareholding company and vice-versa, provisions on subsidiaries and branches, resolutions, employees, the company's general duties, shareholders and the shareholders' meeting. The company registration forms a whole chapter (Chapter 2). The last chapter titled "Supplemental Provisions" only contains further definitions, and the law's transitory regime.

1770 We will first address miscellaneous basic provisions, followed by provisions applying to shareholders and the shareholders meeting. Liabilities, which will regroup various provisions scattered around Chapter 1 of the law, will be outlined in the last subsection of this chapter of the book.

A. Basic Provisions (Within the General Provisions)

To start with *definitions*, "company" in the Company Law is to be understood as a limited liability company or a shareholding company registered in China (Art. 2). It is further defined as an enterprise enjoying legal personality and, as such, owning assets, on all of which it is liable (Art. 3)[784]. 1771

The company *bylaws* (A.K.A. articles of association) must comply with the law; they bind the company itself, as legal subject, together with its shareholders, directors, supervisors, and senior executives[785] (Art. 5). Among other things, they mention the company *domicile*, which is the place of its principal office (Art. 8; s. also Chinese Civil Code, Art. 63 and above, §129), and its *business scope*, which can be only be modified by the bylaws, subject to the approval of the competent authority (Art. 9). 1772

A company must have a *name*, which must comply with the law and is protected by the same (Art. 6). In English, a Chinese limited liability company must include either the abbreviation "Ltd." or its short name "Limited" in its name; a shareholding company "Corp." or "Corporation" (Art. 7). Comparatively, Chinese writing does not allow for abbreviations or acronyms the way Latin languages do; it only provides for short names. Therefore, in Chinese, a limited liability company must include, in its name, either the full name of its form, 有限责任公司 yǒuxiàn zérèn gōngsī, which literally translates as "limited liability company" (while in English "limited" suffices), or its short name, 有限公司 yǒuxiàn gōngsī, which is the equivalent of "Ltd." In English, "Sàrl" in French and "GmbH" in German (Art. 7); a shareholding company must include, in its name, either the full name of its form, 股份有限公司 gǔfèn yǒuxiàn gōngsī, "Corporation", or its short name 股份公司 gǔfèn gōngsī, which is the equivalent of "Corp." in English, "S.A." in French and "A.G." in German (Art. 7). 1773

A company is represented by its *legal representative* (法定代表人, fǎdìng dàibiǎo rén), who must concurrently be one of its directors and may be its chairman (Art. 10). The regime governing the relationships between the legal representative, the company and third parties as well as their mutual liabilities towards one another mirrors Art. 61 and 62 of the Chinese Civil Code, which form the legal basis of Art. 10 and 11 of the Company Law (s. above §§133 to 1774

784 About related terminology issues, s. above §1749.

785 On the definition of senior executive, s. below §§1860 and 2057.

136). The latter provisions further rest on the general regime of the agency contained in Chapter 7 of the First Book on general provisions of the Chinese Civil Code (Art. 161 ff.; s. above Chap. 2 §11, Agency), and that of civil liability.

1775 Art. 10§1 of the Company Law almost paraphrases Art. 61§1 of the Chinese Civil Code; it only differs by implying, rather than directing, that the legal representative should be a "director" (董事 dǒngshì) or a "manager" (经理 jīnglǐ)[786]; although such representative is typically the chairman, another member of the board, the chief executive officer or another senior manager[787], this provision does not mandate it; however, in practice, the registration authority will demand it. The legal representative capacity must conform with the bylaws and the law, even though, unlike Art. 60§1 of the Chinese Civil Code, Art. 10§1 of the Company Law only mentions the bylaws.

1776 Art. 10§2 of the Company Law complements Art. 61 of the Chinese Civil Code by adding that the resignation of the legal representative as an officer of the company carries his capacity as legal representative, and that the company must nominate a replacement within 30 days.

1777 The deeds of the legal representative bind the company (Company Law, Art. 11§1 and Chinese Civil Code, Art. 61§2) which is liable under the law of civil liability for any damage he may have caused (Company Law, Art. 11§3, 1st sentence and Chinese Civil Code, Art. 62§1); any restriction of his powers may not be opposed to against a *bona fide* party (Company Law, Art. 11§2 and Chinese Civil Code, Art. 61§3); the company may recover from its legal representative any loss it suffered by his fault; it may only do so after having indemnified the aggrieved third party however (Company Law, Art. 11§3 *in fine* and Chinese Civil Code, Art. 62§2).

1778 The name of the legal representative is registered and publicly available (s. below §1817). This information appears on the company business license (s. below §1824), which is accessible online on NECIPS (s. below §1822).

1779 However, the scope of the legal representative's powers, such as whether they can sign alone or must sign jointly with another director, is not explicitly registered or detailed in the NECIPS or on the business license. The legal representative is generally authorized to act on behalf of the company and bind it by

786 On the related terminology, s. below §§1858 to 1861.

787 Although this provision is frequently but incorrectly translated as mentioning the "president" or a "director", it literally refers to a "director" or a "manager"; it other words, it does not mandate or imply any requirement that the legal representative must be the chairman or a member of the board of directors. About related terminology issues, s. preceding note.

signing contractual documents, but the specific limitations or requirements for joint signatures are determined by the company's articles of association or internal governance documents, not by public registration. Therefore, depending on the interests at stake or in case of doubt, the third party is advised to seek appropriate assurance from the company. Moreover, while the legal representative is the official representative of the company, it is not necessarily the only one: the company can empower other representatives, subject to the bylaws and the law of agency; however, these other representatives are not listed on the System either.

Comparatively, the Swiss *register of commerce* systematically mentions 1780
whether the representative is entitled to sign alone or must sign with another authorized representative. Moreover, it mentions other authorized representatives and the extent of their powers as defined by law[788]. That said, as will be outlined below, the Chinese System provides other information the Swiss register does not.

As far as FIEs in China are concerned, there is no legal requirement that the 1781
legal representative be a Chinese national, or that he be domiciled in China. However, from a practical point-of-view, it is advisable, not to say necessary, that the company be also represented in China by an adequately empowered officer. Comparatively, in Switzerland, while there is no requirement either that the board members be Swiss citizens or domiciled in Switzerland, the company must register at least one local representative[789].

In case of *transformation* of a limited liability company into a shareholding 1782
company or the other way round, the new company is subject to the law applying to its new form. Furthermore, the Company Law provides for *company succession*, by which the new company inherits the rights and obligations of the old company (Art. 12). These rules are complemented, among other provisions, by Art. 108 (s. below §1946).

The Law further provides the right of the company to create both subsidiaries 1783
and branches (Art. 13). A *subsidiary* (Zh.: 子公司 zǐ gōngsī; Fr.: "filiale"; Ger.: "Tochtergesellschaft") possesses a legal personality independently from its principal or parent; as such it assumes its liabilities independently, namely, from the parent company which controls it, but with which it only forms an economic, not legal, entity, even though they necessarily have legal relationships, let alone because the parent is invested in its subsidiary, but also because they usually enter into mutual transactions such as extending loans or supplying

788 These other authorized representatives are governed, among other provisions, by CO Art. 458 to 465.

789 For the Swiss limited liability company, s. CO Art. 813§3; for the Swiss shareholding company, s. CO Art. 718§4.

goods or services to each other, etc.; however, such relationships are contractual, not organic like between a branch and its parent.

1784 Comparatively, a *branch* (Zh.: 分支 fēnzhī or 分支机构, fēnzhī jīgòu, branch office; Fr.: "succursale"[790]; Ger.: "Niederlassung") does not enjoy a legal personality independently from its principal: its liabilities are, therefore, assumed by its principal. In that respect, the Chinese and the Swiss regimes are similar. The right of setting up a branch mirrors Art. 74§1, 1st sentence of the Chinese Civil Code (s. above §130). *Foreign* branches are specifically governed by Chapter 13 of the Company Law (s. below, Chap. 9 §64.XI, Branches of Foreign Companies).

1785 It may be noted that Swiss law only provides for branches and, as far as the latter are concerned, only for their registration (CO Art. 931 and 952); it does not regulate their operations, which are governed by company law, depending on their form, like any other company. Moreover, unlike the Chinese Company Law, the Swiss Code of Obligations does not even mention subsidiaries, which are occasionally acknowledged in secondary legislation, however.

1786 The provision following that entitling a company to create a subsidiary confirms that a company has the right to *invest* in another "enterprise[791]" (Art. 14§1). Actually, setting up a subsidiary already represents one form by which a company invests in another enterprise. Therefore, Art. 14§1 is to be understood as giving the right to a company to invest in other enterprises other than by creating subsidiaries; namely, it may invest in other enterprises it may not control, and in enterprises which are not "companies", i.e., neither a limited liability nor a shareholding company, which in practice adds the partnership enterprise, even though, as noted, the notion of enterprise is undefined and it is not clear if it extends beyond or is limited to such corporate forms[792].

1787 The second subsection of this provision also serves as a reminder that, in certain cases, the law prohibits the investor from becoming *jointly and severally liable* for the debts of the target. While this provision falls short of identifying any such prohibition, conceivably, for example, antitrust law[793] may prevent such agreements whenever they are deemed to amount to a concentration hampering free competition.

---

790 The literal translation of "branch" in French, "branche", is not used in Swiss French legal language and may, in the common French language, point indistinctively either at a "succursale" or at a "filiale".

791 About the notion of "enterprise", s. above §1750.

792 S. preceding note.

793 Antitrust law is not covered in this book.

Resolutions are the form of juristic acts in which companies formally issue their declarations of will or decisions; they can be adopted either by the board of directors, or by the shareholder's meeting (Art. 15). Art. 15 subjects resolutions to elaborate conditions, which we discuss below in the next subsection about shareholders and the shareholders' meeting (s. below §§1793ff.) 1788

The Company Law generally mandates companies to protect their *employees* (Art. 16), which have the right to set up labor unions (Art. 17)[794]. The company must also set up a cell of the Chinese Communist Party (Art. 18). 1789

Companies must comply with the law and embrace social responsibility. Both notions are liberal. *Compliance* (Art. 19) is not limited to observing laws and regulations but includes accepting the supervision of not only the authorities, but also the general public[795] (e.g., in matters of consumer protection), while it stretches to vague notions including social morality (which can differ from the same notion as understood in other jurisdictions), business ethics and good faith. Likewise, *social responsibility* (Art. 20) is a far-reaching concept relating to the interests of its employees (already mentioned by Art. 16), consumers, "other stakeholders", ecological and environmental protection, and "other public interests". While these norms are to be understood as general injunctions to be clarified and put into practice by secondary legislation, they also leave ample room to the authorities for discretionary interpretation, which they have proven to use whenever they deem that the public interest so commands. 1790

B. *Shareholders and the Shareholders' Meeting*

The last set of provisions (Art. 21 to 28) is the largest of Chapter 1 of the Company Law and addresses shareholders and the shareholders' meeting. The law affirms the foundation of *shareholders' basic rights and liabilities* in its first articles by stating that shareholders are entitled to their share of the company's profit, to participate in important decisions, and to select managers (Art. 4§2). In return, shareholders are liable towards the company's debts: limited liability shareholders are liable to the extent of their subscribed capital contribution, while shareholding company shareholders are liable to the extent of their subscribed shares (Art. 4§1). 1791

This provision is complemented by Art. 21 which recalls the *shareholder's general duties*, namely, compliance with the law and the bylaws, in particular upholding shareholders' rights, and not harming the company (Art. 21). These 1792

794 Company Law Art. 17, which is already detailed, is complemented by the Labor Contract Law which extensively addresses the role of labor unions, s. above §1452.

795 S. above note 689.

injunctions extend to controlling shareholders[796], actual controllers[797], directors, supervisors and senior managers, who may not use their influence or "take advantage" of their "affiliation"[798] or connections against the company's interests (Art. 22). Their liability is discussed in the next section (s. §§1809ff.) It is worth noting that Art. 180§1, which pertains to Chapter 8 of the Company Law on the qualification and duties of directors, etc., is almost identically drafted as Art. 22, but prohibits abuses of "power" instead of "affiliation". The difference between these two provisions is discussed further down (s. §1809).

1793 *Resolutions* are, because they closely, but not only, relate to the shareholders' meeting, already addressed by Art. 15, as noted above (s. §1788). This provision subjects them to somewhat surprisingly elaborate conditions in a chapter dedicated to general provisions and containing general principles rather than detailed operational rules. That level of detail and the position of this provision in the first articles of the Company Law reflects the legislator focus on *corporate governance* and its concern to set safeguards to prevent corporate abuses, which have often proven to be widespread ever since China's Opening.

1794 Art. 15 subjects the *validity* of resolutions to several prescriptions. First and foremost, resolutions must comply with the bylaws. Other than that, as outlined, depending on their subject-matter, resolutions must be adopted either exclusively by the shareholders' meeting, exclusively by the board of directors, or may be adopted indifferently by either.

1795 Specific requirements related to the mode of convocation, the quorum or the majority required for a meeting to be validly held, or a resolution validly adopted, are left to the bylaws, and may be detailed further down in the law, in the chapters dedicated to the limited liability company and the shareholding company. Irrespective of the type of company however, a meeting, whether the shareholders meeting, a meeting of the board of directors, or of the board of supervisors, can be held, and a resolution voted, by "electronic communication" (Art. 24), an expression liberal enough to allow for video conference, e-mail or IM[799].

1796 Thus, a resolution regarding an *investment* to be made by the company in another enterprise can be adopted either by the board of directors or by the shareholders' meeting.

---

796 On the definition of controlling shareholder, s. below §2057.

797 On the definition of actual controller, s. preceding note.

798 On the definition of affiliation and the relationship with the abuse of power and Art. 183, s. below §§2070ff.

799 On the general problematic of electronic communications and declarations of will, s. above, Chap. 2 §10.III, Declarations of Will.

The same applies, in principle, to resolutions on any *security* to be provided by the company "for others", which one should understand as meaning provided by the company to a third party (the creditor) to the benefit of another third party (the debtor). However, there are *exceptions* to this principle: if the debtor is a shareholder or an actual controller of the company, then the resolution can only be adopted by the shareholders' meeting (Art. 15§1). Moreover, in such case, said shareholder or actual controller may not vote on the resolution (Art. 15, 1st sentence). Finally, the resolution must be adopted at the majority of the shareholders present at the meeting (*ibid.*, 2nd sentence). 1797

Both investments and securities must comply with any *limits* on the maximum amount of investment or securities set in the bylaws. 1798

The Company Law protects the shareholders, the company and third parties by providing for several cases in which the law renders resolutions *ineffective* in either of the following three ways: they can be revoked, deemed as being void, or as not having formed. 1799

Thus, any shareholder can petition at court for the *revocation* of any resolution if the latter violates the law or the bylaws, or if such shareholder was not regularly notified of the shareholders' meeting at which said resolution was adopted (Art. 26). In the first case (violation of the law or the bylaws), minor defects, i.e., not having a substantive effect, do not qualify for revocation, however. In both cases, the right to petition is subject to a 60-day time limit from the adoption or, in the second case (irregular notification), from the day the shareholder should have known, but latest within one year from the adoption. 1800

Resolutions are deemed as *not having formed* and are, consequently, non-existent in case they were tentatively adopted: without holding either a shareholders' meeting or a meeting of the board of directors; without a vote; while there was no quorum; or while the majority was not attained (Art. 27). 1801

Finally, the content of any resolution, however regularly formed and adopted, violating the law is deemed to be *void* (Art. 26). In other words, such violation does not void the resolution itself which, unlike a resolution which has not formed, exists and keeps existing, but voids that part of its content which violates the law. However, depending on the resolution's content, the extent to which the resolution is voided can conceivably result in effectively voiding the whole resolution. 1802

While Art. 26 expressly provides that the revocation of a resolution results from a court declaration following an application by a shareholder, it is not clear which party is entitled to apply for a declaration that a resolution has not formed or is void. Given the nature of the cases resulting in the resolution deemed not to have formed, Art. 27 implies that shareholders have such right, but does not 1803 rule out that third parties may. Art. 25 is equally silent; however, its nature suggests that any party with a legitimate interest should have the right to apply.

1804 If the resolution has resulted in a registration with the company registration authority, once the court a rendered the declaration mentioned above, the company must reapply to the company authority to the effect of undoing any such ill-founded registration.

C. *Liabilities*

1805 Chapter 1 of the Company Law on general provisions extensively addresses liabilities; however, the related provisions are scattered around the chapter; we regroup them in this subsection. These provisions are further addressed in Chapter 14 of the law, which is dedicated to liabilities and will be discussed later in this book.

1806 The liability regime contained in the Company Law is to be regarded as a *lex specialis* as compared to the general regimes of liability which are civil liability in general (Chap. 2 §12, Civil Liability), contractual liability (Chap. 4 §27, Liability for Breach of Contract) and liability for illicit acts (Chap. 8 , Liability for Illicit Acts ("Torts")), all of which may, depending of circumstances, complement that of the Company Law.

1807 To start with and as mentioned above, it should be recalled that corporate liability rests on the following two fundamental tenets, i.e., that a company is liable for its debts on all its assets (Art. 3§1 *in fine*; s. above §1771), while shareholders are liable for the company's debts: limited liability shareholders are liable to the extent of their subscribed capital contribution, while shareholding company shareholders are liable to the extent of their subscribed shares (Art. 4§1; s. above §1791).

1808 As noted, the company is liable for any damage caused by its *legal representative* (Art. 11§3, 1st sentence and Chinese Civil Code, Art. 62§1); in turn, the latter is liable towards the company for any loss it suffered by his fault (Company Law, Art. 11§3 *in fine* and Chinese Civil Code, Art. 62§2; s. above §1777).

1809 The Company Law further addresses various specific cases of liability, namely, *abuse of power*: a shareholder is also liable if, by abusing its shareholder's rights, it causes any loss to the company or to other shareholders (Art. 21§2). The controlling shareholder, the actual controller, the directors, supervisors and senior managers are equally liable towards the company if they harm the company by taking advantage of their position (Art. 22§2). This latter provision thus indirectly entitles, by implication, harmed shareholders to petition the court to invalidate resolutions adopted by the shareholders' meeting or the board of directors that violate the law, administrative regulations or the bylaws.

Art. 23 further seeks to prevent *fraud* by providing for two more cases of liability. First, a shareholder which seeks *debt evasion* by abusing the company for incurring personal debts, thus aimed at both escaping personal liability and limiting its shareholder's liability to its contribution, shall be jointly and severally liable for the damage he so caused to the company (Art. 23§1). If that shareholder uses more companies to that effect, each other company is liable for the damage caused to the first (Art. 23§2). This provision thus introduces both *vertical and horizontal veil-piercing*[800], consistently with global standards. 1810

Second, in case of suspected *appropriation* by a sole shareholder of the company assets, the former shall be "jointly and severally" liable for the debts of the company, unless it can prove that its allegedly own assets are independent from the company assets (Art. 23§3). Evidently, a sole shareholder cannot be "jointly and severally" liable with itself. What the law means is that, if the company assets are insufficient to satisfy its creditors, they may claim his personal assets in accordance with the "penetration principle[801]". 1811

As noted above, beyond these general provisions, corporate liability is further addressed extensively in Chapter 14 of the Law (s. below Chap. 9 §64.XII, Liability of the Company). 1812

D. *Company Registration*

Chapter 2 of the Company Law (Art. 29 to 41) is dedicated to company registration. The purpose of this section of the book is not to outline registration procedures: the law is explicit enough, and the purpose of this book is not to provide practical advice. Instead, we will outline some salient features foreign investors ought to be aware of. 1813

In China, legal entities, i.e., mainly, the limited liability company, the shareholding company and the partnership enterprise[802], must register with the competent registration authority, which is the State Administration for Market Regulation (SAMR) 国家市场监督管理总局 guójiā shìchǎng jiāndū guǎnlǐ zǒngjú. Previously, company registrations were handled by the State Administration for Industry & Commerce (SAIC) 国家工商行政管理总局 guójiā 1814

800 This principle is known, in English, as "piercing the corporate veil" and, in Chinese law, as the "penetration" principle (透析原则 tòuxī yuánzé; s. above §1606).

801 S. preceding note.

802 S. above §789.

gōngshāng xíngzhèng guǎnlǐ zǒngjú, which was merged into the SAMR in 2018. In practice, reference to the local Administration for Market Regulation (AMR) 市场监督管理局 shìchǎng jiāndū guǎnlǐ jú (often referred to in English as AMR "Bureau") is used at the provincial and municipal levels.

1815 Foreign investors are subject to special, extensive additional registration requirements applying to *foreign-invested enterprises* which are detailed in the FIL and have been outlined above (s. Chap. 1 §5.V, Registration). These requirements do not replace the registration regime contained in the Company Law but complement it.

1816 The first articles of Chapter 2 of the Company Law are concerned with the registration application (Art. 29 to 32); they are detailed and explicit.

1817 It is worth noting that the registration is *published* on NECIPS (s. below §1822), which as explained is the equivalent of the register of commerce (like, e.g., in Switzerland) or of companies (like, e.g., in the Hong Kong SAR) in other jurisdictions. The information disclosed includes: the company name, domicile, registered capital and business scope, as well as the names of the legal representative, of the shareholders of a limited liability company, and of the founding shareholders (designated in the Company Law as "promoters"[803]) of a shareholding company (Art. 32).

1818 Art. 32 is complemented by Art. 40 which details the former's requirements. Thus, Art. 40§1, item 1) further requires the publication of the amounts of subscribed capital *contribution* and paid-in capital contributions of each shareholder, as well as of their *form*, of their *date* in the case of a limited liability company, and of the number of subscribed *shares* of each promoter in the case of a shareholding company. The reason why this provision does not require the date of the capital contribution for a shareholding company is evident, since a promoter can only contribute at its inception (s. below §§ 1818, 1922 and 1925), while the law does not require the publication of the names or shares of subsequent shareholders; in contrast, it requires the publication of the names and shares of the shareholders of a limited liability company, whether initial or subsequent, which explains why the date of their contribution is needed. In other words, the subsequent shareholders of a shareholding company enjoy anonymity, while its promoters and the shareholders of a limited liability company do not.

803 The Company Law designates the founding shareholders of a shareholding company as "promoters" (发起人 fāqǐ rén) and those of a limited liability company simply as "shareholders" (股东 gǔdōng), not promoters; the Law does not specifically refer to the founding shareholders of a limited liability company.

1819 This understanding is confirmed by Art. 40§1, item 2 which also requires the publication of any *modifications* of equity or shares of (any, initial or subsequent, which this provision does not individualizes) shareholders in the case of a limited liability company, and that of promoters (but not of shareholders, which this provision does not mention) in the case of a shareholding company. The law does impose additional publication requirements to the shareholding company, in particular to listed ones, however, including to non-promoters or subsequent shareholders, which will be mentioned together with the shareholding company regime (s. below §§1999 and 2000).

1820 Likewise, Art. 40§1, item 3 requires the publication of any *license* the company may have been granted, as well as of any modification or cancellation "among others", which indicate that any other information significantly affecting the license should also be published. Finally, Art. 40§1, item 4 generally requires the publication of any other information which may be mandated by other laws or regulations.

1821 The omission to publish such information, the publication of incomplete or untrue information and the omission to publish modifications are subject to administrative *penalties* (Art. 251; s. below §2197).

1822 As briefly mentioned above (s. §§52 to 55), there are two such databases or "systems" which can be equated, to some extent and with some differences, to the register of commerce or of companies found in most other jurisdictions: the *Enterprise Registration System* (ERS) 企业登记系统 qǐyè dēngjì xìtǒng and the *National Enterprise Credit Information Publicity System* (NECIPS) 企业信用信息公示系统 qǐyè xìnyòng xìnxī gōngshì xìtǒng[804]: Both systems serve distinct but complementary purposes[805]: the first (ERS) manages information related to the company registration and its business license. The second (NECIPS) is designed to provide public access to the company's registration, credit-related information[806] and its regulatory records. Only NECIPS is public; it is freely accessible online. The registered data is shared by the authorities

804 NECIPS is commonly known, in Chinese, under the short name of 企信网 qǐ xìn wǎng.

805 Both systems are managed by SAMR. MOFCOM and SAMR jointly oversee the system, which streamlines reporting and avoids duplicate submissions to different agencies.

806 NECIPS provides information about a company's operations, legal compliance, administrative penalties, and public credit records. It does not assign an explicit credit score or rating, but discloses data-such as blacklists, redlists, annual reports, and regulatory violations that can be used to assess a company's creditworthiness and trustworthiness.

through a third system known as the *Departmental Information Sharing System* (部门信息共享系统, bùmén xìnxī gòngxiǎng xìtǒng)[807].

1823 Comparatively, the Swiss register of commerce publishes the same information than Art. 32, including the names of the shareholders of a limited liability company, but not of the shareholders, founding or not, of a shareholding company[808]. However, it is possible to know the names of the founders of a shareholding company by requesting a copy of the foundation act, which contains the names of the founding shareholders, to the register of commerce; no legitimate interest is needed. Moreover, the register does not publish any of the information requested by Art. 40 either, except changes of partners of a limited liability company. The Swiss register of commerce also publishes the names, position and signatory powers of the directors or the board and of the managers empowered to act as representatives of the company however, which NECIPS does not. In contrast, unlike the latter, the Swiss register of commerce does not publish information related to the creditworthiness[809] of the company, other than the registered capital and whether bankruptcy proceedings are pending. Creditors can obtain a list of pending claims from the debt recovery and bankruptcy office, provided they can demonstrate a legitimate interest[810] however.

1824 The company registration notably results in the issuance of its *business license* (营业执照 yíngyè zhízhào; Art. 33). The business license has far more significance in China than in other jurisdiction, namely, in Switzerland, where only a limited number of industries subject to enhanced supervision by the authority[811] must comply with stringent licensing requirements. Under the Chinese Company Law, the date of issuance of the business license is the date of formation of the company (Art. 33§1 in fine), whose civil capacity as a legal person simultaneously comes into existence (Chinese Civil Code, Art. 59; s. above §128). The business license mentions the name, address, registered capital and legal representative of the company (Art. 33§2). It can be issued either in printed or in electronic format (Art. 33§3).

1825 Any *modification* of the business license must be registered (Art. 34§1), in compliance with the requirements detailed at Art. 35, resulting in the issuance

---

807 NECIPS was implemented in 2014; the Departmental Information Sharing System in 2016; the Enterprise Registration System in 2022. The information sharing system is referred to, for example, in the Regulation on the Registration of Resident Representative Offices of Foreign Enterprises (2024 Revision) (Art. 5§2; s. below §2361).

808 The shareholder of a limited liability company is known, in Swiss law, in French as "associé" and in German as "Gesellschafter"); that of a shareholding company as "actionnaire" and "Aktionär".

809 S. above note 806.

810 LP Art. 8a.

811 For example, banks, insurances, certain healthcare providers, public transports, etc.

of a new, updated business license (Art. 36). The formation of a *branch* (Art. 38; s. above §§130 and 1784) and the *termination* of the company (Art. 37) must also be duly registered.

The requirement of a business license is recalled to foreign investors in the FIL (s. above Chap. 1 §5.IV, Business License). However, before applying for a business license, any foreign investment must be pre-approved (s. above Chap. 1 §5.III, Pre-approval). In particular, any investment falling into the Negative List will result in the business license not to be issued (s. above §§40 to 42). 1826

In addition to the business license proper, most activities in China are subject to additional, specific, industry-related licenses. However, "business license" as referred to by the Company Law only refers to the license issued with the registration of the company. Certain activities across more than one industry may call for more than one specific license. 1827

Any fraud in the registration of the company shall result in the revocation of the business license (Art. 39). Failure to register a modification cannot be opposed to a *bona fide* third party (Art. 34§2). Frauds are further punishable under Chapter 14 of the Company Law on the company liability (s. below §2196). 1828

III. Limited Liability Company

The regime governing the limited liability company is divided into two chapters: Chapter 3 bears on the formation and the organization of the limited liability company; Chapter 4 focuses on shares transfer. In Chapter 3, the formation and the organization each correspond to one section. Once again, the purpose of this chapter of the book is not to comment on the regime of limited liability company in every detail, but to explicit its structure and draw the attention of foreign investors on certain salient features of particular significance to them. It will also highlight key differences between the limited liability and the shareholding company. 1829

A. Formation

A limited liability company may be formed by a sole shareholder or up to 50 *shareholders* (Art. 42). Comparatively, the shareholding company may be formed by up to 200 promoters (Art. 92)[812]. Unlike Art. 92, which specifies outright that half of the promoters of a shareholding company must be 1830

812 There is no such maximum in Swiss law.

domiciled in China, the Company Law is silent about any such *domicile* requirement for the limited liability company, which suggests that all the shareholders may be domiciled abroad[813].

1831 The two next provisions (Art. 43 and 44) are concerned with the *liability* of the sole shareholder or of the shareholders relating to the company *formation*. The drafting of Art. 44 is rather convoluted and may be clarified as follows. The law distinguishes between whether the company has been formed eventually, and whether its formation failed. Thus, if the company *succeeds* in being formed, it is liable for any damage related to its formation (Art. 44§1). If, on the contrary, the company *fails* to be formed, then its sole shareholder is liable, or its shareholders are jointly and severally liable (Art. 44§2).

1832 Furthermore, when a shareholder acted in its own name, but for the formation of the company (which eventually succeeded in being formed), the victim or creditor is free to hold either the shareholder or the company liable (Art. 44§3). The company and the non-faulty shareholders may recover any loss from the faulty shareholder (Art. 44§4). In order to facilitate the settlement of any such liability, the shareholders can, before the formation, and are advised to indeed, enter an *agreement* governing their liability related to the formation (Art. 43), which conforms with the general regime of liability (s. above §320).

1833 The formation of the limited liability company revolves around a set of basic *corporate documents* which are the bylaws, the shareholders register, related minutes of shareholders meetings, related resolutions adopted at the meetings of the board of directors, related resolutions adopted at the meetings of the board of supervisors, and the financial accounting reports, as well as the shareholders or contribution certificates.

1834 The *bylaws* are to be drafted in the course of the company formation by the shareholders (Art. 45) who must sign (or seal[814]) them (Art. 46§2). The bylaws must comply with the law; they bind the company (Art. 5; s. above §1772). Their content is mandated by law. Other than the items already mentioned in the general provisions of the Company Law (*ibid.*), they must contain the names of the shareholders, the amount, form and date of their capital contribution[815] (Art. 46§1, items 4 and 5), the company organization, and the designation of the legal representative[816].

---

813 About the domicile of the *legal representative*, which is not to be confused with that of shareholders, under Chinese and Swiss law, s. above §1781.

814 S. above §581.

815 This information is published, s. above §§1817 and 1818.

816 S. above note 815.

The company *organization* must be detailed: the bylaws must not only describe 1835
its structure (board of directors, management, committees, etc.), but also the function and formation of its various components, as well as the internal regulations by which they are governed (Art. 46§1, item 6). The regulations related to the legal representative must address both its designation and change (*ibid.*, item 7). They extend to the shareholders meeting's deliberation and voting procedure (Art. 66§1; s. below §1867), as well as to the election of the directors (Art. 68; s. below §1871). The shareholders meeting may add other items (Art. 46§1, item 8).

The company must maintain a *shareholders register* (Art. 56). This document 1836
is materially important since it entitles the shareholders registered in it to claim their shareholder's rights. The information it must contain is detailed and includes, other than the name and address of each shareholder, the amount of both their subscribed and paid-in capital contribution, as well as their form and date; the serial number of the *shareholder or contribution certificates*, which the company must issue to each shareholder and whose content is also prescribed by law (Art. 55), and the date at which they obtained or lost their status of shareholder.

The company management further takes minutes of shareholders' meetings, 1837
issues the resolutions adopted at the meetings of the board of directors, the resolutions adopted at the meetings of the board of supervisors, and keeps financial accounting reports. All of these, together with the bylaws and the shareholders' register, are subject to the *right of consultation* of the shareholders, which have also the right to copy them (Art. 57§1).

The shareholders further enjoy an *extended right of consultation* of the account 1838
books and accounting vouchers (Art. 57§2, 1st sentence). This right is subject to a written and motivated request (*ibid.*, 2nd sentence), which the company may refuse if it believes that it is abusive; if so, it must motivate so in writing, within 15 days of the request (*ibid.*, 3rd sentence). The shareholders may file at court against such refusal, whether explicit or silent (*ibid.*, 4th sentence). Besides, the shareholders may mandate a third party, such as an accounting firm or a law firm, to consult such records (Art. 57§3). They must respect the secrecy of any information the records may contain (Art. 57§4). The right of consultation extends to subsidiaries (Art. 57§5).

Other than the above, the section on formation is chiefly concerned by the *pay-* 1839
ment of the capital contribution and the consequences of its non-payment.

The *registered capital* is the total of the capital contributions subscribed by the 1840
shareholders and registered with the registration authority (Art. 47§1, 1st sentence). Each shareholder must complete the payment of the share it subscribed within the time schedule set in the bylaws (Art. 49§1). The registered capital

must be paid within *five years* of the formation, subject to the bylaws (Art. 47§1, 2nd sentence). The drafting of this provision suggests that the bylaws can provide for certain payment modalities and for a time limit shorter than five years, but not extend it beyond five years. Moreover, if the company is in default, its creditors may request the shareholders to complete the payment of their contribution earlier than set by the bylaws (Art. 54).

1841 The five-year time limit for capital contribution was introduced by the 2024 revision of the Company Law (which simultaneously abolished minimum registered capital requirements for the limited liability company and the shareholding company, s. below §1844). In the past, the 2005 Company Law had set a time limit which was generally of two years. That limit was abolished with the 2014 Revision, upheld by the 2018 Amendment. Shareholders could freely agree among themselves and specify the period for capital contribution in the bylaws; there was no legal maximum; some companies set payment terms to ten, 20 or more years, or even left them indefinite. The Chinese legislator eventually acknowledged that that freedom had led or could lead to abuses, and reintroduced a time limit in the 2024 Company Law, which it set to five years.

1842 The *transitory regime*[817] at the end of the 2024 Company Law (Chapter 15, Supplemental provisions, Art. 266) provides for a voluntary gradual adjustment for companies registered before it came into effect of 1 July 2024, but whose capital contributions have not yet been entirely paid. However, if such adjustment is unreasonable, the competent authority can order it.

1843 There is no such time limit for the shareholding company since the promoters' contributions must be fully paid before the company can be registered (s. below §1925); nor is there one for the other subscribers (s. below §1939 and 1941)[818]. The time limit related to the limited liability company reflects the Chinese legislator's intent to be more flexible for the limited liability company than for the shareholding company owing to the former's smaller size, while ensuring that the capital contributions will eventually be paid.

1844 The law or the authorities can alter such limits and subject the registered and the *paid-in capital* to specific rules, namely, to a minimum *registered capital amount*[819], however (Art. 47§2). This reservation is to be regarded as exceptional. The 2024 revision of the Company Law abolished the general requirement for a minimum registered capital amount, both for the limited liability

817 S. also above, note 7.

818 Therefore, although Art. 266 refers to "companies", practically, this provision only applies to the limited liability company.

819 Such minimum is the sole rule Art. 47§2 specifies among rules it may subject the registered capital to, but only mentions generically, suggesting that it may impose rules other than a minimum to the paid-in capital.

company[820] and for the shareholding company[821]. That said, issues to consider to the effect of determining the amount of the registered capital are discussed below about the shareholding company (s. §§1916 to 1918), where they may be more acute considering that the capital of a shareholding company is typically much larger than that of a limited liability company.

The *contribution* must be paid on a bank account opened in the limited liability company's name (Art. 49§2, 1st sentence). The contribution can be remitted in renminbi or in convertible foreign currencies. 1845

Alternatively, the Company Law expressly permits contributions to be paid *in kind* (A.K.A. "non-currency" contributions; Art. 48§1). Such contributions can take the form of intellectual property (licenses, transfer of technology, technical support, etc.), land use rights, equity (equity swaps), and "claims". As indicated by the expression "such as" on the beginning of this enumeration, this list is not exhaustive; likewise, the liberal reference to "claims" suggests that any form of contribution is permissible, provided it meets the two following conditions however: first, any such contribution is subject to a mandatory[822] *appraisal*, which the registration authority will closely scrutinize, while the applicant can expect the authority to be conservative to the effect of verifying that such contribution is neither under- nor over-evaluated (Art. 48§2, 1st sentence). Other laws or regulations may provide for such appraisal[823] (Art. 48§2 *in fine*). Second, it must be legally *transferred* (Art. 48§1): a mere commitment is insufficient[824]. Second, the law can exclude certain forms of contributions (Art. 48§1 *in fine*). If either of these conditions is not fulfilled, the contribution 1846

---

[820] This amount was of RMB30'000 for a sole shareholder limited liability company, and of RMB100'000 for a multiple shareholders company. Comparatively, Swiss law mandates a minimum of CHF20'000 for the limited liability company (irrespective of whether there is a sole or there are multiple shareholders), which must be entirely paid-in at the registration (CO Art. 773).

[821] S. below §§1915ff.

[822] Such appraisal is optional for the partnership, s. below §2226.

[823] That is typically the case of mergers and acquisitions (s. Interim Provisions on the Takeover of Domestic Enterprises by Foreign Investors, Art. 14§1), where the law also provides, among other things, for equity swaps (*ibid.*, Art. 27).

[824] Chinese law has not always been so liberal. Under the 1993 Company Law, contributions in kind could not exceed 20% of the registered capital and were limited to "industrial" property rights and "non-patent" technologies, along monetary and physical assets contributions. The 2005 Amendments expanded them to "intellectual" property rights; they retained the 20% limit but introduced flexibility by requiring only 30% minimum cash contribution (indirectly limiting in-kind contributions at 70%). The 2013 reforms removed the 20% limit and allowed for contribution up to 100% of the registered capital. Finally, while a proper assessment of the in-kind contributions had always been required, the 2023 revision qualified it by requiring a monetary valuation, together with legal transfer of such contributions.

will be deemed invalid, and expose the shareholders' liability (Art. 49 *in fine* and 50 *in fine*; s. below §1849).

1847 Art. 49§2 requires shareholders to "complete property rights transfer procedures under applicable laws". The Company Law itself does not detail such procedures: they are governed by other specific laws, depending on the type of asset. To name but a few typical in-kind contributions subject to registration requirements, one may mention real property and land use rights; patents and trademarks assignment agreements; equity pledges and secured transfers of movable assets, etc. (s. above §438). For each of these areas of the law, the reader is invited to refer to those chapters of the book detailing the related procedures; detailed registration procedures exceed the scope of this book and will, therefore, not be covered.

1848 Shareholders remain liable towards the company as long as they have not fully paid their share (Art. 49§3). The Company Law provides for a detailed mechanism in case of a shareholder's *default*, i.e., if it fails to fully and timely pay its contribution: first, after the formation, the board of directors must *check* whether any contribution is missing (Art. 51§1). If so, it must issue a formal *demand* (*ibid.*, *in fine*). If such demand fails, the company must set a *grace* deadline for payment, of minimum 60 days from the demand (Art. 52§1, 1st sentence). If the shareholder fails again, the board may take a resolution by which the company issues a notice of *forfeiture*[825] to the defaulting shareholder forfeiting the latter from its equity from the day of the notice (Art. 52§1, 2nd and 3rd sentences). The company must then either *transfer* the equity to another shareholder, or *cancel* it and *reduce* its registered capital accordingly (Art. 52§3). The defaulting shareholder may resist forfeiture by filing at court within 30 days of the notice (Art. 52§4).

1849 Failure to comply with the registered capital payment mechanism results in several cases of *liability*. The defaulting shareholder is liable towards the company (Art. 49 *in fine*), whether it did not pay in full, or whether the value of its in-kind contribution is insufficient (Art. 50). However, the other shareholders are jointly and severally liable for the shortcoming (Art. 50 *in fine*). Yet if the board of directors fails to comply with its obligation to check the contributions and issuing a demand to any defaulting shareholder, the directors are liable towards the company for any damage resulting thereof (Art. 51 *in fine*). If, in case of forfeiture, the defaulting shareholder's share is not transferred and the registered capital not reduced, the other shareholders are, according to the principle mentioned above, also liable for compensating the missing contribution,

[825] On the notion of forfeiture, s. above §§337 to 339.

in proportion to each share (Art. 52§3 *in fine*). In addition, failure to contribute results in *administrative penalties* (Art. 252; s. below §2198).

After the registered capital has been entirely paid, shareholders are prohibited to "illegally" *withdraw* their contribution (Art. 53§1); this pleonasm implies that they may do so, but only if any such withdrawal has been permitted by the shareholders meeting or the board of directors acting within the scope of their competences. If not, the shareholder must return its contribution (Art. 53§2, 1st sentence); if it fails to, it shall be liable, together with any director, supervisor or senior manager who facilitated such withdrawal (Art. 53§2). This precaution addresses abuses by which unscrupulous shareholders frequently left the company like an empty shell after its formation, to the detriment of its creditors. Like failure to contribute, illegal withdrawals result in *administrative penalties* (Art. 253; s. below §2198). 1850

Like a shareholding company, a limited liability company can also issue *bonds*. Their offering is governed by Chapter 10, which is outlined below (s. Chap. 9 §64.VII, Corporate Bonds). 1851

B. *Organization*

The second section (Art. 58 to 83), which constitutes roughly half of the first chapter on the limited liability company, is dedicated to its structural organization. It revolves around the three main corporate bodies of the limited liability company, which are the shareholders meeting, the board of directors and the board of supervisors. 1852

The *shareholders meeting* (Art. 58 to 66) is the supreme body of the limited liability company (Art. 58). It is composed of all the shareholders (*ibid.*) A sole shareholder limited liability company is, evident that may seem, dispensed of the meeting (Art. 60). 1853

The shareholders meeting and the shareholders' basic rights and obligation are subject, in the first place, to the general provisions of the Company Law contained in its first chapter, in particular Art. 21 to 28 (s. above Chap. 9 §64.II.B, Shareholders and the Shareholders' Meeting), which are complemented by the provisions outlined below, that specifically apply to the limited liability company. 1854

The shareholders meeting's *powers* stem out of two sources: the Company Law and the bylaws. Even though the Company Law does not explicitly affirm it, the powers it grants to the meeting are to be understood as *minimum* powers. While the shareholders can complement them in the bylaws (Art. 58§1, item 9), they cannot delegate them to the board of directors, even though the principle 1855 of such delegation is provided by the Company Law (Art. 67§2, item 10). Indeed, considering the nature of such powers, such delegation would effectively amount to relinquishing them, except for a single exception, which permits the shareholders meeting to delegate, to the board of directors, an offering of corporate bonds (Art. 59§2).

1856 These minimum powers compare to those prevailing in most jurisdictions. They include electing and replacing directors[826] and supervisors and deciding their remuneration[827]; discussing and approving the reports of the board of directors, of supervisors, as well as profit distribution and loss compensation plans; deciding the increase or reduction of the registered capital, offering corporate bonds, the merger[828], division, dissolution, liquidation of the company or the modification of its form, and amending the company bylaws (Art. 59§1, items 1 to 8)[829]. As noted, the bylaws, which are issued by the shareholders (Art. 45; s. above §1834), can allow for additional powers (Art. 59§1, item 9).

1857 In principle, the shareholders must formally meet to decide any such matters; however, if they unanimously agree before such meeting, they may issue a resolution without *meeting*, provided such resolution is signed or sealed by all of them (Art. 59§3). While dispensed of holding a meeting (s. above §1853), a sole shareholder must also issue and record formal resolutions (Art. 60).

1858 The Company Law sets out the *modalities* of the shareholders' meetings in detail (Art. 61 to 66). At this point, it is suitable to clarify the *terminology* used in Chinese law for the company officers, which poses both issues of *translation* and *definition*. The following paragraphs aim at dispelling frequent misunderstandings resulting from inaccurate translations in English, as well as from false friends in French and German.

1859 A *director* in the sense of member of the board of directors of the company is designated in *Chinese* as 董事 dǒngshì. The *board* of directors is, therefore, quite logically, called 董事会 dǒngshìhuì, where 会 huì stands for "board". Likewise, the *chairman* of the board of directors is known as 董事长 dǒngshì zhǎng, which literally translates as the "important" director in the sense of the Latin expression *primus inter pares* ("first among peers"). The *general*

---

826 Cf. Art. 68 *in fine*.

827 Art. 129 further imposes a shareholding company to regularly disclose, to its shareholders, the information on the remuneration received by its directors, supervisors and senior executives, while Art. 136§2 sets additional requirements to listed shareholding companies (s. below §1978).

828 S. Art. 219, which provides for exemptions however (s. below §2128).

829 A qualified majority of two-thirds is required for amending the bylaws, increasing or reducing the registered capital, and for a merger, division, dissolution, or modification of the form of the company (Art. 65§3; s. below §1867).

manager of the company, who is not a member of the board but an executive officer, is merely called, in the Company Law, 经理 jīnglǐ or "manager", but contextually designated as 公司经理 gōngsī jīnglǐ[830], i.e., literally, "company manager"; however, in common Chinese language, a general manager is called 总经理 zǒng jīnglǐ where 总 zǒng stands for "general"; finally the *deputy general manager* is designated as 副经理 fù jīnglǐ where 副 fù stands for "deputy" or, contextually, as 公司副经理 gōngsī fù jīnglǐ, "company deputy manager".

In *English*, "director" (of the board) is also translated as "member" of the board; 1860
"chairman" of the board of directors as "president"[831]; "manager" as "officer", "senior officer", "executive", "executive officer" or "senior executive officer", when not used indistinctively for both managers and directors; "general manager" as "chief executive officer" or "CEO", and "deputy general manager" as "deputy CEO". Inaccurate translations, namely, confusions between board and executive positions, abound; therefore, foreign investors and lawyers are advised to refer to the Chinese terminology. In this book, we will refer, in English, to "director" for 董事 dǒngshì, "chairman" for 董事长 dǒngshì zhǎng, "CEO" for 总经理 zǒng jīnglǐ, and "manager" for 经理 jīnglǐ.

French and German, specifically Swiss legal French and German, are other 1861
sources of confusion. In Swiss law, a director is known as "administrateur" in French and "Verwalter" in German; the board of director as "conseil d'administration" in French and "Verwaltungsrat" in German, i.e., literally "administration council"[832], whereas a mangager is called "directeur" in French and "Direktor" in German which, confusingly, does not mean, and is never used in the sense of "director" (of the board) in English. The chairman is called "président" in French and "Präsident" in German[833].

The *definition* of certain of these positions, i.e., of directors, supervisors and 1862
senior executives, as well as of the related notions of "controlling shareholder" and "actual controller" is further addressed in Chapter 8 of the law on the qualification and duties of directors, supervisors, and senior executives of a company as well as in the last chapter (Chapter 15) on supplemental provisions. They will be discussed about the former chapter (s. below Chap. 9 §64.VI, Qualification and Duties of Directors, Supervisors, and Senior Executives).

---

830 S. Art. 67§1, item 8, Art. 75 and 128. It is worth noting that 公司经理 gōngsī jīnglǐ is frequently but incorrectly translated as "president", which adds to the confusion.

831 S. above note 830.

832 In Swiss law, a director of the board can also be designated as "membre du conseil d'administration" or "Mitglied des Verwaltungsrats", i.e., literally, as *member* of the board of directors.

833 S. above note 830.

1863 That said, a shareholders' meeting must be properly *convened* by the board of directors (Art. 63§1) 15 days in advance (Art. 64§1), unless the bylaws provide, or the shareholders have agreed otherwise (Art. 64§1). Absent specification, this notice is to be understood as applying both to regular and special meetings (s. below §1866). The law does not specify whether a resolution adopted during a meeting which was not, not timely or otherwise not properly convened is subject to *revocation* (Art. 26; s. above §1863).

1864 Other than that, the Company Law does not set specific conditions as to the form of the convocation, which the shareholders are free to choose and is usually defined in the bylaws, as the formulation of Art. 64§1 suggests ("except as otherwise prescribed in the company bylaws")[834]. However, the shareholders must be "notified" (Art. 64§1), which suggests a minimum degree of formalism. Be that as it may, while, in the past, shareholders meeting were typically convened by registered mail, it can be said that, nowadays, especially in China, convocations by e-mail have become the rule, as expressly permitted by Art. 24 (s. above §1795). Eventually, the issue is one of proof since, unless the company can prove that a meeting was properly convened, it exposes any resolution taken in the course of such a meeting to revocation[835].

1865 The Company Law provides in detail, by prescribing a pecking order, where the shareholders' meeting[836] cannot be presided over by its chairman, or is not convened by the board of directors, in which case the vice-chairman or a director shall replace the chairman, the supervisors convene the meeting in place of the directors, and the shareholders replace the supervisors in case the latter default, subject to defined majority rules (Art. 63).

1866 There are three types of shareholders' meetings: regular meetings, special meetings and the initial meeting. *Regular meetings* are held according to the bylaws (Art. 62§2); they are typically held at least once a year. *Special meetings* are foreseen by the law and must be held whenever one or several shareholders representing at least tenth of the voting right, at least one third of the directors, or the board of supervisors call for it (Art. 62§3). The *initial meeting* is, as its name makes clear, the first meeting held after the formation of the company; because the bylaws have, in principle, not yet been adopted, the law prescribes that it is convened and presided over by the majority shareholder (Art. 61).

---

[834] Company Law Art. 46, item 6, which mandates the contents of the bylaws, refers, in the most general terms, to "rules of procedure".

[835] On the general problematic of electronic communications and declarations of will, s. above, Chap. 2 §10.III, Declarations of Will.

[836] About the meetings of the *board of directors*, s. below §1875.

The *deliberation* and *voting* procedure is to be defined in the bylaws, unless the Company Law provides otherwise (Art. 66§1). The latter does not prescribe deliberation procedures; however, it does set, in certain cases, qualified majorities. Unless a qualified majority applies, resolutions are adopted at the *simple majority* of voting rights (Art. 66§2)[837]. *Voting rights* are proportional to the capital contribution of each shareholder; however, the bylaws may provide otherwise (Art. 65)[838]. Thus, a *qualified majority* of two-thirds is required for amending the bylaws, increasing or reducing the registered capital, and for a merger, division, dissolution, or modification of the form of the company (Art. 66§3). The resolutions taken by the shareholders meeting must be recorded in *minutes*, which must be signed or sealed by the shareholders which attended the meeting (Art. 64§2). 1867

It is worth noting that the Company Law falls short of requiring a *quorum*[839], i.e., a minimum number or proportion of shareholders or voting rights attending the shareholders' meeting as a precondition to the *voting*'s validity. That is explainable by the fact that the law does not refer to the votes or voting rights of shareholders attending the meeting, but merely to "voting rights", i.e., to the 100% of the voting rights of the company. As such, the number or proportion of shareholders attending the meeting is irrelevant. 1868

Anyway, the Company Law expressly permits *distant voting* by electronic communications Art. 24; s. above §1795), which renders the notion of quorum, that dates back to the days before modern communication means, when it was still necessary to physically attend a meeting or to be formally represented to vote, largely obsolete, since it is now possible to attend a meeting online from virtually anywhere, with as little as a smartphone which have, nowadays, become a commodity. 1869

Moreover, by referring to "shareholders *representing* (so many, e.g., two-third) of the voting rights", the law implies that shareholders attending the meeting shall not only vote for themselves but may also "represent" (by "proxy") absent shareholders' voting rights. Since the law is silent about them, the modalities of any such representation (which could, conceivably, also restrict it) are to be 1870

---

837 However odd, the law also prescribes that, even in the case of a sole shareholder limited liability company, resolutions must be sanctioned by its vote (Art. 66§2).

838 Unlike the shareholding company regime (s. below §§1953 and 1990ff.), the limited liability one does not specifically provide for *class shares*. However, Art. 65 suggests that, by permitting non-proportional voting rights, the bylaws could effectively create shares comparable to class shares.

839 Company Law Art. 73§2 and 80§3 do mention a quorum in relation with the boards of directors and of supervisors.

prescribed in the bylaws. Be that as it may, nothing prevents the shareholders' meeting to provide for a quorum in the bylaws.

1871 The *board of directors* is regulated by Art. 67 to 75. Its composition is detailed by Art. 68. In principle, it must consist of at least three members, but small limited liability company may dispense with a board and have only one director who doubles as chairman (Art. 75); the law does not define what "small" is deemed to be, however. One of the directors must act as chairman[840]; the board can have one or more vice-chairmen; the election procedure is defined in the bylaws[841].

1872 The *powers* of the board of directors compare to those in most other jurisdictions and include convening shareholders' meetings, reporting to the same and executing its resolutions (generally by delegating such execution to the management); deciding the business and investment plans; formulating plans for profit distribution, loss compensation, increase or reduction of the registered capital, offerings of corporate bonds, merger, division, dissolution, or modification of the form of the company (and submit them to the shareholders' meeting's approval, s. Art. 59 and above §1856); deciding the internal management structure and developing a management system, the hiring or dismissal and the remuneration of the CEO; and approving the hiring or dismissal and the remuneration of the deputy CEO, as well as of the CFO proposed by the CEO (Art. 67§1, items 1 to 9). The bylaws or the shareholders' meeting can provide for additional powers (*ibid.*, item 10).

1873 Like for the legal representative (s. above §1777 as well as Art. 61§3 and 11§2), any restriction on the powers of the board of directors imposed by the company bylaws may not be set up against a *bona fide* opposite party (Art. 67§2).

1874 The *term of office* of a director can end in three cases: it reached three years or a shorter[842] limit provided by the bylaws (Art. 70§1), he resigned (Art. 70§3) or was removed[843] by the board of directors (Art. 71§1). However, the director must continue to perform his duties even after the time limit or after he resigned as long as the quorum of the board of directors (Art. 73§2; s. next paragraph) is not met and an election has not been held (Art. 70§2 and 3).

1875 *Meetings* of the board of directors[844] are to be convened and chaired by the chairman; if he defaults, by a vice-chairman, or a director recommended by the

---

[840] A company is represented by its legal representative, who must concurrently be one of its directors who, in turn, can, but must not, be its chairman (Art. 10; s. above §1774).

[841] So must the designation procedure of the legal representative (Art. 46§1, item 7; s. above §1834).

[842] The bylaws may not extend the three-year limit set by the law, however.

[843] Company Law Art. 71 *in fine* entitles a removed director to compensation.

[844] About the *shareholders* meeting, s. above §1865.

majority of his peers (Art. 72). Decisions are taken at the simple majority of directors attending the meeting (Art. 73§2 *in fine*), each of whom has one vote (Art. 72§3); however, unlike to the shareholders' meeting (s. above §§1868ff.), the Company Law does set a quorum, which must be of more than half of the directors (Art. 73§2, 1st sentence). As for the shareholders' meeting, meetings of the board of directors must be recorded in minutes and signed by the directors who attended (Art. 73 *in fine*). Other than that, deliberation and voting procedures are essentially left to the bylaws (Art. 73§1).

1876 The Company Law does not regulate the *management*, other than recalling that the limited liability company may have a "manager"[845] or CEO, which the powers of the board of directors already implies (s. Art. 67, item 8 and above, §1872), and which or who is not mandatory. The management or the manager's powers are defined by the bylaws or the board of directors to which the CEO reports. The manager may attend the meetings of the board of directors, which he shall "observe", although the Company Law suggests that, by doing so, he is mostly to play a passive role[846] (Art. 74§2).

1877 The single feature which distinguishes the Chinese from the Swiss limited liability company is that of *supervisors*. While supervisors have no equivalent in Swiss law, they are mandated by the Chinese Company Law (Art. 76§1); their cost must be borne by the company (Art. 82).

1878 As aptly formulated by Art. 79, a supervisor may "observe"[847] meetings of the board of directors and raise questions or offer recommendations regarding the matters to be resolved by the board of directors. The board of supervisors may, if it discovers any abnormal operations of the company, conduct an investigation and, when necessary, as a preliminary step, engage an accounting firm, among others, to assist in the investigation at the expense of the company. "May" is not to be understood as an option, but as a right and an obligation simultaneously. If the accounting firm, etc. discovers any abnormal operations during the meeting, it should then report to the board of supervisors which, as provided by Art. 79, 2nd sentence, may then decide to conduct an investigation; it may also, based on such observations, ask the board of directors to submit reports on their activities; the latter must honestly cooperate, and may not obstruct the board's endeavors (Art. 80).

1879 The *powers* of the board of supervisors include inspecting the financial affairs of the company, supervising the activities of the directors and senior executives;

---

845 On terminology, s. above §§1859 to 1861.

846 The notion of "to observe" is defined at Art. 187 which hardly helps since it only provides a circular definition. Moreover, it applies to the shareholders' meeting, where the director, etc. shall answer questions from the shareholders.

847 S. above note 846.

recommending the removal of directors and senior executives who violate a law[848] or administrative regulations, the bylaws, or a resolution of the shareholders' meeting (Art. 80, items 1 to 3), and instituting action against the same upon qualified request from the shareholders (Art. 80, item 6, Art. 188 and 189§1, 1st sentence[849]); requiring a director or senior executive whose conduct harms the company to remedy it; proposing the board of directors to convene a special shareholders' meeting (Art. 62; s. above §1866) and, if the board of directors fails to, doing it in its stead; and making proposals at the shareholders' meeting (Art. 80, items 4 and 5). Like for the other bodies of the limited liability company, the bylaws may provide for additional powers and duties (*ibid.*, item 7).

1880 The functioning of the board of supervisors compares in most respects to that of the directors. It consists of three or more members (Art. 76§2, 1st sentence), elected for three years (Art. 77§1, 1st sentence), who may be neither a director nor a senior executive (Art. 76 *in fine*), and includes one or more representatives of the shareholders (Art. 76§2, 2nd sentence). It has a chairman who is elected by the majority of supervisors, and may be replaced by another, recommended by the same majority, if he fails (Art. 76§4). The supervisors' term can be extended like that for directors (Art. 77; s. above §1874). The meetings of the board of supervisors compare to those of the board of directors (Art. 81; s. above §1875).

1881 A limited liability company may dispense with a board of directors in two cases: first, its bylaws may provide for an *audit committee* composed of directors to exercise the same powers than the board of supervisors (Art. 69); inasmuch, the audit committee circumvents the prohibition, signified by Art. 76 *in fine*, to directors to serve concurrently as supervisors. Second, like for the board of directors, small limited liability companies may have only one supervisor, or dispense with it altogether if, in the latter case, the shareholders unanimously agree to (Art. 83). Therefore, in practice, a sole shareholder is not required to have any supervisor. Be that as it may, whenever small companies may consider eliminating supervisors, they should balance the risk of removing one layer of control, thus exposing the liability of the shareholders, directors and senior executives, or making them more vulnerable to frauds. Generally speaking, supervisors reflect the Chinese legislator's concern to reinforce corporate governance, to which they should be considered a valuable addition.

1882 The Company Law further grants special protection to the representation of *employees* within the company's bodies, by mandating that a limited liability company having more than 300 employees must have either one employees'

[848] Such violations include, among other things, noncompliance with Art. 80, s. above §1878.

[849] On Art. 188 and 189, s. below §§2077ff.

representative on the board of directors (Art. 68§1), or representatives on the board of supervisors forming minimum one third or more, as per the bylaws, of the supervisors (Art. 76§2, 2nd sentence ff.) Both provisions detail their election.

C. Equity Transfer

The transfer of the equity of a limited liability company is governed by Chapter 4 of the Company Law (Art. 84 to 90). The transfer regime varies depending on the circumstances in which it takes place. The law contemplates five such cases: freely between shareholders, freely to an outsider, by enforcement, by the company upon request of a shareholder (A.K.A. "buyback"), or upon a shareholder's death. 1883

The *first case* is also the easiest: it is that of the free transfer of equity *among shareholders*, which the law does not subject to any condition (Art. 84§1) other than the updating of the shareholders' register (s. above §1836). 1884

The *second case* is that of the free transfer of equity from a shareholder *to a third party not being a shareholder* (or outsider); it is more demanding. The shareholder must *notify* the other shareholders, which may refuse and instead buy the share themselves (Art. 84§2, 1st sentence). The notification must be detailed and mention the size of the share, its price and the way it will be paid; this list is not exhaustive, as the expression "among other things" indicates (*ibid.*) The other shareholders enjoy a right of first refusal or *preemption*[850] resulting in giving them the right to buy the share at the same conditions it was offered to the outsider (Art. 84§2 *in fine*). The refusal does not need to be motivated. Indeed, because of the accrued personal nature of the limited liability company as compared to the shareholding company, the law protects the other shareholders by entitling them to refuse a new shareholder and stay among themselves, unless they have been provided with sufficient information enabling them to convince themselves that such new shareholder matches their interests and is, therefore, acceptable. It has no equivalent in the shareholding company regime which aims, in contrast with the limited liability company, at ensuring the liquidity of its shares. 1885

The law provides complementary rules in case the other shareholders keep silent, or if more than one of them exercises such right (Art. 84§2, 3rd sentence). Thus, they are deemed to have foregone it if they do not reply within 30 days from the notification, while in case multiple shareholders exercise their right, the purchase is to be proportional to their share if they fail to agree (Art. 84§2, 1886

[850] S. above note 602.

4th sentence). Last but not least, the bylaws may regulate the transfer to outsiders otherwise (Art. 84§3).

1887 The same regime applies to the *third case* which is that of *enforcement*, i.e., in case the transfer is to be enforced by a court pursuant to a judiciary decision, with two differences, which is that the notification is to originate from the court, and that the time limit for exercising the right of first refusal is reduced from 30 to 20 days (Art. 85).

1888 In the *fourth case* and in four circumstances or sub-cases, a shareholder has the right to request the company to *buy back* its share. Three of these circumstances consist in the fact that the *dissenting shareholder* has voted against a resolution adopted by the majority of the shareholders. These resolutions must result either in a decision not to distribute profit, in a merger or acquisition, or in the continuation of the company beyond its statutory duration or dissolution. The fourth circumstance is met when the majority shareholder abuses its rights.

1889 In the *first sub-case* (no distribution of profit), the resolution deciding not to distribute profit must have been approved while the company had not distributed *profit* to its shareholders for five consecutive years, even though it was beneficiary during the same period of time (Art. 89§1, item 1). This provision adds that the profit distribution should meet the conditions set by the Company Law (*ibid., in fine*). Such conditions are to be found further down in the law, in Chapter 10 containing provisions on financial affairs and accounting, which are common to the limited liability company and the shareholding company (Art. 210 to 212; s. below Chap. 9 §64.VIII, Financial Affairs and Accounting of a Company). The law further gives the board of directors of the limited liability company the power to make proposals to the shareholders' meeting to that effect (Art. 67§2, item 4) and, to the latter, that to approve them or not (Art. 59§1, item 4).

1890 In the *second sub-case* (M&A), the transaction approved by the resolution must result in the *merger* of the company with-, or its *acquisition* by-, or the *transfer* of the majority of its equity to another company (Art. 89§1, item 2).

1891 In the *third sub-case* (continuation), the shareholders' meeting approved the continuation of the company despite its *duration*, set in the bylaws, had expired, alternatively, despite a cause of *dissolution* prescribed in the bylaws had occurred, but the resolution adopted amended the bylaws to the effect of extending such duration or overcoming such cause of dissolution (Art. 89§1, item 3).

1892 The *fourth and last sub-case* (abuse) occurs when the majority or controlling shareholder abuses its rights, thus causing damage to the company or the other shareholders, and entitling them to a so-called *oppression-based buyback*. The harm must be "serious". If so, the other shareholders may also request the company to buy their shares (Art. 89§3).

The shareholder and the company must agree on the buy-back. If they have not within 60 days of the resolution, the shareholder must file at court within another 30 days[851]. The systematic of Art. 89§2 and 3 is puzzling. It suggests that those limits only apply to the first three cases, not to the fourth, which appears not to be subject to any such limit. It can be explained by the fact that, absent a resolution as in the first three cases, there is no clear *dies a quo* in the fourth. Moreover, while Art. 89§2 implies that the parties must agree, Art. 89§3 requires a "reasonable price", which Art. 89§2 falls short to. Likewise, one may speculate that the legislator's intent was to stress the protection of shareholders facing an abusive controlling shareholder, although "reasonable" is undefined; anyway, one could not see, in the case of Art. 89§2, the parties agreeing on an unreasonable price. Eventually, in both cases, if the parties cannot agree, the court shall use its discretion. 1893

Finally, in the last and *fifth case* of *death* of a natural person shareholder, the latter is succeeded by his heirs. However, the bylaws may provide otherwise (Art. 90). 1894

The transfer *modalities* including the modification of the shareholders' register, the cancellation of the capital contribution certificate of the transferor, its issuance to the transferee, the latter's shareholder's rights and the related amendment of the bylaws are explicitly detailed in the law (Art. 86 and 87) to which we refer. In any of the four cases of Art. 89, whenever the purchase has been executed, whether consensually or by court order, the shares must be transferred or cancelled within six months (Art. 89 *in fine*). These amendments need not being voted on by the shareholders' meeting (Art. 87 *in fine*). If the company fails to act accordingly, the transferor or the transferee may institute action at court to that effect (Art. 89 *in fine*). 1895

The law specifically contemplates the case where the share is transferred while the *capital contribution* subscribed by the original shareholder has not been paid. The topical provision (Art. 88) distinguishes between whether the transfer takes place before or after the time limit set by the bylaws for completing the contribution. The drafting of Art. 88 is complex and worsened by inaccurate and deceiving translation issues. It can be clarified as follows. 1896

If the transfer occurs *before*, the transferee is liable to pay the contribution or its unpaid balance by said time limit. However, if the transferee defaults, the transferor remains liable for the unpaid portion, even after the transfer. If the transfer occurs *after* the expiry of the time limit, the transferor and the 1897

[851] Art. 89§2 mentions 60 and 90 days respectively. This drafting is deceiving. Both counts start from the resolution; the 90-day limit does not start from the expiry of the 60-day one, as an inattentive reading could mislead. Thus, the shareholder has another 30, not 90 days, for filing at court after the expiry of the 60-day limit.

transferee are jointly and severally liable. However, if the transferee was of good faith, the transferor is solely liable.

1898 Therefore, on balance, it can be said that the law emphasizes the transferor's liability, which cannot simply change its mind after it subscribed and dispose of its share before paying while avoiding liability, unless the transferee was fully aware of the liability it was transferred and pays in the stead of the transferor. This regime applies irrespectively of whether the contribution was entirely unpaid, partly unpaid, untimely paid, or whether the actual value of any in-kind contribution (Art. 48§1; s. above §§1846 and 1847) is inferior to that of the subscribed capital contribution.

1899 Many, if not most, of the features of the limited liability company are replicated, and often elaborated, in the shareholding company regime forming the next two chapters of the Company Law. We may, therefore, frequently refer to the limited liability company while outlining the shareholding company.

IV. Shareholding Company

1900 The shareholding company is governed by Chapters 5 and 6 of the Company Law (Art. 91 to 167). Their structure slightly differs from that of the limited liability company: like for the limited liability company, the first section of the shareholding company regime starts with formation; however, while the limited liability company regime contains one section about the company organization, Chapter 5 of the shareholding company divides the organization regime in two subsections, addressing separately the shareholders' meeting and the board of directors. In addition, a third section contains special provisions on the organizational structure of a listed shareholding company. Finally, like the second chapter of the limited liability company, Chapter 6 of the shareholding company regime addresses shares transfer.

1901 As noted, generally speaking, the shareholding company regime replicates most of the features of the limited liability company, while elaborating and adapting them to the characteristics of the shareholding company. In that regard, it is worth noting that the shareholding company regime contains several *references* to the limited liability company regime, instead of repeating the latter's provisions. However, these references are scattered around Chapter 5 on the formation and organizational structure of the shareholding company, and may be somewhat difficult to identify: therefore, we regroup them here. These are: Art. 98§2 (referring to Art. 48 and 49§2), 107 (referring to Art. 44, 49§3, 51, 52 and 53), 110§2 (referring to Art. 57§2, 3 and 4), 112§1 (referring to Art. 59§1 and 2), 112§2 (referring to Art. 60), 120§2 (referring to Art. 67, 68§1, 70 and 71), and 130§5 (referring to Art. 77).

A. Formation

The difference between the limited liability company and the shareholding company is highlighted from the first provision of the chapter, which states that a shareholding company may be formed either by promotion, or by flotation (Art. 91§1), whereas a limited liability company can only be formed by subscription (s. above Chap. 9 §64.III.A, Formation). 1902

Formation by *promotion* means that a corporation is formed by the promoters subscribing all the shares issued at the time of the formation (Art. 91§2 and 97§1). Inasmuch, in case of formation of a shareholding company by promotion, the promoters do not fundamentally differ from the subscribers of a limited liability company. 1903

The difference in terminology between "promoter" and "subscriber"[852] is justified by the other mode of formation of a shareholding company, which is the formation by *flotation* (also translated as "by fundraising"; Art. 91§3). Indeed, unlike the formation by promotion, the formation by flotation occurs in two stages: in a first stage, the promoters subscribe a portion of the shares issued before the formation, while in a second stage, after the promoters have fully paid their subscribed shares (Art. 96§1, 2nd sentence)[853], the promoters publish a *prospectus*[854] (Art. 100, 1st sentence) together with subscription forms (*ibid.*), and offer the remaining shares to specific offerees or to the public[855] which, if they subscribe, become subscribers, not promoters, and have to pay their shares (Art. 100 *in fine*). 1904

Therefore, a promoter is an original subscriber of the shareholding company that undertook its formation (Art. 93), which distinguishes it from the other subscribers to which the promoters may have offered a portion of the share, whether these other subscribers were selected offerees or the public. No such distinction exists in the limited liability company, where the subscribers are, by 1905

---

852 Formation by promotion is expressed with the verb 发起 fāqǐ, which translates literally as "to initiate"; that by flotation by 募集 mùjí, which translates as "to raise".

853 Moreover, the promoters must fully pay their subscribed shares before the formation (Art. 98§1; s. below §1925). Therefore, until they have paid, they may neither offer shares to the public, nor form the company.

854 The content of the prospectus is described at Art. 154 (Art. 100, 2nd sentence; s. Art. 154§1, items 2 and 3, and below §2008). A prospectus is an invitation to offer (Chinese Civil Code Art. 473; s. above §2009).

855 While the section on the company formation contains certain provisions on the public offering of shares directly related to the formation, the offering is mainly addressed in the first section of the next chapter of the law (Art. 142 ff.), to which one shall refer for issues related to the offering not addressed in this section (s. below Chap. 9 §64.IV.F.1, Offering of Shares).

definition, the original subscribers; there are none others; namely, the law does not provide for the possibility that the original subscribers of a limited liability company offer a portion of the shares to selected offerees or to the public.

1906 The law imposes a double requirement on promoters: they may not exceed 200, half of which must be domiciled in China (Art. 92). Comparatively, while the limited liability company regime also imposes a maximum number of shareholders, it does not impose any such domicile requirement (s. above §1830)[856]. A shareholding company may have a sole shareholder (Art. 92).

1907 As noted above, the promoters are tasked with the formation of the shareholding company (Art. 93§1). They must enter a *promoters agreement* defining their mutual rights and obligations in that respect (Art. 93§2).

1908 Like for the limited liability company, the first task of the promoters is to draft the *bylaws* (Art. 94). Other than the content mandated by the general provisions of the Company Law (s. above §1772), that of the bylaws of a shareholding company is identical to that of a limited liability company (s. above §1834), but for the following differences: because, unlike the limited liability company which only provides for a unique method of formation, while the shareholding company provides for two, the bylaws of a shareholding company must mention the *method of formation*, i.e., whether it was formed by promotion or by flotation (Art. 95, item 3).

1909 Likewise, the bylaws must mention, in addition to the registered capital, both the total number of *shares* issued and, among these, the number issued at the time of formation, as well as the value per share of shares having the same value, known as *par value* shares (Art. 95, item 4; s. below §1987). If particular *classes* of shares (A.K.A. "preferred shares" as opposed to "common shares") are issued, they must mention the number of shares of each such class and their related rights and obligations (*ibid.*, item 5). While the bylaws of the limited liability company must mention the amount of capital contribution of each shareholder, those of the shareholding company must mention the number of subscribed shares of each promoter (*ibid.*, item 6).

1910 The law does not request the bylaws of a shareholding company to detail its *organization*, i.e., to mention "the components of the company and their respective formation methods, functions, and rules of procedure", because such components, formation methods and functions (about the rules of procedure, s. next paragraph) are detailed further down in the law, while they are not in the

[856] There are no such requirements, be it of maximum number or of domicile of the shareholders, in Switzerland either (s. above note 789). About the domicile of the *legal representative*, which is not to be confused with shareholders, under Chinese and Swiss law, s. above §1781.

regime governing the limited liability company. That difference reflects the fact that the limited liability company, which is intended for smaller companies than the shareholding company, is subject to less stringent corporate governance requirements than the shareholding company, and that the shareholders of a limited liability company are, therefore, left more freedom to define its organization.

In contrast, as to its organization and, in particular, its rules of *procedure*, the bylaws of a shareholding company must specifically detail the composition, powers, and rules of procedure of the board of directors (Art. 95, item 7) and of that of supervisors (*ibid.*, item 9), as well as its methods of notification, none of which are required in the bylaws of a limited liability company. 1911

Finally, unlike the bylaws of a limited liability company, those of a shareholding company must include the method of *profit distribution* of the company (Art. 95, item 10), as well as the causes of dissolution and the method of its *liquidation* (*ibid.*, item 11). 1912

Other items which are required to be mentioned in the bylaws for both the limited liability company and the shareholding company include the name and address of the company (Art. 95, item 1), its business scope (*ibid.*, item 2), registered capital (*ibid.*, item 4), the name of the promoters (but not that of the other subscribers) and the form and (although only implicitly) amount of their capital contribution (*ibid.*, item 6), the method of selection of the legal representative and that of his replacement (*ibid.*, item 8), and other matters which the shareholders meeting may consider necessary (*ibid.*, item 13). 1913

As compared to the limited liability company, the *registered capital* of a shareholding company is defined as the capital corresponding to the total of the shares (Art. 96§1), while in the case of a limited liability company, the law refers to the total of contributions (Art. 47§1; s. above §1840). 1914

It should further be stressed that, unlike in other jurisdictions, among which Switzerland, Chinese law does not mandate a *minimum* registered capital for the shareholding company. Historically, Chinese law and regulations mandated such minimum for the limited liability company[857], the shareholding company[858] and FIEs. These requirements were abolished with the 2014 reforms of, 1915

---

[857] S. above §1844.

[858] For shareholding companies, the minimum registered capital requirement was historically of RMB5 million. In Switzerland, it is of CHF100'000, of which minimum CHF50'000 or 20% (whichever is higher) must be paid-in at registration (CO Art. 621 and 622). It may be noted that that requirement was, in China, a multiple of what it is in Switzerland and that its abolishment should, therefore, encourage foreign investment. Comparatively, as noted, it was only of RMB30'000 for the limited liability company (s. above note 820), which also shows China's past emphasis on the latter over the

among other laws, company law. The 2024 revision of the Company Law did not reintroduce these minimums but required the shareholders of a limited liability company to pay their subscribed capital within five years at most[859]. Minimum requirements have been maintained for specific industries however[860]. Therefore, companies are *free* to determine their registered capital based on operational needs and the expectations of stakeholders such as clients, suppliers, and investors. They have to determine such amount themselves. However, such capital must be *adequate*; unless it is, the registration authority, using its discretion, may reject the registration application.

1916 The determination of an adequate registered capital amount is complex as it depends on numerous factors. If insufficient, an inadequate amount may prevent a company from covering its costs, namely, in its initial phase, before it becomes profitable or, for example, to be eligible for certain tax incentives, or for participating to certain tenders. On the contrary, if excessive, it may unnecessarily mobilize financial resources. Moreover, the increase or decrease of the registered capital is, in China, a demanding, lengthy, cumbersome procedure, while injections of cash other than by capital increase may raise tax issues, and returns of cash to the company's foreign investor other than by capital decrease will raise the scrutiny of the foreign exchange authorities, among other potential issues. The shareholders' liabilities, which are commensurate with that amount, are also to be considered. Specialized advisors assist foreign investors to determine it.

1917 Moreover and notably, the amount of registered capital of an FIE may be indirectly determined by the amount of *debt* a company may borrow. That latter amount is apprehended, in Chinese law, by the concept of *total investment*. The related framework only applies to FIEs; it does not apply to-, and there is no equivalent for domestic-invested companies: therefore, it is not addressed by the Company Law, but by secondary legislation dedicated to foreign investment.

1918 The total investment results from the addition of the registered capital and of the amount a company may borrow proportionally to such capital. This regime aims at capital made available by foreign, not domestic, investors or lenders. It was initially governed by the Provisional Regulations on the Proportion of

shareholding company; this difference is much less pronounced in Switzerland than it was in China.

859 Art. 47§1, 2nd sentence; s. above §1840. For the shareholding company, s. below §1925.

860 Regulations imposing minimum registered capital typically relate to industries such as securities, banking or insurance.

Registered Capital to Total Investment of Sino-Foreign Joint-ventures and related regulations issued by MOFCOM and SAFE.

These regulations set maximum ratios between registered capital and foreign debt[861]. In 2017, they were complemented by the so-called "macro-prudential method"[862], which is a formula intended to calculate such ratios, and may yield results that may differ from the ratios of the Provisional Regulations. However, in practice, to this date, the Chinese authorities have been keeping applying the ratios set by the above-mentioned Provisional Regulations most of the time. 1919

Foreign debt must be *registered*, which subjects it to the authorities' scrutiny. In this context, it is also worth being aware that, under the so-called "Thin Capitalization Rules", the Corporate Income Tax Law and its implementing regulations limit the *deductibility of interest* on related-party debt if the debt-to-equity ratio exceeds certain levels[863]. The "equity" in this context is similar to net assets. This measure purports at deterring companies to turn to easy money by borrowing at no cost. 1920

Once the company has determined the registered capital amount and applies for registration, the registration authority will review whether the registered capital is adequate considering the business scope the company simultaneously applied for; if the authority deems that the registered capital is obviously 1921

861 Currently, these ratios range from 70% of registered capital and 30% of debt for a total investment of up to USD3 million, to 1/3 of registered capital and 2/3 of debt for a total investment of USD36 million or more. In other words, the minimum proportion of registered capital decreases gradually as the debt increases. If it would not, foreign investors would have to comply with unsustainable levels of registered capital, and would be practically prevented to borrow large amounts of debt. The full ratios range is not reproduced here as ratios may be subject to change, local practice, the macro-prudential method, and particular cases. Investors are advised to check with the competent authority.

862 This method bases the calculation of the foreign debt limit on the assets and net assets of the company, and apply a leverage ratio, subject to SAFE approval. It can sometimes allow greater leverage than the traditional foreign debt quota. The legal basis of this method is the Notice on Matters Related to Macro-Prudential Management of Cross-Border Financing issued by the PBOC on 11 January 2017 (adjusted on 7 January 2021).

863 Currently, under these rules, companies may not deduct interest on related-party debt if the debt-to-equity ratio exceeds 2:1 for most industries (5:1 for financial institutions). These rules are not explicitly named as such in the Company Law, but derive from a combination of company law provisions on registered capital, administrative measures on capital sufficiency, and specific tax rules addressing debt-to-equity limits in corporate finance. Depending on the context, they are referred to as 资本稀释规则 zīběn xīshì guīzé, 稀释资本规则 xīshì zīběn guīzé, 资本稀释规定 zīběn xīshì guīdìng or 资本薄弱化规定 zīběn bóruò huà guīdìng.

insufficient for its intended purpose, it may reject the application or require alterations.

1922 As noted above (s. §1905), the promoters may not offer, to the public, the remainder of the shares they did not subscribe (Art. 96§1, 2nd sentence) before they entirely paid the shares they subscribed. Offering shares to the public before they have done so may result in penalties, conceivably for endangering public interest (s. below §2202).

1923 Art. 97§1 paraphrases Art. 91§2 (s. above §1903) by reiterating that, where a corporation is formed by promotion, the promoters shall fully subscribe the shares that shall be issued at the time of formation of the corporation. The only difference is that Art. 97§1 adds "as prescribed in the bylaws" which, one should understand, refers to the number of shares issued at the time of formation, which number the bylaws must mention (Art. 95, item 4, 3rd phrase).

1924 If the company is formed by flotation, the promoters must subscribe at least 35% of the total number of shares to be issued at the time of formation. However, the law reserves the cases where it, or administrative regulations, may provide otherwise (Art. 97§2).

1925 As noted (s. above §§1905 and 1922), the promoters must fully pay their subscribed share before the company can be formed (Art. 91§2 and 98§1). This requirement applies to both modes of formation, whether by promotion or by flotation. Inasmuch, the shareholding company differs from the limited liability company since, under the limited liability company regime, the shareholders must pay their share within the time limit set by the bylaws, which can extend up to five years after the formation of the limited liability company (s. above §§1840ff.) Therefore, the registration authority will not register the shareholding company unless the promoters bring proof that they have fully paid their subscribed shares[864].

1926 Furthermore, Art. 98§2 expressly refers to Art. 48 and 49§2 which pertain to the regime of the limited liability company, but which Art. 98§2 applies *mutatis mutandis* to the *form of the contribution* to the registered capital corresponding to the shares they subscribed. Art. 48 and 49§2 provide that a shareholder may contribute either by a monetary (or "currency") payment or in kind (or by a "non-currency" contribution), with a focus on the modalities of in-kind contributions. For detailed comments, we refer to preceding chapter about the limited liability company (s. above §§1846 and 1847).

864 For the time limit within which other subscribers must pay their capital contribution, s. below §§1939 and 1941.

The shareholding company regime provides for the same mechanism, *mutatis mutandis* again, as the limited liability company regime in case of *default* of the promoters or subscribers, whenever they fail to fully pay their capital contribution. Thus, Art. 99, which applies to the shareholding company and provides that, in case of default of one of the promoters, the other ones are jointly and severally liable for the shortcoming, paraphrases Art. 50 that applies to the limited liability company (s. above §1849). Art. 107 further refers directly, without paraphrasing them, to Art. 44 (liability of the shareholders resulting from the formation of the company; s. above §§1831 and 1832), to Art. 49§3 (liability of the shareholders for paying their share; s. above §§1848), to Art. 51 and 52 (forfeiture in case of default of a shareholder to pay its share; s. above §§1848 and 1849) and, eventually, to Art. 53[865] (illegal withdrawal of registered capital; s. above §1850) of the limited liability company regime, to which we equally refer the reader. 1927

Art. 107 mentions that Art. 44, 49§3, 51, 52 and 53 also apply to the "shareholding company", without distinguishing between promoters and other subscribers, thus suggesting that they apply indistinctively to both. However, Art. 99 only mentions the promoters, which implies that the other subscribers are not jointly and severally liable for the shortcomings of one of them. Likewise, because Art. 44 applies to the liability of the shareholders resulting from the formation of the company, it does not apply to subscribers either, since they are not involved in the formation. 1928

In contrast, Art. 49§3 (liability of the shareholders for paying their share), Art. 51 and 52 (forfeiture in case of default of a shareholder to pay its share), and Art. 53 (illegal withdrawal of registered capital[866]) do also apply to the subscribers, being reminded that they must fully pay the shares they subscribed (Art. 100 *in fine*). The shareholders' default or illegal withdrawals also results in *administrative penalties* (Art. 252; s. below §2198). 1929

The payment of the shares offered to the public must be verified by a so-called *capital verification agency*. Such agencies must be legal institutions, and are typically accounting firms (i.e., certified public accountants or CPAs), law firms or other institutions specializing in assets appraisal. They must be specifically licensed to that effect. They incur civil liability and administrative penalties in case of damageable error or omission, intentional or by negligence (Art. 257; s. below §2199). 1930

Once the agency has verified such payments, it issues a *certificate* (Art. 101). This provision does neither specify the content of such certificate, nor to whom 1931

865 Art. 107 does not refer to Art. 50 since the latter is, as noted, mirrored by Art. 99.

866 While this prohibition is restated, for the shareholding company, by Art. 105§2, 1st phrase, the related liability regime is that of Art. 53.

it should be issued. It is, however, not a payment receipt issued to the shareholders, since such receipt is to be issued by the bank entrusted by the company for collecting such payments (Art. 156§2, 2nd phrase). Therefore, one should understand that that certificate confirms that all the shares have been paid, and that it is issued to the company, i.e., to its board of directors.

1932 The drafting of Art. 101 is somewhat confusing for another reason since it literally reads: "after the shares offered to the public are fully paid for, the capital shall be verified..." Such drafting may seem illogical, as it is the mandate of the agency to verify whether the shares have been fully paid or not. The confusion resulting thereof can be clarified by placing this provision in the context of Art. 156, which rules that the company must entrust a bank for collecting the shares payments (Art. 156§1), which bank, after the collection has completed, must not only issue a receipt to shareholders as noted above, but also issue a *certificate of receipt* to "the relevant department" (Art. 156§2). In practice, such relevant "department" is the verification agency which, after double-checking the payments, shall issue in turn, to the company, the certificate foreseen by Art. 101. Finally, upon receipt of the latter certificate, the board of directors issues an announcement once the shares have been fully paid (Art. 156§3).

1933 It is to be further noted, in the same context, that the law only mentions the end of the offering (Art. 151§1, item 3 and 154§1, item 6), not the time limit within which such payment must be made. One may, therefore, assume that it is a matter which the board of directors typically addresses as it decides on an offering (Art. 153).

1934 After the payment of the capital has been verified, the promoters must hold a *formation meeting*. They must do so within 30 days after the capital has been paid (Art. 103§1, 1st sentence). Although the law does not specify it, one may consider that this time limit starts from the company announcement that the shares have been fully paid (Art. 156§3; s. above §1932 *in fine*).

1935 The formation meeting is subject to further requirements. Subscribers must be notified 15 days in advance, and a quorum of more than half of the voting rights must be reached. The law does not specify if online attendance is compliant, but it does not prohibit it either, while expressly leaving the detail to the bylaws or the promoter agreement (Art. 103§2), which suggests that both are possible, considering that the general provisions of the Company Law expressly permit it (Art. 24; s. above §1795), and provided either the promoter agreement or the bylaws or both provide for either (or do not prohibit it). In practice, both are common.

1936 The agenda of the formation meeting includes deliberating the report of the promoters on the formation, namely, on the related expenses, adopting the bylaws, electing the directors and the supervisors, examining the value of the contributions in-kind and, in extreme cases (force majeure or lack of a material condition), renouncing the formation (Art. 104§1). Decisions are made at simple majority of the shareholders present, being reminded that the latter must represent at least half of the voting rights (Art. 104§2 and 103§1 *in fine*; s. above §1935). Once the meeting is completed, the board of directors must direct a representative to apply for the company registration within 30 days (Art. 106).

1937 The formation of a shareholding company by flotation differs from both its formation by promotion and from that of the limited liability company in one remarkable respect: whenever all the shares offered to the public have not been subscribed, the subscribers have the right to request the promoters to *return their payment*. The rationale behind this feature is arguably that, because the subscribers, unlike the promoters, have not been involved in the formation, they deserve greater protection than the latter in case the company is not adequately capitalized. The refund must include interest (Art. 105§1 *in fine*).

1938 Other than the exception mentioned in the preceding paragraph, the promoters and the subscribers may only withdraw their payments or in-kind contributions if the company is not formed eventually (Art. 105§2).

1939 Questions arise where some of the subscribers did not pay their shares, or not entirely. Art. 107 refers, among other provisions, as far as the default of a subscriber is concerned, to Art. 51 and 52 (forfeiture in case of default of a shareholder to pay its share; s. above §§1848 and 1849). This mechanism provides *mutatis mutandis* for the promoters to issue a *demand* for payment, but the law does not set any time limit, neither for paying the shares after their subscription and before any such demand (s. above §1933), nor after such demand has been issued (Art. 51§1), nor for such payment after that demand (Art. 51§2), where the payment should simply be "timely".

1940 If the demand is ignored, the company may (but "must" not) set a *grace period* which must be a minimum 60 days from the demand. If the default still persists, the corresponding shares may be *forfeited* and transferred to another subscriber, or the registered capital shall be *reduced*. In other words, in case a subscriber does not pay, several months can elapse before the capital of the shareholding company formed by flotation can be declared to be fully paid.

1941 It is only then that the promoters will be able to hold the *formation meeting*, which they will have to do within 30 days of full payment (Art. 103§1; s. above §1934). Therefore, in practice, where the shares are fully subscribed, but one or some shareholders fail to pay, the other subscribers will most likely not be entitled to exercise their right to claim the refund of their shares under Art. 105§1 before several months later, since the 30-day time limit will only start after the capital has been fully paid which, as explained, may, in practice again, take a considerable amount of time. Inasmuch and as noted, the situation fundamentally differs from that of the limited liability company, where the subscribers must pay their contribution within maximum of five years (s. above §§1840ff.)

1942 Even though those provisions governing the formation of the shareholding company and addressing the offering of shares to the public do not generally refer to it, the offering of shares is mainly detailed in the first section of the next chapter of the law on the offering (and transfer) of shares of a shareholding company (Art. 142 ff.), since such offering can occur not only upon the formation of the company, but also at a later stage. One should, therefore, turn to it for any matter not addressed in the section applying to the company formation. The section on the public offering of shares will be outlined below (s. Chap. 9 §64.IV.F.1, Offering of Shares).

1943 The *company records* of the shareholding company include, as with the limited liability company, the bylaws, the shareholders register (Art. 102), the minutes of shareholders' meetings (s. also Art. 119 and below, §1957), of the board of directors and of the board of supervisors, the financial accounting reports and the bondholders register. They must be kept at the company (Art. 109) and the shareholders must be able to consult and copy them (Art. 110), to the exception of the bondholders register, which this provision falls short to mention.

1944 The shareholders may also, as they consult those records, offer *recommendations* or ask *questions* about the operations of the company. The law further provides for *extended access* to the company account books and accounting vouchers. However, whereas the limited liability company regime offers extended access, to any shareholder, to the company books (Art. 57), the shareholding company regime, while referring to Art. 57, restricts it to shareholders holding not only at least 3% of the shares rights, but having also held them for three consecutive months at the time of their request to access the books.

1945 These shareholders may either hold such share alone or form a group whose aggregate share reaches that threshold and request extended access in the name of the group (Art. 110§2). The bylaws may lower that threshold however, and provide for lesser access requirements (Art. 110§2 *in fine*). The modalities of the extended right of consultation have been detailed about the limited liability company. to which we refer (s. above §1838).

1946 While Art. 12 outlined the general principles applicable to the *transformation* of the limited liability company into a shareholding company and vice-versa (s. above §1782), Art. 108 complements them for the case of the transformation of a limited liability company into a shareholding company specifically. Thus, after the transformation, the paid-in capital may not be higher than the net asset value of the shareholding company (Art. 108, 1st sentence). The rationale behind this provision is to ensure that the transformation does not result in an overstatement of the company's capital, which may induce a wrong perception of the company's financial standing, thereby protecting creditors. Moreover, if such transformation implies a capital increase of the shareholding company and a shares offering to the public, the transformation does not exempt the company from complying with the ordinary rules applying to any such offering (*ibid.*, 2nd sentence; s. also above §§1904, 1922, 1924 and 1930ff., as well as Art. 142 ff. and below Chap. 9 §64.IV.F.1, Offering of Shares).

B. Shareholders' Meeting

The shareholders' meeting of the shareholding company largely mirrors that of the limited liability company, with some differences which we highlight above. As with the limited liability company, it is the supreme power of the company (Art. 111); their powers are identical (Art. 112 referring to Art. 59§1 and 2). 1947

Unlike the limited liability company (Art. 62§2, 1st sentence), which holds so-called regular meetings according to the bylaws, the shareholding company must hold each year a meeting aptly known as *annual meeting* (Art. 113§1, 1st sentence). *Special meetings* must be held within two months in the following circumstances: the number of directors is less than two-thirds of the number prescribed in the law or the bylaws; the loss "not covered" (i.e., exceeding the corresponding profit) of the company reaches one-third of the total (registered) share capital; a shareholder holding alone-, or shareholders holding an aggregate ten percent or more of the shares of the corporation request the holding of a special shareholders' meeting; the board of directors considers it necessary; the board of supervisors proposes the holding of a special shareholders' meeting; or other circumstances set out in the bylaws (Art. 113). Comparatively, under the limited liability company regime, a special meeting is proposed by a shareholder or shareholders representing one-tenth or more of the voting rights, one-third or more of the directors, or of the board of supervisors; no special circumstances such as those listed at Art. 113 are required. 1948

Art. 114, which regulates how the shareholders' meeting of the shareholding company shall be convened and chaired, only differs from the limited liability company regime (Art. 63) in two respects: first, in order for shareholders to convene and chair the meeting in case both the board of directors and of supervisors failed to, they need not only to hold at least 10% of the shares but, in addition to the limited liability company regime (Art. 63§2), to have held them for 90 or more consecutive days (Art. 114§2). Second, Art. 114§3, which has no equivalent in the limited liability company regime, provides that, when 1949 shareholders holding at least 10% of the shares request a special meeting, the board of directors must reply to them within ten days.

1950 While the shareholders of a limited liability company must be convened 15 days before a shareholders' meeting, whether regular or special (Art. 64), those of a shareholding company must be convened 20 days before the annual meeting and 15 days before a special meeting (Art. 115).

1951 Unlike for the limited liability company, the shareholding company regime provides for *ad hoc proposals,* entitling the shareholders to make them (Art. 115§2). In order to be entitled to do so, they must represent a minimum of one percent of the shares. The proposal must be submitted in writing ten days before a shareholders' meeting; it must have a clear topic and purport at resolving specific matters. The board of directors must notify the shareholders thereof within two days of its receipt, except if it is illegal, contrary to the bylaws, or out of the scope of powers of the shareholders' meeting. The law grants special protection to the right of *ad hoc* proposals by prohibiting the company from increasing the one percent threshold.

1952 If the shareholding company offers shares to the public, it shall notify the shareholders' annual meeting, special meetings and *ad hoc* proposals in the form of *announcement* (Art. 115§3). Any such announcement must contain an *agenda*; in the absence thereof, the shareholders' meeting is prohibited from adopting resolutions on matters not stated therein (Art. 115§4). There are no such requirements for the limited liability company.

1953 As compared to the limited liability company where the *voting rights* of the shareholders are proportional to their share, the shareholders of a shareholding company have one vote per share (Art. 116§1, 1st phrase). *Class shares*, which designate special categories of rights enjoying certain privileges that may be created among the shares of a shareholding company, may carry out more voting rights (Art. 144§1, item 2 and 116§1, 2nd phrase)[867]. The shares held by the company do not carry out voting rights (Art. 116§1, 2nd sentence). The *ordinary majority* for the adoption of resolutions is the simple majority of those present at the shareholders meeting (Art. 116§2). However, a *qualified majority* of two-thirds of those presents must be reached in the following cases: amend the bylaws, increase or reduce the registered capital, merger, division, dissolution or transformation of the company (Art. 116§3).

1954 The shareholding company regime further contains a unique feature, which is the so-called *cumulative voting system* (Art. 117). The shareholders' meeting may adopt this system for the election of directors and supervisors, in accordance with the company bylaws or a resolution of the shareholders' meeting.

---

[867] Class shares are further elaborated about their public offering, s. below §1990ff.

Such system means that, in the election of directors and supervisors at the shareholders' meeting, the number of voting rights per share is the same as the number of directors or supervisors to be elected, and that each shareholder may cumulate them on the same candidate or candidates. For example, if five directors are to be elected, one shareholder holding one share could cast five votes for the same director, and none for the four left.

This system enhances the minority shareholders' influence by enabling strategic votes allocation. In the same example, a shareholder with 10'000 shares could cast 50'000 votes for one director. Votes can also be split among multiple candidates (e.g., three votes for candidate A and two for candidate B). This mechanism contrasts with so-called *straight voting systems*, where shareholders must spread votes equally among candidates. Cumulative voting is particularly impactful in shareholding companies with dispersed ownership, as it mitigates the majority shareholders' dominance in board elections. Because of the difference in scale between the shareholding company and the limited liability company, where such problems tend to be less acute, it has no equivalent in the latter. 1955

Representation of the voting rights of a shareholder by another (where the representative is known as "proxy") is possible and contemplated by Art. 118. It is subject to strict formal requirements: the powers of the proxy must be authorized by a formal POA issued by the represented shareholder. This power must specify the matters for which the proxy is authorized to use it and its duration, and must be submitted to the company. 1956

The decisions of the shareholders' meeting must be recorded in *minutes*, which must be signed by the directors present (Art. 119, 1st sentence). They must be kept at the company (Art. 109; s. above §1943) together with the sign-in book or *attendance sheet* of the shareholders present at the meeting, and the proxies' POAs (Art. 119, 2nd sentence). 1957

C. Board of Directors and Manager

Whereas the board of directors of the limited liability company is governed by provisions (Art. 67 ff.) contained in the organization section of the limited liability company regime, those related to the shareholding company are contained, like for the shareholders' meeting and the board of supervisors, in a dedicated section (Art. 120 to 129). Moreover, four provisions pertaining to the limited liability company regime (Art. 67 (powers of the board), 68§1 (composition of the board), 70 (term of office of directors) and 71 (removal of a director); s. above §§1871ff.) apply *mutatis mutandis* to the board of directors of the shareholding company. 1958

1959 Both the limited liability company (Art. 69) and the shareholding company (Art. 121) provide for an *audit committee* to the same effect, but the shareholding company regime is more detailed. Moreover, the law sets additional requirements for listed shareholding companies (Art. 137; s. below §1980). The law allows both companies to form an audit committee as a substitute to the board of supervisors (Art. 69, 1st sentence and Art, 121§1). The shareholding company regime further specifies the composition of the audit committee to the effect of ensuring it will use an independent and objective judgment: the audit committee consists of three or more members, more than half of whom shall neither hold any position other than directorship in the company, nor have any relationship with it which may affect his independence or the objectiveness of his judgment (Art. 121§2, 1st sentence). In both the limited liability company and the shareholding company, a representative of the employees may sit on the audit committee (*ibid.*, 2nd sentence).

1960 The shareholding company regime prescribes that each member of the audit committee has one vote (Art. 121§4) and that resolutions are to be adopted by the simple majority of its members (*ibid.*, § 3), i.e., not only of the members in attendance, which further reflects the legislator's concern that no member may outweigh the others, thus threatening the committee's independence and objectiveness.

1961 The bylaws may provide for additional rules (*ibid.*, § 5) and *other committees* (A.K.A. as "special" committees, s., e.g., Art. 136§2) under the board of directors (*ibid.*, § 6). The law sets additional requirements for special committees to listed shareholding companies (Art. 136§2; s. below §1978).

1962 In principle, a shareholding company has a *manager* (经理, jīnglǐ) who is in charge of operational matters. The difference with the limited liability company lies in the fact that, in the latter case, the manager is optional (s. Art. 74§1 prescribing that a limited liability company "may" (可以 kěyǐ) have a manager), whereas it is in principle mandatory in that of the shareholding company (s. Art. 126§1 providing that a shareholding company "has" (设 shè, lit. "to establish") or shall have a manager). Like for the limited liability company, that manager is hired and dismissed by the board of directors to which he reports and whose meetings he "observes"[868]. His powers are also defined by the bylaws or the board of directors (Art. 126§2).

1963 Alternatively, like the limited liability company (Art. 75), a director may concurrently serve as manager (Art. 127). Small companies may have only one director and a manager, or a director who may simultaneously serve as manager (Art. 128). The terminology used for designating the manager gives rise to

[868] S. above note 846.

much confusion, which we attempted to dispel about the limited liability company and to which we refer (s. above §§1858 to 1861).

The law sets out detailed rules about the rhythm of the meetings of the board of directors, summons, quorum, special meetings, resolutions voting, minutes, proxies, and liabilities. The board of directors must meet at least twice a year (*ordinary* meetings; Art. 123§1), and the directors and supervisors must be summoned at least ten days in advance. 1964

A shareholder or shareholders representing one-tenth or more of the voting rights, one-third or more of the directors, or the board of supervisors may propose the holding of a *special* meeting; if so, the chairman must convene and preside over the meeting within ten days (Art. 123§2). The fact that the law conflates "convene" and "preside" suggests that the chairman must, within ten days, do both, i.e., that the ten-day advance notice mandated for ordinary meetings in the preceding subsection does not apply to special meetings and that, practically, the chairman must summon it immediately after it was validly proposed since, if he is indolent, he might find himself either in violation of the unwritten yet general duty to convene a meeting reasonably in advance, or of holding it within ten days. Acknowledging this issue, the law further prescribes that the method and time limit for summoning special meetings may be determined "otherwise", which suggest again that it may be so either in the bylaws, or on a case-by-case basis, when such meeting is proposed. 1965

The law imposes a *quorum* of *more than half*[869] the directors for a meeting to be valid, while *resolutions* shall equally be validly adopted by the votes of *more than half* of them (Art. 124§1). Each director has one vote (*ibid.*, § 2). Resolutions must be consigned in *minutes* (*ibid.*, § 3). Directors must personally attend meetings of the board; however, they may attend by proxy, which must be in writing (Art. 125§1). 1966

Last but not least, the directors are responsible for their resolutions: if any is in violation of a law, an administrative regulation, the bylaws, or a resolution of the shareholders' meeting, causing any serious loss to the company, the directors having participated in its adoption are *liable* towards the company. However, a dissenting director may be *exempted* if he can prove that his dissent was consigned in the minutes (Art. 125§2). 1967

The law sets additional requirements on directors for *listed* shareholding companies (Art. 136§1; s. below §§1975 and 1977). Moreover, it mandates listed 1968

869 Such quorum implies that, in case of boards counting an even number of directors, it shall not be attained if only half are attending.

shareholding companies to have a secretary (Art. 138; s. below §1981), which it neither mandates nor prohibits for non-listed shareholding companies.

D. Board of Supervisors

1969 As with the board of directors, owing to the difference in scale between the two companies, the regime applying to the board of supervisors of the shareholding company (Art. 130 to 133) compares to that of the limited liability company (Art. 76 to 83; s. above §§1877 to 1880) to which we refer, while pointing out at their differences. Generally speaking, these differences reflect the fact that shareholding companies are typically bigger than limited liability companies and call, therefore, for somewhat more elaborate features, namely, to the effect of protecting the shareholding company's shareholders and creditors, than for the limited liability company.

1970 Reflecting the foregoing, the limited liability company generally enjoys greater flexibility than the shareholding company with respect to the supervisory board: thus, notably, small limited liability companies can opt for a *single* supervisor or, with unanimous shareholders' consent, *no* supervisor at all (Art. 83), whereas shareholding companies can reduce it to a single supervisor but cannot fully dispense with supervision (Art. 133); moreover, only the limited liability company is explicitly allowed to establish an *audit committee* within the board of directors as an *alternative* to a board of supervisors (Art. 69); the shareholding company may not. Other than that, the two regimes are similar, if not identical.

E. Special Provisions on the Organizational Structure of Listed Companies

1971 A listed company is defined as a shareholding company whose shares are publicly listed and traded on a stock exchange (Art. 134). The implications resulting from this definition are not as obvious as they may seem. There are currently three stock exchanges in China: the Shanghai Stock Exchange (SSE), the Shenzhen Stock Exchange (SZSE) and the Beijing Stock Exchange (BSE). While Hong Kong is a Special Administrative Region of the PRC, the Hong Kong Stock Exchange (HKEX) is not, legally speaking, a "Chinese" stock exchange since, although it serves as a bridge between mainland China and foreign investors, it is governed by Hong Kong law, not Chinese law, and as a result operates under a different regulatory regime.

The Company Law applies to companies formed under it and registered in China. Therefore, Art. 134 ff. apply to *Chinese* (including foreign-invested-), not to foreign (i.e., not registered in China, even though they may operate on Chinese territory[870]), *companies*. Moreover, it applies to Chinese companies listed *both in China and overseas*, Hong Kong included. In that regard, it is to be noted that Chinese companies may list overseas without being listed in China and frequently do. In such case, they remain subject to Art. 134 ff. 1972

Despite it is, at this stage, still a mostly theoretical question, since in practice *foreign companies* do not yet list in China, although they are not strictly speaking prohibited to do so[871], because Art. 134 ff. apply to Chinese companies only, they will not apply to foreign companies which may be *listed in China* in the future; however, whenever they will, those foreign companies shall have to comply with demanding regulatory requirements under Chinese law and regulations[872], whose effects will equate to those Art. 134 ff. have on listed Chinese shareholding company. In contrast, *Chinese shareholding companies listing abroad* have to comply not only with Art. 134 ff. of the Chinese Company Law, but also with any *foreign* regulatory requirements such foreign stock exchange may impose to the companies listed on its board. 1973

Section 5 on special provisions on listed companies is concerned with enhancing *corporate governance* in order to match the risk accrual typically resulting from the listing of a company, and the resulting expansion of its financial capacity. Thus, it protects the company's *creditworthiness* by subjecting, to a resolution adopted by a *qualified majority* of two-thirds of the shareholders present at the meeting, the purchase or the sale of assets or the provision of security to third parties exceeding 30% in a year of the company's total assets (Art. 135). 1974

It further directs the shareholding company to have *independent directors*, a requirement the law had only developed so far for the members of the audit committee (Art. 121§1; s. above §1959). This requirement is qualified further down at Art. 139, where the law addresses the *affiliation* of a director with third party interests related to the company, but not necessarily compatible with the 1975

---

870 For example, airlines or shipping companies.

871 Foreign companies cannot currently be directly listed on stock exchanges in mainland China. While there is no explicit legal prohibitions to that effect, in practice, no foreign-incorporated companies have been listed due to significant legal and regulatory hurdles, particularly around reconciling different jurisdictions' laws. Chinese authorities have considered establishing an "international board" to allow overseas companies to list directly on the main boards of Chinese exchanges but, as of now, it has not been implemented. Therefore, while the legal framework does not explicitly forbid foreign company listings, the current regulatory and practical environment means that foreign companies are not listed on mainland Chinese stock exchanges.

872 S. below §1977.

latter's interests. In such case, whenever such affiliated party is involved in a matter to be resolved at a meeting of the board of directors, the director shall timely submit a written report to the board of directors (Art. 139, 1st sentence).

1976 The related resolution is then subject to a *double qualified majority* and a *double quorum* requirement: *quorum* wise, first, the meeting of the board of directors at which the resolution related to the affiliated party is to be deliberated may only be held if more than half of the unaffiliated (i.e., independent) directors attend the meeting[873] (Art. 139, 3rd sentence). That first quorum requirement is reinforced by a second quorum requirement by which, even if the first requirement is met, if the number of unaffiliated directors attending the meeting is less than three, the matter must be referred to the shareholders' meeting for deliberation (*ibid.*, 4th sentence). *Majority* wise, first, the affiliated director is deprived of his voting right on the related resolution; such restriction extends to any proxy on behalf of another director (*ibid.*, 2nd sentence). Second, the resolution must be adopted by more than half of the unaffiliated directors, whether in attendance or not (*ibid.*, 3rd sentence, 2nd phrase).

1977 While Art. 136 prescribes that a shareholding company must have independent directors, it further refers to specific *administrative measures* prescribed by the securities regulatory agency of the State Council, which is the CSRC. These measures are extensive and cover areas such as listing procedures, ongoing disclosure obligations, mergers and acquisitions, etc., as well as corporate governance, that is mainly regulated in the CSRC Corporate Governance Code for Listed Companies, which contains complementary provisions about, among other things, directors' independence, and to which we refer the reader.

1978 Art. 136§2 also mandates the bylaws of listed shareholding companies to mention, in addition to the basic requirements applying to a non-listed shareholding company (Art. 95; s. above §§1908ff.), the *composition and powers of the special committees* under the board of directors, and the *remuneration assessment mechanisms* for directors, supervisors and senior executives. This provision thus strengthens the ordinary shareholding company regime: indeed, while Art. 121§5 provides for special committees (mentioned as "other" committees, i.e., other than the audit committee), Art. 95 does not list them among the items to be contained in the bylaws (cf. Art. 95 *a contrario* and above §1960).

1979 Likewise, the ordinary regime only requires *remuneration* matters to be decided by the shareholders' meeting or the board of directors, but not to be mentioned in the bylaws (cf. Art. 95 *a contrario* and above §§1908ff.; Art. 59§1,

[873] This double requirement implies that, if more than half of the unaffiliated directors attend and more than half of the attendees approve the resolution, but represent less than half of the unaffiliated directors, including those unaffiliated directors who did not attend, the resolution shall fail.

item 1 applicable by the reference of Art. 112 and above §1856; Art. 67§2, item 8 applicable by the reference of Art. 120§2). Finally, Art. 136 also reserves other matters in accordance with the law and administrative regulations, which also potentially points at the CSRC Corporate Governance Code for Listed Companies mentioned in the preceding paragraph.

The *audit committee* (s. above §1959) of a listed shareholding company is subject to a qualified majority of more than half of its members, in attendance or not, for the matters including engaging and dismissing the accounting firm that undertakes the audit of the company, hiring and dismissing the CFO, and disclosing financial and accounting reports (Art. 137, item 1 to 3). The CSRC may impose additional requirements (*ibid.*, item 4; s. above §1977). 1980

Unlike for a non-listed shareholding company to which the law neither mandates nor prohibits it, a listed company is required to have a *secretary* for the board of directors. The secretary is responsible for the preparation of the shareholders' meeting and of the meetings of the board of directors; of the preservation of the related documents (namely, the minutes, s. above §1957); of the management of shareholders' documents (namely, the company records, s. above §1943); of handling company information disclosure; and of other affairs of the company (Art. 138). 1981

The law further subjects a listed shareholding company to enhanced *information disclosure* duties. One shall recall, to start with, that the registration of a shareholding company is published on NECIPS (which is the Chinese equivalent of the register of commerce or of companies) and that the information disclosed includes, among other things, the names of the promoters of the shareholding company (Art. 32; s. above §1817). These duties, which already exceed those imposed by Swiss law[874], are extended in the case of a listed company, which shall, in addition, disclose information on the shareholders and actual controller (Art. 140, 1st phrase). 1982

As it does so, Art. 140 merely refers to the law. As a matter of fact, such extended duties are to be found in a comprehensive *legal and regulatory framework*. The principal requirements stem from the Company Law itself, the Securities Law, CSRC Measures for the Administration of Information Disclosure by Listed Companies (2025 Revision), CSRC's Code of Corporate Governance mentioned above (s. §1977) and, for FIEs, foreign investment rules. These collectively ensure that listed companies must identify, record, and publicly disclose information on their shareholders and actual controllers, especially in cases of significant shareholding, changes in control, or related-party transactions. Among the secondary legislation, and without ambitioning 1983

874 S. above §1823.

to be exhaustive given the limited scope of this book, it is worth highlighting the above-mentioned 2025 revised CSRC Measures as the primary administrative rules implementing disclosure obligations, which it sets in great detail. In addition, stock exchanges may have their own listing rules.

1984 Art. 140, 2nd sentence prohibits *nominee shareholding*, A.K.A. *proxy shareholding*, in listed shareholding companies, "in violation of the law": this somewhat unclear formula actually means that nominee shareholding is *tolerated*, provided it does not amount to circumventing the law. Indeed, a nominee shareholding is an arrangement by which one person (the nominee shareholder) holds shares in a company on behalf of another party (the beneficial owner), which is the true owner of the shares, and entitled to the economic benefits and rights associated with them. The nominee shareholder's name appears on the company's official shareholder register and public records, but the beneficial owner effectively controls the shares. Nominee shareholding is commonly used for various reasons, which may be legitimate, such as privacy, regulatory restrictions, or to circumvent legal limitations on certain types of investors (e.g., foreign investors in restricted industries). However, these arrangements can create legal risks and disputes, especially if the nominee shareholder refuses to cooperate, misuses their position, or if the arrangement is used to bypass regulatory requirements. While nominee shareholding is legally recognized, it is considered by the Chinese Company Law as a risky structure potentially raising issues of transparency and compliance, particularly in listed companies. Therefore, however legal *per se*, it is prohibited if it effectively amounts to a violation (or a circumvention amounting to such violation) of the law[875].

1985 Finally, a *non-wholly owned subsidiary* of a listed company may not acquire any shares of the listed company (Art. 141§1). The purpose of this provision is to prevent the company from abusing its power by using, as proxy, a subsidiary it controls. Nevertheless, a non-wholly owned subsidiary of a listed company may also hold shares of the listed company for legitimate reasons, such as in view of a combination between the company and its subsidiary, or as a pledge, namely, before the revised Company Law became effective. If so, the law prevents such abuse anyway by restricting the subsidiary from exercising the voting rights carried out by the shares of the listed company it holds, and by compelling it to dispose of such shares within a timely manner (*ibid.*, § 2).

---

[875] Such prohibition conforms with the general prohibition of *abuse of law* contained in the basic provisions of the Chinese Civil Code (s. above §116 and note 96).

F. *Offering and Transfer of Shares of a Shareholding Company*

1. Offering of Shares

The liquidity of the shares, whether offered to specific offerees or to the public (s. above §1905, is a distinctive feature of the shareholding company over the limited liability company, owing to the latter's personal nature, which is reflected, among other things, by the fact that the limited liability company, contrary to the shareholding company, does not offer shares to the public. Therefore, Chapter 6 on the shareholding company dedicates a first section to the *offering of shares* (Art. 142 to 156) before addressing their transfer, which the limited liability company regime also regulates, in the next (Art. 157 to 167). This section focuses on the following issues: no-par shares, shares classes, shares certificates, new shares and public offering. 1986

The capital of a shareholding company is divided into shares, which may be either *par value shares* or *no-par shares* (Art. 142§1, 1st sentence). "Par value shares" mean that the shares have a predetermined, set or fixed nominal (A.K.A. face-) value assigned by the company at issuance. "No-par shares" mean that they have not: instead, their value is determined by the market, i.e., by how much investors are willing to pay; there is no predetermined or minimum price (A.K.A. "baseline") value. Whether the shares to issue are to be par or no-par, the value of the first, and their number, is determined by the bylaws (*ibid.*, 2nd sentence), which may also provide whether the company has the right to *convert* all the issued par value shares into no-par shares or vice versa (Art. 142§2). If the shares are par value, each has the same value (Art. 142§1, 3rd sentence). 1987

The focus of this provision is set on no-par value shares. Indeed, the 2023 revision of the Company Law introduced a requirement that, if a shareholding company issues no-par shares, at least half of the proceeds from the issuance must be included as registered capital (Art. 142§3). Previously, the law did not specifically address the allocation of proceeds from no-par value shares, *a fortiori* to the registered capital. 1988

The rationale behind the requirement of Art. 142§3 is to ensure that the adoption of no-par value shares does not erode the capital of Chinese companies. By requiring that at least half of the proceeds from no-par shares be included in the registered capital, the law upholds its integrity, protects creditors, and aligns with international best practices, while still allowing companies great flexibility in structuring their equity. Indeed, absent such a requirement, companies could minimize their registered capital, for example, to the effect of enjoying regulatory or tax advantages, while still benefiting from large amounts 1989 of capital resulting from the no-par shares' proceeds, thus potentially threatening the interests of creditors and minority shareholders.

1990 Shares shall be offered under the principles of fairness and impartiality, and each share of the same *share class* shall carry out the same *share rights* (Art. 143§1). While a shareholder present at a shareholders' meeting has in principle one voting right per share (Art. 116§1, 1st sentence; s. above §1909)[876], Art. 143§1 implies that shares of different classes may carry out different rights, namely, more voting rights, as confirmed by Art. 144§1, item 2 and 116§1, 2nd phrase (s. above §1953). It should also be reminded that the shares held by the company do not carry out voting rights (Art. 116§1, 2nd sentence; s. above §1953). The number of shares of each class and their related rights and obligations are to be mentioned in the bylaws (Art. 95, item 5; s. above §1909 and below §1995).

1991 The offering conditions and *price per share*, whether set or paid, must be the same for the shares of the same class in any particular issue (Art. 143§2).

1992 The *shares classes*, i.e., the shares rights attached thereto, are subject to a *numerus clausus*, i.e., they are exhaustively listed by the law, which defines three of them: shares with a preferential or subordinated right to the distribution of profit or to residual property[877]; shares each carrying out more or less voting rights than those carried by common shares; and shares subject to transfer restrictions, such as transfer subject to the consent of the company (Art. 144§1, items 1 to 3). Other classes may be prescribed by the competent authority, which is the State Council, however (*ibid.*, item 4).

1993 Class shares are subject to further restrictions. First, the last two classes (shares each carrying out more or less voting rights than those carried by common shares; shares subject to transfer restrictions, such as transfer subject to the consent of the company; Art. 144§1, item 2 and 3) may only be offered to the promoters. In other words, they may be offered to them either in case of formation by promotion or, in case of formation by flotation, before the offering of shares to the public (Art. 144§2; on the formation, s. above, §§1903 and 1904).

1994 Second, in case of the class of shares carrying out more or less voting rights than those carried by common shares (Art. 144§1, item 2), whenever the

[876] Comparatively, the shareholders of a limited liability company enjoy voting rights proportional to their share (Art. 65; s. above §1867). However, s. above note 838.

[877] "Residual property" relates to the preferential rights a shareholder holding that class of share enjoys in case of liquidation of the company. It specifically refers to the remaining assets of a company after it has settled all debts. That residual property is distributed to shareholders according to the rights corresponding to the class of the shares they hold. These rights are defined in the bylaws (cf. Art. 144§1 *in fine* and 145).

shareholders' meeting has to vote on the election and the replacement of the supervisors and of members of the audit committee, each share of that class must carry out the same number of voting rights as each common share (*ibid.*, § 3).

The rights attached to each shares class must be detailed in the bylaws, which shall mention the profit distribution order or that of the allocation of the residual property; the number of voting rights carried by each share of each class; the restrictions on the transfer of the shares for each class, as the case may be; and the related measures taken by the company for protecting the rights and interests of minority shareholders. The bylaws may contain additional rules as deemed necessary by the shareholders' meeting (Art. 145). 1995

Aside to the shareholders' meeting which assembles all shareholders, irrespective of whether they are ordinary or class shareholders and of the shares class the latter may own, class shareholders may debate matters exclusively related to their class at *class meetings*, whose attendance is restricted to the shareholders of a particular shares class. Whenever such class meetings takes place, the qualified majority applying to certain matters to be voted on by the ordinary shareholders' meeting also applies to class meetings whenever the rights of the class shares' shareholders may be affected (Art. 146§1). These matters are: amending the bylaws, increasing or reducing the registered capital, and the merger, division, dissolution or transformation of the company (Art. 116§3; s. above §1953). The bylaws may provide for other cases of qualified majority for certain shares classes (Art. 146§2). 1996

Shares are represented in the form of a *shares certificate* (A.K.A. stock certificate; Art. 147, 1st sentence). Such certificate proves both the existence of the shares and the ownership of their holder (Art. 147, 2nd sentence). While Art. 147, 2nd and 3rd sentence refers to certificates issued by the shareholding company, which the law directs to immediately issue after its formation (Art. 150, 1st sentence) while being prohibited to do so before (Art. 150 *in fine*), specifically, they are issued by the capital verification agency mandated by the shareholding company, once the agency has verified the shares' payment (Art. 101; s. above §1930). 1997

Certificates must be registered (Art. 147 *in fine*) in the *shareholders register* (Art. 102; s. above §1943). A certificate contains the name and date of formation of the shareholding company or the time of the offering, namely, in case of subsequent offering (s. below §§2003ff.), the class, par value and number of shares represented by the certificate or, in case of no-par shares, their number (Art. 149§2). It must bear a serial number and be signed by the legal representative of the shareholding company (*ibid.*, § 3). Certificates held by promoters must expressly mention it (*ibid.*, § 3). 1998

1999 Even though it does not expressly result from the list set out at Art. 149§2 that the certificate should also contain the name of the shareholder, this requirement indirectly results from Art. 147, 2nd sentence which states that the certificate certifies the shares held by a shareholder (s. preceding paragraph); it is observed in practice. Art. 32§1, item 6 only mandates the names of the shareholders of a limited liability company and of the promoters of a shareholding company to be *published* on NECIPS (s. above §§1817 to 1819 and 1823). However, the names of all shareholders, be them promoters or not, whether shares have been offered to the public or not, and whether such shares have been offered at the formation of the shareholding company or subsequently, must be registered in the shareholders register (Art. 147§2; s. above §1998).

2000 In addition, secondary legislation may mandate the public disclosure of *major shareholders*, who are not only controlling shareholders but are also defined as shareholders holding as little as 5% or more of the shares of a listed shareholding company, to be published[878]. However, such information is not listed on NECIPS, but through the Chinese stock exchanges (s. above §1971) and CSRC. We will not elaborate on such requirements. The purpose of these comments is to stress that China has, nowadays, considerably extended the transparency requirements applying to *economic beneficiaries* (designated in the Company Law as "actual controllers"[879]) of capital companies. The reader is invited to consult specialized literature or seek professional advice for additional detail.

2001 The certificates are in principle in printed *form*; however, the competent authority, which is the CSRC, may authorize "other forms" (Art. 149§1), that in practice are electronic or digital certificates (s. below §2017). Such certificates are widely used in China, in line with the general trend of the Chinese government towards paperless administration. The *endorsement* of the certificate in case of transfer of shares is addressed in the next section of the law (Art. 159; s. below §2016).

2002 While historically *bearer shares* were allowed in China, they were prohibited as of 2022[880], namely, as part China's efforts to comply with international anti-money laundering standards by enhancing transparency in corporate ownership;

---

878 S., for example, Measures for the Administration of the Takeover of Listed Companies (2025 Amendment), Art. 13 and 14; 2025 Provisions on the Administration of Information Disclosure of Listed Companies (s. above §1983), Art. 2, 35 and 36; 2025 Securities and Futures Laws Application Opinion No. 19, Opinion on the Application of Articles 13 and 14 of the Measures for the Administration of the Takeover of Listed Companies, requiring the reporting of major shareholders, also in case of subsequent change of ownership.

879 For the definition of actual controller, s. below §2057.

880 Bearer's shares were prohibited, in Switzerland, as of 2019.

the Company Law does not mention them anymore and requires shares to be registered.

After it has issued its initial offering of shares and been formed, a shareholding company may, in the course of its existence, be willing to increase its capital, which it may do by offering *new shares*. Such offering is subject to double approval: by the shareholders' meeting and by the board of directors. In principle (s. below §2005), such new offering must be decided by a resolution adopted by the shareholders' meeting (Art. 151§1); moreover, once the shareholders' meeting has authorized the board of directors to proceed with the new offering, the decision of the board of directors itself is subject to a qualified majority of two-thirds of the directors, attending or not (Art. 153). 2003

Very much like for the initial offering, the *resolution* must address the class and amount of the new shares, their offering price, the beginning and ending dates of the offering, the class and amount of new shares offered to original shareholders and, if no-par shares are offered, the amount of offering proceeds included in the registered capital (*ibid.*) The law suggests that the shareholding company is relatively free to determine the related *pricing scheme* "based on its operations and financial condition" (Art. 151§2). However, before issuing it, the company will have to apply for approval of its offering. Listed companies must apply before CSRC, irrespective of whether the offering is private or public; so do non-listed companies offering shares to the public (cf. Art. 154§1; s. below §2007). Non-listed companies not offering shares to the public have, in principle, to apply before the local authority, depending on the nature of the offering and the scope of the applicable secondary legislation. Both authorities may reject the application if they deem that such operations and financial conditions do not justify the scheme[881]. 2004

However, the bylaws or a resolution of the shareholders' meeting can also provide the board of directors in advance with a generic *anticipated authorization* to issue new shares, thus giving it more flexibility by enabling it to decide such new issuance without having to first refer to the shareholders' meeting, which can be a time-consuming process. Yet the company is not entirely free to anticipate such issuance: first, it can only authorize the board of directors to do so within three years. The law does not specify the starting point of these three years. It can be understood as that of the resolution authorizing in advance the board of directors to do so or, in case such authorization is contained by the bylaws, from the formation of the company. Second, the authorization may authorize the board of directors to issue new shares up to a maximum of 50% of the existing shares. Third, in case of in-kind contribution, a topical resolution 2005

[881] S. also Art. 154§2, item 3 about the purpose of the proceeds resulting from a public offering, which provides for a different but comparable safeguard (s. below §2008).

of the shareholders' meeting is required anyway (Art. 152§1). The qualified majority of two-thirds of the board of directors (Art. 153; s. above §2003) also applies in case of anticipated authorization.

2006 Once the new shares have been issued, the bylaws must be updated (cf. Art. 95, item 4; s. also above §1909). In principle, these changes should be approved by the shareholders' meeting (Art. 59§1, items 5 and 8 applicable by the reference of Art. 112§1). However, in case of new shares, the law dispenses with such approval (Art. 152§2).

2007 As noted, in case of *public offering*, whether such offering occurs upon the formation of the company or subsequently, and whether the company is listed or not, the shareholding company must apply before CSRC for approval. It must also publish a prospectus and prepare shares subscription forms, like in case of formation by flotation (Art. 100§1; s. above §1904), whose content is detailed at Art. 154§2 and 3 and Art. 100§1, 2nd sentence, 2nd phrase.

2008 The *prospectus* must mention information including the total number of shares offered and, at the formation, that subscribed by the promoters, the par value and the offering price of par and no-par shares, the rights and obligations of subscribers, the class of shares and the related rights and obligations, the beginning and ending dates of the offering, and a statement that the subscribers may withdraw their subscriptions if the shares offered are not fully subscribed after the end of the offering. In addition and notably, it must mention the *purpose of offering proceeds* (Art. 154§2, item 3) which implies that, if the regulatory authority deems that such purpose runs counter the interests of the shareholders and the company's creditors, it may, like for the pricing scheme (Art. 151§2; s. above §2004), reject the application.

2009 It is also worth remembering, for a sound understanding of its legal effects, that, from the point of view of contract law, the prospectus is, contractually, an *invitation to offer* (Chinese Civil Code, Art. 473; s. above §591).

2010 When a shareholding company offers shares to the public, they must be underwritten by a licensed securities company known as an *underwriter*, with which the shareholding company shall enter into a formal underwriting agreement (Art. 155). The securities company, which are typically investment banks, acts as an intermediary and risk manager, ensuring the successful issuance and sale of shares to the public, while providing legal and financial safeguards for all parties involved. Specifically, its role consists in assessing the risk related to the intended shares issuance, setting their price by consultation with the board of directors of the company, guaranteeing the shares' sale in total or in part, and distributing them[882].

2011 Finally, as already outlined with regard to the capital verification agency (s. above §§1930 to 1932), a shareholding company that offers shares to the public shall enter into an agreement with a bank on the *collection of payments* for shares on behalf of the company. The bank must collect and hold the payments on behalf of the company, issue receipts to subscribers who have paid, and issue a certificate of receipt to the "relevant department", which in practice is the capital verification agency[883]. Once the latter has, in turn, issued to the company a certificate stating that the capital has been verified, the corporation shall issue an announcement that the shares have been fully paid. This announcement is of material importance, since it is the starting point of the 30-day time limit within which the formation meeting must be held (Art. 103§1, 1st sentence; s. above §1934).

2012 One should recall, in this context, that, as noted (s. above §1933), the law does not mention the time limit within which the payment of the subscribed shares must be made. One may, therefore, assume that it is a matter which the board of directors addresses as it decides on an offering (Art. 153).

2. Transfer of Shares

2013 Although shareholders of a shareholding company are, in principle, free to transfer their shares (Art. 157, 1st phrase), such transfer is subject to several *restrictions*, contained in the ten following articles (Art. 158 to 167). But for such restrictions, shareholders are free to transfer their shares in or out of the company, i.e., to their fellow shareholders, or to third parties not already being shareholders (Art. 157, 1st phrase). Restrictions may result from the bylaws (*ibid.*, 2nd phrase) and from the other provisions forming the second section of Chapter 6 of the Company Law on the offering and the transfer of shares of a shareholding company, namely, Art. 158 (stock exchanges), 159 (certificates), 160 (lock-up; directors, etc.; pledges), 162 (buybacks), 163 (financial aid) and 167 (inheritance), while the remaining provisions of the section provide for various related, mostly ancillary, rights and obligations.

2014 The first of such restrictions requires shares be transferred on a "legally formed securities trading venue" or in "any other manner prescribed by the State Council" (Art. 158). Legally formed securities trading venue are the Chinese *stock*

[882] On the civil and administrative liability of such institutions in case of error or omission, intentional or by negligence, s. Art. 257 and below §2199.

[883] S. preceding note.

exchanges (s. above §1971). *Prima facie*, the related requirement only applies to listed shareholding companies, which must list and trade their shares and disclose the relevant information in accordance with the law, relevant administrative regulations and internal regulation of stock exchanges (Art. 165 and 166).

2015 Yet *non-listed* shareholding companies are still subject to Art. 158: their shares' transfers must also comply with the procedures and venues prescribed by law, which may include regional equity markets or other methods approved by the State Council. Therefore, non-listed shareholding companies fall under the "other manners" mentioned by Art. 158, which the Company Law does not identify however, and may be set by administrative regulations or specific State Council directives. Examples include court proceedings, and special regulatory approvals[884].

2016 Traditionally, shares are transferred by endorsement of the *shares certificate* (Art. 159, 1st phrase; about the certificate, s. above §§1997ff.) The endorsement is typically written or stamped on the back of the printed (as opposed to electronic-, s. next paragraph) certificate and contains a statement to the effect of transferring the share or shares represented by the certificate from their holder or transferor to the transferee. It is signed by the transferor or both; the related modalities are generally detailed in the bylaws.

2017 However, and again, Art. 159 (2nd phrase) also reserves "other manners" prescribed by the State Council. Such manners primarily relate to the recent, yet widespread use of *electronic certificates*: whenever the shares are dematerialized, the transfer is executed by registration in the securities registration and clearing system, such as the China Securities Depository and Clearing Corporation. The transfer is completed by updating the shareholder register maintained by the relevant securities depository, in accordance with securities law and the relevant administrative regulations. Further manners relate to those mentioned in the preceding paragraph.

2018 Once the endorsement, hence the transfer, has occurred, the company must update the *shareholders register* accordingly (Art. 159§1, 2nd phrase; s. above §1998). However, Art. 159 strictly restricts the *timing* of modifications of the shareholders register: they may not occur within 20 days before a shareholders' meeting, or within five days before the record date decided by the company for distribution of dividends.

---

884 For example, court-mandated transfers, typically as a result of enforcement proceedings, and special regulatory approvals, such as regional equity markets or pilot programs for specific types of securities or companies.

These restrictions purport at ensuring the certainty and stability of the shareholders' identity and at protecting their rights, namely, at times typically critical during the life of a corporation, against last-minute changes, which may otherwise not be timely noticed. Specifically, these restrictions aim at determining voting rights, clarifying dividend entitlements, preventing manipulation and fraud, and at administrative efficiency. Indeed, by freezing changes to the shareholder register shortly before a shareholders' meeting, the company can accurately determine who is entitled to attend and vote. This prevents disputes over voting eligibility and ensures the orderly conduct of meetings. 2019

For *dividends distributions*, the company must establish a clear record date to identify which shareholders are entitled to receive dividends. Restricting register changes immediately before the record date for dividends payment avoids confusion or disputes about who should be paid them. These restrictions also help preventing last-minute transfers intended to improperly influence voting outcomes or gain unfair access to dividends. Finally, they allow the company sufficient time to prepare meeting materials, verify shareholder identities, and execute dividend payments without the complication of ongoing changes to the register. 2020

The law, administrative regulations or CSRC may provide for *exceptions* for listed shareholding companies, however. They reflect the more dynamic nature of public securities markets. 2021

The law further provides for the *invalidation* of the shares certificate whenever the latter has been lost, stolen or has been destroyed (Art. 164). 2022

Beyond the general principle of freedom of the shareholding company's shares transfer of Art. 157 and the general restrictions posed by Art. 158 and 159 about the trading venue and the method of transfer, Art 160 addresses *three specific cases of restrictions*: the one-year lock-up period on the transfer of pre-IPO shares, the sale of shares by senior company officers, and pledges. 2023

First, Art. 160§1 prescribes that the shares a shareholding company has issued before it offers or offered shares to the public may not be transferred within one year from the day when the company is listed and traded on a stock exchange. In other words, this provision institutes a *one-year lock-up period on the transfer of pre-IPO shares* after a company is listed. The purpose of this restriction is to protect market stability and investor confidence during the critical period following a public offering. 2024

Specifically, this restriction aims at preventing immediate selloffs, aligning the interests of old and new investors, and preserving market confidence. Indeed, if founders, early investors, or controlling shareholders were allowed to sell their shares immediately after listing, it could lead to a large volume of shares flooding the market, which in turn could cause significant price volatility or a 2025 sharp decline in the share price, undermining the IPO's success and the interests of new public investors. Moreover, the lock-up period ensures that key shareholders remain invested in the company long-term performance, aligning their interests with those of new investors, and demonstrating their confidence in the company prospects. Finally, by restricting immediate transfers, the rule reassures public investors that insiders cannot quickly exit their positions, which helps build trust in the fairness and stability of the market during the company transition to public ownership.

2026 However, Art. 160 provides for an exception for the transfer of shares of a listed company by its shareholders or its actual controller, if so provided by the law, administrative regulations or the CSRC (Art. 160, 2nd sentence). This exception purports at balancing market stability with legitimate corporate needs, while maintaining regulatory oversight.

2027 *Second*, Art. 160§2 addresses the *transfer of shares by directors, supervisors or senior executives*. This long and somewhat convoluted provision breaks down in several restrictions. To start with, the officers so designated must declare to the company any shares they hold (*ibid.*, 1st phrase).

2028 They further must declare any change (Art. 160§2, 1st phrase), i.e., whether they sell part or all their shares or buy other shares. In any case, any such transfer is limited both in volume and frequence. Volume wise, such officers may not transfer more than 25% of their shares (*ibid.*, 2nd phrase). By transfer, even though this provision does not specify it, one should understand sale, not purchase. The 25% threshold applies to the total number of shares they hold, not to the total number of shares of the company, and to the shares' number, not to their value. Such volume is yearly. The starting point of the yearly period begins at the time the officer officially takes office (*ibid.*, 3rd phrase; namely, as set by the resolution confirming such officer's hiring or, possibly, in his contract of employment, if the resolution did not specify it).

2029 Moreover, and in any event, even though the officer complies with the foregoing, two additional restrictions apply: he may not transfer his shares within one year from the listing and trading of the company shares (Art. 160§2, 4th phrase); and he may not transfer such shares six months after he leaves office (*ibid.*, 5th phrase). Last but not least, the bylaws may contain additional restrictions (Art. 160§3). This provision evidently aims at strictly restraining insider trading.

2030 *Third* and finally, Art. 160§3 addresses *pledges*: where any shares are pledged during the period of transfer restriction prescribed by a law or administrative regulation, the pledgee may not exercise the pledge during the period of transfer restriction.

The three restrictions prescribed by Art. 160 conform to global standards and denote China's commitment to abide by them. They are detailed by a vast array of secondary legislation, administrative regulations and internal regulations (namely, of Chinese stock exchanges) which exceed the scope of this book: we refer the reader to specialized literature and professional advice in that regard. 2031

In addition to the restrictions on transfer outlined above, Section 2 on the transfer of shares of a shareholding company contains provisions providing for certain rights and obligations related to such transfer. Art. 161 and 162 address *buybacks*. The first of these two provisions apply to the right of *shareholders*, in certain circumstances, to buy back their shares (s. next paragraph and ff.) The second applies to restrictions on other cases of buybacks, i.e., spontaneously performed by the shareholding *company*, or upon request of a shareholder but absent such right (s. below §§2040ff.) 2032

In the first of those two groups of buyback cases (*shareholder's* buyback), like Art. 89 for the limited liability company (s. above §§1888 to 1895), Art. 161 entitles shareholders to request the company to buy back their shares. Both provisions are mostly identical, with the following differences. 2033

Art. 89 provides for four circumstances in which a shareholder may exercise this right, while Art. 161 contemplates three such circumstances. In both regimes, they consist in the fact that the *dissenting shareholder* has voted against a resolution adopted by the majority of the shareholders. These resolutions must result either, *first*, in a decision not to distribute profit (Art. 161§1, item 1), or, *second*, in the continuation of the company beyond its statutory duration or dissolution (*ibid.*, item 3). 2034

In addition, and *third*, whereas the limited liability company regime also provides for a resolution approving a merger or acquisition, the shareholding company regime slightly differ by contemplating the *transfer of the majority of the company* (*ibid.*, item 2): indeed, while any merger or acquisition may run counter the personal nature of the limited liability company, thus justifying such right, it does not for a shareholding company, considering the more liquid nature of its shares, until their majority is transferred. 2035

Finally, the limited liability company regime provides for a *fourth* circumstance known as *oppression-based buyback* (Art. 89§3; s. above §1892), which is met when the majority shareholder abuses its rights: Art. 161 does not provide so for the shareholding company, however. The reason for this discrepancy is to be sought, once again, in the personal nature of the limited liability company, whose regime seeks to preserve a balanced relationship among its partners, who are directly involved in the company operation. That is not the case with the shareholding company, whose shareholders are, in their majority, not involved, and are, therefore, not given a right as radical as demanding the 2036 company to buy back their shares. Instead, the law provides for other mechanisms to protect their rights against abuses of controlling shareholders. Still, while Art. 161 does not provide for a buyback right comparable to that of Art. 89, it does offer a robust set of remedies through litigation, fiduciary duties, joint liability and enhanced information rights, as discussed elsewhere in this book[885].

2037 The circumstances entitling to buyback mentioned above need to be detailed as follows. In the *first* case (profit distribution), as for the limited liability company, the resolution deciding not to distribute profit must have been approved while the company had not distributed *profit* to its shareholders for five consecutive years, even though it was beneficiary during the same period of time (Art. 161§1, item 1). This provision adds that the profit distribution should meet the conditions set by the Company Law *(ibid., in fine)*. Such conditions are to be found further down in the law, in Chapter 10 containing provisions on financial affairs and the accounting common to the limited liability company and the shareholding company (Art. 210 to 212; s. below §§2114ff.) The law further gives the board of directors of the limited liability company the power to make proposals to the shareholders' meeting to that effect (Art. 67§2, item 4) applying to the shareholding company by the reference of Art. 120§2) and, to the latter, that to approve them or not (Art. 59§1, item 4 applying to the shareholding company by the reference of Art. 112§1).

2038 In the *second* case (continuation), the continuation of the company must have been approved despite its *duration*, set in the bylaws, has expired, alternatively despite a cause of *dissolution* prescribed in the bylaws, has occurred, and the resolution adopted has amended the bylaws to the effect of extending such duration or overcoming such cause of dissolution (Art. 161§1, item 3). The *third* and last case (majority transfer), M&A, has been mentioned above (*ibid.*, item 2; s. §2034).

2039 The shareholder and the company must *agree* on the buyback. If they have not within 60 days of the resolution, the shareholder must file at *court* within another 30 days[886] (Art. 161§2 replicating Art. 89§2). In any of the three cases of Art. 161§1, whenever the purchase has been executed, whether consensually or by court order, the shares must be transferred or cancelled within six months (Art. 161§3).

---

885 S. above Art. 22 and 23 (§§1809 and 1810) and below, Art. 180, 189 and 192 (s. §§2062ff. and 2080ff.)

886 Art. 89§2 mentions 60 and 90 days respectively. This drafting is deceiving. Both counts start from the resolution; the 90-days limit does not start from the expiry of the 60-days one, as an inattentive reading could mislead. Thus, the shareholder has another 30, not 90, days, for filing at court after the expiry of the 60-days limit.

In the second of those two groups of buyback cases[887] (*company buyback*, i.e., spontaneous buyback from the company or upon request of a shareholder not enjoying a buyback right) and other than the cases mentioned above, the purchase by a shareholding company of its own shares or buyback can occur for numerous reasons, including: to increase shareholder value, improve financial ratios, signal confidence, return excess cash, and for various strategic and operational reasons, such as defending against a takeover, employees incentive plans, or treasury stock. Conversely, they are restricted to promoting market transparency, ensuring fair taxation, protecting shareholders, and preventing potential abuses by corporations and insiders. Buybacks are permitted under the Company Law, but exceptionally so, and confined within strict boundaries, which are detailed at Art. 162. 2040

Thus, in principle, a shareholding company is *prohibited* to buy its own shares (Art. 161§1, 1st phrase); the law only provides for a limited number of *exceptions* (*ibid.*, 2nd phrase). Moreover, the law subjects company buybacks to several requirements: before the buyback, after the buyback, applying to listed shareholding companies, and related to pledges. 2041

The exceptional cases in which a shareholding company may buy its own shares include: the reduction of its registered capital; a merger with any other company holding shares of the shareholding company considering a buyback; using the shares for employee stock option plans or equity incentives; dissenting shareholder's buybacks (Art. 161; s. above §§2034ff.) relating to a merger or a division; using the shares for the conversion of the convertible corporate bonds offered by the company; and the need for a listed company to maintain its value and protect its shareholders (Art. 162§1). 2042

It should be noted that while, in case of transfer of the majority of the company's assets, Art. 161§1, item 2 entitles a shareholder to compel the company, if necessary by filing at court, to buy back its shares (s. above §2039), in case of *merger or division*, Art. 162§1, item 4 authorizes the company to buy back such shares, but does not entitle the shareholder to force the company to do so. 2043

Before the buyback, any such buyback is subject to strict approval requirements with respect to the approving body, the majority and the quorum. The two first cases (reduction of the registered capital; merger with any other company holding shares of the shareholding company) are subject to the most stringent conditions, by requiring a resolution by the shareholders meeting (Art. 162§2, 1st sentence). 2044

The three next cases (using the shares for employee stock option plans or equity incentives; using the shares for the conversion of the convertible corporate 2045

[887] S. above §2032.

bonds offered by the company; need for a listed company to maintain its value and protect its shareholders) are subject to a decision of the board of directors provided, however, it has been authorized to do so by the bylaws or the shareholders meeting; if so, the board of directors shall adopt any such resolution provided a quorum of two thirds of its members in attendance is met (Art. 162§2, 2nd sentence). The law does not mention the related majority; therefore, one may assume that a simple majority applies, unless the bylaws or the shareholders meeting has provided otherwise.

2046 Finally, Art. 162 does not mention any such requirement for the last case (dissenting shareholder's buybacks relating to a merger or a division), which suggests that a mere decision of the board of directors at the majority of those present (subject to more stringent requirements of the bylaws) may suffice, being recalled that, as mentioned in the preceding paragraph, the shareholder does enjoy a right to have its shares bought back.

2047 *After the buyback*, the company must meet certain obligations (Art. 162§3), which depend on the case considered and may be somewhat confusing since they do not recoup the cases addressed in the preceding paragraph. In the first case (capital reduction), the company must cancel the purchased shares within ten days (*ibid.*, 1st sentence, 1st phrase); in two more cases (merger; dissenting shareholder), it shall cancel the purchased shares within six months (*ibid.*, 2nd sentence); in the three remaining cases (employees incentive plan; convertible corporate bonds; company value), the company is subject to a double requirement: it may not hold more than 10% of the total issued shares, and it must transfer or cancel the purchased shares within three years (*ibid.*, 3rd and 4th phrases).

2048 In case of buyback, *listed shareholding companies* are subject to additional requirements (Art. 161§4): they must comply with special disclosure requirements under the Securities Law (*ibid.*, 1st sentence). Moreover, in three cases (employees incentive plan; convertible corporate bonds; company value), they have to purchase their shares "in a public and centralized trading manner" (*ibid.*, 2nd sentence). This latter expression means that buybacks by listed companies must be conducted openly, through the main stock exchange where their shares are traded, rather than through private, off-market or negotiated transactions.

2049 Finally, a corporation may not accept its own shares as the collateral of a *pledge* (Art. 161§5).

2050 The next restriction on the transfer of shares applies to *financial assistance* granted by the shareholding company to third parties. Thus, a shareholding company may not provide any gift, loan, security or other financial assistance to others to acquire shares of the company. The prohibition extends to the company's parent, i.e., a shareholding company may not provide financial assistance to a third party for buying shares of the company that controls it either (Art. 163, 1st phrase). This prohibition evidently aims at preventing the circumvention of the restrictions applying to company buybacks.

Art. 163 provides for two *exceptions*. First, employee stock ownership plans (ESOP) are exempted from that prohibition (Art. 163 *in fine*). Second, the shareholders meeting or, if so empowered by the bylaws, the board of directors, may authorize such assistance. However, any such decision is subject to two restrictions: cumulative assistance may not exceed 10% of the issued shares capital and, if the related resolution is to be adopted by the board of directors, it is subject to a qualified majority of two-thirds of the directors, present or not (Art. 163§2). If the company suffers damage as a result of the inobservance of the foregoing, the responsible officers shall be liable (Art. 163§3). 2051

The last restriction relates to *inheritance*: in case of death of a shareholder, while, in principle, his lawful successor succeeds the deceased shareholder status, the bylaws may restrict such transfer (Art. 167). 2052

The offering of *bonds* is governed by Chapter 10 which is outlined below (s. Chap. 9 §64.VII, Corporate Bonds). 2053

V. Special Provisions on the Organizational Structure of State-owned Companies

Chapter 7 of the Company Law (Art. 168 to 177) is dedicated to the organizational structure of State-owned companies (SOEs; 国有企业 guóyǒu qǐyè). An SOE can be wholly or partly State-owned (Art. 168§2, 1st phrase). It takes the form of a limited liability company or of a shareholding company. As clearly mentioned from the outset by its first article, the other provisions of the Company Law apply if Chapter 7 is silent (Art. 168). 2054

Even though foreign investment in an SOE is possible (and had occasionally occurred, namely, before 2020, in the form of Sino-foreign JV which, since JVs have been abolished by the FIL as of 2025, now typically take the form of a shareholding company or of a limited liability company), such cases are marginal and, therefore, not the focus of this book. In any event, in practice, given the probable balance of power in favor of the State party, a foreign investor in an SOE will unlikely have much say with respect to the latter's organizational structure, although it may, however, wish to familiarize itself with it. Be it as it may, we will not discuss this chapter of the law to which we refer the reader, as well as to specialized literature or professional advice. 2055

VI. Qualification and Duties of Directors, Supervisors, and Senior Executives

2056 Notably relevant to foreign investors is Chapter 8 of the Company Law (Art. 178 to 193) on the qualification and duties of directors, supervisors, and senior executives of a company, be it a limited liability company or a shareholding company. While the limited liability company and the shareholding company regimes already contain several provisions specifically related to the topical regime as far as the duties of the directors, etc.[888] and their liability in case of infringement are concerned, Chap. 8 contains provisions of a more general nature, applicable both to the limited liability company and the shareholding company, which are, for those reasons, of great significance. As such, they exemplify the Chinese legislator commitment to solidify corporate governance, and foreign investors' trust in it.

2057 Chapter 8 is concerned by directors, supervisors, and senior executives[889]. *Directors* obviously refers to directors of the board, which is governed, mainly, by Section 3 of Chapter 5 of the law on the formation and organizational structure of a shareholding company (Art. 120 ff.; s. above Chap. 9 §64.IV.C, Board of Directors and Manager). *Supervisors* are governed by Section 4 of the same chapter (Art. 130 ff.; s. above Chap. 9 §64.IV.D, Board of Supervisors).

2058 The notions of "senior executive" as well as those of "controlling shareholder" and "actual controller", which are related, are defined at the very end of the law, in Chapter 15 on supplemental provisions (Art. 265), as follows: "*senior executive*" means the president, vice president, or chief financial officer of a company, the secretary for the board of directors of a listed company, or any other person prescribed as senior executive (or, arguably, any denomination implying such position) in the company bylaws (*ibid.*, item 1). "*Controlling shareholder*" means a shareholder contributing more than 50% of the total capital of a limited liability company, or holding more than 50% of the total share capital of a corporation, or a shareholder with a capital contribution or shareholding ratio of less than 50% whose voting rights corresponding to its capital contribution or shareholding ratio are, however, sufficient to enable the shareholder to exercise significant influence on the resolutions of the shareholders' meeting (*ibid.*, item 2); finally "*actual controller*" is defined as a person able to actually dominate the conduct of a company through investment relations,

---

888 The short name "directors, etc." used by convenience in this chapter of the book refers to "directors, supervisors and senior executives"; it does include neither controlling shareholders nor actual controllers.

889 About related *translation* issues, s. above §§1858 to 1861.

agreements, or other arrangements (*ibid.*, item 3). These notions are repeatedly referred to in the Company Law.

The law is further concerned by *family ties* and erects extensive guardrails whenever such ties are involved. As such, the duty to report personal transactions outlined below (Art. 182; s. §2065) is extended to the following parties: to close relatives[890] of a director; to third party enterprises controlled by such a director, etc.; to enterprises controlled by a close relative of a director, etc.; and to third parties affiliated to a director, etc. By doing so, Chinese law acknowledges the particular significance of family ties in Chinese business culture, and complies with global corporate governance standards. 2059

The directors', etc. general duties may consist in either what they must do or, on the contrary, not do, as well as their liability if they infringe such prohibitions, and the corresponding rights shareholders may rely upon holding those directors, etc. liable in case of any such infringement. 2060

Starting with their *duties*, most generally, not surprisingly, directors, etc. must comply with the law, administrative regulations and the company bylaws (Art. 179). Those general duties match those to be found in most jurisdictions nowadays; they mainly consist of two fundamental duties: the duty of loyalty and the duty of diligence, from which most other duties (or, conversely, prohibitions) are derived, as outlined below. 2061

The *duty of loyalty* to the company (Art. 180§1, 1st phrase) is not clearly defined by the law; instead, its mention is complemented by a series of corollary duties which are twofold: the duty of adopting measures to avoid *conflicts of interests* between the directors, etc. own interests and those of the company (*ibid.*, 2nd phrase); and the prohibition to *take advantage of their powers* to seek any improper interests (*ibid.*, 3rd phrase). In addition, both corollaries are developed in separate provisions, which we discuss below (s. §§2069ff.) 2062

Next to the duty of loyalty, the *duty of diligence* towards the company is further qualified as the duty of exercising the due care that a manager ordinarily exercises in the best interest of the company in executing its functions (Art. 180§2). 2063

As the title of the chapter makes clear, these duties apply primarily to directors and senior executives. However, when the *controlling shareholder* or *actual controller* of a company practically executes the affairs of the company, even though he does not serve as a director of the company, both the duty of loyalty and that of diligence extend to them (Art. 180§3). 2064

---

890 The notion of "close relative" is defined at Art. 1045§2 of the Chinese Civil Code (s. above note 603).

2065 Among the duties deriving from those of loyalty and diligence, one should add the *duty to report personal transactions*. This duty applies to a director, etc. who enters into a contract, or conducts a transaction with the company, i.e., to which he is personally, as a natural person, a party, and the company his contractual counterpart. It applies both in case of direct or indirect involvement. Such transactions are permitted, but subject to the above-mentioned duty to report to the board of directors or the shareholders' meeting, following which the board of directors or the shareholders' meeting shall adopt a resolution on the same, in accordance with the company bylaws (Art. 182§1). Although the law does not specify it, one may suppose that the board of directors or the shareholders' meeting may either approve or reject such transaction or subject it to certain conditions. As noted above (s. §2059), Art. 182§2 extends the application of Art. 182§1 to the close relatives of a director, etc. Besides, any revenue perceived by such director, etc. deriving from a violation of that duty belongs to the company (Art. 186).

2066 These duties are reflected in a series of *prohibitions* which we outline below. To start with, a person is *prohibited to serve as a director*, etc. in several cases: where that person lost his civil capacity; where, in certain cases, he has been condemned for a criminal penalty; where, as director, etc. or factory director, he has, in certain cases, been involved in a bankruptcy; where, as legal representative, his enterprise forfeited[891] its license or was ordered to shut down (s. below Art. 260§1 and 261, and §§2195 and 2201); and where it is, in certain cases, listed as a "dishonest debtor"[892] by a court (Art. 178§1). This provision provides detail for each particular case. The contemplated cases focus on economic crimes such as embezzlement of public or private property, bribery, misappropriation of property, or disruption of the order of the socialist market economy and are subject to certain conditions of time. If any such person is appointed or elected as director, etc., such appointment or election shall be void (*ibid.*, § 2), and if any such circumstance occurs after such appointment or election, the director, etc. shall be removed from his office (*ibid.*, § 3).

2067 Other than the prohibitions already mentioned together with the corollaries defining the duties of loyalty and diligence in general terms, the duty of loyalty is detailed in two complementary provisions: Art. 181, which specifies several

---

891 On the notion of forfeiture, s. above §§337 to 339.

892 The legal framework for listing "dishonest debtors" in China centers on the Several Provisions of the Supreme People's Court on Issuing the Information on the List of Dishonest Judgment Debtors (2017 Amendment), which establishes a credit discipline system to enforce court judgments. This framework operates under the broader Civil Procedure Law, namely, Art. 255, and involves coordinated sanctions across government agencies.

prohibitions, and Art. 183, which focuses on the abuse of power[893], without expressly mentioning it however (s. below §2070ff.)

2068 Thus, owing to several special *prohibitions* ancillary to the general duty of loyalty, a director, etc. is prohibited to: embezzle any property or misappropriate any funds of the company; deposit any funds of the company in an account opened in his own name or in the name of any other individual; commit bribery or accept any other illegal revenue by taking advantage of his powers; accept and pocket commissions on transactions between others and the company; and illegally disclose any confidential information of the company (Art. 181, items 1 to 5). The law adds a general prohibition to otherwise violate the duty of loyalty, without offering further definitions however, which are thus left to the discretion of the judge, as the case may be (*ibid.*, item 6).

2069 *Abuse of power*, which is already mentioned in general terms at Art. 180§1 *in fine* and, specifically, at Art. 181§1, item 3 in relation to bribery, is further developed at Art. 183. Thus, a director, etc. is subject to the *prohibition of taking advantage of his position to seek any business opportunity* belonging to the company for himself or any other person (who, although the law only implies it, is assumed to be related one way or the other to that director, etc.), except under any of the following two circumstances: first, the director, etc. reported it, and such opportunity was approved as mandated by Art. 182 for personal transactions (Art. 183, item 1; s. above §2065); second, the law, an administrative regulation or the bylaws prevent the company from exploiting the business opportunity[894] (*ibid.*, item 2).

2070 The relationship between Art. 183 and *abuse of power* deserves additional comments, however. First, it is worth noting that Art. 22 (s. above §1792), which pertains Chapter 1 of the Company Law on general provisions and addresses the abuse of *affiliation*, is almost identically drafted as the last phrase of Art. 180§1. However, while Art. 22 prohibits those officers, etc., to take advantage of their "affiliation" to harm the company, Art. 180§1 *in fine* refers to their "powers".

2071 An *affiliation* is defined by Art. 265, item 4 as the relationship between the controlling shareholder, actual controller, directors, supervisors, and senior executives of a company and the enterprise directly or indirectly controlled by them respectively, as well as any other relationship that may cause the transfer of any interest of the company. In contrast, the directors', etc. powers are, in principle, defined by the law, the bylaws, or granted by a resolution of the shareholders' meeting. Arguably, beyond the similarity of their drafting, these

---

[893] We distinguish the abuse of power (singular form; of a director, etc.) from the abuse of powers (plural form) or excess power (of a *falsus procurator*).

[894] This drafting suggests that if neither the law, nor an administrative regulation, nor the bylaws prevent the company to exploit the business opportunity at stake, but that the company does not exploit it anyway, that condition is not met either.

scopes do not overlap: "affiliation" under Art. 22 targets ethical conduct applying to conflicts of interest in related-party relationships, while "powers" under Art. 180§1 regulate compliance with the scope of authorized duties. The two concepts operate in *complementarity* towards each other, but do not overlap.

2072 Second, Art. 183 does not expressly mention "abuse of power" as Art. 180§1 *in fine* but "taking advantage of one's position". Nor does it refer to "affiliation" as Art. 22. Yet one could reasonably submit that taking advantage of one's position is a form of abuse of power, whereas the exploitation of such advantage frequently involves an affiliation.

2073 Beyond those fine lines, we believe that all three provisions, Art. 22, 180§1 *in fine* and 183, however not identical, are different forms of (infringements to) the duty of loyalty, which complement each other. What foreign investors should retain is that the definition of the duty of loyalty under Chinese law should be considered as extensive, and that most forms of violation will likely be considered as illegal, especially since, as noted, Art. 181, item 6 introduces a general prohibition of violating the duty of loyalty, without offering further definitions than those contained in Art. 180§1 and 181, items 1 to 5, thus leaving its appreciation to the discretion of the judge, who can be generally expected to rule conservatively.

2074 A director, etc. is further under the *prohibition to compete with the company*, i.e., to engage in the same kind of business as the company for his own account or for the account of any other person, unless he reports to the board of directors or the shareholders' meeting, and either adopts a resolution authorizing it (Art. 184).

2075 It is interesting to note that, while the mechanism is the same like for personal transactions (Art. 182; s. above §2065), i.e., that both are permitted provided they are reported and approved, personal transactions are mentioned in the form of a generally *licit* behavior, subject to a duty to report and to approval, while competition is mentioned in the form of a generally *prohibited* behavior, yet possibly licit subject to the same duty and approval. This difference in drafting suggests that the Chinese legislator may have been intent in putting more emphasis on the prohibition of certain behaviors than others, subject to the court's appreciation mentioned in the preceding paragraph.

2076 Finally, an affiliated director is constrained by the *prohibition from voting* on any resolution implying (or "affiliating") him in any of the circumstances addressed by Art. 182 through 184 (personal transaction, taking advantage, competition; Art. 185, 1st sentence). This provision only applies to the resolutions of the board of directors, not to those of the shareholders' meeting, where the affiliated director, if also a shareholder, would not be prevented to vote, but where his vote would be diluted and could not, as a result, have the impact it would have within the board of directors. Art. 185, 1st sentence further adjusts the related voting modalities by clarifying that that affiliated director's vote is not counted in the total voting rights, and that if the number of independent directors, i.e., not affiliated or implicated in the circumstances at stake, is less than three, then the matter is to be referred to the shareholders' meeting (*ibid.*, 2nd sentence).

The remaining provisions of Chapter 7 of the Company Law on the qualification and duties of directors, etc. are chiefly concerned with their *liability* as a consequence of the violation of their duties. The basic principle of such liability is expressed by Art. 188, which affirms that a director, etc. of a company who violates a law, an administrative regulation or the bylaws in (not) performing his duties, causing any loss to the company, is liable for damages. Some provisions establishing the liability of directors, etc. are to be found elsewhere in the Company Law: as recalled, Art. 22§2 provides for their liability in case of abuse of their affiliation (s. above §2070). Besides, Art. 51 (missing capital contributions of a limited liability company; s. above 1849); 53 (abuse of capital contributions of a limited liability company; s. above §1927) , 125§2 (illicit resolution of the board of directors of a shareholding company; s. above §1967); 163 (financial assistance of a shareholding company; s. above §2051); and 211 (profit distribution; s. below §2077; this list is not exhaustive) address specific cases of liability, to which one may add Art. 99, which provides for the liability of the promoters of the shareholding company (s. above §1927). Other than that, Chapter 1 on general provisions mainly provides for the liability of shareholders, while Chapter 14 focuses on the liability of the company itself. 2077

As for the general duties of directors, etc., their general liability is detailed in several special liabilities. The regime of directors', etc. liability is complex and needs to be broken down to be soundly understood. It depends on several *factors*, including who is the author; who is the victim; who has the right to challenge the author's liability; which duties have been violated; if such violation needs to be faulty or not; and which remedies are available. 2078

Authors can be a director, a supervisor, a senior executive, a controlling shareholder, an actual controller, or anyone else. Victims can be the company, a subsidiary, a shareholder, or anyone else. Right holders can be the company, its shareholders or a third party. Duties can be the specific duties of directors, etc., or general duties imposed by the law. Violations can be intentional or result from negligence. Remedies can be internal or external, i.e., available within the structure of the company, or before a court; in other words, they can be indirect, i.e., whenever they are resorted to through such structure, for example, through the board of directors, or direct, i.e., when they are resorted to without resorting to such structure, for example, when a shareholder files at court directly. 2079

Authors, i.e., directors, supervisors and senior executives, are held accountable under various circumstances by Art. 188 through 189 and 192, as well as 186. 2080

Directors and supervisors only are under Art. 190 and 191, which do not apply to supervisors. Controlling shareholders and actual controllers are under Art. 192. The company is under Art. 191. Third parties are under Art. 189§3.

2081 *Victims* are the company, which is protected by Art. 186, 188, 189 and 192; shareholders, by Art. 190 and 192; and third parties, by Art. 191.

2082 *Right holders* are either the company (represented by its board of directors or of supervisors) in the case of Art. 186, 189 and 192, or shareholders if, in the case of Art. 189, the board of directors or of supervisors neglects to act; shareholders are also entitled under Art. 190. Third parties are entitled under Art. 191.

2083 *Duties* whose violation causes such liabilities are mostly specific to directors, etc. (Art. 186, 188, 189, 190 and 192), but the violation of other general duties not consisting in the violation of duties specific to the directors, etc. can also result in liabilities under Art. 191.

2084 The law does not mention if the liability resulting from the violations at stake is objective or subjective, i.e., whether their authors need to have committed a *fault*, or whether a mere violation, even non faulty, results in their liability anyway. It does not specify either if, in case such fault is needed, whether it should have been intentional, or if it suffices that it has been committed by negligence. We submit that, considering the nature of the infraction considered, most of them can only be committed intentionally; where they have not, negligence should amount to a violation of the directors, etc., duty of diligence; hence, by definition, such negligence should result in their liability.

2085 In any event, their liability is of a contractual nature, therefore it is, to that extent, objective, but they should be able to exonerate themselves by proving that they have not committed any fault, whether intentionally or by negligence (s. above §794). Only Art. 191, 2nd sentence tempers this assessment by rendering directors, etc. liable *jointly and severally* with the company only if they acted intentionally or by gross negligence, thus sheltering them in case of light negligence (but not preventing the company to claim back, from its director, the damage the company suffered as a result of the compensation the company may have had to pay to the victim, even in case of that director's light negligence, for violation of his duty of diligence towards the company).

2086 Internal or indirect *remedies* consist, in a first stage, in the shareholders requesting the board of directors or of supervisors to take action (Art. 189). External or direct remedies consist in filing at court (Art. 190). It is the board of directors or of supervisors that must file at court in the second stage; however, shareholders may do so directly too, if the board of directors or of supervisors fails to (Art. 189).

Those distinctions being clarified, one may systematically analyze the four provisions forming the liability regime of directors, etc. The first three (Art. 189 to 191) are to be distinguished from the last (Art. 192) by their *author*, who is, for the first three, a *director*, etc. while it is, for the last, a *controlling shareholder* or an *actual controller*. Among the first three, a further distinction is to be made depending on the *victim*: Art. 189 applies in case of damage to the *company*; Art. 190 to *shareholders*; Art. 190 to *third parties*. 2087

As mentioned, the *first* liability case relates to damage to the *company* and is regulated by Art. 189. It is the longest and the most complex of these provisions. It mainly provides for the right of shareholders to internally challenge directors, supervisors or senior executives. Art. 189 refers from the outset to Art. 188, which renders directors, etc. liable if they violated the law, an administrative regulation or the bylaws, and caused thereby damage to the company. 2088

If the shareholders are challenging a *director or senior executive*, they may request the *board of supervisors* to file at court against such director or senior executive (Art. 189§1, 1st sentence). Conversely, if challenging a *supervisor*, the shareholders may request the *board of directors* to file (*ibid.*, 2nd sentence). 2089

Not any shareholder can do so: in a fashion comparable, although not identical, to the right of extended consultation of the company papers (Art. 110; s. above §1944), such request is subject to *qualifications*; they differ for the limited liability company and the shareholding company. For a limited liability company, any shareholder qualifies. For a shareholding company, such shareholder must hold at least one percent of the shares; however, a group of shareholders qualifies too if their added up (or "aggregate") shares qualify; in all cases, the shareholders, whether of a limited liability company or a shareholding company, must have held their shares for at least 180 consecutive days[895] (Art. 189§1, 1st sentence). The request must be formed in writing (*ibid.*, § 2). 2090

The board of directors or of supervisors must file within 30 days; however, in case of emergency, they must file immediately. If it fails to, the shareholder or shareholders may file at court directly, in his or their name (Art. 189§2). 2091

In other words, shareholders may not file at court directly against a director, etc.; they must act through the company; only if the latter fails to act can they file directly. The same regime applies if shareholders intend to file against a *third party* having allegedly harmed the company (Art. 189§3). 2092

Likewise, it applies to the *subsidiary* of a company if the author is either a director, a supervisor or a senior executive of the subsidiary, or a third party, 2093

---

[895] Comparatively, Art. 110 on the right of extended consultation requires 3%; it also sets a threshold of 180 days.

and the victim is the subsidiary: in such case, the right holders are the shareholders of the company; provided they qualify, they have to act indirectly through the board of directors or of supervisors of the subsidiary, unless such board neglects to act (Art. 189§4). Art. 189§1 otherwise applies *mutatis mutandis*.

2094 The *second* liability case relates to damage to *shareholders* and is regulated by Art. 190. Unlike in case of damage to the company, where shareholders can only act through the board of directors or supervisors (Art. 189), they can file at court directly in case the director's, etc. violation of his duty not to harm the interests of shareholders (Art. 190). There is a fine line between the harm to the company and that to the interests of shareholders since, indirectly, any harm to the company eventually results in harming the interests of shareholders. Absent any clarification in the law, one may suppose that Art. 190 requires such harm to be somehow direct, and that that notion, which is relative, is left to the judge's appreciation. Like for Art. 188 and 189, the director, etc. must have caused such damage by having violated the law, an administrative regulation or the bylaws. One could say that the shareholders' right to file at court directly in case of damage to the company if the board of directors or supervisors neglects to act can be equated to that of Art. 191 since, in case of passivity of the board, damage to the company somehow translates into damage to the shareholders.

2095 The *third* liability case relates to damage to *third parties* and is regulated by Art. 191. While the damage must have been committed by a director, etc. performing his function, it must not necessarily result from a violation of the law, etc. Where such harm is inflicted, the company, not the director, is liable in the first place. However, if the director has acted intentionally or by gross negligence, he shall be jointly and severally liable along with the company. We further refer to the discussion above about the implications related to the fault (s. §2084).

2096 Finally, the *fourth* liability case relates to *controlling shareholders* and *actual controllers* and is regulated by Art. 192. Whenever the controlling shareholder or actual controller instructs or, more accurately, *instigates* a director, etc. to engage in any conduct harming the interests of the company or of shareholders of the company, the controlling shareholder or actual controller is jointly and severally liable together with such director.

2097 A *fifth* case of liability, however ancillary to the preceding cases, which has already been mentioned about Art. 181 (personal transaction; s. above §2065), may be added: any *revenue resulting from a violation of the directors, etc. duties*, i.e., of the latter provisions as well as of Art. 182 through 184 (personal transaction, taking advantage, competition) belongs to the company (Art. 186).

A company may contract *liability insurance* for its directors, etc. and must report to its shareholders about it (Art. 193). 2098

VII. Corporate Bonds

Corporate bonds are governed by 13 articles contained in Chapter 9 of the 2099 Company Law (Art. 194 to 206). They are defined as marketable securities offered by a company that, as agreed, repays the principal and pays interest as scheduled. They may be offered publicly or not (Art. 194). At the risk of restating the obvious, compared to shares, bonds make the bondholder a creditor to the company issuing the bond, offering fixed income and lower risk, but no ownership or voting rights, while shares make the shareholder a stakeholder, offering potential for higher returns and voting rights, but with higher risk and volatility.

As the preceding chapter of the law, Chapter 10 applies both to the limited 2100 liability company and the shareholding company: the typically smaller size of the limited liability company does not prevent it to issue bonds too. Be that as it may, the bond regime presents some similarities with that of shares, as well as some notable differences, which we highlight thereafter. To start with, other than the Company Law, bonds are, like shares, also governed by the *Securities Law* (cf. Securities Law, Art. 2). However, the Securities Law only applies to ancillary or regulatory aspects of the rights and obligations related to shares[896]; most of their offering and trading is regulated by the Company Law. In contrast, as far as bonds are concerned, their offering and trading is primarily governed by the Securities Law, which Chapter 9 of the Company Law mentions in its first article (Art. 194 *in fine*). Other administrative regulations, which the law does not specify, apply too (*ibid.*)

Like for the public offering of shares of a shareholding company (Art. 154; s. 2101 above §2004), the company must *register the offering* with the competent authority, which is the CSRC, and issue a *prospectus* (Art. 195§1). The differences between the shares prospectus[897] (Art. 154§2) and the bonds prospectus include the following: by definition, bonds can only be offered with a par value; moreover, unlike the shares prospectus, the bonds prospectus must mention: the method for determination of the interest rate for the bonds; the time limits and methods for repayment of the principal and payment of interest; the security provided for the bonds; the net asset value of the company; the total amount

[896] The Securities Law is only mentioned, as far as shares are concerned, in relation with the company's disclosure duty in case of buyback (s. Art. 162§3; s. above §2047).

[897] S. above note 854.

of corporate bonds issued but not due; and the underwriter of the bonds (Art. 195§2; s. below §2106).

2102 Compared to the shares certificate (Art. 149; s. above §§1885 and 1886), the *bonds certificate* shall mention the par value, interest rate, and time limit for repayment (Art. 196); moreover, it must be registered in the *bondholders register* (Art. 197 and 198§1), which shall mention, among the other usual information, the total interest rate, as well as the time limits and methods for both the repayment of the principal and the payment of interest (Art. 198§2).

2103 Bonds certificate may be *transferred* freely, at the price agreed between the parties, by endorsement, and the updating of the bondholders register (Art. 200 and 201), like for shares certificates, except that the latter, unlike bonds, may be subject to restrictions (Art. 157; s. above Chap. 9 §64.IV.F.2, Transfer of Shares).

2104 Like the limited liability company shareholders meeting (Art. 62; s. above §1866), the shareholding company formation meeting (Art. 103; §§1934ff.), the shareholding company shareholders meeting (Art. 133; s. above §§1948ff.) and the shareholding company class shareholders meetings (Art. 146; s. above §1996), in case of public offering, the law mandates a *bondholders meeting* at which the bondholders have the opportunity to settle matters interesting them. The meeting gathers holders in the same issue of bonds. The related procedures must be detailed in the prospectus (Art. 204§1). Its resolutions are binding on all holders of the same bonds issue, but the prospectus may provide otherwise (*ibid.*, § 2).

2105 A distinctive feature of bonds is that they may be converted into shares. To be publicly offered, *convertible bonds* (Art. 202 and 203) must have been authorized, be it by a resolution of the shareholders' meeting, or by a resolution of the board of directors adopted as authorized by the company bylaws or by the shareholders' meeting (Art. 202§1, 2nd phrase). The resolution must specify the conversion method (*ibid.*, 2nd phrase). Such listing must be registered with CSRC, like an ordinary one (Art. 202§1, 2nd sentence; s. above §2101). They must be clearly marked, both on the certificate and in the register (*ibid.*, § 2). Once convertible bonds are offered, the holder may freely choose to convert, but the company may not: it is bound by such choice; however, the law or an administrative regulation may provide otherwise (Art. 203).

2106 The issuance of listed bonds is severely regulated. Not only does it need to be registered with the supervisory authority, the CSRC; the issuing company must also mandatorily rely on qualified, licensed external operators, including one or more underwriters, a clearing house and a trustee. A *bond underwriter*[898] acts as a key intermediary between the bond issuer and investors, ensuring the success and smooth execution of the bond issuance process; it is only incidentally mentioned among the prospectus' contents (Art. 195§2, item 10). Although the law does not expressly mention whether such underwriter is mandatory, in practice, it is, i.e., the CSRC will not authorize the listing, unless the company retains an underwriter.

The registration and clearing institution, A.K.A. *clearing house* (such as the China Securities Depository and Clearing Corporation), ensures the smooth processing and settlement of bond trades: it establishes rules on the registration, deposit, interest payment, and redemption, among other things, of bonds (Art. 199). Likewise, the law falls short of mentioning whether a clearing house is mandatory, although in practice, like the underwriter, it is. 2107

A *bond trustee* represents and protects the interests of bondholders: in case of public listing, it must be appointed by the company, and handles the acceptance of debt repayments, the protection of claims, bond-related litigation, participation in bankruptcy proceedings of the debtor, and other matters for bondholders (Art. 205). 2108

Such operators are typically investment banks, other financial institutions, or law firms. They must be specifically licensed to that effect. The dual role of both underwriter and bond trustee can, under certain conditions, exceptionally be held by the lead underwriter[899]. However, the clearing house cannot simultaneously serve as the underwriter or bond trustee for the same bond issuance. Likewise, all three roles cannot be combined. Other than the underwriter[900], these operators are specific to the issuance of bonds; as outlined, the issuance of shares relies on other processes (s. above Chap. 9 §64.IV.F.1, Offering of Shares). 2109

VIII. Financial Affairs and Accounting of a Company

Chapter 10 of the Company Law contains eleven articles (Art. 207 to 217); one is duty bound to stress from the outset that they do not exhaustively address the 2110

[898] The shareholding company must equally mandate an underwriter in case of public offering of shares (Art. 155; s. above 2010).

[899] As permitted by the Guidelines on the Trustee Business for Non-Financial Enterprise Debt Financing Instruments in the Interbank Bond Market (Trial) issued by the National Association of Financial Market Institutional Investors (NAFMII) on 27 December 2019.

[900] S. preceding note.

financial affairs and accounting of a company, however; they only set basic rules applying to certain related aspects including reporting, profit distribution, reserves, audit, books and accounts. The detailed regulation of the financial affairs and accounting of a company are further contained in a wealth of secondary legislation, which would not only exceed the scope of this book, but also that of Chinese law strictly speaking, to enter the realm of accounting and finance. Beyond such principles, readers are advised to consult with an accounting firm.

2111 That said, as far as the Company Law is concerned, first and foremost, a company must establish a *system* for managing its financial affairs and accounting. This system must comply with the laws, administrative regulations and the provisions issued by the finance department of the State Council (Art. 207).

2112 A company shall, at the end of each fiscal year, prepare a financial accounting *report*. Such report must be *audited* by an accounting firm. Both the report's content and the role of the accounting firm must comply with the law, etc. (Art. 208). The chapter contains additional provisions about such accounting firms, which we will address further below (s. §2122).

2113 The limited liability company is subject to additional requirements: it must deliver its report to each shareholder within the time limit prescribed in the bylaws and place it at the company for consultation by the shareholders 20 days before the annual shareholders' meeting. The report must mention any public offering of shares (Art. 209).

2114 *Profit distribution* is governed by rather extensive regulations (Art. 210 to 212). By regulating whether profit may be distributed, used to cover losses, or set aside, the law distinguishes statutory reserves from discretionary reserves and, in case of distribution, the limited liability company from the shareholding company. Reserves are further regulated by Art. 213 and 214 (s. below §§2120).

2115 Where a company distributes its after-tax profit for the current year, it must set aside 10% of the profit as funds of the *statutory reserve* of the company (Art. 210§1, 1st sentence). It may, however, discontinue setting aside such funds if their cumulative amount is 50% or more of its registered capital (*ibid.*, 2nd sentence). Furthermore, a special rule applies in case of conversion (Art. 214§3; s. below §2121).

2116 Where the statutory reserve of a company is not sufficient to cover *losses* from the previous years, the profit of the current year shall be used for covering losses before the funds of the statutory reserve are set aside (Art. 210§2). The covering of losses is further regulated by Art. 214§2 (s. below §2121).

2117 If after-tax profit remain after they have been set aside to the statutory reserve funds or used to cover any losses, a company may either keep or distribute them.

In the second option, a company may, upon resolution of the shareholders' meeting, set the excess aside to a *discretionary reserve* (*ibid.*, § 3).

In the second option, the *distribution* of the remaining after-tax profit, i.e., after the loss is covered and reserve funds have been set aside, differs for the limited liability company and the shareholding company. The limited liability company may distribute it in proportion to the paid-in capital contributions of shareholders, unless all the shareholders agree that profit are not distributed in proportion to their capital contributions. In contrast, the shareholding company may distribute it in proportion to the shares held by the shareholders, except as otherwise prescribed in the bylaws (*ibid.*, § 4). A company may not distribute to itself the profit corresponding to its own shares however (*ibid.*, § 5). 2118

If profit have been distributed in violation of Art. 210, the shareholders must return them and are *liable* for any loss together with any responsible director, supervisor or senior executive (Art. 211)[901]. The distribution must occur within six months from the shareholders' resolution, if any (Art. 212). 2119

As noted, reserves are regulated in further detail by Art. 213 and 214. These provisions address a third type of reserve (cf. Art. 214§2), designated as the *capital reserve*. Thus, other than excess profit, certain financial assets are, by law, to be considered as capital reserve, while their use is equally regulated. They include the premium obtained by a company from an offering of shares at an offering price above the par value of stock, as well as the portion of proceeds from an offering of no-par shares, which is not included in the registered capital. The competent authority, which in this case is the finance department of the State Council, may provide for other such items (Art. 213). 2120

Art. 214 applies to the three types of reserves: it provides for the use of the capital reserve and additional uses of the statutory and of the discretionary reserves. Either of the three reserves may be allocated to either of two uses: for covering losses and expanding production and other operations of the company, or to being converted to increase the registered capital (Art. 214§1). In the first option (loss cover and production expansion), when used to cover losses, the law sets a pecking order: the statutory and the discretionary reserves shall be used first and, if they are insufficient, the capital reserve thereafter (Art. 214§2)[902]. In the second option (conversion), a special rule applies to the 2121

[901] Such liability complements the general regime of shareholders' liability governed by Chapter 1 of the Company Law (s. above Chap. 9 §64.II, General Provisions), as well as that of directors', etc. by Chapter 8 (s. above Chap. 9 §64.VI, Qualification and Duties of Directors, Supervisors, and Senior Executives). On the liability regimes within the Company Law, s. above §2077.

[902] The law poses additional conditions for the use of a registered capital reduction for covering losses, s. Art. 225 and below §§2137ff.

statutory reserve only: where it is converted, its remainder may not be less than 25% of the registered capital before the conversion (Art. 214§3).

2122 *Accounting firms* undertaking the *audit* of the company are also subject to certain regulations aimed at protecting their independence and fostering corporate governance. Their engagement or dismissal must be decided by the shareholders' meeting or the board of directors or of supervisors in accordance with the bylaws (Art. 215§1); in case of *dismissal*, the accounting firm must be allowed to present its opinion (*ibid.*, § 2). Moreover, the company must provide it with truthful and complete accounting vouchers, account books, financial accounting reports, and other accounting materials; it may not decline providing any such material, concealing any, or providing any false materials (Art. 216). A company, i.e., its directors, etc., which would so act would be *liable* for any damage to the company, shareholders or third parties resulting thereof (s. above Chap. 9 §64.VI, Qualification and Duties of Directors, Supervisors, and Senior Executives).

2123 Likewise, and beyond its duties towards its auditor, a company may not create any account books other than the statutory account books; neither may company funds be deposited in any account opened in the name of an individual.

IX. Combination, Division and Capital Increase or Reduction of a Company

2124 As its title makes plain, Chapter 11 (Art. 218 to 228) of the Company Law is concerned by four issues: the combination, the division, the capital increase and the capital reduction of a company. These provisions complement the regimes of the limited liability company and the shareholding company which, while they may briefly mention any of those issues, do not develop them.

2125 The first issue is concerned with *mergers and acquisitions* (Art. 218 to 221). It is worth mentioning from the outset that, as far as *foreign investors* are concerned, M&As are primarily governed by the Interim Provisions on the Takeover of Domestic Enterprises by Foreign Investors (2006 Revision). The Interim Provisions extensively detail the M&A process, while the Company Law only contains four articles on this topic. The former are not covered in this chapter, however; the reader may consult specialized literature on this topic, a selection of which is listed in the bibliography featured in this book.

2126 That said, Chapter 11 of the Company Law poses outright *terminology* issues as far as M&A are concerned. In order to address them, it is worth recalling that, in common M&A language, a *merger* in a strict sense refers to two companies of similar size combining to form a new legal entity, after which both original companies cease to exist. Such merger is also known as a merger by *consolidation* or "merger of equals". Comparatively, an *acquisition* refers to one company purchasing and absorbing another, after which the acquired company ceases to exist, while the acquiring company survives. Such merger is also referred to, although less frequently given the risk of confusion with a merger *stricto sensu*, as merger by *absorption*, where "merger" is used in the wider sense. Unlike the common legal English language, Chinese law does not use a different word than "merger" to refer to an acquisition; it uses "merger" for both types and qualifies either, as the case may be. Thus, "merger" is expressed by 合并 hébìng or, specifically, by 公司合并 gōngsī hébìng or "company merger"; merger *stricto sensu* or by absorbtion, by 新设合并 xīn shè hébìng or, literally, "new company establishment merger"; merger *lato sensu* or by consolidation, by 吸收合并 xīshōu hébìng, which as explained commonly translates in legal English as acquisition. Inasmuch the title of Chapter 11 which starts, in Chinese, by 公司合并 gōngsī hébìng or "company merger", may lead to some confusion since it may be wrongly understood as only referring to mergers *stricto sensu*, and is arguably best translated by the neutral word of "combination", since the latter expression may refer to both merger (by absorption) and acquisition.

These preliminary clarifications further help to correctly understand the *definitions* given by the law to such combinations, which are described either as merger by absorption, or as merger by combination (Art. 218§1). This provision further matches the notions outlined above by defining, on one hand, a merger by absorption (or acquisition) as where a company is merged into another company and the merged (i.e., acquired) company is dissolved and, on the other hand, a merger by consolidation as where two or more companies are combined to form a new company and all the parties to the combination are dissolved (*ibid.*, § 2). 2127

In principle, a merger must be *approved* by the shareholders' meeting of both the limited liability company and the shareholding company (Art. 59§1, item 7 for the limited liability company, applicable to the shareholding company by the reference of Art 112§1) upon proposal from the board of directors (Art. 67§2, item 6 for the limited liability company, applicable to the shareholding company by the reference of Art. 120§2); in addition, the law sets the limited liability company a qualified majority (Art. 66§3). However, the law provides for two *exemptions* (Art. 219): if either the controlling company holds 90% or more of the controlled one, or the price it paid does not exceed 10% of its assets. 2128

In the first case (90% or more stake), the "merged company" is not required to obtain a resolution of its shareholders' meeting, but shall notify the other shareholders, which may request the company to purchase their equity or shares at a 2129 reasonable price (Art. 219§1). Although this provision does not make it plain *prima facie*, the scenario contemplated by the law is that of a merger by *absorption* by a controlling shareholder, typically of a parent absorbing its subsidiary. In such situation, the "merged company" is the controlled entity or subsidiary while, after the merger, only the absorbing entity or parent survives. For the sake of clarity, one may add that the controller must hold the 90% or more stake *before* the merger; that stake is not the one the acquirer may purport at acquiring through the merger.

2130 In the second case (price not exceeding 10%), a resolution of its shareholders' meeting is not required, except as otherwise prescribed in the bylaws (Art. 219§2). The assets referred to are those of the acquiring company. In that case, unlike in the first one, the law does not impose any notification duty, nor does it entitle the dissenting shareholders to a buyback (s. above §2035). Finally, in both cases, the power of executing the merger is left to the board of directors (*ibid.*, § 3).

2131 The law further subjects M&As to general guidelines purporting at the *protection of shareholders and creditors*: where companies are combined, the parties shall enter into an M&A agreement; they shall prepare balance sheets and lists of property to that effect. Each company shall, within ten days of adoption of a resolution regarding the combination, *notify* the creditors, and within 30 days, issue an *announcement* in a newspaper or on NECIPS[903]. The creditors may, within 30 days of receipt of the notice, or within 45 days of issuance of the announcement if they fail to receive the notice, require the company either to repay debts, or to provide corresponding security (Art. 220).

2132 Finally, after a merger, a *legal succession* occurs, by which the surviving company or the newly formed company succeeds in the claims and debts of the parties to the combination (Art. 221)[904].

2133 *Division* is addressed by the next two articles (Art. 222 and 223). Like a merger, a division must be approved by the shareholders (s. above, §2128). Art. 223, which we mention first since it explains Art. 222, prescribes that, after the division, the companies resulting thereof are jointly and severally liable for the debts of the company before the division. A written agreement on debt repayment reached between the company and the creditors may provide otherwise however, provided it was reached before the division.

2134 Art. 222 provides for requirements similar to those of Art. 220 for a merger (s. above §2131), but alleviated: given the intrinsic difference between a merger

---

903 S. above §1782.

904 The same solution applies in case of company transformation (s. Art. 12 and above §1782; Art. 108 and above §1946).

and a division where, in the latter case, the protection of shareholders and creditors is arguably a lesser concern than in case of merger, Art. 222, unlike Art. 220, does not entitle creditors to require the company to repay their debts or provide security. The rationale behind that difference in treatment is that, in case of merger, creditors face a change of debtor, hence a potentially accrued risk, so the law gives them a direct right to demand repayment or security, while in that of division, creditors are protected by the joint and several liability of all successor companies provided by Art. 223. Indeed, at the peril of restating the obvious, it should be recalled that, in case of division, unlike in case of reduction, there is no reduction of the substance of the company, which is merely divided among jointly and severally liable smaller companies. Besides, given that, in case of division, unlike in case of merger, there is no counterpart, no agreement such as the merger agreement is needed.

Reduction is governed by the next set of provisions (Art. 224 to 226). The re- 2135
duction this regime is concerned with is that of the *registered capital* of the company. It must equally be approved by the shareholders (Art. 59§1, item 5 for the limited liability company, applicable to the shareholding company by the reference of Art 112§1). Art. 224§1 and 2 provides for exactly the same requirements as Art. 220 in case of merger (s. above §2131), but for an agreement, for the same reasons as for a division.

Where a company reduces its registered capital, the law provides for different 2136
regimes for the limited liability company and the shareholding company. For a limited liability company, it must proportionally reduce the capital *contributions*, except if otherwise agreed by all the shareholders. For a shareholding company, it must proportionally reduce the *shares*, except if otherwise prescribed in the bylaws. The law may provide for additional exemptions (Art. 224§3).

The law further focuses on the use or *allocation* of capital resulting from the 2137
reduction for covering losses[905]. As outlined above, Art. 214§2, to which Art. 225§1 expressly refers, provides that, when reserves are used to cover the

[905] The reduction means that the company formally decreases its registered capital or shares value and uses the reduced amount to write off losses. For example: a limited liability company has accumulated losses of RMB2 million. After using all available reserves, RMB1 million losses remain. The limited liability company's registered capital is RMB5 million. The shareholders pass a resolution to reduce the registered capital to RMB 4million, thus reducing the value of the limited liability company by RMB1 million and, simultaneously, using that amount, by accounting compensation, to write off the remaining losses in its balance sheet. Alternatively, a shareholding company with a share capital of RMB1 million and losses of RMB200'000 reduces the nominal value of its shares from RMB10 to RMB8 per share, thus equally reducing the value of the shareholding company and writing off the corresponding losses. The company then files the change with the registration authority and updates its business license.

losses of a company, the discretionary and statutory reserves shall be first used; and if they are insufficient for covering those losses, the capital reserves may be used according to the "applicable provisions" (s. above §2121). Art. 225 is one of these provisions. Thus, when the losses cannot be fully covered by the discretionary and statutory reserves, the company may reduce its registered capital to cover them (Art. 225§1, 1st phrase).

2138 Such reduction is subject to *restrictions*: first, the company may neither distribute the reduction to the shareholders, nor exempt them from the obligation of making capital contributions or paying their shares, if such contributions or payments are still due (Art. 225§1, 2nd phrase). Second, after reducing its registered capital under the preceding two paragraphs, a company may not distribute profit before the cumulative amount of the statutory and discretionary reserves reaches 50% of the registered capital of the company (*ibid.*, § 3).

2139 Besides, in such case, the company is exempted from the notification requirements mandated by Art. 224§2 (s. above §§2135 and 2131), and the creditors may not request the company to repay its debts or provide security. However, the company must also *announce* the reduction in a newspaper or on NECIPS within 30 days of adoption of the resolution of the shareholders' meeting to reduce (Art. 225§2).

2140 If the reduction occurs in violation of the law, the latter provides for the same *remedy* as in case of illegal distribution of after-tax profit (Art. 211; s. above §2119 and note 901): the registered capital must be restored to its level before the reduction, meaning that, if shareholders have been wrongfully distributed the reduction, they must return the amounts so received; if they have been wrongfully exempted from contributing, they must contribute; and if their contribution has been wrongfully reduced, such reduction must be annulled, and they must contribute fully. Finally, if any loss is thus caused to the company, the shareholders and responsible directors, etc. are *liable* for damages (Art. 226).

2141 The last set of provisions applies to registered capital *increase* (Art. 227 and 228). Like a reduction, an increase must be approved by the shareholders (Art. 59§1, item 5 for the limited liability company, applicable to the shareholding company by the reference of Art 112§1). Other than that, and once again, the limited liability company and the shareholding company are treated differently. Where a limited liability company increases its registered capital, the shareholders enjoy a *right of preemption* to subscribe capital contributions in proportion to their paid-in capital contributions. The offer to contribute must be extended under the same conditions to all shareholders; however, they may unanimously derogate to the requirement of proportionality (Art. 227§1). In contrast, where a shareholding company offers new shares to increase its registered capital, the shareholders do, in principle, not enjoy such preemptive right to subscribe the new shares, unless the bylaws so provide or the shareholders' meeting adopts a resolution to that effect (*ibid.*, § 2). The regimes governing either the capital contributions of a limited liability company (s. above Chap. 9 §64.III.A, Formation) or the payment of shares of a shareholding company (s. above Chap. 9 §64.IV.A, Formation, and Chap. 9 §64.IV.F.1, Offering of Shares) apply to any such increase, as the case may be (Art. 228).

X. Dissolution and Liquidation of a Company

After briefly enunciating the causes of dissolution, Chapter 12 on the dissolu- 2142
tion and liquidation of a company (Art. 229 to 242) focuses on detailing the liquidation process. Among the *causes* of dissolution, a company may be dissolved because its duration expires, another cause of dissolution foreseen by the bylaws occurs, the shareholders so resolve[906], a merger or division requires it, the company loses its business license, or a court orders it (Art. 229§1 and 231).

Even though the drafting of Art. 229§1, item 4 is not entirely clear, a company 2143
may lose its *business license*, voluntarily or not, because it forfeits it, or because the authority cancels it, while the authority may order the company to *dissolve* (also translated as "close down") or dissolves (also translated as "abolish") it itself (Art. 229§1, item 4; compare with Art. 233§2).

A court may order such dissolution upon petition of the *shareholders* when the 2144
company encounters difficulties which are so serious that its continuous existence will cause major losses to the shareholders and cannot be solved by other means. The petition is subject to a qualified majority of 10% of the voting rights (Art. 231).

If the dissolution is to occur because the company has reached its statutory 2145
duration or because it was decided by the shareholders but its assets have not yet been distributed, the shareholders may *extend* the company's existence by amending its bylaws[907] or a resolution (Art. 230§1), both subject to a qualified majority of two-thirds of the voting rights for a limited liability company[908]

---

906 As permitted by Art. 59§1 for the limited liability company, item 7, applicable to the shareholding company by the reference of Art 112§1.

907 This provision conforms with the powers conferred to the shareholders' meeting by Art. 67§1, item 6, applicable to the shareholding company by the reference of Art. 120§2.

908 This provision conforms with Art. 66§2.

and of the voting rights represented at the meeting for a shareholding company[909] (Art. 230§2).

2146 The law provides for *three procedures* leading to the liquidation of the company, whose basic features can be distinguished as follows. Even though the law does not make it clear from the outset, once a dissolution cause has occurred, there are *two paths* to liquidation and, eventually, deregistration: the *ordinary* and the *simplified* procedure. Moreover, the ordinary procedure itself subdivides into *two sub-procedures*, depending on whether the company is solvent or not: if it is, the liquidation shall proceed under the ordinary procedure detailed in Chapter 12; if not, it shall shift procedure, and fall under the *bankruptcy* procedure governed by bankruptcy law.

2147 The *ordinary* procedure is chiefly concerned with the protection of the company's creditors. In contrast, if a company has not incurred any debt during its existence or has paid off all its debts, the registration of the company may be cancelled through the *simplified* procedure detailed at Art. 240. In the latter case, there is no need to follow the elaborate steps mandated by Art. 232 ff. to protect creditors, since there are none.

2148 If the company has *no debts*, the only matter left over to resolve is that of the *distribution of the company assets* to its shareholders. As a matter of fact, that concern is hardly expressed in Chapter 12 of the law which, once again, is primarily concerned with the protection of creditors, to a lesser extent of that of the company at large, therefore, indirectly, of that of its shareholders, but only incidentally addresses the distribution of the company assets to its shareholders, if the company has no debts.

2149 It does so by mentioning that the company may be deregistered under the *simplified* procedure "upon undertaking by all the shareholders", which only implies that, among other things, they may distribute the company assets, if there are any left, among themselves, before applying for its deregistration under the simplified procedure. Thus, within the ordinary procedure, the law only mentions such distribution to the effect of prohibiting it before any continuation of the company's existence, or before all debts have been paid off (Art. 230§1 and 234, item 6). The shareholders may decide on such distribution by virtue of Art. 59§1, item 7 (for the limited liability company, applicable to the shareholding company by the reference of Art 112§1).

2150 Alternatively, in case the company does have *debts* and must, therefore, subject to the *ordinary* procedure, it must comply with all the steps mandated by the same, including the formation of a liquidation group, which shall comply with numerous

[909] This provision conforms with Art. 116§3.

duties including forming a liquidation committee, notifying creditors, settling all debts, and submitting a liquidation report before deregistration can be completed.

Having outlined the basic distinctions between the ordinary, the simplified and the bankruptcy (s. above §2147) procedures, we will detail them below, in the same order. 2151

Under the *ordinary procedure*, the dissolution *process* starts by the mandatory *publication*, by the company, on NECIPS (s. above §53), within ten days of its occurrence, of any cause of dissolution (Art. 229§2). 2152

The *liquidation* of the company must ensue as a consequence of any of the causes enumerated above, but in case of merger or division (Art. 232§1, 1st sentence). 2153

The directors of the company are, by law, put in charge of the liquidation and, as such, designated as *liquidation obligors* (*ibid.*, 2nd sentence, 1st phrase). They are liable if they fail to conduct the liquidation or to do so untimely, thus causing damage to the company or any creditor (Art. 232§3) although, as mentioned in the next paragraph, the liquidation obligors may change. It should be noted that such liability relates to the *formation* of the liquidation group. The liability regime applying to the latter's *performance* is covered by Art. 238 and subject to different standards (s. below §§2170 to 2172)[910]. 2154

The directors must, within 15 days from the occurrence of the cause of dissolution, form a *liquidation group* to conduct the liquidation (Art. 232§1 *in fine*). The law distinguishes the formation from the composition of the liquidation group: while the latter is necessarily formed by the directors and is, in principle, composed of the same, the bylaws may prescribe or the shareholders may decide another composition (Art. 232§2). Therefore, it is conceivable that other officers of the company not being directors (e.g., a senior executive), or a third party (e.g., an external accountant), be appointed to sit with the directors, or even to replace them. 2155

If the liquidation group is not timely formed, or the liquidation does not proceed, *any interested party* may petition the court to form a liquidation group and organize the liquidation (Art. 233§1). In the case of Art. 229§1, item 4 (forfeiture, etc.), the *authority* may (*ibid.*, § 2). The law also provides a special rule in case of forfeiture, etc. if the company eventually neglects to apply for its deregistration (Art. 241; s. below §2163). 2156

---

910 For other cases of liability under the regime of dissolution and liquidation of a company, s. below §§2173 and 2174.

2157 The *powers* and, indeed, although the law does not formulate it as such, duties[911] of the liquidation group include identifying the company's assets, preparing a balance sheet and a list of property; notifying creditors and issuing an announcement; handling the unfinished business of the company related to liquidation; identifying and paying the taxes owed and the taxes arising in the process of liquidation; identifying and disposing of claims and debts; distributing residual property after the debts of the company are paid off; and participating in civil litigation on behalf of the company (Art. 234).

2158 Once the liquidation group has been formed, it shall both *notify* the creditors and *publish* such notification in a newspaper or on NECIPS (Art. 235§1, 1st sentence). Although the first sentence of this provision mandating the notification does not specify its content, its second sentence implies that the notification should invite creditors to declare their claim to the liquidation group.

2159 The direct and the public notifications are not subject to the same *time limits*: the first shall occur within ten days of the liquidation group's formation; the second within 60 days. Moreover, the publication on NECIPS mandated by Art. 235§1, 1st sentence is not to be confused with that of Art. 229§2: first, the subject-matter of the latter provision is the existence and nature of a dissolution cause, while that of the former an invitation to creditors to declare their claims; second, Art. 229§2 mandates such publication on NECIPS only while Art. 235§1, 1st sentence offers the option between NECIPS or a newspaper.

2160 Once notified, the creditors have 30 days from receipt of the notice or 45 since the publication if they were not directly notified to declare their claim (Art. 235§1, 2nd sentence). They must further motivate and prove them, and the liquidation group must register them (*ibid.*, § 2). The company may not pay any claim as long as those time limits have not expired (*ibid.*, § 3).

2161 The liquidation group shall then prepare a *liquidation plan* and submit it to the shareholders' meeting[912] or the court (s. above, §2156), as the case may be, for confirmation (Art. 236§1).

---

[911] Indeed, the disregard, by the liquidation group, of such "powers" would expose its liability (s. below §2170).

[912] The law empowers the board of directors to prepare a plan for the "dissolution" of the company (Art. 67§1, item 6 for the limited liability company, applicable to the shareholding company by the reference of Art. 120§2) and the shareholders' meeting to approve it (Art. 59§1 for the limited liability company, item 7, applicable to the shareholding company by the reference of Art 112§1); however, the latter provision hardly overlaps with, or contradicts Art. 236§1 empowering the liquidation group to prepare a "liquidation" plan and submit it to the shareholders' meeting for approval, since the liquidation group is, in principle, formed of directors anyway, whose composition the bylaws or shareholders' meeting may modify (Art. 232; s. above §2155).

After completion of the liquidation, the liquidation group shall prepare a *liquidation report*, submit the report to the shareholders' meeting or at court for confirmation, submit the confirmed report to the company registration authority, and apply for *cancellation of the company's registration* (Art. 239). 2162

In case the company forfeited its business license, was ordered to close down or was abolished (Art. 229§1, item 4; s. above §2143), the company registration authority may issue an announcement through the NECIPS. If so, the publication must last at least 60 days. If no objection is raised upon expiry of that period, the authority may cancel the registration (Art. 241§1). Even though the law does not specify it, such objection could be raised, conceivably, by a creditor, a shareholder, an officer of the company or an authority (typically, although not only, the tax authority). 2163

Because numerous time limits apply and are calculated from varying starting points, it may help to tentatively recapitulate them in cumulated figures from a single *dies a quo* or starting point. All the limits mentioned thereafter apply to the ordinary procedure; they are calculated from the occurrence of the dissolution cause and are maxima, i.e., they can be shortened but not extended. 2164

Thus, the company must publish the cause of dissolution on NECIPS within *ten days* from its occurrence (Art. 229§2; s. above §2152). The liquidation obligors must form the liquidation group within *15 days* (Art. 232§1 *in fine*; §2155). The liquidation group must notify the creditors directly within *25 days* (Art. 235§1, 1st sentence; s. above §§2158 and 2159). The creditors must announce their claims within *55 days* in case they have been notified directly (Art. 235§1, 2nd sentence; s. above §2160). They must also be informed by way of publication within 90 days. Those which were not notified directly must announce their claims within *135 days* (*ibid.*) The notification must be published until at least *150 days* after the occurrence of the dissolution cause (Art. 241§1; s. above §2163). 2165

The limits mentioned in this paragraph are not a substitute to the law, however. Indeed, the reader must be warned that, if the law sets the starting point of a limit other than from the dissolution cause, and that that starting point has been effectively shortened, the limit resulting thereof may be *shorter* than the limit mentioned in this paragraph. 2166

The *bankruptcy procedure* substitutes to the ordinary one, however, if the liquidation group discovers that the property of the company is insufficient for paying off debts after identifying the property of the company and preparing the balance sheet. In such case, it must file at court for bankruptcy liquidation and transfer the liquidation to the bankruptcy administrator designated by the court (Art. 237). Where a company is declared bankrupt, bankruptcy 2167 liquidation is instituted and conducted in accordance with the law on the bankruptcy of enterprises (Art. 242).

2168 Finally, as explained above, the *simplified procedure* is only available if the company has not incurred any debts during its existence or has paid off all its debts. If so, the company may dispense with the ordinary liquidation procedure described above (Art. 229§2 ff.); after a dissolution cause has occurred, it may proceed straight to the deregistration.

2169 The cancellation of its registration shall be *announced* through NECIPS, but not sooner than 20 days after the occurrence of the dissolution cause. This announcement is not to be confused with the publication mandated by Art. 229§2 (s. above §2152), which only applies in case of ordinary procedure. If there is no objection raised upon expiry of the period of announcement, the company may, within 20 days, apply to the company registration authority for the cancellation of its registration.

2170 The regime of the dissolution and liquidation of companies contains several special cases of *liability*. Thus, the members of the *liquidation group* are subject to the same duty of loyalty and diligence (Art. 238§1) as directors. etc. (s. above Chap. 9 §64.VI, Qualification and Duties of Directors, Supervisors, and Senior Executives). In case of liquidation, that duty is *qualified*; besides, it is enhanced in case of damage to the company but comparatively alleviated in case of damage to creditors. Thus, those members shall be liable for breach of their duties (s. above §§2157ff.), notably in case of *delay*, i.e, if, by the mere fact of having performed them too slowly, they caused a damage to the *company* (Art. 238§2, 1st sentence). However, if they caused damage to *creditors*, they shall only be liable if they acted intentionally or by gross negligence (*ibid.*, 2nd sentence), a threshold, in the latter case, the mere fact of having acted slowly may not reach. In other words, in case of damage to the company, the members' liability requires no intention, while a light negligence, such as acting slowly or staying passive, shall suffice.

2171 One may wonder why creditors do apparently not deserve the same degree of protection as the company. It has been argued that the law imposes a stricter standard (intent or gross negligence) for creditors' claims to avoid excessive liability for directors by being unduly exposed to minor claims, while for the company itself, a lower threshold encourages diligent internal management and protects the company's assets during liquidation, by holding them accountable to the company for any lack of diligence in fulfilling their duties.

2172 Be that as it may, as noted, the regime of Art. 238 is applicable to the liquidation group's *performance*. The liability regime related to the group's *formation*, which applies to the liquidation obligors, who may not necessarily be the same as the members of the liquidation group, is covered by Art. 232§3 and not subject to the same standards (s. above §2154).

Besides, where the registration of a company is cancelled through the simplified procedure, the *shareholders* making untrue statements to the effect that a company has not incurred any debt during its existence or paid off all the debts, as required by Art. 240§1 to be eligible for the simplified procedure, are jointly and severally liable for the debts of the company before the cancellation of registration (Art. 240§3). 2173

Finally, where the registration of a company is cancelled pursuant to Art. 241§1 (forfeiture, etc.; s. above §2163), the liabilities of the original shareholders and liquidation obligors of the company are not affected (Art. 241§2). 2174

The liability of third parties or so-called *institutions*, typically external auditors, etc., appointed by the company for the liquidation, undertaking assets appraisal or other verifications and delivering, intentionally or by negligence, reports, etc. containing material omissions or untrue statements, and having thereby caused a damage to creditors of the company, are liable under Chapter 14 of the Company Law on the administrative liability of the company (Art. 257; s. below §2199). 2175

Moreover, the company shall incur administrative liability resulting in *administrative penalties* if, during the liquidation, it failed to notify the company creditors (Art. 255; s. below §2197), concealed any assets, made false statements in the balance sheet or list of assets, or distributed any company assets before paying off its debts (Art. 256; s. below §2200). 2176

The dissolution of the *branch of a foreign company* is also governed by Chapter 12 (Art. 249; s. below §2186). 2177

XI. Branches of Foreign Companies

Foreign companies are not to be confused with *foreign-invested companies* (s. above §§6 to 8). The former are defined as formed outside of China under foreign laws (Art. 242). Chapter 13 of the Company Law (Art. 243 to 249) applies to their branches in China. Branch is expressed in Chinese as 分支 fēnzhī ("branch") or 分支机构 fēnzhī jīgòu ("branch office"); in French as "succursale" and in German as "Zweigniederlassung". 2178

Further and foremost, branches of foreign companies are not to be confused with *representative offices of foreign enterprises* (s. below Chap. 9 §67, Representative Offices). While both share the common, distinctive feature of not enjoying legal personality, the main difference is that a representative office of 2179 a foreign enterprise is prohibited, in principle, to engage into for-profit activities (although there are exemptions), while the branch of a foreign company does not face such restriction, provided it is compliant otherwise. Also, the permitted scope of representative offices is more limited than that of branches. As mentioned (s. above §1760), we will elaborate those comparisons at the end of the chapter of this book on representative offices (s. below §§2386ff.)

2180 That said, it should be recalled that the Chinese Civil Code gives the right to any legal person to establish *branches*, whose establishment must be compliant (Chinese Civil Code, Art. 74§1; s. above §130). That rights is reiterated in the general provisions of the Company Law, which also asserts that of establishing *subsidiaries* (Art. 13; s. above §§1783ff.) Subsidiary[913] is expressed in Chinese as 子公司 zǐ gōngsī, in French as "filiale" and in German as "Tochtergesellschaft"[914].

2181 Both the notions of branch and subsidiary are defined by Art. 13: according to the legal definition, which is perfectly apt, a subsidiary has the status of a legal person, and assumes civil liability independently, while the civil liability of a branch, which does not have the status of a legal person, shall be assumed by its *parent*, as already prescribed by the Chinese Civil Code which specifies that, alternatively, while the assets of the branch may be used for meeting any such liability, the assets of its principal shall be used for covering any portion not covered by the branches' assets (Chinese Civil Code, Art. 74§2; s. above §143). For the sake of dissipating any doubts as far as foreign branches are concerned, Chapter 13 reiterates that foreign branches do not enjoy any special status in either regard, i.e., be it as to their lack of legal personality or liability; namely, the foreign parent is liable for its Chinese branch (Art. 247) which must comply with Chinese law (Art. 248).

2182 The notions of branch and subsidiaries and their corollaries have been further discussed above with the general provisions of the Company Law; we refer the reader to the topical paragraphs (s. §§1783ff.) Chapter 13 of the Company Law only applies to branches, not to subsidiaries, however.

2183 We also believe worth recalling that, comparatively, Swiss law regulates branches to a limited extent (CO Art. 931 and 952[915]; s. above §1785), but not subsidiaries, and that the literal translation of "branch" in French, "branche",

913 About the distinction between a branch and a subsidiary, s. above note 101.

914 Unlike English, the Chinese, French and German denominations all three share the meaning of "child company".

915 Art. 952§2 is the only provision applying specifically to branches of foreign companies. It requires the branch to mention, in its registered name, its foreign parent corporate form and the place of the latter's incorporation.

is not used in Swiss French legal language while it may, in common French language, point indistinctively either at a "succursale" or at a "filiale".

Branches of foreign companies must be properly *registered* in China (s. above Chap. 9 §64.II.D, Company Registration) and obtain a *business license* (s. above §§1824ff.) in order to be authorized to operate (Art. 244). Absent it, the foreign company shall face administrative penalties and be ordered to close its branch down (Art. 261; s. below §§2195 and 2196). Art. 244 also describes the related procedure in broad terms; Chapter 13 contains additional prescriptions, such as related to the company name (Art. 246). They must have a *legal representative* in China (Art. 245§1, 1st phrase; s. above Chap. 2 §8.III.C, Legal Representative). Because a branch has no legal personality, such representative shall be employed by the foreign parent. The branch must be adequately *funded* (*ibid.*, 2nd phrase); the authorities may prescribe minimum amounts (*ibid.*, § 2). 2184

The registration requirement implies that branches of foreign companies fall under the scrutiny of the *Foreign Investment Law* (s. above Chap. 1 §5, Management), which expressly applies to "investment through other legal means" (FIL Art. 2§2, item 4; s. above §6). 2185

When a foreign parent closes down its subsidiary in China, the latter must be *liquidated* like any other company in China (Art. 249, 1st sentence, 2nd phrase; s. above Chap. 9 §64.X, Dissolution and Liquidation of a Company). In particular, the parent must pay all the debts related to its Chinese branch's operations (*ibid.*, 1st phrase). It should be stressed, in this latter regard, that the parent will not be authorized to transfer any assets out of China before it has paid off all its debts (*ibid.*, 2nd sentence). 2186

XII. Liability of the Company

Before systematically commenting on the provisions of the penultimate chapter of the Company Law, one needs to put it in context. Although simply titled "legal liability", Chapter 14 of the Company Law is chiefly concerned by the *administrative* liability of the *company*. As such, it is to be distinguished from the civil liability of the company, as well as from the civil and, as the case may be, administrative liability of shareholders, subscribers, promoters, controlling shareholders, actual controllers, directors, supervisors, senior executives, committee members, other officers or employees, liquidation obligors, members of the liquidation group, third parties[916], the parent company, branches and 2187

[916] Among third parties whose liability may be invoked in connection with the company, one may mention, in particular, *institutional* third parties such as those involved with the issuance of shares of a shareholding company (s. above Chap. 9 §64.IV.F, Offering

subsidiaries, etc., governed by provisions scattered around the Company Law, by other chapters of the same, or by other laws, namely, the Chinese Civil Code.

2188 As far as the *Chinese Civil Code*[917] is concerned, one should consider that the relationship between the shareholders, the company officers and contractual third parties on one hand, and the company on the other, are fundamentally of a contractual nature and, therefore, subject to the general regime of *contractual liability* governed by the Chinese Civil Code (Art. 577 ff.; s. above Chap. 4 §27, Liability for Breach of Contract)[918], keeping in mind that, according to the Roman law adage *lex specialis derogat leges generali* (Chinese Civil Code, Art. 12; s. above §117), special provisions of the Company Law may supersede general provisions of the Chinese Code of Obligations.

2189 In particular, all the officers of the company are, in principle, bound to the latter by a labor contract and subject, as a result, to the *Labor Contract Law*, which also contains a liability regime that we commented together with labor law (Art. 80 ff.; s. above Chap. 6 §51, Liabilities). The law of *other contracts*, such as, for example, that of the contract of mandate binding an external auditor to the company[919], may apply of course, all of which contain a liability regime to some extent. Typical contracts are contained in Section 2 of Part 3 of the Chinese Civil Code on contract law (Art. 595 ff.); atypical ones are governed by the general regime of contractual liability (Chinese Civil Code, Art. 577 ff.)

2190 Besides, the liability of *third parties* not being bound by a contractual relationship to the company such as actual controllers or non-contractual third parties is, in case of damage caused by an illicit act, fundamentally governed by the regime of *liability for illicit acts* equally contained in the Chinese Civil Code (Part 7, Art. 1164 ff.; s. above Chap. 8 , Liability for Illicit Acts ("Torts")), while special provisions contained in the Company Law may also apply.

2191 Likewise, beyond the regime of its liability contained in the Company Law, the *company* may also be liable for illicit acts, namely, under the Chinese Civil Code including *special liability regimes* such as product liability (Art. 1202 ff.; s. above §§1701ff.), liability for environmental pollution and ecological damage (Art. 1229 ff.; s. above §§1710ff.), and high-risk liability (Art. 1236 ff.; s.

---

and Transfer of Shares of a Shareholding Company), with the audit (s. above §2112), and with the issuance of bonds (s. above Chap. 9 §64.VII, Corporate Bonds), among others. Such liabilities are partly addressed by Chapter 14 of the Company Law nevertheless (s. below §2199).

917 S., for the liability of legal persons, above Chap. 2 §8.III.D, Liability; for the liability of partners exceeding their powers, s. above Chap. 2 §11.III, Powers of Agency and Agents Without Power.

918 Cf. Art. 257§2 (s. below §2193).

919 S. above note 916.

above §§1727ff.), or *other laws*, such as, typically, the law of consumer protection, the Unfair Competition Law, etc. Most of these various regimes and provisions have been commented throughout this book, therefore we refer the reader to its topical parts.

While a company (and its officers) may incur *criminal liability* under Chinese law, it is neither the topic of Chapter 14 of the Company Law, which refers[920] to criminal law to that effect (Art. 264), nor that, by definition, of Chinese civil law at large; it will not be covered in this book. That said, Chapter 13 of the Company Law imposes numerous *fines* for violation of its provisions, where such fines may be considered of a penal administrative nature, as confirmed by Art. 263 referring to "administrative or criminal fines". 2192

Last but not least, Chapter 14 is not exclusively concerned with the administrative liability of the company, but also, although occasionally, with that of certain *shareholders* (Art. 253; s. below §2198), of the *authority* (Art. 258; s. below §2196), of certain *third parties* (Art. 257§1; s. below §2199), as well as of "*directly responsible persons in charge or of other directly responsible persons*", a formula broad enough to accommodate officers of the company, officials and third parties; moreover, it extends to *unregistered* companies or entities (Art. 259; s. below §2196) and to *foreign* parents (Art. 261; s. below §2196 and note 922). Besides, on one occasion, it concerns itself with certain third parties' *civil* liability (Art. 257§2; s. below §2199). Those liabilities are to be regarded as marginal compared to the administrative liability of the company regulated by the bulk of the provisions forming Chapter 14 of the Company Law, however. 2193

That said, Chapter 14 of the Company Law (Art. 250 to 264) is concerned with violations related to company registration, publications, capital contributions, capital use, accounting, notifications, liquidation, company assets, business licenses, branches, national security and public interest. 2194

In most cases, Chapter 14 prescribes that the authority shall order the company to take *corrective action* and, as noted, that it may impose a *fine* within a certain range, or proportional to the amount at stake; it occasionally sets higher penalties for serious violations: we refer to the law, which is clear, for the detail. In two cases, it may result in the company's *business license forfeiture* (Art. 260§1 and 262; s. below §2201), a *prohibition to operate* (Art. 259; s. next paragraph) or an *order to close down* (Art. 261; *ibid.*)[921] 2195

---

[920] Although Art. 264 does not explicitly refer to criminal law but to "the law", it does expressly refer to criminal liability.

[921] A forfeiture or an order to close down may result in a prohibition to serve as director of the company (Art. 178§1; s. above §2066).

2196 Specifically, not only *registration* fraud (Art. 250) but also operating, without being registered, a limited liability company or a shareholding company (Art. 259) or a branch (Art. 261)[922], as well as neglecting to announce, to the authority, modifications of the registration (Art. 260§2), are all punishable. Moreover, where the registration fraud had succeeded because of a *corrupt or negligent official*, the latter shall be administratively punished, together with any other responsible officer or third party (Art. 248). Registration fraud is already sanctioned in Chapter 2 of the Company Law on registration by the cancellation of the business license (Art. 39; s. above §1823).

2197 The omission to *publish* mandatory information on NECIPS or the publication of untrue information is also punishable (Art. 251). The information the law refers to is that mandated by Art. 40 (s. above §§1818 to 1820). So is the failure to *notify* creditors or to publish a merger, division, reduction of registered capital or liquidation (Art. 255).

2198 During the formation of the company, not contributing, partly contributing, untimely contributing or false *contributions*, whether currency or in-kind contributions, by a promoter or a subscriber[923], are all punishable[924] (Art. 252). After the formation of the company, so is the *misappropriation* of capital by a promoter or shareholder after it was contributed (Art. 253).

2199 *Accounting* fraud consisting of, namely, *double accounting*, i.e., creating an account book other than those required by law, as well as making false statements or concealing material facts in a *financial report* are punishable under the Accounting Law. So is it about company *assets appraisal*, *capital verification* or any other such statutory verification performed by a third-party accountant or a similar qualified *institution*, all of which are punishable under the Assets Appraisal Law and the Certified Public Accountant Law (Art. 257§1). In addition, any such institution shall incur *civil liability* for any damage resulting thereof (*ibid.* § 2). In case of false statement, the fault of the institution is presumed, consistently with its *contractual liability* (s. above §794; to free itself from its liability, the institution must prove that it was not at fault (*ibid., in fine*).

---

922 Branches of foreign companies must be registered in compliance with Chapter 13 of the Company Law. If they fail to, Art. 260§2 empowers the registration authority to order the foreign parents to comply or close down the branch, and to impose a fine.

923 The civil liability of the subscriber of a limited liability company for default and illegal withdrawals is governed by Art. 49 to 53 (s. above §§1849 and 1850); for that of the promoter, s. above §§1927ff.; for that of the subscriber of a shareholding company, s. above §§1939ff.

924 Art. 252 actually mentions "shareholder" 股东 gǔdōng, not "subscriber" 认股人 rèngǔrén. However, a subscriber who has not yet contributed cannot, legally, be a shareholder. One should, therefore, read "subscriber", not "shareholder". In contrast, Art. 253, which applies after the formation, correctly refers to a shareholder.

Beyond the general purpose provisions mentioned in the preceding paragraph, the law pays special attention to accounting fraud in the course of a company *liquidation* where, in the process of liquidation, a company conceals any property or makes any false statement in the balance sheet or list of property, along with, in addition, distributing any property of the company before paying off its debts, all of which are punishable (Art. 256). 2200

Surprisingly perhaps as compared to other jurisdictions where dormant companies abound, in China, a company must operate, i.e., being a *going concern*. If it does not, after six months at most, however temporarily, it must announce the suspension of its business to the registration authority, which results in a suspension or cancellation of its business license. Therefore, under Chapter 14 of the Company Law, if a company fails to commence business six months after its formation without good cause, or suspends business on its own initiative for six or more consecutive months after commencing business, the authority may impose a *forfeiture*[925] *of the business license* of the company, unless it has undergone business suspension formalities with the authority (Art. 260§1). 2201

The same consequence may arise in cases of serious illegal conduct endangering *national security* or the *public interest* conducted in the name of a company (Art. 262). Finally, as noted (s. above §2196), *registration* fraud is also sanctioned in Chapter 2 of the Company Law on registration by the *cancellation of the business license* (Art. 39; s. above §1824). 2202

XIII. Supplemental Provisions

The last chapter of the law contains "supplemental" provisions merely consisting in two such provisions; they apply to certain definitions (Art. 265; s. above §2058) and the transitory regime (Art. 266; s. above §1842); both have been addressed above. 2203

§65. The Partnership Enterprise

I. Introduction

As outlined above in this book in the introduction to company law (s. §1752), Chinese and Swiss law share the same fundamental distinction between *capital companies* (Fr.: "sociétés de capitaux"; Ger.: "Kapitalgesellschaften") and 2204

925 On the notion of forfeiture, s. above §§337 to 339.

partnerships (Fr. "sociétés de personnes"; Ger.: "Personengesellschaften"). In Chinese law, the first category includes the limited liability company and the shareholding company; the second the partnership enterprise. The difference between those two regimes is outlined below (s. §2225).

2205 The partnership enterprise (合伙企业 héhuǒ qǐyè) is not to be confused with the *partnership contract*, A.K.A. *contractual partnership*, which is, as its name makes clear, a contract, not a form of company. The partnership contract is a typical contract governed by the Chinese Civil Code; as such, it has been outlined in the contract law chapter of this book (s. above Chap. 5 §41, Partnership Contract). However, because it shares common features with the partnership enterprise, it will also be addressed in this chapter of the book (s. below §§2215 and 2217).

2206 Likewise, despite they share certain features, neither the partnership enterprise, nor the partnership contract are to be confused with the former *contractual joint-venture* (CJV), i.e., whether before the FIL abolished them as of 1 January 2020 (s. above §30) or thereafter, after they transformed into a limited liability CJV or a contractual CJV. Their similarities and differences will be discussed further down, in the chapter of this book dedicated to JVs (s. below §§2340, 2345 to 2348 and 2353).

2207 Finally, a partnership is not an *association* (s. above §152), which is a non-profit organization, either.

2208 The partnership enterprise is governed by the law of the same name, the Partnership Enterprise Law. The latter was initially enacted in 1997 and last revised in 2006. Unlike the Company Law, which was initially promulgated in 1993, the Partnership Enterprise Law did not undergo the profound revision the Company Law was last subjected to in 2023, in the aftermath of the reform of foreign investment law in 2019 and the promulgation of the Chinese Civil Code in 2020: it remained untouched since its last revision.

2209 It can generally be said that, like in many other jurisdictions providing for similar forms of companies, as compared to the limited liability company and the shareholding company, the partnership is typically intended for smaller ventures. Namely, the partnership enterprise, unlike the limited liability company and the shareholding company, does not have a registered capital (s. below §2225), thus reflecting the lesser concern of the legislator, given the generally smaller size of a partnership enterprise's business, to protect its creditors, and the emphasis of the partnership (whether enterprise or contractual) on its *personal* nature primarily reflected in the personal liability of its partners[926].

Like the limited liability company and the shareholding company, the partnership enterprise is open to *direct foreign investment*, to the conditions set forth by the FIL and the related regulatory framework (s. above Chap. 1, Foreign Investment Law)[927] which is reserved at the end of the Partnership Enterprise Law (Art. 108). It is noteworthy that a Chinese partnership can be formed of foreign partners only. There is no requirement of a minimum number or proportion of Chinese nationals. 2210

The Chinese partnership enterprise entails two primary sub-forms, the first of which contains yet another secondary sub-form: the first form, the *general partnership*, corresponds, in Swiss law, to the "société en nom collectif" in French and the "Kollektivgesellschaft" in German; the other form, the *limited liability partnership*, corresponds to the "société en commandite" in French and to the "Kommanditgesellschaft" in German. In addition, unlike Chinese law, Swiss law provides for an alternative form of the limited liability partnership, enabling it to divide its capital in shares, and to be organized like a shareholding company: the "société en commandite par actions" in French and the "Kommanditaktiengesellschaft" in German; Chinese law does not enable it. As noted, the general partnership entails itself a sub-form, the *specialized general partnership*, which does not have any specific equivalent in Swiss law. These forms are detailed below. 2211

Chapter 1 of the Partnership Enterprise Law (Art. 1 to 13) contains general provisions applicable to all types of partnership enterprises. They are mainly 2212

---

926 This general comment does not imply that partnership enterprises are necessarily small. Namely, they can be used as the basic corporate form for structuring *private equity investment funds*, which often manage very large assets. Although such funds can also rest on limited liability or shareholding companies, partnership enterprises are frequently preferred because of their personal nature. Such funds are subject to strict supervision under the Securities Investment Fund Law (s. Art. 12§1), the Provisional Measures as well as the Regulations on the Supervision and Administration of- and the Measures for the Registration and Filing of Private Equity Investment Funds, which this book will not detail, however.

927 Foreign invested partnerships used to be specifically governed by the Administrative Measures for the Establishment of Partnership Enterprises within China by Foreign Enterprises or Individuals 外国企业或者个人在中国境内设立合伙企业管理办法 wàiguó qǐyè huòzhě gèrén zài zhōngguó jìngnèi shèlì héhuǒ qǐyè guǎnlǐ bànfǎ issued by the State Council on 25 November 2009. It was repelled as of 29 November 2020 in the wake of the Foreign Investment Law, which established a level-playing field for foreign invested and domestic enterprises (s. above §§17 and 18).

concerned with the definitions of such types, the partnership agreement, the partnership enterprise's protection and its establishment.

2213 A *general partnership* (普通合伙 pǔtōng héhuǒ) is defined as a partnership comprising of *general partners* with unlimited joint and several liability for the debts of the partnership (Art. 2§2, 1st sentence and § 3, 2nd sentence, 1st phrase). In contrast, a *limited liability partnership* (有限合伙 yǒuxiàn héhuǒ) is composed of general partners and *limited liability partners*: unlike general partners, limited liability partners bear liability for the debts of the partnership to the extent of the capital contributions they have subscribed for (Art. 2§3, 2nd sentence, 2nd phrase).

2214 The Partnership Enterprise Law implies, rather than expressly states, that the partnership enterprise rests on a *partnership agreement*. Such an agreement is a prerequisite for the partnership enterprise's establishment (Art. 9 applicable to both the general and the limited liability partnership; Art. 14, item 2 applicable to the general partnership and to the limited liability partnership by the reference of Art. 60; and Art. 63 applicable to the limited liability partnership). It must be concluded through consultation between the partners, in compliance with the law (Art. 4 and 7), and the principles of voluntariness, equality, fairness and good faith (Art. 5). Its violation results in liability (Art. 103§1; s. below §2316).

2215 At this stage, two distinctions must be recalled. First, the partnership *enterprise* (合伙企业 héhuǒ qǐyè) is, as noted above (s. §2205), not to be confused with the partnership *contract* (合伙合同 héhuǒ hétóng) or contractual partnership: the former is a company (*lato sensu*, not in the sense of the Company Law, which so designates the limited liability company and the shareholding company), i.e., a corporate form, while the latter, as its name makes clear, is a contract, i.e., a typical contract, governed by Art. 967 ff. of the Chinese Civil Code.

2216 The main difference between the two is that the partnership enterprise enjoys *legal personality*; the partnership contract does not. Therefore, unlike the partnership enterprise (s. below §2220), a partnership contract cannot be registered with the SAMR (s. above §1814). Therefore, the law expressly states that the partners of a partnership enterprise shall individually pay *taxes* on the partnership's incomes derived from production, business operation and other incomes (Partnership Enterprise Law, Art. 6); the enterprise itself is not subject to the enterprise income tax as a separate entity.

2217 Second, the partnership *agreement* (合伙协议 héhuǒ xiéyì) prescribed by the Partnership Enterprise Law is also to be distinguished from the partnership *contract* (合伙合同 héhuǒ hétóng) mentioned in the preceding paragraph: yet despite Chinese law uses slightly different names for designating the one and the other, both regimes actually refer to the *same* legal institution, where the

Partnership Enterprise Law is concerned with the partnership agreement in relation with the formation and operation of the partnership and, as *special law*, derogates, as the case may be, to the Chinese Civil Code which, in return, as *general law*, applies for supplementing the Partnership Enterprise Law whenever contract law issue relating to the partnership agreement arise and the Partnership Enterprise Law is silent. The partnership contract has been addressed in detail in the chapter on typical contract of this book (s. above Chap. 5 §41, Partnership Contract), to which we refer the reader.

In Swiss law, the contractual partnership corresponds to the "société simple" 2218
in French and the "einfache Gesellschaft" in German. Although the French and the German names of the contractual partnership both deceivingly contain the name "company" (Fr.: "société"; Ger.: "Gesellschaft"), the Swiss contractual partnership, like the Chinese partnership contract, cannot be registered either as corporate entity on the Swiss register of commerce.

Partnerships, irrespective of their type, may be established by natural persons, 2219
legal persons or "other organizations"[928] (Art. 2§1). However, SOEs, whether wholly or partly State-controlled, listed companies, i.e., limited liability companies or shareholding companies, as well as "public welfare institutions and social groups"[929] may not become general partners (Art. 3). This drafting suggests that they could become limited liability partners, however.

The establishment of a partnership enterprise is subject to *registration* (Art. 9 2220
to 13). However, the related requirements are alleviated as compared to the limited liability company and the shareholding company: if the application is in order, the business license should, if possible, be granted on the spot (Art. 10§1); if not, the registration authority must make a decision within maximum 20 days; refusals must be motivated (Art. 10§2). Even though the law does not expressly mention it, such motivation entitles the applicant to request the authority to reconsider, possibly after having complemented or altered its application, or to file at court against such decision. Changes must be registered within 15 days (Art. 13). A partnership enterprise may establish branches[930], which must be registered (Art. 12). The registration is partly *published* (s. below §2229). Fraud and omissions in the registration are punishable and result in civil liability (Art. 93 and 95§2; s. below §2313).

Finally, the law proclaims that it protects the lawful property and rights and 2221
interests of the partnership and its partners (Art. 8).

---

928 S. above note 97.

929 One understands that the law refers to associations, s. above §§2207 and 152.

930 For branches of foreign companies, s. above Chap. 9 §64.XI, Branches of Foreign Companies.

II. General Partnership

2222 As mentioned above (s. §2213), *general partnership* is defined as a partnership comprising of *general partners* with unlimited joint and several liability for the debts of the partnership (Art. 2§2, 1st sentence and § 3, 2nd sentence, 1st phrase).

2223 Chapter 2 on the general partnership of the Partnership Enterprise Law (Art. 14 to 59) is the most substantial of the law and also applies to the limited liability partnership whenever the chapter dedicated to the latter, which only applies to residual aspects, is silent (Art. 60, 2nd sentence). It is divided into five sections. which cover the establishment of the partnership, its property, the execution of its affairs, the relationships between its partners and with third parties, joining the partnership, withdrawing, and specialized general partnerships.

A. Establishment

2224 As noted, the establishment of the partnership in general is already addressed in the general provisions of the law (Art. 9 to 13; s. above §2220), which the general partnership regime complements. Thus, and evidently so, to be established, a general partnership must have at least two partners, but the law does not set any maximum (Art. 14, item 1), unlike for the limited liability partnership (s. below §2279). Other notable conditions for its establishment include a *partnership agreement*, which must be in writing (*ibid*., item 2), and a *capital* (*ibid.* item 3). It must also have a *name*, which must be followed by the Chinese characters "general partnership" (普通合伙 pǔtōng héhuǒ; *ibid*., item 4 and Art. 15); omissions are punishable (Art. 94; s. below §2313). A partnership is established, i.e. comes into legal existence, with the issuance of its business license (Art. 11§1). Conducting business without the latter is punishable (Art. 95§1; s. below §2313).

2225 A major difference with the limited liability company and the shareholding company is that, while as for those two the subscribed contributions to the *capital* of the partnership enterprise must be paid (s. below §2227), unlike for them the capital of the partnership enterprise does not have to be *registered* with the authority and, consequently, disclosed to the public[931]. The capital of the partnership enterprise does not need to be entirely *paid out* either for the partnership enterprise to be established; it suffices that it has been subscribed (Art. 14,

[931] About limited or indirect exceptions to this principle, s. below §2287 however.

item 3). This regime applies by default to any type of partnership (Art. 55§3 and 60, 2nd sentence).

Like for the limited liability company and the shareholding company, contributions may be financial or *in kind*, i.e., physical items like machines, equipment, premises, etc., IPR, land use rights, other property rights, labor or services (Art. 16§1 *in fine*). Likewise, the value of in-kind contribution must be appraised; however, the related requirements are less stringent than for a limited liability company or a shareholding company (s. above §§1846, 1847 and 1926): indeed, such value can be determined by consultation among the partners, while an official appraisal is mandatory for limited liability companies and shareholding companies. Alternatively, for physical items, IPR, land use rights and other property rights, the partners can entrust a licensed evaluation institution to that effect, while for labor or services, the method of evaluation must be clearly mentioned in the partnership agreement (Art. 16§2). 2226

Contributions must be paid according to the partnership agreement (Art. 17§1), and the property of in-kind contributions transferred to the partnership according to the law (*ibid.*, § 2; s. above §1847)[932]. They can be subsequently modified, i.e., increased or decreased, if the partnership agreement so provides, or all the partners so agree (Art. 34). 2227

The *partnership agreement* is the equivalent, for the partnership enterprise, of the bylaws (or articles of association) of the limited liability company or the shareholding company (cf. Art. 19§1, 2nd sentence). Its minimum content is prescribed by law and must include the following information or provisions regulating the following topics: the name of the partnership and the location of its principal business; its objectives and the partnership business scope; the names and domiciles of the partners; the form, amount and time limit of the capital contributions; profit distribution and loss sharing; execution of partnership affairs; joining or withdrawing from the partnership; dispute resolution; dissolution and liquidation; and liability for breach of contract (Art. 18). 2228

The Partnership Enterprise Law only specifies that the partnership agreement, among other things, needs to be registered (Art. 9§1; s. above §2220); it falls short of prescribing whether it should also be published. In practice, part of the partnership agreement's content is *published* on NECIPS (s. above §52), including: the registered name, the registered address, the business scope, the 2229

[932] Unlike the regime of limited liability partnership (Art. 65, 2nd sentence; s. below §2286), that of general partnership falls short from mentioning the partner's liability for payment default. However, because it rests on the partnership contract, it is implied in Chapter 5 on legal liability under Art. 103§1 and 106 (s. below §§2316 and 2318) as well as, more generally, the regime of contractual liability (s. above Chap. 4 §27, Liability for Breach of Contract).

partners' names, and the amount, form and date of the capital contributions. The other items are not published. These requirements compare to those applying to the limited liability company and the shareholding company (s. above §§1817 and 1818). A notable exception is the legal representative of the partnership enterprise who, unlike for the limited liability company and the shareholding company[933], does not need to be published or even registered in the NECIPS.

2230 The substance of the matters generically listed as mandatory content is to be agreed upon by the partners, as implied by Art. 19§3, 1st sentence. So are the changes to the partnership agreement, unless agreed otherwise (*ibid.*, § 2). If the partnership agreement is silent and absent a consensus, the law applies (*ibid.*, § 3). Even though that provision simply refers to "other relevant laws" or administrative regulations and does not specify them, any such vacuum were to be filled by the law of the *partnership contract* in the first place since, as explained, the partnership agreement and the partnership contract are the same (s. Art. 19§3, last sentence; above §2217). Of course, other laws may apply, depending on the subject matter.

B. Property

2231 As already stated in the general provisions, the *property* of the partnership is protected (Art. 8; s. above §2221). The regime of such property is further detailed in Section 2 (Art. 20 to 25) of Chapter 2 on general partnership of the law. Such property comprises the partners' capital contributions, its profit and any other property legally acquired by the partnership (Art. 20).

2232 Section 2 is otherwise concerned with the use of the shares, be it by division, abuse, assignment or pledge. No *division* may take place before the partnership enterprise's liquidation (Art. 21§1). However, if abuse occurs, that prohibition may not be used against a *bone fide* third party (*ibid.*, § 2).

2233 The *assignment* of a share to a third party may only occur if the assignor has notified its partners (Art. 22§2) and with their consent, unless the partnership agreement permits it (*ibid.*, § 1); moreover, such assignment is subject to the other partners' right of first refusal or preemption right[934] at the same conditions (Art. 23). The assignee becomes a partner and enjoys the corresponding rights and obligations upon amendment of the partnership agreement (Art. 24).

---

933 Cf. Company Law, Art. 32§1, item 5 and § 2; s. above §1817.

934 S. above note 850.

The *pledge* of a share is equally subject to the other partners' consent; absent it, the pledge is invalid (Art. 25, 1st sentence and 2nd sentence, 1st phrase). If the *bona fide* third party (which, although the law does not specify it, should be the pledgee or, alternatively, the creditor) suffers damage as a result thereof, the pledgor partner shall be liable for it (*ibid.*, 2nd sentence, 2nd phrase). 2234

C. *Partnership Affairs*

1. General Provisions

Section 3 on the *execution of partnership affairs* (Art. 26 to 36) is, together with Section 5 on joining and withdrawing from the partnership, the most substantial of Chapter 2 on the general partnership. Section 3 is concerned with the rights of the partners, the partnership's representative, its managing partners, decision making, prohibited activities, profit and losses, modification of the capital contributions, employees, and management systems. 2235

In accordance with the principles of voluntariness, equality, fairness and good faith at the core of the partnership (Art. 5), all partners enjoy *equal rights* in the execution of partnership affairs (Art. 26§1). 2236

The partnership may have one or several *representatives* and *managing partners*. It results from the drafting of the law that the power of a representative does not necessarily extend to managing the affairs for which it represents the partnership, and that the power of a managing partner does not necessarily extend to representing the partnership for the affairs it manages. They may be either representative, or managing partner, or both, as defined by the partnership agreement or entrusted by the partners (Art. 26), which can unanimously terminate their appointment (Art. 29§2). If the managing partner is an organization, the management is executed by the organization's own representatives (*ibid.*, § 2)[935]. Excess power results in liability (Art. 98; s. below §2314). 2237

Managing partners must regularly *report* to the other partners on the current operations and finances (Art. 28§1, 1st sentence). The latter enjoy a *right of supervision* (Art. 27§2), i.e., to consult the books, and to check the operational and financial status of the partnership. However, that right does not extend as far as *interfering* with the management (Art. 27§1). If they do so, any managing partner may oppose it and the execution of the affairs interfered with must be suspended (Art. 29§1, 1st and 2nd sentence); any dispute resulting thereof shall 2238

---

[935] On the registration and publication of the partnership enterprise's legal representative, s. above §2229.

be settled by a partners' resolution (Art. 29§1, 3rd sentence and Art. 30; s. next paragraph).

2239 *Decisions* related to the partnership are to be taken in the form of a resolution. The method applying thereto, i.e., the voting method, majority, quorum, etc. is to be specified in the partnership agreement (Art. 30§1, 1st sentence). If not, or if the agreement is unclear, the law prescribes a default method which is the simple majority of all the partners (*ibid.*, 2nd sentence), unless the Partnership Enterprise Law mandates otherwise (Art. 30§2), namely, unanimity for certain matters, including a change of the name, scope or main business premises of the partnership, the disposal of its real property, the assignment or disposal of its IPR or other property, the provision of a guarantee to a third party, and the engagement of persons other than the partners as managers (Art. 31). Acting without authorization results in liability (Art. 97; s. below §2314).

2240 The law further prohibits the partners from conducting certain activities including *competition*, by cooperating among themselves or with third parties, with the partnership (Art. 32§1), *business transactions with the partnership* unless authorized by the partnership agreement or by the all partners (*ibid.*, § 2)[936], and any other activity which may harm the partnership (*ibid.*, § 3). Either case results in liability (Art. 99; s. below §2314). The limited liability partnership regime is more liberal in those regards (s. below §§2290 and 2291).

2241 The proceeds derived from the execution of the partnership affairs belong to the partnership, as already prescribed by Art. 20 (s. above §2231). The latter further bears the expenses or losses resulting therefrom (Art. 28§1, 2nd sentence). *Profit and losses* are shared[937] according to a cascading regime: first, between the partners according to the partnership agreement (Art. 33§1, 1st sentence); however, the agreement may not grossly advantage or discriminate certain partners, i.e., it may not provide that all profit shall be distributed or all losses be attributed to certain partners and not to others (Art. 33§2)[938]. Second, if the agreement is silent or unclear, the partners shall reach an agreement by consultation (Art. 33§1, 2nd sentence); if such consultation fails, the law

---

936 The prohibition to engage into business transactions with the partnership may be derogated to by the partnership agreement or the other partners (Art. 32§2); that of competing may not however (*ibid.*, § 1 *a contrario*).

937 The law actually mentions the *distribution* of profit and the *sharing* of losses (s. Art. 18, item 5 and Art. 33). This wording suggests that the profit may be distributed or not, depending on the partnership agreement or the partners' decision; their sharing only occurs once they are to be distributed. In contrast, the losses, once shared, are to be borne by the partners (s. Art. 33).

938 The limited liability partnership regime is more liberal in this respect, as it allows the partnership agreement to derogate to that prohibition (Company Law, Art. 70 *in fine*; s. below §2289).

provides by default for a two-steps mechanism, which form the third and fourth levels of the cascade: third, *pro rata* sharing in proportion of each partner's contribution to the partnership capital (*ibid.*, 3rd sentence); fourth and last, if such contributions cannot be determined, equally among all partners (*ibid.*, 4th sentence).

One is duty bound to note, however, that it is unlikely that the partnership may be silent, since the method of profit distribution and loss sharing must mandatorily be mentioned in the partnership agreement (Art. 18, item 5; s. above §2228); absent it, the registration authority should refuse to register the partnership, reminding that such registration is a preliminary condition to the establishment of the partnership (s. above §2224), and invite the applicant to complement the partnership agreement. It is, however, conceivable that the latter may be unclear or fails to specifically address some sort of profit or loss: if so, the default mechanism may be helpful. 2242

Capital *contributions* (s. above §§2225 to 2227) can be subsequently modified, i.e., increased or decreased, if the partnership agreement so provides or all the partners so agree (Art. 34). 2243

The partnership management must establish and rely on a financial and accounting *system*. It may employ *managers* (not to be confused with *managing partners*, who are not employed by the partnership enterprise but, as their name makes clear, partners of the partnership enterprise, and may hire employed lower-level managers) whose powers must be defined (Art. 35§1). They are liable towards the partnership if they harm the partnership by exceeding them or otherwise, intentionally or by gross negligence (*ibid.*, § 2). 2244

2. Liability Towards Third Parties

Section 4 (Art. 37 to 42) of Chapter 2 on the general partnership of the Partnership Enterprise Law, which is somewhat vaguely titled "Relationship Between Partnership and Third Party", focuses on the partnership's *liability for debts* towards third party creditors. 2245

This set of provisions provides for cascading liabilities. First, a partnership shall pay its debts with its own property[939] (Art. 38 and 20). Second, if that does not suffice, its partners bear *unlimited* (s. next paragraph), *joint and several* liability (Art. 39). Third, if one partner pays more than its share as prescribed by Art. 33§1 (s. above §2241), it has the right to recover the excess from its partners (Art. 40). 2246

[939] About the notion of partnership property, s. above §2231.

2247 *Bona fide* third parties are protected: a partnership may not invoke internal power restrictions to escape its liabilities (Art. 37)[940]. This is consistent with the general regime of agency governed by the Chinese Civil Code (s. above Chap. 2 §11.III, Powers of Agency and Agents Without Power) and with that of excess power in the Partnership Enterprise Law (Art. 98; s. below §2314).

2248 As mentioned, the partners' liability is not only joint and several; it is *unlimited* (Art. 39). Even though the law falls short from elaborating, that single qualifier embeds the fundamental difference between a general and a limited liability partnership: it implies that, in a general partnership, if the partnership's assets and the partners' share is insufficient, the partner shall bear liability on the *personal assets*. In contrast, the liability of the partners of a limited liability partnership is limited, as its name clearly implies, to their share.

2249 The law further sets out a special regime for *partners' debts unrelated to the partnership*. Whenever so, the creditor may not mix its claims towards a partner with those it may have towards the partnership, neither by offsetting them, nor by subrogation, i.e., by exercising the rights of such partner against the partnership (Art. 41).

2250 If that partner's own assets and share of the partnership's profit are insufficient to pay such debts, the creditor may ask the court to enforce the *liquidation* of its share (Art. 42§1). The court shall notify the other partners which may choose among the following four options: either, approve that share's assignment to a new partner (1st option); or refuse it and either buy the withholding partner's share (2nd option), reduce (3rd option) or cancel (4th option) it, and compensate that partner accordingly, so it can pay its debts. The other partners enjoy a preferable *right of first refusal* or preemption right[941] over such proposed assignment (1st option), provided their offer is subject to equivalent terms, in which case they must choose one of the other three options. The reduction or cancellation (3rd and 4th options) are subject to Art. 51 (s. below §§2259ff.)

3. Joinder and Withdrawal

2251 Section 5 on joining and withdrawing from the partnership (Art. 43 to 54) is the other substantial section of Chapter 2 on the general partnership of the

940 That protection is further qualified for limited liability partners, s. Art. 76§1 and below §2294.

941 S. above note 602. A right of first refusal generally consists in a preemption right (2nd option); however, in this case, it also entitles, alternatively, to other rights (3rd and 4th options).

Partnership Enterprise Law. It focuses on withdrawing. Joining is only addressed by a couple of provisions. The remaining set of provisions applying to withdrawing is roughly divided between causes and consequences.

Joining a partnership is subject to the consent of all the partners and the conclusion of a written *joinder agreement* (Art. 43§1). While the law permits the partnership agreement to dispense with it, it seems hardly conceivable in practice, and in any event not to be recommended. Upon joining, the existing partners must truthfully *inform* the new partner of the state of business operations and the financial status of the partnership (*ibid.*, § 2). In principle, new partners enjoy *equal rights* with the existing partners, unless the joinder agreement provides otherwise, which is frequent in practice (Art. 44§1), since existing partners may want to retain some privileges over new partners, taking into account the goodwill to which they contributed before a new partner joins. Such equality also means that the new partners become jointly and severally *liable* with the existing ones; moreover, it is important to note that their liability extends to the partnership's debts incurred *before* they joined (*ibid.*, § 2). 2252

As noted, the regime of *withdrawal* from the partnership details both the causes (Art. 45 to 49) and the consequences (Art. 50 to 54). The law further distinguishes, among the *causes*, voluntary or optional from compulsory ones, and causes for expulsion. Optional causes vary depending on whether the duration of the partnership is fixed or not. 2253

If the duration of the partnership is *specified* in the partnership agreement, a partner may withdraw if a cause for withdrawal provided in the partnership agreement has occurred; if all the other partners consent; if any other cause resulting in making it "difficult" (难以 nányǐ) for that partner to remain in the partnership occurs; or if other partners violated the partnership agreement (Art. 45). 2254

If the duration of the partnership is *not specified* in the partnership agreement, a partner may withdraw with a simple 30-day advance notice to the other partners, provided, however, that its withdrawal does not adversely impact on the partnership's affairs (Art. 46). If it does, or if the withdrawing partner has violated Art. 45, it shall be liable for any damage (Art. 47). 2255

In contrast, a partner *must* (as opposed to may as for Art. 45 and 46) withdraw from the partnership in the following cases, or any such case shall result in that partner's withdrawal: he died; became insolvent; as an organization, its business license is revoked, ordered to close down, is dissolved or declared 2256 bankrupt; is not qualified anymore as required by law or the partnership agreement; or all its shares are enforced (Art. 48§1)[942].

2257 Finally, a partner may be *expelled* by the other partners if it fails to pay its capital contribution; causes losses to the partnership intentionally or by gross negligence; conducted "improper" (不正当 bù zhèngdàng) activities; or because any other cause foreseen by the partnership agreement occurred (Art. 49§1).

2258 The expulsion may not be arbitrary, however. It must be formally notified to that partner (*ibid.*, 1st sentence). While the law only requires that it be notified in writing (*ibid.*), it implies that it should be motivated to some extent. Indeed, the expelled partner has the right to oppose it at court (*ibid.*, § 3); absent such motivation, an expulsion would be duty bound to be annulled. In that regard, it is to be noted about the third cause of expulsion (*ibid.*, § 1, item 3) that the law uses the qualifier "improper", not "illegal", thus leaving a certain discretion to the other partner to deem what is improper to the point it justifies an expulsion, and what does not reach that threshold which is, therefore, relatively subjective. The expulsion, which results in the withdrawal from the partnership, becomes effective upon receipt of the notice (*ibid.*, § 2, 2nd sentence), from which the expelled partner has 30 days to file at court (*ibid.*, § 3).

2259 The *consequences* of withdrawal (Art. 50 to 54) may result from any of the causes foreseen by Art. 45 to 49. The general consequences of withdrawal are governed by Art. 51 to 54; death (Art. 48§1, item 1) is specifically governed by Art. 50.

2260 Generally, in case of withdrawal (other than resulting from the partner's death), the other partners must *settle* its share with the departing partners and return it (Art. 51§1). The share of the withdrawing partner shall be settled either according to the method specified in the partnership agreement or, absent such method, as determined by all the partners (Art. 52, 1st sentence). This provision falls short of offering a solution in case the partnership agreement is silent, unclear or inadequate and the partners fail to agree. If so, one may suppose that Art. 33 on the sharing of profit and losses apply (s. above §§2241 and 2242). This is supported by Art. 54, which refers to Art. 33 in case the partnership's assets are insufficient for compensating the departing partner (s. next paragraph *in fine*).

2261 The point of time at which such share's *value* is to be taken into account is that at which the withdrawal becomes effective (Art. 51§1, 1st sentence). However, if there is outstanding business at the time of the withdrawal, the settlement

942 Moreover, a partner losing his civil capacity may become a limited liability partner, subject to his partners' agreement (Art. 48§2). Absent such agreement, the former must withdraw (*ibid.*, *in fine*), unless he is a limited liability partner (Art. 79).

shall be carried out after such business' conclusion (*ibid.*, § 2). The withdrawing partner bears unlimited joint and several liability for the debts of the partnership resulting from causes having arisen before its withdrawal (Art. 53). Moreover, any loss it may have caused to the partnership shall be deducted from its share (Art. 51§1, 2nd sentence). Such liability mainly results from the partnership enterprise's general provisions (Art. 2§2, 1st sentence and § 3, 2nd sentence, 1st phrase and above, §2213) and from the regime of its or its partners' liability for debts towards third parties (s. above Chap. 9 §65.II.C.2, Liability Towards Third Parties). Finally, if the partnership's assets are insufficient for reimbursing the withdrawing partner, it shall share the corresponding loss proportionally (Art. 54). In either case, the withdrawing partner's share shall be reduced accordingly. That share may be returned in currency or in kind (Art. 52, 2nd sentence).

In case of *death* of a partner, the latter is not replaced outright within the part- 2262
nership by the successor inheriting his share. Such replacement depends on either the partnership agreement, or the unanimous consent of all the other partners. If such replacement is permitted, however, that successor is vested in the rights of the deceased, subject always to the partnership agreement or the decision of the other partners, from the point of succession (Art. 50§1). Alternatively, such replacement may not occur against the will of such successor (*ibid.*, § 2, item 1), or if he does not meet the qualifications required by the law or the partnership agreement (*ibid.*, items 2 and 3)[943]. In such cases, the deceased partner's share shall be settled under Art. 50 to 54 as described in the two preceding paragraphs, and its proceeds remitted with its successor: although the law does not say so expressly, such reference results from its structure.

III. Specialized General Partnership

While Section 6 on the specialized general partnership (Art. 55 to 59) forms the 2263
last section of Chapter 2 on the general partnership of which it is, therefore, structurally, a sub-type, the features of the specialized general partnership (特殊普通合伙 tèshū pǔtōng héhuǒ), whose characters must follow its name (Art. 56)[944], actually place it in between the general partnership and the limited liability partnership forming Chapter 3 of the law.

The characteristic feature of a specialized general partnership is its *special lia-* 2264
bility regime, which partly derogates from the ordinary liability regime of the general partnership (Art. 55§2). In order to outline it, one has to distinguish its

943 Art. 50§3 addresses the special case in which the successor lacks civil capacity.
944 Omissions are punishable (Art. 94; s. below §2313).

external effects (towards third party creditors) from its internal ones (towards the partnership).

2265 From the point of view of *external liability*, as in a general partnership, the partners of a specialized general partnership are jointly and severally liable towards third party creditors for the debts of the partnership (Art. 39; s. above §2246). That liability is, in principle and subject to the exception which follows, *unlimited* (*ibid.* and above §2248, as well as Art. 57§2 and below §2271), meaning that the partners may be held liable on their personal assets if the partnership's assets or their share do not suffice.

2266 The difference with the general partnership is that, in a specialized general partnership, in case the latter incurs debts as a result of one partner's *wrongful act* committed *intentionally* or by *gross negligence*[945], only that partner shall bear unlimited liability towards that third party creditors for such debts, while the other partners' liability shall be *limited.* Even though the law does not expressly state it, what it implies is that while, as reminded in the preceding paragraph, the faulty partner's liability is unlimited, that of its innocent partners is limited to their *share*, like in a limited liability partnership (s. below §2278). They may not be held liable on their *personal* assets, even by *bona fide* third-party creditors; inasmuch, the specialized general partnership liability regime derogates from that of the general partnership (cf. Art. 37; s. above §2248).

2267 The mere fact that one partner intentionally caused the partnership to incur a debt does not, as such, result in limiting the liability of the other partners. The act having caused such debt must fulfill two cumulative conditions, the second of which is alternative: it must be wrongful and have been committed either intentionally or by gross negligence. By wrongful, one should understand that the act was committed either in breach of the law, or of the partnership agreement, and without the other partners' approval. In other words, if such act was compliant, or if the other partners approved it, they shall not be entitled to shelter themselves behind their limited liability. Likewise, they shall not either if the act resulted from light negligence. The special liability regime of the specialized general partnership derogates from the ordinary regime of the general partnership which protects *bona fide* third parties (Art. 37; s. above §2247); therefore, such derogation should be interpreted narrowly.

2268 In practice, a third party creditor may request the faulty partner to bear full liability; if its share and personal assets are insufficient, such third party creditor may request the *partnership* to use its assets (Art. 38 and 20; s. above

945 Some translations omit "wrongful" while other use "serious" instead of "gross negligence". We believe that translation we propose is the most adequate.

§§2231 and 2246) and the innocent partners to pay any outstanding balance, but those partners' liability shall be limited to their shares.

From the point of view of *internal liability*, if and after the partnership has paid any such debts to third party creditors, the faulty partner is liable towards the partnership for any damage resulting thereof (Art. 58). In other words, the former must reimburse to the partnership the debts the latter may have paid to third party creditors. The extent of the faulty partner's liability towards the partnership is determined by the partnership agreement (*ibid.*, *in fine*). 2269

If several (but not all) partners have been committing a wrongful act intentionally or by gross negligence, they shall bear unlimited liability jointly and severally both towards the third-party creditors and the partnership (Art. 57§1 and 58). 2270

If the partnership incurs debts which did not result from any wrongful act committed by a partner intentionally act or by gross negligence, the partnership bears unlimited, joint and several liability (Art. 57§2). 2271

In other words, the specialized general partnership is a *hybrid* partnership, mixing the general and the limited liability enterprise's regimes, while limiting the limited liability regime to innocent partners in case of debts resulting from a wrongful act committed intentionally or by gross negligence. It is typically used by and, as the case may be, mandatory for *law firms*, *accounting firms* and other highly specialized service providers delivering high added-value services entailing significant economic risks, to the effect of protecting innocent partners from the misdeeds of faulty partners. 2272

A specialized general partnership must set up *practice risk fund* and purchase *professional civil liability insurance* (Art. 59§1). The practice risk funds are to be used for paying off the debts incurred by partners in their business activities. A separate account for such fund must be opened and managed separately (*ibid.*, § 2) in order to prevent mingling them with other funds and effectively emptying them by using them to other ends. 2273

Other than the *lex specialis* described above, the general regimes of the partnership and of the general partnership apply as *lex generalis* (Art. 55§3). Besides, when a *contractual specialized partnership* transforms into a partnership enterprise, the liability of the former's partners shall be governed by the specialized general partnership regime (Art. 107)[946]. 2274

---

[946] This provision (Art. 107) is not contained in Section 6 on the specialized general partnership of Chapter 2 on the partnership but, oddly, in Chapter 6 on supplementary provisions, which is the last chapter of the Partnership Enterprise Law.

IV. Limited Liability Partnership

2275 Chapter 3 on the limited liability partnership (Art. 60 to 84) of the Partnership Enterprise Law is a subsidiary regime which modifies or complements the regime of the general partnership and Chapter 1 on the general provisions, both of which apply whenever the regime of the limited liability partnership is silent (Art. 60; 2nd sentence).

2276 As already explained (s. above §2213), while a general partnership (普通合伙 pǔtōng héhuǒ) is defined as a partnership comprising of general partners with unlimited joint and several liability for the debts of the partnership (Art. 2§2, 1st sentence and § 3, 2nd sentence, 1st phrase), a limited liability partnership (有限合伙 yǒuxiàn héhuǒ), whose characters must follow its name (Art. 62)[947], is composed of general partners and *limited liability partners*: unlike general partners, limited liability partners bear liability for the debts of the partnership to the extent of the capital *contributions* they have subscribed (Art. 2§3, 2nd sentence, 2nd phrase).

2277 The main feature distinguishing the general partnership, the specialized general partnership and the limited liability partnership is, as the latter's name spells out, liability. However, such distinctions may be less straightforward than they seem. Two potential misconceptions may be dispelled at this stage. First, unlike its name suggests, in an limited liability partnership, as compared to a general partnership, not all partners bear limited liability: the limited liability partnership's liability regime is, in fact, a *hybrid* regime: it provides for both partners with limited and unlimited liability; there must be at least one general partner, i.e., with unlimited liability (Art. 61§2), which implies that there can be more than one general partner.

2278 Second, as already outlined, the limited liability partnership and the specialized general partnership's regimes compare inasmuch as both provide for partners with limited and unlimited liability. The difference is that, in the specialized general partnership, the liability of certain partners is limited in specific circumstances only, i.e., if one or several partners committed a wrongful act, intentionally or by gross negligence, causing the specialized general partnership to incur debt (s. above Chap. 9 §65.III, Specialized General Partnership), while in the limited liability partnership, the liability of limited liability partners is *permanently* limited, not subject to specific circumstances or conditions, least a wrongful act.

---

947 Omissions are punishable (Art. 94; s. below §2313).

Unlike for the general partnership, the *number of partners*, whether limited liability partners or general partners, of a limited liability partnership is limited to maximum 50 partners (Art. 61§1). 2279

The *affairs* of the limited liability partnership must be executed by the general partners: the limited liability partners may not (Art. 67, 1st sentence), subject to certain exceptions (s. below §2288). Acting without power results in liability (Art. 98; s. below §2314). Representation is outlined below (s. §2288). 2280

One may deduct from the foregoing that, because the law imposes a minimum of one general partner but no *maximum* while limiting the maximum number of partners of a limited liability partnership, nothing would prevent, in theory, a limited liability partnership to be formed of up to 49 general partners and only one limited liability partner. Two reasons suggest that such an outcome may be unlikely, however: first, because the general partner or partners are in charge of the affairs of the company, the law, while not setting a maximum of general partners in a limited liability partnership, clearly envisions the limited liability partnership to typically have not less than, but either only one general partner, or a small number of general partners relatively to the number of limited liability partners, like the manager of a limited liability company, or the general manager and the senior management of a shareholding company relatively to the shareholders (s. above §§1876 and 1962). Second, even though the law does not set a maximum, the registration authority would probably frown upon extreme proportions where general partners would outnumber limited liability partners and invite the applicant to consider registering a general partnership instead of a limited liability partnership. 2281

In contrast, while there is no maximum of general partners, if the *minimum* of one general partner mentioned above (Art. 61§2; s. above §2277) is not complied with anymore (supposedly because all the general partners withdrew), the limited liability partnership must be dissolved and transformed into a general partnership (Art. 75). 2282

To complement the liability regime of the limited liability partnership, a limited liability partner may *transform* into a general partner or vice versa, subject to the unanimous consent of all the other partners or the partnership agreement (Art. 82). It is worth noting that, if a limited liability partner transforms into a general partner, it shall *lose* retroactively the benefit of having been a limited liability partner and bear unlimited joint and several liability for the debts of the partnership incurred during the period when it was a limited liability partner (Art. 83). The reciprocal statement is not true, however: if, conversely, a general partner transforms into a limited liability partner, it shall retain unlimited joint and several liability for the debts of the partnership incurred during the period when it is a general partner (Art. 84). 2283

2284 The transformation of a partner is not to be confused with that of the partnership enterprise: in the former case, the fate of the partner's liability is governed by Art. 83 and 84. In the latter case, unlike in the former, the enterprise is dissolved and replaced by a new one; the fate of the dissolved enterprise is governed by Chapter 4 of the law on the dissolution and liquidation of the partnership (s. below Chap. 9 §65.V, Dissolution and Liquidation of Partnerships).

2285 The law adds some requirements specific to the limited liability partnership to the content of the *partnership agreement* described in the general provisions of the law (Art. 18), to which it refers (Art. 63). In particular, it is concerned by the partnership's *affairs*, whose execution is mentioned at Art. 18 (item 6) without further detail, while Art. 63 elaborates them by requesting the qualifications of the managing partners (who are, as mentioned above, the general partners of the limited liability partnership) and the procedure for their selection, the limits of their powers, the measures for handling any breach of contract they may commit in performing their duties, and their termination and replacement (*ibid.*, items 2, 3 and 4). Art. 63 also requires the partnership agreement to detail the procedure for *conversion* of a limited liability partner into a general partner and vice versa (item 6). While Art. 63 mentions a few other items, they merely reformulate *mutatis mutandis* items already mentioned at Art. 18. The names and capital contributions of the limited liability partners are specifically addressed by Art. 66 (s. below §2287).

2286 Like in a general partnership (Art. 17§1; s. above §2226), a limited liability partner must pay its *capital contribution* (Art. 65, 1st sentence). However, unlike in a general partnership (Art. 16§1; s. above §2226), a limited liability partner may not contribute to the capital of the limited liability partnership in the form of *labor services* (Art. 64§2). If a limited liability partner fails to pay, it shall be liable towards the other partner (Art. 65, 2nd sentence)[948].

2287 The law expressly requires the names of the limited liability partners and the amount of their contribution to be *registered* (Art. 66)[949]. The general provisions and the general partnership regime, which apply by default, already provide so, albeit indirectly: indeed, the partnership agreement must be registered (Art. 9§1; s. above §2220), while the latter must contain both items (Art. 18, items 3 and 4). Moreover, Art. 18 does not seem to be limited to general partners, since it only mentions "partners"; therefore, it should also apply to limited liability partners, thus arguably removing the necessity of Art. 66. Yet one may note that Art. 63 which complements, for the limited liability partnership, the mandatory content of the partnership agreement already listed at Art. 18 for the

[948] The general partnership regime falls short from mentioning such liability (s. Art. 17§1 and above, §2227). It is implied however (s. above note 932).

[949] The capital of a partnership as such needs not to however (s. above §2225).

general partnership, only mentions the limited liability partners' names, not their capital contributions (Art. 63, item 1). Art. 66 could then be understood as complementing Art. 63. Finally, and in any event, Art. 66, like Art. 9, falls short of specifying whether the limited liability partners' capital contribution should be not only registered but also *published*, as the protection of the public interest should command given that, by definition, their liability is not, like for general partners, unlimited. Again, like for the general partnership, in practice, the capital contributions of limited partner is published on NECIPS as it should *a fortiori*, since those of general partners are (s. above §2229). Therefore, Art. 66 may be understood as emphasizing, if only by implying it, that the limited liability partners' capital contribution must be not only registered, but also published.

As mentioned, the affairs of the limited liability partnership must be executed 2288
by the general partners: the limited liability partners may not do so (Art. 67, 1st sentence; s. above §2280). In particular, limited liability partners may not *represent* the partnership towards third parties (Art. 68§1). However, certain activities *derogate* to that prohibition. They include: deciding the joinder or withdrawal of a general partner; offering suggestions on the business operations and management; selecting an auditor; obtaining the audited financial and accounting reports; consulting the accounting books and other financial documents of the partnership if that partner's personal interests are involved, as well as, if so, challenging the liability of other partners and filing at court; urging the managing partners to exercise their rights for protecting the interests of the partnership if they neglect doing so, or filing at court if they do not do so, and offering a guarantee to the partnership. Acting without power or excess power results in liability (Art. 98; s. below §2314).

As a default rule, the *profit* may not be distributed to certain partners, but not 2289
to others; however, the partnership agreement may provide otherwise (Art. 69). Insofar, the limited liability partnership regime is more liberal than the general partnership's, since the latter expressly prohibits the partnership agreement to derogate to that prohibition (Art. 33§2; s. above §2241). The reason for this discrepancy is that, while general partnerships require equal opportunity to share profit among all partners due to their equal and unlimited liability, limited liability partnerships allow for differentiated profit sharing because limited partners may have different levels of involvement, risk, and capital contribution. In practice, even though the law does not specify it, the partnership agreements of a limited liability partnership frequently provide that limited liability partners are entitled to a lesser share of profit than general partners. Inasmuch, that repartition may also take into account the fact that the managing partners (who are, as noted, by law, general partners; Art. 67, 1st sentence; s. above §2280) are entitled not only to be remunerated for managing the partnership

affairs, but also that such remuneration be expressly mentioned in the partnership agreement (Art. 67, 2nd sentence).

2290 While, as noted above, the limited liability partners' rights may be occasionally restricted as compared to those of general partners (management, contribution in the form of labor services, representation, distribution of profit; s. above §§2280, 2286, 2288 and 2289), the limited liability partnership's regime is also *more liberal* towards limited liability partners where the general partnership's one imposes restrictions on general partners' rights.

2291 Thus, where, as a matter of principle, a general partner may not engage into *business transactions with the partnership* or only subject to his partners' unanimous consent (Art. 32§2; s. above §2240), a limited liability partner may (Art. 70). Likewise, while a general partner may not *compete* with the partnership (Art. 32§1; s. above §2240), a limited liability partner may (Art. 71)[950]. Where a general partner may not *pledge* his shares without the unanimous consent of his partners (Art. 25; s. above §2234), a limited liability partner may (Art. 72). Finally, where a general partner may only *assign* his shares subject to the unanimous consent of his partners and subject to their preemption right (Art. 22 and 23; s. above §2233), a limited partner only has the obligation to notify his partners 30 days in advance (Art. 73); he does not need their consent. While most of the related rights and obligations may be restricted or alleviated in the partnership agreement[951], the legislator's intent clearly is to compensate for limited liability partners' lesser role in the limited liability partnership by a greater freedom.

2292 The limited liability partnership's regime complements the *liabilities* regime of the general partnership by adding specific provisions applying to debts unrelated to the partnership, third parties, unauthorized transactions, and debts before and after the partnership.

2293 The liability of a limited liability partner for debts towards third parties *unrelated to the partnership* is the same, *mutatis mutandis*, than that of general partners (Art. 74 and 42), with one exception: while, in case of court enforcement, the mandatory drafting of Art. 42§2, 2nd sentence suggests that the court may

---

[950] While Art. 71 expressly mentions that a limited liability partner may compete with the partnership alone or with "others" without specifying whether, if the latter are other partners, they should be limited liability or general partners, Art. 32§1, which prohibits general partners to compete without providing for any derogation in the partnership agreement, implies that limited liability partners, while competing with the partnership together with other partners, may only do so with other limited liability partners.

[951] Of all the provisions mentioned in this paragraph, only two, both pertaining to the general partnership's regime, Art. 25 (pledge) and 32§1 (competition) may not be altered by partnership agreement.

impose a withdrawal- or a share decrease settlement to the other partners (s. above §2250), that faculty is not mentioned in the limited liability partnership regime (s. Art. 74 *a contrario*).

The general partnership's regime, which applies by default to the limited liability partnership, already protects *bona fide third parties* (Art. 37; s. above §2247). The limited liability partnership's regime complements that general protection by providing that, where a *bona fide* third party reasonably believes that the limited liability partner with whom it does business is a general partner, that limited liability partner shall bear the same liability as a general partner (Art. 76). As noted about the general partnership (s. above §2247), this is consistent with the general regime of agency governed by the Chinese Civil Code (s. above Chap. 2 §11.III, Powers of Agency and Agents Without Power) and with that of excess power in the Partnership Enterprise Law (Art. 98; s. below §2314). 2294

While the general partnership's regime only implies it (s. above Chap. 9 §65.II.C, Partnership Affairs), thus resting on the general regime of liability of Chapter 5 of the Partnership Enterprise Law, namely, Art. 98 (s. below §2314), the limited liability partnership's one expressly renders any limited liability partner liable for *unauthorized transactions*, i.e., for any damage caused to the partnership because it entered into any such transaction without being authorized to do so (Art. 76§2)[952]. 2295

Like the general partnership's regime (Art. 44§2), the limited liability partnership's one prescribes that the liability of a limited liability partner extends to the debts incurred by the partnership *before its admission*; however, unlike for general partners, such liability is *limited* to that limited liability partner's capital contribution (Art. 77). 2296

Likewise, as a general partner (Art. 53; s. above §2261), a limited liability partner which withdrew bears unlimited joint and several liability for the debts of the partnership resulting from causes having arisen *before its withdrawal* (Art. 81). 2297

The liability of partners *transforming* from limited liability partners to general partner and vice versa has been outlined above (s. §2283). 2298

A limited liability partner shall *withdraw* or be deemed to have withdrawn from the partnership in case of death, if, as a legal person, its business license was revoked, it was ordered to close down or was declared bankrupt, or its share was enforced (Art. 78 referring to Art. 48§1, items 1, 3 and 5). In other words, it is worth noting that, unlike for general partners, insolvency and 2299

952 This liability is reaffirmed at Art. 97; s. below §2314.

incompetence, i.e., the loss of qualifications required by law or the partnership agreement, do *not* constitute causes for the withdrawal of a limited liability partner (*ibid.*, *a contrario* and Art. 48§1, items 2 and 4)[953]. The *succession* of a limited liability partner follows the regime of the general partnership (Art. 80 and 50; s. above §2262).

V. Dissolution and Liquidation of Partnerships

2300 Chapter 4 of the Partnership Enterprise Law (Art. 85 to 92) is a set of guidelines applying to the dissolution and liquidation of partnerships. It is concerned with the circumstances in which a partnership should dissolve, the appointment of the liquidators, the affairs they should settle, notifications to the creditors, the partnership's assets distribution, reporting, liabilities and bankruptcy.

2301 A partnership must be dissolved upon the expiration of its duration unless the partners decide to continue it; if any cause for dissolution specified in the partnership agreement arises; if all the partners decide to dissolve; if their number does not meet the statutory requirements[954] for 30 days; if the objectives of the partnership specified in the partnership agreement have been achieved or if it is impossible to achieve them; if its business license is revoked, it is ordered to close down or is dissolved by law; or for any other reasons specified by law or administrative regulations (Art. 85).

2302 However obvious it may seem, the liquidation must be formally entrusted to *liquidators* (Art. 86§1). They are appointed at the simple majority of the partners. There can be one liquidator or more. They can be either partners or third parties. Until the partners agree on such appointment, all of them are liquidators (*ibid.*, § 2). The appointment must occur within 15 days of the cause of dissolution. Unless it does, any partner of interested third party may apply at court to that effect (*ibid.*, § 3).

2303 The liquidators are entrusted with identifying the partnership's assets and establishing an inventory thereof as well as a balance sheet; handling the pending partnership affairs related to the liquidation; pay off taxes; settle the partnership's receivable and debts; dispose of the residual assets of the partnership after paying off its debts; and represent the partnership in litigations or arbitrations (Art. 87).

---

953 In case a limited liability partner loses his civil capacity, s. above note 942.

954 These requirements are: a minimum of two partners (Art. 14§1 and 61§1; s. above §2224); for limited liability partnerships, a minimum of one general partner (Art. 61§2; s. above §2277), and a maximum of 50 partners (Art. 61§1; s. above §2279).

The liquidators must *notify* the partnership's creditors in order to enable them to declare their credits. Such notification must occur directly within ten days after the liquidator's (or liquidators') appointment; in addition, they have to do so indirectly, in a newspaper, within 60 days (Art. 88§1, 1st sentence). In turn, creditors must declare their credits within 30 days from such notice or, if they did not receive it, 45 days after the publication (*ibid.*, 2nd sentence): in other words, such declaration should occur at most 40 days after the liquidator's appointment in case of direct notification and 105 days in case of publication. Creditors have to prove their claim, which the liquidator must register (Art. 88§2). 2304

The partnership continues to exist during the liquidation (Art. 88§3, 1st sentence). However, it may not engage in any business unrelated to the liquidation (*ibid.*, 2nd sentence). The *distribution* of its assets, i.e., of their remainder, if any, to the partners may only occur after the liquidation costs, salaries, social insurance premiums, employees' statutory indemnities, taxes and debts owed by the partnership, as the case may be, have been paid (Art. 89). Such distribution is regulated by Art. 31§1 (s. above §2241). 2305

Once the liquidation is completed, the liquidator must issue a *liquidation report*, file it with the registration authority within 15 days after it has been signed by all partners or sealed and apply for deregistration (Art. 90). *Fraud* or *negligence* in the liquidation must be corrected and result in the *liability* of the liquidator (Art. 100 to 102; s. below §2315); criminal liability is reserved (Art. 105; s. below §2317). 2306

If the partnership is unable to pay its debts, it must be stressed once again that the partners remain *liable* even after the deregistration (Art. 91) or bankruptcy (Art. 92§1) of the partnership. While the law expressly recalls that, in both cases, general partners retain unlimited, joint and several liability (*ibid.*), it is implied that limited liability partners equally remain liable, although up to their capital contribution (s. Art. 2§2, 1st sentence and § 3, 2nd sentence, 1st phrase; Art. 78 referring to Art. 48§1, items 3 and 5; Art. 81 and above, §§2276, 2297 and 2299). Creditors are, therefore, entitled to file at court either for *bankruptcy* of the partnership, or against the partners personally (Art. 92§1). 2307

VI. Liabilities

Chapter 5 of the Partnership Enterprise Law (Art. 93 to 106) governs liability for a range of infringements. These provisions may apply to the partnership as such, its partners individually, whether general partners, managing partners, or limited liability partners, to third parties, civil servants, and liquidators. They provide both for civil and administrative liability, as well as public liability, 2308 and reserve criminal liability. The infringements they address range from registration to the partnership's name, its business license, assets, partners' powers, competition, liquidation, the partnership agreement, abuse of office, as well as any infringement to other provisions of the Partnership Enterprise Law indeed. Most of these provisions have already been pointed out above.

2309 Chapter 5 of the law is not comprehensive, however. Some of the provisions pertaining to the liability regime at large of the partnership enterprise are not contained in it, but in its preceding chapters. These include: *in general*, liability for debts of the partnership (Art. 37 to 42; s. above Chap. 9 §65.II.C.2, Liability Towards Third Parties, §§2245 to 2250, as well as Art. 57§2, 91 and 92§1; s. above §§2213, 2222, 2265 to 2271 2276 to 2278 and 2307); liability of the limited liability partners (s. above §§2293 to 2298); liability for violation of the partnership agreement (Art. 18; s. above §2229); liability of partners of a specialized general partnership (s. §§2264ff.); and *in particular*, the partners' liability for pledge (Art. 25, 2nd sentence, 2nd phrase; s. above §2234); the (non-partners) managers' liability (Art. 35§2; s. above §2244); new partners' liability (Art. 44§2 and 77; s. above §§2244, 2252 and 2295); liability for withdrawal (Art. 47, 51§1, 2nd sentence and 53; s. above §2255 and 2261); liability in case of transformation (Art. 83 and 84; s. above §2283); liability for capital contribution default (Art. 65, 2nd sentence; s. above §2286); and liability for unauthorized transactions (Art. 76§2; s. above §2295).

2310 This list is not exhaustive, namely because, on one hand, the limited liability enterprise's regime *refers* to that of the general partnership enterprise by default (Art. 60, 2nd sentence; s. above §§2223 and 2275); therefore, certain liability cases of limited liability partners may not be expressly mentioned in the limited liability partnership regime. On the other hand, certain cases of liability may be *implied*, notably, they may be expressly mentioned in one regime, whether that of the general partnership, the specialized general partnership or of the limited liability partnership but only implied in another. Whenever so, we have done our best, if not comprehensively, to signal it in the paragraphs referred to in the preceding one.

2311 Conversely, certain provisions contained in Chapter 5 of the law may double with others already contained in the law's other chapters; alternatively, the general scope of such provisions may cover more specific provisions. We have also endeavored to highlight them, both above and below.

2312 Finally, it should not be forgotten that the partnership enterprise's liability regime at large relates to other liability regimes contained elsewhere in Chinese law. Above all, the partnership mainly rests on the partnership agreement;

therefore, as noted, the *partnership contract* regime[955] (Chinese Civil Code, Third Book, Chapter 27, Art. 967 to 978; s. above Chap. 5 §41, Partnership Contract) should also be taken into consideration, namely, whenever a violation of the partnership agreement is at stake. Furthermore, like any contract, the partnership is, generally speaking, subject to the *contractual liability* regime, i.e., to the regime of liability for breach of contract governed by Chapter 8 (Art. 577 ff.) of the Third Book on contacts of the Chinese Civil Code (s. above Chap. 4 §27, Liability for Breach of Contract), which implicitly refers itself, by default, to the *civil liability* regime (s. above §317, 790 *in fine* and above Chap. 2 §12, Civil Liability[956]). Lastly, while the partnership enterprise's liability regime only opportunistically mentions its *administrative liability* (s. next paragraph), it extends neither to its *criminal liability*, although it expressly reserves it (Art. 105; s. below §2317), nor to its *liability for illicit acts* (s. above Chap. 8 , Liability for Illicit Acts ("Torts")), which it does not mention, and is governed by the Seventh Book (Art. 1164 ff.) of the Chinese Civil Code, if relevant.

Reverting to Chapter 5 of the law, fraud in the *registration* (Art. 9 to 13; s. above §2220), whether at the time of the application (Art. 93) or by omission of registering changes (Art. 95§2), results in *administrative liability*, must be corrected and is punished by a fine; in addition, any damage caused by such omission entitles the victim, be it the partnership, other partners or a *bona fide* third party, to compensation (*ibid.*, § 3). So does the omission of mentioning, in Chinese, "general partnership", "limited liability partnership" or "specialized general partnership" after the *name* of the enterprise (Art. 94, 15, 56 and 62; s. above §§2224, 2263 and 2276) shall also be corrected and fined. Doing business without a *license* may result in business suspension and a fine (Art. 95§1). 2313

Any *appropriation* by both managing partners and non-partner managers of the partnership's assets must return them and are liable for compensation (Art. 96). Any partner executing the affairs of the partnership either *without power* (Art. 98; s. above §§2237, 2280 and 2288[957]) or, however empowered, *without* 2314

---

[955] The partnership contract regime is not specific about liability, however. The only provision mentioning it (Chinese Civil Code, Art. 973) merely mirrors the basic liability regime already provided by the Partnership Enterprise Law, i.e., that the partners are jointly and severally liable for the debts of the partnership, and that a partner who paid any of them has the right to claim compensation from his partners proportionally to their share.

[956] S. also, for the liability of legal persons, above Chap. 2 §8.III.D for the liability of partners exceeding their powers, s. above Chap. 2 §11.III, Powers of Agency and Agents Without Power.

[957] For *bona fide* third parties, s. also §§2247 and 2294.

authorization where such affair is subject to the partners' unanimous approval (Art. 97; s. above §§2239 and 2295), is liable towards the partnership for any damage[958]. Besides, the proceeds of any illicit[959] *competition* or *business transaction* with the partnership belongs to the latter, which is consistent with Art. 20 and 28§1, 2nd sentence which prescribe that the proceeds resulting from the partnership affairs belong to the latter (s. above §§2231 and 2241). Although it does not specify it, this provision only applies to general partners however (cf. Art. 32§1 and 2 and above §2240), since limited liability partners are expressly authorized to compete or engage into business with the partnership (Art. 70 and 71; s. above §2291). Finally, and in any event, consistently with Art. 32§3 (s. above §2240), if a partner causes *damage to the partnership*, it is liable for it (Art. 99).

2315 In the *liquidation* of the partnership (s. above Chap. 9 §65.V, Dissolution and Liquidation of Partnerships), failures in the liquidation report (Art. 100), assets appropriation (Art. 101) or their distribution before having paid the partnership's debts (Art. 102) result in the liability of the liquidator, who may be ordered to rectify the report or return such assets, and compensate for any damage to the partnership, others partners or creditors.

2316 Any violation of the *partnership agreement* (s. above §2214) results in liability (Art. 103§1). As noted, this provision, which generically refers to the law, implicitly refers to, mainly, the partnership contract law, and that of contractual liability (s. above §2312). It further provides for three-tier cascading *remedies*: consultation or mediation, followed, in case of failure, by arbitration, eventually litigation (Art. 103§2).

2317 The law also provides for the *public liability* of civil servants or the authorities: any violation of the Partnership Enterprise Law, abuse of power, seeking private benefits, corruption, or other infringement of the rights or interests of a partnership, is subject to administrative sanctions (Art. 104). Moreover, as noted, whenever the violation of the Partnership Enterprise Law may amount to a crime, it reserves its author's, irrespective of the latter's capacity, *criminal liability* (Art. 105).

2318 Finally, whenever any such liability results in both compensation and a fine, and the author is not solvent enough to pay both, the law sets a *priority* order, by which compensation should be paid first (Art. 106).

---

[958] For limited liability partners, such liability is already foreseen by Art. 76§2 (s. above §2295).

[959] S. above note 936.

§66. Joint-ventures

2319 A JV can be generically defined, irrespective of Chinese law or of any other jurisdiction, as a business arrangement by which two or more parties collaborate to pursue a specific project or objective, typically sharing resources, risks, profit, and control without fully merging their operations.

2320 Sino-foreign JVs; (中外经营企业 zhōngwài jīngyíng qǐyè) have been the first form of FIEs after China's Opening. They have existed from 1 January 1980 until 31 December 2024 (s. preceding paragraph), in the form of either (Sino-foreign-) *equity* joint-venture (EJV; 中外合资经营企业合同 zhōngwài hézī jīngyíng qǐyè hétóng, or that of *contractual* (also frequently translated as "co-operative") joint-venture (CJV; 中外合作经营企业合同 zhōngwài hézuò jīngyíng qǐyè hétóng; s. below §2329), under the laws of the same name, the Sino-Foreign Equity Joint-venture Law and the Sino-Foreign Contractual (or Cooperative) Joint-venture Law.

2321 As explained in this book about the FIL, the new foreign investment regime instituted by the FIL put an end to FIEs and placed them on a level-playing field with domestic enterprises (s. above §31). Therefore, as of 1st January 2020, the FIL mandated FIEs, which had existed so far in the form of EJV, CJV or WFOE, to *transform* into one of the corporate forms available to domestic investors, i.e., either a limited liability company or a shareholding company under the Company Law, or a partnership enterprise under the Partnership Enterprise Law (FIL, Art. 31). Furthermore, the reference to "other laws" silently but effectively permitted purely contractual CJVs (s. below §2326) to transform, alternatively, into a (non-corporate) *contractual* partnership (s. above Chap. 1 §5.I, Corporate Form).

2322 As a result, the three laws which had applied to FIEs until the inception of the FIL, including the two JV laws, were *abolished* by the FIL as of its promulgation, i.e., on 1st January 2020 (FIL, Art. 42§1). However, FIEs enjoyed a *transitory period* of five years, until 31 December 2024, to transform. Meanwhile, JVs kept being governed by the same laws, i.e., the EJV and the CJV laws, however abolished (FIL, Art. 42§2)[960]. Therefore, since 1st January 2025, JVs do not exist in China as companies or corporate forms, i.e., as registrable legal entities, anymore.

2323 The latter status conforms with the general provisions of the Chinese Civil Code, which define a *legal person* as an organization enjoying civil capacity (Art. 57). In order to exist, it must meet the conditions set forth by the law for its establishment (Art. 58); a legal person only starts to exist after it has been

960 S. also below note 968.

established (Art. 59; s. above §§127 and 128). As already noted, in China, generally speaking, aside a limited number of very specific, seldom used forms which are generally out of reach to foreign investors and exceed the scope of this book[961], only the limited liability company, the shareholding company and the partnership enterprise enjoy legal personality, can register as a company, and are accessible to foreign investors as of 1 January 2025.

2324 Meanwhile, Art. 467§2 of the Chinese Civil Code, which was promulgated on 28 may 2020 shortly after the FIL and became effective as of 1st January 2021, provided that "the law of the People's Republic of China" shall apply to "a *contract* for a Chinese-foreign equity JV, a contract for a Chinese-foreign contractual JV, or a contract for Chinese-foreign cooperative exploration and exploitation of natural resources performed in the People's Republic of China". However, Title 2 on typical contracts of the Third Book of the Chinese Civil Code on contract law does not contain any contract named "joint-venture contract". Yet the first paragraph of Art. 467 of the Chinese Civil Code prescribes that, for a contract not expressly provided for in the Code or any other law, the general provisions of the First Book shall apply, and that the provisions on the most *similar* contracts in that Book or any other law may apply *mutatis mutandis* (Chinese Civil Code, Art. 467§1).

2325 Therefore, by expressly referring to the Sino-foreign EJV "contract" and the Sino-foreign CJV "contract"[962], Art. 467§2 of the Chinese Civil Code expressly acknowledges the existence of *JV contracts*, while implicitly acknowledging that, *combined* with the limited liability company, the shareholding company and the partnership enterprise which have substituted the former corporate form of pre-2025 JVs, JV contracts have replaced the latter.

2326 While, despite a widespread but enduring misconception to the contrary ignoring the recent developments recalled above, JVs are not, legally speaking, a corporate form anymore, they remain (in the common sense of a venture invested by both foreign and Chinese investors, as opposed to a 100% foreign-invested one) an important institution of Chinese business law. They persist, as explained, in the form of *sui generis corporate-*, i.e., mixing corporate and contractual features, or *purely contractual* entities, although, since the reform of the FIL, Chinese law hardly expressly names JVs anymore. While not confined to foreign investment anymore, they retain a significant relevance for foreign

961 S. above §124.

962 Contracts for Chinese-foreign cooperative exploration and exploitation of natural resources performed in China will not be covered in this book. About foreign investment in SOEs, s. above Chap. 9 §64.V, Special Provisions on the Organizational Structure of State-owned Companies.

investors. As such, they deserve a dedicated chapter in the company law chapter of this book.

In order to discuss JVs under the new, post-2024 regime, several notions and distinctions must be apprehended, under both the old and the new regime. They include: terminology; the types of JVs; the distinction and the relationship between the corporate and the contractual aspects; the laws governing them; and the related registration requirements. 2327

Before any discussion, it is necessary to clarify the *terminology* of several distinct but deceivingly similar notions which will be recurrently referred to in this chapter. Thus, a *limited liability company contractual joint-venture* is to distinguish from a *purely contractual joint-venture*: although being the same main form of JV (the other one being the EJV), the first sub-type is registered (as corporation), while the second is not. The purely contractual JV is, in turn, to be distinguished from the *joint-venture contract*, which is the contract internal and common to both the EJV and the limited liability company CJV binding its partners and focuses on the contractual aspects typical of a JV. The latter is, again, to be distinguished from the *bylaws*, which regulate the corporate aspects within a limited liability company or a shareholding company. The *partnership enterprise* is to be distinguished from the *partnership agreement*, which can be said to play for the former the same role as the JV contract for the JV. Finally, the partnership agreement is to be distinguished from the *partnership contract* or *contractual partnership*, which can be said to be to the partnership enterprise what the purely contractual JV is to the limited liability company CJV. All these notions will be developed in context below. 2328

Generally speaking (irrespective of the jurisdiction to which JVs may pertain), the main difference between the two main types of JVs, *equity* joint-venture and *contractual* joint-venture is that, in the EJV, each partner is liable in proportion to its *contribution* to the registered capital of the limited liability company, while in the case of a CJV, the parties may *contractually* agree on the apportionment, which may depart from the proportion of their contribution, of their liability. 2329

In JVs, while the JV itself may (s. next paragraph) be a legal person governed by *corporate law*, the relationship between partners is of a contractual nature which may, therefore, also be subject to *contract law*, whenever corporate law does not extend to all contractual aspects of the JV. 2330

In China, before 2021, EJVs had to be registered as limited liability company and enjoyed, henceforth, legal personality. CJVs could alternatively take the 2331 form of either a *limited liability company*, or that of a *contract*[963] or purely contractual CJV; in both cases, the contractual aspects used to bear more weight in a CJV than in an EJV. In other words, there were three forms of JVs, the EJV, the limited liability company CJV and the purely contractual CJV, or two main types, the EJV and the CJV, while the CJV subdivided in two sub-types.

2332 As limited liability company, the *corporate* aspects of the EJV and the limited liability company (as opposed to the purely contractual) CJV were, internally, governed by their *bylaws*. That said, both the EJV and the limited liability company CJV (as opposed to the purely contractual CJV) required the parties to be bound by a *joint-venture contract* (EJV Law, Art. 3; CJV Law, Art. 5) separate from those bylaws, thus acknowledging that limited liability company JVs were governed both by a *corporate* and a *contractual* regime.

2333 As a result, under the old regime, the CJV and EJV laws applied to both the corporate and the contractual regimes of the EJV and the limited liability company CJV while, as far as the *corporate* aspects of the JV were concerned, the Company Law residually applied to aspects not covered by the JV laws[964].

2334 Because the contract of partnership was only introduced by the Chinese Civil Code (s. above §1343), which simultaneously abolished the JV laws, it did, therefore, not apply, even residually, to the *contractual* aspects of JVs; neither did the Partnership Enterprise Law, despite it briefly mentions the partnership agreement (s. above §2214)[965]. The general provisions of the former Contract Law may have, however, whenever the JV laws may have been silent on contractual issues.

2335 Finally, while the *purely contractual* CJV was also governed by the CJV Law, the latter's application was limited to its contractual regime, and by the Contract Law, to the extent mentioned in the preceding paragraph.

2336 It is also worth, at this stage, to clarify that, under the old regime, there were *two types of registration* : a corporate one, if applicable, and, in both cases, a contractual one. This distinction matters to the effect of dispelling the confusion by which, because a CJVs could abstain from registering as limited liability company[966], it could abstain to register altogether: it could not. Indeed, JVs, i.e., the EJV in any case, and the limited liability company CJV, had to register

963 CJV Law, Art. 2§2; CJV Detailed Rules, Art. 14. These provisions subjected the formation of a CJV as limited liability company to meeting the conditions applying to the registration of a limited liability company.

964 CJV Detailed Rules, Art. 55 and 56.

965 About the applicable law under the new regime, s. below §§2344ff.

966 S. above note 963.

as corporate entities, i.e., as *limited liability company*, while the purely contractual CJV had not. However, as FIEs falling under FIL, all three had to register the JV *contract* in any case and obtain the authority's approval independently of the registration of either JV as a limited liability company, as the case may be (EJV Law, Art. 3; CJV Law, Art. 5)[967].

As recalled, the legal regime applicable to JVs fundamentally changed since the inception of the FIL and that of the Chinese Civil Code. Thus, between 1st January 2020 and 31 December 2024, EJVs and CJVs kept being governed by the EJV Law and the CJV Law, despite these two laws were abolished by the FIL as of 1st January 2020[968]. The question, which is not straightforwardly addressed by Chinese law, is that, as of 1 January 2025, of the fate of, i.e., the *new regime* applying to old, *pre*-2020 JVs beyond their transformation into another form, none of which is specifically designed for accommodating features typical of a JV as the EJV and CJV laws did, i.e., and that applying to new, *post*-2020 JVs. 2337

To reply that question, among pre-2020 JVs, one shall distinguish two cases: EJVs and CJVs which were already registered as limited liability company (1st case), on one hand, from, on the other hand, purely contractual CJVs (2nd case). Among the first case, one should further distinguish EJVs and CJVs which retained their limited liability company form, or transformed into a shareholding company, on one hand (1st case, 1st option) from, on the other hand, those which transformed into a partnership enterprise (1st case, 2nd option). 2338

As far as the *first case, first option* is concerned (formerly registered JV remaining a limited liability company, or transforming into a shareholding company), the JV regime of the former JV features could subsist, theoretically, in the company's *bylaws*. However, the bylaws, whose content generally follows templates dedicated to such companies forms, not to JVs, may be ill-suited to accommodate features specific to a JV. That is especially true for Sino-foreign JVs since, as wanted by the new foreign investment regime, neither the limited liability company, nor the shareholding company are specifically intended for FIEs. 2339

---

967 About registration under the new regime, s. below §§2350 and 2352.

968 In principle, residual aspects not covered by the EJV or CJV laws and relating to contractual obligations born after 1st January 2021 have been governed by the Third Book on contracts of the Chinese Civil Code ever since the Code's entry into force, however. The (abrogated) Contract Law may keep applying to contractual obligations having born before that date. The extension granted up to 31st December 2024 to the application of the EJV and CJV laws did not apply to the Contract Law, which was repelled by the Code as of 1st January 2021 (Art. 1260). The solution to such conflicts of laws, as the case may be, may not always be obvious and, if the parties cannot agree, may have to settled before Chinese courts, as provided by Art. 142§1 and 466§1 (s. above Chap. 4 §23.II, Contractual Interpretation)

2340 Therefore, the JV features of the former JV which may not be adequately incorporated in the bylaws may, instead, be restructured in a *contractual* form (like the former JV contract, s. above §2332), along with its new corporate form, to complement the new corporate regime, and be qualified as a *partnership contract* operating within the new corporate form chosen. It will, as such, be governed by contract law, i.e., by Chapter 27 of the Second Title on typical contracts of the Third Book of the Chinese Civil Code on contract law (Art. 967 ff.; s. above Chap. 5 §41, Partnership Contract)[969] and, for any matter not covered by the latter, by the First Title on general contractual provisions of the Third Book (s. above Chap. 4 §20, General Rules to Chap. 4 §27, Liability for Breach of Contract).

2341 It should also be mentioned that former JVs already registered as limited liability company and retaining such form did not need applying for any *change* of registration solely because of the new law, provided, however, their existing form was fully compliant with the revised 2023 Company Law (s. above Chap. 9 §64.I, Introduction). Typically, certain features inherited from pre-2020 limited liability companies often proved to be inconsistent with the requirements of the Company Law; whenever so, a change to the bylaws, etc. may have been necessary and, accordingly, filing for the modification of the registration was mandatory. That is now part of the past[970], since JVs which omitted to comply by 31 December 2024 were prevented to apply for registration changes, exposed themselves to sanctions, and to be ordered to cease to operate and to the publication of the same (s. above §§2143 and 2163).

2342 As far as the *first case, second option* is concerned (formerly registered JV transforming into a partnership enterprise; s. above §2338), two risks of confusion should, again, preliminarily be dispelled or recalled (s. above §§2214 to 2217). First, as already noted about the partnership enterprise (s. above §§2215 and 2217), the latter is not to be confused with the partnership *contract* (Chinese Civil Code, Art. 967 ff.) which is, as its name makes clear, a typical contract, while the partnership enterprise is a company or corporate form: unlike the former, the latter enjoys legal personality.

2343 Second, the partnership *agreement* (合伙协议 héhuǒ xiéyì), which is prescribed by the Partnership Enterprise Law[971], is to be distinguished from the

[969] In case of R&D JV, the JV agreement may also rely on the regime of the technology cooperative development contract (s. above §1296).

[970] Major changes related to the supreme body, voting majority, State approval, the JV contract, minimum duration and equity transfer.

[971] Partnership Enterprise Law, Art. 9 applicable to both the general and the limited liability partnership, Art. 14, item 2 applicable to the general partnership and to the limited liability partnership by the reference of Art. 60, and Art. 63 applicable to the limited liability partnership.

partnership *contract* (合伙合同 héhuǒ hétóng) mentioned in the preceding paragraph: yet despite Chinese law uses slightly different names for designating the one and the other, both regimes actually refer to the *same* legal notion, if not institution (s. above §1345). The partnership agreement plays for the partnership enterprise the same role as the *joint-venture contract* played for the JV (s. above §2332): both govern the relationship between partners, which is of a contractual nature and may, therefore, be also subject to contract law, whenever corporate law does not extend to all contractual aspects of the JV (s. above §2330).

The partnership agreement is primarily governed by the Partnership Enterprise Law which applies as *special law* and it derogates, as the case may be, to the Chinese Civil Code which, in return, as *general law*, applies for supplementing the Partnership Enterprise Law to contract law issues whenever the latter is silent. 2344

Therefore, where a former JV transforms into a partnership enterprise (FIL, Art. 31; s. above §30), the JV features of the former JV can be reflected in the *partnership agreement* provided for by the Partnership Enterprise Law. Indeed, given its similarity with the partnership contract, the partnership agreement is adequately suited to accommodate the contractual features of a JV: a separate partnership contract is unnecessary. 2345

If so, residual aspects are covered, as mentioned in the penultimate paragraph, by the law of the partnership contract (Chinese Civil Code, Art. 967 ff.) and, in case the latter does not suffice, by the First Title on general contractual provisions of the Third Book on contract law, both being applicable by virtue of the general reference of Art. 19§2, 2nd sentence of the Partnership Law ("other relevant laws"). 2346

Both the partnership contract (s. above §2340) and the partnership agreement (s. penultimate paragraph) *contents* may typically match that of the JV contract formerly required by the JV laws (s. above §2332), i.e., among other things, provisions regulating the investment or conditions for cooperation, the distribution of earnings or products, the sharing of risks and losses, the mode of operation and management and the ownership of the property at the time of the termination of the CJV (Art. 2), the sharing of profit or products, risks and losses (*ibid.*, Art. 21), and dispute resolution (*ibid.*, Art. 26). Because of the contractual freedom (s. above §554) they enjoy, the parties are, as they were under the JV laws, free to determine their scope, provided always, however, that, in case the JV was transformed into a limited liability company or 2347 shareholding company, the partnership contract does not run counter the Company Law as noted (s. above §2341)[972].

2348 Now as far as the *second case* is concerned (purely contractual CJV retaining its status; s. above §2338), purely contractual CJVs which were not registered as limited liability company have ceased to be governed by the CJV law since 1 January 2025 and are, effectively, even though the law does not explicitly states it, governed henceforth by the law of the *contractual partnership* under the Chinese Civil Code (Art. 967 ff.; s. above Chap. 5 §41, Partnership Contract) ever since; the general provisions of contract law equally apply residually.

2349 In other words, the generic reference of Art. 467§2 of the Chinese Civil Code to "the laws of the People's Republic of China" is flexible enough to accommodate the relatively complex change of regime described above. In all cases, a clear, comprehensive applicable law clause is advised, however.

2350 Finally, under the *new regime*, not only is the approval of the JV contract not required anymore as it was under the JV laws, subject to foreign investment law however (s. below §2352); moreover, no separate JV contract is required as it was under the JV laws either, in case the JV has transformed into a limited liability company or a shareholding company[973], although it remains optional, not to say advisable (s. above §§2339 and 2340).

2351 To summarize, since 1 January 2025, a JV is, in China, neither a corporate form, nor a typical contract, but a *sui generis* legal entity mixing both corporate and contractual features. It is to be understood, depending on the circumstances described above (s. §§2338ff.), as a limited liability company or a shareholding company regulated by the Company Law, whose JV regime is governed by the bylaws and a partnership contract under Art. 967 ff. of the Chinese Civil Code; alternatively, as a partnership enterprise. In the latter case, its JV features will be embedded in the partnership agreement under the Partnership Enterprise Law, which may be complemented by the law of the partnership contract. Purely contractual CJV which were not registered as limited liability company under the old regime are now governed by the partnership contract law. Lastly, the general provisions of contract law of the Chinese Civil Code apply to contractual aspects where the aforementioned regimes may be silent. Therefore, we refer, for the detail, to the law of the limited liability company, of the

---

972 The most authoritative international guidelines for JV contracts are generally considered to be the International Chamber of Commerce (ICC) Model Joint-Venture Contract. UNCITRAL's Legal Guide on Drawing Up International Contracts for the Sale of Goods offers supplementary guidance on JV-related clauses.

973 In case of transformation of the JV into a partnership enterprise, s. above §2345.

shareholding company, of the partnership enterprise, of the enterprise contract and to contract law for further detail.

Moreover, as far as foreign investors are concerned, Sino-foreign JVs are subject, in addition and in any event, to the scrutiny of the *Foreign Investment Law*. Namely, purely contractual JVs in the form of contractual partnership may not be used for circumventing the requirements typically applying to registered FIEs (s. above §§1349ff.) 2352

In conclusion, it is important to stress that, in China, since 1 January 2025, JVs, including Sino-foreign JVs, are not specifically regulated by Chinese law anymore, either as companies or as contracts, that they can still be setup in another form nevertheless, and that the parties are free to agree on their related rights and obligation, provided they comply with the framework of existing laws, the most relevant of which have been recalled in the preceding paragraph. 2353

§67. Representative Offices

Representative offices of foreign enterprises in China are, together with branches of foreign companies (s. above Chap. 9 §64.XI, Branches of Foreign Companies and below, §§2386ff.), the only corporate form dedicated to FIEs surviving in China since the FIL placed both foreign invested and domestic enterprises on the same level playing field and abolished both JVs and WFOEs as of 1 January 2020 (s. above Chap. 1 §5.I, Corporate Form). 2354

Initially regulated by the Procedures for the Registration and Administration of Resident Offices in China of Foreign Enterprises of 15 March 1983, they are currently governed by the Regulation on the Administration of Registration of Resident Representative Offices of Foreign Enterprises (2024 Revision), whose initial version was issued in 2010 and replaced the 1983 Procedures. The Regulation only underwent minor, unsubstantial revisions, in 2010 and 2013, ever since; namely, it was left untouched by the 2019 FIL. 2355

Representative office, also colloquially known as "rep of" or abbreviated "RO", is the short name for its official designation of 外国企业常驻代表机构 wàiguó qǐyè cháng zhù dàibiǎo jīgòu, meaning permanent (or resident) representative offices of foreign enterprise. 2356

It often escapes unexperienced foreign investors that representative offices are not the cheap, quick and easy alternative to registering a proper company in China, but that their scope is dramatically, and deliberately so, *limited*, in three notable ways: first, they may not earn profit; second, they have no legal personality and may not, as such, for example, hire employees directly or sign contracts; and third, they are gradually phased out, and as such discouraged by 2357 the government, which is gradually making their establishment and operation less attractive through regulatory, tax, and practical restrictions, thus encouraging foreign companies to opt for more robust corporate entities like limited liability companies, shareholding companies and partnership enterprises, which are easier for Chinese authorities to regulate and tax.

2358 Although representative offices are still legally allowed, and while those hurdles make them impractical or unsustainable for many purposes, they may still be appropriate for limited *scopes* compliant with such restrictions such as liaison, market research, marketing, sourcing or support to their parent. While phasing out representative offices is an established policy, the Chinese government has not announced any plan to abolish them at the time of drafting this book.

2359 As its name makes clear, the law is chiefly concerned by the *registration* of representative offices. The Regulation, which is relatively short with 45 articles, contains seven chapters, four of which focus on the registration application, its modification and cancellation, and are complemented by the three last on liability, general and supplementary provisions.

2360 The *general provisions* start by stressing two defining characteristics of representative offices which are, as noted, that, beyond representing foreign enterprises, they are not-for-profit[974] and are deprived of legal personality (Art. 2). Foreign enterprises are defined in the *supplementary provisions* as for-profit enterprises registered outside of China (Art. 42). The Regulation extends to representative offices of companies registered in the SAR of Hong Kong and Macau, and in Taiwan (Art. 44).

2361 The Regulation further designates the competent registration (which is the AMR, s. above note 15) and regulatory authorities (Art. 5§1 and 43), and promotes information sharing among their agencies, thus referring to the Information Sharing System established by the government (Art. 5§2; s. above §1822).

2362 Representative offices must keep an accounting according to legal standards (Art. 7§1) and file annual reports. The report must provide evidence of the existence of the foreign parent, detail the activity of the representative office and its development, file audited proofs of its expenses and any other relevant information. The Regulation even specifies that the report must be filed between March and June (Art. 6). The Regulation further insists that accounting must be independent; it cannot be incorporated in that of another enterprise, organization or individual (Art. 7§2). Finally, the Regulation reminds that the representative office's personnel must abide by the law and specifically,

---

974 This prohibition is reiterated at Art. 13§1 (s. below §2366).

although not exhaustively, mentions administrative regulations on departure and entry, residence, employment, taxation, and foreign exchange registration.

Chapter 2 of the Regulation, which is rather vaguely titled "registration matters", contains in fact *general registration provisions* addressing issues such as the name of the representative office, its representatives, activities, location, term, registration publication, certificates, and supervision. The registration procedure proper is governed by Chapter 3. 2363

The law both mandates and prohibits certain components of the *name* of a representative office. Its mandatory content includes its name in Chinese, the nationality of the foreign parent, the name of its registered address' city and the characters 代表处 (dàibiǎo chù, "representative office"). Any illegal[975] content is evidently prohibited and includes, among other things, anything adverse to the public interest[976], and the name of any international organization (Art. 10§1). 2364

A representative office may appoint up to three *representatives*, one of whom must be the chief representative[977] (colloquially known as "chief rep"; Art. 11 §1, 1st sentence and § 2). Because the representative office has no legal personality, its representatives must, like for foreign branches (s. above §§2181 and 2184), be employed by the foreign parent. The law makes clear that, while the chief representative may sign the application for the registration of the representative office, he may only do so while duly empowered by the foreign parent, and on the latter's behalf (Art. 11§1, 2nd sentence), which is coherent with the fact that the representative office does not enjoy legal personality. Representatives are subject to the registration authority's scrutiny, and their appointment will be rejected if their standing is deemed incompatible with such position (Art. 12)[978]. The hiring of representative is not to be confused with that of *local Chinese workers* which is subject to a separate, and much more constraining, regime (s. below §§2376ff.) 2365

Prohibited activities include any *for-profit* activity, as already mentioned at Art. 2; this prohibition is expressly reiterated at Art. 13§1. However, the second subsection of this provision expressly reserves international treaties which may 2366

975 The Regulation generically refers to the law. One may find guidance on prohibited contents, among other things, in the Trademark Law (Art. 9 ff.)

976 Art. 10§1, item 1 also mentions the national security, although one may have difficulty to figure out a name threatening it.

977 The maximum of three representatives is not to be understood in addition to the chief representative, but including him. In other words, a representative office may not have up to four representatives, chief representative included, but *three*.

978 Motives of rejection include any criminal sentence for harm to the public interest, and if the appointee served as representative of a representative office and was suspended for the same motives less than five years before the application.

provide for *exemptions*, subject to any reservation which China may have declared (*ibid.*, § 2). Notable exemptions include foreign law firms, civil aviation and accounting firms. Under China's commitment towards the WTO and certain bilateral agreements[979], foreign law firm in China, which are governed by a specific regulation[980], may provide for-profit service, but are otherwise severely restricted. The same applies to accounting firms. Representative offices of foreign airlines in China can engage in profit-making business, such as selling tickets and cargo services; this exception stems from specific bilateral aviation agreements[981]. These derogations do not dispense from approval or registration, which are distinct notions (s. below §§2368 and 2373ff., together with Art. 23§3 specifically applying to international treaties).

2367 *Permitted activities* include *verbatim* "market research, presentation and publicity activities related to the products or services of foreign enterprises, and liaison activities related to the product sales, service delivery, domestic purchase and domestic investment of foreign enterprises" (Art. 13§1). Again, the fact that an activity may be permitted does not dispense from approval or registration (s. next paragraph and 2373ff.)

2368 The notion of permitted activity, including for-profit, is not to be confused with that of *approval*, namely, before registration. Indeed, despite it may enjoy a derogation such as for-profit (s. above §2366), the beneficiary representative office may be subject to preapproval before being eligible for applying for registration (Art. 14§2). Like the notion of permitted activity is distinct from that of approval (s. above §2370), the latter is also to be distinguished from that of registration. The approval requirement depends on the industry and business scope of the representative office considered. Examples include: finance and insurance (requiring approval from the PBOC); sea transport and ocean cargo agents (requiring approval from the Ministry of Communications); air transport (requiring approval from the State Aviation Administration); trade, manufacturing and forwarding agents (requiring approval from MOFCOM); industries related to national security (defense industry) and sectors such as major agricultural products, energy, infrastructure, and key technologies (all requiring higher-level approvals and subject to national security review[982]); and legal

979 S., for example, the Sino-Australian FTA or the Sino-Singaporean FTA.

980 Regulations on the Administration of Foreign Law Firms' Representative Offices in China (2024 Revision).

981 S., for example, the Sino-Swiss agreement on air services (Fr.: Accord entre le Conseil fédéral suisse et le Gouvernement de la République populaire de Chine relatif aux services aériens; Ger.: Abkommen zwischen dem Schweizerischen Bundesrat und der Regierung der Volksrepublik China über den Luftverkehr of 1 March 2011, effective as of 10 June 2011 (RS 0.748.127.192.49), Art. 13.

982 S. above §§66ff.

services (law firms; requiring approval from the Ministry of Justice; s. above §2366 and note 980). This list is not exhaustive. Industries not considered as restricted or sensitive do not require prior approval: they may register directly.

As far as the representative offices of *Swiss* parents are concerned, questions 2369
may arise as to the compliance of the Chinese for-profit and approval requirements outlined above from the point of view of the reciprocal protection and treatment commitments taken by both countries, in this case by China towards Switzerland, in the Sino-Swiss agreement on the promotion and reciprocal protection of investments (BIT), namely, the *most-favored-nation* (MFN) clause (s. above §17) contained therein (Sino-Swiss BIT, Art. 4), and is a standard in most BITs. Indeed, arguably, Chinese companies incorporating in Switzerland face no such restrictions. This argument may not stand for the following reasons however: first, there is no equivalent to Chinese representative offices in Switzerland (s. above §§1759 and 1760), so that a Swiss investor could not quite claim inequality of treatment. Second, there is an equivalent to Swiss branches (Fr. : "succursale"; Ger. : "Zweignierlassung") in China, which are branches of foreign companies (*ibid.*), that do not suffer, in China, the same restrictions like representative offices, thus offering equality of treatment with their Swiss counterpart. Third, the restrictions imposed to representative offices and, as the case may be, to FIEs (s. above Chap. 1 §5, Management and, for branches, §2185) are expressly legitimated, in the Sino-Swiss BIT, by China's reservations (Protocol to the Sino-Swiss BIT, *ad* Art. 4§2 and 3), which in turn the Regulation expressly reserves (Regulation, Art. 13§2 *in fine*). Fourth, as noted, Switzerland, like many other countries, enjoys certain exemptions (s. above §2366 and note 981).

A representative office is free to choose the *location* of its registered offices, 2370
but that location must be adequate in the eyes of the registration authorities, which can require the representative office to "adjust" it, if it deems that such location threatens the national security or the public interest (Art. 15)[983].

The *term* of a representative office cannot exceed that of its foreign parent 2371
(Art. 16).

As outlined, representative offices are subject to tight supervision from the au- 2372
thorities. Notably, the law expressly entitles the registration authority to *investigate*[984] and *punish* representative offices (Art. 21). Although the law subjects

983 Typically, foreign representative offices may be prohibited to be located in the immediate vicinity of certain sensitive State buildings (e.g., army premises), and may be requested to regroup in certain areas.

984 Such investigation powers, which are extended, are detailed by the law and include interviews, consulting, copying and taking away documents, accounts or items such as tools, products, etc. (Art. 21, items 1 to 4).

such investigation to some suspicion of violating the law, in practice, it gives the authorities discretionary power to keep a close watch on representative offices. Generally speaking, the set of provisions described above highlights, by contrasting them, the narrow scope consented to representative offices and the close supervision to which they are subjected.

2373 Chapter 3, 4 and 5 of the Regulation apply to the *registration procedure* proper, to its modification and to its cancellation. As already mentioned, a representative office must be registered (Art. 4§1); as outlined above (s. §2368), if the representative office's intended activity subjects it to *approval*, the foreign parent must obtain it before it may apply for registration of its representative office.

2374 If a representative office is subject to preapproval (s. above §2368), once it has been approved, the foreign parent must apply for *registration* within 90 days (Art. 23§2); even though the law falls short from mentioning it, if the foreign parent fails to do so timely, the approval will lapse and the foreign parent will have to repeat its application for approval.

2375 Once the registration authority has accepted the application, it must make a decision within 15 days. Once it has, it must, within five days, either, in case of acceptance, issue the certificate of registration, which is the equivalent of a business license for a not-for-profit entity or, in case of rejection, motivate it (Art. 24§1). The representative office is deemed to come into legal existence on the date of the certificate (*ibid.*, § 2). Its representative must then immediately comply with the various formalities following the registration related to matters such as its residence, employment, taxation registration, foreign exchange registration, etc.

2376 It is to be stressed, in those latter respects, that *employment* is another distinctive feature of representative offices: as noted, like foreign branches (s. above §§2181 and 2184), because representative offices do not enjoy legal personality, they cannot hire local Chinese personnel. Nor can their foreign parent (which must employ its appointed foreign representatives, however, s. above §2365). A representative office can only hire local Chinese personnel through its foreign parent and a so-called *temp agency*[985], which is an agency licensed by the Chinese government whose mission is to make workers available to, among others, representative offices: to that effect, a triangular relationship, known as *labor dispatch*, is established, by which a contract for the provision of work services is entered into between the foreign parent and the agency, which in turn places the local Chinese workers with the rep of.

985 The main of these agencies is Beijing Foreign Enterprise Human Resource Service Co. (known as FESCO). Its Shanghai counterpart is Shanghai Foreign Service (Group) Co., Ltd. (FSG). There is a small number of others.

The whole contractual relationship, known as "temp work" or "labor dispatch", which is peculiar, is not governed by the Regulation on the Registration of Resident Representative Offices of Foreign Enterprises, but by labor law, i.e., the Labor Contract Law. It has been comprehensively discussed in detail in the labor law chapter of this book, to which we refer the reader (s. above Chap. 6 §50.II, Labor Dispatch.) 2377

As far as the representative office is concerned, the only contract of employment is passed between the agency and the worker; neither between the foreign parent, nor the rep of, and the worker. There is no contract between the employee and the rep of; the employee is merely bound to the rep of by the latter's instructions (which it legally issues on behalf of the foreign parent) to the former, whose inobservance amounts to a breach of the contract of employment with the agency. Those instructions can be either specific, on a day-to-day basis, or general, in the form of internal staff regulations, staff code of conduct, etc. Such constraints do not apply to the foreign representatives themselves (s. above §2365). 2378

In case of *modification* of any of the information registered with the registration authority, the foreign parent must apply for its update (Art. 26 and 29). Such information includes, but is not limited to, the foreign parent, namely its signatory powers, registered capital and business scope, as well as any changes of its representative office's representatives (Art. 31). The foreign parent must do so within 60 days (Art. 27§1). If preliminary approval is required, that time limit is shortened to 30 days from such approval (*ibid.*, § 2). Such application is also to be made 60 days before the expiry of the term of residence (Art. 28). The time limits for approval or rejection are shortened to five days (Art. 30). 2379

Finally, the foreign parent must apply for *cancellation* in case it closes down its representative office, the representative office is to disrupt its activity at the expiry of the term of residence, the foreign parent is dissolved, the representative office's certificate is cancelled, or the representative office ordered to close down (Art. 32). The application must be filed within 60 days (*ibid.*) The documents to file are listed at Art. 33. The authority must make a decision within ten days and notify the applicant within five days thereafter (Art. 34). 2380

The representative office's registered information is *published* (Art. 17) on NECIPS, which is the Chinese equivalent of the register of commerce or of companies (s. above §58). In addition, the foreign parent must *announce* the establishment of the representative office on media designated by the registration authority, as well as in case of modification, cancellation or revocation (Art. 20). 2381

The importance of the representative office's *certificates* is emphasized by a detailed regulation. The representative office's registration results in two of them: a registration certificate (Art. 24§1), which legitimates the representative 2382 office's legal existence, and a representative certificate (Art. 19§1), which legitimates its representative or representatives' powers. The registration certificate must be prominently displayed (Art. 18). If it is lost or damaged, it must be replaced (Art. 19§2). They are automatically invalidated in case of modification, cancellation or revocation (*ibid.*, § 3).

2383 Chapter 6 on legal liabilities (Art. 35 to 41) is chiefly concerned with the *foreign parent's administrative liability* for its own deeds or those of its representative office or representatives which it details in great length, so confirming the legislator's intent to strictly contain representative offices. Any of the following infringements may result in an order to cease and desist or to correct, a fine, confiscation, the cancellation or revocation of the certificates: establishing a representative office or doing business without registration (Art. 35), making profit (Art. 36), fraud (Art. 36; fraud related to certificates is specifically governed by Art. 20 and 36§3), out-of-scope activities (Art. 37), failing to report, to use the registered name while doing business, to adjust the residence location, to make an announcement or to register as mandated by the law (Art. 38); or harm to the national security or to the public interest (Art. 39§1). In addition, in the latter case, or in that of serious illegal activity, the foreign parent shall be barred from establishing another representative office within five years of the cancellation (*ibid.*, § 2).

2384 The law is also concerned with the administrative or *public liability* of its *civil servants* in case of all manners of illegal activities related to their duties such as abuse of power, negligence, fraud, etc. (Art. 40).

2385 The *criminal administrative liability*[986] and the *criminal liability* , if applicable, of any author, is reserved (Art. 41).

2386 Before concluding this chapter, given their similarities, it may be worth to discuss the differences between representative offices of foreign enterprises and *branches of foreign companies* (s. above Chap. 9 §64.XI, Branches of Foreign Companies). The latter are governed by Chap. 13 of the Company Law (Art. 243 to 249). Indeed, among their similarities, both represent foreign parents, which are liable for their deeds; and both are deprived of legal personality, despite being registered. It is, therefore, not obvious to understand what distinguishes those regimes from one another.

2387 The main differences are that branches, unlike representative offices, may earn *profit*, while the latter are, in principle, prohibited to (s. above §§2357, 2360 and 2366). As a result, the *scope* of representative offices is, as described above, dramatically limited to specified activities (Regulations, Art. 13§1; s. above

986 The Regulation expressly refers to violations of the public security administration, governed by the Public Security Administrative Punishments Law (Art. 41).

§§2358 and 2367), while that of branches is only constrained by the general framework imposed to foreign investment (s. above Chap. 1 §5, Management) and the conditions which may be attached to the issuance of the business license (s. above Chap. 1 §5.IV, Business License) and its use (s. above §§40 to 42), depending on the industry, location or other relevant factors related to the activity contemplated.

Yet the prohibition made to representative offices to earn profit is, as outlined, 2388 subject to *exemptions* (s. above §2366), which then raises the question of the comparative advantages of registering an exempted, for-profit representative office as compared to a branch.

That question raises in turn another preliminary question, which is whether a 2389 representative office authorized to earn profit is subject to the regime applying to branches. Although there does not seem to be a straightforward answer, we understand that representative offices and branches are governed by their own regime, i.e., that representative offices are governed by the Regulation and branches by the Company Law, and that they do not overlap. Mostly, exempted representative offices have been operating in China for decades so that, in practice, little doubt remains.

Turning now to the question of the *comparative advantages* of for-profit rep- 2390 resentative offices versus branches, a foreign enterprise might still choose to register a representative office in China despite the restrictions described above for several practical reasons: registering a representative office is generally faster, simpler, and less costly than setting up a branch, a limited liability company, a shareholding company or a partnership; it does not require abiding by complex incorporation procedures. Moreover, a representative office allows a foreign enterprise to establish a presence in China to conduct activities limited to market research, promotion, networking and liaison, without committing to full commercial operations. Thus, if that enterprise's purpose in China is limited to not-for-profit activities such as marketing, quality control, after-sales support, or maintaining relationships with clients and suppliers, a representative office suffices. Representative office are also often used as a test before investing in larger, more permanent structures such as a branch, a limited liability companies or shareholding companies. Also, notably, unlike limited liability companies and shareholding companies, representative offices are not subject to minimum registered capital requirements, while branches must be "adequately funded" and the authority may prescribe them minimum amounts (s. above §2184).

These relative advantages have to be balanced with the inconveniences typi- 2391 cally related to representative offices, above all the fact that, unless exempted, they cannot earn profit, and that, while their administrative burden may be lighter compared to branches, it may be relatively heavier considering their limited scope, in particular if they are not-for-profit. A notable advantage of branches, among other things, is that, unlike representative offices (s. above §§2376 and 2378), their foreign parent may hire personnel directly: it does not have to use an intermediary licensed temp agent such as FESCO. That said, many if not most exempted representative offices (such as those of airlines) use that form simply because it is provided by international treaties (s. above §§2366 and note 981), which effectively rules out the option of a branch.

§68. Variable Interests Entities

2392 Although it is not strictly speaking a legal form of enterprise under Chinese law, but rather a corporate and contractual investment *structure* resting, at least in part, on Chinese law, we will briefly outline variable interests entities because of their relative importance in foreign investment in China.

2393 A *variable interest entity* (VIE) can be described as a cross-border corporate and contractual structure used both by foreign investors to access sectors where foreign investment in China is *restricted or prohibited*, and by Chinese investors to access such foreign capital.

2394 Because VIEs are not acknowledged *per se* by Chinese law as a legal person or a typical or nominate contract, there is no official translation or even a consensus on their name in Chinese; therefore, *terminology* variations abound. Thus, VIEs may be addressed as VIE 架构 VIE jiàgòu (VIE architecture) or VIE 结构 VIE jiégòu (VIE structure, i.e., both expressions using the English acronym and appending 架构 jiàgòu, architecture or 结构 jiégòu, structure); 协议控制 xiéyì kòngzhì, contractual control, where "contractual control" may be declined as 协议控制安排 xiéyì kòngzhì ānpái, contractual control arrangement, 协议控制架构 xiéyì kòngzhì jiàgòu, contractual control arrangement architecture, or 协议控制结构 xiéyì kòngzhì jiégòu, contractual control arrangement structure; as well as 可变利益实体 kě biàn lìyì zhǔtǐ, variable benefits (or interests) entity; 可变权益实体 kě biàn quányì shítǐ, variable rights (or interests) entity, or 可变利益主体 kě biàn lìyì zhǔtǐ, variable benefits (or interests) subject. The 2015 draft FIL soberly used 实际控制 shíjì kòngzhì which translates as "actual control", but that reference was dropped from the final version.

2395 Since the foreign investment sector targeted is restricted or prohibited, the VIE uses contractual arrangements between a *Chinese operating company* and an *offshore*[987] *holding*[988]. Since the Chinese company operates in a sector restricted or prohibited to foreigners, it must be controlled[989] by Chinese nationals.

Meanwhile, the offshore entity controlling the Chinese company can be invested by foreigners, which *directly control* the holding, thus, through the holding, *indirectly control* the Chinese operating company, in which they would be restricted or prohibited to invest directly. Even if the foreign investors only hold a minority investment in the holding, they can still enjoy certain rights entitling them to a share of the Chinese operating company's profit, to which they could otherwise not be directly entitled. In counterpart, the Chinese partners enjoy *indirect access to foreign capital*, which could otherwise not be directly invested in China. 2396

Such control is achieved through *contracts*, such as service agreements, option agreements, voting proxy agreements, etc.) Moreover, if the partners to a VIE elect to subject their overarching partnership agreement to Chinese law, they may do so under a *partnership contract* (Chinese Civil Code, Art. 967 ff.; s. above Chap. 5 §41, Partnership) whose flexibility (s. above §1355), combined with the contractual freedom acknowledged by Chinese law (s. above §554), would leave them with ample liberty, within the applicable regulatory framework which, especially in financial matters, can prove constraining however. 2397

The offshore company is frequently *listed* on a foreign stock exchange, where the VIE structure typically aims, among other things, at facilitating listings overseas and attracting foreign investment, while listing in China is still regarded as a comparatively less attractive option. 2398

In other words, VIEs aim at legally *circumventing* foreign investment restrictions or prohibitions. Even though their legality has been questioned, they have been *tolerated* by the Chinese authorities so far, subject to certain boundaries. Still, such tolerance still falls short of an unambiguous acknowledgment of their legality. 2399

Namely, VIEs became more scrutinized after the promulgation of China's FIL and the Negative List in 2020: indeed, as outlined in the FIL chapter of this book, the FIL provides that contractual arrangements might be treated as foreign investment if they result in "actual control" by foreigners, thus subjecting 2400

---

987 Both distant offshore jurisdictions such as the Cayman Islands or the British Virgin Islands and Greater China ones such as Hong Kong and Taiwan are frequently favored.

988 Such holdings are frequently referred to as *special purpose vehicles* (SPVs), although SPVs are not confined to that role.

989 In certain cases, the Negative List allows the foreign investor to hold a majority share but imposes a Chinese minority share (s. above §37). A VIE to the effect of lowering or eliminating the Chinese minority share would also be conceivable in such case.

the VIE to the Negative List restricting or prohibiting foreign investment in certain economic sectors.

2401 Namely, in February 2023, the CSRC introduced new requirements for *overseas listings*, including those using VIE structures, requiring the Chinese companies being the operating entity of a VIE to file with CSRC for the overseas listing of the offshore entity controlling them. As such, the Chinese company must also report to CSRC certain changes or investigations resulting from their holding's overseas market presence.

2402 That said, it is important to stress once again that, to date the Chinese government has never formally codified the legitimacy of VIEs, thus confining their legal existence in a grey area. They are, therefore, subject to *regulatory risks* and policy changes. As noted, even though authorities generally tolerate VIEs controlled by Chinese nationals, foreign control may face greater scrutiny and future regulation with unpredictable consequences. Namely, enforcement of contracts and changes in sectoral restrictions are key ongoing risks, while new foreign investment laws may involve additional national security reviews in sensitive sectors. Despite risks, VIEs remain a major strategy for accessing foreign capital in restricted sectors[990].

2403 A detailed commentary of VIEs would exceed the scope of this book, although the corporate and contractual basis on which such structures rest are, as far as Chinese law is concerned, detailed therein. For more specific or actual information, the reader is invited to consult topical literature or to seek specialized advice.

990 Notable examples include Alibaba and Tencent.

Index

The index refers to page numbers.